AF173478

Reflections on the International Association for Media and Communication Research

Jörg Becker • Robin Mansell
Editors

Reflections on the International Association for Media and Communication Research

Many Voices, One Forum

palgrave
macmillan

Editors
Jörg Becker
Political Science
Philipp's University of Marburg
Marburg, Hessen, Germany

Robin Mansell
Media and Communications Dept.
London School of Economics and
Political Science
London, United Kingdom

ISBN 978-3-031-16382-1 ISBN 978-3-031-16383-8 (eBook)
https://doi.org/10.1007/978-3-031-16383-8

© The Editor(s) (if applicable) and The Author(s), under exclusive licence to Springer Nature Switzerland AG 2023
This work is subject to copyright. All rights are solely and exclusively licensed by the Publisher, whether the whole or part of the material is concerned, specifically the rights of translation, reprinting, reuse of illustrations, recitation, broadcasting, reproduction on microfilms or in any other physical way, and transmission or information storage and retrieval, electronic adaptation, computer software, or by similar or dissimilar methodology now known or hereafter developed.
The use of general descriptive names, registered names, trademarks, service marks, etc. in this publication does not imply, even in the absence of a specific statement, that such names are exempt from the relevant protective laws and regulations and therefore free for general use.
The publisher, the authors, and the editors are safe to assume that the advice and information in this book are believed to be true and accurate at the date of publication. Neither the publisher nor the authors or the editors give a warranty, expressed or implied, with respect to the material contained herein or for any errors or omissions that may have been made. The publisher remains neutral with regard to jurisdictional claims in published maps and institutional affiliations.

This Palgrave Macmillan imprint is published by the registered company Springer Nature Switzerland AG.
The registered company address is: Gewerbestrasse 11, 6330 Cham, Switzerland

Preface

From 1957, the International Association for Media and Communication Research (IAMCR)—Asociación Internacional de Estudios en Comunicación Social (AIECS)—Association Internationale des Études et Recherches sur L'information et la Communication (AIERI)—has facilitated international exchanges and research collaborations among academics, journalists, and other practitioners in the field of media and communication. Established in an era of Cold War politics, the publication of accounts of IAMCR's history is timely in view of continuing geopolitical, global, regional, and national struggles for peace and recognition. The challenge to IAMCR, as historically, is to ensure that contemporary struggles against hegemony in the Global North and in the Global South do not occlude the enormous diversity of scholarly traditions in the media and communication field. Throughout its history, IAMCR has sought an international membership with the ambition of addressing media and communication problems, focusing initially on the mass media, including the press, and later embracing all kinds of mediated communication.

With early-career researchers and established scholars from the East and West and the Global North and South, IAMCR has close to 3000 members based in 93 countries. The association's statutory aims in 2022 include the ambitions to "improve media and communication research, policy and practice, especially from international and interdisciplinary perspectives, with attention to their ethical nature" and to "guarantee, at every level of the Association, the diversity that characterizes the global academic community of media and communication scholars, to ensure their respectful and balanced presence, and to actively strengthen the academic communities which have been underrepresented". IAMCR also aims "to contribute … to the development and improvement of the education and training of journalists and other media professionals and to promote and defend the freedom and independence of their work" and "to defend the professional interests of academic media and communication researchers, to help the improvement of their training, and to promote and defend the freedom and independence of academic work in media and communication research".

At Jörg Becker's suggestion, during IAMCR's 2018 Oregon Conference, a group of members was commissioned to research the association's history. This group was created and endorsed by IAMCR's Executive Board under the leadership of then President, Janet Wasko and, later, by President Nico Carpentier. The Commission's mandate was to "prepare an edited collection of papers recounting crucial turns and developments of our association, based on personal memories or topical examinations". This edited volume accompanies a monograph in preparation on IAMCR's institutional history by Cees J. Hamelink and Kaarle Nordenstreng. This present collection of chapters amplifies their insights into the making of an international academic association from the perspectives of IAMCR members who undertook a variety of roles.

The Commission members were Binod C. Agrawal, India; Cees J. Hamelink, Netherlands; Robin Mansell, United Kingdom; Kaarle Nordenstreng, Finland; Sandra Ristovska, United States; and Eduardo Villanueva-Mansilla, Peru. For a time, the group included Ulla Carlsson, Sweden, and Annabelle Sreberny, United Kingdom. The group was expanded to include Usha Raman, India and, throughout, the Commission was supported by Bruce Girard, Uruguay, IAMCR's Executive Director.

The Commission met multiple times between 2018 and 2022 in person and then in Zoom sessions to discuss a structure for this collection in consultation with IAMCR members, and to oversee author invitations and manage the chapter peer review process. The Commission is proud to present this edited collection as the result of its collective work.

This book highlights how IAMCR's members contributed to the development of an international association in the field of media and communication studies. The association attracts researchers and practitioners who engage in critical analysis of contemporary media and communication. Not content simply to understand developments in the media and communication field, the membership has sought to influence theory and practice through published research and participation in global, regional, national, and local debate. Several articles with accounts of the association's history are available, including those by Hamid Mowlana (2022) who served as IAMCR's President (1994–1998) and by Michael Meyen (2014, 2015) and Kaarle Nordenstreng (2008). There are also book-length histories of the field of media and communication which discuss IAMCR in a chapter or mention it in passing (Park & Pooley, 2008; Simondson et al., 2013).

This volume is organized in several parts following an introduction which provides a concise overview of IAMCR's institutional history. *Part I: Scholarly Traditions in Media and Communication* highlights prominent areas of research that have attracted the interest of scholars and the association's efforts to be inclusive of early-career scholars. *Part II: IAMCR Scholarship and the Political* includes chapters bringing to light political struggles of a membership, engaging in research across divides—East and West, global North and global South. These chapters provide insights into how members have contributed to initiatives aimed at fostering a more inclusive and equitable international information and communication order. *Part III: IAMCR and National and Regional Scholarship* turns to accounts of how members from selected countries and regions have contributed to the association and the opportunities as well as the barriers they have faced in securing an equitable standing in the association. Finally, *Part IV: Reflections on People* highlights the significant scholarly and institution-building contributions of James D. Halloran, IAMCR's President (1972–1990) and other prominent contributors to the study of culture and the political economy of media and communication (George Gerbner, Stuart Hall, Herbert I. Schiller, and Dallas W. Smythe), each of whom shaped the focus of the association through their research and activism. Hall's, Schiller's, and Smythe's scholarship is recognized by the awarding of prizes in their memory to students and early-career scholars for papers that reflect the critical traditions embodied by their work. These chapters show how these academics sought to build bridges across cultural, political, and economic divisions and how they sought to achieve respect for intellectual difference.

* * *

As Chair of the IAMCR History Commission and as co-editor (Jörg Becker), I reflect here on IAMCR from a perspective based on almost 50 years of membership—my entire academic and professional life. I became a member in 1976 and it is tempting to say that IAMCR became a part of my family. I made a great many personal friends within IAMCR; some friendships went so far as to mean that I was invited to weddings. To this day, I receive regular private visits. This network of relationships has become so intense that I now go to IAMCR conferences primarily to meet friends rather than for scientific engagement. To say that IAMCR has become a part of my family is as trivial as it is banal, but after such a long membership of an association, it does become part of the family.

Membership in a scientific association and participation in its conferences also means participating in the academic merry-go-round of vanity and one's own self-marketing in search of opportunities and career development. In an international association such as IAMCR, however, this does not apply in the same way for those from all countries. The academic placement market is often national with people looking for jobs in their own country, although the growth of English language teaching programs means that border crossing is increasingly common. As an international association, IAMCR members from larger countries have been underrepresented as those looking for an academic position tended to go to their own national scientific association's conferences. This means that scholars from larger countries such as France, Germany, or the United States have been underrepresented in IAMCR, relative to the size of their respective academic communities. Academics from smaller countries with more modest-sized academic markets in the global North such as Denmark, Finland, or Netherlands, have been better represented. Because of the challenges of getting a job at home, they were more likely to gravitate toward an international arena from the beginning of their careers. As a result, historically, those who became members of IAMCR from larger countries have tended to have intrinsic, rather than career, motivations. This may explain why the proportion of idealists among IAMCR members often has seemed greater than that of careerists. It is also precisely the reason that there have been so many unconditional internationalists in IAMCR.

Older IAMCR members often cultivate an image of IAMCR as an association that helped to build a bridge between East and West in the midst of the Cold War; that it was, in effect, a forerunner of the Commission on Security and Cooperation in Europe (CSCE), which was founded in 1975. They regard IAMCR as having been exemplary of the peaceful coexistence of diverse cultural, political, and economic systems and of the capacity to bring diverse social scientists to the same table. IAMCR's commitment to encouraging dialogue among those advancing different intellectual traditions and normative commitments is well-illustrated by a debate between Ithiel de Sola Pool and Herbert I. Schiller, moderated by Cees J. Hamelink, which occurred in 1980 and which we republish in this volume.

This account may be partly accurate, but it is also a myth. This is because IAMCR was developed, and to an extent, controlled, by a small club of members who pursued their activities as left-wing intellectuals and in the shadow of Moscow. In my experience, these activities, for example, cooperations between conservative Noelle-Neumann from West Germany and communist Dusiška from East Germany were concerned principally with their own academic-political reputational power and structures. The prevailing power structures within IAMCR meant that innovative members such as Dallas W. Smythe would be excluded from various IAMCR roles and initiatives such as the founding of the Political Economy Section, would be hindered and suppressed, at least for a time.

I gave two lectures at my first IAMCR Conference in Leicester in 1976, one on racism in children's books and the other on enemy images in parliamentary speeches. Reflecting now on what I argued then, after 50 years very little has changed. There is still racism in the media and, at the time of writing during the Ukraine-Russia War, media images of the enemy are proliferating. This does not mean that scholarly orientations do not change. In my own work, for instance, I made the leap from analysis of media content to the analysis of media structures early on when I began asking why structures of media organizations favor certain kinds of content. IAMCR accompanied me very well on my research path (my shift from content to structure was addressed in *Medien im Krieg—Krieg in den Medien* [Media at War—War in the Media], 2016).

IAMCR has provided a very important meeting place between the East, the West, and the North and the South for years. The worlds of Eastern Europe communism, of European and United States capitalism and the socio-economic and political orders of lower-income countries, met controversially together. Before the end of communism in Eastern Europe, IAMCR was a highly fertile place for learning about political controversies, akin to the Habermasian ideal of a place for communication free from domination, which I did not find anywhere else. In the middle of the Cold War, the Wall in East Berlin was not just a wall that prevented people from going from East to West, but, also from West to East. In West Germany, there was a professional ban on all academics who had close contacts with scientists in communist Eastern Europe. As a West German, I was keenly interested in what kind of communication science existed in East Germany, that is, in the German Democratic Republic. I looked forward to IAMCR conferences because I could meet scientists from communist countries only there, and I fully enjoyed these opportunities for engagement. My friendships with some 20 IAMCR colleagues from communist Eastern Europe broke off abruptly with the end of Eastern European communism. Many of these colleagues became "free" market economists, preferring to be in contact with conservative colleagues in West Germany who had ignored me earlier, precisely because of these communist colleagues.

The image that sometimes circulates of IAMCR as a left-liberal association needs to be put into perspective in the light of my experience. First, left-liberal cultural hegemony was a worldwide phenomenon between 1965 and 1990 (with women's, peace, and ecology movements) and, particularly, during the 1968 student movement. IAMCR echoed these developments. Second, IAMCR, with its conferences in Pamplona in 1968 (Barrera, 2019) and in Buenos Aires in 1972 (Cimadevilla, 2021), twice managed to come to terms with fascist governments, at least to the extent that the conferences could be hosted by local organizers in these cities. Third, from around 1990 with the end of Fordism and the end of communism in Eastern Europe, and in the wake of a growing prevalence of cultural studies in contrast to political economy in the social scientific study of media and communication, IAMCR began following another global political trend. Research consistent with the dominance of neoliberalism and new identity politics became the predominate climate for research in the field, with an increasing need to defend research in the political economy tradition.

* * *

My (Robin Mansell) initial encounter with IAMCR was its Prague conference in 1984 where I presented a paper on "Contradictions in Canadian Information Policies". Much to my surprise, once I got past the fear of a first presentation at an international conference, I found there was time for discussion and there was interest in developments beyond the United States. Trained in the political economy of media and communication at Simon Fraser University in Canada, on the advice of my PhD supervisors, William (Bill) H. Melody and Dallas W. Smythe, I gave my attention to what is now the Communication Technology and Policy Section of IAMCR. This section had been led by Dallas as the Satellites Section from 1970, later becoming the Technology and Satellites Section led by Emil Dusiška in 1976, followed by Dallas again in 1978. In 1980, it would become the Communication Technology Section, led by Bill Melody until 1990. When I was elected as Section Head in 1990, I changed the name to Communication Technology Policy Section to signal that the section should attract scholars with critical perspectives to offer on technology, including those drawing from political economy and those from the then nascent field of science and technology studies. I served as IAMCR President (2004–2008) and remain active in various capacities, including as Chair of IAMCR's Clearinghouse for Public Statements.

IAMCR became my main intellectual home. At my first conference in 1984, I found a hugely welcoming community. With a fellow PhD student from Simon Fraser University, we worked up the courage to introduce ourselves to senior scholar Cees J. Hamelink who chatted with us for a time—rather than nodding and passing by as we had expected and we felt included. I met my co-editor, Jörg Becker, who was similarly friendly and would later invite me to participate in a conference he organized in Moscow in 1990 on "a Common European House". I was invited to give opening plenary comments on a paper by James D. Halloran at the IAMCR Ljubljana Conference in 1990. My research was on the political economy of the (tele)communication industry and, at the time, there were very few women working in this field. I found my work being acknowledged and rewarded at IAMCR. Although women and early-career scholars faced challenges in being heard, my experience of the association was nowhere near as exclusionary as other association conferences I had attended.

Intellectually, too, IAMCR was different. Coming from a research training context at Simon Fraser University where strenuous debate about the respective strengths and weaknesses of liberal pluralist and Marxist theories in the media and communication field was a daily occurrence and where a research horizon starting and ending in North America was strongly discouraged, IAMCR challenged me to learn to listen, to seek out those who came from different contexts, and to be receptive to difference. I cannot claim to have learned fully how to do this, but IAMCR offered a remarkable opportunity to work with scholars from around the world, including with members of the History Commission and the contributors to this volume. My hope is that the accounts of IAMCR's historical development in this book can offer a touchstone for those who work toward the association's renewal, expansion, and commitment to critical research with the purpose of "changing the world" in whatever organizational form emerges in the future.

* * *

A history of any organization, and indeed, an academic professional association, is a reflection of the experiences and memories of its members. The history recounted in this collection is inevitably selective and readers will identify gaps and imbalances. IAMCR's History Commission sought to include a mix of research traditions, but we were not able to encompass the richness of all of IAMCR's sections and working groups. The History Commission invited contributions from a range of countries and regions. We aimed to achieve a reasonable gender balance and to represent scholars located in the global South and North, the result being 30 male and 17 female contributors, but only 9 of 34 chapters authored by contributors whose work originates in the global South. There is much work to do to achieve inclusivity, a theme emphasized strongly in several chapters.

Readers will find not only a history of an academic professional organization, but insights into the controversies, conflicts, failings and achievements of IAMCR members who have worked very hard to develop the field of media and communication research and journalism practice. The substantial contemporary importance of media and communication for sustaining reciprocity and mutual respect means that we hope the insights in this book will resonate with the many current challenges to media and communication research and practice today.

Solingen, Germany — Jörg Becker
London, United Kingdom — Robin Mansell
April 2023

References

Becker, J. (2016). *Medien im Krieg—Krieg in den Medien* [Media at war—War in the media]. SpringerLink.

Barrera, C. (2019). Cold War, press freedom and journalism education: Paradoxes of the untypical 1968 IAMCR conference in Pamplona. *Javnost—The Public*, *26*(4), 420–434.

Cimadevilla, G. R. (2021). Milicos, gestores y literatos: La historia jamás contada del IX congreso de la IAMCR en Buenos Aires (1972). *Revista Latinoamericana de Ciencias de la Comunicación*, *20*(36), 36–48.

Meyen, M. (2014). IAMCR on the East-West battlefield: A study on the GDR's attempts to use the association for diplomatic purposes. *International Journal of Communication*, 8, 2071–2089.

Meyen, M. (2015). 'The IAMCR story: Communication and media research in a global perspective'. In P. Simonson & W. W. Park (Eds.), *The international history of communication study* (p. 90–106). Routledge.

Mowlana, H. (2022). Paradigmatic debates, theoretical diversity, and the IAMCR. In M. Yoshitaka & J. Yin (Eds.), *The handbook of global interventions in communication theory* (p. 42–60). Routledge.

Nordenstreng, K. (2008). Institutional networking: The story of the International Association for Mass Communication Research (IAMCR). In D. W. Park & J. Pooley (Eds.), *The history of media and communication research: Contested memories* (p. 225–248). Peter Lang.

Park, D. W., & Pooley, J. (Eds). (2008). *The history of media and communication research: Contested memories*. Peter Lang.
Simonson, P., Peck, J., Craig, R. T., & Jackson, J. P. (Eds). (2013). *The handbook of communication history*. Routledge.

Acknowledgments

Acknowledgments are due to numerous colleagues. During its four years of work, IAMCR's History Commission lost several colleagues. While working on his chapter on IAMCR and Latin America, Rafael Roncagliolo of Peru died in May 2021. IAMCR lost one of its most eminent Latin American sociologists and communication scholars who tirelessly campaigned for an independent media policy in Latin America; independent of external influences. Roncagliolo, Peruvian Minister of Foreign Affairs (2011 to 2013), was a member of IAMCR's International Council from 1980, serving as IAMCR Vice President from 1984 to 1988. We are grateful to his family for the permission granted to Eduardo Villanueva-Mansilla to complete the chapter which appears in this volume. We also remember Annabelle Sreberny, who died unexpectedly and much too soon on 30 December 2022. She was not only President of IAMCR from 2008 to 2012 but also a temporary member of our IAMCR History Commission. We appreciated her always dedicated and special intellect. Binod C. Agrawal, the meritorious initiator of IAMCR's Conference in New Delhi in 1986, initially was an active contributor to this book. He withdrew from the project for health reasons and very sadly died on 28 March 2023.

We also acknowledge the work of Usha Raman, IAMCR Vice President, who greatly assisted us with managing the chapter review process and other tasks. Bruce Girard provided needed encouragement along the way and helped with sourcing some archival material, ensuring it was collated and available to us and to IAMCR's members. We give our heartfelt thanks to Shruti Singhal for her highly professional and timely editing of chapters prior to submission to the publisher and we acknowledge financial support by IAMCR for this work. We especially thank contributors to this book for their work which ensured that the Commission could fulfill its task. We thank them for their patience over an extended period.

Thank you to Oxford University Press for permission to republish Chap. 33 'Perspectives on Communications Research: An Exchange'. We thank the following institutions and people for permissions to publish photographs: the

Open University UK (Chap. 33), Nico Carpentier, IAMCR President for archived photographs, Jörg Becker, Ranji Cherian, Robin Mansell, Divina Frau-Meigs, Claudia Padovani, Padma Rani, Dan Schiller, and Eduardo Villanueva-Mansilla for graphics and photographs appearing in various chapters. Every effort has been made to trace copyright holders and obtain permission to reproduce material that appears in this book. Please get in touch with the editors for any enquiries or any information relating to the material in this book.

Lastly, we thank Lauriane Piette, our Palgrave editor, for her enthusiasm and commitment to this publication. We are also grateful to Samriddhi Pandey and colleagues for being very responsive to our many queries.

Contents

Notes on Contributors

Binod C. Agarwal (1942–2023) was Professor and Director General TALEEM Research Foundation, Ahmedabad (2008–2015), Vice-Chancellor, Himgiri Zee University, Dehradun, Uttarakhand (2005–2012), Founding Director, Mudra Institute of Communications, Ahmedabad (1993–1994) and Professor, Manipal Academy of Higher Education (MAHE).

Sara Bannerman Canada Research Chair in Communication Policy and Governance, is an Associate Professor of Communication Studies at McMaster University, Canada. She researches and teaches communication policy and law. She is an IAMCR past Co-Vice-Chair of the Law Section and a past Co-Chair of the Emerging Scholars Network.

Jörg Becker is Professor of Political Science at Marburg University, Germany and an IAMCR member since 1976. He works in the fields of international media politics, media technologies, peace, military and the media, and the history of the German labor movement.

Deepti Bharthur is a Senior Research Associate at ITforChange in Bengaluru, India, where she contributes to academic, action, and policy research in the areas of data economy, platforms and digital exclusions, and digital citizenship. She also manages the alternative media platform, *Bot Populi*. Deepti received her doctorate from Bowling Green State University in the United States.

Sanjay Bharthur is Professor of Communication at the Manipal Institute of Communication, MAHE, India. His teaching and research span four decades in several institutions across the country. He is an active member of IAMCR with interests in the Political Economy, Journalism Education Research, and International Communication Sections. He focuses on holistic issues and institutional relations regarding communication and media in India and comparative perspectives.

Andrew Calabrese is a Professor of Media Studies and was Associate Dean in the College of Media, Communication and Information at the University of

Colorado Boulder, United States. His articles and books focus on communication and social justice.

Colin Chasi is Professor and Director, Unit for Institutional Change and Social Justice, at the University of the Free State, South Africa. Past-President of the South African Communication Association, he is interested in the philosophy of communication. His latest book is *Ubuntu for Warriors* (2021).

Marjan de Bruin moved to the Caribbean in 1987, leaving The Netherlands behind to start a career at The University of the West Indies' Caribbean Institute of Media and Communication, Jamaica. With IAMCR, Marjan has been engaged in various positions, including co-Chair as well as founding Chair of several sections and working groups; elected Vice-President, International Council member, and is an active member of IAMCR's Publication Committee and its Scholarly Review Committee.

Ithiel de Sola Pool was Sloan Professor of Political Science and Director of the Research Program on Communications Policy at the Massachusetts Institute of Technology, United States.

Aditya Deshbandhu is Lecturer of Communications (Digital Media Sociology) at the University of Exeter, United Kingdom. His research interests include new media studies, digital cultures, various conceptions of the digital divide, and the emerging field of video game studies. He is the author of *Gaming culture(s) in India: Digital play in everyday life* (2020) and *The 21st Century in a Hundred Games* (forthcoming).

Divinia Frau-Meigs is Professor of Media Sociology at Université Sorbonne Nouvelle, France. She is a specialist in Cultural Diversity, Internet Governance, and Media and Information Literacy (MIL), and her research examines media uses and practices of young people and information disorders (radicalization, disinformation, hate speech). She was IAMCR Assistant Secretary General (2000–2004), Vice-President (2004–2008), and Head of the Media Education Research Section (2009–2015). Current Head of the European chapter of the Global Alliance on Media and Information Literacy (GAPMIL), she holds the UNESCO Chair—Savoir-devenir in sustainable digital development.

Margaret Gallagher is an independent researcher in Ireland, specializing in gender, media, and communication. She serves on the editorial boards of *International Communication Gazette*, *Feminist Media Studies*, and *Media Development*. She is an Advisory Board member of the European Communication Research and Education Association (ECREA), and an international steering committee member of the Global Alliance on Media and Gender (GAMAG).

Peggy Gray was born in London in 1934, graduating in Sociology from Exeter University in 1956, United Kingdom. After meeting James D. Halloran in 1968, she held a full-time research post at the Centre for Mass Communication Research, Leicester University, and from 1974, served as Administrative

Assistant for more than 20 years, working as the main contact for IAMCR members, conference organizer, and bridge to the President. She was awarded the IAMCR Distinguished Contribution Award 2016.

Peter Gross is Professor Emeritus, School of Journalism and Electronic Media, College of Communication and Information, University of Tennessee, United States, serving as Director (2006–2016). He is also Non-Resident Fellow, Center for Media, Data and Society, Central European University, columnist at Transitions Online, and co-editor, *Journal of Romanian Studies.*

Cees J. Hamelink is Emeritus Professor of International Communication at the University of Amsterdam, Netherlands, Honorary President of IAMCR, and editor-in-chief of the *International Communication Gazette*. He has written 19 monographs on human rights, culture, and technology, *Communication and Peace* (Palgrave Macmillan, 2020), and *Communication and Human Rights* (forthcoming).

Stewart M. Hoover is Professor of Media Studies and Director of the Center for Media, Religion, and Culture in the College of Media, Communication, and Information at the University of Colorado Boulder, United States. A theorist of media audiences and audience research, his research is located at the intersection of religion and modern media of communication.

Tom Jacobson is a Professor in the Klein College of Media and Communication at Temple University in Philadelphia, United States where he serves as Director of Temple's Master of Science in Communication for Development and Social Change. He is Chair of IAMCR's Scholarly Review Committee.

Deqiang Ji is a Professor of International Communication and Vice-Dean of the Institute for a Community with Shared Future at the Communication University of China, People's Republic of China. He has served as the Vice-Chair of the International Communication Section of IAMCR since 2016.

Friedrich Krotz is Professor Emeritus in Communication and Media at the University of Bremen, Germany. He works in the fields of digitalization, mediatization research, media sociology, methodology and theories of communication and the media. He served as Mediated Communication, Public Opinion & Society Section Head and two terms as elected member of IAMCR's International Council.

Philip Lee is General Secretary of the World Association for Christian Communication (WACC) and Editor of its international journal, *Media Development*. Based in Canada, his publications include *The Democratization of Communication* (Ed.) (1995); *Many Voices, One Vision: The Right to Communicate in Practice* (Ed.) (2004); *Communicating Peace: Entertaining Angels Unawares* (Ed.) (2008); *Public Memory, Public Media, and the Politics of Justice* (Ed. with Pradip N. Thomas) (2012); and *Expanding Shrinking Communication Spaces* (Ed. with Lorenzo Vargas) (2020).

Louise Luxton is an Economic and Social Research Council-funded PhD candidate at Newcastle University, United Kingdom. Her research focuses on gender, political communication, and party politics. She is completing a thesis on the concerns of women's parties and the media representations of their candidates.

Robin Mansell is Professor Emerita of New Media and the Internet, Department of Media and Communication, London School of Economics and Political Science, United Kingdom. Her research addresses issues of digital media governance and its consequences. She is former IAMCR President (2004-2008), and is Chair of IAMCR's Clearinghouse for Public Statements and member of the Scholarly Review Committee. She received the IAMCR Distinguished Contribution Award in 2017.

Armand Mattelart is Professor Emeritus at Paris 8 University Vincennes-Saint-Denis and Rennes II universities, France. Following a career in Chile addressing social planning and communication policies during Salvador Allende's regime, he was active in the French university system and the Ministry of Scientific Research at the time of François Mitterrand, and internationally. His books include *How to Read Donald Duck* (with Ariel Dorfman), *Thinking about the Media* and *History of Communication Theories* (both with Michèle Mattelart), *La communication-monde, L'invention de la communication*, *History of the Planetary Utopia*, *For a World View* (with Michel Sénécal), and *The Profiling of Populations* (with André Vitalis), with translations in numerous languages.

William H. Melody is Visiting Professor, Center for Communication, Media, and IT (CMI), Aalborg University Copenhagen, Denmark and Emeritus Professor, Delft University of Technology, Netherlands. His festschrift book addresses his work: Mansell R., Samarajiva, R., & Mahan, A. (Eds.) (2002) *Networking Knowledge for Information Societies: Institutions and Intervention*, Delft: DUP Science.

Bingchun Meng is Professor in the Department of Media and Communications at the London School of Economics and Political Science, United Kingdom. Her research interests include gender and the media, political economy of media industries, communication governance, and comparative media studies. She is author of *The Politics of Chinese Media: Consensus and Contestation* (Palgrave, 2018) and she is working on a monograph about AI industries in China.

Bernard Miège is Emeritus Professor of Information and Communication Sciences at the University of Grenoble Alpes, France, in the GRESEC Laboratory. He was first holder of a UNESCO Chair in International Communication and served as Director of Research and as President of his University. He is author of more than 400 published works with many translations, with 21 books, including *The Society Conquered by Communication* (1989, 1997, 2007), addressing the cultural and creative industries, the development of digital information and communication techniques, changes in public space, and the epistemology of information—communication.

Graham Murdock is Emeritus Professor of Culture and Economy at Loughborough University, United Kingdom. He was a founding member of IAMCR's Political Economy Section and served as IAMCR Vice-President. His critical analysis of the material and symbolic organization and impact of contemporary communications has been translated into 21 languages.

Bruce Mutsvairo is a Professor and Chair in Media, Politics, and the Global South at Utrecht University's Department of Media and Culture Studies, Netherlands, where he studies the intersection of social media and politics in non-Western societies.

Kaarle Nordenstreng is Professor Emeritus of Journalism and Mass Communication at Tampere University, Finland. He has been Vice-President of IAMCR (1972–1988) and President of the International Organization of Journalists (IOJ, 1976–1990). His research has focused on communication theory, international communication, and media policies.

Claudia Padovani is Associate Professor in Political Science and International Relations at the University of Padova, Italy. Her main areas of interest concern global political transformations, with a special focus on gender equality issues, communication rights, and social justice. She is Co-Chair of the UNESCO UniTWIN Network on Gender Media and ICT and member of the IAMCR Task Force on GAMAG.

Fernando Oliveira Paulino is Professor at the University of Brasilia, Brazil. IAMCR member since 2009, he has been President of the Brazilian Federation of Scientific and Academic Communication Association (SOCICOM) and Vice-President of the Latin American Communication Researchers Association (ALAIC), CNPq Researcher 1B.

Victor Pickard is C. Edwin Baker Professor of Media Policy and Political Economy at the University of Pennsylvania's Annenberg School for Communication, United States, where he co-directs the Media, Inequality & Change (MIC) Center. He has written six books, including *America's Battle for Media Democracy* (2014) and *Democracy Without Journalism? Confronting the Misinformation Society* (2019).

Marc Raboy is Professor Emeritus in the Department of Art History and Communication Studies at McGill University, Canada. He taught at the universities of Concordia, Laval, and Montreal, and has been a visiting scholar at universities in Stockholm, New York, Oxford, and London. He was a member of IAMCR's International Council from 2000 to 2012.

Usha Raman is a Professor in the Department of Communication, University of Hyderabad, India. Her research and teaching span the areas of journalism pedagogy, critical studies of science, health, and technology, feminist media studies, and digital culture. She was elected Vice-President of IAMCR (2020–2024) and is co-founder of FemLab.Co, an IDRC-funded initiative on feminist futures of work.

Padma Rani is Director and Professor at the School of Communication, Manipal Institute of Communication, Manipal Academy of Higher Education.

Wajiha Raza Rizvi is Director, Film Museum Society, Associate Professor, School of Media & Mass Communication, Beaconhouse National University, Pakistan, member of IAMCR's International Council, and Co-Chair of the Gender and Communication Section. She is President of the Pakistan National Association of Fulbright Alumni, a FCOSAS/Chevening/GIMD research scholar and a documentary filmmaker.

Ylva Rodny-Gumede is the Head of the Division for Internationalisation and a Professor in the School of Communication at the University of Johannesburg, South Africa. She is a Past President of the South African Communication Association. Ylva has served on a wide range of consultancy projects that make use of her scholarly interests in journalism, communication, and media studies.

Rafael Roncagliolo-Orbegoso (1944–2021) was a Peruvian journalist and social scientist, author of multiple books and papers on Latin American communication policy. Visiting Professor at a number of universities during his lifetime, he was Vice-President of IAMCR (1982–1986), President of AMARC (1995–1998), as well as founder of Transparencia, an electoral observation NGO. He served as Foreign Affairs Minister of Peru from 2011 to 2013.

Naomi Sakr is Professor of Media Policy at the Communication and Media Research Institute (CAMRI), University of Westminster, United Kingdom, focusing on the political economy of Arab media. She started covering the MENA region as a business journalist in 1974 and gained insights into censorship as a consultant for ARTICLE 19 in the 1990s.

Katharine Sarikakis is Professor of Communication Science specializing in media governance, media organization, and the media industries, at the Department of Communication, University of Vienna, Austria, where she leads the Media Governance and Industries Research Lab. She is co-editor of the *International Journal of Media and Cultural Politics*, founding and twice-elected Chair of ECREA's Communication Law and Policy Section, and has been elected member of ECREA's Executive Board and IAMCR's International Council.

Herbert I. Schiller (1919–2000) was Professor of Communications at the University of California at San Diego, United States.

Franziska Scholz is a doctoral candidate at the Institute of Communication Studies, Communication University of China, People's Republic of China.

Slavko Splichal is Professor of Communication and Public Opinion at the University of Ljubljana, Slovenia, member of the Slovenian Academy of Sciences and Arts and Academia Europaea; founder and director of the European Institute for Communication and Culture, and editor of its journal *Javnost-The Public*. He was a member of IAMCR's International Council, and served as Deputy Secretary General and Chair of ECREA's Advisory Board.

Hans-Jörg Stiehler is Professor Emeritus of Empirical Communication and Media Research at the University of Leipzig, Germany. His research has included the relationship between sports and the media, the media system of the former GDR, and media use in East Germany. In 1999, he was one of the organizers of the Leipzig meeting of IAMCR.

Gregory Taylor is an Associate Professor in the University of Calgary's Department of Communication, Media, and Film, Canada. He is author of *Shut Off: the Canadian Digital Television Transition* (2013) and co-editor of *Frequencies: International Spectrum Policy* (2020).

Ilinca Ungureanu-Burlan is a PhD student at the College of Journalism and Mass Communication, University of Bucharest, Romania.

Eduardo Villanueva-Mansilla is Professor in the Communications Department, Pontificia Universidad Católica del Perú, Peru. His interests center on digital politics, specifically on the relationship between digital media and political transformations, and cultural expression in digital media.

Janet Wasko is Professor in Media Studies at the University of Oregon, United States. She is author or editor of 23 books, including *Understanding Disney: The Manufacture of Fantasy*, 2nd ed. (2020); *A Companion to Television*, 2nd ed. (2020) with Eileen R. Meehan; *Global Media Giants* (2017) with Benjamin Birkinbine and Rodrigo Gómez; and *The Handbook of Political Economy of Communications* (2011) with Graham Murdock and Helena Sousa. She is a Past President of IAMCR, and former Knight Chair in Communication Research.

Garry Whannel is Emeritus Professor at the University of Bedfordshire, United Kingdom. His most recent book is *Understanding the Olympics*, 3rd ed. (2020) with John Horne. He has been writing about popular culture, sport, and politics for over 40 years and previous books include *Blowing the Whistle* (1983); *Fields in Vision* (1992); *Media Sport Stars, Masculinities and Moralities* (2002); *Culture Politics and Sport* (2008), and with Deborah Philips, *The Trojan Horse* (2013).

Abbreviations

AEJ	Association for Education in Journalism
AEJMC	Association for Education in Journalism and Mass Communication
AGEMI	Advancing Gender Equality in Media Industries, project
AIECS	Asociación Internacional de Estudios en Comunicación Social
AIERI	Association Internationale des Études et Recherches sur L'information et la Communication
ALAIC	Latin American Communication Research Association
AMCAP	Association of Media and Communication Academic Professionals, Pakistan
AMIC	Asian Media, Information and Communication Center
APC	Association for Progressive Communications
ASC	Annenberg School of Communication, Pennsylvania
ATS	Applications Technology Satellite
AUC	American University in Cairo, Egypt
AUD	Audience Section, IAMCR
BFI	British Film Institute
BND	West German Federal Intelligence Service
BOC	Bureau of Outreach and Communication, India
BPfA	Beijing Declaration and Platform for Action
BRI	Belt and Road Initiative, China
CANA	Caribbean News Agency
CARIMAC	Caribbean Institute of Mass Communication, now Caribbean School of Media and Communication
CCA	Chinese Communication Association
CCCS	Centre for Contemporary Cultural Studies, Birmingham
CDCE	Convention on the Protection and Promotion of the Diversity of Cultural Expressions
CDMC	Centre for Digital Media Cultures, Brighton
CECMAS	Centre d'Études des Communications de Masse, France
CEM	Cultural Environment Movement
CETSAP	Centre for Transdisciplinary Studies: Sociology, Anthropology, Politics, France

CETSAS	Centre for Transdisciplinary Studies: Sociology, Anthropology, Semiology, France
CIA	Central Intelligence Agency, United States
CIESPAL	International Center for Superior Studies in Journalism for Latin America
CLO	Comité de Liaison, UNESCO
CMCR	Centre for Mass Communication Research, Leicester
CNN	Cable News Network, United States
COMECON	Council for Mutual Economic Assistance, Eastern bloc countries
CRIS	Communication Rights in the Information Society
CSCE	Conference on Security and Cooperation in Europe
CNSAS	National Council for the Study of the Securitate Archives, Romania
CPTPP	Comprehensive and Progressive Agreement for Trans-Pacific Partnership
CSW	Commission on Status of Women, United Nations
DGPuK	German Communication Association
DKP	German Communist Party
EACA	East African Communication Association
ECCR	European Consortium for Communications Researchers
ECOSOC	Economic and Social Council, United Nations
ECREA	European Communication Research and Education Association
EKD	Protestant Church in Germany/Evangelische Kirche Deutschland
ESF	European Science Foundation
ESN	Emerging Scholars Network, IAMCR
ESRC	Economic and Social Research Council, United Kingdom
EU	European Union
EURICOM	European Institute for Communication and Culture
FBI	Federal Bureau of Investigation, United States
FCC	Federal Communications Commission, United States
FELAFACS	Latin American Federation of Communication Schools
FRG	Federal Republic of Germany
FTA	Free Trade Agreement
GA	General Assembly, IAMCR
GAMAG	Global Alliance on Media and Gender
GAPMIL	Global Alliance for Partnerships in Media and Information Literacy, renamed MIL Alliance
GATT	General Agreement on Tariffs and Trade
GCRA	Global Communication Research Association
GDPR	General Data Protection Regulation, European Union
GDR	German Democratic Republic
GEM	Comparing Gender and Media Equality Across the Globe, project
GEN	Gender and Communication Section, IAMCR
GLC	Greater London Council
HIV/AIDS	Human Immunodeficiency Virus/Acquired Immunodeficiency Syndrome
HUAC	House Committee on Un-American Activities, United States
IAMCR	International Association for Media and Communication Research
ICA	International Communication Association
ICDC	Indian Committee for Development of Communication

ICT	Information and Communication Technology
IC	International Council, IAMCR
ICANN	Internet Corporation for Assigned Names and Numbers
IDRC	International Development Research Centre, Canada
IFCCD	International Federation of Coalitions for Cultural Diversity
IFEX	International Freedom of Expression Exchange
IFLA	International Federation of Library Associations
IFP	Institut Français de Presse
IIMC	Indian Institute of Mass Communication
IMC	International Music Council
INC	International Communication Section, IAMCR
INCD	International Network for Cultural Diversity
IOJ	International Organization of Journalists
IP	Intellectual Property
IPAL	Institute for Latin America, Peru
IPDC	International Programme for the Development of Communication, UNESCO
IS	Islamic State
IT	Information Technology
ITU	International Telecommunication Union
ISA	International Sociological Association
J&MC	Journalism and Media and Communication, programs
JRE	Journalism Research and Education Section, IAMCR
LGBTQIA	Lesbian, Gay, Bisexual, Transgender, Intersex, Queer and/or Questioning, and Asexual and/or Ally
MCS	Media, Culture and Society journal
MDG	Millennium Development Goals
MeCCSA	Media, Communication and Cultural Studies Association, United Kingdom
MENA	Middle East and North Africa
MILID	Media and Information Literacy and Intercultural Dialogue, UNESCO
MPS	Mediated Communication, Public Opinion & Society Section, IAMCR
MSU	Moscow State University
NAFTA	North American Free Trade Agreement
NAM	Non-Aligned Movement
NANAP	Non-Aligned News Agencies Pool
NASA	National Aeronautics and Space Administration, United States
NATO	North Atlantic Treaty Organization
NCA	National Communication Association, United States
NGO	Non-Governmental Organization
NIIO	New International Information Order
NLR	New Left Review
NWICO	New World Information and Communication Order
OECD	Organisation for Economic Co-operation and Development
OPEC	Organization of the Petroleum Exporting Countries
OSS	Office of Strategic Services, United States
PCL	Polytechnic of Central London

PCR	Participatory Communication Research Section, IAMCR
PCRN	Participatory Communication Research Network Working Group, IAMCR
PCWG	Popular Culture Working Group, IAMCR
PHEC	Punjab Higher Education Commission, Pakistan
PLO	Palestinian Liberation Organization
PRC	People's Republic of China
PUCRS	Pontifícia Universidade Católica do Rio Grande do Sul, Brazil
RCEP	Regional Comprehensive Economic Partnership
ROAM	Rights, Openness, Accessibility, Multi-stakeholder actors, UNESCO
SACA	South Asian Communication Association
SACOMM	Southern African Communications Association
SBC	Swedish Broadcasting Corporation
SDG	Sustainable Development Goals
SED	Socialist Unity Party of Germany, GDR
SEFT	Society for Education in Film and Television
SIC	Sciences de l'information et de la communication
SITE	Satellite Instructional Television Experiment, India
SFU	Simon Fraser University
TRIPS	Agreement on Trade-Related Aspects of Intellectual Property Rights
TPRC	Telecommunication Policy Research Conference/Research Conference on Communications, Information, and Internet Policy, United States
UDC	Union for Democratic Communications
UERJ	Rio de Janeiro State University, Brazil
UFF	Federal University of Fluminense, Brazil
UFJR	Federal University of Rio de Janeiro, Brazil
UN	United Nations
UNESCO	United Nations Educational, Scientific and Cultural Organization
UniTWIN	University Twinning and Networking Scheme, UNESCO
USC	University of Southern California
USMCA	United States-Mexico-Canada Agreement
USSR	Union of Soviet Socialist Republics
VDJ	GDR Union of Journalists/Verband der Journalisten der DDR
VoA	Voice of America
WACC	World Association for Christian Communication
WIPO	World Intellectual Property Organization
WJEC	World Journalism Education Council
WPFC	World Press Freedom Committee
WGIG	Working Group on Internet Governance
WTO	World Trade Organization
WSIS	World Summit on the Information Society

List of Figures

List of Tables

CHAPTER 1

Introduction: Overview of the Institutional History of IAMCR

Cees J. Hamelink and Kaarle Nordenstreng

Introduction

The press release of UNESCO on 23 December 1957 begins as follows:

> Fifty experts on information media, from 15 countries, have just completed in a two-day session at Unesco House, Paris, the task of establishing the International Association for Mass Communication Research. Created with the co-operation of Unesco, the new association, which is independent, has its headquarters in Paris, in the offices of the Institut Français de Presse of the University of Paris, 27 rue St. Guillaume. Its function is the promotion throughout the world of the development of research on problems related to press, radio, television and films. The association's membership list includes about 200 names of institutes, educational establishments and individuals. Educators in journalism are the most numerous on the individual list of educators and sociologists.

C. J. Hamelink (✉)
University of Amsterdam, Amsterdam, Netherlands

K. Nordenstreng
Tampere University, Tampere, Finland
e-mail: kaarle.nordenstreng@tuni.fi

© The Author(s), under exclusive license to Springer Nature Switzerland AG 2023

J. Becker, R. Mansell (eds.), *Reflections on the International Association for Media and Communication Research*,
https://doi.org/10.1007/978-3-031-16383-8_1

The history of IAMCR goes back to the first years of UNESCO.[1] Its Committee on Technical Needs in the Mass Media drafted in 1946 a constitution for an "International Institute of the Press and Information, designed to promote the training of journalists and the study of press problems throughout the world." The United Nations Conference on Freedom of Information, held in 1948 at Geneva, took note of the proposal and resolved that such an Institute could be conducive to the improvement of the quality of information, requesting "the Economic and Social Council to invite Governments and professional organizations, national and international, to examine together the possibility of implementing this proposal and, if it is found practicable, to co-operate in carrying it out."

Actively involved in the 1948 UN Conference were Fernand Terrou (first President of IAMCR 1957–1958), Jacques Kayser (Deputy President 1957–1958), and Jacques Bourquin (President 1964–1962). They also played an important role in the drafting of Article 19 on freedom of information of the Universal Declaration of Human Rights.

Fernand Terrou, Director of the Institut Français de Presse, was a leading advocate of the idea that an international association should be created "responsible for promoting throughout the world the development of the scientific study of problems relating to the important sources of information (press, cinema, radio, TV, etc.)." Terrou considered that no scientific progress was possible without extensive international exchange and collaboration. A parallel momentum was developing among academic centers of journalism education which also looked for international cooperation.

The 1952 UNESCO General Conference authorized the Director General to proceed with the proposal, and as a result, two lines of action developed. One culminated in the establishment of training centers for journalists, the first being established in Strasbourg in 1956. The other development led to the establishment of a separate international organization for the promotion and exchange of scientific research. In 1953, a UNESCO expert meeting began the compilation of a list of projects in mass communication research around the world, and in 1955, a report entitled "Current Mass Communication Research" was published. In November 1956, the UNESCO General Conference authorized the Director General "to promote the coordination of activities of national research institutes in the field of mass communication in particular by encouraging the establishment of an international association of such institutes." In December of that year, an international conference took place at Strasbourg, where a committee (Fernand Terrou with Mieczyslaw Kafel from

[1] This account of IAMCR's history is a work in progress excerpted from a longer text which can be accessed at IAMCR's website—https://iamcr.org/history Accessed 15 June 2022. It gives a summary of the institutional history of the association which will be presented in a forthcoming book authored by Cees J. Hamelink (IAMCR member 1974–, President 1990–1994) and Kaarle Nordenstreng (IAMCR member 1966–, Vice President 1972–1988). Appendices A and B in this volume have been updated by Kaarle Nordenstreng and the IAMCR Secretariat. The main sources are available in the association's digital archive—https://iamcr.org/digital-archive Accessed 15 June 2022.

Poland, Marcel Stijns from Belgium, and David Manning White from the United States) was formed and prepared an assembly of what was to become IAMCR.

This constituent assembly took place on 18 and 19 December 1957, at UNESCO headquarters. Fernand Terrou of France was elected as the first president with Jacques Kaiser (France) as deputy president and Jacques Bourquin (Switzerland) and Raymond B. Nixon (US) as vice-presidents, and the following as members of the Permanent Bureau: Claude Bellanger (France), Mieczyslaw Kafel (Poland), and Marcel Stijns (Belgium). It is remarkable that at the high time of the East-West ideological confrontation, colleagues from both sides worked together in the establishment of this international research organization; in addition to Kafel from Warsaw, Vladimir Klimes from Prague was an active participant. Also academics from developing countries were involved from the beginning, including Danton Jobim from Brazil. Hifzi Topuz attended the founding conference as a young Turkish journalist.

The main aim of the association was to facilitate exchanges of methods and findings between research institutes and to promote personal contacts among individual members. A related objective was to seek recognition for mass communication as a subject for independent scientific investigation.

The first IAMCR General Assembly (GA) after the founding conference was held in October 1959 in Milan, where Raymond B. Nixon became president. The first leaders of the association came mainly from journalism, journalism training, and the print media, particularly from European countries. The enrollment of researchers from various disciplines and the widening of geographical representation were among the first priorities.

Between 1959 and 1979, the association grew from 30 countries and 100 individuals to 60 countries and 1000 members. In the course of the 1990s, further expansion resulted in the representation of some 80 countries (Fig. 1.1).

In 1958, the first Section to be established was Historical Research, confirmed by the General Assembly in Milan 1959, which also established sections for Legal and Political Research, Psychological and Sociological Research, as well as Economic and Technical Research. Since then, IAMCR has regularly expanded the scope of its scientific domains; by 2023, it had 15 Sections and 18 Working Groups (WGs).

Since its foundation in 1957, the association has organized every second year a scientific conference in connection with its statutory GA. From 1970 onwards, the conferences were successively held in Western Europe, Eastern Europe, and the Third World. Table 1.1 includes the venues of the biennial conferences and the presidents elected.

Since 1991, the association also held a scientific conference in the years between the biennial statutory assemblies, first with smaller conferences focusing on a particular topic and later with full-size conferences, including section and WG sessions. These venues are shown in Table 1.2.

Fig. 1.1 IAMCR Conference 1984, Prague Reception. (From left to right) **Robin Cheesman**—IAMCR International Council 1976–1978, 1988–1992, Secretary General 1992–1994, Working Group Head—Materialist 1976–1978, Section Head—Political Economy 1978–1986, Section Head—Bibliography 1990–1992; **Kaarle Nordenstreng**—IAMCR Executive 1970–1972, Vice President 1972–1986, International Council 2004–06, Section Head—Developing Countries 1972–1974, Section Head—Professional Education 1990–1996, Chair Section/Scholarly Review Committee 1996–2010; **Cees Hamelink**—International Council 1976–1980, Vice President 1980–1988, President 1988–1994, Section Head—Law 1988–2000, Chair—Legal Committee 1990–1994, 1996–2000, Chair—Elections Committee 2002–2006, Chair—Future IAMCR Scenarios 2012; **Peggy Gray**—Administrative Assistant to President James Halloran 1974–1990. (Courtesy of IAMCR)

Over six decades, the aims and scope of the association remained focused on the creation of a global forum where researchers and others involved in media and communication could meet and exchange information about their work. The association works to stimulate interest in media and communication research, to disseminate information about research, and to create a broad constituency of researchers, practitioners, and policymakers.

Throughout its history, the association has adopted public statements on such issues as the protection of journalists, the right to communicate, the freedom of research, the support for international communication policies in the service of democratic development, and the need to contribute to the improvement of communication facilities in the Global South. The concern about the public presence of communication research and its role in public life has been a leading motive throughout the years. This became very concrete in the contributions of IAMCR to the United Nations World Summit on the Information Society (WSIS) in 2003 (Geneva) and in 2005 (Tunis).

Table 1.1 IAMCR Conference venues and presidents elected, 1957–2022

1957	Paris (France), Fernand Terrou (France)
1959	Milan (Italy), Raymond B. Nixon (US)
1961	Vevey (Switzerland)
1964	Vienna (Austria), Jacques Bourquin (Switzerland)
1966	Herceg Novi (Yugoslavia)
1968	Pamplona (Spain)
1970	Konstanz (West Germany)
1972	Buenos Aires (Argentina), James D. Halloran (UK)
1974	Leipzig (East Germany)
1976	Leicester (England)
1978	Warsaw (Poland)
1980	Caracas (Venezuela)
1982	Paris (France)
1984	Prague (Czechoslovakia)
1986	New Delhi (India)
1988	Barcelona (Spain), Cees J. Hamelink (Netherlands)
1990	Bled (Yugoslavia)
1992	Guarujá (Brazil), Hamid Mowlana (US)
1994	Seoul (South Korea)
1996	Sydney (Australia), Manuel Parés i Maicas (Spain)
1998	Glasgow (Scotland)
2000	Singapore (Singapore), Frank Morgan (Australia)
2002	Barcelona (Spain)
2004	Porto Alegre (Brazil), Robin Mansell (UK)
2006	Cairo (Egypt)
2008	Stockholm (Sweden), Annabelle Sreberny (UK)
2010	Braga (Portugal)
2012	Durban (South Africa), Janet Wasko (US)
2014	Hyderabad (India)
2016	Leicester (England)
2018	Eugene, Oregon (US)
2020	Tampere (Finland, online), Nico Carpentier (Belgium)
2022	Beijing (China, online)

Table 1.2 IAMCR Conference venues between statutory assemblies, 1991–2021

1991	Istanbul (Turkey)
1993	Dublin (Ireland)
1995	Portoroz (Slovenia)
1997	Oaxaca (Mexico)
1999	Leipzig (Germany)
2001	Budapest (Hungary)
2003	(scheduled in Taipei but cancelled due to SARS epidemic)
2005	Taipei (Taiwan)
2007	Paris (50th anniversary of IAMCR)
2009	Mexico City (Mexico)
2011	Istanbul (Turkey)
2013	Dublin (Ireland)
2015	Montreal (Canada)
2017	Cartagena (Colombia)
2019	Madrid (Spain)
2021	Nairobi (Kenya, online)

PART I

Scholarly Traditions in Media and Communication

CHAPTER 2

Dialectical Imagination: Frankfurt School and IAMCR

Bingchun Meng

Introduction[1]

In the age of hashtag activism and TikTok videos, it seems completely out of fashion to revisit Adorno's and Horkheimer's (Adorno & Horkheimer, 1972) scathing critique of the culture industry. After all, the contemporary media landscape has become so diverse and fragmented that it is now difficult to imagine the consciousness industry (Enzensberger, 1974) as a whole perpetuating some form of mass deception. In the meantime, the ways in which media companies and digital platforms sustain inequality and injustice on various fronts offer little cause for celebration. While it is convenient to dismiss the uncompromising criticality of the Frankfurt School as either overly pessimistic or irredeemably elitist, their impact on the agenda of critical communication research has been profound. In fact, critics of the Frankfurt School are often preoccupied with their alleged lack of empirical rigor (e.g., Stevenson, 1983), yet fail to engage with their work at epistemological and theoretical levels. Such delegitimization of critical research serves an ideological function without admitting to it, which is exactly why Adorno rejected positivism in the study of culture and ideology. As Martin Jay (1973) points out in his intellectual history of the Frankfurt School, "to the Institute, one of the fundamental

[1] The author would like to thank Professors Jörg Becker, Graham Murdock, and Terhi Rantanen for their helpful suggestions.

B. Meng (✉)
London School of Economics and Political Science, London, UK
e-mail: b.meng@lse.ac.uk

© The Author(s), under exclusive license to Springer Nature Switzerland AG 2023

J. Becker, R. Mansell (eds.), *Reflections on the International Association for Media and Communication Research*,
https://doi.org/10.1007/978-3-031-16383-8_2

characteristics of a non-ideological theory was its responsiveness to the interrelationships of past history, present realities, and future potentialities, with all the attendant mediations and contradictions" (Jay, 1973, p. 195). In pursuit of objectivity, a narrow conceptualization of empirical evidence that is deprived of historical context and alienated from its theoretical positioning would only end up conforming to extant power relations.

From its inception, IAMCR has aligned itself with the strand of critical communication research. Several key factors were at play during the early decades of the organization that contributed to IAMCR's overall intellectual profile as well as its ideological affiliation. First, the historical connection between IAMCR and UNESCO has been well documented (Hamelink & Nordenstreng, 2016; Mowlana, 1997). Founded in the aftermath of World War II, UNESCO's strong initiative in promoting freedom of information represents "the idealism that had inspired the founding of the United Nations (UN) itself" (Hamelink & Nordenstreng, 2016). Such idealism, on the one hand, recognizes the unequal flow of information internationally, and on the other hand, aspires to bridge the East-West divide (Meyen, 2014; Mowlana, 1997), rather than reinforcing the split between the "free world" and the "communist world."

As a result of the orientation of UNESCO, Eastern European scholars were involved in IAMCR from the very beginning. For example, scholars from Czechoslovakia, Poland, and Yugoslavia were present at the first general assembly in 1959 (IAMCR Bulletin, 1959). Walery Pisarek from Poland and Yassen Zassoursky from the Soviet Union joined in the 1960s (Hamelink & Nordenstreng, 2016). Irena Tetelowska of Poland became head of a new Section on bibliography, and the first woman to hold a leading position in the association (Nordenstreng, 2008). Emil Dusiška, a journalism professor at the University of Leipzig in East Germany, became IAMCR's Secretary General and did most of the association's paperwork from 1972 to 1978 (Meyen, 2014). Their participation signals that, in contrast to similar research associations established in the US during the Cold War,[2] IAMCR has much closer affinity with Marxism, even though its members undoubtedly have different takes on a Marxist analysis of media and communication.

Third, the European lineage of IAMCR has important implications for the epistemological inclination of the organization, which differs from its US counterparts, steeped as they are in the philosophical tradition of Anglo-American empiricism and which identify strongly with a positivist approach to social science. Combining the dual influence of German Idealism and Marxist historical materialism, the Frankfurt School sought to distinguish their aims,

[2] Despite the involvement of Eastern European scholars, IAMCR was not immune to Cold War politics. The association's second President Raymond Nixon actively recruited mainstream American scholars, including Paul Lazarsfeld and Wilbur Schramm, whose 1954 book *The Process of Effects and Mass Communication* was prepared under government contract as training materials for US Propaganda programs. Schramm was also known for reporting on Dallas Smythe to the FBI during the McCarthyism witch-hunt when Smythe was working at the Institute of Communication Research, University of Illinois.

methods, theories, and forms of analysis from both natural science and conventional social science. For the founding members of IAMCR who were wary of US dominance not only in the media and communication industries (as manifested in debates about media imperialism) but also in scientific research, Critical Theory provided an important foundation for building an alternative research agenda.

Repudiating Positivism

As is well-known in the field of media and communications, the dichotomy of critical versus administrative research arose from the unsuccessful collaboration between Adorno and Lazarsfeld on the Rockefeller-funded Princeton Radio Project in the late 1930s. Putting aside the consensus on Adorno's personality which was that he was very difficult to work with (Jay, 1973; Morrison, 1978), the intellectual cleavage runs deeply between Critical Theory and the kind of empiricist research Lazarsfeld advocated. The Princeton Project needed to figure out what exactly audiences were listening to on the radio and Adorno directed the research on music programs. He later recalled:

> I was particularly disturbed by the danger of a methodological circle: that in order to grasp the phenomenon of cultural reification according to the prevalent norms of empirical sociology one would have to use reified methods as they stood so threateningly before my eyes in the form of that machine, the program analyzer. When I was confronted with the demand to 'measure culture', I reflected that culture might be precisely that condition that excludes a mentality capable of measuring it. (Adorno, 1969, p. 347)

Lazarsfeld was equally aware of their incompatibility, if less sentient about its root cause. In a sharp-tongued letter he wrote in the summer of 1939, voicing disappointment with their association, Lazarsfeld expressed frustration over Adorno's "grave deficiencies of elementary logical procedure" (cited in Jay, 1973, p. 223). He also criticized Adorno's arrogance and naivete when it came to verification techniques: "your disrespect for possibilities alternative to your own ideas becomes even more disquieting when your text leads to the suspicion that you don't even know how an empirical check upon a hypothetical assumption is to be made" (Jay, 1973, p. 225). On the surface, their differences lie in divergent methodological choices. For Adorno, however, the problem with the positivist approach of hypothesis testing is not just trying to measure things that cannot be measured, but also asking the wrong question altogether. Even more importantly, by only raising questions within the ideological parameters of the status quo and through identifying linear correlations without regard to the totality of history, positivist research ultimately was understood to serve the conservative function of reinforcing the hegemonic political order.

Either deliberately or unconsciously, scholars who identify with positivism often fail to recognize the political implications of epistemological orientation and methodological choice. In his 1941 piece that canonized the label of critical versus administrative research, Lazarsfeld called for the integration of the two perspectives by assigning the role of theorist to the former and that of empiricist to the latter. He proposes that,

> if it were possible in the terms of critical research to formulate an actual research operation which could be integrated with empirical work, the people involved, the problems treated and, in the end, the actual utility of the work would greatly profit. (Lazarsfeld, 1941, p. 14)

Elihu Katz, who, among many other achievements, is famous for working with Lazarsfeld on developing the two-step flow of communication model, expressed a similar sentiment decades later when revisiting the famous debate. Even though Katz and Katz (2016) acknowledge that the rift between Adorno and Lazarsfeld has an ideological dimension, they narrowly interpret the ideological difference as whether "we need to question the ulterior motives of those who posed these questions to researchers and respondents" (Katz & Katz, 2016, p. 8). Katz seems to understand administrative research at face value by referring to the practice of an external funding body setting the agenda for researchers. The real issue for critical scholars, however, is the extent to which researchers have internalized capitalist values through positivist training so that they lose the ability to ask the most important questions.

For scholars who associate more closely with the Frankfurt School tradition, this epistemological tension is always at the forefront even as they advocate for pluralism in research approaches. James Halloran, the longest-serving President of IAMCR, cautioned against "the positivistic/behavioristic blindness" when making a case for critical eclecticism. Halloran's view of critical researchers excludes "those who are not even aware, who are unable to recognize or unwilling to accept that value assumptions are implicit in every research question and that such assumptions enter into the formulation of every research design" (Halloran, 1983, p. 274). George Gerbner, another long-term member of IAMCR who joined the organization in 1967 (Hamelink & Nordenstreng, 2016), readily admits that "the long and checkered history of empiricism certainly produced fractured positivistic fantasies based on real data abstracted from their historical context" (Gerbner, 1983, p. 362). He reminds researchers who aspire to retain criticality not to "surrender authority to some critical mystique based on the assumption that methodological chastity and terminological purity are the best guarantees of truth" (Gerbner, 1983, p. 362). In fact, the whole "Ferments in the Field" special issue published in the *Journal of Communication* in 1983 is organized around the critical versus administrative research debate. In addition to Halloran and Gerbner, many contributors who sided with the critical camp were IAMCR members, including for example,

Armand Mattelart, Cees Hamelink, Jeremy Tunstall, William Melody, Robin Mansell, Dallas Smythe, and Herbert Schiller.

In their co-authored piece for the special issue, Smythe and Van Dinh (1983) singled out Adorno's *The Authoritarian Personality* as a representative case of institutional administrative research, which addresses "institutionally framed problems with either a critical or a seemingly 'neutral' ideological perspective" (p. 121). Funded by a large Jewish organization during the early period of the Cold War, the study led by Adorno found that the leftists (socialists and communists) had attitudes close to the polar opposite of those held by persons high on the "F" (fascist) scale. Smythe points out that by using the scaling technique developed in conventional social psychology, the study is devoid of any historical, institutional analysis of the social process that led to the ascendance of fascism. What is particularly noteworthy is that, while Smythe regards *The Authoritarian Personality* as failing to understand the characters of individuals in relation to the social totality, Lazarsfeld considers it a major success of integrating critical and administrative research, which even prompted his self-criticism for not being able to achieve the same with the Princeton Radio Project (Jay, 1973).

While Smythe's attack on Adorno reflects his general discontent with Western Marxism for what he considered as an overemphasis on ideology and the neglect of the concept of commodification, *The Authoritarian Personality* should be understood in relation to the Frankfurt School's wider program of research into the roots of Fascism. In fact, in the first major study the Institute of Social Research at the University of Frankfurt produced under Horkheimer's directorship, the group explicitly stayed away from "developing a theory of specifically political authority," because to do so would have implied a fetishization of politics as something apart from the social totality. Horkheimer wrote at that time -

> A general definition of authority would be necessarily extremely empty, like all conceptual definitions which attempt to define single moments of social life in a way which encompasses all of history ... General concepts, which form the basis of social theory, can only be understood in their correct meaning in connection with the other general and specific concepts of theory, that is, as moments of a specific theoretical structure. (Cited in Jay, 1973, p. 118)

Even though many scholars made clear that critical media and communication research is neither purely theoretical nor has anything against empirical work per se (e.g., Murdock, 2017) the misconception persists in the field. Youchi Ito, one of the few Asian scholars in the leadership of both IAMCR (International Council Member, 1988–1996) and ICA (Board-member-at-large, 1997–2000), chose the latter as his favorite association, because "My approach is basically empirical. In that sense, ICA suits me better than IAMCR" (Meyen, 2012, p. 1665). Roderick Hart, another ICA fellow and a political communication scholar based at the University of Texas, Austin, when being asked to draw a landscape of communication worldwide, readily admitted that "I just don't know much about people who attend IAMCR. There are more progressive groups in IAMCR and a lot of South American institutions" (Meyen, 2012, p. 1652). Putting these two pieces of comments together, one might wonder whether, from the vantage point of ICA core members, IAMCR is composed of critical scholars who do not care as much about empirical rigor. But as Smythe and Van Dinh (1983) point out, critical and administrative research should be differentiated based on three inter-relating features, "the type of problem selected, the research method employed, the ideological perspective as identified by the researchers' treatment of the results of the analysis as well as the choice of problems and tools" (p. 118). In other words, within the paradigm of critical theory, methodological choice is always a political decision. Positivism excludes the "unspeakable" from the domain of scholarly inquiry by restricting reality to that which could be expressed with established protocols. As a result, the existing order becomes reified through unreflective acceptance of "facts" as well as the separation of data and value.

The Dialectics of Ideology

As a multilayered, hugely complex, and fiercely uncompromising intellectual enterprise, the Frankfurt School defies any form of reductionism and reification. For one thing, there are plenty of debates among its main theorists on many important issues. For another, key figures of the Frankfurt School, including Horkheimer, Adorno, Benjamin, Marcuse, Lowenthal, and so on, engage with Marxist philosophy via a different entry point and with their own analytical focus. Instead of focusing narrowly on whether and how the works of the Frankfurt School are cited in the publications of IAMCR members, I highlight how they offer crucial intellectual resources for envisioning a broad research agenda that examines media and communication as part of a social totality.

The notion of social totality comes from Marx, whose theory of political economy combines historical materialism and dialectical materialism. Critical Theory's conceptualization of social totality is different from orthodox Marxism which emphasizes the centrality of the economic base in the functioning of capitalist society. For Horkheimer and his colleagues at the Institute of Social Research, a cultural phenomenon is not an ideological reflex of class interests. In Adorno's (1983) words,

> the task of criticism must be not so much to search for the particular interest-groups to which cultural phenomena are to be assigned, but rather to decipher the general social tendencies which are expressed in these phenomena and through which the most powerful interests realise themselves. Cultural criticism must become social physiognomy. (p. 30)

In addition, core members of the institute started to engage with psychology and psychoanalysis as early as the 1930s. The first task Horkheimer outlined for the institute under his leadership was a study of workers' and employees' attitudes toward a variety of issues in Germany and the rest of developed Europe. He particularly stressed the role of social psychology in bridging the gap between individual and society (Jay, 1973). Erich Fromm's *Escape from Freedom* is considered one of the founding texts of political psychology. Lowenthal calls mass culture "psychoanalysis in reverse," and Marcuse later wrote the highly influential *One-dimensional Man* (1964) by combining Marxism with Freudian psychoanalysis. These two important points of departure from Marxist political economy, together with the Frankfurt School's consistent emphasis on dialectics and social totality, make Critical Theory particularly generative and capacious in setting the research agenda of an interdisciplinary field.

Perhaps as crucial as the discussion of critical versus administrative research in shaping the contours of our field is the debate between political economy and cultural studies within the subfield of critical media and communications research. These polemic exchanges may have created the impression that the two approaches are incompatible. But a careful reading of the Frankfurt School provides a unique vantage point to view political economy and cultural studies as not only complementary, but also equally indispensable. A founder of the field of political economy of communication, Dallas Smythe once made scathing comments on the Frankfurt School for their lack of attention to the material conditions of the Consciousness Industry (Enzensberger, 1974). In *Dependency Road*, Smythe (1981) disparages previous Marxist scholarship, including that of Gramsci and the Frankfurt School, for being "idealist" and "subjective," because he argued they focus too much on what goes on in people's minds, yet do not pay nearly enough attention to the economic function that the media industries serve in capitalism. It is understandable that Smythe wanted to make the case for political economy by critiquing the Frankfurt School scholars, who, after all, were the principal interlocutors in these debates due to the significant theoretical contributions they made to Marxism.

Moving beyond Smythe's rhetoric, which is partially for the sake of argument, one finds that not only had Marxist political economists such as Henryk Grossman and Friedrich Pollock played a pivotal role in the early decades of the Institute, but so also did Horkheimer include economics as an important part of the interdisciplinary research program he formulated after taking over the directorship in 1930 (Fuchs, 2012). Even on the concept of commodity fetishism, which seems primarily "idealist" and "subjective," Adorno (1983) insists upon a dialectic view by stressing that "the fetish character of commodities is not a fact of consciousness, but dialectic in the eminent sense that it produces consciousness" (p. 85). For him,

> commodity fetishes are not merely the projection of opaque human relations into the world of things. They are also the chimerical deities which originate in the primacy of the exchange process but nevertheless represent something not entirely absorbed in it. (p. 86)

In other words, it is a social reality rather than a psychological reality. In this sense, a political economy of communication is neither rejecting the theoretical premises nor the fundamental concerns of the Frankfurt School. It is extending the inquiries of Critical Theory into new realms.

From the other side of the debate, cultural studies is often the anchor point around which critiques of the Frankfurt School are formulated. As the conventional wisdom goes, by decrying the Culture Industry as instigators of mass deception, the Frankfurt School's view of contemporary media culture is structurally functionalist, pessimistic, and elitist. In contrast, by recognizing the polysemy of media texts and the audience capacity for decoding, cultural studies opens up a space for agency, hope, and progressive social change. Such a simplistic juxtaposition, on the one hand, reduces the Frankfurt School's dialectic and holistic understanding of culture into the single most influential piece by Adorno and Horkheimer (1972), while, on the other hand, it ignores the theoretical tensions among different strands of cultural studies.

Although compared with other associations in the field, IAMCR is most distinct for its commitment to critical political economy, cultural studies has also been part of the agenda. Among the three memorial awards that IAMCR has set up so far, two are named after prominent political economists (Herbert Schiller and Dallas Smythe) and the third is for commemorating the achievements of Stuart Hall, whose relationship with Marxism deserves more thorough consideration than what is currently visible even in the celebration of Hall's work. Despite their obvious disagreement on various fronts, including for example Adorno's and Hall's opposing verdict on Jazz music, and the fact that Hall makes scarce reference to the Frankfurt School even when discussing the problem of ideology, they converge on several important issues as a result of their common affinity with Marxism (see also Chap. 30, 31 and 33 in this collection).

First, studies of aesthetics and ideology should always be situated within historicized materialist premises. Horkheimer made clear that the materialist theory of society that he proposed is predicated on dialectic interactions between the subject and the object, between the material base and the superstructure. But he also expressed aversion to the tendency of vulgar Marxists to "elevate materialism to a theory of knowledge, which claimed absolute certainty the way idealism had in the past" (Jay, 1973, p. 53). Similarly, Hall (1986) is of the view that ideas arise from and reflect the material conditions and circumstances in which they are generated. By the same token, one detects social relations and social contradictions from thoughts emerging at a given historical conjuncture. What he meant by "arise" and "reflect" is not a mechanical correspondence, but a non-linear process fraught with tension and discrepancy. No one would have accused British Cultural Studies of promoting economic reductionism. Significantly though, in his last interview with Sut Jhally in 2012, Hall reserved his warning for those who became detached from the materialist premise, commenting that this is "much more damaging than that in its attempt to move away from economic reductionism, it sort of forgot that there was an economy at all" (Hall, 2012). To do so would mean for cultural studies to lose its political edge.

Second, media industries play a central role in percolating the "common sense" about contemporary capitalist society. The overtly pessimistic tone of *Culture Industry: Enlightenment as Mass Deception* (Adorno & Horkheimer, 1972) often leads to the misconception that the Frankfurt School simply regards commercial media industries as producers of "false consciousness" and that the masses are being duped. In fact, Adorno argues that a dialectical, or "immanent" critique of art, "takes seriously the principle that it is not ideology in itself which is untrue but rather its pretension to correspond to reality." (Adorno, 1983, p. 32) What is less well-known than the unsuccessful Princeton Radio Project is the television research project Adorno directed while at the Hacker Foundation of Beverly Hills, California. In an article published after the completion of this project, Adorno (1954) argues that,

> the psychoanalytic concept of a multi-layered personality has been taken up by cultural industry, but that the concept is used in order to ensnare the consumer as completely as possible and in order to engage him psychodynamically in the service of premeditated effects. (p. 223)

Noticing that George Gerbner was one of the research assistants for this study, one cannot help wondering whether Cultivation Theory was, to a certain extent, Gerbner's attempt to support this argument with systematic empirical data. Further, the incorporation of psychoanalysis by scholars like Marcuse and Fromm opened up new lines of inquiry, which generated nuanced insights into how exactly mass media function as new forms of social control.

Praxis-oriented Social Science Research

Whether it is the repudiation of positivism or an emphasis on social totality, regardless of the analytical focus on either the political economy of communication industries or the media culture of our times, the dialectical imagination that the Frankfurt School fosters is "not mere contemplation but praxis" (Adorno, 1983, p. 150). For the Institute of Social Research, the possibility of transforming social order through human praxis lies in combining philosophy and social analysis, in exposing the incongruence between ideology and material reality, and in critiquing the corrosive power of instrumental rationality in late stage capitalism. The concern over the ideological impact and the political influence of media and communication industries naturally lead to further inquiry into alternative institutional arrangements that could avoid the pitfalls of an advertising-driven and profit-oriented commercial model. For many IAMCR members who conduct research on policy and governance, the writings of Jürgen Habermas not only offered important conceptual tools, but also set out key normative principles toward which an ideal speech environment is oriented.

As an academic association dedicated to critical research on media and communication, IAMCR's orientation toward praxis manifests in scholars' involvement in media activism and policy research (Melody & Mansell, 1983), in raising the consciousness of younger generations through education (Wasko & Wiedemann, 2015) and in preserving—in its comprehensive research agenda—the yearning for and the imagination of another kind of society beyond the status quo.

References

Adorno, T. W. (1954). How to look at television. *The Quarterly of Film Radio and Television, 8*(3), 213–235. https://doi.org/10.2307/1209731

Adorno, T. W. (1969). Scientific experiences of a European scholar in America. In *The intellectual migration* (p. 338–370). Harvard University Press.

Adorno, T. W. (1983). *Prisms.* MIT Press.

Adorno, T. W., & Horkheimer, M. (1972). The culture industry: Enlightenment as mass deception. In J. Cumming (Trans.), *Dialectic of enlightenment* (p. 349–383). Seabury Press.

Enzensberger, H. M. (1974). *The consciousness industry: On literature, politics and the media.* Seabury Press.

Fuchs, C. (2012). Dallas Smythe today—The audience commodity, the digital labour debate, Marxist political economy and critical theory. *TripleC: Communication, Capitalism & Critique. Open Access Journal for a Global Sustainable Information Society, 10*(2), 692–740. Retrieved 15 June 2022, from, https://doi.org/10.31269/triplec.v10i2.443

Gerbner, G. (1983). The importance of being critical—In one's own fashion. *Journal of Communication, 33*(3), 355–362. Retrieved 15 June 2022, from, https://doi.org/10.1111/j.1460-2466.1983.tb02435.x

Hall, S. (1986). The problem of ideology: Marxism without guarantees. *Journal of Communication Inquiry, 10*, 28–44.

Hall, S. (2012). *The last interview: Stuart Hall on the politics of cultural studies.* Retrieved 15 June 2022, from https://www.mediaed.org/transcripts/The-Last-Interview-Transcript.pdf

Halloran, J. (1983). A case for critical eclecticism. *Journal of Communication, 33*(3), 270–278.

Hamelink, C., & Nordenstreng, K. (2016). *Looking at history through the International Association for Media and Communication Research (IAMCR).* Retrieved 15 June 2022, from https://iamcr.org/node/3578

Jay, M. (1973). *The dialectical imagination.* University of California Press. Retrieved 15 June 2022, from https://www.ucpress.edu/book/9780520204232/the-dialectical-imagination

Katz, E., & Katz, R. (2016). Revisiting the origin of the administrative versus critical research debate. *Journal of Information Policy, 6*, 4–12. Retrieved 15 June 2022, from https://doi.org/10.5325/jinfopoli.6.2016.0004

Lazarsfeld, P. F. (1941). Remarks on administrative and critical communications research. *Studies in Philosophy and Social Science, 9*, 2–16.

Lazarsfeld, P. F., & Schramm, W. L. (1954). *The process of effects and mass communication.* University of Illinois Press.

Marcuse, H. (1964). *One-dimensional man: Studies in the ideology of advanced industrial society*. Routledge & Kegan Paul.

Melody, W. H., & Mansell, R. E. (1983). The debate over critical vs. administrative research: Circularity or challenge. *Journal of Communication*, *33*(3), 103–116. Retrieved 15 June 2022, from https://doi.org/10.1111/j.1460-2466.1983.tb02412.x

Meyen, M. (2012). 57 Interviews with ICA Fellows: Table of contents. *International Journal of Communication, 6*, 1451–1886.

Meyen, M. (2014). IAMCR on the East-West battlefield: A study on the GDR's attempts to use the association for diplomatic purposes. *International Journal of Communication, 8*, 2071–2089.

Morrison, D. E. (1978). Kultur and culture: The case of Theodor W. Adorno and Paul F. Lazarsfeld. *Social Research, 45*(2), 331–355.

Mowlana, H. (1997). *A historical perspective*. Retrieved 15 June 2022, from https://iamcr.org/node/2948

Murdock, G. (2017). Critical theory. In K. Y. Yun (Ed.), *The international encyclopedia of intercultural communication* (pp. 1–14). Wiley-Blackwell. Retrieved 15 June 2022, from https://doi.org/10.1002/9781118783665.ieicc0207

Nordenstreng, K. (2008). Institutional networking: The story of the International Association for Media and Communication Research (IAMCR). In D. Park & J. Pooley (Eds.), *The history of media and communication research: Contested memories* (p. 225–248). Peter Lang.

Smythe, D. W. (1981). *Dependency road: Communications, capitalism, consciousness, and Canada*. Ablex Publishing Corporation.

Smythe, D. W., & Van Dinh, T. (1983). On critical and administrative research: A new critical analysis. *Journal of Communication*, *33*(3), 117–127. Retrieved June 15, 2022, from https://doi.org/10.1111/j.1460-2466.1983.tb02413.x

Stevenson, R. L. (1983). A critical look at critical analysis. *Journal of Communication*, *33*(3), 262–269. Retrieved 15 June 2022, from https://doi.org/10.1111/j.1460-2466.1983.tb02427.x

Wasko, J., & Wiedemann, T. (2015). *Janet Wasko: I really do have a lot of questions*. Biografisches Lexikon der Kommunikationswissenschaft. Retrieved 15 June 2022, from http://blexkom.halemverlag.de/iamcr-wasko/

CHAPTER 3

Contested Critique: The Political Career of the Political Economy Section

Graham Murdock and Janet Wasko

Introduction

The idea for a new IAMCR section dedicated to the critical interrogation of the media industries and their relations to the exercise of power and resistance was first discussed in an informal meeting at the 1976 Leicester Conference, developed in subsequent meetings of interested members, and formally approved at the 1978 Warsaw Conference. While various strands of economic analysis have informed contributions to a number of IAMCR sections and initiatives, a general account lies outside the scope of this chapter, which focuses on the Political Economy Section, detailing its formation and development, and the political contexts in which it evolved (Fig. 3.1).[1]

[1] This chapter was partially prepared from a review of available Political Economy Section's programs for past IAMCR conferences, as well as personal recollections by various members who have been active in the Section. For a shorter overview of the Section's history, see Wasko (2013). See also Chap. 2 for discussion of Frankfurt School and Chaps. 30, 31 and 33 on Dallas W. Smythe, Herbert I. Schiller, and Stuart Hall in this collection.

G. Murdock
Loughborough University, Loughborough, UK
e-mail: G.Murdock@lboro.ac.uk

J. Wasko (✉)
University of Oregon, Eugene, OR, USA
e-mail: jwasko@uoregon.edu

© The Author(s), under exclusive license to Springer Nature Switzerland AG 2023

J. Becker, R. Mansell (eds.), *Reflections on the International Association for Media and Communication Research*,
https://doi.org/10.1007/978-3-031-16383-8_3

Fig. 3.1 IAMCR Conference 1982, Paris, Political Economy Section gathering. (Clockwise) Oscar Gandy, Jr. [*no name available*], Noreene Janus, Anna Zornosa, James Miller, Graham Murdock, Karen Paulsell, Janet Wasko, Vincent Mosco, Tim Haight. (Courtesy of IAMCR)

Retrieving Integrative Inquiry

Naming the new IAMCR section "Political Economy" announced a return to the integrative analysis that had directed efforts to characterize Western modernity formed by the consolidation of capitalism and the emergence of nation states and representative government. 1776 saw both—the publication of *The Wealth of Nations*, Adam Smith's enduringly influential defense of minimally regulated markets as the only viable basis for the new economic order, and England's American colonies rejecting monarchical rule and declaring a republic based on popular political participation. This double transformation set an agenda for political economic analysis centered around relations between markets and states, and tensions between corporate ambitions and the public realm, private interests and the common good. Communication systems assumed a central role in debates as both essential infrastructural supports for economic activity and resources for popular participation in social life.

Smith's foundational vision of a market-based system, often now designated as "classical" political economy, was most forcefully countered by Marx's root and branch critique of the structural exploitation, inequalities, and ideological mystifications of a production system rooted in private property and driven by the search for ever-expanding corporate profits. His writings and later commentaries building on his ideas and insights are central to the critical tradition of political economy and have provided departure points, provocations, and theoretical resources for the work developed by section members. At the same time, the impetus to integration has also mobilized critical work in sociology, political philosophy, and a range of other strands of social inquiry, including heterodox currents within economic analysis. This openness stands in marked opposition to the intellectual enclosure that has dominated the academic study of economics.

The rise of the modern university at the turn of the twentieth century saw the study of capitalist society parceled out into distinct disciplines that aspired to the status of sciences. Mainstream analysis of economic life continued to promote "free" markets but was separated from sociology and political science and focused on the "economy" redefined as a relatively self-contained domain of action governed by dynamics that could be expressed in mathematical models claiming to be value free. Political economy's original articulation to moral philosophy and the constitution of the good society was jettisoned, and critical inquiry, inspired by Marx, progressively marginalized within the academy.

The section's retrieval of integrative inquiry has been defined by four core characteristics (Golding & Murdock, 1991). Firstly, it is holistic, approaching capitalism not simply as an economic system, but as a social and cultural formation that aspires to global reach and is marked by multiple inequalities, conflicts, and contradictions. Secondly, it takes the long view, relating contemporary events to fundamental structural changes as they unfold over long loops of time. Thirdly, it defines the "political" in political economy as centrally concerned with the role of government in regulating corporate activity and financing publicly owned and operated utilities and services and with the relations between communication, democracy, and the articulation of popular demands. Fourthly, it reconnects analysis to critical political economy's original relation to moral philosophy. Concepts of justice, equity, care, and the public good are deployed as criteria for evaluating prevailing systems and contributing to movements pressing for change.

Internationalism and Realpolitik

The struggle to establish the section was fundamentally shaped by the tension between IAMCR's declared commitment to creating a genuinely international community of scholarship and practice and the intensifying competition for ideological advantage within a shifting and conflicted global arena. This contest was framed by the wider struggle for control between the declining European imperial powers and the rising power of the US and the Soviet Union. This battle begins in earnest in the inter-war period with new international cultural agencies coming to play a central role.

The 1914–1918 War demonstrated the destructive power of two new sets of weapons: the mechanized slaughter inflicted by armored tanks, aerial bombardment, and improved artillery, and the mass public opinion engineered by the saturation propaganda carried by posters, popular newspapers, and films promoting nationalist and racist stereotypes. The League of Nations was launched in 1920 as an ambitious international initiative to secure a lasting peace based on reducing stockpiles of weaponry and replacing the "nationalistic mentality of the past" with "a general mentality among the peoples of the world more appropriate to cooperation" (Laqua, 2011, p. 224). This aim of "moral disarmament" would be pursued through scholarly exchange, "the meeting of minds," and mentality found a prominent and influential proponent "practical intellectual cooperation" (Laqua, 2011, p. 243) led by a committee of eminent writers, artists, scientists, and intellectuals. At the first meeting of the League's International Commission for Intellectual Cooperation, the eminent French philosopher Henri Bergson declared its unwavering commitment to "the grand ideal of fraternity, of solidarity, of agreement among men [sic]" (Pemberton, 2012, p. 37). These ideals would be promoted and popularized through "meaningful lines of communication with the wider public" (Pemberton, 2012, p. 38) established through concerted press publicity (Nordenstreng & Seppa, 1986) and "research into the role played by radio [and] cinema in encouraging international understanding" (Pemberton, 2012, p. 43). In 1935, the League awarded Walt Disney a special medal for creating Mickey Mouse as "an international symbol of goodwill."

The disengagement from arguments around cultural colonization signaled by this citation pointed to a wider refusal to confront the politics of imperialism and the shifting organization of global order. US President Woodrow Wilson was awarded the Nobel Prize for Peace for his leading role in founding the League but was unable to persuade the US to become a member. Following the Bolshevik victory in the Russian Civil War, the Soviet Union established a rival international association, the Communist International (Comintern) in 1919, dedicated to generalizing the communist revolution. It was disbanded in 1934 and the Soviet Union joined the League but was expelled in 1939 after invading Finland. Without the world's two rising powers, the League's pursuit of cultural internationalism was primarily organized around the interests and conceptions of the established European colonial powers led by France and Britain. The roster of intellectual notables included representatives from India and Latin America, but the underlying definition of culture was securely rooted in Western European understandings.

The League ceased activities with the outbreak of war, but the armistice saw the launch of a new international agency, the United Nations (UN), designed once again to secure a lasting peace. The headquarters were in New York, but the division responsible for education, science, and culture, UNESCO, was located in Paris. Charged with continuing the League's encouragement of "intellectual co-operation, exchange and endeavour" as an essential support for "humanity's capacity to renew itself" after the devastation of global war (Morgan, 2014, p. 53), it adopted many aspects of its predecessor's "organisational model and ethos" (Pemberton, 2012, p. 42). By then, however, the nexus of Western power within the global arena had shifted decisively to the US.

In an event charged with symbolism, in April 1956, following defeat by the North Vietnamese liberation army at Dien Bien Phu two years before, French troops finally left Vietnam marking the end of France's once extensive Indo-Chinese empire. In November, the US dispatched military advisors to train South Vietnamese soldiers, initiating a protracted and rapidly escalating commitment to a war fought under the banner of halting communist incursion. Alongside direct military interventions, the US deployed the global reach of Hollywood and American popular culture to promote a capitalist model of "development" based on minimal state involvement, competing private companies, market choices, and the pleasures of consumerism.

After a brief flirtation with internationalism, the US came to see UNESCO as a useful platform for promoting a pro-capitalist, pro-market consensus (Graham, 2006, p. 231–232), a goal that intensified once the Soviet Union joined in 1954, following Stalin's death the year before.

In April 1957, UNESCO formally recognized the establishment of IAMCR as a new association to encourage international scholarly exchange in communications research and journalism. Fernand Terrou, President of the French Association of Communication Sciences and Director of the French Ministry of Information, was appointed its first president. Despite long-standing traditions of European research and debate on communication, including critical currents rooted in Marxism, the leading post-war centers of empirical research in mass communication were based in the US. And in 1959, Raymond Nixon, professor of journalism at the University of Minnesota, became IAMCR President, a position he held until 1964.

In the spirit of inclusiveness, Nixon visited over 40 countries and claimed to find "workers on both sides of the so-called 'Iron Curtain' eager for 'closer contact'" (Nixon, 1960, p. 228). In Moscow, Yassen Zassoursky, who taught journalism at the city's State University, remembered him being "instrumental" in creating an "atmosphere of trust and mutual respect of the IAMCR" (Meyen & Wiedemann, 2018). At the same time, Nixon made every effort to persuade prominent US communication researchers to join the association. They included Paul Lazarsfeld, director of the Bureau of Applied Social Research at Columbia University, America's premier center of empirical inquiry in mass communications, who served on IAMCR's Executive Committee from 1961 until 1966. Discussion of research in the social sciences was concentrated in the Psychology and Sociology Section headed by Wilbur Schramm, director of the Institute of Communication Research at the University of Illinois and "a zealous Cold Warrior who had been showered with contracts from the State Department, military, and CIA" (Pooley, 2017, p. 9).

Cold War, Intellectual Chill

While a myth has arisen that IAMCR was always a center of critical research, it is clear from its history that this is not the case. As Britain's war-time leader, Winston Churchill noted in 1946 in a phrase that came to define the era, an

"Iron Curtain" had descended on Europe, and by extension the world, separating the Capitalist West from the Communist East. The early years of the association were marked by the politics of the ensuing Cold War organized around the contest for global ascendency between the US, championing "free" market capitalism and the Soviet Union, promoting centralized state management. Command over the organization of communication systems was seen as central to the battle for hearts and minds in the former Western colonies struggling for national independence.

North America

Influential early members of IAMCR vigorously promoted "free" markets as a core ideological support for capitalism and supported interventions to limit critique as a necessary curb on communist influence. At the same time, critical political economists working in American universities were subject to covert surveillance and restricted in what they could publish.

In their hugely influential 1956 book, *Four Theories of the Press*, Schramm and his co-authors presented the liberal promotion of markets as the only viable guarantor of media freedom against the repression of Soviet communism (Siebert et al., 1956). It was an ideological manifesto masquerading as social analysis. As Dallas Smythe observed in an unpublished note at the time, conceptions of freedom and control are never simply matters of abstract doctrine. They are indelibly shaped by "class and power structures" forcing inquiry to ask "*whose* freedom is protected in the service of *what value patterns or policies*, against restraints from *what sources*" (Smythe, 1959, p. 98) (italics in the original).

Smythe was active in IAMCR in the 1970s and served on the Executive Bureau. (His involvement is detailed in Chap. 30 of this collection.) He was an early and enthusiastic supporter of proposals to form a Political Economy Section, but his major influence on members stemmed from his writings, particularly his 1977 article *Communications: Blindspot of Western Marxism* (Smythe, 1977), applying Marx's analysis of commodification to audiences for commercial media. The fact that his long-standing engagement with Marxist theory appeared in print almost 30 years after taking up his first teaching position and that over the decades much of his critical commentary remained unpublished is evidence of the chilling effect of anti-communism.

The search for suspected communists and "fellow travelers" working in American universities, the media, and public service was dubbed "McCarthyism" after the grandstanding performances of Republican Senator Joseph McCarthy, chair of the Senate Permanent Subcommittee on Investigation. The best-known cases, however, were pursued by the House Un-American Activities Committee (HUAC), operating from 1945 to 1975 which McCarthy was never a member of.

After serving as Deputy Chief Economist at the Federal Communications Commission (FCC), Smythe was appointed as a professor at the University of

Illinois in 1948 where he established the first named university course in the political economy of communication (Smythe, 1960). He left the university in 1963 and moved back to Canada. His FBI file, obtained under a Freedom of Information request, confirmed that he had been under almost constant surveillance while there, with Schramm making regular contributions. During Smythe's active involvement in IAMCR, he did propose a new section, but it focused on satellite communication and not political economy.

In October 1957, the Soviet Union successfully launched Sputnik, the first artificial earth satellite, moving the Cold War into space. Sputnik was confined to a low earth orbit, but the possibility of placing communication satellites in the higher geostationary orbit directly above the equator, with transmission footprints covering huge areas of the earth's surface, had been under discussion since the 1940s. As Smythe noted in a paper, they offered the technological potential to "organize the integration of Western culture in space-time in ways which are serviceable" for social development (Smythe, 1962, p. 14).

The first live satellite television broadcast in June 1967 attracted a global audience estimated at between four hundred and seven hundred million, rekindling the prospect of a new era in international cultural exchange and understanding. Smythe's proposal for a new IAMCR section to explore the issues was endorsed at the association's General Assembly in Constance in 1970.

It was soon clear, however, that satellites were part of a broader push for corporate and governmental command over emerging communications technologies. In October 1974, reporting on the section's activities to James Halloran, who had been elected IAMCR president at the 1972 Buenos Aires Conference, Smythe admitted that the initiative had run its course and something more ambitious was needed.

> As a section devoted to appreciating the startling possibilities opened up by communication satellites, it had done its job ... But the "gee whiz" phase of satellites quickly passed. [What is needed now is] analysis of the consequences, implications, and problems created by communications technologies in all its manifestations. (Smythe, 1974)

Following an interim period, the International Council at the 1980 Caracas Conference agreed to rename the section "Communication Technology."

The "marriage of economics and electronics" as the driving force, replacing the old European colonial powers and installing the US at the center of the new global order, also had been a central focus of Herbert Schiller's path-breaking 1969 book, *Mass Communication and American Empire* (Schiller, 1969), which included a preface by Smythe. Schiller had joined the Illinois faculty in 1963 and later assumed responsibility for teaching political economy. Through his writings and riveting public lectures, he was a major influence and inspiration for younger scholars. Elected as IAMCR vice president in 1972, he was a vocal supporter of the proposed Political Economy Section, but never took a leading role in organizing its activities. (See more on Schiller in Chap. 31.)

Schiller's book was greeted by Edward Herman as "a landmark in the post-McCarthyite revival of critical social science research" (Herman, 1970, p. 113). However, hailing a "post-McCarthyite" revival proved overly optimistic. With the Vietnam War escalating, major academic publishers remained wary of critical work and after-serial refusals, Schiller's manuscript eventually found a home with a "small, one-man operation" trading in reprints of classical economics and philosophy texts (Maxwell, 2013, p. 31). Herman and his long-standing collaborator, Noam Chomsky, later published a key contribution to the critical political economy of communications, *Manufacturing Consent: The Political Economy of Mass Media* (Herman & Chomsky, 1988), but had earlier experienced open political censorship themselves. Their 1973 book on US media coverage of conflicts in Indo-China, *Counter Revolutionary Violence: Bloodbaths in Fact and Propaganda* (Chomsky & Herman, 1973), had been abruptly withdrawn by the publisher, Warner Module Publications, a division of the WarnerMedia conglomerate, and the remaining copies pulped.

Europe: Germany

European intellectual life was also strongly marked by opposition to critical inquiry. Split internally between West and East with a wall erected in 1961 bisecting Berlin, Germany was positioned as the continent's "'front line' in the Cold War." Anti-communism played a central role in the country's domestic politics (Graf, 1984, p. 164). In 1977, scholars interested in forming an IAMCR Political Economy Section assembled informally in Paris (at a meeting discussed later in this chapter). Horst Holzer, a key figure in developing the critical political economy of communication in Germany, was invited. He had attended IAMCR's 1974 Leipzig Conference but was unable to come to Paris because he was due to defend the case brought against him under the *Berufsverbot* provision introduced in Germany in 1972, excluding those holding radical views from public service employment. As a member of the German Communist Party, he was barred from his professorship and confined for the rest of his academic career to temporary and insecure positions (Fuchs, 2017). Lacking a solid institutional base and access to funding, he was unable to participate fully in IAMCR, leaving critical German work underrepresented in the Political Economy Section.

With the partial exception of Dieter Prokop, none of the other major contributors to materialist communications inquiry in Germany (Hoffmann, 1983) were active in the section. Prokop had included an early essay by Graham Murdock on corporate ownership and control in his edited collection on media production (Prokop, 1972), the first of three volumes of readings on mass communications research that became standard fixtures on university reading lists; he also presented a paper at IAMCR's 1980 Caracas Conference. But apart from a programmatic essay in *Media Culture and Society* (Prokop, 1983) and a contribution to the Festschrift for Herb Schiller compiled by Jörg Becker and other IAMCR members (Prokop, 1986), few of Prokop's writings were translated and his important work extending the early critical political economy of the Frankfurt School remained unknown to English-speaking readers.

In marked contrast, conservative currents within West German communications research secured a prominent platform within IAMCR. In 1972, Elisabeth Noelle-Neumann, described by one of her critics as "by any standard, one of the most prominent European analysts of mass communication" (Simpson, 1996, p. 150), joined the association's Executive Committee and remained on its successor body, the International Council, until 1981. Since its launch in 1947, the Allensbach Institute, the private research center she founded with her husband, had "served as the primary polling service and public communication advisor for Germany's ruling Christian Democratic Party" (Simpson, 1996, p. 150). Despite her vociferous denials, many of her core preoccupations were continuous with the views she had expressed as a well-regarded journalist and apologist writing for Nazi newspapers, including *Das Reich*, the weekly tabloid launched by Goebbel's propaganda ministry (Simpson, 1996; Becker, 2013).

Commissars and Cosmopolitans

Representation in IAMCR from Central and Eastern Europe gathered momentum in 1968 when the original plan to meet in Oxford fell through, and the Journalism School at the University of Navarra stepped in to host IAMCR's Conference in Pamplona. Franco's Spain was still a fascist dictatorship, but 12 of the 27 foreign conference attendees came from communist countries that had supported the Republican forces in the Spanish Civil War. They had the symbolic satisfaction of seeing flags carrying the hammer and sickle, hastily made by local nuns, flying over the conference venue (Barrera, 2019, p. 426).

The Cold War mentality found a prominent and influential proponent in Emil Dusiška, head of East Germany's only journalism training school, based in Leipzig. Elected IAMCR's secretary general in 1972, a position he held until 1978, he was a practitioner and party functionary, a commissar, not an intellectual. He came from a proletarian rather than a professional family and never attended university. Starting out as a print worker, he became a journalist and in 1955, a member of the party agitation commission responsible for formulating propaganda policy. After 14 months of study at a party think-tank, he was awarded a doctorate and appointed a full professor in 1965.

Until September 1973, when it was finally admitted to the UN, East Germany (officially, the German Democratic Republic or GDR) had been more or less isolated, recognized only by socialist countries and some Arab and African states. Bringing IAMCR's 1974 Conference to Leipzig offered an opportunity "to demonstrate to the world that the GDR was a legitimate and fully competent player in the international arena" (Meyen, 2014, p. 2075). In his conference report to the Communist Party's central committee, Dusiška stressed that in addition to promoting "Marxist-Leninist views" and publications on the mass media and "addressing bourgeois theories of the press and information freedom," the meeting aimed to provide "the opportunity for young Marxist-Leninist and Leftist academics from capitalist European countries to criticize the capitalist system" (Meyen, 2014, p. 2079). In language with strong echoes of Lenin's 1920 pamphlet, *Left Wing Communism: An Infantile Disorder*, attacking eminent Marxists who failed to follow the party line, Dusiška dismissed Dallas Smythe as a "left wing radical" and presented young Western Marxists as unrealistic and unreliable idealists. Their promotion of Marxism, however, made them useful idiots, a judgment summed up in his favorite saying reported by Zassoursky: "In the West, the blind educate the naïve" (Meyen & Wiedemann, 2018).

The absence of an official IAMCR journal as a shop window for the range of research and theorizing conducted by members had been a bone of contention within the association for some time. George Gerbner, a University of Pennsylvania professor, originally from Hungary and active in IAMCR for a number of years (see also chapter 29 in this collection), had offered the newly launched *Journal of Communication*, but the proposal was turned down as likely to be viewed as too close to US interests. Dusiška, seeing an opportunity, offered to launch a journal based and edited from Leipzig, but was rebuffed. Elsewhere within the Soviet sphere of influence, however, there was support for more open exchange and dialog.

In his memoir included in this volume, Slavko Splichal recounts his surprise at being detained and thoroughly searched at the East German border while driving to the Leipzig IAMCR Conference. Coming from Slovenia, then part of the Socialist Federal Republic of Yugoslavia, he was used to visa-free travel to Austria and Italy and an intellectual milieu at the University of Ljubljana that was strongly influenced by Western scholarship, including critical research. Dallas Smythe had lectured in his department.

If Slovenia was among the most open countries in Central and East Europe, East Germany was arguably the most closed, with an estimated 90,000 employees working for the State Security Services (the Stasi), supported by over 100,000 unofficial informants primed to report on ideological backsliding among colleagues and neighbors. In the remaining territories, the balance varied over time.

In February 1956, Nikita Krushchev had denounced Stalin's crimes and repressions in a coruscating speech to a closed session of the 20th Congress of the Soviet Communist Party. Once confirmed as party secretary, he embarked on a reformist program of peaceful coexistence with the West, opening the domestic market to selected Western films, books, and cultural collaborations. In July 1959, the American National Exhibition opened in Moscow as a showcase for consumer lifestyles. Two months later, Krushchev became the first Soviet leader to visit the US, spending time at the Twentieth Century Fox studios in Los Angeles and exploding with anger when a scheduled trip to Disneyland was canceled on security grounds. This "thaw" in relations ended in 1966 when an amendment to the Russian Criminal Code was introduced banning the preparation and circulation of any material "discrediting the Soviet state and social system."

Cosmopolitanism was not entirely eradicated, however. The Central and East European attendees at the Pamplona IAMCR Conference were headed by Yassen Zassoursky, by then Dean of Moscow State University's Journalism School (Meyen, 2014, p. 2078). Zassoursky was a scholar and internationalist, who reluctantly accepted the deanship at the urging of colleagues, anxious that the position be filled by a teacher and researcher rather than a party functionary. He came from a solidly professional family. His father was an engineer and his mother a physician. In 1939, his father had visited the US and his letters home from New York aroused his young son's interest, reinforcing his later decision to focus his academic studies on twentieth-century American literature. He knew a number of American authors personally and after joining IAMCR formed a strong personal friendship with Herbert Schiller, whom he regarded as "very knowledgeable in international problems" with a nuanced understanding of Cold War politics from his time serving with the American Administration in Berlin, immediately after the War. Zassoursky's election as an IAMCR vice president at Pamplona gave him a platform at the center of the association.

His cosmopolitan outlook, knowledge of US culture, and familiarity with foreign journalism, which he taught in Moscow, led him to see his main task as contributing to building a transnational professional community of mass communication scholars and teachers of journalism, dedicated to principled inquiry into issues of common concern, detached, as far as possible, from immediate political agendas. As Zassoursky told an interviewer, looking back on his time in IAMCR, "I really tried to stop the Cold War mentality and I'm against it even now. I was never supportive of any confrontational tactics and activities" (Meyen & Wiedemann, 2018; also see Chap. 19 in this volume.)

Elsewhere in Central and Eastern Europe, Krushchev's condemnation of Stalin had permanently undermined "faith in the party's collective infallibility, political wisdom and moral integrity" and fueled the "search for alternatives to official policies and, for some, alternatives to the political system and its ideology" (Bociurkiw, 1970, p. 74). Reformist movements led to open confrontation with Moscow in Hungary in 1956 and Czechoslovakia in 1968, but dissent remained mostly behind closed doors. As Robin Cheesman, the first Chair of the Political Economy Section, recalled, as a visiting scholar at the Hungarian Institute for Public Opinion Research in Budapest, it was only in "small seminars and meetings" in the private office of the Director, Tamás Szecskö, that "ideological ruptures appeared and were admitted" (Cheesman, 2019).

Old and New Lefts

Critical political economy was still an underdeveloped field in Western Europe in 1968 but was gathering momentum. During the early 1970s, the rediscovery of Marx and Western Marxism gave new impetus to critique. Media dismissals of opposition movements around the war in Vietnam, trade union militancy, feminism, and anti-racism promoted renewed scrutiny of the control over public culture exercised by the major commercial operators. Proposals for alternatives proliferated but were often in tension and opposition to the mainstream policies of the major Left parties.

In August 1968, Russian troops invaded Czechoslovakia and removed the reforming government of Alexander Dubček. Images of Soviet tanks once again in a major East European city revived memories of November 1956, when Russian troops had moved to suppress the reformist Hungarian government of Imre Nagy, occupying the center of Budapest. The ensuing armed resistance left 2500 Hungarians dead and 20,000 injured; Nagy was arrested and executed.

The brutal intervention in Hungary prompted mass resignations from Western communist parties allied to Moscow and drew younger activists and intellectuals toward emerging social movements. As Stuart Hall who went on to play a central role in the development of British cultural studies (detailed in Chap. 33 of this book) recalled: "Hungary had fractured the old politics… Out of this emerged our 'between/against both camps' position and the hope for the creation of an independent popular left politics" (Hall, 2018, p. 228). *New Left Review*, launched in 1960 under Hall's editorship, gave this project a name and a platform.

Military intervention against Dubček prompted a second break with Moscow by Western Communists. Some hoped to reform parties from within, drawing on the democratic socialist traditions promoted by the emerging Eurocommunist movement. During his research leave in Budapest in 1984, Cheesman recalled the tensions:

> At this time I defined myself as a "euro-communist." I joined the Danish communist party (DKP) in spite of its close ties to USSR. I wrongly assumed that things would soon change. While in Budapest I was asked by the party daily if I would write an article on the media situation in Hungary. I did so and mentioned the "communication between the lines" and the [plethora] of *samizdat* publications. The article was refused as I refused to "correct my errors." A few months later I left the party. (Cheesman, 2020)

Others on the Left campaigned for change through the trade union movement and the radical wings of the major socialist and Labour parties. Nicholas Garnham, a founding member of the Political Economy Section, had been a program producer at the BBC and actively involved with both the *Report on Nationalising the British Film Industry*, published by the main film and television union, and *The People and the Media* manifesto, issued by a radical group within the British Labour Party (Garnham, 2005, p. 473). Others were active within the new social movements. In the US, Vincent Mosco, later to chair the Political Economy Section, was a committed supporter of civil rights, student activist, and conscientious objector to the war in Vietnam (Tracy, 2006).

These various oppositional strands were grouped together under the umbrella of the New Left. Theoretically, they drew on a range of intellectual sources, but Marx and Marxism played an important role. As Dallas Smythe later noted:

> Political economy by reason of its long, consistent history stands at the cutting edge of critical theory. Is it necessary to be a political economist to be a critical theorist? My answer is, no, but it helps. .... By the same token, it is not necessary to be a Marxist political economist in order to work with critical theory, but it helps. (Smythe, 1984, p. 211)

Rereading Marx, Rediscovering Critique

Vincent Mosco remembers being introduced to Marx and Engels' *The German Ideology* by a fellow undergraduate student and thinking it "was one of the most profound works I had ever encountered." As a postgraduate at Harvard, taking Daniel Bell's course on Marxism, he was surrounded by classmates "keenly eager to pursue a Marxian analysis of society" (Tracy, 2006, p. 10).

Between 1973 and 1976, Penguin Books published a series of new authoritative translations of Marx's key works, including his 1857 notebook, the *Grundrisse*, previously virtually unknown to English language readers. The ensuing revival of interest prompted a more open engagement with his central arguments. His core insights remained central to critique, but as starting points and provocations to be read as Stuart Hall later noted "without guarantees" and always in relation to changing circumstances (Hall, 1983).

These circumstances were dominated by the disappearing prospects for radical change promised by the "events" of May 1968 in Paris, which had seen student occupations of campuses and public buildings and a general workers' strike met by violent confrontations with the paramilitary police. Within weeks, the conservative President General Charles de Gaulle, who had briefly left the country at the height of the clashes, was returned to power in a landslide election. This restoration promoted renewed interest in the generation of Marxists who had witnessed the great reversal that followed World War I, with the defeat of short-lived communist insurgencies in Germany and Hungary, and the rise of fascism.

An essay on the "Culture Industry" written by the leading members of the Frankfurt Institute for Social Research, Max Horkheimer and Theodor Adorno (exiled in California) and published in English for the first time in 1973, was particularly influential (Horkheimer & Adorno, 1973). Their central argument—that the drive to minimize risks and maximize profit pushed commercial production toward a reliance on styles and formats with proven market appeal that reproduced prevailing values and viewpoints—offered a useful starting point for a renewal of critical inquiry into the relations between economic dynamics, production processes, and ideological reproduction. However, this emphasis was not universally welcomed.

In his seminal "Blindspot" essay, Dallas Smythe argued that Western Marxism's focus on ideology ignored the defining role of commercial media in assembling audiences as commodities for sale to advertisers and setting them to work learning "to buy particular 'brands' of consumer goods" and "simultaneously reproducing their own labour power" (Smythe, 1977, p. 6). Like the free salted peanuts provided in cocktail bars to encourage patrons to order more drinks, Smythe presented commercial media content as an inducement for audiences to stay around and view the ads in a receptive mood.

As Graham Murdock argued in response, this characterization of commercial television's political economy ignores two key points (Murdock, 1978). Firstly, it does not apply to public service media funded from taxation, where relations with the state and government are central to any analysis. Secondly, as Smythe conceded, to say that commercial programming is a "free lunch" offered as an inducement "is not to obscure the agenda-setting function of the 'editorial' content" (Smythe, 1977, p. 5). It was the connections between levels of economic organization and systems of signification and ideology that many members of the Political Economy Section set out to unpack.

In Paris, American-born Seth Siegelaub, a major figure in the conceptual art movement, was assembling an archive of books, manuscripts, and artifacts to support this project. It included a wide range of Marxist and socialist writings from Europe and the US, together with posters and even a cobblestone from the 1968 student demonstrations (Gotz, 2016, p. 478). In 1973, Siegelaub launched the International Mass Media Research Center, located in his house in Bagnolet (a communist stronghold on the outskirts of Paris) and open to anyone. Those interested but unable to visit could search for relevant sources in the bibliographic guides published under the title, *Marxism and the Mass Media: Towards a Basic Bibliography* (IMMRC, 1980). Selected readings were later collected in two volumes as *Communication and Class Struggle* (1979 and 1983), jointly edited with Armand Mattelart and published by International General (IG), Siegelaub's independent press. IG had earlier published the English translation of Mattelart's hugely influential dissection of imperialist ideology in Disney comics, *How to Read Donald Duck* (1975), written jointly with Ariel Dorfman. Banned in Chile after the right-wing coup, it had been turned down by major English language publishing houses.

New Centers, New Research

As noted earlier, until the late 1960s, the critical political economy of communication was confined to the margins of American academia, developed by scattered practitioners led by Dallas Smythe and Herbert Schiller, for whom IAMCR provided an intellectual home. Marginality was even more pronounced in Britain, where there were no university degree programs in communications and no stable research hubs.

In 1966, Leicester University agreed to support a research program in communications proposed by James Halloran, who had been teaching in the adult education department. Housed in a new Centre for Mass Communication Research (CMCR), it set out to examine the social processes of communication from production to reception. The planned mass march in London against the Vietnam War in October 1968 offered an opportunity to investigate the production of news, the main source of public information on contentious events. The resulting study, *Demonstrations and Communication*, based on ethnographic observations in the newsrooms of major national newspapers and broadcasting organizations, detailed how coverage of an overwhelmingly peaceful expression of mass opinion was dominated by images of atypical violent confrontations with police, shifting attention away from arguments against the war and delegitimizing direct political action (Halloran et al., 1970).

The study inevitably raised wider questions about the role of media concentration, press ownership, commercialism, and the relations between broadcasters and the state, in shaping dominant accounts. These issues were taken up by Graham Murdock, one of the researchers on the study, in a paper written jointly with Peter Golding, who had joined the Leicester Centre to work on a comparative transnational study of news production. The essay *For a Political Economy of Mass Communication* (Murdock & Golding, 1974) appeared in the annual *Socialist Register*, co-edited by one of Britain's leading Marxists, Ralph Miliband. It launched critical political economy as a strand within the Leicester Centre's research portfolio.

In the same year, Nicholas Garnham became Head of the newly created Department of Communication at the Polytechnic of Central London (later to become the University of Westminster), launching the first named British degree in Media Studies in 1975. He built on his previous critical work as a union activist and commentator on communications policy to revisit Marx in a programmatic essay, later published as *Contribution to a Political Economy of Mass Communication* (Garnham, 1979).

Meanwhile, in Smythe and Schiller's former program at Illinois, Smythe's one-time student, Thomas Guback, who had presented a paper at the Leipzig Conference on the economic and political aspects of the American film industry, was attracting a group of graduate students working within the political economy tradition. Inspired by Guback's IAMCR participation, some of these students began attending the association's conferences. They included Janet Wasko, later chair of the Political Economy Section. As she recalled, meeting with British, European, and (a few) Latin American scholars working within different intellectual and media environments to the formative figures in the US was "very influential" in confirming the reach and relevance of critical political economy's concerns and approach (Prodnik & Wasko, 2014, p. 15).

Contested Terrain: Forming the Section

On Kaarle Nordenstreng's initiative, an informal meeting was convened during the 1976 Leicester Conference to explore the possibility of forming a "special interest group" in political economy. The meeting attracted 27 participants, bringing together critical researchers from Britain, the US, Western Europe, and the Eastern bloc, including Yassen Zassoursky and Emil Dusiška. There was a lively discussion over possible names for the group. Roque Faraone, originally a lawyer in Uruguay forced to leave in 1973 following the US-backed military coup and working at the time in Paris as a correspondent for Agence France Presse, suggested "Marxist Communication Theory." This was strongly opposed by Dusiška who argued that it would antagonize conservative IAMCR members and make establishing the group impossible. Eventually, "Materialist Communication Theory" was agreed on as a working title, although this still carried strong associations with Marxism (Hoffmann, 1983).

Writing afterwards to Dallas Smythe, who was unable to attend the conference, Nordenstreng reported that "One of Leicester's positive items was a get-together of Marxist scholars ... not a prepared meeting ... but still a good start. There is a nucleus generating quite weighty stuff." He asked if Smythe was interested "in contributing to such an enterprise" and invited him to circulate the draft of his "Blindspot" paper, adding that "my own participation in the circumstances will be limited to acting as an agent only" (Nordenstreng, 1976).

Nordenstreng had been elected president of the International Organization of Journalists (IOJ) in 1976, a position he held until 1990. Originally launched in Copenhagen in 1946 as a comprehensive world association of journalists, as the Cold War intensified, journalists allied to the West broke away in 1952 to form the International Federation of Journalists and the IOJ (based in Prague) came under the direction of the Central Committee of the Czechoslovak Communist Party. Recruiting journalists in newly independent states, opposing US global power, and fostering criticism of the distortions of communications under capitalism were central to its remit (Nordenstreng, 2020).

As previously noted, the initial Leicester meeting revealed a solid base of support for a political economy group and a follow-up meeting was arranged for March 1977 in Paris, organized jointly by Robin Cheesman and Fernando Perrone. Twelve people, all paying their own way, attended, including Nicholas Garnham and Graham Murdock from Britain, Janet Wasko from the Illinois group, and Roque Faraone, Josiane Jouet, and Seth Siegelaub, based in Paris. Cheesman agreed to assume responsibility for organizing future meetings and Murdock took on the role of secretary. Writing to Nordenstreng and Zassoursky, Cheesman reported that participants saw the meeting as "very positive because we really felt a common need to continue and because we could see some promising perspectives" (Cheesman, 1977). They agreed to apply "to be constituted as a section" within IAMCR but emphasized that "the group will not remain limited to the 'West'."

The problems of including members from the East were underlined by the absence of Lothar Bisky from the GDR. Bisky had attended the initial meeting in Leicester and been invited to Paris. His 1974 survey of the dominant tendencies in Western mass communications research converged at key points with work being developed by critical researchers in Europe and North America (Bisky, 1974). Replying to Cheesman's invitation however, he regretfully noted that "unfortunately I have no possibility to support the work of the 'Materialist Theory Group'" (Bisky, 1977). The phrase "no possibility" points to a major schism.

The son of refugees from Polish Pomerania, Bisky grew up in West Germany, but his experience of discrimination persuaded him, at the age of 18, to cross into East Germany. He entered the free university system, majoring in media and culture and secured a teaching position at Leipzig. He became a member of the official Socialist Unity Party (SED) in 1963 but was never entirely trusted. Working under Dusiška, a Party hard-liner, hostile to "scholars with broader world views" (Meyen & Wiedemann, 2018), he was denied the promotion that his abilities merited. His commitment to expressive diversity found practical expression in his later role as Rector of the Babelsberg Film and Television Academy in Potsdam (from 1986–1990), where he supported students in their battles against censorship.

Recognizing the restrictions imposed on East European scholars wanting to attend conferences in the West led the Paris planning meeting for the Political Economy Section to propose that future meetings "should preferably be held in a socialist country" (Cheesman, 1977). This did not address the problem of political surveillance, however. Formal presentations by Eastern European scholars were rigorously vetted in advance for "correctness" and candid "off the record" conversations were only possible in situations of mutual trust. But suspicions that someone may be reporting on conversations were never entirely banished. Later, CIA inspections of the files of the East German secret police, the Stasi, suggest that Bisky had been an informer. He denied this, but admitted communicating with the intelligence services, arguing "that in his position he had no choice" (Hockenos, 2011).

Bisky's politics were on open display on 4 November 1989, when he joined the crowd on Berlin's Alexanderplatz and read a statement calling for the radical renewal of the GDR as a democratic socialist state. It marked his move from scholar to politician. Following the dismantling of the Berlin Wall and the purge of hard-liners, he chaired the successor to the SED, the Party of Democratic Socialism, served in the Brandenberg Parliament, and later led the Left Party coalition in the European Parliament.

Following the Paris meeting, Nordenstreng met informally with Cheesman and Perrone in November 1977, during a symposium on "Mass Communication and Structures of Peace" in Finland and announced that it was possible to finance a meeting of the group in Prague, providing participants covered their own travel expenses. Cheesman agreed to contact selected group members to discover who might be interested and able to attend. In January 1978, Nordenstreng received confirmation from the Czech union of journalists that his request for support had been approved. The union would fully fund a four- to five-day meeting of up to 15 group members in their boarding center, Castel Rostez, 60 kilometers outside Prague.

The meeting, held between the 17 and 22 April 1978, was attended by Kaarle Nordenstreng and group members from earlier meetings, including

Garnham, Faraone, and Jan Eckecrantz (Sweden). They were joined by Giuseppe Richeri, who had written to Cheesman volunteering to be the contact for the group in Italy and offering the newly launched journal, *IKON*, as a publication outlet. Guback, Murdock, and Schiller were invited, but unable to attend. Discussion focused on organizing the group's presentations for the forthcoming IAMCR Conference in Warsaw in September.

The week before, however, IAMCR's International Council at its meeting in Leipzig had invited Tamás Szecskö to "take the necessary initiatives" to explore "possibilities with a view to establishing" a new section "in Economics" (IAMCR, 1978a, p. 5). Labeling the envisioned section "Economics" suggested a move on the part of conservative IAMCR members to pre-empt the Materialist Group from achieving section status.

At the Warsaw Conference, group participation was listed in the official program as organized jointly by the "Materialist theory of communication" and "The economics of mass media communications," under the co-supervision of Robin Cheesman and Tamás Szecskö (IAMCR, 1978b, p. 20). Members presented 12 papers attracting substantial audiences. A total of 54 people crowded into the session based on papers by Garnham and Smythe, outlining their conceptions of political economy's core concerns. As Cheesman later recalled, writing to section members in 1980, "We were not really prepared for such a large public" (Cheesman, 1980).

The unexpected level of interest confirmed the group's earlier decision to seek section status. To pre-empt expected opposition, the proposed name was changed from "Materialist Theory" to "Political Economy." Recognizing the politics underpinning Szecskö's brief from the International Council, the section's aims were described in deliberately general terms as improving "theoretical analysis of the economics of mass communications production, distribution and consumption" and developing "the empirical study of the economic structure and development of mass communications institutions."

Nevertheless, James Halloran, the association's President at the time, was less than enthusiastic. His politics were solidly Labour but centrist, favoring pragmatism and distrusting theory. His "disrespectful remarks about Marxist contributions" at the Leipzig Conference had been noticed and noted in Emil Dusiška's report to the East German Communist Party (Meyen, 2014, p. 2079). Conservative IAMCR members were even more strongly opposed. During the Warsaw Conference, Dusiška met privately with two prominent West German members of the International Council, Martin Löffler and Otto Roegele, both of whom he had earlier classified as "pronounced anti-communists," to persuade them to withdraw their objections. He was successful and after a lengthy discussion in the international council meeting, the proposal was finally approved and then ratified by the association's General Assembly. Robin Cheesman and Tamás Szecskö were confirmed as joint Section Heads.

Gaining Ground: Expanding Networks, Increasing Visibility

The section's launch coincided with other developments, giving critical political economy more prominence within Anglo-American academia. During the late 1970s, a group of graduate students from Stanford University (including Oscar Gandy, Noreene Janus, Timothy Haight, and others) organized a number of critical communications conferences on the West coast. Around the same time at Illinois, Guback supported a group of graduate students (including Martin Allor, Sara Douglas, Fred Fejes, Eileen Meehan, Jennifer Slack, and Janet Wasko), who launched *Communication Perspectives*, a newsletter started in 1978 to explore ideas and activities related to critical communication research. And, in March 1979, this group organized a small informal gathering in Illinois to discuss critical theories and methods, which was attended by Dallas Smythe and Vincent Mosco.

Representatives from these two groups met periodically over the next two years, resulting in the launch of the Union for Democratic Communication (UDC) in Philadelphia in 1981. The UDC provided a forum for discussing emerging research in critical communication and a base from which to build bridges with media workers, media producers, policy makers, and grassroots communications activists (Bettig & Heresco, 2013). At the UDC's annual conference in San Diego in 1990, Schiller was presented with a Lifetime Achievement Award in recognition of his pioneering contribution to reinvigorating critical political economy. In 1992, following Smythe's death, the award was named after him.

Mosco and Wasko (1983) had already introduced American readers to European work in political economy through the annual book series they edited under the title *The Critical Communications Review*. The second volume, *Changing Patterns of Communications Control* (1984), carried contributions from Smythe and Schiller, alongside essays from younger US scholars, including Noreene Janus and Manjunath Pendakar (who later chaired the IAMCR section), and Western European writers active in the section, including Giovanni Cesareo and Graham Murdock (Mosco & Wasko, 1984).

Work in the critical political economy of communications was also gaining greater visibility through the publications associated with the "Mass Communication and Society" course offered between 1977 and 1983 by the British Open University's part-time degree program. The pedagogic strategy of the course actively encouraged students "to follow the history of debates between Marxists and liberal pluralists over the media," opening a space for engagement with critical political economy's concerns (Gurevitch et al., 1982). Murdock contributed a core module on corporate ownership and media power (Murdock, 1982) and, together with Peter Golding, the opening essay in the official course reader, outlining critical political economy's distinctive approach (Murdock & Golding, 1977). "Like other Open University texts [it] was available to students and academics outside the Open University," and over the next decade, was reprinted nine times reaching "an audience far wider than …initially intended" (Curran & Gurevitch, 1991, p. 7).

Political economy perspectives were also reaching a wider readership through the journal, *Media, Culture and Society* (MCS), launched in 1979 under Nicholas Garnham's editorship and frequently carrying translations of leading European work. Between 1987 and 1996, over a quarter of the contributions to MCS (25.8%) could be classified as critical, rising to almost a third (32.7%) in the years between 2007–2016, with issues around political economy providing the dominant strand. In contrast, critical perspectives were still largely absent from major US-based journals (Splichal & Mance, 2018).

Patterns of Participation: Geographies and Histories

Venue choices for IAMCR conferences inevitably imposed constraints on section participation, excluding members without access to institutional funding for travel and conference attendance. One consequence was a persistent overrepresentation of papers from scholars from relatively well-resourced universities in the Northern Hemisphere and Australasia. Despite strong traditions of critical inquiry, contributions from France and Germany also remained underrepresented.

One of the most influential early contributions to the development of critical political economy came from Bernard Miège and his co-researchers at Grenoble University, who produced a novel classification of media industries based on their rhythms of production, labor processes, and income streams (Miège, 1987; Flichy, 1980a). Their contrast between the logics of "publishing" typified by novel writing and "flow" represented by daily news production was widely adopted and deployed (Fitzgerald, 2012). An English translation of Miège's essays was published in English by Seth Siegelaub's International General press as *The Capitalization of Cultural Production* (Miège, 1989) and he periodically presented at IAMCR conferences. Neither he nor his colleagues were regular attendees, partly because sessions were normally conducted in English, but also pointing to a degree of national self-enclosure. As Patrice Flichy noted, while there is "a certain similarity between some of the work being carried out …French researchers have few contacts with their Anglo-Saxon equivalents" (Flichy, 1980b, p. 187).

Outside North America and North Europe, the most consistent contributions to the section came from Latin American scholars. Participation was facilitated by the Latin American Communication Research Association (ALAIC) and boosted when IAMCR conferences were located in Spanish- and Portuguese-speaking venues. The 2002 Barcelona Conference included papers on developments in Mexico, Argentina, Venezuela, and Chile, and a major re-reading of Marx's work on intellectual labor from Brazil's leading critical political economist, César Bolaño.

Political economy enjoyed a prominent position within Latin American communication studies, generating a rapidly growing corpus of work (Bolaño et al., 2012). Researchers engaged with formative North American and European theorizing, while measuring their distance from it, lodging reservations and critiques, and insisting on the need to develop a distinctive Latin American approach grounded in the region's particular political and intellectual histories (Bolaño, 2014; Califano, 2021).

Critical Political Economy and Critical Sociology

IAMCR's Political Economy Section entered an intellectual field where critical perspectives were steadily gaining ground elsewhere in the social sciences, particularly within sociology. On the one hand, these interventions offered frameworks for analysis. In his widely used summative text, *The Political Economy of Communication* (1996), Vincent Mosco, a former Chair of the section, drew on his sociological training to organize his presentation around the concepts of structuration and spatialization, alongside the core Marxist emphasis on commodification. On the other hand, critical engagement with communications within sociology's major professional associations generated alternative claims on time and commitment. Some IAMCR members moved between both spheres. In 1974, Tamás Szecskö was elected to the board of the International Sociological Association's (ISA) Research Committee on Mass Communication. In 1978, the year the Political Economy Section was formally approved, he became the committee's vice president. Nicholas Garnham and Slavko Splichal both served on the ISA Media Committee between 1990 and 1994.

For others, ISA became the primary international intellectual arena. Lothar Bisky and Dieter Prokop were elected to the ISA board in 1978. Bisky remained a board member until 1990, Sociology's less immediately politically contested intellectual profile offered him a more flexible operating space than the Political Economy Section. Prokop launched a Working Group on international media concentration and co-directed a sociology of cinema group, an area with no specifically designated intellectual home within IAMCR (International Sociological Association, 2022).

In 1995, a new division was launched within the European Sociological Association to provide "a platform for critical research and debate on questions of power, inequality, identity and social change in increasingly mediatized societies" (European Sociological Association, 2022). Headed by Peter Golding until 2008, it regularly featured work in critical political economy, but most members were not regular attendees at IAMCR conferences.

Critical Political Economy and Cultural Studies

Critical political economy's emergence as a legitimate area of research also coincided with the growth of cultural studies. As Stuart Hall recalled in his final interview: "what cultural studies was trying to do was to understand the ensemble of relations between the economic, the political, the cultural, the ideological, and the social" (Jhally, 2016, p. 7).

Developing an integrated and holistic analysis was also central to critical political economy, but the competition for resources and status within the academy led some advocates of cultural studies to present the two approaches as antagonistic and mutually exclusive rather than complementary. This opposition was typified by the exchange between James Lull and Vincent Mosco at the IAMCR Seoul Conference in 1994. Drawing on his ethnographic work in China, Lull insisted that audience responses are always actively constructed and "cannot be controlled by social forces from right or left" and that "this theoretical assertion stands in contrast to the (imperialistic!) universalist pretenses of conventional political-economic theory" (Lull, 1994). In reply, Mosco (1994) pointed out that the "political economy critique is not about whether audiences are active. They are." But he insisted that "this activity cannot be fully understood without analysing the economic forces determining the distribution of material, social and symbolic resources for interpretation and response." Unpacking these relations had been central to the work on youth subcultures conducted at the Centre for Contemporary Cultural Studies at Birmingham University under Hall's direction. Published as *Resistance Through Rituals*, with an invited contribution by Murdock, it became one of cultural studies' key texts (Hall & Jefferson, 1975).

The Seoul debate led to a round table at the Sydney Conference in 1996, sponsored jointly by the Political Economy Section and the Network for Qualitative Audience Research, and to a collection, *Consuming Audiences?* edited by Ingunn Hagen and Janet Wasko (2000), exploring relations between political economy, ethnography, and audience research.

The wider disagreement over critical political economy's contribution to communications and cultural research was on full display in an ill-tempered exchange in 1995 between Nicholas Garnham and Larry Grossberg, who had spent time at the Birmingham Centre and taken a leading role in promoting cultural studies in the US (Garnham, 1995; Grossberg, 1995). Grossberg dismissed Garnham's reading of Marxism as overly reliant on a simplistic concept of economic determination that reduced the production process to "the institutional contexts of capitalist manufacturing." This was a misrepresentation. As Garnham later noted, his early career as a film critic and television program maker had made him "very conscious that the intentions of authors and producers" mattered but were shaped in crucial ways by "social determinants and transformed in the material labour of production itself" (Garnham, 2005, p. 473).

This revisionist conception of determination was developed in an influential intervention by Raymond Williams, one of the central figures in defining British cultural studies, and the subject of one of Garnham's television documentaries. In William's formulation "the reality of determination is the setting of limits and the exertion of pressures, within which variable social practices are profoundly affected but never necessarily controlled" (Williams, 1974, p. 130). As Stuart Hall noted, the pressure exerted by "the structure of ownership and control," while -

> not a sufficient explanation of the way the ideological universe is structured, ... is a necessary starting point. It gives the whole machinery of representation its fundamental orientation in the value-system of property and profit. It prevents new kinds of grouping, new social purposes and new forms of control from entering in a central way, into the production of culture. (Hall, 1986, p. 11)

In his dispute with Garnham, Grossberg claimed that "cultural studies is returning to questions of economics in important and interesting ways" (Grossberg, 1995, p. 80). A decade later, Stuart Hall saw little evidence of this and lamented the retreat from the original integrative project. As he noted in his last interview:

> ...in its attempt to move away from economic reductionism, [cultural studies] sort of forgot that there was an economy at all. You have to look at the articulation between culture and...economic interests. (Jhally, 2016)

Political Economy and Cultural Production

The articulations between culture and the economic interests are negotiated and struggled over within concrete sites of production. It is in the newsrooms, studios, and agents' offices that the general relations between capital and labor are translated into decisions over whose voices to relay and which information, imagery, and narratives to privilege. Studies of labor processes in specific sites of production or sectors of employment are essential to demonstrating how the logics and strategies of "larger level operations" shape the contours of public culture. Critical political economy's commitment to a comprehensive and integrated interrogation of communications under capitalism requires both. Detailed empirical research on production, however, remained a blank space in Hall's own work and in much of cultural studies more generally.

This neglect is now being addressed. Policy promotion of the "creative" and "cultural" industries as generators of growth and employment in post-industrial capitalism has prompted a flurry of academic entrepreneurship, presenting production studies as a new area of research. This call is often bolstered by claims that critical political economy has failed to address it. The proposal for a new field of "Critical Media Industries Studies" advanced by Timothy Havens and his colleagues is typical in arguing that critical political economists predominantly and consistently -

> focus on the larger level operations of media institutions, general inattention to entertainment programming, and incomplete explanation of the role of human agents (other than those at the pinnacle of conglomerate hierarchies) in interpreting, focusing, and redirecting economic forces that provide for complexity and contradiction within media industries. (Havens et al., 2009, p. 235)

This characterization presents levels of analysis as separate domains of inquiry. It ignores entirely the substantial body of detailed empirical research on media (including entertainment) production conducted by critical political economists (Wasko & Meehan, 2013; Murdock & Golding, 2016), together with wider analyses of labor processes in the communication industries (Maxwell, 2015). As Marx insisted, sites of production are also always sites of struggle over control and exploitation. Communicative labor is no exception, but these contests are missing from much recent work on the cultural industries. In sharp contrast, members of the Political Economy Section have consistently charted resistance and unionism within the communication industries and actively supported demands for workers' rights. This commitment informed Vincent Mosco and Janet Wasko's 1983 collection, *Labor, the Working Class and the Media* and has been built on in a range of later interventions, including Mosco's work on labor activism in the information industries (Mosco & McKercher, 2009).

The Return of Adam Smith: Markets and Platforms

It is important to note that the Political Economy Section's formal launch in 1978 coincided with a major transformation in the organization of capitalism and the world system. The mid-1970s saw a deepening crisis of accumulation in the advanced capitalist economies of the West. Market fundamentalists blamed the regulatory regime and public management of core resources that underpinned the social contract of the post-war period and advocated a return to Adam Smith's vision of minimal state intervention. In Margaret Thatcher in Britain (elected in 1979) and Ronald Reagan in the US (president from 1981–89), they found enthusiastic political champions for a new, neoliberal, re-emphasis on markets governed by entrepreneurial initiative and consumer choice. Communication systems were assigned a central role in restoring profitability and boosting consumption. Public telecommunications systems were deregulated and sold to private investors. Public service broadcasters faced intensified competition from new commercial cable and satellite services. Meanwhile, the relaxation of regulations allowed leading media companies to increase their market share and expand into new regions and markets, creating multimedia conglomerates with unprecedented reach. This pattern was later repeated with the platform capitalist corporations that colonized the World Wide Web, which was launched publicly in April 1993, creating de facto monopolies in social media (Facebook), search and video (Alphabet), and electronic shopping (Amazon).

Marketization was not confined to advanced capitalist economies and in the 1990s, it achieved global reach. In the space of less than a year, the three major economies of India, China, and Russia that had been uncoupled from global capitalist circuits to varying degrees throughout the post-war period rebalanced relations between states and markets. In 1991, as conditions for granting a loan, the World Bank required India to deregulate, sell off public assets, and accept foreign direct investments. In December that same year, the Soviet Union finally collapsed and in January 1992, during his "Southern Tour,"

Deng Xiaoping relaunched his market-oriented reforms in China. Section members were among the first to offer analysis of the new marketized communications landscape. In 2007, a volume dedicated to the memory of Herbert Schiller was assembled under the title *Media in the Age of Marketization* (Murdock & Wasko, 2007) and in 2011, a comprehensive summation of available research and theorizing in key areas of critical political economy was edited by three long-standing section members (Wasko et al., 2011). In 2013, section members Peter Thompson and Wayne Hope launched the open access journal *The Political Economy of Communication*, offering a dedicated space for exploring unfolding issues.

The retreat from public interest regulation also prompted renewed interest in the power exercised by the new megacorporations. In 2017, section members published the first comprehensive survey in *Global Media Giants* (Birkinbine et al., 2017). Covering both established media companies and new platform operators, it built on pioneering past work by members typified by Janet Wasko's influential research on Disney (2001) and Scott Fitzgerald's detailed anatomies of Time Warner, Bertelsmann, and News Corporation (Fitzgerald, 2012).

In addition, the relations between public communication and participatory politics acquired a new centrality with the double transition to marketization and democratization in the former communist countries of Central and Eastern Europe. The section offered an early forum for debate, especially at the 1990 IAMCR Conference held in Bled, as Slovenia was only months away from breaking away from Yugoslavia to form an independent Republic. Selected contributions were later published in *Communication and Democracy*, jointly edited by Slavko Splichal and Janet Wasko (1993). At the IAMCR 1994 Seoul Conference, with other "post-socialist" transitions gathering momentum, two of Central East Europe's leading communications scholars, Karol Jakubowicz (1994, 2001) and Slavko Splichal (1994a), presented papers to the Political Economy Section, pointing to emerging tensions and contradictions. Splichal's paper summarized developments expanded on in his 1994 book, *Media Beyond Socialism* (Splichal, 1994b), with aggressive commercialization hollowing out the public sphere, and re-nationalization, nationalistic, and religious exclusivism cementing the control of new political elites. As he noted in a later piece, these trends created "almost unmanageable obstacles to the development of more democratic systems in the region" (Splichal, 2000, p. 5). His pessimism has been vindicated by the subsequent rise of authoritarian populism and "illiberal democracy" across Central and Eastern Europe, with governments systematically attacking independent media and curbing journalists' freedoms, as well as business elites buying up news outlets to defend their political and economic interests (Štětka, 2015).

While the unprecedented concentrations of power commanded by the digital majors raised familiar issues of corporate abuses, new challenges were presented by their innovative business models granting users cost-free access to their platforms in return for monopoly rights to collect, collate, and sell the personal data they generate through their online engagements. Section members were early contributors to debates on the corporate misuse of personal data. At the Barcelona Conference in 2002, Oscar Gandy presented his pioneering work on data mining and surveillance as key elements in "the management of risk in the marketing of goods and services" (Gandy, 2002), an area that has since become central to the analysis of "surveillance capitalism" (Zuboff, 2019) raising urgent questions around public regulation and users' rights.

Section members have also been prominent in arguing and campaigning for interventions to build bulwarks against commercial enclosure and guarantee universal access to the full range of cultural resources required for participatory citizenship, revisiting the case for public investment and democratic accountability in public interest journalism, public service broadcasting, and the construction of a public service internet (Pickard, 2021; Fuchs & Untenberger, 2021).

Importantly, the global reach of marketization has invested critical political economy with a new indispensability to analysis. Issues around the concentration of corporate power in both "legacy" and platform media, the relations between media ownership and control over public culture, the ubiquity of advertising and consumerist ideology, the regulatory role of states, the case for public ownership and subsidy, and the idea of a digital commons are now actively discussed everywhere. The section has continued to attract new members researching these areas in a widening range of locations. Recent years have seen increasing participation in the section by Chinese scholars grappling with China's unique and continually shifting relations between private enterprise and state management, and intensified interest in the next generation digital technologies organized around artificial intelligence and quantum computing as prime engines of economic growth.

Marx is Back—But Whose Marx?

The negative social and cultural impacts of marketization and the financial crash of 2008 have prompted a resurgence of interest in Marx's writings as a resource for analyzing contemporary capitalist control over information, symbolization, and connectivity. Under Christian Fuchs' editorship, the open access journal *Triple C*—which under its original title "cognition-communication-cooperation" had provided a general outlet for work in the science of information—marked its tenth anniversary in 2013 by relaunching as *Communication, Capitalism, Critique*, signaling its explicit commitment to promoting critical perspectives. An extended issue entitled *Marx is Back*, edited jointly by Christian Fuchs and Vincent Mosco, carried a wide range of contributions debating core issues in Marxist analysis (Fuchs & Mosco, 2012).

The terms of online engagement have prompted researchers to revisit Dallas Smythe's (1977) seminal essay on the audience commodity and the surplus value generated by the unpaid labor of watching television. Once again, it has become a focus of debate with Christian Fuchs' influential extension of Smythe's argument to digital spaces (Fuchs, 2012), countered by César Bolaño's insistence that the labor generated by the internet is done by workers employed by the digital corporations and not by users (Bolaño, 2014). Once again, disagreement centered on differential readings of Marx.

Re-evaluating Marx took another founding member of the section, Nicholas Garnham, in a different direction and a shift in focus from the constitution of public culture and participation to the role of "dynamics within production in general" in driving the "development of information goods, services and communication networks" (Garnham, 2011, p. 52). He discounted core "concepts of ownership, control and ideological domination" as "not useful in understanding the processes and stakes involved" (Garnham, 2011, p. 59) and dismissed much critical political economy as "a euphemism for a vague, crude, and unself-questioning form of Marxism, linked to a general and self-satisfied, if often paranoid, radicalism" (Garnham, 2011, p. 42). This blanket condemnation rehearsed the standard dismissal of the field from the Right and broke with much of Garnham's earlier work on public culture, including his strong defense of public service broadcasting as an essential support for the public sphere required by deliberative democracy (Garnham, 1986). It also misrepresented the variety of critical research and theorizing conducted by section members over the years.

Within IAMCR, from an early point, critical analysis of the communication systems had been divided between the Political Economy Section and the Technology Section founded, as we noted earlier, by Dallas Smythe. Separating content from carriage was always an institutional rather than an intellectual division and members, including Nicholas Garnham, straddled both. In 1972, he was involved in campaigns in the UK around the future of cable services and the fourth broadcast channel and was introduced to North American debates on telecommunications policy by Smythe, who was visiting London, researching systems for radio spectrum allocation. Garnham's growing sense "that broadcasting was, from both an economic and technology policy point of view, entirely marginal" and that the key economic and policy struggles were "over telephone and data networks" was confirmed by attending a lecture in 1976 on developments in Britain's national telecommunications network (Garnham, 2005, p. 478). He carried this conviction into the early planning meetings for the Political Economy Section, alongside interests generated by his earlier experiences as a film critic, television producer, and activist. His later marginalization of media's ideological role has been comprehensively countered by subsequent developments, not least the avalanche of hyper-consumerism, misinformation, and conspiracy promoted on social media platforms. However, by insisting on the need to interrogate the links between communication systems and the general organization of capitalist production, Garnham's intervention posed an important challenge.

Materialist Theory Revisited

The COVID-19 pandemic and the accelerating climate crisis have confirmed in the starkest terms that the connectivity demanded by both corporations and consumers depends on assemblies of infrastructures and devices organized around networks of cables, masts, and satellites and delivered on smartphones, large screen televisions, laptops, and gaming consoles. Recognizing this reconnects the analysis of communication to the general industrial organization of extraction, manufacture, transportation, retailing, and disposal (Murdock, 2021).

The Political Economy Section began as the Materialist Theory Working Group. Its future will depend in large part on its contribution to developing a materialism that anchors choices over the future of public communication not only in decisions over the organization and funding of production and the diversity and accessibility of content, but also in policies that take full account of environmental and social impacts. This must include the costs of obtaining the minerals and materials that media infrastructures and machines are made of; the labor processes involved in their manufacture, transportation, and operation; the energy, water, and other resources they consume in use; and the levels of pollution and waste generated when they are discarded. Some section members have been early contributors to these debates (Maxwell & Miller, 2012, 2020; Brevini & Murdock, 2017).

Critical political economy's grounding in moral philosophy has always placed promoting social justice, equality, and mutuality at the center of evaluations of prevailing conditions and proposals for change. It is crucial that a fourth criterion be added: environmental care and repair.

References

Barrera, C. (2019). Cold war, press freedom and journalism education: Paradoxes of the untypical 1968 IAMCR conference in Pamplona. *Javnost—The Public, 26*(4), 420–434.

Becker, J. (2013). *Elisabeth Noelle-Neumann: Demoskopin Zwischen NS-ideologie udn Konservatismus.* Schoningh.

Bettig, R. V., & Heresco, A. (2013). The history of union for democratic communication through the Democratic Communiqué. *Democratic Communiqué, 26*(1), 29–45.

Birkinbine, B. J., Gomez, R., & Wasko, J. (Eds.). (2017). *Global media giants.* Routledge.

Bisky, L. (1974). *Zur kritik der bürgerlichen massenkomunikationsforschung.* VEB Deutscher Verlag der Wissenschaften.

Bisky, L. (1977). Letter to Robin Cheesman Zentralinstitut Fur Jugendforschung Leipzig, 6 November.

Bociurkiw, B. R. (1970). Political dissent in the Soviet Union. *Studies in Comparative Communism, 3*(2), 74–106.

Bolaño, C. (2014). Latin American communication thought and the challenges for the XXI century: Theoretical points for a collective and critical new research agenda. *Journal of Latin American Communication Research, 4*(1), 3–11.

Bolaño, C., Mastrini, G., & Sierra, F. (2012). *Political economy, communication and knowledge: A Latin American perspective.* Hampton Press.

Brevini, B., & Murdock, G. (Eds.). (2017). *Carbon capitalism and communication: Confronting climate crisis.* Palgrave Macmillan.

Califano, B. (2021). Economia politica de la communicacion: De sus origines a la consolidacion del campo en America Latina. *Perspectivas de la Communicacion, 14*(2), 57–94.

Cheesman, R. (1977, March 28). Letter to Kaarle Nordenstreng and Yassen Zassoursky.

Cheesman, R. (1980, March 12). Letter to IAMCR members who had expressed an interest in the Political Economy Section. Roskilde Universitet Centre.

Cheesman, R. (2019, October 31). My love affair with Tömegkommunikációs Kutatóközpont. Personal Communication.

Cheesman, R. (2020). Personal communication.

Chomsky, N., & Herman, E. S. (1973). *Counter-revolutionary violence: Bloodbaths in fact and propaganda.* Warner Modular Publications.

Curran, J., & Gurevitch, M. (1991). Introduction. In J. Curran & M. Gurevitch (Eds.), *Mass media and society* (pp. 7–11). Edward Arnold.

Dorfman, A., & Mattelart, A. (1975). *How to read Donald Duck: Imperialist ideology in the Disney comic.* Pluto Press.

European Sociological Association. (2022). RN18-Sociology of Communication and Media Research. Retrieved 15 June 2022, from https://www.europeansociology.org/research-networks/rn18-sociology-communications-and-media-research

Fitzgerald, S. (2012). *Corporations and cultural industries: Time Warner, Bertelsmann and News Corporation.* Lexington Books.

Flichy, P. (1980a). *Les industries de l'imaginaire.* Presse Universitaires de Grenoble/Institut National de L'audiovisuel.

Flichy, P. (1980b). Current approaches to mass communication research in France. *Media, Culture & Society, 2*(2), 179–188.

Fuchs, C. (2012). Dallas Smythe today—The audience commodity, the digital labour debate, Marxist political economy and critical theory. Prolegomena to a digital labour theory of value. *tripleC, 10*(2), 692–740.

Fuchs, C. (2017). The forgotten Marxist theory of communication and society: Horst Holzer. *tripleC, 15*(2), 686–725.

Fuchs, C., & Mosco, V. (Eds.). (2012). Marx is back—The importance of Marxist theory and research for critical communication studies today. *tripleC, 10*(2), 127–632.

Fuchs, C., & Untenberger, K. (Eds.). (2021). *The public service media and public service Internet manifesto.* University of Westminster Press.

Gandy, O. H. (2002, July 22). *Data Mining and Surveillance in the Post 9-11 Environment* [Paper Presentation]. IAMCR: Political Economy Section, Barcelona, Spain.

Garnham, N. (1979). Contribution to a political economy of mass-communication. *Media, Culture and Society, 1*(2), 123–148.

Garnham, N. (1986). The media and the public sphere. In P. Golding, G. Murdock, & P. Schlesinger (Eds.), *Communicating politics: Mass communications and the political process* (p. 37–53). Leicester University Press.

Garnham, N. (1995, March). Political economy and cultural studies: Reconciliation or divorce? *Critical Studies in Mass Communication, 12*(1), 62–71.
Garnham, N. (2005). A personal intellectual memoir. *Media, Culture & Society, 27*(4), 469–493.
Garnham, N. (2011). The political economy of communication revisited. In J. Wasko, G. Murdock, & H. Sousa (Eds.), *The handbook of political economy of communications* (p. 41–61). Wiley-Blackwell.
Golding, P., & Murdock, G. (1991). Culture, communications, and political economy. In J. Curran & M. Gurevitch (Eds.), *Mass media and society* (p. 15–32). Edward Arnold.
Gotz, L. (2016). Unpacking Siegelaub's library: The collection of IMMRC at the International Institute of Social History. In *Seth Siegelaub: Beyond conceptual art* (p. 478–486). Stedelijk Museum.
Graf, W. (1984). Anti-communism in the Federal Republic of Germany. In R. Miliband, J. Saville, & M. Liebman (Eds.), *The socialist register 1984: The uses of anti-communism* (p. 164–212). Merlin Press.
Graham, S. E. (2006). The (Real)politiks of culture: U.S. cultural diplomacy in UNESCO, 1846–1954. *Diplomatic History, 30*(2), 231–251.
Grossberg, L. (1995, March). Cultural studies vs political economy: Is anyone else bored with this debate? *Critical Studies in Mass Communication, 12*(1), 72–81.
Gurevitch, M., Bennett, T., Curran, J., & Wollacott, J. (Eds.). (1982). Introduction. In *Culture, society and the media* (p. 1–3). Methuen.
Hagen, I., & Wasko, J. (2000). *Consuming audiences? Production and reception in media research.* Hampton Press.
Hall, S. (1983). The problem of ideology: Marxism without guarantees. In B. Matthews (Ed.), *Marx: A hundred years on* (p. 57–85). Lawrence and Wishart.
Hall, S. (1986). Media power and class power. In J. Curran, J. Ecclestone, G. Oakley, & A. Richardson (Eds.), *Bending reality: The state of the media* (p. 5–14). Pluto Press.
Hall, S. (2018). *Familiar stranger: A life between two islands.* Penguin Books.
Hall, S., & Jefferson, T. (Eds.). (1975). *Resistance through rituals: Youth subcultures in post-war Britain.* Hutchinson.
Halloran, J., Elliott, P., & Murdock, G. (1970). *Demonstrations and communication.* Penguin Books.
Havens, T., Lotz, A., & Tinic, S. (2009). Critical media industry studies: A research agenda. *Communication, Culture and Critique, 2*(2), 234–253.
Herman, E. S. (1970, Spring). Review: *Mass communications and American empire. AV Communication Review, 18*(1), 113–115.
Herman, E. S., & Chomsky, N. (1988). *Manufacturing consent: The political economy of mass media.* Pantheon Books.
Hockenos, P. (2011, April). Director of the left. *Politico.* Retrieved 15 June 2022, from https://www.politico.eu/article/director-of-the-left/
Hoffmann, B. (1983). On the development of a materialist theory of mass communication in West Germany. *Media, Culture & Society, 1*, 7–24.
Horkheimer, M., & Adorno, T. W. (1973). The culture industry as mass deception. In M. Horkheimer & W. T. Adorno (Eds.), *The Dialectic of Enlightenment* (p. 120–167). Allen Lane.
IAMCR. (1978a, April 10–11). *Minutes of the meeting of the International Council.* Karl Marx University, Leipzig.

IAMCR. (1978b, September 4–9). *Mass media and national cultures: Programme and timetable*. XI Congress, Warsaw, Poland.

IMMRC (International Mass Media Research Center). (Ed.). (1980). *Marxism and the mass media: Towards a basic bibliography 6–7*. International General (and see earlier issues).

International Sociological Association. (2022). RC14 sociology of communication, knowledge and culture: History. Retrieved 15 June 2022, from https://www.isa-sociology.org/en/research-networks/research-committees/rc14-sociology-of-communication-knowledge-and-culture/rc14-history

Jakubowicz, K. (1994). *Changing perspectives on social communication in Central and Eastern Europe* [Abstracts, p. 206]. IAMCR Conference: Seoul, South Korea.

Jakubowicz, K. (2001). Rude awakening: Social and media change in Central and Eastern Europe. *Javnost—The Public, 8*(4), 59–80.

Jhally, S. (2016). The last interview: Stuart Hall and the politics of cultural studies. Retrieved 15 June 2022, from https://www.mediaed.org/transcripts/The-Last-Interview-Transcript.pdf

Laqua, D. (2011). Transnational intellectual co-operation, The League of Nations, and the problem of order. *Journal of Global History, 6*, 223–247. Retrieved 15 June 2022, from https://doi.org/10.1017/S1740022811000246

Lull, J. (1994). *Mediating the political economy: Reception research and historical context* [Abstracts, p. 241]. IAMCR Conference: Seoul, South Korea.

Mattelart, A. & Siegelaub, S. (Eds.). (1979). *Communication and class struggle: An anthology. Vol. I: capitalism, imperialism*. International General.

Mattelart, A. & Siegelaub, S. (Eds.). (1983). *Communication and class struggle: An anthology, Vol. II: liberation, socialism*. International General.

Maxwell, R. (2013). *Herbert Schiller*. Rowman & Littlefield Publishers.

Maxwell, R. (Ed.). (2015). *The Routledge companion to labour and media*. Routledge.

Maxwell, R., & Miller, T. (2012). *Greening the media*. Oxford University Press.

Maxwell, R., & Miller, T. (2020). *How green is your smartphone?* Polity Press.

Meyen, M. (2014). IAMCR on the East-West battlefield: A study on the GDR's attempts to use the association for diplomatic purposes. *International Journal of Communication, 8*, 2071–2089.

Meyen, M., & Wiedemann, T. (2018). Yassen Zassoursky: 'I Tried to Stop the Cold War Mentality'. In M. Meyen & T. Wiedemann (Eds.), *Biografischer lexicon der kammunikationswissenschaft*. Herbet von Halen.

Miège, B. (1987). The logics at work in the new cultural industries. *Media, Culture & Society, 9*(3), 273–298.

Miège, B. (1989). *The capitalization of cultural production*. International General.

Morgan, W. J. (2014, January). UNESCO: A social philosophy for the 21st century? *Planet: The Welsh Internationalist*, 52–58.

Mosco, V. (1994). *There's the beef: Back to basics* [Abstracts, p. 242]. IAMCR Conference: Seoul, South Korea.

Mosco, V. (1996). *The political economy of communication: Rethinking and renewal*. Sage Publications.

Mosco, V., & McKercher, C. (2009). *The labouring of communication: Will knowledge workers of the world unite?* Lexington Books.

Mosco, V., & Wasko, J. (1983). *The critical communications review, Volume 1: Labor, the working class, and the media*. Ablex Publishing.

Mosco, V., & Wasko, J. (1984). *The critical communications review, Volume II: Changing patterns of communications control.* Ablex Publishing.
Murdock, G. (1978). Blindspots about Western Marxism: A reply to Dallas Smythe. *Canadian Journal of Political and Social Theory, 2*(2), 109–119.
Murdock, G. (1982). Large corporations and the control of the communication industries. In M. Gurevitch, T. Bennett, J. Curran, & J. Woollacott (Eds.), *Culture, society and the media* (p. 118–150). Methuen.
Murdock, G. (2021). Dark materials: Media, machines, markets. In J. Swartz & J. Wasko (Eds.), *Media: A transdisciplinary inquiry* (p. 44–64). Intellect Books and University of Chicago Press.
Murdock, G., & Golding, P. (1974). For a political economy of mass communication. In R. Miliband & J. Saville (Eds.), *The socialist register 1973* (p. 205–234). The Merlin Press.
Murdock, G., & Golding, P. (1977). Capitalism, communication and class relations. In J. Curran, M. Gurevitch, & J. Woolacott (Eds.), *Mass communication and society* (p. 12–43). Edward Arnold.
Murdock, G., & Golding, P. (2016). Political economy and production studies: A reply to Dwyer. *Media, Culture & Society, 38*(5), 763–769.
Murdock, G., & Wasko, J. (2007). *Media in the age of marketization.* Hampton Press.
Nixon, R. B. (1960). Current developments: International cooperation in mass communication research. *Audiovisual Communication Review, 8*(4), 224–228.
Nordenstreng, K. (1976). Letter to Dallas Smythe 5 October.
Nordenstreng, K. (2020). *The rise and fall of the International Organisation of Journalists based in Prague 1946–2016: Useful recollections part III.* Charles University Karolinum Press.
Nordenstreng, K., & Seppa, T. (1986, August 27). *The League of Nations and the mass media: The rediscovery of a forgotten story* [Paper Presentation]. IAMCR conference: New Delhi, India.
Pemberton, J. (2012). The changing shape of intellectual cooperation: From the League of Nations to UNESCO. *Australian Journal of Politics and History, 58*(1), 34–50.
Pickard, V. (2021). From the ashes: Imagining a post-commercial future for media. *The Political Economy of Communication, 9*(1), 79–83.
Pooley, J. (2017). Wilbur Schramm and the 'Four Founders' history of U.S. communication research. Retrieved 15 June 2022, from https://www.jeffpooley.com/pubs/pooley-schramm-2018.pdf
Prodnik, J. A., & Wasko, J. (2014). Professor Janet Wasko: An interview with the president of the IAMCR and one of the key representatives of the political economy of communication approach. *tripleC, 12*(1), 14–27.
Prokop, D. (1972). *Massenkommunikationsforschung 1: Produktion.* Fischer Taschenbuch Verlag.
Prokop, D. (1983). Problems of production and consumption in the mass media. *Media, Culture & Society, 5*, 101–116.
Prokop, D. (1986). Towards a psychoanalytical critique of mass communication. In J. Becker, G. Hedebro, & L. Paldan (Eds.), *Communication and domination: Essays to honour Herbert I Schiller* (p. 96–103). Ablex Publishing.
Schiller, H. I. (1969). *Mass communications and American empire.* Beacon Press.

Siebert, F. S., Peterson, T., & Schramm, W. (1956). *Four theories of the press: The authoritarian, libertarian, social responsibility and Soviet Communist concepts of what the press should be and do.* University of Illinois Press.

Simpson, C. (1996). Elisabeth Noelle-Neumann's "spiral of silence" and the historical context of communication theory. *Journal of Communication, 46*(3), 149–173.

Smythe, D. W. (1959). Freedom of the press doctrine in its class and politico-economic context. In T. Guback (Ed.), *Dallas Smythe: Counterclockwise-perspectives on communication* (p. 96–106). Westview Press.

Smythe, D. W. (1960). On the political economy of communications. *Journalism Quarterly, 37*(4), 563–572.

Smythe, D. W. (1962). Time, market and space factors in communication economics. *Journalism Quarterly, 39*(1), 3–14.

Smythe, D. W. (1974). Letter to James Halloran October 3rd. *SFU archive collection F-41, Dallas Smythe collection.* Retrieved 15 June 2022, from https://atom.archives.sfu.ca/f-41

Smythe, D. W. (1977). Communications: Blindspot of Western Marxism. *Canadian Journal of Political and Social Theory, 1*(3), 1–27.

Smythe, D. W. (1984). New directions for critical communications research. *Media, Culture & Society, 6*, 205–217.

Splichal, S. (1994a). *Postsocialism and the media: Between paternalism and pluralism* [Abstracts]. IAMCR conference: Seoul, South Korea, p. 208.

Splichal, S. (1994b). *Media beyond socialism: Theory and practice in West-Central Europe.* Westview Press.

Splichal, S. (2000). Reproducing political capitalism in the media in East-Central Europe. *Medijska Iskrazizanja, 6*(1), 5–17.

Splichal, S., & Mance, B. (2018). Paradigm(s) lost? Islands of critical media research in communication journals. *Journal of Communication, 68*, 399–414.

Splichal, S., & Wasko, J. (Eds.). (1993). *Communication and democracy.* Ablex.

Štětka, V. (2015). The rise of oligarchs as media owners. In J. Zielonka (Ed.), *Media and politics in new democracies: Europe in a comparative perspective* (p. 85–98). Oxford University Press.

Tracy, J. F. (2006). On Mosco street: An interview with Vincent Mosco. *Democratic Communique, 20*, 1–24.

Wasko, J. (2001). *Understanding Disney: The manufacture of fantasy.* Polity Press.

Wasko, J. (2013). The IAMCR political economy section: A retrospective. *The Political Economy of Communications, 1*(1), 4–8.

Wasko, J., & Meehan, E. R. (2013). Critical crossroads or parallel routes? Political economy and the new approaches to studying media industries and cultural production. *Cinema Journal, 52*(1), 150–157.

Wasko, J., Murdock, G., & Sousa, H. (Eds.). (2011). *The handbook of political economy of communication.* Wiley-Blackwell.

Williams, R. (1974). *Television, technology and cultural form.* Fontana.

Zuboff, S. (2019). *The age of surveillance capitalism: The fight for a human future at the new frontier of power.* Profile Books.

CHAPTER 4

Popular Culture and IAMCR

Garry Whannel and Graham Murdock

Introduction

The launch of the Popular Culture Working Group (PCWG) at Barcelona in 2002 marked the formal recognition of a constellation of interests IAMCR members had been engaged in since the association's foundation. IAMCR's inauguration in 1957 coincided with two major changes to capitalism's media landscape: the rise of television and the growing popularity of rock and roll. Both developments rekindled long-standing concerns around the negative impact of commercialized popular culture on young people. The search for direct links between media consumption and delinquent behavior followed successive moral panics, dating back to Victorian campaigns against sensationalist "Penny Dreadful" comics. This "effects" agenda was contested within IAMCR and papers exploring young people's active engagement with popular media became a recurrent feature of conference programs. There was also early interest in the systematic study of popular music and comic books.

Whereas other areas of interest within IAMCR have drawn primarily on traditions of inquiry from economics, political science, social psychology, and sociology, work on popular culture takes insights and methods from cultural and social history, literary studies, folklore studies, textual analysis, and ethnography. Over time, approaches became increasingly informed by the distinctive

G. Whannel
University of Bedfordshire, Luton, UK
e-mail: garry.whannel@beds.ac.uk

G. Murdock (✉)
University of Loughborough, Loughborough, UK
e-mail: G.Murdock@lboro.ac.uk

© The Author(s), under exclusive license to Springer Nature Switzerland AG 2023

J. Becker, R. Mansell (eds.), *Reflections on the International Association for Media and Communication Research*,
https://doi.org/10.1007/978-3-031-16383-8_4

cluster of concerns and traditions developed within cultural studies, which, from modest beginnings in Britain has become institutionalized in university departments, degrees, and research centers across the globe, supported by an expanding range of dedicated journals and scholarly associations.

The emergence of cultural studies as an intellectual field coincided with the launch of IAMCR but it was not until the launch of the PCWG that its perspectives secured a regular institutional home within the association.

In this chapter, we sketch a map of the roots and trajectories of this tradition of inquiry and trace its impact, initially in the UK where it gained traction and momentum earlier than elsewhere and established a distinctive agenda of study that has achieved international currency.

From Cultural Commentary to Cultural Analysis

The syntheses now underpinning popular culture analyses took time. Early writing on popular culture appeared primarily in essays as part of wider intellectual commentary on social and cultural change. This was particularly vigorous in England, the first industrializing nation, running from the early nineteenth-century essays of Hazlitt to George Orwell's incisive observations in the 1940s. Conservative commentary viewed the new urban working class as continually open to the attractions of cheap and disreputable mass entertainment and the blandishments of political demagogues. This fear of the crowd crystallized in the presentation of popular culture as catering to an undifferentiated and susceptible "mass," prompting moral panics and elevating education to the frontline in the battle for youthful hearts and minds.

This condemnatory current in cultural commentary found an influential academic advocate, from the 1930s onwards, in F. R. Leavis, Professor of English at Cambridge University. Leavis and followers, grouped around the journal *Scrutiny,* voiced a deep suspicion of the adverse impacts of popular culture and developed practices designed to protect people while educating their tastes toward the worthiness of literature and art, represented in the reconfigured cultural canon they championed.

Dismissive attitudes to popular culture were also articulated on the Left. The "Culture Industry" essay by Frankfurt School members Adorno and Horkheimer, during war-time exile in the US in the 1940s, has been influential as a negative reference point within cultural studies (Adorno & Horkheimer, 1972; Jay, 1973). Their depiction of commercialized media as a machine for closing off radical critique and aesthetic innovation, by endlessly reproducing a limited repertoire of marketable cultural forms, typifies, in cultural studies commentary, an economic determinism that neglects the layered nature of popular media and the complexity of responses. This over-easy characterization, though, misrepresents both the wider work of Adorno and the Frankfurt Group and the critical tradition of research in the political economy of culture.

Alongside condemnation and critique, commentary on popular culture also offered celebration: charting, recording, and registering popular cultural manifestations, as epitomized by the work of Ray Browne and the group of scholars that developed around Bowling Green State University from the mid-1960s.

American cultural essayists, from Edmund Wilson to Susan Sontag and Tom Wolfe, while highly diverse, provided more complex responses to culture and popular culture often characterized by a sharp and often anthropological ear and eye, through which they noticed the unnoticed, and interrogated the taken-for-granted aspects of everyday cultural practices and artifacts. Charting the shift from cultural commentary to cultural analysis as an academic mode of enquiry, however, needs to focus on "its institutional underpinnings in educational contexts and relations" (Bennett, 1996).

Cultural Studies and Conflicted Change

Two 1958 texts played a central role in establishing cultural studies. Both were written by British literary scholars who had grown up in working class communities and taught workers in the adult education system, experiences that gave them a more nuanced appreciation of the interplay between lived experiences, vernacular culture, and popular media (Steele, 1997).

Culture and Society, by Raymond Williams (1958), provided a critical review of English cultural commentary since the emergence of industrial capitalism in the late eighteenth century. *The Uses of Literacy*, by Richard Hoggart (1958), charted the incursion of the new post-war consumerism into working class communities and its impetus to "unbend" the springs of collective action. It was partly a lament for the disappearing culture of his childhood. At the same time, his experience as an adult education tutor confirmed that solidarity and distrust of ruling authorities remained central to working class culture. This revisionist approach replaced blanket condemnation and uncritical celebration by asking how far media artifacts displayed creative integrity and spoke honestly to the complexities of lived experience.

The transitions and tensions Hoggart identified were the latest manifestations of an extended process of change that Raymond Williams named in his landmark book, *The Long Revolution* (1965). Williams identifies the reorganization of cultural life around successive innovations in communications as a third dimension of the fundamental changes shaping contemporary life, alongside the ascendency of industrial capitalism and the installation of representative democracy. In a pioneering venture into a history neglected by professional historians, he traces how the growth in literacy, fostered by compulsory schooling, supported an explosive growth in popular newspapers, magazines, and fiction. In later work, he turned to the development of audio-visual technologies and particularly television, as potent sources of new sensations, pleasures, and points of connection (Williams, 1974).

For Williams, innovations in popular communication, and their complex entanglements with commerce and democracy, are always and everywhere the site of continuous struggles over control and use. This insistence on approaching culture as an arena of contest has supported two defining characteristics of cultural studies: it reconnects the study of popular representations with analysis of ideology, and it focuses attention on popular creativity, refusal, and resistance.

Williams borrows from anthropology to present cultural activity as a defining dimension of everyday life, in which people reaffirm and express beliefs and values that give meaning to their lives through objects they surround themselves with, symbolic systems they engage with, and social practices and rituals they participate in. This places social stratification at the heart of analysis, directing attention to social locations and experiences that provide resources for responses to professionally made symbolic materials and support self-organized vernacular cultural formations. Williams ends *Culture and Society* by celebrating the "very remarkable cultural achievement" of core institutions created by working class struggle—trade unions, co-operatives, and political parties (Williams, 1958, p. 313)—but adds a cautionary note, observing that "it is difficult to feel that the working class movement" has made sufficient room for "not only variation, but even dissidence, within a common loyalty" (Williams, 1958, p. 319).

He was writing in the context of a major transformation in the English class structure, as traditional industries declined, and the salience of fractures generated by generation, gender and sexuality, and ethnicity became more visible. Negotiating these intersections was central to the emerging politics of the "New Left" which underpinned the intellectual trajectory of cultural studies in its foundational phase. The New Left's platform was widely disseminated in *The May Day Manifesto,* originally published in 1967 and reissued as a Penguin paperback in 1968 (Williams, Hall & Thompson, 1968).

The Cultural Politics of the New Left

The early New Left in Britain was shaped by imperial decline, the fiasco of Suez, the disillusion with the Labour party, and above all, the collapse of intellectual support for the Communist Party after the Soviet invasion of Hungary, and revelations about the tyranny of Stalin's period. In this context, the New Left developed modes of political analysis that took culture/s and cultural history seriously, as can be seen in the journal *Universities and Left Review* (1957–1959) and its successor *New Left Review* (NLR) launched in 1960, after a merger with *The New Reasoner.* Stuart Hall, NLR editor 1960–62, introduced the inaugural issue by declaring that popular culture was "directly relevant to the imaginative resistances of people who have to live within capitalism," and that the "task of socialism is to meet people where they *are*" (Hall, 1960).

Reevaluating Commercialized Culture

Culture and politics were central to evaluations presented by Stuart Hall and Paddy Whannel in their landmark study, *The Popular Arts* (1964). Both were engaged practically with popular education. Stuart Hall was teaching in London's secondary schools; Paddy Whannel, a former secondary school art teacher, was Head of Education at the British Film Institute (BFI). The BFI Education Department sought to promote film culture and teaching by supporting Film Studies lectureships and establishing adult evening classes in film and from 1980, television (Nowell-Smith & Dupin, 2012). It was, arguably, in film study, that popular culture was first taken seriously as an object of analysis.

During the 1950s, the French journal *Cahiers du cinema* outlined and developed a "politique des auteurs" (later fetishized and de-contextualized in Anglophone criticism as "auteur theory") presenting designated Hollywood directors as employing popular genres to craft distinctive personal visions. The BFI developed close, if uneasy, relations with the Society for Education in Film and Television (SEFT), which began running day schools on themes such as realism, pleasure, comedy, and horror (Bolas, 2009). By the early 1970s, BFI Education began developing slide sets, alongside teaching notes, resources that were of huge influence on the generation of teachers and lecturers who introduced the teaching of film and media into schools and colleges.

BFI and SEFT, along with the SEFT journals *Screen* and *Screen Education*, played a significant role in the introduction of semiotics/semiology into the anglophone world. In January 1967, Peter Wollen discussed cinema and semiology in a BFI Education seminar series (Wollen, 1967), probably the first public discussion of Barthes in the UK. Later in 1967, an English translation of Barthes' *Elements of Semiology* (Barthes, 1967) became available in Britain and in 1969, Peter Wollen's highly influential *Signs and Meaning in the Cinema* (Wollen, 1969) was published.

Ideology Revisited

The English publication of Roland Bathes' *Mythologies* (1972), containing provocative dissections of French popular culture and the methodological essay, introduced him to a wider audience, and marked the entry of semiology into the mainstream of popular cultural analysis. Barthes went beyond the close reading of oral and written texts to examine popular visual imagery and the relation between word and image. His argument that ideology operates primarily through chains of association (connotations) was widely applied to media imagery, from front page news photos to advertisements (two examples Barthes himself offers). As Barthes points out, despite producers' best efforts to direct viewers toward the desired interpretation, the connotative level of meaning holds open the possibility of a variety of responses, depending on the cultural resources viewers bring to them. This focus on ideological analyses provided new points of entry for analyses of images of women, and hence patriarchal relations, and of racialized imagery, establishing presences in a field hitherto dominated by class perspectives. From 1970, French structuralist and post-structuralist theories (e.g., Althusser, Metz, Foucault, Kristeva, Derrida, and Lacan) had a growing influence on semiologically inspired analyses of ideological signifying practices in the anglophone world.

In 1971, an English translation, *Prison Notebooks,* (Gramsci, 1971) introduced the 1930s' writings of jailed Italian communist activist, Antonio Gramsci. Gramsci compares popular consciousness to geological strata laid down over time, with historically sedimented beliefs and prejudices coexisting with faith in the latest innovations. In this conception, ideology operates by selecting from these elements and combining them into a configuration that presents itself as "common sense" expressing what "right-thinking" people already know, the very opposite of an alien ideology imposed by distant others. Stuart Hall was later to employ this framework in his influential analysis of the authoritarian populism of the Thatcher governments (Hall, 1979). Popular culture was conceptualized as a relay between common sense and organized political discourse.

Popular Culture and Popular Experience

The Centre for Contemporary Cultural Studies (CCCS) was launched in 1964, when Richard Hoggart became Chair in English at Birmingham University and recruited Stuart Hall. As he noted in his manifesto for the Centre: "Even the apparently most processed forms of mass art are more complex constructions than the usual formulations suggest, complex in themselves and in their relations to their readers or audiences" (Hoggart, 1969, p. 12). The Centre's early work pursued this program, exploring the ways mass media engaged with popular experience and aspiration, generating projects which culminated in books: *Paper Voices* (Smith, 1975), an analysis of two leading popular newspapers; and *Images of Women* (Millum, 1975). Richard Dyer, another doctoral student at CCCS in the late 1960s, subsequently produced the highly influential *Stars* (Dyer, 1979).

Later work at Birmingham contributed to a vibrant current of research focusing on popular media as resources for constructing gendered identities. Angela McRobbie's (1978) readings of magazines for teenage girls and Dorothy Hobson's (1982) ethnographic work with women watching popular soap operas were important early additions to a growing volume of research that moved feminist perspectives, not without resistance (see *Women Take Issue,* CCCS, 2012) into the mainstream of popular cultural analysis.

Searching for Refusal and Resistance

In 1969, Stuart Hall took over as CCCS Director. Umberto Eco, another semiotician, had, since 1965, been exploring plural codes and diverse decodings in popular media. In a keynote speech at the Prix Italia festival, he argued, "we must now ask ourselves if there are hidden subordinate autonomous cultures, with their own differently organized codes, each able to supply competence rules ... in understanding the expressions of others" (Eco, 1974, p. 56). Stuart Hall, who was in the audience, took up the argument at a subsequent colloquium on reading television language organized by the Council of Europe. *Encoding and Decoding in Television Discourse* (Hall, 1973) became a key text in popular television studies and continues to be a major reference point. The interplay between professional and popular codes was pursued in work at CCCS analyzing the nightly current affairs program *Nationwide* and audience readings of it, searching for the social roots of popular distrust and skepticism, and outright rejections of official positions (Brunsdon & Morley, 1978; Morley, 1980).

Attention to class was central to research on youth subcultures in *Resistance Through Rituals* (Hall & Jefferson, 1976) and Dick Hebdige's *Subcultures* (1979), which combined an ethnographic sense of everyday life and lived experiences and the semiological analysis of meaning production. The two volumes became points of reference in popular culture studies.

The problem with the celebration of subcultures as nodes of resistance is that it confines opposition to the sphere of consumption. As Paul Willis (1978, p. 225) noted in *Profane Culture*, by creatively reworking standard commercial artifacts, the motor bike boys and hippies he studied "were striking back at the heart of the whole commodity form and its detailed domination of everyday life." But they were not challenging the productive system that manufactured those commodities. In his hugely influential ethnography, *Learning to Labour*, Willis (1977) details how thoroughly young working-class males had internalized the school's message that they were fit only for menial work.

CCCS analyses elaborated on ideological theories, drawing on the work of Gramsci, Althusser, and Poulantzas (Hall, 1983). Hall's original "encoding/decoding" schema had included relations of production within the cultural industries and the infrastructures that supported them as the starting point for analyzing the circuit of cultural activity. This crucial level of analysis was rarely pursued at CCCS. The result was a radical asymmetry. The creative work of audiences was interrogated, while the creative labor of cultural workers and their negotiations with dominant ideological frames was left unexplored.

Cultural Analysis and Political Economy

It was, however, taken up elsewhere, for example, at the Polytechnic of Central London (PCL). In 1975, the department launched a BA in Media Studies; Britain and the world's first named undergraduate degree in the area, giving "extensive attention to the analysis of popular culture," and drawing on critical social theory, social and cultural history, literary studies, anthropology, and philosophy. As one of its primary architects, James Curran (2013, p. np) noted, "In effect, Britain reinvented communications in a new form, and gave it a new label, media studies."

In 1979, Department Head Nicholas Garnham and colleagues launched a journal, *Media, Culture and Society,* offering a wider platform for their interdisciplinary approach. From the outset, it played an important role in making available key innovations in European work, in particular that of Bourdieu (1984) and Habermas (1989). Bourdieu's work was first introduced to English readers in an essay for *Media, Culture and Society,* co-written by Nicholas Garnham and Raymond Williams (1980).

Garnham made major contributions to policy studies and critical political economy. He was one of the founders of the Political Economy Section within IAMCR and was key in introducing Habermas's public sphere concept to English readers, before an English translation (Habermas, 1989). Habermas's analysis dealt primarily with the political public sphere, but deliberation presupposes the ability to imagine the world as others see it. Jim McGuigan (2005) subsequently directed attention to the central role played by drama, comedy, and entertainment in addressing contemporary issues, a complex he usefully named the "cultural public sphere."

Recovering History from Below

The turn toward "history from below" prompted by Edward Thompson's *The Making of the English Working Class* (1963) and extended beyond class in Sheila Rowbotham's path-breaking feminist history of women's lives and struggles, *Hidden from History* (Rowbotham, 1975), it acquired new momentum in the 1970s. The Feminist Library opened in 1975 and the Museum of London opened in 1976, with extensive documentation of working-class life. The History Workshop movement organized by Raphael Samuel developed during the 1970s, with events, conferences, and its journal *History Workshop*, launched in 1976.

Nicholas Garnham was a consultant for the Greater London Council (GLC) during Ken Livingstone's (1981–86) radical Labour administration. It pioneered an arts policy that moved the margins to the center, celebrating working class, women's, black, and youth histories, and supporting their contemporary expression. After increasing antagonism from Conservative commentators and politicians, the GLC was abolished by Margaret Thatcher in 1986.

Folklore studies made major contributions to charting the lived development of popular culture but focused on rural lives and traditions on the point of disappearing. The new social and cultural history directed attention to lives and struggles forged by conditions in the industrial cities and became an essential resource for understanding the interplay between change and continuity in popular culture. It was an explicitly political project intended to recover past struggles in order to create a politics of the present and was enthusiastically embraced by younger scholars as a critical riposte to dominant accounts, organized around the actions of the powerful.

Staff at PCL made significant contributions to rewriting mass media history “from below.” James Curran’s research on the illegal, “unstamped” press of the early nineteenth century underlined the central role of working-class movements in forging modern journalism (Curran & Seaton, 1981). Paddy Scannell and David Cardiff’s *A Social History of Broadcasting* (Scannell and Cardiff, 1991) explored the BBC’s early years, probing the tensions between the impetus to cultural paternalism and program forms offering opportunities for public participation and vernacular cultural expression.

The Politics of Production

Questions of media institutions and production were also addressed in studies produced by the other pioneering research center in Britain, the Centre for Mass Communication Research at Leicester University. This originated in a small research group led by James Halloran, established in 1963, for a government inquiry into the impact of television on young people. In 1966, Halloran was appointed Director of the new Centre.

The relation between news, politics, and the media constituted a focus for research (Halloran, Elliott & Murdock, 1970). From the outset, studies of production were a major research focus. Initiated by Phillip Elliott’s (1972) path-breaking ethnography of the making of a television documentary series on prejudice, they examined creative ambitions and practical choices informing the production of news, drama, and comedy, and the ways professional practices and ideologies were framed by the economic and political pressures, generated by the changing political economies of the cultural industries. Significant work on popular media production was also being conducted by the BFI with case studies of popular television drama designed to provide teaching materials.

Popular Culture in its Own Right

In 1982, the Open University launched its innovative interdisciplinary course on popular culture (U203). The planning team sought and relied on the guidance of BFI Education, experienced in designing teaching materials for use in adult education (Bennett, 1996). Key figures from SEFT, the CCCS, and PCL also played significant roles in the development of the course design and content.

Planning meetings for a cross-disciplinary course on popular culture (U203) commenced in 1977 and over 50 lecturers were involved in setting it up. Although it constituted only one-sixth of a full degree, it contained enough substance for a degree course in its own right and marked the establishment of the first systematic curriculum for popular culture at the degree level. Raymond Williams was appointed as the external assessor.

Stuart Hall had joined the Open University in 1980 as Professor of Sociology when work on the course was already well underway, but his conception of popular culture as a site of struggle, neither imposed from above nor generated spontaneously from below, developed during his time at CCCS, exerted considerable influence on course design.

It only ran from 1982–87 but was studied by nearly 5000 students and taught by over 100 people (Easthope, 1991). It reached people who would not otherwise have encountered university-level education. For many tutors, it functioned as an apprenticeship, advanced schooling, and career opportunity. It brought together people who had been trying, in isolation, to work on popular culture without the support of colleagues and constructed a dispersed scholarly community. Its impact was immense. It marked a watershed—a culmination of the accumulated and convergent roots of the systematic study of popular culture—but also a bridgehead and a base for future developments.

Reckonings with Empire

In 1972, James Halloran was elected President of IAMCR, a post he held for almost two decades, until 1990. In 1976, the association's conference was held in Leicester, attracting a number of the Leicester center's staff and students and British scholars. Many became active members and later held executive positions, but the association's international reach had the more general effect of directing attention to popular culture as a global phenomenon.

The aftermath of the long, and often bloody, struggle to dismantle the empires of Britain and the other European powers raised two major questions for popular culture studies: race and immigration; and cultural imperialism and Americanization. The emergence of cultural studies, as an academic field coinciding in Britain with a growing volume of migration from the former colonies in the Caribbean and Indian subcontinent, met with a rising tide of popular racism, grounded in an essentialist view of the nation as an imagined community defined by its shared white ethnicity and "Englishness." As a Black British citizen born in Jamaica, Stuart Hall was acutely aware of this gathering climate of hostility. It was explored analytically at Birmingham in Paul Gilroy's *There Ain't No Black in the Union Jack* (1987) and in the collaborative project *Policing The Crisis* (Hall et al., 1978), detailing the press-fueled moral panic around a spate of street muggings and the official tilt toward authoritarianism, and at Leicester in Paul Hartmann and Charles Husband's exploration of popular responses to racial stereotypes in *Racism and the Mass Media* (Hartmann & Husband, 1974). All three books remain essential resources for interrogating popular racism.

The Popular Culture Working Group: Formation and Development

The emergence of cultural studies' distinctive approaches to popular culture took time to permeate IAMCR and did so in a rather patchy fashion. The Political Economy Section, launched in 1978, offered a place for critical theoretical perspectives on culture and economy. From the late 1980s, with pressure from the newly formed Women's Network (Robinson, 2002), women members began to break through the IAMCR glass ceiling. The establishment of a Gender and Communications Section offered another space for popular cultural analysis.

A Working Group on Mass Media and Popular Fiction had been formed in 1988, and subsequently contributed to conferences during the 1990s. At the end of 1999 (*IAMCR Newsletter* 9 (1): Nov), the group, with a new convenor, changed its name to the Film and Television Fiction Working Group, but did not contribute to subsequent conferences. Recognizing that this meant a neglect of popular culture across the range of media, some IAMCR members proposed, in 2000, that a new Working Group in Popular Culture be established, and Garry Whannel agreed to be its first convenor. The group sought to have a gender balance among contributors, to represent a range of media and popular cultural topics, and to extend the range of contributors beyond the UK, North America, and Australia. To achieve this with limited program space was a challenge.

Until 2008, Working Group sessions were limited. The 2002 PCWG program featured eight papers, but by 2008, with more slots, there were 16. Between 2004–08 there were significantly more papers presented by women than men, but contributors came mainly from core academic centers in the Global North. By 2008, the group's mailing list had almost 100 contacts, and regular attenders were beginning to emerge. Garry Whannel stood down as convenor and was replaced by Barry King (University of Auckland, New Zealand). Over the subsequent decade, IAMCR conferences thrived, and the PCWG grew considerably in scope and size, with 477 papers between 2010 and 2019. In 2016, Tonny Krijnen joined Barry King as co-convenor, and in 2018, Barry stood down. The group established a Facebook page, continues to pursue becoming a section, and is planning a handbook.

Of the 15 sessions at Madrid 2019, seven were framed partly around issues of identities. Another five addressed politics and power in one form or another. Identity politics raises new questions about power relations. The group provides a forum in which politics and identity are discussed together, rather than as distinct and separate perspectives. This welcome diversification, however, presented challenges. How far cultural studies' original agenda of inquiry can accommodate the realities of "whole ways of life" in the Global South is an open question.

Reconsiderations: De-Westernizing Analysis

Together with other areas of human and social sciences, cultural studies has been increasingly and rightly challenged to move beyond its original frames of reference and engage with histories, conditions, and issues in the Global South. In the context of the committed internationalism that has defined IAMCR from the outset, de-Westernizing the analysis of popular culture is a necessary, urgent, and continuing project.

As the first continent to emancipate itself from European colonization, only to be defined as a zone of particular strategic interest by the US, Latin American writing played a formative role in debates. Ariel Dorfman and Armand Mattelart's *How to Read Donald Duck* (1975) excavated the coercive ideology concealed by the seemingly innocent pleasures provided by the Disney Corporation. As Janet Wasko's (2020) analysis confirms, Disney's continuing global reach and expanded portfolio, acquiring the Marvel comics and Star Wars franchises, and opening a theme park in Shanghai ensure the continuing relevance of critical popular cultural analysis.

American popular culture domination has been challenged by the rise of new regional production hubs. India's Bollywood film industry and Brazilian and Mexican popular television have been joined by the "Korean Wave" in popular music and television, the emergence of Nigeria (Nollywood) as a major center of popular filmmaking, the turn to commercialism in Chinese television, and the proliferation of localized musical styles.

Writing from the Global South underlines the continuing importance of peasant cultures, indigenous peoples, and religion in organizing popular cultural practices. Religious practices of pilgrimage, ritual, and everyday rites have been missing from the cultural studies research agenda. The recent resurgence of fundamentalist religious movements, from Donald Trump's militant evangelical base to Modi's Hindu nationalism, raises urgent questions around the relations between popular culture, popular belief, and political action that can no longer be avoided.

Convergences

In the influential *Hybrid Cultures* (1990), Canclini draws on Latin American experience to explore contemporary culture. His later book (2001), *Consumers and Citizens,* singles out tensions between consumer culture's possessive individualism and the civic solidarities of citizenship. This is a universal fracture.

During the last 40 years, capitalist economies responded to the structural profitability crisis of the 1970s by pursuing and exporting neo-liberal policies. With the collapse of Soviet Communism, India's retreat from self-sufficiency, and China's embrace of markets, the three major economic zones that had operated outside the global capitalist system have all become major players within it. Competition for national advantage in the global arena has translated civic solidarities of nation-building into increasingly militant nationalisms.

Social media platforms have boosted commodity culture by expanding the space available for product advertising and promotion and enabling the fine tuning of target audiences through monopoly control of personal data.

At the same time, self-organized user communities are collaborating to produce and distribute material that speaks to their interests. Struggles around competing popular cultural economies and modes of expression are increasingly being fought out online, though stark digital divides in access and use, within and between countries, should caution against excessive new media focus. The lived experience of popular culture continues to occupy multiple other private and public spaces.

Resources of Hope

Recent years have seen early champions of cultural studies express increasing disillusion over its current direction of travel (e.g., Miller, 2020). Under pressure from the marketization of higher education, careerism, subject to incorporation within the dominant neo-liberal project, the field, it is argued, has been subject to a degree of de-politicization and the mission, drifting away from its critical edge.

Mounting challenges from widening social inequalities, ever-increasing flows of migrants and displaced persons, accelerating climate change, recurrent pandemics, and the next generation of digital innovation around artificial intelligence and robotics pose urgent new questions.

Raymond William's last essay collection was *Resources of Hope* (1989). Continuing to build on popular culture analysis as a pivotal arena of struggle over the distribution and deployment of resources for self-understanding and social agency remains a key contribution to the search for a more just, equitable, and ecologically sustainable social order.

References

Adorno, T., & Horkheimer, M. (1972). *Dialectic of enlightenment.* Herder and Herder.

Barthes, R. (1967). *Elements of semiology.* Jonathon Cape.

Barthes, R. (1972). *Mythologies.* Jonathan Cape.

Bennett, T. (1996). Out in the open: Reflections on the history and practice of cultural studies. *Cultural Studies, 10*(1), 133–153.

Bolas, T. (2009). *Screen education: From film appreciation to media studies.* Intellect.

Bourdieu, P. (1984). *Distinction: A social critique of the judgement of taste.* Routledge.

Brunsdon, C., & Morley, D. (1978). *Everyday television: Nationwide.* British Film Institute.

Canclini, N. G. (1990). *Hybrid cultures: Strategies for entering and leaving modernity.* University of Minnesota Press.

Canclini, N. G. (2001). *Consumers and citizens: Globalization and multicultural conflicts.* University of Minnesota Press.

CCCS (Centre for Contemporary Cultural Studies). (2012). *Women take issue; Aspects of women's subordination.* Routledge.

Curran, J. (2013). Mickey Mouse squeaks back: Defending media studies (Keynote address). MeCCSA Conference, Derry.

Curran, J., & Seaton, J. (1981). *Power without responsibility*. Fontana.

Dorfman, A., & Mattelart, A. (1975). *How to read Donald Duck*. International General.

Dyer, R. (1979). *Stars*. British Film Institute.

Easthope, A. (1991). *Literary into cultural studies*. Routledge.

Eco, U. (1974). *Does the public hurt television?* (RAI, broadcasters and their audiences: Vol.1. Introductory reports). Proceedings of the XXV Prix Italia Colloquium, Venice, Italy, 1973, p. 49–64). Edizioni Radio Televisione Italia.

Elliott, P. (1972). *The making of a television series: A case study in the sociology of culture*. Constable.

Garnham, N., & Raymond, W. (1980). Pierre Bourdieu and the sociology of culture: An introduction. *Media, Culture & Society, 2*(3), 209–223.

Gramsci, A. (1971). *Selections from the prison notebooks of Antonio Gramsci* (Hoare, Q., & Smith, N., Eds. & Trans.). Lawrence & Wishart.

Gilroy, P. (1987). *There ain't no Black in the Union Jack: The cultural politics of race and nation*. Hutchinson.

Habermas, J. (1989). *The structural transformation of the public sphere: An inquiry into a category of bourgeois society*. Polity.

Hall, S. (1960). Introducing NLR. *New Left Review, 1*(Jan-Feb). https://newleftreview.org/issues/i1/articles/stuart-hall-introducing-nlr Accessed 15 June 2022.

Hall, S. (1979, January). The great moving right show. *Marxism Today*, p. 14–20.

Hall, S. (1973). *Encoding and decoding in television discourse* (Paper Presentation). Council of Europe Colloquy on Training in the Critical Reading of Television Language, Council and CMCR, University of Leicester, Leicester, England.

Hall, S. (1983). The problem of ideology-Marxism without guarantees. In B. Matthews (Ed.), *Marx: A hundred years on* (p. 57–85). Lawrence and Wishart.

Hall, S., & Whannel, P. (1964). *The popular arts*. Hutchinson.

Hall, S., & Jefferson, T. (1976). *Resistance through rituals: Youth subcultures in post-war Britain*. Hutchinson.

Hall, S., Critcher, C., Jefferson, T., Clarke, J., & Roberts, B. (1978). *Policing the crisis: Mugging, the state and law and order*. Macmillan.

Halloran, J. D., Elliott, P., & Murdock, G. (1970). *Demonstrations and communication: A case study*. Penguin.

Hartmann, P., & Husband, C. (1974). *Racism and the mass media*. Davis-Poynter.

Hebdige, D. (1979). *Subculture: The meaning of style*. Methuen.

Hobson, D. (1982). *Crossroads: The drama of a soap opera*. Methuen.

Hoggart, R. (1958). *The uses of literacy*. Penguin Books.

Hoggart, R. (1969). *Contemporary Cultural Studies: An approach to the study of literature and society*. Centre for Contemporary Cultural Studies (CCCS).

Jay, M. (1973). *The dialectical imagination*. Heinemann.

McGuigan, J. (2005). *The cultural public sphere*. Routledge.

McRobbie, A. (1978). *Jackie: An ideology of adolescent femininity*. Stencilled Occasional Papers, Birmingham: CCCS.

Miller, T. (2020). Immigration and climate change might just matter more than getting that next grant. *European Journal of Cultural Studies, 23*(6), 970–988.

Millum, T. (1975). *Images of women*. Chato and Windus.

Morley, D. (1980). *The nationwide audience*. British Film Institute.

Nowell-Smith, G., & Dupin, C. (2012). *The British Film Institute, the government and film culture 1933-2000.* Manchester University Press.

Robinson, G. (2002, July 21-25). *IAMCR then and now: Lessons from gender research* (Paper Presentation). IAMCR conference.

Rowbotham, S. (1975). *Hidden from history.* Pluto Press.

Scannell, P., & Cardiff, D. (1991). *A social history of British broadcasting.* Blackwell.

Smith, A. C. H. (1975). *Paper voices.* Chatto and Windus.

Steele, T. (1997). *The emergence of cultural studies.* Lawrence & Wishart.

Thompson, E. P. (1963). *The making of the English working class.* Victor Gollancz.

Wasko, J. (2020). *Understanding Disney* [2nd Edition]. Polity Press. (Original work published 2001).

Williams, R. (1958). *Culture and society.* Chatto and Windus.

Williams, R. (1965). *The long revolution.* Penguin.

Williams, R. (1974). *Television: Technology and cultural form.* Fontana Collins.

Williams, R. (1989). *Resources of hope: Culture, democracy, socialism.* Verso.

Williams, R., Hall, S., & Thompson, E. (Eds.). (1968). *The May Day manifesto.* Penguin Books.

Willis, P. (1977). *Learning to labour.* Saxon House.

Willis, P. (1978). *Profane culture.* Routledge.

Wollen, P. (1967, January 26). *Cinema and semiology: Some points of contact* (Seminar). *BFI Education Seminar Series*, London, United Kingdom.

Wollen, P. (1969). *Signs and meaning in the cinema.* Secker and Warburg.

CHAPTER 5

IAMCR's Engagement with Participatory Communication

Tom Jacobson

Introduction

This edited collection reports the many ways in which IAMCR has engaged with both scholarship and wider publics since it was established in 1957. This chapter covers IAMCR's engagement with the topic of participatory communication.[1] Participatory communication can refer to communication processes that facilitate agency at any number of levels of social organization, ranging from participation in small groups, to communities, to nations, and to global institutions. Agency refers to self-reliance, self-determination, autonomous social development, democratic processes, and more. Communication includes face-to-face interaction in groups, community deliberations, multi-stakeholder collaborations among institutions, social movements, and mass as well as social media use.

In terms of scholarship, many of IAMCR's sections and working groups (WG) have addressed such processes. The Political Communication Section addresses political processes, many of which are concerned with citizen participation in

[1] Thanks to Jan Servaes, Rico Lie, and Satarupa Dasgupta for supporting historical materials. Thanks also to Cees Hamelink and Kaarle Nordenstreng for their invaluable *Basics of IAMCR History* as well as the IAMCR and Participatory Communication Research Section digital archives, at https://iamcr.org/digital-archive and https://iamcr.org/s-wg/section/pcr, respectively. Both accessed 15 June 2022.

T. Jacobson (✉)
Temple University, Philadelphia, PA, USA
e-mail: jacobson.thomas@temple.edu

© The Author(s), under exclusive license to Springer Nature Switzerland AG 2023

J. Becker, R. Mansell (eds.), *Reflections on the International Association for Media and Communication Research*,
https://doi.org/10.1007/978-3-031-16383-8_5

democratic institutions and the role of media in these processes. Among the many topics studied within the International Communication Section, global institutions and processes must be included, as well as issues related to the participation, and often exclusion, of the Global South in these institutions. The Gender and Communication Section interrogates issues such as gendered constructions of women's access to power, resources, and opportunities for communication. IAMCR has one research group, the Participatory Communication Research Section, that is devoted entirely to the subject of communication and its role in participation.

In terms of wider, non-academic, communities, IAMCR has a rich legacy of contributions to citizen participation in education, media, policy-making, and broad matters of public import. These non-academic efforts have been reflected in actions taken by the association itself in training activities, policy statements, collaborations with other organizations, and in other ways. This chapter addresses IAMCR's engagement with participatory communication as an organization of the whole, as well as engagement reflected in the scholarly work of its Sections and WGs, while focusing on the accomplishments of the Participatory Communication Research Section (See Footnote 1).

Communication, Participation, and National Development

The Rise and Fall of the Dominant Paradigm: Communication and Participation in Post-World War II National Development Efforts

An understanding of IAMCR's engagement with participatory communication requires some background related to broad, global historical dynamics following World War 2. These involve both an explosive growth in the number of new countries in the Global South, resulting from struggles of decolonization, and the geopolitics of the superpowers during this period. Considerable research during this time concerned prospects for establishing and evolving the new countries and with policy stances taken among high-income countries in relation to their development.

Both academics and policy-makers addressed the prospects of the newly established countries through the lens of modernization theory. Academically, modernization theory comprised, during the 1950s, 1960s, and 1970s, a collection of studies ranging across the social sciences which shared the assumption that "traditional societies" must transition rapidly to democratic "modern societies" by pursuing explosive economic growth (Rostow, 1960). This explosive growth was understood to require related social transformations, including increased reliance on technological and scientific development, the separation of church and state, increased social mobility, citizen literacy, growth of capital accumulation, and other features (Black, 1966).

The idea of citizen participation was among these transformations. This was seen chiefly as participation in the institutions of representative government, free speech, and media use. The most prominent political scientist addressing such matters was Daniel Lerner. For Lerner, consumption of print and broadcast media should be treated as "media participation." Media participation would, in turn, make possible "political participation" in the form of involvement in party politics and voting (Lerner, 1958, p. 43–75). Participation in this form was widely considered to be an important part of modernization as communication for development. One influential study of political development at the time characterized modernizing societies as undergoing a "participation explosion" (Almond & Verba, 1963, p. 4).

In many ways, events failed to corroborate modernization theory's predictions. The disappointments in modernization economics have been analyzed in an extensive critical literature (Amin, 1997; Frank, 1984; Galtung, 1971; Wallerstein, 1979). Rapid economic growth produced highly uneven results, including massive income disparity within countries, crushing national debt burdens, social dislocation, and other problems. Even where economic growth was relatively strong, citizen participation, whether media participation or political participation, was often limited where it existed at all.

IAMCR and the Rise of Critical Scholarship on Communication and National Development

Critical studies of economic development theory were accompanied by critical studies of media and communication for development (Inayatullah, 1973; Hedebro, 1982; Matta, 1986; Mattelart, 1979; McAnany et al., 1981). These studies shifted from the modernization viewpoint that saw commercial mass media as supporting citizen participation in democracy to a view holding that mass media could often undermine democracy. Luis Ramiro Beltrán held that the concepts of communication embedded in modernization theory were foreign to social conditions in the Third World and in Latin America, in particular. They were "alien" and oriented toward diffusion of Western ways rather than toward democratic emancipation. He urged more horizontal communication (Beltrán, 1980). Herbert Schiller tracked the global promotion of modernization theory's version of free speech and media principles, equating them with American pursuit of media markets abroad (Schiller, 1976).

Many of the scholars contributing to this passing of modernization styled communication theory were active members of IAMCR who reported their studies at its conferences, including Herbert Schiller, Luis Ramiro Beltrán, Juan Diaz-Bordenave, Armand Mattelart, and many others. As explained by Cees Hamelink and Kaarle Nordenstreng:

> IAMCR members offered a critical analytical approach, seeking to achieve a balance between those with proprietary interests in employing the concept of human rights as an instrument to justify globalization for commercial purposes, and those with democratic interests, championing fundamental freedoms in pursuit of enhancing civil society and its media in the post-Cold War world. (Hamelink & Nordenstreng, 2020, p. 33)

This critical turn in post-modernization scholarship concerned not only development studies but also a critical analysis of media more generally, advanced again by many members active in IAMCR, including Dallas Smythe, Robin Cheesman, Graham Murdock, Nicholas Garnham, and Janet Wasko, among others. "The thematic focus of IAMCR's 1990 Bled Conference on democracy signaled the beginning of critical reflection on the larger significance of communication—its technology, its institutions—to worldwide efforts to strengthen democratic systems of governance" (Hamelink & Nordenstreng, 2020, p. 28). These scholars, even when studying media institutions of the North, shared a global understanding of media and political institutions. Appreciation for the importance of genuine citizen participation in democratic institutions and criticism of media aligned with hegemonic political powers that undermined this participation were themes that ran throughout much of their work.

IAMCR's Engagements with Participatory Communication as an Organization

In addition to contributions of critical scholarship made by its individual members during this period, IAMCR itself contributed organizational efforts that advocated for the democratic operation of the media. One place that IAMCR's engagement with participatory communication can be seen is in its efforts to facilitate the participation of scholars from across the globe in communication research. IAMCR has frequently held conferences in the Global South, in countries such as Argentina, Brazil, Venezuela, India, Mexico, Egypt, South Africa, and others. Additional meetings have been held in non-NATO European countries, including Yugoslavia, which was a founding IAMCR member, the German Democratic Republic (GDR), Poland, Czechoslovakia, and others. Combined, these conferences total nearly half of all IAMCR meetings.

As critical scholarship flourished throughout the decolonization period, policy initiatives, and debates over them, were entertained within the United Nations' (UN) system, the non-aligned movement, and other multilateral organizations. UNESCO was a particularly active venue for thinking and policy-making on participatory communication for development during this period in the context of calls for a New International Information Order (NIIO), later called the New World Information and Communication Order (NWICO), which would redress disparities in global information flows and domination of these flows by commercial interests in the industrialized North (Masmoudi, 1979).

IAMCR and its member scholars were much engaged in these discussions. During the association's 1966 annual conference in Herceg-Novi, Yugoslavia, mass media and national development were among the topics of discussion. As the NWICO debates later evolved, IAMCR and member scholars followed events keenly and contributed in a number of ways. Throughout the period of the MacBride Commission's work, IAMCR members, including its then President Jim Halloran and Vice President Yassen Zassoursky, contributed background papers to the Commission's efforts (Hamelink, 1980; MacBride Commission, 1980).

The NWICO debates within UNESCO waned following this period, but IAMCR's interest remained in the form of engagements with related policy issues. One such issue addressed by the association and its members was the idea of a "Right to Communicate". At the association's 1993 conference in Dublin, members received reports about the recent presence of the association at the UN World Conference on Human Rights in Vienna where the "Right to Communicate" had been promoted. Preceding the world conference, sections of the association organized a seminar on "The Right to Communicate" in Bratislava. Participants in the seminar adopted a Bratislava Declaration that was fed into diplomatic negotiations at the Vienna Conference.

Another of IAMCR's engagements with global issues concerning communication and participation was work related to the globally evolving digital information system. Some of the issues addressed in the NWICO debates were carried forward in meetings of the World Summit on the Information Society (WSIS), with meetings in Geneva in 2003 and Tunis in 2005. For many in global NGO and policy communities, the WSIS was a forum in which disparities in information access between and within countries could be addressed, and hopefully redressed. At IAMCR's Barcelona Conference in 2002, a WSIS task force was established to coordinate IAMCR's involvement in the WSIS process. The commitment was reaffirmed during the 2004 Porto Allegre Conference where a task force was formed to represent the association in the second phase of the WSIS in Tunis.

> Throughout its history the Association has adopted public statements on such issues as the protection of journalists, the right to communicate, the freedom of research, the support for international communication policies in the service of democratic development, and the need to contribute to the improvement of communication facilities in the Third World. (Hamelink & Nordenstreng, 2020, p. 7)

Communication, Participation, and Social Change

Participatory Communication for Development and Social Change

The critical analysis of media and related policies was one important theme of research in the post-modernization era. A second important theme was concerned less with how citizen participation in communication could be marginalized by commercial media and concerned more with the kinds of communication that might be required to redress this marginalization. In this line of thinking, there was less concern with criticizing undemocratic practices of commercial media and more concern with the kinds of communication that could be generated by citizens and communities themselves in pursuit of self-reliance and grassroots social change (Diaz-Bordenave, 1976; Fraser & Restrepo-Estrada, 1998; Melkote, 2012; Moemeka, 1994; O'Sullivan-Ryan & Kaplan, 1982; Servaes, 1985, 1989, 2020). The catchword for such processes was "participatory communication."

The single most important theoretical touchstone for this version of participatory analysis was the work of Paulo Freire. Freire was a Brazilian educator identified with an approach to teaching that would broaden education's goals from acquisition of information to personal transformation and liberation (Freire, 1968). The key characteristic of his pedagogical approach was its emphasis on dialog for *conscientização*, or critical consciousness. This pedagogy advocated the use of dialog devoted to understanding the social contradictions of unjust power and to developing critical consciousness that could then be directed toward radical humanization. Freire's pedagogy has found application in a wide range of development settings where dialog can be devoted to participatory social change (McLaren & Lankshear, 1994). It has been employed in projects ranging from the implementation of new agricultural practices to collective management of local radio stations to local production of videos conducted in a dialogic, participatory fashion, and more.

The breadth of development and participatory social change practices used in the field today is considerable, and more varied, than Freire's ideas alone would suggest, but all have been informed by Freire's thinking. A minimal list of commonly employed techniques would include Participatory Rural Appraisal, Media Advocacy, Social Mobilization, Entertainment Education, Social Marketing, Social Media for Participation, Participatory Needs Assessment, and Implementation and Evaluation. Some of these techniques are interpersonal; some are mediated; and some are more participatory than others (Carpentier, 2011; Hemer & Tufte, 2005; Quarry & Ramirez, 2009; Thomas & van de Fliert, 2015; Tufte, 2017; Wilkins et al., 2014). However, all are used today in conjunction with participation at least on occasion, such has been the influence of Freire's thinking on participation.

IAMCR's Sections, Working Groups, Task Forces, and the Participatory Communication Research Section

Scholarship into processes of participatory communication can be seen in many of IAMCR's research groups. This includes the work of sections such as the Political Communication Section noted above, the Community Communication and Alternative Media Section, and the Journalism Research and Education Section. It can also be seen in the activities of WGs such as the Public Service Media Policies Working Group.

While many of IAMCR's Sections and WGs address participatory communication in one way or another, they do vary in the extent to which they engage with subjects related to communication for participation in the sense covered here. There is one section whose work has been entirely dedicated to research and practice related to participatory communication, the Participatory Communication Research (PCR) Section. Established in 1994, the PCR Section grew over time to be among the larger of the association's sections, and highly productive of both research outputs and collaborations. The Section's work must figure prominently in any treatment of IAMCR's engagement with participatory communication and its work is covered in the body of what remains of this chapter.

Meetings on participatory communication had been conducted during the late 1980s under the auspices of the association's International Communication Section. Topics discussed included broad trends in development communication but devoted considerable attention as well to project-level interventions, community processes, and regional efforts to facilitate local participation in the design of development planning and social change efforts. The first formal meeting discussing participatory communication in this sense took place at the Bled Conference in 1990, convened under the name of the Participatory Communication Research Network (PCRN) Working Group. At this time, the emphasis not only included participatory treatments of communication among citizens but also emphasis on participation among theorists and practitioners; on making these exchanges operate in a two-way fashion between them, rather than a one-way fashion moving from theorists to practitioners.

Subsequent PCRN meetings took place at IAMCR's Istanbul and Guarujá Conferences. In 1993, the PCRN launched a *PCR-Newsletter*. Newsletter contents from that time indicate the focal concerns of the WG. The lead article in the newsletter's inaugural issue was *Communication and Development: Freirean Cultural Politics in a Post-Modern Era*, written by Pradip Thomas, later a PCR Section Head, who at that time was with the World Association of Christian Communication (WACC) based in London. A second piece comprised *A Selected Bibliography on Participatory Communication Research*, prepared by Daniele Mezzana who worked for the CE.R.FE, Research and Documentation Center, Rome (PCR-Newsletter, 1993). This established a pattern for subsequent newsletters with content comprising one or two substantive pieces followed by bibliographies, announcements of upcoming relevant meetings or events, notices of ongoing research, new publications, and abstracts from that year's annual conference.

The PCRN applied for status as a Section within the association and was authorized as the Participatory Communication Research (PCR) Section during the Seoul Conference in 1994. Jan Servaes, who had been the animating force in launching both the PCRN network and the PCR Section, was its first Section president (as Section heads were then called). The new Section's mission statement represented the mix of theoretical and practical aims that had developed within PCRN meetings.

> ...the work of the Participatory Communication Research Section/Network (PCRN) is not based on any specific definition of participation. Rather, participation is a term used to refer to a number of social and planning processes occurring in many different places and in many different contexts. The Network exists to help support people working across this variety of participatory contexts, by providing contacts, by locating relevant information sources, and by working toward theoretical clarification. (PCR-Newsletter, 1993, p. 1)

The Section undertook scholarly efforts such as book publishing projects that collected papers presented during Section meetings at IAMCR conferences, including *Participatory Communication for Social Change* (Servaes et al., 1996) and *Theoretical Approaches to Participatory Communication* (Jacobson & Servaes, 1999). The Section was also involved in practice and policy-related collaboration, such as helping organize UNESCO-IAMCR and inter-agency Roundtables on Development Communication.

It is not possible here to catalog all the Section's activities over the past 25 or so years. Nevertheless, the early years established a pattern. As the Section grew and stabilized within IAMCR, its activities concerned theoretical analysis, case studies, methodological studies, seminars joining academics and practitioners, and engagements with multilateral organizations and non-profits. This work was led over time by a sequence of regularly elected series of heads of Section continuing until today. Jan Servaes (Belgium), Tom Jacobson (United States), Ullamaija Kivikuru (Finland), Rico Lie (Netherlands), Pradip Thomas (Australia), Satarupa Das Gupta (United States), Nico Carpentier (Czech Republic), and Ana Duarte Melo (Portugal).

Selected highlights show the continuity of this work over time. PCR Section activities at IAMCR's 1998 Glasgow Conference included 48 individually submitted papers, presented in six sessions. The PCR program that year demonstrated the Section's collaboration with other research groups within IAMCR. One session was jointly convened by PCR and IAMCR's Human Rights Committee on the topic of "The People's Communication Charter." Another was convened with the Gender and Communication Section, entitled, "In our own Image: Using media to represent ourselves." Sessions were co-sponsored as well with the International Communication and then Local Radio and Television Sections. A different set of sessions in the Glasgow meeting comprised the PCR Section's collaboration with groups outside the association. One was co-sponsored by PCR and the African Council for Communication Education on "Social Change: Principles and Strategies." Another session convened the Third IAMCR-UNESCO Roundtable on Development Communication, whose theme was "Communication and Poverty Alleviation: Grassroots Development through Participatory Communication."

At the association's 2000 Conference in Singapore, the Indian Committee for Development of Communication (ICDC) began supporting the Section's efforts. The ICDC provided travel grants for a number of years to promising young Indian scholars to present papers in PCR Section meetings at the association's conferences.

The PCR Section program in Puerto Alegre in 2004 covered what had become its customary range of both applied and theoretical matters, but also addressed the increased relevance of digital media in a substantial way. As reported by Ullamaija Kivikuru, Section Head during this meeting:

> The scope of topics was quite large as usual, ranging from case studies based on projects to theoretical considerations around communicative action and Foucault's perception of power. The majority were more empirically oriented, but not only descriptive, basing on a theoretical frame, quite often that of Habermas' public sphere. Reflections of the conference theme (democracy) were also quite common. ... There were also quite a few papers which had cultural studies as a point of departure. The concept of community media, especially community radio received fairly much attention, but several papers elaborated also on the new forms of alternative media such as weblogs and co-links. (Kivikuru, 2002, p. 23)

The PCR Section had a productive conference at IAMCR's 50th anniversary meeting in Paris in 2007, including panel and poster presentations by individuals from 25 countries. A session on the history of participatory communication research reflected on both theory and practice (Servaes, 2007).

In Stockholm, in 2008, the PCR Section had a large program including a number of fully pre-formed panel sessions, including one arranged by colleagues from the London School of Economics and Political Science on "Public Participation," referring not to project interventions, but to political participation in the wider sphere of politics. Another panel session promoted and celebrated the global launch of ØRECOM, "a new bi-national (Denmark and Sweden) research platform in the field of Communication for Development" (Lie, 2008, p. 17).

The PCR Section has continued or expanded its publishing and collaborations over recent years. In 2016, the Section organized and delivered a PhD Winter School on Participation and Communication, in cooperation with Jinan University's College of Journalism and Communication in Guangzhou, China.

In 2017, the PCR Section hosted a seminar entitled "Imagine Europe," in Roskilde, Denmark. And it organized an event on participatory advertising in

Bogota leading up to the association's Cartagena meeting. Papers from this seminar were developed into a published book, *ParticipAD—Participatory advertising: A global perspective with a Latin American focus* (Duarte Melo & Duque, 2018). During the Cartagena Conference, PCR introduced a notable institution in the Section's history, a PCR Section keynote speaker presentation to be held annually at subsequent IAMCR conferences.

The PCR Section had 42 papers at the Eugene meeting in 2018, presented in 12 panels, three of which were mixed language English/Spanish. Another PCR Section activity that year was involvement in a conference on "Post-Representative Participations" co-hosted by the MeCCSA Postgraduate Network, the IAMCR PCR Section, and the Centre for Digital Media Cultures (CDMC) at the University of Brighton.

During 2019, the Section co-organized the event "Participatory communication and the struggle over human rights," in Rio de Janeiro, with a number of Brazilian institutions, including the *Laboratório de Comunicação Dialógica* at Rio de Janeiro State University (UERJ), the Institute of Educational Technology for Health at the Federal University of Rio de Janeiro (UFRJ), and the Research and Production Centre in Communication and Emergence at the Federal University of Fluminense (UFF). It also completed a journal publishing effort. Section officers Ana Duarte Melo and Nico Carpentier co-edited with Fábio Ribeiro Volume 36 of the Portuguese journal *Comunicação e Sociedade*, entitled, *Rescuing Participation.* In addition, communication among Section members was enhanced during this period by the re-launch of a *PCR Section Newsletter*, in place of the *PCR Newsletter* which had ceased publication some years earlier (https://iamcr.org/s-wg/section/pcr).

The IAMCR 2020 and 2021 annual conferences were profoundly impacted by the COVID-19 crisis and conducted online. The Section had, for a number of years, been among the association's innovators in efforts to explore interactive, online scholarly modalities and took this opportunity of these meetings to push its online programming further (Participatory Communication Research Section, 2021).

Closing

This chapter of the present volume addressing IAMCR's history covers the association's engagement with the topic of participatory communication. As the foregoing pages demonstrate, this engagement has been broad and deep, comprising the work of the association's individual member scholars as well as its Sections and WGs, together with initiatives undertaken by the association as a whole. This engagement should be expected to continue. In terms of scholarship, democratically oriented research continues to be advanced throughout many, if not all, of IAMCR's Sections and WGs. And the PCR Section remains vigorous.

At the organizational level, the association continues to reach out for engagement opportunities. Ongoing engagements include periodic releases from IAMCR's Clearinghouse for Public Statements and the work of its occasional task forces. Task forces related to past WSIS meetings have already been noted. In addition, the association has two currently active task forces that liaise with the Global Alliance on Media and Gender (https://gamag.net) and the Global Alliance for Social and Behavior Change (https://globalallianceforsbc.org). The association is clearly maintaining its historical practice of participating in matters of practice and policy that concern media and communication.

Given the challenges facing the global community at the time of this writing, such research and practice will perhaps be even more relevant in the future than it has been in the past. Citizens must be involved and heard. Their viewpoints must be taken on board by governments. International collaborations aiming to face these challenges will be required, with fully global participation of all countries in mechanisms dedicated to face them. In such venues, democratic representation not only relies on, but in many ways fully consists in, dialogic or participatory communication among citizens and stakeholders, academics, policy-makers, and politicians. There is, therefore, every reason to expect not only that IAMCR and its scholarly units will continue to be engaged with the subject of participatory communication, but also every reason to expect that this work will continue to be relevant to democratic aspirations globally.

References

Almond, G. A., & Verba, S. (1963). *The civic culture: Political attitudes and democracy in five nations*. Princeton University Press.

Amin, S. (1997). *Capitalism in the age of globalization: The management of contemporary society*. Zed Books.

Beltrán, L. R. (1980). Farewell to Aristotle: Horizontal communication. *Communication, 5*, 5–41.

Black, C. E. (1966). *The dynamics of modernization: A study in comparative history*. Harper & Row.

Carpentier, N. (2011). *Media and participation: A site of ideological-democratic struggle*. Intellect.

Diaz-Bordenave, J. (1976). Communication of agricultural innovations in Latin America: The need for new models. *Communication Research, 3*(2), 135–154.

Duarte Melo, A. D., & Duque, M. (Eds.). (2018). *ParticipAD – Participatory advertising: A global perspective with a Latin American focus*. University of Minho Center for Communication and Society Studies.

Frank, A. G. (1984). *Critique and anti-critique: Essays on dependence and reformism*. Praeger.

Fraser, C., & Restrepo-Estrada, S. (1998). *Communicating for development: Human change for survival*. I. B. Tauris.

Freire, P. (1968). *Pedagogy of the oppressed*. Herder and Herder.

Galtung, J. (1971). A structural theory of imperialism. *Journal of Peace Research, 2*, 81–116.

Hamelink, C. (Ed.). (1980). *Communication in the eighties: A reader on the "MacBride Report"*. IDOC.

Hamelink, C., & Nordenstreng, K. (2020). *Basics of IAMCR history* (2nd ed.). Retrieved 15 June 2022, from https://iamcr.org/sites/default/files/basics_of_iamcr_2nd_ed_rev2.pdf

Hedebro, G. A. (1982). *Communication and social change in developing nations: A critical view*. Iowa State University Press.

Hemer, O., & Tufte, T. (2005). *Media and glocal change: Rethinking communication for development*. Clacso Books / NORDICOM.

Inayatullah, C. (1973). Western, Asian, or global models of development: The effect of the transference of models on the development of Asian society. In W. Schramm & D. Lerner (Eds.), *Communication and change: The last ten years – And the next* (p. 241–252). University Press of Hawaii.

Jacobson, T., & Servaes, J. (Eds.). (1999). *Theoretical approaches to participatory communication*. The Hampton Press.

Kivikuru, U. (2002). Participatory communication research section report. *IAMCR Newsletter, 13*(2), 23–24.

Lerner, D. (1958). *The passing of traditional society: Modernizing the Middle East*. The Free Press.

Lie, R. (2008). Participatory communication research section report. *IAMCR Newsletter, 18*(1), 17–18.

MacBride & Commisioners. (1980). *Communication and Society Today and Tomorrow: Many voices, one world. Towards a new, more just and more efficient world information and communication order*. Kogan Page, Unipub, UNESCO.

Masmoudi, M. (1979). The new world information order. *Journal of Communication, 29*(2), 172–179.

Mattelart, A. (1979). *Multinational corporations and the control of culture: The ideological apparatuses of imperialism*. Harvester Press.

Matta, F. R. (1986). Alternative communication: Solidarity and development in the face of transnational expansion. In R. Atwood & E. McAnany (Eds.), *Communication and Latin American society: Trends in critical research, 1960–1985*. University of Wisconsin Press.

McAnany, E., Schnitman, J., & Janus, N. (1981). *Communication and social structure: Critical studies in mass media research*. Praeger.

McLaren, P., & Lankshear, C. (Eds.). (1994). *Politics of liberation: Paths from Freire*. Routledge.

Melkote, S. (2012). *Development communication in directed social change: A reappraisal of theory and practice*. Asian Media Information and Communication Centre.

Moemeka, A. A. (Ed.). (1994). *Communicating for development: A new pan-disciplinary perspective*. State University of New York Press.

O'Sullivan-Ryan, J., & Kaplan, M. (1982). *Communication methods to promote grass-roots participation: A summary of research findings from Latin America, and an annotated bibliography*. UNESCO. Retrieved 15 June 2022, from https://unesdoc.unesco.org/ark:/48223/pf0000043552

Participatory Communication Research Section. (August, 2021). *Newsletter*. Retrieved 15 June 2022, from https://iamcr.org/s-wg/section/pcr/august-2021-newsletter

PCR-Newsletter. (1993). An occasional publication, *1*(1). Retrieved 15 June 2022, from https://iamcr.org/s-wg/section/pcr

Quarry, W., & Ramirez, R. (2009). *Communication for another development: Listening before telling*. Zed Books.

Rostow, W. W. (1960). *The stages of economic growth: A non-Communist manifesto*. Cambridge University Press.

Schiller, H. (1976). *Communication and cultural domination*. Routledge.

Servaes, J. (1985). Towards an alternative concept of communication and development. *Media Development, 4*, 2–5.

Servaes, J. (1989). *One world, multiple cultures*. Acco Press.

Servaes, J. (2007). Participatory communication for development and social change: Some reflections and suggestions. *Journal of Development Communication, 18*(2), 11–23.

Servaes, J. (Ed.). (2020). *Handbook of communication for development and social change*. Springer.

Servaes, J., Jacobson, T., & White, S. (1996). *Participatory communication and social change*. Sage Publications.

Thomas, P. N., & van de Fliert, E. (2015). *Interrogating the theory and practice of communication for social change*. Palgrave Macmillan.

Tufte, T. (2017). *Communication and social change: A citizen perspective*. Polity.

Wallerstein, I. (1979). *The capitalist world economy*. Cambridge University Press.

Wilkins, K. G., Tufte, T., & Obregon, R. (2014). *The handbook of development communication and social change*. John Wiley & Sons.

CHAPTER 6

IAMCR's Legacy in Scholarship on Religion

Stewart M. Hoover

Introduction

Media and communication research has undergone great change in the decades since the founding of IAMCR. This change has featured an evolution from early reliance on predecessor disciplines, including psychology, history, sociology, economics, and politics, through a period of refinement and narrowing, as the academic assemblies that emerged sought to refine this research into narrowed and domesticated compartments, fitted more to institutional demands than to intellectual exploration. But this rather narrow view then began to open again, as scholars started to engage intellectual and other resources from a broad range of fields in order to explain the ever-expanding geographies of media and communication.

This broadening was also driven by a growing appreciation, among these scholars, of the need to build knowledge about the ways that media and communication were critically implicated in the large social and cultural trends that define local, regional, and global life within the range of "modernities" that define the history of the present. Questions of class, gender, colonialism, and decoloniality, of the economics of neo-liberal globalization and the rise of new forms of authoritarian populism and ethno-nationalism, are not easily explained without robust engagement with the systems, economies, and processes of media and communication. The scholars and discourses within the association

S. M. Hoover (✉)
University of Colorado Boulder, Boulder, CO, USA
e-mail: Hoover@colorado.edu

© The Author(s), under exclusive license to Springer Nature Switzerland AG 2023

J. Becker, R. Mansell (eds.), *Reflections on the International Association for Media and Communication Research*,
https://doi.org/10.1007/978-3-031-16383-8_6

have risen to the challenges of theory and methodology directed at this ever-expanding field of endeavor.

The Question of Religion

Throughout this developing legacy, perhaps no question has been more complex and challenging than the question of religion. In the last century, academic scholarship rooted in social theory tended to assume the so-called secularization paradigm. In its simplest form (and unfortunately that has been the way it has been tacitly passed down across intellectual generations), it held that as modernity progressed, religion would gradually fade in importance. The logic assumed that as publics became increasingly educated, as their economic prospects evolved, and most importantly, as modernity gradually rationalized and instrumentalized traditional social ties, they would no longer turn to religious belief, practice, and explanation (Berger, 1967; for a critique specifically addressed to the field, see Morgan, 2013). It was therefore thought that attention to religion would be a waste of time and energy as its influence would fade and that, by the turn of the twenty-first century (as one of my senior colleagues once told me), it would be a "residual category" that would have lost theoretical significance.

This of course has not happened. Religion has not "gone away" (Calhoun et al., 2011). Even before the end of the twentieth century, there were signs that new forms and instantiations of "the religious" were emerging and gaining in importance in new ways and in new contexts, not least in realms of national and global politics. The Islamic Revolution in Iran and the rise of conservative Christian politics in the United States and elsewhere were but two of a growing number of ways that religion was asserting itself. These trends have only accelerated in the twenty-first century. First came the attacks in New York, London, and Madrid. Then religion became more prominent in emerging politics in locations as diverse as India, Brazil, Russia, Myanmar, and China. Most recently, religion has become an important dimension of a rising ethno-religious nationalism being felt from Europe to North America, to the Antipodes. The attacks on the German Reichstag in 2019 and the US Capitol building in 2021 were driven by this emerging political dynamic where nostalgia for remembered pasts has become a potent political ideology, one that is increasingly inflected with a religious sensibility. And media, mediation, social media, and media imaginaries are central to these developments, placing them squarely on the agendas of media scholars (Hoover, 2020).

This has substantially altered a landscape where religion was already increasingly subject to media and to the media sphere. Religious institutions, practices, and—most importantly—religious *authority* today operate in local, national, and global contexts where the media are determinative. Things exist through and in media, both in legacy media coverage and in the circulations of the digital and social media. In important ways, religions today exist in and through media, and new forms and deployments of "the religious" absolutely depend on—and are made meaningful in modernity by—media practices, systems, and circulations.

Non-Binary Religion and Media Studies

IAMCR was a pioneering site for the consideration of the question of religion in media scholarship. Beginning with a forum session at the Prague Conference in 1984, interest and efforts in IAMCR gradually developed into a stable scholarly unit. The conversations at conferences across these years (including in particular at the meetings in Dublin, Seoul, Guarujá, Sydney, Glasgow, and Barcelona) showed an evolution of thought, theory, and methodology. In the early years, most observers thought of relations between religion and media in terms of the "effects" of one upon the other. In this way, scholarly discourse about religion in the association was not that dissimilar from work in other interest areas, such as in the then Social Psychology Section. For most of the early years of its development, the field of media studies (often under the rubric of "mass communication") was driven by an instrumentalist approach, where "effects" of media on individuals and groups were thought of largely in terms of potential pathologies.

When looked at in this way, the objectives of research on religion were similar to those in other areas of interest. There were questions of what happens when "religion" uses "media," as in the case of religious broadcasting or other sectarian communication (Horsfield, 1984). Then there were questions of what happens when "media" cover "religion," as in journalistic treatment of religion (Hoover, 1998) or the presence of religious themes and tropes in television or film. The IAMCR Religion Working Group also devoted some time and attention to questions of media and theology in later years.

But the simple binary of religion and media as separate and distinct spheres came to be seen as too narrow, because it fundamentally misunderstood religion and misunderstood media. Religion is more than the simple expression of history, doctrine, or theology (Casanova, 1994). And the entire project of IAMCR has been to substantially deepen and broaden our understanding and knowledge of media as being more than just the transmission of messages or intelligence. The instrumentalist paradigms that focused some scholarship took place in the association in a context where history, policy, consciousness industries, globalization, and colonial/decolonial discourses were also part of the overall project. This broader context was important as it became increasingly obvious that as media and religion have each evolved in modernity, they have become increasingly implicated in one another. IAMCR's influence was particularly present in the evolution of interests in the field away from the early instrumentalist "binary" approach. An important turning point was the collection *Rethinking Media, Religion, and Culture* (Hoover & Lundby, 1997) which featured a number of the association's scholars in its pages. That book remains one of the most important milestones in the evolution of the study of media and religion. Its introduction has been described as the most widely read and widely circulated basic resource in the field of media and religion, internationally (Lundby, 2007).

Rethinking laid out a new disciplinary focus for research on media and religion, one that centered questions of *what was produced* by the inter-relationships between media and religion, rather than objectifying them as separate spheres. It changed the subject, as it were, directing scholarly attention toward the question of what new things were being produced as media and religion increasingly engaged one another in modernity. The book pointed to "culture" as the object, and—along with the discourses in the association—opened the door to entirely new ways of thinking about these relations.

But IAMCR's contribution did not end there. As the first truly *international* scholarly organization in the field, its scholars insisted that there was much to be learned from a broad view not bound by intellectual blinders that privileged any particular national or cultural context (such as—for a prominent example—that of the continuing global colonial powers) (Collins et al., 2004). This suggested both comparative and broadly critical perspectives, and the study of media and religion has benefitted from this re-positioning. Today, we can assume that there is much to be learned by focused case studies from outside the Organisation for Economic Co-operation and Development (OECD) countries.

This legacy also traces IAMCR's influence in the development of contexts where scholarship on media and religion has increasingly found a home in allied professional associations such as the International Communication Association, the American Academy of Religion, the Society for the Scientific Study of Religion, and the British Association for the Study of Religion. This influence is also clear in the international professional group focused specifically on this field, the International Society for Media, Religion, and Culture, which has held biennial meetings (beginning in 1996) in Edinburgh, Louisville, Stockholm, Eskisehir, São Paulo, Boulder, and Toronto. Work presented in these contexts clearly shows the marks of IAMCR's legacy. In particular, there are no important voices in the field of media and religion that do not take the paradigm seriously and/or that fail to recognize that a fully international and intercultural view is essential to understanding the critical issues.

The international context is more important than simple comparativism however. It demands that scholars engage the question of the location and circulation of media and communication in the broadest sense. This points to new approaches to research that are layered both historically and conceptually. Rethinking the dominance of Western imperialism in social and political space has of course demanded its critical review in scholarly and conceptual spaces as well. The legacy of the association's internationalism has been the mandate to take seriously the project of "provincializing" theory and research in media and in media and religion (to borrow the powerful concept from Chakrabarty, 2000). This means that scholarship does not deny the Western project and, specifically, the legacies of the media of the North Atlantic West. Instead, it contextualizes them, opening up promising and productive avenues for research and scholarship, as has been demonstrated by the evolving scholarships focused on "decoloniality" (Mignolo, 2011).

Conclusion

IAMCR's legacy in media and religion thus points to an evolving scholarly agenda that includes some significant features. My purpose in presenting this account is not to produce a canon for the field or an axiomatic taxonomy, but instead to illustrate the broad range of possibilities for critical research on media and religion and to suggest the disciplinary and methodological resources that might helpfully be brought to the effort as work in this area continues to develop.

First, there does seem to be value in continued historical work on the evolution of media practices in religion and the framing of religion by media. There is much we do not know about this history, and we would all benefit from such knowledge as we encounter a time when mediated religion is increasingly important in culture and politics (Campbell, 2012).

Second, it remains important for us to understand how religion and religions are constructed and shaped by their representation in media of various kinds. Biases and stereotypes, such as in the case of "Islamophobic" journalism, continue to contribute to both understanding and misunderstanding at a time when the world is increasingly interconnected (WACC, 2016).

Third, it is also important to account for the ways that technological and industrial change in the media sphere alters the terms and references through which religions and religious sensibilities function today. Most notably, the rise of digital media and the so-called social media has led to epistemic change in the location and circulation of the whole range of interests and impulses we once identified as uniquely the province of religion. This condition is increasingly theorized as "hypermediation" (Echchaibi, 2017).

Fourth, entirely new forms of religion and of religious influence are being produced by and through the media. This is most obvious today in ways that media imaginaries increasingly define social and cultural meaning-making (Alma & Guido, 2018). It is also very obvious in the emergence of contemporary ethno-nationalist politics in contexts as diverse as India (Thomas, 2021), Brazil (Cunha, 2021), Russia (Staehle, 2021), and the United States (Hoover, 2021).

Finally, evolving research and scholarship in media and religion must be conscious of the layered complexities of relations in the field. One of the most important learnings from the recent development of work on decoloniality is the value of understanding the complex historiographies that have produced the legacies of modernity. The evolution of media and communication took place through a complex interplay of economic, political, cultural, and social forces. Technology has not been uniquely determinative. Instead, it has interacted with these other spheres in ever more entangled ways. Technology both afforded power and has been the instrumentality of that power. We understand today, however, that to fully appreciate, and to be able to critically engage with the versions of modernity and the diverse modernities that have resulted, we need a scholarship that can account for these complexities. This is true across the range of scholarships in media and communication. It is even more true of scholarships of religion in media and communication. We have long known, for instance, that the media have been deeply engaged in religious evolution in the North Atlantic West from at least the time of the Protestant Reformation. And we have understood the role that those forces played in the imperialist project. Still, we have not yet developed a broad and nuanced history that connects media and communication, power and religion. This is only one domain in which critical scholarship in media and religion continues to be of utmost importance to scholarly knowledge production moving forward, and thus remains a central challenge and agenda of IAMCR.

References

Alma, H., & Guido, V. (Eds.). (2018). *Social imaginaries in a globalizing world.* DeGruyter.

Berger, P. (1967). *The sacred canopy: Elements of a sociological theory of religion.* Doubleday.

Calhoun, C., Mark, J., & van Antwerpen, J. (Eds.). (2011). *Rethinking secularism.* Oxford University Press.

Campbell, H. (2012). *Digital religion.* Routledge.

Casanova, J. (1994). *Public religions in the modern world.* University of Chicago Press.

Chakrabarty, D. (2000). *Provincializing Europe: Postcolonial thought and historical difference.* Princeton University Press.

Collins, E., Jensen, M., Kanev, P., & McCall, M. (2004). Shifting power: U.S. hegemony and the media. *International Journal of International Studies, 2*, 21–49.

Cunha, M. (2021). Media, religion, and the fabric of culture and communication in contemporary Brazil. In S. Hoover & N. Echchaibi (Eds.), *Media and religion: The global view* (pp. 125–140). DeGruyter.

Echchaibi, N. (2017). *Hypermediation as an argument* (Seminar Series). Center for Media, Religion, and Culture. University of Colorado, .

Hoover, S., & Lundby, K. (Eds.). (1997). *Rethinking media, religion, and culture.* Sage.

Hoover, S. (1998). *Religion in the news: Faith and journalism in American public discourse.* Sage.

Hoover, S. (2020). Myth today: Reading religion into research on mediated cultural politics. *International Journal of Communication, 14*, 4508–4532.

Hoover, S. (2021). Media, religion, and politics in the Capitol siege. https://stewart-hoover.wordpress.com/2021/01/31/media-religion-and-politics-in-the-capitol-siege-part-3/ Accessed 15 June 2022.

Horsfield, P. (1984). *Religious television: The American experience.* Sage.

Lundby, K. (2007, May). *Rethinking media, religion, and culture* (Conference Remarks). International Communication Association, San Francisco.

Mignolo, W. (2011). *The darker side of Western modernity: Global futures, decolonial options.* Duke University Press.

Morgan, D. (2013). Religion and media: A critical review of recent developments. *Critical Research in Religion, 1*(3), 347–356.

Staehle, H. (2021). *Media and religion in Russia: How digital criticism is driving transformation of the Russian Orthodox church.* Routledge.

Thomas, P. (2021). Religion, media & culture in India: Hindutva and Hinduism. In S. Hoover & N. Echchaibi (Eds.), *Media and religion: The global view* (p. 205–218). DeGruyter.

WACC (The World Association for Christian Communication). (2016). *How do the media fuel Islamophobia?* https://waccglobal.org/how-do-the-media-fuel-islamophobia/ Accessed 15 June 2022.

CHAPTER 7

Women, Gender, Feminism: Status, Scholarship, and Advocacy

Margaret Gallagher, Louise Luxton, and Claudia Padovani

Introduction

In this chapter, we look at the trajectory of women, gender, and feminist issues within IAMCR since its birth in 1957. The first section traces the history of women as actors in the association from its earliest days until the election of the first female president in 2004. Next, we consider the research themes that have been the focus of work within the Gender and Communication Section, analysing how these themes have reflected a broadening of conceptual approaches in the field over time. In the third section, we examine the engagement of women and feminist scholars in IAMCR with gender and communication issues within global policy debates, showing how knowledge and scholarship have been used to advocate for change. A short final section sums up the chapter's main themes and the challenges facing the association in this area.

M. Gallagher (✉)
Independent Researcher, Dublin, Ireland
e-mail: Margaret@mgallagher.eu

L. Luxton
Newcastle University, Newcastle upon Tyne, UK
e-mail: L.Luxton1@newcastle.ac.uk

C. Padovani
University of Padova, Padova, Italy
e-mail: claudia.padovani@unipd.it

© The Author(s), under exclusive license to Springer Nature Switzerland AG 2023

J. Becker, R. Mansell (eds.), *Reflections on the International Association for Media and Communication Research*,
https://doi.org/10.1007/978-3-031-16383-8_7

From the Margins to the Presidency[1]

Almost half a century after its founding in 1957, IAMCR elected its first female President—Robin Mansell. The year was 2004. At first a reluctant candidate, Mansell later spoke of her "astonishment" at having won. The result was historic not just in returning a woman as president, but in electing women to both of the vice presidential positions. As the all-female top team—Robin Mansell, Divina Frau-Meigs, and Annabelle Sreberny—walked up to acknowledge the results of the vote, they heard a male colleague complain loudly that their election meant "doom" for IAMCR.

Happily, IAMCR survived. Indeed by the end of Mansell's term in 2008, thanks largely to her efforts, it was on a considerably stronger footing. In 2004, the membership renewal system was in deep disarray and income was in dramatic decline. Faced with a tangled internal situation, Mansell set in place a new membership process and system which would later develop into the permanent administrative unit that many in the association had long called for. Between 2004–2005 and 2007–2008, membership income increased seven-fold.

The female triumvirate proved itself a good team, spearheading important initiatives that included the launch of new book series, an International Researchers' Charter for Knowledge Societies, preparations for the World Summit on the Information Society (WSIS), and much more. Far from meeting its "doom," the organization flourished under its first female president. As if to underline the point, women would go on to lead IAMCR for three more consecutive terms, with the presidencies of Annabelle Sreberny (2008–2012)[2] and Janet Wasko (2012–2020). But though the electoral barrier had been broken, the breakthrough had been a long time in the making.

Early Days—a Very Male Environment

In its first decade, IAMCR was led entirely by men. Until 1968, all members of both the Bureau and the Executive Committee were male—despite the fact that, even at that time, the field of mass communication research included a small body of notable female professionals. For instance, Elisabeth Noelle-Neumann, co-founder and director of the Allensbach Institute for Public Opinion Research in Germany, presented a paper at the international symposium held in association with the first General Assembly (GA) in 1959. She

[1] Unless referenced otherwise, quotes used in this section of the chapter are taken from communications with Marjan de Bruin, Peggy Gray, Cees Hamelink, Ullamaija Kivikuru, Madeleine Kleberg, Olga Linné, Robin Mansell, Kaarle Nordenstreng, Wajiha Raza Rizvi, Gertrude J Robinson, Karen Ross, Ramona Rush, Katharine Sarikakis, the late Annabelle Sreberny, and Liesbet van Zoonen. We are grateful to all of them. Given the mobility of members over time, institutional affiliation and geographic identification are included only when pertinent.

[2] This was also a landmark election, in which two of the three candidates were women, with Divina Frau-Meigs polling in second place.

would eventually become a member of the Executive Committee (later known as the International Council), but not until 1970. Meanwhile, in 1968, Irena Tetelowska, Director of the Krakow Press Research Centre, became Chair of the newly formed Bibliography Section, and thus a member of the Executive Committee.[3]

With these two exceptions, IAMCR documents from the 1960s and early 1970s describe an almost exclusively male world. Jacques Bourquin, in his presidential letter of 27 April 1967, addresses a presumed male membership: "you are all men of science, research men."[4] Women, if mentioned at all in these documents, are routinely denied a professional or institutional title. The presidential letter of 31 December 1971 notes that "member Mrs E. Blum (Urbana)" had contributed to the Bibliography Section. This member was Dr Eleanor Blum, Professor of Library Science at the University of Illinois. To some extent, this effacement of women reflected conventions of the era, but as the 1970s wore on, it began to be challenged.

1972 marked not just the beginning of James D. Halloran's tenure as President, but the arrival on the IAMCR scene of Peggy Gray, then a researcher at the University of Leicester. Halloran asked her to be his administrative assistant for his first conference as president (Leipzig, 1974), and for the next 18 years, she would be conference organizer, problem solver, advisor, and "organisational genius" (Robinson, 1997, p. 43). Though Gray's role throughout the Halloran presidency was crucial, it typified the contribution of many talented women at that time: low-key, behind-the-scenes, and away from the spotlight.[5]

At the 1974 IAMCR GA in Leipzig, plans began for the next conference in two years' time. It would be held in Leicester and was to be called "Mass Media and Man's View of Society."[6] The taken-for-granted male-based normativity of this title did not go unnoticed by some members, and at least one—George Gerbner—spoke out. James Halloran's presidential letter of December 1974 reports that Gerbner cautioned the all-male conference planning committee to take care to avoid a sexist interpretation of "Man's View." The leadership's response was to include a woman—Elisabeth Noelle-Neumann—on the planning committee, and in his next presidential letter (April 1975), Halloran described the conference theme as "Mass Media and Man's/Woman's View of Society." Despite this nod to inclusivity, the original conference title was not

[3] Less than a year later, in April 1969, Irene Tetelowska tragically died in a plane crash near Krakow.

[4] All cited IAMCR presidential letters in this chapter are available at https://iamcr.org/node/10510. Accessed 15 June 2022.

[5] Much later, Peggy Gray's immense contribution to IAMCR would be publicly acknowledged. In 2007, at the 50th anniversary Conference in Paris, she was appointed an honorary member of the association; at the 2016 Conference in Leicester, she received the IAMCR Distinguished Contribution Award (see Chap. 34 in this collection).

[6] The title was one of several study themes proposed by an International Advisory Panel on Communication Research set up by UNESCO in 1971. The panel and its work, which continued until 1975, is described in Nordenstreng (1994).

changed. The presence of Noelle-Neumann—not known as a supporter of women—on the planning committee did not upset the male-dominated list of conference speakers: only one of the 14 "main papers" was presented by a woman (Noelle-Neumann herself), and just two of the 17 discussants were women. The planning committee for the following conference in 1978 was again all-male.

Nevertheless, the 1976 Leicester event was a landmark. Ramona Rush—attending her first IAMCR conference, and a discussant in the opening plenary session—had recently completed one of the first studies of women in journalism education for the Association for Education in Journalism (AEJ). She presented some of this work in a workshop paper on "Women and the Media"—the first reported discussion of the topic at an IAMCR conference.[7] And the 22-member Executive Committee (EC) was replaced by an International Council (IC) comprising 28 members (as well as the Section Heads), of whom nine were women (up from two on the EC). They included Anita Werner, a pioneer of gender-sensitive research, as well as strong supporters of women's status and scholarships like Gertrude J. Robinson, Breda Pavlič, Nelly de Camargo, and Olga Linné. Both Olga Linné and Ramona Rush would later run for IAMCR presidency—Linné in 1992 and Rush in 2000. A new generation of women was arriving and change was on the way.

Women Claim Their Space

Madeleine Kleberg joined the Department of Journalism, Media, and Communication Studies at Stockholm University in 1976. By 1980, she had attended two IAMCR conferences—Warsaw (1978) and Caracas (1980)—and was "astonished and fed up with all the males taking the floor everywhere."[8] Just before the Caracas Conference, she and her colleague Anne-Margrete Wachtmeister of the Swedish Broadcasting Corporation (SBC) had been to the non-governmental forum of the UN Women's Conference in Copenhagen, where a vast gathering of activists and academics had debated—*inter alia*—male dominance in communication structures, bias in information systems, and the need for feminist networking. By 1980, there was a vast amount of research, in almost all regions, on aspects of women's relationship to the media.[9] A lot was happening—but not, it seemed, in IAMCR. Talking with other women at the Caracas Conference, Kleberg and Wachtmeister found they were not alone in thinking it was time to act. At a meeting attended by 30 people, a decision was taken to organize a Working Group (WG) at the 1982 IAMCR Conference in Paris, using a newsletter to call for papers. That first newsletter—*Sex Roles*

[7] See IAMCR Presidential Letter, December 1976.

[8] The Caracas Conference was typical of IAMCR Conferences at that time. For instance, the presidential letter of November 1980 reports that all eight papers at the plenary sessions were presented by men.

[9] Documented in publications such as Gallagher (1981), as well as in later accounts of the history of feminist communication scholarship, including Rakow (1992), Rush, et al. (2004).

within the Mass Media[10]—was mailed to a list of 90. The WG on Sex Roles in Mass Media was born.

The WG was headed by Kleberg along with Wachtmeister until 1983, and then with Ulla Abrahamsson, also from the SBC. Within two years, the mailing list included over 200 names; by the time of the last newsletter in 1993, it had reached almost 500. The WG's gatherings in IAMCR expanded quickly. At its first meeting in 1982, there were six papers, on disparate topics, from five countries. By the third meeting in 1988, there were 23 papers by researchers in 17 countries, organized into four themes and presented in two half-day sessions. Kleberg recalls that the announcement of the project in 1980 attracted some demeaning comments—"was this scholarly?"—and there were complaints that the WG work lacked a theoretical framework. But by the second meeting in 1984, a sympathetic male colleague acknowledged that this field of research was "here to stay—and to be developed."[11] And so it proved: the WG's calls for papers, from the mid-1980s onwards, demonstrate the emergence of a feminist consciousness and a search for feminist theoretical models.

As the WG expanded, its identity evolved. In November 1989, the newsletter became the *Newsletter—Gender & Mass Media*. The move from "sex roles" to "gender," said Kleberg and Abrahamsson, was a shift away from terminology that had come to signify "biological determinism" towards terminology that embraced an understanding of "culturally determined patterns and practices."[12] At the same time, a proposal was submitted to IAMCR to transform the WG into a permanent section called Gender and Mass Communication—the title being chosen to reflect the name of the association, then known as the International Association for Mass Communication Research. The word "mass" was dropped by the IC, and the new Gender and Communication Section—to be headed by Madeleine Kleberg—was confirmed by the GA in August 1990.

The 1980s was the decade when women's voices began to be heard within IAMCR. At the 1984 Conference in Prague, for the first time, a feminist analysis was included among the plenary papers.[13] Women's place in the leadership structures of IAMCR was helped by the historic overturning—at the Barcelona Conference in 1988—of IAMCR's established system of elections. As per tradition, the Nominations Committee presented a "slate" of names for the IC, to be adopted by the GA. In an unprecedented move, the GA delegates in

[10] From the outset, the newsletter was designed to reflect a broader constituency than IAMCR itself. It was a truly international resource on women's/feminist communication scholarship. Each of the 13 issues—some of which ran to more than 70 pages—included reports on research projects, books, meetings, and conferences from around the world.

[11] See *IAMCR Newsletter, Sex-Roles Within Massmedia*, November 1984, p. 12.

[12] Discussion on the merits of this move actually began three years earlier in the December 1986 issue of the newsletter.

[13] The paper (Gallagher, 1984)—one of several presented in the first plenary session after the main address by Johan Galtung—was invited at the suggestion of Olga Linné, Chair of the Sociology and Social Psychology Section, and a member of the Conference Planning Committee.

Barcelona rejected the slate, and called for an actual vote. This resulted in the election of eight women to the 30-member IC. The vote, recalls Annabelle Sreberny, was "a pivotal moment in democratising the organisation." Gertrude Robinson, reflecting on the progress of women after Barcelona, saw it as a lesson in the need for transparency: "women's participatory chances were increased as soon as organisational rules were spelled out" (Robinson, 1997, p. 43).

The Barcelona vote—"the first time the organisation had actually voted for anything!" says Sreberny—heralded a new era for IAMCR. The introduction of open electoral processes brought much wider participation in running the organization which, in turn, made space for new ideas. The search for diversity in membership and leadership—until then defined in geographical terms—now expanded to embrace gender as well as age. For instance, section heads were asked to propose papers from potential discussants for the opening plenary of the 1990 Conference in Bled. This led to a gender-balanced discussant slate of three men and three women, the latter comprising Robin Mansell, Trine Syvertsen, and Janet Wasko—two of whom would be future presidents.

The association was changing and another wave of women was arriving—vocal and influential. Among those elected to the IC in 1988 was the late Brenda Dervin. In 1986, she had become the first female President of the International Communication Association (ICA), devoting her inaugural presidential lecture to the subject of feminist scholarship and communication (Dervin, 1987). Feminist scholars were increasingly prominent within the organization. For instance, Liesbet van Zoonen, whose *Feminist Media Studies* (1994) would become one of the most widely read texts in the field, was elected to the IC in 1992. The 1990s was to be a decade of intense organizing, data gathering, and networking that would enhance women's visibility and build women's case for recognition as leaders and scholars.

Challenging the System

By the time of its transition from WG to Section, the Gender and Communication Section had become the forum for analyses of the gender and communication relationship from "different theoretical positions, in contrasting cultural and political contexts and diverse media situations."[14] Liesbet van Zoonen, Chair of the Section from 1994 to 1996, described it as a "haven for young researchers, mostly female at the time." But its focus was still relatively narrow. Marjan de Bruin (Co-Chair 1996–2000) remembers the "excitement of discovering" the section, though she gradually felt distanced from its discussions—dominated as they were at the time by an essentially binary approach to gender and a narrower conceptualization of feminism than was typical of debates in her Caribbean experience.

[14] *IAMCR Newsletter*, October 1992, p. 9.

In the next part of this chapter, we analyse how the research focus of the Section has changed over time. This shift coincided with the arrival of a more culturally diverse generation in the Section and its leadership, which for many years had been chaired mainly by scholars from Europe and North America. Among the earliest incomers from other regions were Gita Bamezai (India), Co-Chair 2000–2008, and Aimée Vega Montiel (México), Co-Chair 2011–2012. Also important was Todd Holden, the only man to co-chair the Section (2004–2012). Though American-born, Holden worked for 26 years at Tohoku University in Japan and had a Japanese family. His immediate predecessor Karen Ross (Co-Chair 1996–2004) credits Holden with opening up spaces for non-binary gendered work, as well as encouraging geographically diverse, non-Western scholarship in the Section. More consistent diversity is evident since 2015, after which the Section was led by a succession of scholars—including Wajiha Raza Rizvi (Pakistan), Mehita Iqani (South Africa), Shweta Sharma (India), and Carolina Matos (Brazil)—who put their own stamp on the calls for papers. This produced not only a broader range of topics and approaches but also, says Rizvi, "plenty of submissions from our individual countries." The Section's 2021 pre-conference symposium "Being Marginal—Performing Raced and Gendered Labour" was an indication of the journey travelled since its inception 30 years earlier.

With the advent of the 1990s and the shift from biennial to annual conferences, the Gender and Communication Section became increasingly important as a focal point for women's strategizing to amplify their influence within the association. Karen Ross, whose first IAMCR Conference was in 1995 (Portoroz), says the Section offered not just "opportunities to hear interesting gender-based scholarship but, more importantly, to network and form relationships with other gender scholars." For instance, at the 1996 Conference in Sydney Virginia Nightingale organized a women's dinner—an idea that was adopted for future conferences. The dinners gave women a chance to enjoy each other's company, but also to discuss the changes they wanted to see in the organization, and to plan for them. Out of these and other conversations emerged IAMCR Womennet. Its aim was to collect data on IAMCR's women members and to create a mailing list that could serve as a network to exchange information and discuss issues around women's status in the association.

Womennet was coordinated by Ullamaija Kivikuru with the help of graduate student Henna Tarjanne at the University of Helsinki, Finland. In late 1995, they carried out the first-ever survey of women members of IAMCR. Apart from basic quantitative information, the survey uncovered the frustration felt by many women who were irritated at the time wasted at conferences by the "power struggles of middle-aged men" (Kivikuru, 1996, p. 23). A major impediment to the survey was the absence of a list of female members to guide distribution of the questionnaire. At the initiative of Gertrude Robinson, IAMCR Treasurer at the time, this led to the creation of new membership forms which, from 1997 onwards, asked for gender identification[15]—a basic element in tracking gender progress and equality within the organization. Using the revised membership base, Karen Ross and Gertrude Robinson went on to produce the 1998 Women's Research Directory—a 30-page indexed compendium of projects and areas for potential collaboration. This was the first directory of members' research interests within IAMCR.

By the end of the 1990s, IAMCR was close to achieving gender balance in the organization's leadership bodies. But this was not reflected in the academic work it chose to showcase at the annual conferences. Despite regular expressions of intent to ensure women's representation among conference speakers,[16] that did not happen and frustration mounted. Marjan de Bruin, who in 2000 became a Vice President and member of the Executive Board (EB), recalls that, at that time, it included "a set of young and outspoken people with innovative perspectives on gender issues." They included Annie Méar (Treasurer), Divina Frau-Meigs (Deputy Secretary General) and Katharine Sarikakis (Vice President). Sarikakis had attended her first IAMCR Conference in 1998 (Glasgow) as a graduate student. Supported and mentored by Ramona Rush, two years later she became the youngest-ever elected Vice President with a remit to increase the number of junior scholars and to widen the participation of women.

In the summer of 2001, Sarikakis launched a discussion via Womennet on what could be done to enhance women's visibility as scholars in the association. The issue of the "unthinking" or taken-for-granted composition of all-male plenaries and panels led to the proposal for an all-female plenary at the next IAMCR Conference (Barcelona, 2002).[17] Titled "Women and communication scholarship" the plenary was organized by Katharine Sarikakis with support from Karen Ross. It was intended to "break the mould" and to make the great and the good within the association "think twice" about the relevance of women's scholarship and its contribution to the field. Sarikakis hoped that, once shown to be possible, the idea would be repeated. This did not happen. However, the "unthinking" selection of all-male speaking lists had been called into question in a memorable way. Two decades later, women's visibility as speakers was not just accepted but expected: the 2018 Conference (Oregon) had a 50:50 gender balance across speakers at its two plenary sessions. Over the same period, plenary interventions by feminists like Taslima Nasrin, Anita Gurumurthy, Fatoumata Sow, and others helped to build credibility for feminist scholarship.

In her presentation to the all-women plenary in 2002, Annabelle Sreberny spoke of the politics of recognition—the process through which achievements

[15] *IAMCR Newsletter*, March 1997, p. 7-8.

[16] For instance, the Conference Committee for the 1996 Sydney Conference announced its intention that "women academics play a prominent role in the plenary sessions as speakers, moderators, chairpersons, or all of these": *IAMCR Newsletter*, November 1995, p. 1.

[17] Details of the conference are reported in *IAMCR Newsletter*, November 2002, p. 14.

and status are recognized. The organizational culture of IAMCR, she argued, was among the reasons why women felt unrecognized (Sreberny, 2002). Despite changes in that culture, 20 years later, the struggle for recognition persists. Looking back, Sreberny concludes:

> It's one thing to bring more women into an organisation and support their work. It's a different trajectory to get feminist theory and argument into not only its niche section but integrated as a critical part of our entire field. We probably did much better in the former than the latter (Sreberny, 2002, p. np).

The Gender and Communication Section and its Contribution to the Field

The Gender and Communication Section reflected, in its name, the shifts in gender-based research that had occurred since the launch of the WG on Sex Roles in Mass Media a decade earlier. It also reflected the aspirations of founding members to establish an open space for research into all facets of the heterogeneous relationship between gender and media. In the Section report for the 1996 Sydney Conference, Karen Ross (Co-Chair 1996–2004) celebrates the range and content of that year's papers: "attending to the gender dimension in all academic endeavour, in all research contexts, [and] in every research study is both possible and desirable."[18] This ethos was a driving force in the Section's early years. Over three decades later, we can offer a brief review of its development as both a conduit for and instigator of diverse gender and communication scholarship.

Growth of the Section

A comparison of conference programs from 1992 and 2019 (see Table 7.1) illustrates the expansion of the Section, both in size, but more significantly in research scope.[19] Members of the newly established Section first presented research at the 1992 Guarajà Conference and the program for this inaugural meeting reveals that, at least in its first years, the scholarly focus remained close to that of the foundations of the earlier WG. The Section hosted two sessions of papers relating to the construction of women in mass media and the role of women as recipients of media communication. Additionally, a joint session on feminist theory and political economy was organized with the Political Economy Section, signalling from the outset the Section's wish to collaborate across research disciplines.

[18] *IAMCR Newsletter*, November 1996, p. 11.

[19] Comparison is made with the 2019 Madrid Conference as the extenuating circumstances of the virtual conferences in 2020 and 2021 meant the Section hosted only one video session of papers, with members invited to upload conference papers to an online portal for others to comment on.

Table 7.1 Gender and Communication Section Sessions at the 1992 Guarujá and 2019 Madrid Conferences

*Guarujá, 1992 **	*Madrid, 2019 ***
Sessions: • The construction of women in mass media • Combined study of media content and study of women as receivers • Joint session with Political Economy Section: Feminist Theory and Political Economy **Panel:** • Gender, public space, and the medium	**Sessions in English:** • Violence against women (I) • Violence against women (II) • Cyber-femme culture • Boys, men, masculinity • Advertising with/against gender • Queer mediations • Migrations, borders, gender • Experiencing #MeToo (I) • Experiencing #MeToo (II) • Rights and responsibilities • Race and racism • Erasures and portrayals • Marriage and maternity • Storytelling online • Patriarchal power • New feminisms? • Public spheres and gender • Regulations and infrastructure • Gendered technology use • Gender and sexuality on TV **Sessions in Spanish:** • Apropiación del discurso y ciberfeminismo • Perspectiva de género y estudios para la diversidad • Narrando violencias y resistencias • Feminismo y espacio político en medios **Panels:** • Misogyny without borders • #MeToo as a global ontology • Gendered online harassment in journalism. • Communicating gendered luxury in Africa

Source: * *IAMCR Newsletter*, October 1992, p. 9 for Guarujá, 1992; ** IAMCR Madrid 2019 conference program. https://iamcr.org/madrid2019/cfp/gec for Madrid, 2019. Accessed 15 June 2022.

In stark comparison, at the 2019 Madrid Conference, the Section hosted 124 papers across 25 sessions (four of which were in Spanish). Session topics in 2019 ranged from the broad, such as "Gendered technology use," to the specific—for example, "Experiencing #MeToo." Several sessions addressed the interaction between gender, media, and issues that were not gender-specific—for instance, "Race and racism." No joint sessions were convened in 2019.[20]

[20] The number of joint sessions with other WGs and Sections has waned in tandem with the Section's growth. The latest joint session was held in 2015 (Montreal) with the WG on Global Media Policy.

This brief comparison immediately highlights the substantial growth of the Gender and Communication Section and its greatly expanded scholarly agenda.

Reflecting and Shaping Gender and Communication Research

The Gender and Communication Section's development over the last three decades can be understood more thoroughly through a combination of quantitative content analysis and an interpretive review of the titles of the Section's conference sessions from 1992–2019.[21] This longitudinal study produces an overview of the Section's relationship with broader trends within gender and media scholarship. It traces the research themes that have remained a focus since the Section's inception and identifies contemporary themes that have emerged and grown in prominence.

Figure 7.1 visualizes the results of the quantitative content analysis, displaying the 100 most common words in conference session titles.[22] Unsurprisingly, "gender(ed)," "women('s)," "media," and "communication" are among the most common words. "Representation(s)," "violence," "culture," "advertising," and "activism" rank highly as some of the most consistently popular topics of research. The high frequency of "feminism/feminist" in session titles reflects the Section's engagement both with feminist theory and feminism as a political movement. This initial analysis indicates that the Section has a consolidated core of traditional gendered media research themes, such as representation. It also recognizes the Section's feminist consciousness and its focus on gender inequalities and the experience of marginalized communities. An interpretive review of conference session titles paints a more detailed picture of the areas of continuity and change within the Section.

Consistent Themes

Production, Representation, Consumption

The gendered production, representation, and consumption of mass media have been core research themes since the Section's outset and have remained a continuous focus over the last three decades. This is typified in the program of the 1997 Oaxaca Conference, where the Gender and Communication Section organized three sessions titled:

[21] Conference programs, calls for abstracts, and IAMCR newsletters were collated, and a database of session titles and paper presentations was produced. Due to a lack of available material, session titles for the following conferences are not included in the quantitative analysis: Budapest, 2001; Porto Alegre, 2004; Cartagena, 2017. In several cases, individual paper titles were instead available and the overall analysis draws together the broad picture provided by session titles with a more nuanced perspective available from the diversity of paper presentations.

[22] Stop words were removed and the frequency of some similar words (for example, "women" and "women's") were combined to provide a summary of the general themes of conference session titles.

Fig. 7.1 100 Most Common Words in Gender and Communication Section Conference Session Titles, 1992–2019. (Prepared by Louise Luxton, 2022)

- Using and producing: making meaning in the media
- Sexing the media: gendered representations in popular media
- Consuming media: new information technologies and women's lives[23]

In terms of production across the years, individual papers have focused on gendered power dynamics in newsrooms, the dearth of female film directors, and women's own media production, including the rise of "mommy blogs." The representation of women and men has been investigated across media, from popular culture to news to magazine advertisements; gradually, papers in this category have adopted an intersectional focus on specific cultures, races, ethnicities, or sexualities. Consumption of media and media effects has been

[23] *IAMCR Newsletter*, November 1997, p. 26.

studied in relation to various groups, including children and teens; these papers have commonly focused on new media technologies, information and communication technologies (ICTs), and social networking. While these three research themes do reflect the traditional concerns of gender and media scholarship, our study shows that Section members have increasingly engaged with them through dynamic analyses typical of contemporary approaches.

Feminism and Activism

The results of the quantitative analysis indicate a long-running interest in the study of marginalized groups and the use of media technologies as tools for activism. Sessions dedicated to research on social activism are often related to the broader conference theme. For example, the 2009 Mexico City Conference theme *Human Rights and Communication* saw the Gender and Communication Section organize several sessions focused on women's right to communication and media representations of women's human rights.[24] Moreover, at the initiative of Aimée Vega Montiel, a member of both the Gender and Communication Section and the 2009 Conference Committee, there was also a plenary presentation on the subject.

Under the umbrella of social activism scholarship, gendered violence, in particular, has emerged as a prominent research theme beginning in the 2010s. Since then, sessions have been organized at several conferences under the broad banner of "violence against women," and members have presented papers on topics ranging from gendered violence within popular culture (and the intersection of race and sexuality in these narratives) to the use of media technologies to aid domestic violence sufferers, and the abuse and harassment of female journalists and political actors.

In part, the emergence of gendered violence as a popular research theme is related to the Section's responsiveness to contemporary issues and debates in the public arena. For example, following the explosion of the #MeToo movement in public discourse in 2017, the 2018 Oregon Conference saw several presentations on the topic; and in Madrid (2019), the Section organized two sessions and a panel to further explore the issue. Other important contemporary issues have included transformations in post-Cold War Eastern Europe, media discourses on HIV/AIDS, and gender issues in the development of internet technologies, such as the growth of internet pornography and the "trolling" of women on social media.

Underpinning this long-running research focus on gendered social activism is an engagement with feminist theory and approaches. Figure 7.1 indicates that many conference sessions have been dedicated to feminist themes over the years and a closer investigation of material finds that individual paper titles containing the words "feminist" or "feminism" span sessions focused on a wide range of topics. This reflects how feminist perspectives are intertwined with

[24] IAMCR 2009 Mexico City Conference program. https://iamcr.org/sites/default/files/PROGRAMME-IAMCR2009-MEXICO.pdf Accessed 15 June 2022.

research throughout the Section. However, while Section members evidently interact with feminist perspectives in their research, conference programs show less engagement with feminist theory and feminist methods *per se*. There is space then in the Gender and Communication Section's research agenda for further dialog about feminist epistemologies and methodologies, as well as feminist issues.

Emergent Themes

Masculinities

As a forum for feminist scholarship, the research of Gender and Communication Section members has predominantly focused on women. However, there have been consistent efforts since the Section's formation to include and promote scholarship concerning masculinities. Calls for abstracts as early as 1994 and as late as 2019 request papers on masculinity and communication, recognizing this as an under-represented theme within the Section. For instance, at the Section's business meeting during the 2002 Barcelona Conference, it was agreed "that we would encourage (again!) the widest possible view of 'gender' to include issues of masculinity and sexuality and to encourage men as well as women scholars to present their work in the Section."[25] Gradually through the 2000s, recalls Marjan de Bruin, "more male members attended the Section's sessions"—a development that could be partly linked to the influence of Todd Holden, the only man to date to co-chair the Section (2004–2012).

The 2010s saw a concerted increase in masculinities research, with the Section organizing at least one session dedicated to masculinities at each conference since 2015. Individual papers have addressed issues such as hegemonic masculinity in newsroom cultures, men's fashion advertisements, and constructions of masculinity in the Disney franchise. Although these reflect the traditional themes of production, representation, and consumption, the Section has also showcased research on emergent topics—for example, narratives of toxic masculinity—another illustration of its role in both reflecting and shaping scholarship within the field.

Intersecting Identities

The section report from the 1996 Sydney Conference laments the "absence of papers relating to sexuality and race."[26] From the earliest days, members of the Section and indeed the WG acknowledged that limited accessibility—the fact that a relatively small number of women, mainly from Western Europe and North America, had the means to attend conferences—had an impact on the sharing and shaping of research. The encouragement of research on marginalized communities and the need to diversify the Section's membership were

[25] *IAMCR Newsletter*, November 2002, p. 21.
[26] *IAMCR Newsletter*, November 1996, p. 11.

constant preoccupations. Through specific calls for research on intersecting identities and cooperation with, for example, the Ethnicity, Racism, and Media WG,[27] the research output of the Section gradually diversified. For instance, at the 2019 Madrid Conference, the Section organized sessions on "Race and racism," "Queer mediations," and "Migrations, borders and gender" (see Table 7.1). Additionally, it has become increasingly common for the Section to call for papers in languages other than English, particularly Spanish.

Of the emerging intersectional research themes, queer research, in particular, has established itself within the Section. As well as dedicated sessions on queer mediations, individual papers across sessions have investigated the intersection of gender and sexuality in mass media, and the use of social media as a tool to facilitate queer relationships. Since the late 2010s, there has also been a burgeoning interest in transgender identities. However, there remains space for growth on these topics within the Section, as research from the Global North still dominates and only a very few conference sessions have been dedicated to intersections of gender with ethnicity or/and race.

Technology

Since the early days of the Section, digital media technologies have received steady academic attention. A session dedicated to "Gender and new information technologies"[28] was held at the 1996 Sydney Conference, and over the next decade, sessions were regularly organized on gender and new technologies, digital media, and ICTs. Since the mid-2000s, the exponential increase of internet use and Web 2.0 technologies has generated significant research interest in digital media, which has transformed into a substantial sub-field within the discipline and within the Gender and Communication Section.

Scholarly attention to digital media continues to grow as contemporary social issues such as the #MeToo movement intensify the focus on online communication environments. Since 2015, the Section has organized between two and six sessions per year on topics ranging from feminist activism on social media to gender and video games. While broadcast media remains the primary focus of research within the Section, as the study of digital media expands in broader gender and communication scholarship, this is likely to be reflected in even more space for this area of enquiry in the Section's future work.

Looking Back, Looking Forward

This longitudinal analysis of conference material shows that at the heart of the Gender and Communication Section lies a consolidated core of traditional gender and media research themes underpinned by an engagement with feminist approaches and issues. Over the years, emergent discourses on masculinities, intersecting identities, and digital technologies also reflect this feminist

[27] This WG was in existence during the 1990s.
[28] *IAMCR Newsletter*, November 1996, p. 11.

consciousness. This commitment to the diversification of research was an acknowledgement that the Section would benefit from moving beyond its role as a space for women's research by women scholars, towards a platform for gender and media scholarship from a heterogeneous membership. Over time, an influx of new voices spurred nuanced analysis of the cultural processes and intersecting identities of gendered communication. Looking back on the evolution of the Section, Marjan de Bruin (Co-Chair, 1996–2000) recounts how the early focus on "body count" studies gave way to an understanding of the interplay between professional ideologies and practices in reproducing gendered outcomes, and how these discussions were reflected in her later, influential work with Co-Chair Karen Ross (de Bruin & Ross, 2004). Two decades later, other scholars are building new discourses. Looking to the future, we can expect to see an ever-growing and diversifying Section offer a platform for the development of research topics such as queer identities and modern technologies, as well as a space for discussion of pressing social issues in gender equality and women's rights, and a more systematic focus on the contributions of media policy intervention and digital governance to media gender equality.

The Last Decade: IAMCR's International Advocacy on Media and Gender[29]

Gender and communication was a well-established theme of scholarly debate in IAMCR when conditions emerged for the association to engage in supranational debates of the twenty-first century. By engaging in these debates, IAMCR was reprising an advocacy role that it had successfully played on previous occasions. The new context provided a major opportunity to contribute to shaping the global policy agenda on gender inequalities in the media and communication arena.

IAMCR, UNESCO, and the Global Alliance on Media and Gender

In 2013, UNESCO announced plans to establish a Global Alliance on Media and Gender (GAMAG). Its aim was to intensify action on achieving gender equality in media systems, structures, and content. From the outset, IAMCR was invited to be part of the initiative, which was welcomed as an opportunity to establish a group of expert scholars who could build bridges between generations of researchers and across the world's regions. This collective was coordinated by IAMCR Vice President Aimée Vega Montiel (2012–2020), who acted as a focal point between IAMCR and UNESCO. It has grown over time as a strong voice within IAMCR, while also becoming visible in different transnational venues.

[29] This section reflects Claudia Padovani's personal account, enriched by a conversation with Aimée Vega Montiel.

The founding moment was a Global Forum on Media and Gender organized in Bangkok, Thailand, as a follow-up to one of the critical areas of concern of the Beijing Declaration and Platform for Action—Women and Media Diagnosis (BPfA, Section J).[30] A gathering of about 350 people, including media executives, journalists, civil society leaders, researchers, journalism educators, and representatives of government, the Forum aimed to add "momentum to gender equality and women's empowerment in and through the media"—a topic expected to "take marked prominence in the post 2015 Millennium Development Goals (MDG) formulation."[31] A number of IAMCR members were invited to participate, including President Janet Wasko and Vice President Aimée Vega Montiel, together with Karen Ross, Claudia Padovani, and Margaret Gallagher (See Fig. 7.2).

The participation of IAMCR members, apart from contributing to the initial "vision" for the Alliance in its founding documents, emphasized the role to be played by the scholarly community in a global effort aimed at involving a range of stakeholders. The Bangkok Forum marked a new phase of international commitment for the association. Since then, IAMCR has positioned itself in the global arena, to serve as an infrastructure for global-level research on women's structural relationships with media systems, and to highlight the policy relevance and implications of ongoing inequalities.

Fig. 7.2 IAMCR Members at the UNESCO Global Forum on Media and Gender, Bangkok, December 2013. (From left to right) **Aimée Vega Montiel**—IAMCR Vice President 2012–2020, Section Head—Gender and Communication 2012–2014, Chair—Task Force on the Global Alliance for Social and Behavioural Change 2020–; **Karen Ross**—Section Head—Gender and Communications 2000–2004; **Margaret Gallagher**—International Council 1992–1996. (Courtesy of Claudia Padovani)

[30] See https://aibd.org.my/2013/12/16/unescos-global-forum-on-media-and-gender-towards-a-global-alliance/

[31] From the Forum booklet and agenda, p. 2.

After the Bangkok meeting, an International Steering Committee (ISC) was set up to guide the GAMAG. Initially chaired by Colleen Lowe Morna (Gender Links, South Africa), it comprised representatives of media organizations, trade unions, journalists' associations, and NGOs from all world regions. As an NGO affiliated with UNESCO, IAMCR positioned itself in the GAMAG as—

> a think tank that would develop and put forward a research agenda in relation to media and gender, which builds on previous and existing research and develops new areas for investigation in response to challenges emerging from contemporary changes in the media environment. (Padovani Interview)

Thanks to the strategic and sustained support of the association's governing body, in 2014, an IAMCR Task Force for GAMAG was constituted. Seen as an opportunity to re-activate and strengthen the relation between IAMCR and UNESCO, the Task Force was mandated to coordinate the association's activities with the Alliance; and to develop a research agenda to both inform existing research and support actions towards expanding women's communication rights. Aimée Vega Montiel has coordinated the Task Force since its establishment.

In December 2014, members of IAMCR's Task Force for GAMAG participated in the first General Assembly of GAMAG in Geneva, Switzerland. The active role of IAMCR was again crucial in discussions about the structure of the Alliance itself.[32] On that occasion, a Research and Policy Committee was established, to be chaired by IAMCR.[33] Carolyn Byerly headed the committee between 2015 and 2019, followed by Carla Cerqueira in 2019 (to-date). Alongside the GAMAG Assembly, an International Development Cooperation Meeting on Gender and Media was organized by UNESCO. It was open to UN agencies, regional development organizations, and international donors, with the aim of establishing an International Development Cooperation Framework on Gender and Media that could support and finance gender and media-related initiatives, including GAMAG. The event fell short of expectations and no cooperation framework was set in place. Nevertheless, the meeting provided a platform to publicize the establishment of a UNESCO UniTWIN Network on Gender, Media, and ICT (see Fig. 7.3). Initially conceived as an "educational branch" of the GAMAG, it inevitably called on

[32] Points on the agenda included overview of GAMAG and UNESCO's role, research agenda, key initiatives, communication guidelines, GAMAG Action Plan, GAMAG structure, GAMAG legal character, and financial responsibilities.

[33] The mandate of the Research and Policy Committee was to establish an online clearinghouse and knowledge community as a central repository on gender and media; to connect other existing platforms; to commission and disseminate research to aid the development of action, including gender indicators to account for the participation of women and girls in the communicative environment; to create regional observatories; to monitor the safety of women working in the media; and to constitute a think tank that would develop and put forward a research agenda in relation to media and gender which develops new areas for investigation in response to challenges emerging from contemporary changes in the media environment.

Fig. 7.3 Founding Moment of the UNESCO UniTWIN Network on Gender, Media, and ICT, December 2015. Aimée Vega Montiel signs the constitutional document. (From left to right) **M. Williams,** Chief Communications & Public Affairs; **A. Shala**, Chair UNESCO IPDC; **Aimée Vega Montiel**—IAMCR Vice President 2012–2020, Section Head—Gender and Communication 2012–2014, Chair—Task Force on the Global Alliance for Social and Behavioural Change 2020–. (Courtesy of Claudia Padovani)

IAMCR researchers to implement its plan of action to integrate a gender perspective in communication and media degrees and courses across the world. Thus, the UniTWIN Network became another space of concrete collaboration amongst IAMCR members. Since then, the network has been actively involved in projects[34] such as assessing the presence of gender perspectives in existing courses in different regions, elaborating educational materials, and organizing training sessions at IAMCR and beyond.[35]

In May 2015, members of IAMCR's Task Force attended the international forum "Gender, Media, ICTs and Journalism. 20 years after the Beijing Platform for Action," convened by Aimée Vega Montiel and held in Mexico City. In fact,

[34] Some of these projects have been funded by the UNESCO International Programme for the Development of Communication (IPDC).

[35] The Network is currently co-chaired by IAMCR members Aimée Vega Montiel and Claudia Padovani, together with Lisa French (RMIT, Australia). The network website is accessible at http://www.unitwin.net. Accessed 15 June 2022.

2015 was a special year, as it marked two decades since the adoption of the Beijing Platform for Action and its Section J on Women and Media. Meanwhile, other initiatives, including feminist interventions in the follow-up process to the World Summit on the Information Society (WSIS+10) and in the consultations on a post-2015 Development Agenda, were ongoing: by this time, IAMCR scholars were well-positioned to take part in such conversations, and they managed to do so with the institutional support of the association (see Fig. 7.4).

Fig. 7.4 International Development Cooperation Meeting on Gender and Media: Towards a Joint Development Cooperation Framework for the Global Alliance on Media and Gender, Geneva, December 2015. (From left to right) **Anita Gurumurthy**—IAMCR Keynote Speaker; **Aimèe Vega Montiel**—IAMCR Vice President 2012–2020, Section Head—Gender and Communication 2012–2014, Chair—Task Force on the Global Alliance for Social and Behavioural Change 2020–; **Claudia Padovani**—IAMCR International Council 2004–2012, 2016–2022, Co-Chair Publications Committee 2012–2018, Co-Chair IAMCR Palgrave Book Series 2010–2022, Co-Chair of WG on Global Media Policy 2008–2012, 2018–2022; **Karen Ross**—Section Head—Gender and Communications 2000–2004; **Margaret Gallagher**—International Council 1992–1996; **Janet Wasko**—International Council 1984–2020, President 2012–2020, Section Head—Political Economy 2002–2010. (Courtesy of IAMCR)

Research Meets Advocacy at IAMCR Conferences

Since 2014, the Task Force has organized GAMAG-related events at IAMCR's international conferences. Thus, IAMCR's annual conference became the institutional space for elaboration and implementation of a scholarly agenda that would inform the work of GAMAG. This was done both by discussing areas where more research was needed—particularly in relation to local-to-global policy developments, increasing concerns about gender-based harassment and violence in the digital environment, and the need for transnational comparative studies—and by highlighting the challenges of engaging with supranational processes focused on gender communication inequalities. The endeavor thus contributed to an ongoing conversation about IAMCR members' responsibilities as public intellectuals. At the same time, the Task Force has helped to raise the profile of the gender and media agenda within the association, playing a complementary role to that of the Gender and Communication Section.

In 2014 (Hyderabad Conference), a panel titled "IAMCR contribution to the Global Alliance on Media and Gender" was convened. On that occasion, a number of knowledge resources were presented, including a thematic e-book produced by IAMCR and published by UNESCO in March 2014: *Media and Gender. A Scholarly Agenda for the Global Alliance for Media and Gender.*[36] Chaired by President Wasko, the panel speakers were Aimée Vega Montiel, Karen Ross, Carolyn Byerly, Claudia Padovani, and Gitiara Nasreen.

The following year in Montreal, a special session was organized, focused on "GAMAG Research Agenda. The follow up." This was chaired by Vice President Vega Montiel and included the late Indrajit Banerjee (Knowledge Societies Division, UNESCO) as respondent. Members of IAMCR's Task Force Lisa McLaughlin, Claudia Padovani, Karen Ross, Carolyn Byerly, and Kaitlynn Mendes discussed major information gaps and identified priority issues for research, together with representatives from civil society initiatives, such as the Global Media Monitoring Project and the International Women's Media Foundation. This contributed to making IAMCR a space where multi-stakeholder conversations could develop.

A key moment to take stock of all that was happening around gender and media issues worldwide was the IAMCR Cartagena Conference in 2017, where another special session was convened on "IAMCR and GAMAG: Research, Knowledge and Activism." At the time, a number of relevant international activities were shaping up, including the UNESCO UniTWIN Network; the European-funded project "Advancing Gender Equality in Media Industries

[36] See https://unesdoc.unesco.org/ark:/48223/pf0000228399. Accessed 15 June 2022. The publication was crucial in outlining ideas on emerging research topics. The main themes were violence of gender, media, and information; women's access to media and information; gender media policies and strategies; and gender, education, and media information literacy.

(AGEMI)"[37]; and a Swedish-funded project, "Comparing Gender and Media Equality Across the Globe (GEM)."[38] Guy Berger, Director of UNESCO's Media Development Division, chaired the session, which featured project-focused contributions by Carolyn Byerly, Claudia Padovani, Karen Ross, Aimée Vega Montiel, and Lisa McLaughlin. Once again, representatives from international and non-governmental organizations—Albana Shala (Chair of the UNESCO IPDC at the time) and Sandra Chaher (Comunicar Igualdad, Argentina)—were invited to be a part of the discussion.

The 2018 IAMCR Conference in Eugene, Oregon, featured another GAMAG Task Force special session on "Gender Mainstreaming in Journalism and Communication Schools: towards an engendered media education IAMCR initiative." Here, the focus was on the absence of gender sensitivity in higher education curricula, where future media and ICT professionals are trained. Moderated by Albana Shala, the session explored good practices and new opportunities to face the educational challenge, with presentations by IAMCR members Aimée Vega Montiel, Soledad Vargas, Pilar Bruce, and Carolyn Byerly, all of whom were involved in the UniTWIN Network's activities.

Over the years, research, education, and advocacy initiatives on gender and media issues found in IAMCR fertile ground for intellectual exchange, opening up paths to engage in policy-oriented cross-cultural dialogs and practice. This had become very clear by 2019 when IAMCR met in Madrid. The AGEMI and GEM projects were coming to a close and could present their output (see Fig. 7.5). The UniTWIN had published its syllabus for journalism educators (UNESCO/UniTWIN Network on Gender, Media and ICT, 2019). The GAMAG (with Aimée Vega Montiel as Chair and Sarah Macharia of WACC as General Secretary) was being reorganized and gaining more autonomy from UNESCO. The international community was preparing to celebrate 25 years since the Beijing Conference.

Against this background, several gatherings were held to discuss different aspects of communication, media, and gender.[39] In addition, two important sessions were organized with a view to contributing to the forthcoming global review of Section J of the Beijing Platform for Action and to critically discuss the 2030 Agenda. The first was a one-day pre-conference devoted to

[37] The project was designed and coordinated between 2017 and 2019 by IAMCR members Karen Ross and Claudia Padovani, and the resulting platform includes a database of good practices, a set of learning units, interviews with professionals and experts, and a global interactive map of relevant organizations. All materials are accessible at: https://www.agemi-eu.org. Accessed 15 June 2022.

[38] The GEM project was developed by IAMCR members and ran between 2017 and 2020. The resulting volume edited by Monika Djerf-Pierre and Maria Edström (2020) is available at https://www.nordicom.gu.se/en/publikationer/comparing-gender-and-media-equality-across-globe. Accessed 15 June 2022.

[39] The UniTWIN Network on Gender, Media, and ICTs held it meeting on July 4; the GEM project invited a number of participating scholars to its first public presentation on July 6; and the Advancing Gender Equality in Media Industries (AGEMI) team organized a hands-on workshop to teach how to make use of its online platform and resources on 10 July.

Fig. 7.5 Presentation of the "Comparing Gender and Media Equality Across the Globe" (GEM) Project, IAMCR Conference, Madrid, July 2019. Participants in the GEM Project. (Courtesy of Claudia Padovani)

"Actualizing Section J through Transnational Collaborations: making gender equality in the media and ICT visible in the 2030 Agenda" (See Fig. 7.6).

On this occasion, IAMCR members expressed their concern that media and communication issues were being marginalized in international debates, which were increasingly marked by narrow understandings of gender inequalities in digital developments. Secondly, a GAMAG special session focused on "Gender and Communication: towards the Beijing Platform for Action +25 and the 2030 Agenda +5 global reviews." Chaired by Aimée Vega Montiel, this session involved Claudia Padovani and Lisa French, Carolyn Byerly and Julie Posetti (Reuters Institute, UK), Anita Gurumurthy (IT for Change, India), and Albana Shala. At the session, UNESCO's Guy Berger announced the publication of two volumes resulting from the collaboration between UNESCO, IAMCR, and GAMAG—*Setting the Gender Agenda for Communication Policy*—and between UNESCO and IAMCR members in the framework of the UniTWIN Network on Gender Media and ICT—*Gender, Media and ICT: New approaches for teaching, education & training*[40] (See Fig. 7.7).

This was the last opportunity for institutional, scholarly, and civil society perspectives to be brought together in the physical space of IAMCR Conferences. Then came the COVID-19 pandemic and plans for events at the

[40] Both volumes are available on UNESCO website at https://en.unesco.org/gamagandunitwin. Accessed 15 June 2022.

Fig. 7.6 "Actualizing Section J through Transnational Collaborations: Making Gender Equality in the Media and ICT Visible in the 2030 Agenda." IAMCR Preconference, Madrid, July 2019 at https://iamcr.org/madrid2019/actualizing-section-j

Fig. 7.7 UniTWIN Network and GAMAG Chairs Pose at IAMCR with Copies of *Gender, Media and ICT. New approaches for teaching, education & training and Setting the Gender Agenda for Communication Policy*—published by UNESCO. (From left to right) **Claudia Padovani**—IAMCR International Council 2004–2012, 2016–2022, Co-Chair Publications Committee 2012–2018, Co-Chair IAMCR Palgrave Book Series 2010–2022, Co-Chair of WG on Global Media Policy 2008–2012, 2018–2022; **Lisa French**, RMIT; **Aimée Vega Montiel**—IAMCR Vice President 2012–2020, Section Head—Gender and Communication 2012–2014, Chair—Task Force on the Global Alliance for Social and Behavioural Change 2020–; **Sarah Macharia,** WACC. IAMCR Conference, Madrid, July 2019. (Courtesy of Claudia Padovani)

2020 and 2021 IAMCR Conferences, expected to take place respectively in Beijing and Nairobi, were moved online.

Engaging at the United Nations Level

Thanks to the prominent role played by IAMCR Vice President Aimée Vega Montiel (2012–2020), as well as to sustained collaboration with UNESCO, starting in 2015 the IAMCR Task Force was able to participate in sessions of the United Nations Commission on Status of Women (CSW), held in New York. GAMAG and the IAMCR Task Force have come to be recognized as an "epistemic community" by agencies such as UN Women as well as by non-governmental advocacy networks. This has happened mainly through the elaboration of position papers and submissions in response to the evolving framework for gender and media at the UN level: the Sustainable Development Goals (SDGs) and Agenda 2030, the Beijing+25 review process, and the most recent Generation Equality Forum fostered by UN Women.

In 2015, IAMCR members collaborated with the GAMAG International Steering Committee in drafting a position paper that called on the UN to include a gender lens on media and ICTs in the SDGs. Presented as an "urgent call by 500 media and freedom of expression organisations across the globe to governments … to get gender and the media on the post-2015 agenda before it's too late!" this was a request to integrate media indicators in the existing goals and targets while making their gender dimensions explicit.[41]

In 2018, colleagues from the association gathered in New York for the 62nd CSW, to take part in parallel and side events and to present a series of statements, elaborated by GAMAG and IAMCR members (See Figs. 7.8 and 7.9). "Media and gender" was the review theme of the CSW gathering that year; this offered a space to exert meaningful influence, not only through the organization/participation in official "side events" and NGO events (12 in total), but

Fig. 7.8 IAMCR Members Contributing to the Seminar Jointly Organized by UNESCO and GAMAG, New York, March 2018. (From left to right) **Carolyn Byerly**—Howard University, US; **Guy Berger**—UNESCO; **June Nicholson**—Virginia Commonwealth University; **Aimée Vega Montiel**—IAMCR Vice President 2012–2020, Section Head—Gender and Communication 2012–2014, Chair—Task Force on the Global Alliance for Social and Behavioural Change 2020–; **Sarah Macharia**—WACC. Commission on the Status of Women (CSW) 62 'The Holistic Gender and Media Agenda,' New York, March 2018. (Courtesy of Claudia Padovani)

[41] The position paper was the basis for two caucus meetings: one with Phumzile Mlambo-Ngcuka, Executive-Director of UN Women; the second with Saniye Gülser Corat, Director of UNESCO's Division for Gender Equality, both of whom supported the GAMAG position. The paper also allowed GAMAG to make a political statement during the side event on Gender and Media held during the 2015 CSW and to call for media and ICTs to be moved to the core of the gender equality agenda.

Fig. 7.9 Chairs of the GAMAG, the UniTWIN Network on Gender, Media and ICT, and the GAMAG Research Committee at UN Premises during CSW 62, New York, March 2018. (From left to right) **Carolyn Byerly**—Howard University, US; **Lisa French**—RMIT, Australia; **Claudia Padovani**—IAMCR International Council 2004–2012, 2016–2022, Co-Chair Publications Committee 2012–2018, Co-Chair IAMCR Palgrave Book Series 2010–2022, Co-Chair of WG on Global Media Policy 2008–2012, 2018–2022; **Aimée Vega Montiel**—IAMCR Vice President 2012–2020, Section Head—Gender and Communication 2012–2014, Chair—Task Force on the Global Alliance for Social and Behavioural Change 2020–. (Courtesy of Claudia Padovani)

also through the official agreed conclusions adopted by member states.[42] A particularly important event, jointly organized by UNESCO and GAMAG, was the seminar titled "The Holistic Gender and Media Agenda." The wide-ranging agenda covered gender equality in media decision-making positions, media policy, gender and freedom of expression, and the rights of women media workers. Key action areas and practical recommendations for member states, as well as for media and ICT companies, were identified. This was also an opportunity for the UniTWIN Network to advocate for the priority of gender perspectives in media and ICT education globally.

After its General Assembly in Madrid in July 2019, GAMAG started a process towards the 25-year review of the Beijing Platform for Action+25. A set of strategic supranational moments was envisioned between 2019 and 2020 where the Task Force could contribute to regional meetings, CSW gatherings,

[42] The Official Agreed Conclusion can be read at https://press.un.org/en/2018/wom2145.doc.htm. Accessed 15 June 2022.

the Generation Equality Forum to be held in Mexico City and in Paris, and the United Nations General Assembly. All such events were inevitably affected by the COVID-19 pandemic, which seriously reduced the possibility for the IAMCR Task Force to fully operate as a collective.

GAMAG engagement continued online, through the elaboration of statements and reports[43] and the preparation of international events. But the main focus of the IAMCR Task Force in this context was the Beijing Platform for Action +25 review process, and the need to keep media and communication on the agenda of what remains the major international mechanism for the achievement of gender equality and women's human rights. To that end, the Task Force joined other GAMAG members to develop national reports, to assess progress and shortcomings in gender and media, and to restate the importance of considering gender, media, and ICT as core to the global discussion on the SDGs.[44]

Women, Gender, Feminism: A Summing Up

It is undeniable that over the past half-century, women's status in IAMCR has changed beyond recognition. That change has been achieved through the struggle of not just the individuals highlighted in this chapter, but through the efforts of countless unacknowledged members who have played important roles in the association and whose contribution is often overlooked. The place of gender issues and feminist scholarship seems assured in IAMCR's work, though it is a moot point whether that place yet enjoys the respect accorded to other academic strands.

As for the GAMAG Task Force and the global positioning of IAMCR advocacy, in spite of some meaningful achievements, the future is not clear. Engaging supranationally is demanding. It requires understanding of complex processes and needs resources—of time, specialized knowledge, and financial support. No *ad hoc* resources were dedicated to the Task Force and its members, who have mostly contributed on a voluntary basis. This has inevitably limited the possibility for wider participation, an aspect that must be considered as the Task Force moves into a "next decade."

[43] This included a Report in 2019 on "Violence against women journalists" addressed to the special rapporteur on Violence Against Women, its Causes and Consequences, and a petition in support of Philippino journalist Maria Ressa; a 'Shadow Report' to the 9th Periodic Review of the Mexican Government before the CEDAW; and the coordination of two official sessions on the BPfA Section J at the Generation Equality Forum in Mexico (March 2021). All GAMAG documents can be found at https://gamag.net. Accessed 15 June 2022.

[44] A series of national position papers was then prepared, spanning Argentina, Australia, Brazil, Burkina Faso, Cameroon, Chile, Colombia, Costa Rica, Cyprus, Ecuador, El Salvador, Italy, Ireland, Morocco, Romania, Spain, Uruguay, and Venezuela. All national reports can be accessed on the GAMAG website at https://gamag.net/2020/01/22/beijing-25-gender-media-and-icts/. Accessed 15 June 2022.

Connecting research with policy engagement may not be a priority for all IAMCR members, but efforts can and should be made to establish stronger connections between the Task Force as an advocacy body, and the Gender and Communication Section where the scholarly knowledge regularly flows. Collaboration between the two entities, possibly arranging an "in-between space of encounter," could help to strengthen both the research and the advocacy communities.

Finally, it is fair to ask to what extent decades of engagement—from the early days of the WG on Sex Roles in Mass Media, through the wealth of reflections hosted in hundreds of panels coordinated by the Gender and Communication Section over 30 years, to the more recent commitment of IAMCR Task Force in international policy fora—have contributed to the transformation of IAMCR in line with feminist principles and goals. These include mainstreaming gender in communication research and initiatives, critically addressing inequalities, and struggling to transform communication practices and related knowledge. As we move on from revisiting the past, taking stock of the many achievements and changes, it remains crucial to (re)consider the extent to which a gendered lens on media and communication, not just as a specific strand of investigation, but as a perspective for understanding and transforming media ecosystems as well as academic institutions, has really become a shared legacy for IAMCR and its membership.

References

de Bruin, M., & Ross, K. (Eds.). (2004). *Gender and newsroom cultures: Identities at work*. Hampton Press.

Dervin, B. (1987). The potential contribution of feminist scholarship to the field of communication. *Journal of Communication, 37*(4), 107–120.

Gallagher, M. (1981). *Unequal opportunities: The case of women and the media*. UNESCO.

Gallagher, M. (1984). *Communication, control and the problem of gender* (Plenary Paper presentation). IAMCR Conference "Social Control and Global Problems," Prague, Czech Republic.

Kivikuru, U. (1996, November). Glass ceiling found in academy: Big-boy games in the association. *IAMCR Newsletter*, 23–24.

Nordenstreng, K. (1994). The UNESCO expert panel with the benefit of hindsight. In C. J. Hamelink & O. Linné (Eds.), *Mass communication research: On problems and policies* (p. 2–19). Ablex Publishing.

Rakow, L. F. (Ed.). (1992). *Women making meaning: New feminist directions in communication*. Routledge.

Robinson, G. J. (1997, November). Up from the footnote (Speech at the 40th anniversary ceremony of the IAMCR, Oaxaca, 7 July). In *IAMCR Newsletter*, p. 10, 38, et passim.

Rush, R. R., Oukrup, C. E., & Creedon, P. J. (Eds.). (2004). *Seeking equity for women in journalism and mass communication education: A 30-year update*. Lawrence Erlbaum Associates.

Sreberny, A. (2002, July). *Gender and the politics of recognition* (Plenary Paper Presentation). IAMCR Conference, Barcelona, Spain.
UNESCO/UniTWIN Network on Gender Media and ICT. (2019). *Gender, media and ICT. New approaches for teaching, education & training*. UNESCO Series in Journalism Education. UNESCO Press.
van Zoonen, L. (1994). *Feminist media studies*. Sage Publications.

CHAPTER 8

Media Technologies and Globalization Arrive at IAMCR

William H. Melody

Introduction

IAMCR is a child of a new medium of communication, television. It was established in 1957 as a UNESCO initiative in response to the introduction of new communication technologies that enabled the broadcast of video signals, and the introduction of television as a new medium for mass communication. IAMCR's mission was to be responsible for "promoting throughout the world the development of the scientific study of *problems* relating to the media"[1] which at the time included press, cinema, radio, and television (Hamelink & Nordenstreng, 2020) in a new era of mass communication, then already dominated by television broadcasting in industrialized countries. The same year, Russia launched Sputnik, initiating an era of global satellite communication that would dramatically change the communication environment, nationally and internationally.

During the 1960s and 1970s, the most important "problem" needing IAMCR research support was the introduction of television in "developing"

[1] Emphasis added by author. The mission in 1957 was to create "une association internationale des études et recherches sur l'information, chargée de promouvoir à travers le monde le développement de l'étude scientifique des problèmes relatifs aux moyens d'information." Minutes and Statutes, 18–19 December 1957, Paris.

W. H. Melody (✉)
LIRNE.net, Copenhagen, Denmark
e-mail: melody@lirne.net

© The Author(s), under exclusive license to Springer Nature Switzerland AG 2023

J. Becker, R. Mansell (eds.), *Reflections on the International Association for Media and Communication Research*,
https://doi.org/10.1007/978-3-031-16383-8_8

countries. Most did not have it, and few had any significant domestic production, relying primarily on re-broadcasts of Euro-North American programs, most often delivered by post. Although researchers from many disciplines were investigating the different dimensions and possible solutions to this problem, there was no evident recognition of it, let alone "promotion throughout the world of the development of research" on the problem by IAMCR.

The research "problems" prioritized by IAMCR were those related to mass media content, primarily television content in Euro-North America. Television, radio, the press, and film were very different media. They were based on the capabilities and limitations of different media technologies, and they were being applied in a variety of ways for various purposes in different countries. The basic model for IAMCR research was adapted from traditional press journalism in Euro-North America—reporting analyses of audiences and critical comments on mass media messages generated in the established media environment, often referred to as "content analysis." IAMCR was functioning administratively and, for most conference presentations, only in English, despite its origins as a bilingual English and French language association. A research journal was not established when the association was launched, and it served essentially as a meeting ground for Euro-North American researchers studying issues relating to mass media content.

This micro-communication research focus had come to prominence in the United States (US) after World War II with the establishment of new centers at leading universities, most notably: the Institute of Communication Research at the University of Illinois (1946), the Institute for Communication Research at Stanford University (1956), and the Annenberg School of Communication, University of Pennsylvania (1958). These focused on communication research, rather than on the traditional communication skills needed to work in the media industries, and their primary purpose was to study the post-war mass media communication environment in the US that had become dominated by commercial television (Schramm, 1983).

IAMCR participants' recognition of communication technology developments as being essential to an understanding of the changing roles and significance of mass media internationally and in societies around the world finally occurred during the 1980s. Only then did IAMCR belatedly expand its research horizon to formally acknowledge research on the implications of communication technologies. In this period, it also started to acknowledge the importance of research communities in countries beyond the Global North in its programs and activities. From the 1980s, it began to live up to its mission.

This chapter begins by briefly documenting IAMCR's historical context, emphasizing that communication technologies have always been important factors influencing the nature of development processes. This discussion identifies some notable research on important communication technologies from ancient times until 1957 when IAMCR was established. The next section then highlights major new electronic communication technologies that were being implemented from 1957 to 1980, here noting selected research relating to their capabilities, applications, policies for implementation, implications for economies and societies, and IAMCR's position in relation to these areas.

This large body of research cuts across many disciplines. A significant part of it related to the "problems" identified in the IAMCR mission statement, but I suggest that this was not recognized as relevant by IAMCR participants. In this period, I was one of the researchers working in national and international communities of economists and other social scientists, policy analysts, and communication technology specialists. Some of my research included interactions and collaborations with leading communication researchers who focused on content, and this sharpened my understanding of the differences between communication technology and content-related research. This understanding is illustrated by relevant developments in my own research career that led me unexpectedly to IAMCR in 1978 and my experience of the association to the end of the 1980s. During this period, communication technologies finally were accepted as an important topic for research, and "developing" country research communities were accepted as full partners in IAMCR conference programs, achievements which the association highlighted as accomplishments in its presidential newsletters.[2]

The research for this chapter benefits from my review of IAMCR public documents and discussions with research colleagues at IAMCR and around the world over the years. Additional documentation relating particularly to international satellite developments and IAMCR debates during the 1960–1980 period was provided to me by Dallas W. Smythe, a highly respected member of IAMCR from its earliest days. The chapter is also informed by my personal experience as a communication technology researcher and policy advisor to international agencies and government authorities in industrialized and other countries, by my participation in establishing and managing several research organizations, and by my membership of IAMCR's International Council (IC) from 1980 to 1990.

Communication Technologies in Historical Context: IAMCR's Heritage

The Era of Transport Technologies: Physical Delivery of Messages

Communication technologies have been an important subject of research and analysis since even before the time that Plato criticized writing because its growth within the population was deemed to be weakening the oral tradition and the strength of Athenian public discourse and democracy (McCoy, 2009). That technologically advanced communication techniques provide enormous military, political, and economic advantages has long been recognized. Information is power and communication techniques have an important

[2] See archived Presidential Letters during the 1980s at https://iamcr.org/node/10510. Accessed 15 June 2022.

influence on the distribution of power within societies as well as on the rise and fall of empires.

Historians, philosophers, and social scientists of all stripes have researched and debated the implications of new communication technologies for societies, economies, major institutions, power structures, social relations, and individuals. They have documented the profound changes that each new medium of communication has enabled, supported, and promoted. They have examined the beneficial and detrimental implications of new mediums, often drawing conclusions about the long-term consequences for societies and civilizations. Communication capabilities, patterns, and structures have been acknowledged as important and often controlling influences in development and change in all societies.

From the Stone Age until the electric telegraph was invented in 1837, communication through time and over distance required the physical transport of people or documents. The major technologies in the ancient world for communicating beyond local communities were ships and roads, with support from horses and homing pigeons which expanded these communication capabilities. In his masterful book, *The Silk Roads: A New History of the World*, Frankopan (2015) documents how the Silk Roads became the centerpiece of "a world that was profoundly interconnected." He observes,

> There was good reason why the cultures, cities and peoples who lived along the Silk Roads developed and advanced: as they traded and exchanged ideas, they learnt and borrowed from each other, stimulating further advances in philosophy, the sciences, language and religion. (Frankopan, 2015, p. xvii)

Historians of the Roman era have documented how the Roman road networks throughout Europe were more important as communication networks enabling the management of the empire than they were as paths for military troop movement and trade. An efficient postal service with "light carriages and fast horses" was part of the advanced communication infrastructure helping to maintain the empire.

Gutenberg's invention of movable type enabled an expansion of reading capabilities, breaking down the monks' monopoly. This invention has been credited with stimulating the Renaissance and the Enlightenment. Improved ship construction, navigation capabilities, and understanding of world geography enabled voyages from Europe by Columbus to the Americas and Vasco de Gama to India in the 1490s. These opened new trade routes that fundamentally changed the structure of international communication, with consequences for all forms of international relations, enabling colonization and the extension of empires. An enabling force for these developments was the application of new communication technologies. The content of messages was not without significance, but that significance was enabled and constrained by the communication technologies, and the extent of their application.

Harold Innis's Analysis: The "Bias" of Media Technologies

Comprehensive research on the implications of communication technologies for the structure of societies and people in those societies was presented in two thought-provoking books by Harold Innis: *Empire and Communications* (1950) and *The Bias of Communication* (1951) (Melody et al., 1981). The first was a historical analysis, focusing particularly on the role communication systems had played in extending the power of empires. Innis observed that in all societies, the media of communication have greatly influenced trading conditions, forms of social organization, patterns of individual association, and the nature of international relations. New competing communication media, he suggested, can alter forms of economic and social organization, enable new patterns of association, develop new forms of knowledge, and often shift centers of power. He concluded that technologies of communication are central to all other societal developments.

In the second book, Innis sought to draw out a common theoretical framework from his historical research. He concluded that any medium of communication is "biased" in terms of its tendency to permit control over extended periods of time or over extended geographical space. The media used in ancient civilizations such as stone, clay, and parchment were durable and difficult to transport. These characteristics, he suggested, are conducive to control over time, but not over geographical space. They are time-biased. In contrast, paper is light, less durable, and easily transportable at a reasonable speed. It is spatially-biased and this has permitted administration over great distances and, therefore, the extension of empires.

Innis argued that the medium of communication, depending on its bias, conferred monopolies of authority and knowledge on religion, through sacred order and moral law, or on the state, via technical order and civil law. He positioned an over-emphasis or monopoly of either time- or space-biased media of communication as the principal dynamic of the rise and fall of empires since a bias toward time or space can produce instability in society. For Innis, a stable society is possible only with the development of mechanisms that preserve a balance between time and space orientations. He concluded that the flowering of ancient Greece, for example, was made possible and maintained by a balance between the time-bias of the oral tradition and the space-bias of writing on easily transportable documents.

The rapid development of communication technologies today, including the internet, artificial intelligence, and robots, is providing for instantaneous communication throughout most of the world and the extension of empires into space itself. Innis's theoretical framework applied in today's context suggests that the world is presently characterized by a powerful space-bias that points toward increased instability in the future and that this is unlikely to lead to a more informed and participatory public communication environment, locally, nationally, or internationally.

Innis observed 70 years ago that

> The ability to develop a system of government in which the bias of communication can be checked and an appraisal of the significance of space and time can be reached remains a problem of empire and the Western world. (Innis, 1950, p. 197)

Innis's historical research has powerful present-day and future implications. Recent research on the international balance of power between the US, China, Russia, and other countries suggests that the extension of power and empire in the future will focus less on military and/or economic competition, but more on control of the communication environment (Cummings et al., 2018). In some respects, this is already reflected on the internet as social media, "fake" news, and alternative reality websites create evermore Orwellian representations of reality. His work presented an important theme for a media and communication technology research agenda that can be ignored only at our peril, and it is one that IAMCR is uniquely positioned to support.

The Modern Era of Electronic Communication

The electronic age in communication began with the invention of the electric telegraph (1837). Television was an advanced electronic technology developed a century later, building on a series of technological developments in the interim, including the wireless telegraph (1895), shortwave radio (1926), and then more reliable high-frequency microwave radio (1946). Microwave technology provided larger capacity communication channels for transmitting television signals, a foundation for television services in the 1930s and color television in the early 1950s. The Sputnik satellite in 1957 announced a new era in international communication where all forms of electronic communication could be transmitted globally.

The research literature on the development and application of these technologies included important areas of debate relating to how television broadcast services could best be provided. It included studies of public versus private ownership, educational versus entertainment programming, monopoly versus competitive networks, alternative financing approaches by viewers, advertisers, or governments, and the implications for social and cultural policies.

Countries adopted different institutional structures for the provision of radio and television services. Notably, the United Kingdom (UK) established the BBC in 1922 to develop and operate radio and later television as a monopoly public corporation, providing diverse public interest programs financed by viewer license fees and some government subsidy. In the US, the private companies developing radio and television technologies were allocated broadcast radio frequencies and operating licenses by a new government regulatory authority, the Federal Communications Commission (FCC), established in 1934. In this case, the television industry structure would be devoted primarily to advertiser-financed entertainment programming. Most countries in the Global South had yet to establish television networks and were seeking advice and support from those countries that had done so.

IAMCR During an Era of Dynamic Change: 1957–1980

When IAMCR was established in 1957, the era of dynamic technological advances in media and communication was well underway. There was a strong need for research on their performance, and there were opportunities for extending the reach of television to those people in many countries who had yet to be able to receive signals or produce programs. For this reason, the timing of UNESCO's support for the establishment of IAMCR was prescient.

In the 1957–1980 period, the pace of change in communication technologies increased with applications of new electronic technologies fundamentally altering the communication environment throughout the world. The Telstar satellite was launched in 1962, the first satellite to relay television programs from one continent to another. Soon thereafter, global communication satellite services became possible and computer-communication (1967) and mobile communication (1973) were introduced. Unfortunately, these new communication media were not seen as relevant by IAMCR members. The association had grown as an insular club with a relatively narrow agenda which was of declining significance or relevance in view of its stated mission.

James D. Halloran became IAMCR President in 1972. He advocated a broadening of the research agenda "beyond the effects" of mass media messages to include social and public policy issues relating to the established media, such as the differences between public and private commercial television (Halloran, 1970, 1973). There was minimal change in the association's research agenda, however, and little activity in promoting research communities in "developing" countries, beyond Halloran's personal UNESCO projects.

A widely read and internationally recognized media and communication research publication of the time was by a former student of Harold Innis. Marshall McLuhan's book *Understanding Media* (1964) popularized a central theme of Innis's research around the phrase, "the medium is the message." He claimed that international communication satellites would provide instant global communication, opening the possibility for creating an electronic "global village." Although many of his idealistic claims were unsupported, his central argument was a direct challenge to a research agenda focused principally on message content which had been adopted by the new university-based media and communication programs in the US and that was favored by IAMCR.

Dallas W. Smythe had been researching the implications of the new television media in the US in this period, examining the possibilities for television transmission and distribution by satellite. He had suggested during the 1960s that IAMCR's research agenda should recognize and support communication satellites as an important research area that could significantly benefit developing countries and would be of interest to developing country researchers. It was not until the 1974 IAMCR Conference in Leipzig, however, that Smythe was able to establish a Satellite Technology Section to discuss the issues and research possibilities. There was little evidence of enthusiasm at IAMCR for "promoting research throughout the world" on this new media technology development.

By 1980, Canada, the US, Europe, and more than 20 other countries had launched communication satellites, including India and Indonesia. Global communication satellites had made television reception possible in many lower income countries, although often by a single second-hand television set in the village community center. Universal access was still a long way off. Nevertheless, the take up of satellite communication did stimulate the growth of media and communication research communities in many of these countries. They looked to IAMCR for the kind of international support promised in its mission statement, but they did not get it. Instead, the new Satellite Technology Section was tolerated within IAMCR as an accommodation to Smythe's special interest.

In the wealthy countries, the continuous improvement in communication technologies, affecting all forms of communication, stimulated a wave of research by historians and researchers from numerous disciplines on the implications of these technologies for societies, economies, most institutions, and individuals. Dallas Smythe and I were part of this rapidly growing research community.[3] Research results were presented in the meetings and publications of many professional organizations, but very little of this research, and, save Smythe, few if any of the researchers made it to IAMCR conferences. IAMCR remained a fringe association in relation to work on the implications of these technologies, focusing instead on the traditional mass media—mostly, the message content of television, radio, and the press in Euro-North America.

Intersecting Communication Technology and Media Content Themes: A Research Career

The absence of intersections at IAMCR between a rapidly developing field of research on the implications of new communication technologies and research principally focused on media content is confirmed by presenting a brief account of my own research career from the 1960s. By the mid-1960s, my research focus was on technology policy in the US. As an economist with the FCC, for five years I undertook research on several timely policy/regulatory matters relating to communication technologies, including international satellites, achieving universal telephone and television access in Alaska, the economics of computer-communication, and efficiency in the allocation and assignment of radio spectrum licenses (Melody, 1972, 1978, 1980). The wave of new communication technologies being introduced was also stimulating research interest at other government agencies in Washington, D.C., relating to the possible benefits for education, health, medicine, defense, libraries, administration, and

[3] The author was an IAMCR member from 1978 to 1990.

other areas. Universities, research institutes, and companies were starting new research programs. For example, in 1972, Washington researchers started an annual conference, the "Telecommunication Policy Research Conference" (TPRC) to promote engagement among researchers from universities, government agencies, industry, and other organizations on telecommunication policy issues raised by the introduction of the new communication technologies.[4] This conference grew to become popular, attracting researchers from many disciplines and countries. Yet, at this time, IAMCR was not seen as a relevant conference for presenting and debating this kind of research.

From 1971 to 1976, I was a faculty member at the Annenberg School of Communication (ASC), University of Pennsylvania. When I read Marshall McLuhan's *Understanding Media* (1964) and discussed it with social science research colleagues, a common view was that the theme of the book, "the medium is the message" was belaboring the obvious. However, while the message content studied by communication researchers can be significant for understanding certain issues, as Frankopan, Innis, and many others have shown, it is media technologies that have helped to shape the course of development of economies, cultures, and societies. The communication media are the infrastructure technologies that enable messaging possibilities and shape the characteristics and patterns of communication in societies, and this was being studied by historians and social scientists.

When George Gerbner, Dean of the ASC, called me in 1970 to enquire about my interest in a faculty position, I suggested that he may have contacted the wrong person. I was studying the technology, economics, and government policies of the media. ASC was mainly concerned with the message content of television and the press at the time, and Gerbner was leading a major study of the effects of violence in television programs on viewer attitudes and behaviors. I soon learned that Gerbner and his colleagues had decided that the new media technology developments warranted a broadening of ASC programs by becoming more multidisciplinary and by introducing media technology issues and research. He expected my research interests on new media technology issues to strengthen ASC's program.

My new multidisciplinary research opportunities at ASC worked surprisingly well. In addition to collaborations with colleagues in ASC, I was able to establish a National Science Foundation Multidisciplinary Research Program on Communication Technologies, Economics, and Law with colleagues from the law and engineering departments. This research examined next-step reforms to the telecommunication infrastructure in the US to accommodate computer-communication and information services. A major conference on these issues at ASC led to a timely book, *Communication Technologies and Social Policy* (Gerbner et al., 1973).

[4]TPRC is now The Research Conference on Communications, Information, and Internet Policy. See http://www.tprcweb.com/. Accessed 15 June 2022.

I also found common ground with my ASC colleagues regarding the content of children's programs on the commercial national television networks when I took up a project to explain why children's programming was subject to intense criticism from parents, teachers, and education researchers. Children's television content in the US contained aggressive saturation advertising of junk food and poor-quality toys to young children, especially at times when research showed an adult was not watching with the child. My book, *Children's Television: The Economics of Exploitation* (Melody, 1973), explained that the primary cause of the problem was the institutional structure of the US commercial television industry, that is, the specific way the technology was being implemented and regulated. With the economic incentives of the commercial networks distorted from the normal incentives in efficient markets, television networks were not selling programs to viewers. They were selling viewers' attention to advertisers (the industry term was "eyeballs") because uninformed and innocent viewers are more susceptible to influence by aggressive advertising, and the networks were merging advertising with program content. In this way, innocent viewers could be schooled as lobbyists for the advertised products, especially if there was no authority present to counter the message.

As the television networks needed a government license to operate and a government allocation of radio spectrum to carry the signals, the three major network operators were provided with enormous barriers preventing the entry of possible competitors that might produce more diverse and attractive content, especially for children. Economic research on oligopoly industries has shown since my early research that under certain conditions three networks will compete on differentiating their content, but not on practices that might reduce their common profit-maximizing activities (OECD, 1999; Adams & Brock, 2001). The television technology, and the way it had been implemented in a commercial market system within a particular set of government policies and regulations in the US, was fostering the programming of message content that exploited the innocence of children and other viewer groups. For communication researchers, these developments provided an important area where media technology research and message content research could be mutually supportive.

While at ASC, I also prepared research reports for the International Telecommunication Union (ITU) and the Organisation for Economic Co-operation and Development (OECD) on the changing global telecommunication landscape and the possibilities for computer-communication technologies and information technology (IT) services. At this time, it was becoming clear that the combination of telecommunication policy changes removing the monopoly of telecommunication operators and IT developments in the computer industry, could bring revolutionary changes in the media of communication, ultimately affecting all forms of electronic communication and especially the traditional mass media. I found a common interest in my research on these projects with American and international colleagues in economics and other social sciences, as well as in telecommunication and computer technology policy forums, but IAMCR was not seen as a relevant or an interested venue for presenting and discussing this research.

In 1976, I returned to my native Canada as Professor and Chair of the Communications Department at Simon Fraser University (SFU) and worked there until 1986, succeeding Dallas Smythe. Unlike the schools and departments of communication research in the US at this time, this department was oriented primarily to the multidisciplinary study of the communication media in society, closer to the tradition of Harold Innis than to the US programs that were still focusing on message content as a standalone subject. At SFU, there was a strong focus on how the implementation of media technologies was shaped by government policies and industry practices to create the environment in which message content is generated. Smythe and I were able to pursue our common interest in satellites as Canada had recently (1972) launched the world's first domestic satellite system, and I had just completed a research project on using satellites to provide universal telephone, television, and education services to remote Alaska villages (Melody, 1978).

New initiatives were being planned and introduced on international, Canadian, and US satellite systems, extending the telephone and television networks to unserved areas in far north mountainous and rural areas, and experiments in tele-medicine, tele-education, and tele-work were being trialed and researched. This, in turn, sparked interest in potential satellite applications to promote economic and social opportunities in lower income countries. Smythe and I began working with Canadian and international agencies on research projects with colleagues in Latin America, who then sent students to our SFU communication program.

Around this time, Smythe suggested I should join him at the next IAMCR conference. He argued that IAMCR would be the best association to present our work at, if its leaders could be convinced to live up to its mission statement. Our SFU communication program needed to find an international association that could benefit our growing international focus on communication and development, including participation from teachers and students from Global South countries. I reviewed IAMCR President James Halloran's 1973 statement outlining plans for updating the research agenda to address the changing global communication environment, and noted that he was undertaking research on communication in countries beyond the Global North. Smythe and I agreed to attend the next IAMCR conference and advocate that the Satellite Technology Section should be broadened to form the Communication Technology Section, and develop a plan to promote it for future IAMCR conferences. The next section highlights my observations about the research agendas being addressed within IAMCR based on my participation in the association, starting with the first conference I attended.

Participating in IAMCR in the Late 1970s and 1980s

Warsaw Conference, 1978

IAMCR reported that 500 people attended this conference from 38 countries and that membership had risen to 1000 people from 50+ countries—much larger than I envisioned. As often happens at large conferences, the most positive part of the meetings was the personal interaction with old and new colleagues outside the formal program. My observation was that it was about 60 percent European, 30 percent North American, with a handful of participants from Global South countries. Presentations were made on a very wide variety of issues from an equally wide variety of perspectives and interpretations of mass communication. It was more like a big tent research *bazaar* offering a smorgasbord of unrelated presentations than a coherent conference, and there was little or no discussion of the presentations. There was almost no evidence of research papers or other documentation being distributed in association with the presentations.

With a few exceptions, the research presented by this eclectic group was more "show and tell" summaries and personal opinions than analytical, empirical, or historical research on the pressing research and policy issues in the field. Several researchers spoke glowingly about the important resolutions IAMCR had adopted at the previous 1976 Conference in Leicester. On probing, I learned that those resolutions stated there was a need for international communication policies in the service of democratic development, and for the support of the universal right to communicate. But no research on these issues was presented at the conference as far as I could detect, and no one could identify any research that had been done by IAMCR researchers or that was in process.

It was common knowledge that there were many undemocratic countries exercising monopoly control over their national media, and that access to television was far from universal in most lower income countries. Universal access to telephone service had not been achieved in most European countries, and in most lower income countries, it was less than 10 percent. There was no mention of satellites (except by Smythe and me) as a vehicle for implementing these resolutions, nor any other action items. What purpose did these resolutions serve? This was self-indulgent posturing and feel-good puffery as far as I could tell; a poor substitute for research on the issues, but an affliction that periodically plagued some IAMCR leaders over the years.

IAMCR President James Halloran and other IAMCR leaders told us that technology issues were new and unfamiliar to most IAMCR participants. With some serious reservations, Smythe and I decided to plan to attend the next IAMCR conference in two years' time in Caracas, Venezuela. We would promote the participation of Latin American researchers working in their home countries or in North America by presenting a variety of research on communication and development issues. We thought this might be the catalyst needed to bring about a significant strengthening of IAMCR toward fulfilling its mandate and facilitating research on new communication technology applications by lower income country researchers.

Caracas Conference, 1980

It was immediately apparent to me that this was a meeting of the Euro-North American IAMCR "mafia" which just happened to take place in Caracas. The participation of Latin American researchers was larger than normal, but not large enough to influence the agenda. Most Latin American researchers could not afford to participate, and the event was dominated by Euro-North American participants. Smythe chaired a session on satellite communication, and I chaired one on communication technologies, each with a small participation of about 20 people, most of whom were interested in the issues but not yet doing research in the area. They provided an insignificant diversion from the major sessions on current Euro-North American media content issues.

A political science colleague, Ithiel de Sola Pool, came to my Communication Technologies Section meeting, his first IAMCR conference. He was preparing a book on *Technologies of Freedom* (1983) in the US. Later in the IAMCR program, he engaged in the highlight event of the conference, a spontaneous debate with long-time IAMCR member Herbert Schiller on the implications of new communication technologies for individual freedom (see Chap. 32 in this volume). But the discussion was all within the framework of the US Constitution and its policy and regulation, unfortunately of little relevance to many other lower income countries and the technologies that could enable an enhancement of their citizens' freedoms. Smythe and I failed to make any significant headway in our mission to broaden the traditional agenda of IAMCR at this conference. However, as I had been invited to join IAMCR's IC, we hoped this would increase the chances for success at future conferences.

Paris Conference, 1982

In 1980, India was the first Global South country to launch its own national television network, transmitted over the Indian national satellite. The US Cable News Network (CNN) was launched the same year as an international service transmitted to most countries by satellite. These events shaped the agenda for our satellite technology session which focused on television broadcasting. The contributions of a contingent of Indian researchers made for a lively and significant meeting for 40 to 50 participants that was informative for researchers from both industrialized and lower income countries. This was our first IAMCR experience where Global South country researchers had an opportunity to take the lead in research presentations and discussions.

As the development and application of digital technologies was continuing to penetrate the communication network and the devices connected to it, this was the theme for the Communications Technology session. Dramatic increases in the productivity of transistors, microchips, and microprocessors were converting the telecommunication network into a giant computer. Personal computers (PCs) had been introduced as had high-capacity fiber optic cable, and plans were underway to link the continents by submarine fiber cable. New satellite technology systems now could provide Direct Assignment Multiple Access (DAMA) signaling to small earth stations, providing telephone and data services in remote areas. But researchers who were working on these issues did not come to IAMCR. Instead, this research was being presented in economics, political science, sociology, and other professional associations, such as TPRC. The 30 to 40 participants attending the IAMCR session were seeking a tutorial on the subject, rather than an opportunity to present and debate research contributions.

Prague Conference, 1984

Smythe and I decided that it might be more useful to researchers who were attending the IAMCR conference to put greater emphasis on technology policy issues, rather than on the opportunities enabled by the new communication technologies. An obvious case was the policies and regulations associated with the launching of Eutelsat 1 in 1983 and Eutelsat 2 in 1984, Europe's first geostationary communication satellites. One of their planned uses was to transmit television signals across Europe, but the conditions had not yet been agreed. European viewers would be able to view some channels of their neighbors, but which ones and under what conditions had not yet been decided. Sensitive issues of competition between Eutelsat and national satellites, such as the Czech satellite launched in 1978, and between the public service broadcasters of different countries, had yet to be settled. Neither had the role of private satellite broadcasters been agreed, nor the conditions for advertising or imports of foreign television channels from outside Europe been determined. Our session generated a lot of interest and discussion, but very little research that might inform these policy issues was brought forward. Participants said the value to them was that they were more informed and better prepared to plan research projects on the issues.

The second timely research area was the reform of national telecommunication monopolies in response to the growth of IT and the necessary digitalization of national networks to accommodate an increasing array of IT services. National monopolies had universally resisted competition at every turn. In the US, AT&T had been charged with anti-competitive practices. The UK was considering establishing a telecommunication regulator (Oftel). In other countries, privatizing the national operator and introducing competition were being considered, as were the possibilities for competition among different technologies—new satellite and mobile companies could compete with the national operator—all these issues were being debated at the time of this conference.

The result was the same as our satellite session at the IAMCR conference. There was lots of interest, but very little research to report, and I concluded that this was the culture of IAMCR. Despite the fact that there was a lot of research on these issues, it was not being presented at IAMCR. I would make the same observation at many IAMCR sessions. The association could be an interesting place to discuss researchable problems, but not a place for critically assessing ongoing and completed research projects.

New Delhi Conference, 1986

I enjoyed discussions with colleagues on the IC, both at IAMCR conferences and often at informal meetings between conferences, though I could not help observing that I was now a member of the Euro-North American "mafia." The rest of the world was encouraged to join our association, but what happened in the end was what was desirable and convenient for us. This was driven home to me when the IC was considering the application from the Indian delegation to hold the 1986 Conference in New Delhi.

After a review of the India conference proposal and a short discussion, the Council concluded it would have to be rejected for several reasons: the proposal was not complete; there was a high risk the Indians would not be able to organize and finance it; attendance would be small as few IAMCR members from Euro-America would attend; the quality of the program would be poor; it would be too hot in New Delhi in the summer; we would prefer to go to a nice place in Euro-North America.

That was not my assessment. I concluded the proposal was equal to those submitted for past conferences. It was not complete and would require assistance from some of us and the IAMCR administration, but I felt we should give this an opportunity since we had always done so with the hosts of other IAMCR conferences. Participation by Indian researchers could be substantial because they would have a very large contingent of researchers, an increasing number of whom were members of IAMCR. Judging from the Indian participation I had seen at recent IAMCR conferences, the quality of the program would be satisfactory. I doubted the location would be determinative of whether Euro-North Americans would go or not. There would be air-conditioning. I did not change anyone's mind on the IC. Yet, when I presented my argument to the later IAMCR General Assembly (GA) at the end of the Prague 1984 Conference, the members voted almost unanimously to approve the Indian proposal. The 1986 Conference was a great success. There were more Indian researchers attending than Euro-North Americans. The session on satellites attracted a large group of Indian researchers reporting on services being provided using the Indian satellite. The session on information and communication technologies (ICTs) was more like a big seminar as we discussed research proposals examining applications that were being generated by research institutes around the world, and proposals by Indian researchers for comparable research in India.

Barcelona Conference, 1988

By this time, the digitalization of the telecommunication networks in industrialized countries was well advanced and the primary focus of research attention had shifted from the necessary policy reforms to enabling digital services to be provided for applications of those services throughout economies and societies. Organizations in banking and finance were establishing advanced global networks, and applications in health, education, and other areas had begun. In 1985, the UK's Economic and Social Research Council (ESRC) decided to establish a network of ICT research centers at six British universities directed to examining the implications of ICTs for UK institutions. As Director of the program, I worked with researchers on developing the centers and projects. Similar research initiatives were being launched in other European countries. The participants in these British and European programs considered the potential of IAMCR as a venue for discussing and debating its research projects, but concluded that the association would not be likely to foster such debates. A new association modeled after the TPRC annual conference in the US was established, the "European Communication Policy Research Conference (Euro-CPR)," as a key venue for discussion, while individual researchers were made aware of IAMCR and encouraged to consider whether IAMCR conference programs were relevant for their research.

For the Barcelona IAMCR Conference, the Communication Technology Section encouraged research contributions on the theme of ICT applications. Although there was considerable interest in the topic, most research projects presented were at an early stage and unable to report conclusions. This did lead to serious discussion of research problem definition, project design, and research methods in this growing field for research. However, the weakness was that the session failed to take up the matter of the implications for lower income countries that did not have the digitalized telecommunication infrastructure necessary to make this research relevant for them. These developments were making the digital divide wider and it was agreed that this should be a priority topic for future research.

Reflections on IAMCR's Mission and Future

By the end of the 1980s, communication technology research had become an active section in the IAMCR conference agenda with significant participation by researchers from both wealthy, industrialized and lower income countries. Its growth and acceptance were followed by the establishment of other new sections examining media-related research issues. IAMCR was persuaded to change its name from "mass communication" to "media and communication" research, which it did formally at its GA in 1996.[5] In 1989, I was appointed Director of a new international ICT research center in Melbourne, Australia. The responsibilities of building a new center prevented me from attending the 1990 IAMCR Conference in Bled, but I was able to send several researchers. My successor as Chair of the Communication Technologies Section, Robin Mansell, updated the Section's name and focus to Communication Technology Policy Section, reflecting the priority need for critical policy research as new communication technologies and services were being widely implemented in the 1990s and the internet was being established.

By 1990, IAMCR conferences had become a much larger research *bazaar*, accommodating a larger smorgasbord of research interests than in 1978. Its strength was in bringing a very diverse spectrum of researchers together to discuss media and communication issues of common interest, but rarely to provide critical reviews and discussions of the substance of research projects as one might find at traditional disciplinary research meetings. My attendance at a few IAMCR conferences in the 1990s reinforced this observation.

The structure of IAMCR now is like a holding company network that coordinates the activities of Sections, Working Groups (WGs), and other workshops to present an annual conference and various occasional events. It has very rarely undertaken or financed research projects on topics other than preparing reports about itself, although this began to change in the 2000s. The substance of research exchange and discussion, in my experience, has remained in the Sections and WGs. IAMCR still interprets its mission of promoting research relating to the media "throughout the world," as accepting membership and conference attendance from anyone who can pay the fees and costs of conference attendance and is prepared to participate most of the time in English. This should be an embarrassment.

IAMCR still maintains a highly centralized management structure with a small central group controlling key administrative and financing decisions, with little change, until very recently, from its initial structure a half-century ago. With membership now many times larger and the substance of IAMCR research activity being provided by the Sections and WGs, it is past time for IAMCR to update its structure to involve the Heads of the Sections and WGs more directly in the major administrative and financing decisions. I am reminded that I have spent a significant portion of my career trying to get university administrators to give researchers more control over the management and finance of their research.

Other research organizations have developed electronic journals for publishing their research. Although some IAMCR Sections and WGs have established initiatives for electronic research exchange, relatively frequent newsletters in several languages can now be done cheaply and efficiently. Almost all the major research by IAMCR researchers is published in professional journals or costly books that are not open access and therefore not available to many

[5] General Assembly Minutes of 20th Meeting, 21 August 1996, Sydney, Australia.

IAMCR members. Summaries in several languages could be readily published by IAMCR as could bibliographies on topical research subjects. And much more.

It is ironic that IAMCR now recognizes communication technologies as a relevant research area in its program, but, at least until the COVID-19 pandemic, it neglected to research possibilities for applying the new technologies to strengthen its capability for fulfilling its mission. In recent years, its website has been significantly improved and it has responded to the pandemic restrictions positively with internet-based events. But a priority research project surely must be to assess how IAMCR can use the internet and related media to maximum effect in fulfilling its mission, especially in relation to supporting research in countries in the Global South. Such a project should identify internet-based services the IAMCR "holding company" can provide for the Sections and WGs, developing country researchers, and research networks throughout the world, such as, LIRNEasia, Research ICT Africa, and organizations throughout Latin America.[6] There is an opportunity for IAMCR to significantly expand its influence in the global media and communication environment by providing essential research support services to the global research community. If it were to do so, it could more robustly fulfill its mission.

References

Adams, W., & Brock, J. (2001). *The structure of American industry* (10th ed.). Prentice Hall.

Cummings, M. L., Roff, H., Cukier, K., Bryce, H., & Parakilas, J. (2018, June 14). Artificial intelligence and international affairs. *Chatham House Report*. Retrieved 15 June 2022, from https://www.chathamhouse.org/2018/06/artificial-intelligence-and-international-affairs

de Sola Pool, I. (1983). *Technologies of freedom: On free speech in an electronic age*. Belknap Press/Harvard University Press.

Frankopan, P. (2015). *The silk roads: A new history of the world*. Bloomsbury.

Gerbner, G., Gross, L., & Melody, W. H. (Eds.). (1973). *Communication technologies and social policy*. Wiley.

Halloran, J. D. (Ed.). (1970). *The effects of television*. Paladin Press.

Halloran, J. D. (1973). *Understanding television* (Paper Presentation). Council of Europe Colloquia, University of Leicester, Leicester, UK.

Hamelink, C., & Nordenstreng, K. (2020). *Basics of IAMCR history* (2nd ed.). IAMCR. Retrieved 15 June 2022, from https://iamcr.org/sites/default/files/basics_of_iamcr_2nd_ed_rev2.pdf

Innis, H. A. (1950). *Empire and communications*. Clarendon Press.

Innis, H. A. (1951). *The bias of communication*. University of Toronto Press.

McCoy, M. B. (2009). Alcidamas, Isocrates, and Plato on speech, writing, and philosophical rhetoric. *Ancient Philosophy, 29*(1), 45–66.

McLuhan, M. (1964). *Understanding media: The extensions of man*. Routledge.

[6] LIRNEasia at https://lirneasia.net/; ResearchICTAfrica at https://researchictafrica.net/. Both Accessed 15 June 2022.

Melody, W. H. (1972). Technological, economic and institutional aspects. In *Applications of Computer/Telecommunication Systems* (Proceedings of Seminar, 1972, November 13). OECD Informatics Studies, Paris, France.

Melody, W. H. (1973). *Children's television: The economics of exploitation.* Yale University Press.

Melody, W. H. (1978). *Telecommunications in Alaska: Economics and public policy.* Alaska Office of Telecommunications, University of Wisconsin-Madison.

Melody, W. H. (1980). Radio spectrum allocation: The role of the market. *American Economic Review, 70*(2), 395–397.

Melody, W. H., Salter, L., & Heyer, P. (Eds.). (1981). *Culture, communication and dependency: The tradition of H. A. Innis.* Ablex Publishing.

OECD. (1999). *OECD roundtables, Oligopoly.* OECD. Retrieved 15 June 2022, from www.oecd.org/competition/mergers/1920526.pdf

Schramm, W. (1983, September). The unique perspective of communication: A retrospective view. *Journal of Communication, 33*(3), 6–17. Retrieved 15 June 2022, from https://doi.org/10.1111/j.1460-2466.1983.tb02401.x

CHAPTER 9

IAMCR's Emerging Scholars Network

Katharine Sarikakis and Sara Bannerman

"This is such an international conference!""Are you enjoying it?""I am, but I was lucky to attend this year; I study in Glasgow. The conference fees are so expensive, I can't see how students might be able to attend every year…""Well, then, you have to change that!""Ok … how?"

Introduction

The opening quotation is ultimately the seed conversation between a graduate student and a senior scholar leading to the establishment of the Emerging Scholars Network (ESN) of IAMCR. ESN is a section with a dual role: it was founded not only to provide academic space for the scholarship of emerging scholars, but also to provide a dedicated space for connection and representation.

ESN was founded during the 21st scientific conference and General Assembly (GA) of IAMCR in Glasgow, Scotland, as the "Graduate Students

K. Sarikakis
University of Vienna, Vienna, Austria
e-mail: katharine.sarikakis@univie.ac.at

S. Bannerman (✉)
McMaster University, Hamilton, ON, Canada
e-mail: banners@mcmaster.ca

© The Author(s), under exclusive license to Springer Nature Switzerland AG 2023

J. Becker, R. Mansell (eds.), *Reflections on the International Association for Media and Communication Research*,
https://doi.org/10.1007/978-3-031-16383-8_9

Network" (GSN) in 1998 with around 30 members.[1] It was renamed the "Junior Scholars Network" (JSN) the next year in 1999 (IAMCR Newsletter, 1999, p. 7). The network was initiated by Katharine Sarikakis, who was supported and inspired by Ramona R. Rush, then Professor of Communication and former Dean of the Graduate School at the University of Kentucky. For over 23 years, the network has fostered a space for academic exchange, debate, and guidance among graduate students, new professors, and "all researchers who feel 'young' in academia." In 2006–2007, the network became the Emerging Scholars Network. Its commitment and objectives remained the same, but the new name signaled the network's openness to emerging scholars, a reference to status rather than age.

The key strategic aim of the ESN has been to open IAMCR to new members, to promote their participation in the organization and its conferences, and to facilitate a more diverse and international mosaic of scholarship while recognizing the work of emerging faculty and granting that work the same recognition as that of established colleagues.

Nearly a quarter of a century after its founding, ESN constitutes a solid pillar of IAMCR, contributing to an inclusive and accessible organization. The network maintains its scope and mission to connect and involve emerging scholars not only from the West but also from the Global South. At the time of writing, ESN had 117 members from different parts of the world.

This chapter, after a brief outline of our research methods, revisits the history of the establishment of ESN as a Section. It discusses some of the main contributions of the network and finally offers reflections by current and past ESN chairs, co-chairs, vice-chairs, mentors, and supporters about the network.

We draw on personal memories and testimonials from the authors' experience with the network and as chairs as well as historical documentary analyses and interviews.[2] The authors of this chapter are Katharine Sarikakis, founder and first Chair of the Emerging Scholars Network and past Vice President-elect with a portfolio to support the promotion of women and young scholars, and Sara Bannerman, Co-Chair of the network between 2008 and 2012. We utilized the digital archive of IAMCR newsletters, reports, and statutory minutes available on IAMCR's website[3] and documents stored by ourselves and past ESN chairs, co-chairs, and vice-chairs in outlining the history of the

[1] Raffaella Benanti, Paula Chakravartty, Jessica Davis, Philip Drake, J. A. Dumas, Lisbeth Egsmose, Kerstin Engstrand, Arild Fetveit, Sara-Jane Finlay, and Audrey Gadzekpo. Dietmar Gattwinkel, Leona Geudens, Aine Haslam, Michael Higgins, Hyun Joo Lee, Kris Jozajtis, Lewis Kaye, Claire Mackie, Philippe Meers, Colm Murphy, Petr Pavlik, Shoba S. Rajgopal, Ellen Riordan, Nandini Sen, John Sullivan, George Terzis, Trond Arne Undheim, and Uta Wehn.

[2] Interviews were conducted in 2021 by Sara Bannerman with Sibo Chen (July 27), Steph Hill (July 27), Rosa Mikael Martey (July 30), Francesca Musiani (July 28), and John Sullivan (July 30). Quotations in text are personal communications.

[3] These URLs link to all IAMCR Newsletters and Bulletins referenced in this chapter, https://iamcr.org/category/newsletter and https://iamcr.org/node/10511. Accessed 15 June 2022.

establishment of the network and its main activities. We used the content analysis software MaxQDA to conduct keyword searches to identify relevant information in the archives.

We conducted interviews in July and August 2021 with five current and past Emerging Scholars Network chairs, co-chairs, and vice-chairs about the network. We asked about the initiatives of the network, the section's membership composition, the concerns and challenges confronted by the network, individuals who have had an impact on the section, the inclusion of underrepresented groups in the section, and the section's accomplishments. We also asked interviewees if they had any advice for emerging scholars today as they embark to join the international community of IAMCR.

The Path to Recognition

The first meeting of the network took place in 1998 in Glasgow, assembling around 30 young scholars who were named the founders of ESN. John Sullivan, Chair of the network from 2000 to 2002, told us in an interview that:

> On the one hand, we were at the [IAMCR conference], but on the other hand, we weren't necessarily a part of the event; we were outsiders—we were interlopers, we were observers, we were there presenting our papers, but no one knew who we were. No one did any kind of outreach to us there, and so we were kind of commiserating in the corner and it was Katharine who helped us turn our commiseration into collective action.
>
> Spurred on by Katharine [Sarikakis], we agreed that we should try and establish an identity for ourselves within this association to make sure that we are never ignored again. (Sullivan, 2021)

ESN sought formal representation in the governing bodies of IAMCR, especially the International Council (IC). A formal proposal was submitted to the IC by the network chair in 1999. As ESN had no seat in IC, member Tom Jacobson conveyed the proposal in the 30 July 1999 meeting. The IC then decided to put this on the agenda of the GA meeting of Singapore in 2000. IAMCR President Manuel Pares I Maicas welcomed the presence of the JSN on IAMCR's IC (IAMCR Newsletter, April/May 2000, p. 24). This engagement was acknowledged in an IAMCR Rejuvenation Report in May 2000: paragraph 4.4.5 stated the need for IAMCR to "embrace new members especially young people, women and colleagues from developing nations."[4] Yet, the same report refrained from providing a recommendation for the network to be given formal recognition in IAMCR; the ESN Chair, a member of the drafting committee, recalls the committee did not reach consensus, and the ESN would not yet gain its own seat on the IC.

Initially, ESN was established as a Working Group (WG) of IAMCR, despite resistance from several established scholars. One such scholar at the Singapore

[4] May 2000 IAMCR Toward Rejuvenation Report, May 2000, https://iamcr.org/node/10512. Accessed 15 June 2022.

GA, in an attempt to belittle the initiative, said, "next we will have a network of scholars with green hair—the Green haired scholars' network." Others reported on their personal desire not to be seen as graduate students by scholars established decades earlier and opposed the network. Although the 1998 *IAMCR in the 21st Century Report* had flagged the need to engage and support young people and other groups in the association, the claim to formally recognize the emerging scholars' arm of IAMCR proved to be controversial. The minutes are not available from the 2000 GA. However, it is in the memory of participants that ESN was given the mandate to continue its activities to "prove" the continuous need for its presence and its sustainability. That year, Katharine Sarikakis was elected to IAMCR Executive Board (EB), the youngest ever elected Vice President, bringing initial realization, in an official form, of the claim of these scholars for equitable and inclusive representation within IAMCR (IAMCR Newsletter, November 2000, p. 7).

Meanwhile, ESN developed its own bylaws (2001). In addition to its aim for transparency in its governance (Article V, Paragraph 3 regulated elections), ESN was unprecedented in including acheivement of a gender and regional balance of co-chairs in its mission (Article V, Paragraph 4). It deployed these aims in relation to other positions as well. In 2002, for example, the network held elections for the positions of academic officer, financial officer, and internal communications officer (IAMCR Newsletter, May–June 2002, p. 29).

In 2005, the JSN submitted a proposal to become a full section, which was pushed back and it remained a quasi-section for the next two years (IAMCR Newsletter, April 2005, p. 10). In 2006–2007, it became the ESN and was recognized as a full section with representation on the IC (IAMCR Newsletter, April 2007, p. 9). See Table 9.1 for those who have led the ESN.

Over the following years, the ESN grew in terms of members, responsibilities, and leadership positions. In 2010, Co-Chairs Stefania Milan and Sara Bannerman created several *ad hoc* positions within the leadership of the network. Running the network required not only the organization and peer review of conference panels, the invitation of discussants, and the organization of social events, but also the organization of a mentorship program, ongoing

Table 9.1 ESN chairs, co-chairs, and vice-chairs, 1998–2022

Term of service	*Past chairs, co-chairs, and vice-chairs of the network*
1998–2000	Katharine Sarikakis, founding Chair, and John Sullivan, Vice-Chair
2000–2002	John Sullivan, Chair, and Rosa Mikael Martey, Vice-Chair
2002–2006	Rosa Mikael Martey, Chair, and Sandor Vegh, Co-Chair/Deputy Chair
2006–2008	Rosa Mikael Martey, Chair
2008–2012	Stefania Milan and Sara Bannerman, Co-Chairs
2012–2016	Sandra Ristovska and Francesca Musiani, Co-Chairs
2016–2018	Ksenia Ermoshina and Sylvia Blake, Co-Chairs
2019	Ksenia Ermoshina, Chair/Co-Chair
2019–2021	Ksenia Ermoshina and Sibo Chen, Co-Chairs, and Steph Hill, Vice-Chair
2022–	Sibo Chen and Steph Hill, Co-Chairs

communications with and advice to members, policy advocacy on issues affecting students (such as conference fees and distance participation), and other activities.

The Contribution of the Emerging Scholars Network

The very *raison d'être* of ESN has been the democratization of IAMCR as a space of intellectual exchange and also as a space for bridging academia and world politics. The ESN was established not out of the simple self-interest of an under-represented category of scholars; the network also intended to bring under-represented voices into the construction of knowledge, and to confront world communication inequities. As the personal is political, individual and group-focused concerns reflected broader issues of inclusion/exclusion, as well as knowledge legitimation and political claims. Opening IAMCR to all categories of scholars who historically had been under-represented in the organization, in particular, those at the beginnings of their careers, was not a "personal" or selfish project, but rather one that was fully in line with IAMCR's declared mission and standing vis-à-vis its commitments to global communication equity.

It became clear to the founding members of ESN very soon after its establishment that age is a category of disadvantage. Younger scholars at the beginning of their careers may have access to fewer resources, including networks, to enable them to produce and present material at conferences; and older and especially female academics may experience a break or delay in their doctoral studies due to care work. Through informal discussions and business meetings, the network identified two major directions in pursuing a more inclusive and representative IAMCR: the lowering of structural barriers to conferences and the creation of spaces. The latter meant activities initiated and run by ESN as well as the cultivation of synergies with such existing spaces.

In 1999, the network held its first graduate student roundtable in Leipzig, Germany, under the theme: "Global Communications: Talking in Future Tense" supported by Wolfgang Kleinwächter. This first discussion emphasized the need for action to encourage and increase the participation and visibility of women, young people, and scholars coming from less-privileged parts of the world in IAMCR. This was followed by a second roundtable in Singapore in 2000 (IAMCR Newsletter, April 2001, p. 12). By the 2001 IAMCR Conference, the network had begun holding its own panels, with 12 papers and works-in-progress presented in 2001 and 31 panel and poster presentations presented in 2002 in Barcelona (IAMCR Newsletter, November 2001, p. 11; May/June 2002, p. 29). While it can be easy for newcomers to an association to feel lost in a huge conference, these panels provided a space where junior or emerging scholars could present with lower levels of pressure—a space that was particularly important for women, LGBTQIA people, and under-represented groups (Sullivan, 2021).

Structural Blockages: The Conference Fees

ESN has long advocated for affordable conference fees as a core structural initiative. In Glasgow in 1998, a group of students at the social event discussed the high cost of the conference. John Sullivan, who would become the second Chair of the ESN, recounts what eventually would be recognized as the first meeting of the GSN in 1998:

> We were in this bar and restaurant with this extremely lavish setting with all this wonderful food and drinks and things like that, and we [students] found each other. [...] We were talking about the ridiculous high cost of the conference as a whole and we kind of agreed at that point. [...] The only way we can have a voice is if we fought, we have to formalize, we have to find ways to make ourselves known to be association as a whole, so it's not just one or two people, one or two voices lone voices complaining. (Sullivan, 2021)

Sullivan recalls that Katharine Sarikakis emphasized the importance of organizing and institutionalizing students at IAMCR in order to have a collective voice on issues such as the affordability of conferences and other concerns of students and emerging scholars. As far back as 1999, the network advocated for lower conference fees (IAMCR Newsletter, 1999, p. 7).

In 2010, 12 years after the initial ESN meeting on fees and representation, the network, led by Co-Chairs Stefania Milan and Sara Bannerman, brought the issue of conference fees back on the IAMCR agenda and initiated a high-level conversation through a letter to the IC.[5] It noted, "The IAMCR this year charged between $318 and $636USD[6] for student registration, and between $190 and $381 USD[7] for students from low income countries. These rates are comparable to a months' rent or more in some places."[8] The letter called for a reduction in conference fees to apply not only to students but also to postdoctoral researchers, independent/low-waged researchers, and contract/low-waged instructors. Milan and Bannerman issued a statement at the meeting of the IC, endorsed by the heads of Sections and WGs, that the reduced fee category should be expanded to encompass those precariously employed, and that IAMCR fees should be set "as low as possible."[9] A motion was passed at the GA in Braga that year. In response, in 2011, a President's Committee on Conference Fees released a report and set of recommendations, noting, "The principle that conference fees should be set as low as possible was endorsed by the GA of the IAMCR in 2010 and is therefore a principle that must be fol-

[5] Milan, S., & Bannerman, S. Letter from the Emerging Scholars Network to IAMCR International Council. July 14, 2010. https://iamcr.org/conf-fees-2. Accessed 15 June 2022.

[6] See https://iamcr.org/conf-fees-2#%5B1%5D. Accessed 15 June 2022.

[7] See https://iamcr.org/conf-fees-2#%5B2%5D. Accessed 15 June 2022.

[8] Milan, S., & Bannerman, S. Letter from the Emerging Scholars Network to IAMCR International Council. July 14, 2010. https://iamcr.org/conf-fees-2. Accessed 15 June 2022.

[9] Milan, S., & Bannerman, S. Letter from the Emerging Scholars Network to IAMCR International Council. July 14, 2010. https://iamcr.org/conf-fees-2. Accessed 15 June 2022.

lowed by conference organizers."[10] Conference fees were, as a result, frozen or reduced for students from 2010 to 2011. Conference fees fell by about 30 percent between 2011 and 2019, particularly for participants from low-income countries (fees fell 49 percent) and students (fees fell 44 percent). Currently, IAMCR offers discounted membership categories, including students and casual laborers.[11]

Sustainability of the Network: Spaces for Scholarship, Mentorship, Collegiality

Since its official recognition as a section in 2007, ESN has held eight to 10 ESN panels typically, including roundtables and special sessions in every IAMCR conference. It has focused on timely topics in the communicational realm, such as war and peace communication, the internet and education, global media policy, theories and practices in the press throughout history, gender and media, identity representations, media and global inequalities, and media and the public good. It has also organized special sessions regarding topics that influence emerging scholars' careers, such as, *inter alia*, academic work and academic jobs, publishing processes, or language barriers in academia.

Moreover, ESN has participated in collaborative projects to develop spaces for discussion among emerging academics and to promote participation of emerging scholars in academic activities internationally. For instance, the network has collaborated with the Spanish Association of Young Researchers in Communication (2002), the Global Internet Governance Academic Network (Giganet) (2013), *Stream: Culture/Politics/Technology*, the graduate journal of the School of Communication at Simon Fraser University (2015), and participated in the IAMCR-Open Society Foundation Rapid Response Grants on Communication Policy for Emerging Media and Communication Scholars in 2013. The network has also organized joint sessions with other sections within IAMCR, such as the Communication Policy and Technology Section, the Community Communication and Alternative Social Media Section, the Law Section, the Gender and Communication Section, and the History Section.

Mentorship Program

Beginning in 2000, Katharine Sarikakis in her role as Vice President advocated the establishment of a mentorship system in IAMCR (IAMCR Newsletter, November 2000, p. 7; IAMCR Newsletter, November 2001, p. 12). The need for such an organization-wide initiative was reflected in the words of Wai Hsien Cheah, a then emerging scholar:

[10] Authors' records.

[11] *IAMCR 2011 Registration Fees*, https://iamcr.org/2011fees; *IAMCR Membership Fees*. https://iamcr.org/membership-fees. Both Accessed 15 June 2022.

> [M]y real passion is in research [but…] I did not know where to start, who to talk to, how to get myself involved in collaborative work with local scholars, for the purpose of generating new knowledge at the local scene […] I have developed the courage to make my voice be heard, and I have also found the support from other junior/young scholars, like myself, through JSN, who share my vision—to do great things for our respective countries in the future. (2001 November Vol 12 No 2, P. 17: 2560) (IAMCR Newsletter, November 2001, p. 17)

Cheah advocated a mentorship program to support the kinds of mentoring necessary for productive research. The next year, Sumati Nagrath also advocated a mentorship group system of online discussion for IAMCR (IAMCR Newsletter, May/June 2002, p. 8, 22). Katharine Sarikakis' proposal to implement an IAMCR mentorship program was endorsed at the 2002 GA in Barcelona (IAMCR Newsletter, November 2002, p. 6). Rosa Mikeal and Sandor Vegh were elected ESN Chairs. Rosa was "really instrumental" in fostering mentorship and "that outreach to other scholars within the organization" (Sullivan, 2021). In 2003, Sarikakis announced that the mentoring system was being developed and tested (IAMCR Newsletter, December 2003, p. 17).

The process of establishing the mentoring system was met with skepticism by some established scholars. For instance, some expressed concern about creating an additional workload, or mentorship becoming an imposed task. However, in 2003, the mentoring program started as an online platform where junior scholars could find valuable resources on the website, as well as a Frequently Asked Questions page where IAMCR senior scholars offered answers to the most popular questions (IAMCR Newsletter, December 2003, p. 9). An initial set of questions was disseminated to senior scholars in the December 2003 IAMCR Newsletter (p. 17).

The mentorship program, an inspiration of ESN founding member Katharine Sarikakis, further came to life in 2008 (Mikael Martey, 2021). The mentorship program had two main goals: firstly, to assist emerging scholars in developing their research, publications, and participation in IAMCR and other academic communities by opening spaces to connect with senior scholars. Secondly, to contribute to an international community of scholarship by promoting the exchange of ideas, perspectives, and research that can enrich the work of ESN members across the world (IAMCR Newsletter, May 2008, p. 19). The program also responded to concerns raised by some members of IAMCR that the existence of the network might bracket off or separate students and junior/emerging scholars from the general membership; the goal of the mentorship program was to integrate junior and senior scholars together (Sullivan, 2021).

The mentorship program is a pillar initiative of the network that has been active for over a decade, except for the interruption of the global COVID-19 pandemic when in-person meetings between mentors and mentees were not possible (Chen, 2021). Mentees meet with their mentors at conferences and can be reachable for basic questions, feedback, and advice via email. Currently, the mentorship program aims to provide mentee guidance, assistance, and advice in relation to their research, publications, conferences, and participation in IAMCR. The program aims to promote the exchange of ideas and viewpoints and to encourage meaningful mentorship relationships by having informal meetings and keeping in communication during the year. Despite the fact that there are sometimes more mentees than mentors, the program continues. Although there was no opportunity for mentors and mentees to meet during the global pandemic, the network Co-Chairs Sibo Chen and Steph Hill continued to answer questions and act as mentors to network members—always an important part of the role of network leaders (Chen, 2021; Hill, 2021; Mikael Martey, 2021). Mentorship also takes place in informal ways during the conference; for example, Francesca Musiani and Sandra Ristovska worked to ensure that panel discussants were chairs of other sections and members of the EB, building mentorship into the conference program itself.

Inter/Sections, the Official Journal of the JSN

A key milestone came in 2001 with the publication of *Inter/Sections*, the JSN official journal. Edited by Katharine Sarikakis and Antonis Skamnakis and produced in cooperation with the European Consortium for Communications Researchers (ECCR), the journal published its first issue in the Summer of 2001. *Inter/Sections*, a journal of global communication and culture, aimed to provide a space for emerging scholars and academics interested in new forms of intellectual discourse that did not necessarily follow conventional patterns of academic scholarship in culture and communications. For the 2002 edition of *Inter/Sections*, a double issue on marginalization as violence was published. *Inter/Sections* was discontinued in the pre-online journal era due to limited available resources.

As part of furthering the spaces of communication and connection, John Sullivan created a website for the network. This site was a key repository of information about the network, including a space for centralized job postings—a useful tool during a time when job postings were less accessible (Sullivan, 2021).

In 2006–2007, the network launched a new website built on the content and mission of the initial one, donated by the Department of Journalism & Technical Communication at Colorado State University and developed by Rosa Mikeal Martey. This new space included online projects, a blog, a listserv, and updated announcements.

In 2008, when Stefania Milan and Sara Bannerman became Co-Chairs of the network, the network's information was posted on the main IAMCR website. A formal IAMCR listserv was established and acted as the main vehicle for network communications. Since then, social media communications and the IAMCR website have become the main formats of communication for the network.

Reflections on the Emerging Scholars Network

ESN leadership initially focused on the structural obstacles (conference fees) and institutional restrictions to participation, first creating space for junior or emerging scholars within IAMCR. It addressed the concern that the network might sequester students and emerging scholars from the broader organization as a whole by encouraging the involvement of and mentorship by senior scholars (Sullivan, 2021). Network leadership continued its work on a number of members' key concerns: the cost of conference attendance (Musiani, 2021); academic labor precarity (Chen, 2021); pragmatic concerns, such as questions about where to publish (Hill, 2021); providing career goal assistance—including paths other than traditional academic career pathways (Musiani, 2021; Hill, 2021); and enrolling the support of senior scholars (Musiani, 2021; Mikael Martey, 2021). All these concerns were always understood as part and parcel of the goals of gender equity and global inclusion.

ESN has played *a continuous and consistent* role in encouraging the inclusion of under-represented groups within IAMCR; indeed, this was one of its goals (Mikael Martey, 2021). Katharine Sarikakis simultaneously promoted the participation of junior scholars and the visibility of women in IAMCR (IAMCR Newsletter, November 2001, p. 11–12). It may be that this dual focus helped to establish the groundwork for the *strong participation of women throughout the history of the network*. In 1999, "marginalized groups were more marginalized," noted John Sullivan. Every scholarly association grapples with issues of marginalization and the establishment of the network was one of the early steps by IAMCR in addressing this (Sullivan, 2021). The leadership of the network has been carried, largely, by women. The network has also been an entry point for emerging scholars from regions other than Europe and North America into the association (Mikael Martey, 2021; Musiani, 2021; Hill, 2021). ESN, under its Chairs, Francesca Musiani and Sandra Ristovska, promoted further linguistic diversity, holding panels in Spanish—one of IAMCR's three official languages—and established a Spanish-language version of the network webpage (Musiani, 2021).

Asked what advice they might have for scholars newly engaging in IAMCR today, Rosa Mikael Martey suggested "do not underestimate the social" aspects of IAMCR, as "non-panel activities of conferences are truly where so much of my learning and connection have happened, both in terms of concrete opportunities for being on a grant team or co-authoring a paper." Francesca Musiani emphasized the importance of conference social events and involvement in multiple sections, such as ESN and one other section, to benefit from both the support of the network and the scholarship and from the specificity of topics in subject-matter sections. John Sullivan suggested taking advantage of peer-to-peer intellectual scholarly engagement, and the ability to meet "others who are going through the same kinds of career and work experiences that you are—granted, with lots of local differences, but there's so much that's similar about our experiences" (Sullivan, 2021).

In addition to the cost of conference attendance which, for network leaders, may or may not be supported by their home institutions, network leaders noted that leading the network appears to involve far more work than organizing other IAMCR sections. This work involves meeting the needs of emerging scholars working at diverse levels and coming from diverse geographical regions (Hill, 2021) through not only regular conference panel and social event organizing, the coordination of panels with other sections, and organizing special topic workshops and roundtables—activities associated with regular IAMCR sections. It also involves a significant amount of mentoring of network members (which comes with its own difficulties as a junior scholar), recruiting senior scholars to attend sessions, running workshops, acting as mentors in the mentorship program, coordinating the mentorship matching program, creating resources for network members, and playing a role in the leadership of IAMCR more broadly.

Playing a leadership role in the network has been a fruitful and rewarding endeavor for many past chairs. Rosa Mikael Martey, in a sentiment echoed by Francesca Musiani, recalls that chairing the network was a wonderful opportunity to take on an academic leadership position, build leadership skills, and to provide a needed service to the academic community. It was an opportunity to learn what she had to offer and "what this leg of my academic life and academic career meant" (Mikael Martey, 2021). Being involved in the leadership of the network has helped chairs to build confidence and is an opportunity to position "yourself and your contributions" (Hill, 2021; Chen, 2021). Chairing the network is a wonderful opportunity to meet great people, to network with and be known by senior scholars, hear about people's concerns, and build one's CV and a path to future leadership positions. Network leaders have been able to see the "back end" workings of IAMCR and help to shape its future (Mikael Martey, 2021; Musiani, 2021; Sullivan, 2021; Hill, 2021). From a research point of view, it is an opportunity to learn about the dynamics of academia, what topics are being researched, what people are interested in, and the direction one's research can or should go in (Chen, 2021).

Importantly, however, it is crucial to remember that none of the "pragmatic" or short-term micro goals alone are sufficient to maintain the motivation and energy required when becoming involved in the nurturing of public spaces such as the ESN. The history of the network and its initiatives have shown that opposition to a trailblazing idea can come with immense force, but peer support and building alliances can result in the construction of sustainable spaces where there were none. Larger, aspiring aims such as constructing new spaces—not as another exclusive clique, but as an expanding space for inclusion—are not only worth the "sweat and tears" involved but benefit all—scholars and, ultimately, IAMCR.

References

Chen, S. (2021, July 27). Interview conducted by Sara Bannerman.
Hill, S. (2021, July 27). Interview conducted by Sara Bannerman.
IAMCR (Various Years). *Newsletters and Bulletins.* Retrieved 15 June 2022, from https://iamcr.org/node/10511
Mikael Martey, R. (2021, July 30). Interview conducted by Sara Bannerman.
Musiani, F. (2021, July 28). Interview conducted by Sara Bannerman.
Sullivan, J. (2021, July 30). Interview conducted by Sara Bannerman.

PART II

IAMCR Scholarship and the Political

CHAPTER 10

The Latin American Critical Tradition of Communication Research and the Early Years of Participation in IAMCR, 1960–1990

Rafael Roncagliolo Orbegoso
and Eduardo Villanueva-Mansilla

Introduction[1]

Latin America started engaging with IAMCR in the 1970s, when both the association and the approach to communications began to change significantly. "Communications" as a knowledge field had started in the region during the

[1] This chapter is the result of a series of conversations with Rafael Roncagliolo, known by his friends and students as Rafo, one of the most important players in the early years of communication research in Peru and in Latin America. These talks took place in late 2019 and early 2020, and were interrupted by the pandemic and, sadly, by Rafo's death in 2021.

While mostly based on his recollections, an attempt has been made to include as much bibliographic support as possible; a number of publications relevant to this period of lively and innovative concern for communication research are not easily available since they were published as papers in short-lived journals, or as books that circulated in the countries where they were printed. Access to Rafo's personal library was planned, although it was not to be.

Rafael Roncagliolo Orbegoso is deceased.

R. Roncagliolo Orbegoso (Deceased)

E. Villanueva-Mansilla (✉)
Department of Communications, Pontificia Universidad Católica del Perú, Lima, Peru
e-mail: evillan@pucp.pe

© The Author(s), under exclusive license to Springer Nature Switzerland AG 2023
J. Becker, R. Mansell (eds.), *Reflections on the International Association for Media and Communication Research*,
https://doi.org/10.1007/978-3-031-16383-8_10

1960s, under a series of influences that brought attention to a different understanding of what used to be seen as an assortment of professions and practices. The intellectual and political context of the 1960s was also relevant to understand the transformation: what Fernando Henrique Cardoso (2009) called "the new form of dependency," identified as a structural cause of underdevelopment. All aspects of social and economic life were understood under this new gaze; including what used to be the practical and professional domain of journalists, filmmakers, and the new activities of advertising and marketing, they came to be seen as expressions of the relationship between the capitalist center and the dependent periphery. The need for a change, of course, was the engine behind new approaches in all the social sciences and for the beginning of communication studies as we understand them today (Fig. 10.1).

The appearance of such demand for a systemic understanding of communications coincided with the aforementioned expansion of technological innovations, as well as demographic transformations, not only by population growth but also by the expansion of urban populations, increasing the market for television. Middle-class expansion brings changes in consumption, both cultural and material, while the urban poor emerges as a new, larger political and social actor. A dispute about what culture means in Latin America, with new professional classes seeing the US as a dominant force and moving away from traditional cultural practices, is confronted by the political influence of national liberation movements and the many different convulsions that affect the region, from Arbenz's government in Guatemala to the Cuban revolution, and the reaction to them: coups and military dictatorships. The media, seen as allies of the status quo, were considered ripe for change; while the industries were controlled by a variety of national entrepreneurs, the control of broadcasting, in particular, was seen as critical for any real transformation, as discussed in many of the books reviewed by Mahan (1995).

As a region, Spanish-speaking Latin America[2] has at least a common language, with little local specificity, thus easily comprehensible to the urban classes. Cultural markets were shaped, during the 1950s, by this reality, as movies, television shows, and music started to shape around the shared experiences of consuming, for instance, content produced in one of the larger national markets; this did not mean that there was no local cultural production; and the news market remained, by necessity, national.

As my role was, once again, to act as the dedicated student taking notes and asking questions when needed—though this time in a privileged one-on-one setting—I decided to maintain a rather conversational tone, reflecting the revisions that Rafo made to the transcriptions of our conversations. I'm grateful to Rafo's children, Santiago, Inés y Tania, for allowing publication of this short paper, the final publication about communication research by Rafo, and one belated collaboration that was a pleasure to share. EVM, November 2021.

[2] Though many contributions to the larger field of social sciences came from Brazil, this chapter deals only with the Spanish-speaking parts of Latin America, as there was less contact in those years with our larger neighbor.

Fig. 10.1 Rafael Roncagliolo-Orbegoso (1944–2021). Member—IAMCR International Council 1980–1984, Vice-President 1984–1986, Working Group Head—South-South Cooperation in Communications 1990–1994, Minister of Foreign Relations, Peru 2011–2013. (Courtesy of Santiago Roncagliolo)

At the same time, certain regional hegemonies appeared: radio melodrama first, and then telenovelas, had production centers in Cuba before the Castro revolution, then México, with Venezuela, Argentina, and Colombia participating at different points in time; sport was dominated by football, with Argentina becoming the most important producer of news content, though Mexico maintained its own dynamic; only Central America and the Caribbean did not follow this trend. Mexican cinema was quite common all around the region until the mid-1960s. In music, Mexico, Argentina, and later, Colombia provided the regional soundtrack, and even when tropical music became a larger presence, it was identified as Latin American, as the combined influences of Cuban, Puerto Rican, and Colombian musicians shaped the style. Before there was Latin American studies, there was Latin American communication.

In this context, the convergence between academic thinking and demands for political action took place. The media sector in the region was, from its beginning, mostly if not completely under private control, with family firms related to local bourgeoisies extending the reach of their power into the symbolic realm and promoting cultural and moral standards that were quite conservative and, in some cases, foreign to the experience of many sectors of societies. If there were non-private broadcasters, they were mostly run by governments, and had to compete with private companies without significant governmental support, financial or political. Modernization and development was seen as a process of Westernization, leaving behind more traditional cultural expressions associated with political and cultural control by landowners.

Simultaneously, media owners promoted Western patterns of consumption while trying to modernize, to a point, their countries; this modernization was concerned with leaving behind any old-fashioned cultural practices but without changing power structures. This meant ignoring cultural expressions originating in the indigenous/urban poor communities and promoting a notional "national culture" based on the localized manifestations of Westernized culture. Media produced content that negated poverty, local cultures, and social and political disputes. Many intellectuals promoted, almost always unsuccessfully, recognition, inclusion, and representation of those who were being left behind.

The Sources

In this context, and taking into account the diversity of social and cultural realities in the region, there were at least four large threads of development of media research in Latin America, presented here in no particular order.

The semiotic tradition was one of the earliest threads, embodied by Eliseo Verón from Argentina. The first translator into Spanish of Claude Levi-Strauss, he was also the founding editor of the *Argentinian Journal of Sociology and Semiotics.* Verón organized in 1967 a seminar in Buenos Aires to discuss Language and Social Communication, which is also the title of the book with the papers presented in the conference (Verón et al., 1969). This quite important early work started a long tradition of semiotic approaches to communication studies in the region, which is notable as many universities in Latin America still offer semiotics as one of the formative courses in their undergraduate programs. This was a clear connection with the academic world that was absent in this early period in other threads, more concerned with politics, policy, and activism.

Another significant thread was the notion that media, and particularly television, could be a force for social advancement: public ownership oriented toward education and good-quality entertainment. Chile, where control of television stations was reserved to universities and the state, started late by the region's standards (1962, in time for the Football World Cup). Likewise, in Venezuela, starting in 1974, Carlos Andrés Pérez's administration started the Radio Televisión Venezolana (RATELVE) project. Venezuela at the time was flush with petrodollars and was also one of the few remaining democracies in the region, and Perez had allowed many progressive intellectuals to work for Venezuelan institutions. In this particular case, Antonio Pasquali, a philosophy professor at Universidad Central de Venezuela, was head of the commission for creating and running a new broadcasting network, running along the lines of European public service broadcasters (Capriles Arias, 1996). Pasquali, a francophile, developed a relationship with UNESCO that led to participation in IAMCR, due to the relationship that both organizations had at the time. He later became deputy director general of UNESCO. Pasquali's time working with RATELVE (design for a new broadcasting policy of the Venezuelan State) led to a body of work related to national communications policies, which went on to influence the development of the New World Information and Communication Order (NWICO), one of the most important and more contentious attempts to propose an alternative to commercial media and communication ever tried.

International cooperation was another impulse for innovation, as the case of Luis Ramiro Beltrán, from Bolivia, shows. Beltrán studied in Michigan after working as a journalist in his birth town of Oruro, and later in the Interamerican Agricultural Institute. As a representative of the International Development Research Centre (IDRC), Canada, in the Bogotá Regional Office, he was involved in many of the original attempts to promote communication research in Latin America. He became involved with the Centro Internacional de Estudios Superiores de Comunicación para América Latina (CIESPAL), originally the UNESCO-sponsored International Center for Latin American Research in Journalism, and in 1965, one of the first institutions calling for a shift in focus toward the larger communications subject. Together with Pasquali, they were some of the earliest participants in IAMCR's conferences, under the auspices of UNESCO. By the early 1970s, Beltrán started building bridges with US researchers on development studies, thus beginning the establishment of *comunicación para el desarrollo* (communication for development) as part of the field, especially working with US academic Elizabeth Fox. These two shifts, from journalism to communication and from media studies to development and communication, were quite transformative, both promoted by UNESCO, and this brought contact with IAMCR as a result of the extant relationship between the two.

Finally, political activism was a really important component of the early development of communication research in Latin America, spurred by the aforementioned perception of a demand for radical change in the political and economic conditions in the region. Many of those involved in activism of this kind came from universities and academic backgrounds, where the influence of the Paris May 68 movement was important; also, a number of young academics came from Europe to Latin America, instead of serving in their nations' militaries and to participate in the intellectual and political fervor of the time. Chile, in particular, at the time a stable democracy with a large left-wing front on the cusp of winning elections, attracted people like Manuel Castells and Armand Mattelart. Mattelart, particularly, came to teach demography at the Catholic University in Chile, an institution seen as a redoubt of conservative thinking; in 1967, in the midst of a political dispute in the University, a group of students posted a banner in front of the main university building, located at the Alameda, the most important thoroughfare of central Santiago de Chile. The banner said, "Chileans, El Mercurio lies!" referring to the paper of record of the country, seen as the representative of bourgeois, conservative thinking. It was the first time that a direct connection between the media and political power was so clearly proposed, especially coming from students of a traditional institution associated precisely with the milieu that produced a newspaper like *El Mercurio*.

Mattelart became a critical participant in the development of a cultural studies approach to communication studies, as well as an activist, Marxist understanding of communication as a political subject embedded in a larger struggle, that of people's liberation. He co-wrote with Ariel Dorfman a classic of political mobilization, *How to Read Donald Duck* (Dorfman & Mattelart, 1972), one of the first examples of an academic book that approached mass communication and particularly, the popular products of "the Empire" (as the US was referred to then by the leftists), and connected the need for decolonization with the demand for a different communication environment. This book, banned during the ensuing dictatorship in Chile, is perhaps the most published ever in the field of communication studies in Latin America.

However, this revolutionary engagement with the subject of communication somewhat clashed with the rather institutional relationship that UNESCO and IAMCR had developed in Latin America. At the same time that Dorfman and Mattelart's classic was published in Chile, Buenos Aires across the Andes and still under a military dictatorship that had begun in 1966 hosted the 9th Congress of IAMCR. Promoted and sponsored by UNESCO, it was held for a rather long time—almost 15 days—during which the panel of international experts (one of which was Luis Ramiro Beltrán) were feted by government officials and academic authorities. The conference itself was focused on what we would now call media studies and communication for development. The scarce information available, collected by Cimadevilla (2020), offers an interesting contrast: while Latin America was in the throes of revolutionary fevers of different intensities, colors, and degrees, the association's officials were hosted by a committee of dignitaries that had very little contact with either academia or the profession of communications, and were connected with governmental circles by social and commercial reasons, as much as by their militant opposition to any leftist politics.

As much as UNESCO had been critical to the development of modern research and education on communications in Latin America, IAMCR, still quite connected to the UN agency, had little if any contact with the people who would become the protagonists of the coming years. Both the regional community of researchers and IAMCR would be transformed in a short time.

Exile and New Order

At the same time that RATELVE was being discussed in Venezuela, the military dictatorship in Peru had decided to start a different kind of communications: socialized media. All the major dailies of the country were taken over from their owners and put into governmental control, allegedly for a year while the "people's organizations" prepared to become the owners of those papers. It was the most radical and the most regressive attempt to change communications in the region, and it significantly shaped Latin American thinking.

The contradictory statement arises from the fact that it was a military dictatorship—though left-wing to a point—that had brought in the need for non-oligarchic media supply. Already controlling television and squeezing economically all newspapers that did not get along with its policies, the Peruvian military presented the decision not as democratization but rather nationalization, in the sense of promoting control of the news media by Peruvians, and instead by allies of international capital. Many of the left-wing intellectuals involved with the supposed transition were exiled about a year after the takeover (including the senior author of this paper), and in the process, converged with many other Latin American intellectuals who went into exile in Mexico, where a long tradition of political asylum and a well-funded public education sector allowed for a welcoming environment; Venezuela, under a generic progressive government, was also hosting many exiles. Both countries had foreign policies shaped by the generic banner of non-alignment, meaning independence from the Cold War poles.

Among the many exiles, some came from Chile, where a democratically elected socialist government had been brutally brought down in 1973; the flourishing criticism of media as an extension of capitalist imperialism had been cut short and, for all practical purposes, the remaining media outlets had become as much unanimous in their support as the Peruvian ones had. By mid-1975, any pretense of "people's ownership" of the news dailies had been transformed into complete governmental control that continued until 1980 when democracy was restored.

If democracy was not able to allow for democratic communications, and the military, even if presenting itself as socialist, would always become authoritarian, what was left to do? The intellectual fervor of the time shifted focus and connected with international discussions around a radical transformation at global level. This also had to do with the non-aligned perspective, which favored multilateral arrangements, not completely controlled by "the empire." IAMCR, associated with UNESCO, was welcoming to representatives of the "second world," that is, the Soviet bloc, as well as the different, less "academic" concerns than those that the International Communication Association (ICA) hosted. Particularly, the shared concern on the need for a political understanding of communications led to a political position about it, and also political consequences—like exile. It was not the kind of political participation that a functional democracy may offer, but rather a more militant and committed concern for radical change in the field of concern. This went beyond public policy, but rather policy as a manifestation of politics, toward changing society and the state.

As many of those involved in communication research at this stage did not see themselves primarily as academics, but rather as "committed intellectuals"—a phrase that alluded to their involvement in politics and activisms on the side of the people—the ICA was alien to their interests, and IAMCR offered something else: a connection with the discussion on a new world order for their concerns.

IAMCR thus appears as an organization fitting the political sensibilities as much as the intellectual interests of this foundational generation from Latin America. Apart from the semiotics community, many of the originators participated in conferences and even as members of IAMCR. At the 1978 Warsaw Conference, the Political Economy Section was started, representing the convergence of political and intellectual interests. In 1980, at Caracas, Rafael Roncagliolo took a regional vice presidency, in an expression of the dispute between the more traditionally minded members of IAMCR and the progressive members more interested in the promotion of the NWICO.

NWICO was the proposal and culmination of a process started earlier in the decade, by UNESCO's Director General Amadou-Mahtar M'Bow. Its main issue was the need for a more democratic communication environment, less dominated by international conglomerates. Though the geopolitical arrangements of the time made NWICO a manifestation of Communist propaganda, clashing with the "free flow of information" rationale that prevailed in the Western world, those promoting this approach ran a wide gamut.

As such, it fit the mode of political transformation underlying the work of the communication scholars from Latin America; while its politics were more generally oriented toward non-alignment, and criticism of what came to be known as *actually existing socialism* through promoting solidarity with revolutionary Cuba, both the diagnosis of the concentrated, for-profit nature of communication industries and the solution, as general as it was, coincided with many IAMCR members' interests in a different model for communications.

While the final product of the NWICO movement, the so-called MacBride Report, came from UNESCO in 1980, the intellectual arguments around at the time had IAMCR as a natural home. For instance, during the Caracas Conference, the Political Economy Working Group had a discussion around the subject using a contribution by the Uruguay scholar Alvaro Barros Lemez. As found in Dallas W. Smythe's papers, the conclusion presented a dilemma as it stated that there was not such a thing as a "new international order" for communication, that the demands that the concept promoted had to be considered specifically at the national level, considering national conditions; and that if such a thing as a New Order was developed, it would be between states and governments, rather than between communities and peoples. Mr. Barros was not part of the intellectual group that had been involved in the regional discussion on the NWICO, but his criticism brought forward both the critical demand of providing a voice to communities and the contradictions of promoting a transformation to be run by states for the benefit of the people.

Indeed, such a dilemma is still standing, but IAMCR allowed for radical proposals that could not be even considered by a politically negotiated committee like the one that created the MacBride Report. Even considering its powerful criticism of the status quo in the communications industry, the report was much more an intellectual exercise than an actual, actionable proposal, facing severe and coordinated criticism from the different businesses involved in communications, and the governments representing them at UNESCO.

The political failure of NWICO came through the neoliberal turn in the US and the UK that took those two countries from UNESCO, as well as coolness from the Soviet bloc, uninterested in the underlying policy agenda. Latin America started emerging from the decade of dictatorship around the same time, and the focus shifted again, with many of the intellectual forces that had converged in exile into international communication coming back to their countries to promote local developments, but with a regional perspective and with IAMCR as a forum to discuss and shape those developments.

Popular Communication and the Community Shift

After the heady days of NWICO and exile, the 1980s was a complex time for communication research. At the same time that democracies were restored, the financial crisis brought high inflation and economic and social upheavals; a turn toward neoliberal options meant that legislation and policy in communications reinforced already existing property structures at the same time that the first steps toward pay television and cellular telephony were taking place. Technological winds of change were apparent while the original issues that concerned scholars had not changed significantly.

This technological innovation reduced state capabilities and moved telecommunications services as well as broadcast media away from the public to the private sector. This diminished the potential for discussing large collective responses to perceived societal needs, as these processes had different rhythms and speeds in different countries. A clear need for local action, combined with the realization that community practices could be harnessed toward a more democratic communication became the focus.

This situation has to be understood in the larger context of a collapse of quality of life standards in the region, which demanded working on a new set of solidarities, based on local experiences. New communication practices, like community radio using megaphones, were significant for the establishment and strengthening of social linkages; this inspired a connection with the political tradition of communication studies, in the wider context of searching for alternative paradigms of democratic and sustainable development (Roncagliolo, 1985). While not under many military dictatorships as in the past decade, political violence takes many different shapes during this period: local convulsions replace the larger narrative of transformation that coexisted with the nascent field two decades before.

Thus, IAMCR continued to be a reference point for expert advice and identification of emerging trends, while the community of researchers settled themselves in different conditions. While in some countries academia was welcomed as part of the democratization process, in others, the preferred mechanism was the non-governmental organization (NGO) financed by bilateral, private agreements. The focus shifted from developing capabilities in 1960, through policy debates in the 1970s, to developing community capabilities under the *comunicación popular* (popular communication) paradigm (Rodríguez, 2001).

Grounded on the works of Paulo Freire, the *comunicación popular* paradigm was fed by the alternative and community communication paradigm present in the Western world, with the particularities of Latin American conditions. It was developed by a number of scholar-activists whose work defined, up until the end of the following decade, what a progressive approach to communication research and practice should be (Barranquero & Treré, 2021).

During these years, working at the different registers of NGO projects and university teaching, many of these scholars continued to develop the relationship with IAMCR, although the conference itself only returned to the region in 1992. This dialog was channeled through two regional associations, Latin American Federation of Communication Schools (FELAFACS) and Latin American Association of Communication Research (ALAIC), which participated, at different levels and with diverse membership, in IAMCR activities.

Another issue emerging in the 1980s is the aforementioned "new technologies," demanding cooperation from international partners, as development and access to the technical underpinnings of these developments were not common in the region and, in many cases, were quite different from the academic and professional backgrounds of those doing research in the region. This cooperation brought experts to the region and allowed the dissemination of critical perspectives regarding the potential benefits and risks of digital technologies, including books translated into Spanish and published by Institute for Latin America (IPAL), run from Lima by Rafael Roncagliolo. Becker (1988) is a prime example of this trend.

By the end of the decade, political developments around the world transformed communication research. The end of the Cold War also defined the end of ideological battles around control of transnational flows of information, and the financial crisis in Latin America ended the era of the state as an economic actor, while reinforcing academic professionalization. While IAMCR continued to be receptive to different approaches and views of the world, it fully became an international learned society; on the other hand, in Latin America, the regional associations redefined themselves, with ALAIC compounding its original intent of being a forum for counter-hegemonic action through intra-regional cooperation (Fuentes Navarro, 2016), with a more conventional role as a learned society.

At the same time, NGOs lost many sources of financing under the change in conditions brought by the global political settlement and new priorities for the countries providing resources. Those working in universities, adapted to changing circumstances.

This process accelerated in the 1990s, a timeframe outside the scope of this paper. The new decade brought new challenges, including the beginning of cultural transformations brought by the internet and different issues to attend to, including debates about what exactly development means in a world with enormous ecological challenges. A certain distance from IAMCR was the end result: there was no one firm, unifying struggle to connect everyone on the progressive side, nor a demand for catching up on larger topics, but rather a collection of professionally shaped demands grounded on the growing demand for university degrees in the field. A new generation of scholars, expecting a more academic context in which to work, learn from the immediate past, and the global dialog, was created through the interaction of the founders of communication research, and understanding that there are many different issues demanding attention.

Of course, this does not mean that the influence of IAMCR disappears. It still allows for a larger diversity of issues, approaches, and work styles than other international associations. The critical tradition of communication research continues its presence at conferences and academic exchanges.

References

Barranquero, A., & Treré, E. (2021). Comunicación alternativa y comunitaria. La conformación del campo en Europa y el diálogo con América Latina. *Revista Chasqui*, 146, 159–182. Retrieved 15 June 2022, from https://revistachasqui.org/index.php/chasqui/article/view/4390

Becker, J. (1988). *Tecnología de la información: Reto para el tercer mundo.* Institute for Latin America.

Capriles Arias, O. (1996). *Poder político y comunicación.* Universidad Central de Venezuela.

Cardoso, F. H. (2009). New paths: Globalization in historical perspective. *Studies in Comparative Development Studies, 44*, 296–317. Retrieved 15 June 2022, from https://doi.org/10.1007/s12116-009-9050-3

Cimadevilla, G. (2020). Milicos, gestores y literatos: La historia jamás contada del IX congreso de IAMCR en Buenos Aires (1972). *Revista Latinoamericana de Ciencias de la Comunicación, 20*, 36–48. Retrieved 15 June 2022, from https://revista.pubalaic.org/index.php/alaic/article/view/690

Dorfman, A., & Mattelart, A. (1972). *Para leer al Pato Donald: Comunicación de masa y colonialismo.* Siglo XXI.

Fuentes Navarro, R. (2016). Cuatro décadas de internacionalización académica en el campo de estudios de la comunicación en América Latina. *Anuario Electrónico de Estudios en Comunicación Social 'Disertaciones', 9*(2), 8–26. Retrieved 15 June 2022, from https://www.redalyc.org/articulo.oa?id=511552709002

Mahan, E. (1995). Media, politics, and society in Latin America. *Latin American Research Review, 30*(3), 138–162.

Rodríguez, C. (2001). *Fissures in the mediascape. An international study of citizen's media*. Hampton Press.

Roncagliolo, R. (1985, January 28). *Welcome Speech* (Speech: As preserved in the Dallas Smythe papers at Simon Fraser University). IPAL's Transnational information flows Seminar, Lima, Peru.

Verón, E., Prieto, L. J., Ekman, P., Friesen, W. V., Sluzki, C. E., & Masotta, O. (1969). *Lenguaje y Comunicación Social.* Nueva Visión.

CHAPTER 11

Germany in IAMCR

Jörg Becker, Friedrich Krotz, and Hans-Jörg Stiehler

The Early Years

IAMCR was founded at UNESCO headquarters in Paris in December 1957. Fernand Terrou from France was elected as the first President and 50 experts from 15 countries attended this meeting. Five participants represented Germany at that time: Wilmont Haacke (University of Social Sciences, Wilhelmshaven), Heinz Braun and Heinz Starkulla (University of Munich), Martin Löffler (Studienkreis für Presserecht und Pressefreiheit (study group for press law and freedom of the press, Stuttgart), and Hermann Budzislawski (University of Leipzig). German individual members who were not present were Emil Dovifat (Freie Universität Berlin), Hans Jessen (Bremen City Library, Bremen), Max Kohlhaas (Public Prosecutor, Karlsruhe), H. W. Lavies (Institut für Filmkunde, Wiesbaden), Eberhard Lutze (Deutsche Presseforschung, German Media Research Center, Bremen), and E. F. Podlach (Stuttgart). German institutional members not present were Martin Löffler's Studienkreis für Presserecht und Pressefreiheit, the Berlin and the Münster

J. Becker (✉)
University of Marburg, Marburg, Germany
e-mail: joerg.becker@komtech.org

F. Krotz
University of Bremen, Bremen, Germany

H.-J. Stiehler
University of Leipzig, Leipzig, Germany

© The Author(s), under exclusive license to Springer Nature Switzerland AG 2023

J. Becker, R. Mansell (eds.), *Reflections on the International Association for Media and Communication Research*,
https://doi.org/10.1007/978-3-031-16383-8_11

Institut für Publizistik (Münster Institute for Media), and the Munich Institut für Zeitungswissenschaft (Munich University's department of print media).

Joining 26 individual members from France, 17 from Italy, eight from Poland, and 47 from the United States (US) in founding IAMCR were also a relatively modest number of members from the Federal Republic of Germany (FRG), with an even more modest number from the German Democratic Republic (GDR). The US's top journalism experts, in effect, represented their country in IAMCR: Alex S. Edelstein, George Gerbner, Harold D. Lasswell, Raymond Nixon, Ithiel de Sola Pool, O. W. Riegel, Wilbur Schramm, and Percy Tannenbaum. However, the influence both Germany and the US would have in IAMCR would change multiple times over the course of this association's history.

From an overall German perspective, founding a research association with FRG and GDR representatives on an equal footing was indeed a unique and novel act. Beginning with the adoption of the Hallstein Doctrine in the middle of the Cold War in 1955, the FRG regarded the establishment of diplomatic relations with the GDR by third countries as an "unfriendly act." Thus, as much as international isolation of the GDR was the official FRG objective, IAMCR pursued exactly the opposite under UNESCO protection. In a certain way, IAMCR was thus an historical precursor to the peace process of the Conference on Security and Cooperation in Europe (CSCE) with its Final Act signed in Helsinki in 1975.

In addition to this productive German-German cooperation in IAMCR, there was, however, also a destructive level that existed from the very beginning, exemplified by the two German founding members, Wilmont Haacke from the FRG and Hermann Budzislawski from the GDR. While Haacke was an opportunistic follower (as well as an anti-Semite) during Nazi times, the Social Democrat and later Communist Budzislawski was forced to flee from the Nazis into political exile in France. The German system conflict (*querelles d'allemand*) between the FRG and the GDR, in this case also between idealistic humanism and historical materialism, was felt in IAMCR for many years. Often enough, the respective German delegations at international IAMCR conferences did not speak to one another or they engaged in furtive attempts to avoid each other. This tense relationship went so far that an FRG attendee at the 1982 IAMCR Conference in Paris crossed out the three words "Federal Republic of" denoting the name of his country "Federal Republic of Germany" printed on his badge, so that it read "Germany" only, and provocatively approached GDR attendees.

Although some German media and communication scientists occasionally attended IAMCR conferences in the 1950s, 1960s, and 1970s (Gerhard Maletzke, Otto Roegele, Franz Ronneberger, Fritz Eberhard, and Alphons Silbermann from the FRG and Günter Heydorn and Wolfgang Rödel from the GDR), IAMCR was in fact a mere low-profile organization in the eyes of German experts.

The very active role played by Stuttgart lawyer Martin Löffler in IAMCR was strongly in contrast to this fact. Löffler was an IAMCR member from 1957 onward, in charge of the Legal Matters Section until 1985, and he took Franco-German relations particularly to heart. The study group he headed, Studienkreis für Presserecht und Pressefreiheit, raised him to a scientific level, giving him the appearance in IAMCR of a researcher and scientist, not the private-sector lawyer he actually was. A look at the series of papers his study group published reveals that all the top FRG communication scientists of the time wrote articles for it. Martin Löffler enjoyed great renown among German lawyers and with the public at large. He published the first major commentary on press law in Germany in 1955 (Löffler, 1955).

Germany's influence in IAMCR increased dramatically when, in 1970, an IAMCR conference attended by around 100 people was held for the first time in Germany—in Constance. The key figures from FRG were the two hostesses Elisabeth Noelle-Neumann from her Allensbach Institute for Public Opinion Polling (Institut für Demoskopie), located nearby in Allensbach am Bodensee, and Birgit Weyl of the regional daily newspaper *Südkurier* from the city of Constance. The latter was active in IAMCR as a member of the FRG UNESCO Commission in Bonn and as a representative of the German Federation of German Newspaper Publishers (Bundesverband Deutscher Zeitungsverleger, BDZV).

Up against the FRG heavyweights, in IAMCR Löffler and later Noelle-Neumann, were the GDR members Hermann Budzislawski, Wolfgang Rödel, and Emil Dusiška as influential IAMCR officials, all three of whom served one after the other as Dean of the Journalism Department at Leipzig University (which FRG cold warriors nicknamed the "Red Monastery"). Dusiška held the key position of IAMCR Secretary General from 1972 to 1982. His predecessor Budzislawski had still embodied the old liberal spirit of the typical popular front emigrant, whereas Dusiška was a strict party cadre of the newly established GDR.

Martin Löffler (born in 1905), Elisabeth Noelle-Neumann (born in 1916), and Brigitte Weyl (born in 1926) were all implicated in the Nazi era in some form or another. Martin Löffler defended the Sturmabteilung (SA) in the Nuremberg Trials and, later, high-profile Nazis such as Josef Hermann Abs and Albert Speer, while Elisabeth Noelle-Neumann worked continuously as a journalist for a number of different Nazi newspapers without any occupational ban during the entire Nazi period. Brigitte Weyl was definitely too young to have incriminated herself in any way during Nazi times. However, her father Johannes Weyl, with whom she co-ran the *Südkurier* daily newspaper in Constance from 1948 onward, had been the head of newspaper distribution for a major Nazi party publisher during the Nazi era. Although all three individuals had actively worked to build up a new GDR after the FRG was created in 1949, their backgrounds also placed all of them at the conservative end of the new FRG political spectrum. It was this very conservative spirit that they brought with them into IAMCR. The tensest position of them all was the conservatism of Elisabeth Noelle-Neumann. After all, it was precisely she who had helped to overcome an idealistic-humanist conservatism à la Wilmont Haacke and Otto Roegele with an empirical conservatism that she had adopted from the US.

The German conservative dominance in IAMCR changed with the IAMCR Conference in Leicester in 1976. In his presidential letter dated December 1976, President James Halloran noted, not by chance, in a passing review of this conference: "The cry for more grass roots participation in the affairs of the Association was frequently heard at Leicester."[1] He was referring not only to unrest in his own institute at the University of Leicester, in which some of his research associates no longer wanted him clipping their wings, but also to an increasing willingness among the younger IAMCR members to engage in confrontation in the period following the 1968 student protests.

Younger colleagues such as Hans-Jürgen Kleinsteuber, Jörg Becker, Thomas Rothschild, Horst Holzer, and Dieter Prokop protested by advocating a new critical communication science in the FRG; the same applied to Lothar Bisky in the GDR, and to Kurt Luger, Benno Signitzer, and Werner Meier in Austria and Switzerland. In terms of ideological tradition, these colleagues were somewhere between FRG conservatism and a communist party line as in the GDR. In the jargon of true party Communists, the protestors were "wild" and "radical" individuals, suffering from Lenin's "infantile disorder of left-wing communism." The move from conservative to critical science in Germany became definite at the IAMCR Conference in Prague in 1978: Instead of Elisabeth Noelle-Neumann, who had long represented FRG on the Executive Board (EB) or in the International Council (IC), Jörg Becker was elected to the IAMCR IC, an office he held until 1986. Moreover, IAMCR President James Halloran noted this shift in scientific approach in Prague in his dramatically formulated presidential letter dated December 1978: "We are no longer a cosy club of armchair elitists playing about on the fringes of society. We are involved, we are at the centre of an international stage where vital issues are being debated."[2] The radical change in Prague had a significant impact on FRG participation in IAMCR as a number of conservative FRG communication scientists resigned from the association thereafter.

IAMCR activities in the late 1970s and 1980s were overshadowed in FRG as well by controversies arising in the UNESCO debates on a New International Information Order (NIIO), or the subsequently renamed New World Information and Communication Order (NWICO). In the context of these debates, for example, the intellectual writings of non-German key figures in the organization, Cees Hamelink from the Netherlands and Herbert Schiller from the US, were well received in the FRG. Herbert Schiller's influence on West German intellectual debates was so great that some of his articles even appeared in *Media Perspektiven*—a marketing journal for public service broadcasting in the FRG (Schiller, 1986, 1988, 1999).

[1] See IAMCR Archive, https://iamcr.org/node/10510. Accessed 15 June 2022.
[2] See IAMCR Archive, https://iamcr.org/node/10510. Accessed 15 June 2022.

From the very beginning, all of IAMCR's research focused on the international aspect—the idea of an international and intercultural exchange and that of an international communication and media policy. For smaller countries such as the Netherlands or Denmark, every type of international cooperation is crucial to their survival. For big countries, the situation is different. They tend to focus on their own matters with no great need for external contacts. This is why there was traditionally little interest in international media policy in the FRG. For years, there were only three scientists working in this field, namely, the conservative anti-communist Hansjürgen Koschwitz (1974) and two left-wing liberal colleagues Hans-Jürgen Kleinsteuber (1973) and Jörg Becker (1979). Although Koschwitz was not active in IAMCR, both of the other two certainly were. It is true that their standing on the communication science scene was not that high as both were political, not communication, scientists, and neither held a professorship in the 1970s. Against this background, the MacBride Report (Macbride, 1981) when published in German translation did not arouse much interest in Germany. It is curious to note that this report was published by a publishing house owned by IAMCR member Brigitte Weyl, since at the IAMCR Conference in Caracas in 1980, Brigitte Weyl was still vehemently opposed to the report's content.

In addition to IAMCR members Hans-Jürgen Kleinsteuber and Jörg Becker, the Protestant Church in Germany (Evangelische Kirche in Deutschland—EKD) and the Friedrich-Ebert-Stiftung under the direction of Reinhard Keune, who was later Chair of UNESCO's International Programme for the Development of Communication, joined in on the NWICO debates in FRG. A sensational event in this context was the international conference entitled "Information Technology and a New International Order," which the EKD along with the World Association for Christian Communication (WACC), had organized in Bonn in 1982 (MacBride, 1984). It was held under the patronage of Nobel Peace Prize and Lenin Peace Prize recipient Seán MacBride. Prominent non-German IAMCR speakers included Cees Hamelink (Netherlands), Enrique Gonzáles Manet (Cuba), Neville D. Jayaweera (Sri Lanka), Noreene Janus (Mexico), and Tran Van Dinh (Vietnam/US).

Of similar significance was the international conference, "Europe Speaks to Europe. International Information Flows between Eastern and Western Europe" held near Frankfurt in 1988 (Brandt, 1989). This conference again arranged by the EKD and the WACC, among other bodies, was jointly organized by Jörg Becker and the Hungarian sociologist Tamás Szecskö, the then IAMCR Secretary General. Prominent IAMCR speakers were Dallas Smythe (Canada), Lothar Bisky (GDR), Werner Meier (Switzerland), Kurt Luger (Austria), Karol Jakubowicz (Poland), András Szekfü (Hungary), Cees Hamelink (Netherlands), Wolfgang Kleinwächter (GDR), and Emil Konstantinov (Bulgaria).

IAMCR's archived meeting minutes for the years prior to 1990 list FRG communication scientist Otto Roegele as interim Deputy Secretary General of IAMCR in the period from 1968 to 1974. The minutes also state that in 1966,

Gerhard Maletzke, and in 1976, Elisabeth Noelle-Neumann, gave the respective opening lectures on the conference topics in these years.

The end of the systemic conflict between Western capitalism and Eastern socialism in 1989–1991 had immediate consequences for the roles the GDR and FRG played in IAMCR. Many conservative West German communication scientists returned to IAMCR in then reunited Germany because they interpreted the collapse of the Eastern bloc states as a victory of the free West over the dictatorial East; and from this point in time onward, they were pleased to cooperate with IAMCR colleagues from Eastern Europe whom they previously avoided, and who for their part—at least some of them—suddenly defined themselves as resistance fighters against the former system of socialism.

Intermezzo: The GDR in IAMCR (1957–1990)

The brief history of the GDR in relation to IAMCR, which can be dated from the association's foundation, until 1990, is characterized firstly by discontinuity, and secondly, by a strong relation to individual researchers.[3] Initially, this had to do with the dominant theory and practice of mass communication. Mass communication, in the understanding of the country's leadership, was no "monologue" and no form of "self-reflection" on society with its own set of principles and mechanisms that needed researching in more detail (Prakke, 1968; Luhmann, 1995). The media—in the tradition of Lenin's media theory—were "instruments of political struggle" considered by the communist party and government as a means of agitation, propaganda, and organization of the masses (Stiehler, 2008). In the prevailing model of "conviction" and transmission of (true) information from "top" to "bottom"—from the party and state to the masses, the problem of communication existed only in the sense of "finding the right words." A rigid control practice and binding rules on media design underpinned the model. Consequently, until the late 1980s, there were only a handful of education and research institutions and only individual scientists that dealt theoretically and/or empirically with mass communication issues. These included, among others, at the institutional level, the journalism section of the University of Leipzig (which, however, only considered itself as a journalism studies faculty and thus concerned itself with merely a part of the mass media system), the research groups in GDR TV and radio (primarily for empirically monitoring the success of their own programs), the Central Institute for Youth Research (*Zentralinstitut für Jugendforschung*) in Leipzig (with a department for cultural and media research), and individual university and academy institutes for international relations (Leipzig, Berlin,

[3] When the GDR is mentioned in this text, this means first and foremost the political and government structures and party and government decision-makers. Decisions concerning memberships and activities in international associations were taken centrally (also due to the foreign currency required). The objectives, expertise, and positions of the individual scientists who assumed the actual memberships and performed the activities in the international organizations did not necessarily coincide with the party or government line.

and Potsdam), cultural studies faculties (e. g., in Berlin) and psychology departments, such as at the Friedrich-Schiller-Universität in Jena. There was no national organization of communication and media research as a potential partner for IAMCR. Such an organization was not founded until the Spring of 1990, and once the GDR became part of the FRG the organization lacked any basis for survival. The main criteria for the existence of communication/media science—first and foremost, were stable institutionalization as a subject area, specialized degree programs, and the existence of a professional body—and thus were not fulfilled.

A system of rule that does not perceive communication as a problem in its own society does not promote communication sciences,[4] or it allows the subject area to occupy but a few "niches." Problems of international, cross-border communication constituted a certain exception. The GDR—particularly given its vulnerability to the uncontrollable influence of foreign electronic media due to its position on the dividing line between the major political blocs—was directly or indirectly (e.g., through Intervision) involved in the policy and technology rules of such communication and pursued its own interests in that context, in aspects ranging from technology to ideological clashes. This resulted in a need for (internal) scientific studies and scientific expertise based on very sound argumentation.[5]

Given the underdeveloped research landscape, what interests might the (official) GDR have had in participating in an international community such as IAMCR/AIERI dedicated to researching information and communication problems? (Meyen, 2014). Firstly, for the GDR, all international-level activities served to promote its national reputation. The West's policy had been denial of GDR state sovereignty and refusal of diplomatic relations for decades. Not until the GDR's admission to international organizations (membership in UNESCO, 1972; admission to the United Nations, 1973) was its international recognition completed. Membership in a UNESCO-related organization such as IAMCR could only have come under consideration as a means of promoting and boosting such recognition, particularly in the years prior to full recognition. And secondly, international organizations were the "stages," on which—in this case in the area of the sciences—presentation of one's own position, that of the "superiority of Marxism-Leninism," could play itself out. As regards

[4] It is no coincidence that the sphere of communication (press and information freedom, dialog, etc.) is highly featured in the slogans and demands of the Peaceful Revolution of 1989. The call to start a civil rights movement *Neues Forum* (September 1989) began with the following diagnosis: "In our country, the communication between state and society is obviously disturbed. […] The disturbed relationship between state and society is paralysing the creative potential of our society and hindering solution of the local and global issues at hand." https://www.chronik-der-mauer.de/material/180971/gruendungsaufruf-des-neuen-forum-10-september-1989 Accessed 15 June 2022.

[5] These studies were initiated and coordinated in the special Communication Section of the GDR UNESCO Commission, an advisory board attached to the Ministry of Foreign Affairs. This body was thus the only, albeit non-public, institution for the coordination of and exchange on scientific research in the field of (political) communication.

IAMCR, such positioning might have encompassed showcasing the country's experiences and its stance on the training of journalists, or in the emerging debates on a new world information order, cross-border communication, etc.[6]

Three cases occurring at different times within the said period are now offered in substantiation of these basic assumptions. The fact that their recounting focuses on individuals is not so much dramaturgical in nature, but due to the fact that the GDR was largely represented by individual scientists.

Emil Dusiška and the 1974 Leipzig Conference

The reasons for early participation in IAMCR were varied. One was the involvement of the GDR Union of Journalists (*Verband der Journalisten der DDR*—VDJ) in the International Organization of Journalists (IOJ) combined with the VDJ's commitment to training journalists from (friendly) developing countries (in its own training center in Berlin). This drew attention to international problems of communication—and created global contacts.[7] The second reason was the attention IAMCR enjoyed in Moscow at the Lomonosov University journalism faculty in the person of Yassen Zassoursky. For the GDR, it was always (politically) helpful at that time to be following in the steps of its "big brother." It can be assumed with a high degree of certainty that Zassoursky introduced his Leipzig "university counterpart" Emil Dusiška—Dean of the journalism faculty in 1967 and, following a higher education reform, Director of the journalism section from 1968 to 1978—to IAMCR. Dusiška ultimately considered IAMCR to be a sub-organization of UNESCO and thus a "stepping stone" for advancing the cause of international recognition of the GDR. Involvement in the organization and arranging the annual conference and the general meeting in the GDR were the options that presented themselves to achieving this end. These options became reality with the resolutions adopted at the general meeting in Buenos Aires in 1972, when the GA elected Dusiška as Secretary General (he held this office until 1982) and accepted his invitation to the 1974 Conference in Leipzig. Emil Dusiška (1914–2002) had, since 1965, held a Leipzig University professorship in the theory and practice of the socialist press, but was by no means a scientist in terms of his education and career path. In contrast to his predecessors Hermann Budzislawski (Schmidt, 2017) and Franz Knipping, Dusiška

[6] The objectives did not, or did not primarily, include scientific exchange. The country's (official) self-image gave credence to the idea of Marxism-Leninism holding the key to scientific truth. There was nothing to learn in the social sciences and humanities, and particularly not from the West. This belief differed markedly from the GDR's commitment to international organizations in technical and natural sciences as well as in medicine. Such involvement meant participation in an international exchange, furnishing or contributing knowledge that could be put to good use in one's own country (knowledge and technology transfer).

[7] The VDJ would later be the GDR's only institutional member in the IAMCR.

represented the "party official" type.[8] He was very well connected in the GDR, and maintained excellent relations with the party and state leadership, above all with the SED Central Committee's Department of Agitation responsible for controlling the GDR media. Dusiška had been a member of this department for ten years.

Dusiška's networks played a key role in IAMCR's invitation to Leipzig. According to GDR custom, the invitation to Leipzig was not extended without political cover. The meeting (as were Dusiška's activities in IAMCR) is likely to have been preceded by extensive informal discussions. The official decision of the SED Central Committee Secretariat (a type of executive body of the party leadership) was not made until December 1972.[9] The formal commitment and provision of financial resources, in particular, the funds for preparing and actually holding the conference, as well as the "foreign hard currency" necessary for hosting the guests, were tied to the corresponding decision by the GDR's Council of Ministers, adopted shortly thereafter.[10] The official documents described the "political and scientific objectives of the conference" as a propaganda show. By way of example, they stated, among other things:

1. Marxist-Leninist theory on the class-related functions of mass media [...] will be expounded in front of a large international group of journalism scientists in the analysis of bourgeois theories of press and information freedom.
2. The works produced in the socialist countries on the tasks, structure, content, and mode of operation of the mass media will be announced to developing country representatives in order to influence their political and scientific orientation.
3. Young Marxist-Leninist or left-wing scientists from West Europe and non-European countries will be given the opportunity for system criticism and a forum for expressing their critical opinions.[11]

The style and use of language in this description were typical for the time, particularly for legitimization of an international meeting project vis-à-vis party

[8] Dusiška, E. Biographische DatenBanken, https://www.bundesstiftung-aufarbeitung.de/de/recherche/kataloge-datenbanken/biographische-datenbanken/emil-dusiska Accessed 15 June 2022. "But Hermann Budzislawski was a real scholar and a very good journalist. He was the creator of the Leipzig school. Franz Knipping was very professional too. Emil Dusiška was much stronger on the ideological side than Budzislawski or Knipping" (quoted by Zassoursky, 2018).

[9] The following comments are taken from the archives of the Journalism Section in the Leipzig University archives (UAL-Sektion_Journalistik_064 and 065), in particular, from Dusiška's two reports on the conference.

[10] No information on the amount of these funds is stated in the archive files mentioned. It was customary at this time for the host of the general meeting and the conference to assume the travel and lodging costs of IAMCR IC members.

[11] Dusiška, E. Information on the international scientific conference of the journalism section on the theme "Mass Communication and Social Consciousness in a Changing World." Leipzig, 1974a (UAL_Sektion_Journalistik_064, sheets 3–12), p. 2 et seq.

and state leadership.[12] This could have been part of the (official) language games in the GDR, behind which other objectives could also have been "hidden." In this case, however, the description resonated with the spirit of the ideological class struggle and the GDR's self-promotion, to which the Journalism Section was committed. Consequently, conference content and organization were very thoroughly prepared, with the conference tailored overall to meet the host country's objectives. Concerning content, efforts were made to generate as many papers from the GDR as possible. This was accomplished primarily by supporting not only Journalism Section employees and staff of other scientific institutions, but also above all, practicing journalists and civil servants in writing their own articles. Moreover, editors from the Journalism Section were employed to rework all contributions submitted from outside the GDR; these editors were tasked with drafting arguments for "objective debate" at the conference.

Organizational preparation comprised activities, such as the search for representational venue space, which apply to all conference organizers, as well as all-round chaperoning (and supervision) activities specific to GDR security requirements. Organization also covered excursions to cultural cities like Dresden and Weimar, a variety of meetings with newspaper editors in Leipzig, Dresden, and Erfurt, and receptions with the journalist association, the rector of the university, and the GDR Council of Ministers. Consequently, there was plenty of opportunity for informal communication and becoming acquainted with the country and its people, something most scientific conferences do not normally offer.

The conference itself took place in Leipzig from 16–21 September 1974. In addition to the Journalism Section of Karl Marx Universität Leipzig and the Verband der Journalisten der DDR (VDJ), the GDR national committee of AIERI, and the AIERI office also acted as organizers.[13] The general theme was "Mass Communication and Social Consciousness in a Changing World," whereby the last words of this title were added at the insistence of the IAMCR IC. The scientific part of the conference comprised mainly a plenary session with the opening by the GDR Minister of Science and Technology, Dr. Weiz, and four keynote addresses. The keynote addresses simultaneously introduced the conference's four parallel Working Groups (WGs) headed by Herbert Schiller ("Economy and structure of the mass media"), Emil Dusiška ("Mass media and participation"), James D. Halloran ("Mass media and socialization"), and Kaarle Nordenstreng ("Mass media and developing nations") to which each was assigned a Journalism Section scientist as a "scientific secretary." An additional conference day was dedicated to reports from the WGs

[12] One can assume that this or similar wording can also be found in the requests submitted for support of the conference and in the resolutions mentioned, thus rendering it binding.

[13] Dusiška, E. Report on the international scientific conference of the journalism section on the theme "Mass Communication and Social Consciousness in a Changing World" and the IX General Conference of AIERI (17–20 September 1974 in Leipzig) (27 September 1974). Leipzig 1974b (UAL_Sektion_Journalistik_064, sheets 13–42).

and a closing plenary session—a review of the conference by Dusiška as representative of the organizers and Halloran as IAMCR President.

With 251 delegates from 39 countries, this was the largest IAMCR Conference until that time: "From the 126 delegates from socialist countries, 79 conference participants came from the GDR[14] (including 27 scientists from the Journalism Section); 125 conference participants came from capitalist and developing nations to Leipzig."[15] These included—in addition to the above-mentioned plenary session speakers—Herbert Schiller (US), Kaarle Nordenstreng (Finland), James D. Halloran (UK), Elisabeth Noelle-Neumann (FRG), Nicholas Garnham (UK) and Robin Cheesman (Denmark), Hamid Mowlana (Iran), Slavko Splichal (Yugoslavia), Dallas W. Smythe (Canada), Cees Hamelink (the Netherlands), Tomas Goban-Klas and Walery Pisarek (Poland), Olof Hultén and Olga Linné (Sweden), Peter Hunziker (Switzerland), George Gerbner (US), and Yassen Zassoursky (USSR), all prominent scientists, many of whom would go on to determine IAMCR's further development. Zassoursky summed up this aspect of the conference in an interview: "He got a lot of money, yes. It was a good conference. Dusiška also succeeded in inviting good people from all over the world" (Zassoursky, 2018, p. np).

In Dusiška's closing reports, the results of the conference read as a triumph in the ideological contest of beliefs and systems:

> The conference was a complete success for the GDR and the other socialist states in political, scientific and organisational terms. [...] Through coordination with the socialist states and long-term preparation of content, the conference managed to offensively present the Marxist-Leninist positions as essential issues of journalism and journalism science that engage with bourgeois theories.[16]

The following, however, was noted in the archived files, which also include many individual reports commenting on participant sentiment and offering assessment of the conference. Even a conference in Leipzig, for which the organizers' central intention consisted of self-promoting the country in a positive light, is still just a conference—with some good and some mediocre speakers, and with debates, networking, informal communication, etc.

[14] This large number could be considered very remarkable or rather astonishing in view of the initial communication and media science situation presented. The GDR's official participants meanwhile included a large number of civil servants and employees of the journalist association, of ministries, parties, and local authorities, as well as journalists and employees of different media, all of whom it would have been difficult to label as acknowledged scientists.

[15] Dusiška, E. Information on the international scientific conference of the journalism section on the theme "Mass Communication and Social Consciousness in a Changing World." Leipzig: 1974 (UAL_Sektion_Journalistik_064, sheets 3–12), p. 4.

[16] Dusiška, E. Information on the international scientific conference of the Journalism Section on the theme "Mass Communication and Social Consciousness in a Changing World." Leipzig: 1974, (UAL_Sektion_Journalistik_064, sheets 3–12), p. 20 et seq.

The conference in Leipzig was a unique event that took place in a special political, personal, and institutional situation. The basic intent for involvement in IAMCR in helping to advance international recognition of the GDR was rendered obsolete at the least with the country's admission to the UN (1973) and the signing of the Final Act of the CSCE on 1 August 1975. The GDR's opportunities for and constraints on participating in the communication policy debates of the time and of staging its own positions shifted to other, more important organizations. Thus, it comes as no great surprise that the (official) GDR was no longer particularly interested in broad participation in further IAMCR activities. It is true that even more scientists attended the conferences in Warsaw (1978) and Prague (1984) (for reasons including inexpensive funding of travel costs and conference fees), but those were exceptions. These conferences had the strongest impact through the partially intended, and partially unintended, establishment of a global network (Meyen, 2014) and generation of greater international attention. Only a few participants saw a window opening to the world and to contacts around the globe. These included Wolfgang Kleinwächter and Lothar Bisky, who in 1974 were just starting their scientific careers. The two men are the most important GDR communication and media scientists, influenced by their participation in IAMCR activities and were able to shape the organization themselves to a certain extent—the former more in the 1970s and the latter later on, in the 1980s and 1990s.[17]

Lothar Bisky and the 1976 Keynote Address

During 1962–1967, Lothar Bisky (1941–2013) had begun his studies in philosophy at Humboldt-Universität zu Berlin, then taking up cultural studies at Karl Marx Universität Leipzig.[18] In 1967, he joined the Central Institute for Youth Research (Zentralinstitut für Jugendforschung) in Leipzig, where he established the mass communication/leisure studies department. Parallel to his work at the institute, Bisky wrote his dissertation A,[19] obtaining his PhD in 1969 (Bisky, 1969). This thesis can—also viewed from the special youth

[17] Beyond these two, Günter Heidorn deserves particular mention. Günter Heidorn (1925–2010) was a lawyer and a historian, who wrote his PhD on "German style newspaper reporting." He was Rector of the Universität Rostock in the 1960s and GDR Deputy Ministry of Higher and Technical Education from 1976 to 1988 https://www.bundesstiftung-aufarbeitung.de/de/recherche/kataloge-datenbanken/biographische-datenbanken/guenter-heidorn. Accessed 15 June 2022. He was presumably the "longest-serving" IAMCR member from the GDR and headed the association's History Section for a long period. In his ministerial function, Heidorn promoted participation of GDR scientists in IAMCR activities.

[18] For an overview, see https://www.munzinger.de/search/portrait/Lothar+Bisky/0/20508.html. Accessed 15 June 2022.

[19] The GDR higher-education reform of 1968–1969 introduced the terms 'dissertation A' and 'dissertation B' borrowed from the terms for academic qualifying theses used in the Soviet Union. The first term applied to a "normal" dissertation and the second term replaced the traditional term typically used until then in German higher education: "Habilitation" or postdoctoral lecturing qualification.

research angle—be considered a type of "charter" for mass communication research in the GDR, as it constitutes a thoroughly critical analysis of communication and mass communication models. The term "communication" had not found its way into social studies in the GDR prior to that time nor had it been comprehensively explained. For this reason, Bisky's thesis and the way of thinking that developed out of it were also suspected of being a "petty bourgeois deviation." His thesis met with considerable skepticism, particularly in the Journalism Section at Leipzig University, where academics were averse to any efforts to modernize theory—especially after the party and state leadership passed their verdict against cybernetics.[20]

Bisky attended the Leipzig Conference in 1974. The conference transcript refers to a contribution in which he critically analyzes Habermas, although there is no mention of this in the archival files cited.[21] In 1975, Bisky defended his dissertation B. The resultant book on the critical analysis of Western communication research and the positions it states on the materialist basis of communication and media science attracted readership in both the East and the West. The book established Bisky as one of the leading communication and media scientists (at least in Eastern Europe) (Bisky, 1976).[22] The overarching theme of the 1976 IAMCR Conference was "Mass Media and Man's View of Society." One conference focus was "the state of the art in communication research." Lothar Bisky, George Gerbner (US), and Peter Golding (UK) were invited as plenary session keynote speakers on "Inventory and Prospects in Mass Media Research." Reconstruction of the chain of events leading to Bisky's invitation is no longer possible. A report by Dusiška, still IAMCR Secretary General at that time, indicates that the IAMCR IC was keen on the idea of gaining representatives from a variety of different places and of different viewpoints to make up this "theoretical inventory." Bisky's contribution to the debate was published in 1978 (Bisky, 1978). The number of international contacts and invitations rose significantly following the Leicester Conference, and they were not limited to IAMCR. In 1980, Bisky moved to the SED Central Committee's academy for the social sciences and became honorary professor at Humboldt-Universität. This meant a certain refocus in research areas, particularly concerning popular and mass culture issues. In 1986, Bisky became rector of the "Konrad Wolff" University of Film and Television in Potsdam-Babelsberg,

[20] The thesis was accepted by the philosophy faculty, to which Journalism Section representatives officially had no access. A report for the MfS (Stasi) later in March 1977 stated: "As already reported and again made known, the director Prof. Dr Dusiška fundamentally questions Dr Bisky's political integrity in relation to the UNESCO cultural study, the mass communication and mass media congress in Leicester, England, and Dr Bisky's image in foreign capitalist countries, etc." (BStU/MfS AP no. 74150/92).

[21] This lecture is entered in the publications list and also published on an archival and memorial website for Lothar Bisky. http://www.lothar-bisky.de/index.php/archiv-gedenkseite/reihe-wissenschaft-theorie/jugend-und-kommunikationsforschung Accessed 15 June 2022.

[22] The Doctoral Thesis, Universität, was completed in 1975. Under the restrictive conditions in the GDR, the book opened up access to the international debate on media and society since, at the same time, it was a critical and comprehensive introduction to the newly emerging subject area.

which involved another shift in the main areas of his work. Lothar Bisky entered politics in the upheaval of 1989–1990. He was party and faction chair of the Party of Democratic Socialism (PDS), a member of Brandenburg Landtag, and, later, of the European Parliament and the Bundestag.

Wolfgang Kleinwächter and the Law Section

Wolfgang Kleinwächter studied journalism, international relations, and international law at Karl Marx Universität Leipzig from 1968 to 1974.[23] Kleinwächter earned his doctorate on political and international law aspects of the Four Power Agreement on Berlin, at the Institut für internationale Studien in 1974 (Kleinwächter, 1974). During preparations for the 1974 IAMCR Conference, Dusiška had invited other section and institute directors of Karl Marx Universität to actively participate in the conference. Professor Walter Poeggel, the then Director of the Institut für Internationale Studien, proposed to Kleinwächter that he prepare a paper on international law aspects of international mass communication. The Soviet Union had submitted a draft convention to the UN in 1972 on preventing direct transmission of satellite television to private homes. Poeggel's proposal sparked Kleinwächter's interest in the subject. There was initially no scientific analysis in the GDR of the debate emerging in the UN and the UNESCO in the 1970s on the New International Information and Communication Order (NWICO). Kleinwächter saw a "niche" for this theme. In 1981, he defended his dissertation B on this very topic. In 1987, Kleinwächter was appointed Professor for International Communication Relations. In 1988, he became Director of the Institut für Internationale Studien at Karl Marx Universität Leipzig.[24]

During his "aspirantura" or postgraduate study period in Moscow (1977), Kleinwächter met Yassen Zassoursky and Kaarle Nordenstreng. Nordenstreng was elected President of the International Organization of Journalists (IOJ) in 1976. Nordenstreng invited Kleinwächter to take part in the newly formed IOJ study group on international communication (Nordenstreng et al., 1986). This was simultaneously Kleinwächter's "admission ticket" to IAMCR. It enabled him—as one of the few GDR researchers—to regularly attend IAMCR Conferences from 1986 to 1990. At the IAMCR Congress in New Delhi in 1986, he was elected as Deputy Section Chair of IAMCR's reactivated Law

[23] Unless otherwise mentioned, the following statements refer to an e-mail personal communication addressed to one of the authors, 5 September 2020.

[24] At the Institut für internationale Studien in the mid-1980s, Kleinwächter set up an interdisciplinary research project on political, legal, economic, and cultural aspects of cross-border communication that dealt, among other things, with the concept of the internet, just emerging at the time. Research group members included Angela Kolb, later Minister of Justice of Saxony-Anhalt, and Karola Wille, later Director of Mitteldeutscher Rundfunk (MDR radio). The Institut für internationale Studien was dissolved in December 1990. Kleinwächter, who was a member of the Media Control Council of the GDR Volkskammer from January to September 1990, went to Tampere University in 1992. He lectured at American University's School of International Service in Washington, D.C. from 1993 to 1995, and at Aarhus University's Department for Information Studies from 1998 until his retirement in 2014.

Section. After the Chair of the Law Section, Cees Hamelink, was elected IAMCR President in Barcelona in 1988, Kleinwächter headed IAMCR's Law Section, remaining Chair until 2000.

In summary, it can be said that the interest of the (official) GDR in IAMCR was selectively limited to the single event of the 1974 Leipzig Conference, which had little long-lasting impact on establishing communication and media science as a discipline in the GDR; instead, it remained more of a tolerated "niche science" (Stiehler, 1993), denied promotion through international contacts outside Eastern Europe. For this reason, the GDR's commitment to IAMCR after 1974 was limited to a few individuals—and such commitment was not free of coincidence.

From 1990 to Now

Even after the Unification Treaty between the FRG and the GDR in 1990, the significance of IAMCR to overall German communication and media science was based on the activities and dedicated efforts of individuals and not on institutionally agreed commitments or cooperations. The highlight of the past three decades, namely Germany as a venue for the annual IAMCR Congress in 1999, deserves mention at this point. Wolfgang Kleinwächter availed himself of the 10th anniversary of the Peaceful Revolution in the GDR and the city of Leipzig's considerable interest at the time in a repeat invitation of IAMCR to the city to host the event in Germany. It is, thanks above all, to Kleinwächter that IAMCR returned to Leipzig a quarter of a century after the 1974 Conference.

This was to remain the last highlight thus far in the relationship between reunited Germany and IAMCR. Preliminary perusal of the available archive materials reveals that only media historian Jürgen Wilke, media lawyer Wolfgang Kleinwächter, and communication researcher Friedrich Krotz, as elected association members representing Germany, have been active in the IAMCR IC since 1990.[25] The records also list the names Wolfgang Donsbach, Christina Holtz-Bacha, and Corinna Lüthje as Heads of Sections. In contrast, there have been and are many more Germans in the governing bodies of the International Communication Association (ICA) as well as the European Communication Research and Education Association (ECREA).

This situation has not changed in the new millennium. Only a limited number of German scientists have continued to participate in IAMCR activities—and this in spite of the field's considerable expansion in Germany since the 1990s. Although the German delegations represented at the annual conferences are usually some of the most numerous, younger German colleagues have noticed that participation in ECREA and ICA activities in the institutional

[25] See, in particular, *IAMCR in Retrospect 1957–2007*, https://iamcr.org/history Accessed 15 June 2022 and Hamelink, C. & Nordenstreng, K. (2016) "Looking at history through the International Association for Media and Communication Research (IAMCR)," https://iamcr.org/node/3578. Accessed 15 June 2022.

network of the major German communication association, Deutsche Gesellschaft für Publizistik- und Kommunikationswissenschaft (DGPuK), plays a bigger role than in IAMCR activities. As a result, there are also only a few institutional IAMCR members in Germany: the current member directory lists only three institutes located in Hamburg, Munich, and Mainz—the same number of institutional members as in Portugal and fewer than in South Africa. By contrast, there are 80 individual paying members from Germany.[26] However, as far as can be observed, there are no institutionalized contacts or references between these members and institutions apart from IAMCR annual conferences, which is due, of course, to participation in IAMCR activities thus far largely being restricted to these annual conferences. Recently, at least, a few themed cooperations of specialized DGPuK groups with thematically related IAMCR Sections have been established.[27]

Such developments must be viewed against the backdrop of complex historical, political, and science-policy interests.

For example, in the German-speaking scientific research field, which evolved not only in Germany but also in Austria and Switzerland, social science-based communication research and theory formation have developed and continue to develop independently of media research and theory formation based on the humanities and literary science.

Both disciplines, social science-based communication science and humanities-based media research, considered themselves independent of each other even before their institutionalization in professional associations. Each established their own organizational formats, journals, and conferences, and even, for instance, separate realms in terms of German research community funding. What is more, German universities seldom have both a communication science and media science institute. Not until undergoing Europeanization, in particular through creation of ECREA in 2005, did these two scientific disciplines begin to take closer note of each other.

This divide was compounded by the fact that multiple areas of specialization had also developed within communication studies in West Germany after World War II. Until the 1960s, FDR communication science had tended to be a rather small, practical discipline focused on journalism and radio research. Germany's domestic scientific debate was determined, on the one hand, by the group of scientists around Elisabeth Noelle-Neumann, who were politically closely aligned with the CDU government, and, on the other, by the Hans Bredow Institut funded by the public law radio broadcasters ARD and ZDF, among other supporters. Moreover, there was never any systematic dealing with the field's Nazi past, other than in individual articles. This is the reason that until today debates are occasionally fired up—particularly by media historians—on such topics as the role that different scientists, also well-known ones in Germany, played in that context.

[26] See https://iamcr.org/member-institutions and https://iamcr.org/member-directory. Accessed 15 June 2022.

[27] See www.dgpuk.de. Accessed 15 June 2022.

Furthermore, a variety of different inter-university organizational structures was established and then evolved, also in German communication and media science. The German communication research society Deutsche Gesellschaft für Kommunikationsforschung (DGKF) has existed since 1961, developing out of the former Gesellschaft für Filmwissenschaft. The DGKF was established as an open-membership association of researchers and practitioners[28] and was dominated for many years by Alphons Silbermann. Today, the society still publishes primarily *the European Journal of Communication Research* ("Communications"). The DGPuK[29] was founded in 1963, largely as an academic professional association, and is today the field's largest professional association in Germany. Since 1980, it has primarily focused on quantitative empirical social research and is thus allied in particular with the US-dominated ICA.

The DGPuK never adopted to any reasonable degree of qualitative and/or interpretative research approaches, as followed in the 1970s, for instance, by Will Teichert (1972) and Karsten Renckstorff (1973) on the basis of symbolic interactionism or, later in the 1990s, cultural studies (Krotz, 1992), which had found its way over and had always played a role in IAMCR, even if a good-sized minority of DGPuK members geared their work to these paradigms. Consequently, communication scientists drifted away from communication science organizations such as the DGPuK, time and again, to enter fields such as sociology, psychology, and media education. Alternatively, they became lonely wolves dedicating their efforts to specific research issues. Marxist positions were excluded from the DGPuK as well (Scheu, 2012).

The decisive impetus to broad-based internationalization extending beyond German-speaking countries and US empirical science came first and foremost with the establishment of the ECREA European professional society, in the context of which German scientists from different research areas also met more frequently with colleagues from other countries.

In actual fact, IAMCR and its topics scarcely played any role in this complex situation. The only IAMCR Conference held before West and East German reunification, in 1970, is listed in the DGPuK tabular chronicle as merely an internal DGPuK work session—the chronicle mentions only a work meeting in Constance: "workshop to discuss training and further education of journalists (following the 7th AIERI congress)."[30]

Nor has the DGPuK taken the matters that characterize IAMCR as a UNESCO-related NGO seriously, that is, apart from those serving science. By way of example: neither the issue of a NWICO debated in the 1970s nor the World Summit of the Information Society (WSIS) hosted by the UNESCO right after the turn of the new century between 2003 and 2005 and focused on creation of a fairer distribution of computer digitalization and mediatization resources to the Global South met with any particular institutional response

[28] See https://dgkf-communications.de. Accessed 15 June 2022.

[29] See www.dgpuk.de. Accessed 15 June 2022.

[30] See https://www.dgpuk.de/de/chronik.html. Accessed 15 June 2022.

from the DGPuK. Nor did the DGPuK direct much attention to and likely did not broadly endorse IAMCR's "Clearing House for Public Statements"—a commission the organization created some years ago to handle statements reflecting its specific political commitment.

One could possibly conclude by assuming that critical and theoretical perspectives of communication and media could represent a potential new area of overlap in topics of importance to IAMCR and to the field of German communication science (beyond the DGPuK). Viewed historically, communication science in Germany was influenced for many years by Critical Theory and the works of Adorno and Horkheimer, an influence that only slowly diminished in the 1980s, although these were also the years in which the critical theories of Jürgen Habermas (1990), particularly the idea of the public sphere as a prerequisite for democracy, spread throughout the global scientific world. Conversely, the importance of theory and criticism in IAMCR was already evident in its awarding of prizes, namely to Dallas Smythe and Herbert Schiller. Political economy, gender research, cultural studies, and research on Global North/South issues, all of which became IAMCR focal areas, constitute a number of critically and/or theoretically based subdisciplines also prevalent in German communication science, albeit rather scattered in part and explored outside the DGPuK.

The fundamental change in the field of communication science today, in other words, computer digitalization, the consequences of which are currently still underestimated in established science, indeed harbors great potential for democracy and people's self-realization. Present developments, however, are determined and driven by huge companies such as Amazon and Facebook, Microsoft and Apple, Google and Uber, and so on and also by state institutions for the purpose of government control, as described by whistleblower Edward Snowden, among others. Communication science must, thus, take a much more critical approach in investigating such developments aimed at colonizing life, everyday activities, and communication in a cross-cultural manner binding for all people around the globe. It might, therefore, be the necessary and theoretically based criticism of digitalization, capitalist-driven artificial intelligence, and, very generally, criticism of an ever more invasive computer regime that could unite the forces of German communication science and IAMCR—along with those of other institutions as well, of course. Criticism also needs to be increasingly directed at companies and governments attempting to bring universities, which are actually civic institutions effectively serving the public good, under their control.

References

Becker, J. (Ed.). (1979). *Free flow of information?* Gemeinschaftswerk der Evangelischen Publizistik.

Bisky, L. (1969). *Massenkommunikation und Jugend. Studie zu theoretischen und methodischen problemen* (Unpublished Doctoral Thesis). Universität Leipzig.

Bisky, L. (1976). *Zur Kritik der bürgerlichen Massenkommunikationsforschung*. VEB Deutscher Verlag der Wissenschaften.
Bisky, L. (1978). Massenkommunikation und soziales Handeln der Massen (Discussion paper on Inventory and Prospects in Mass Media Research). *Communications, 4*, 289–301. Retrieved 15 June 2022, from https://doi.org/10.1515/comm.1978.4.3.289
Brandt, W. (1989). Preface. In J. Becker & T. Szecskö (Eds.), *Europe speaks to Europe. International information flows between Eastern and Western Europe*. Pergamon Press.
Habermas, J. (1990). *Strukturwandel der Öffentlichkeit*. Suhrkamp.
Kleinsteuber, H. J. (1973). *Kommerzielles fernsehen in den USA und Großbritannien*. Hoffmann & Campe.
Kleinwächter, W. (1974). *Politische und rechtliche Aspekte der Westberlin-Frage nach dem Inkrafttreten des vierseitigen Abkommens vom 3. September 1971*. Doctoral Thesis, Universität Leipzig.
Koschwitz, H. (1974). *Publizistik und politisches system. Die internationale Presse der Gegenwart und ihre Entwicklungstendenzen in unterschiedlichen Herrschaftsordnungen*. Piper.
Krotz, F. (1992). Kommunikation als Teilhabe. Der "Cultural Studies Approach". *Rundfunk und Fernsehen, 40*, 412–431.
Löffler, M. (1955). *Presserecht*. Beck.
Luhmann, N. (1995). *Die Realität der Massenmedien*. Westdeutscher Verlag.
MacBride, S. (1981). *Many voices, one world: Communication and society, today and tomorrow*. Report by the International Commission for the Study of Communication Problems to UNESCO, Universitätsverlag, Konstanz.
MacBride, S. (1984). Preface. In J. Becker (Ed.), *Information technology and a new international order*. Studentlitteratur.
Meyen, M. (2014). IAMCR on the East-West battlefield: A study on the GDR's attempts to use the association for diplomatic purposes. *International Journal of Communication, 8*, 2071–2089.
Nordenstreng, K., Gonzales-Manet, E., & Kleinwächter, W. (1986). *New international information and communication order: Sourcebook*. International Organization of Journalists.
Prakke, H. J. (1968). *Die kommunikation der gesellschaft*. Regensberg.
Renckstorf, K. (1973). Alternative Ansatze der Massenkommunikationsforschung: Wir kungs- vs. Nutzenansatz. *Rundfunk und Fernsehen*, 2–3, 183–197.
Scheu, A. M. (2012). *Adornos Erben in der kommunikationswissenschaft. Eine Verdrängungsgeschichte*. Herbert von Halem.
Schiller, H. (1986). Die Kommerzialisierung der kultur in den Vereinigten Staaten. *Media Perspektiven, 10*, 659–672.
Schiller, H. (1988). Disney, Dallas und der elektronische Informationsfluss. *Media Perspektiven, 12*, 782–790.
Schiller, H. (1999). Kultursponsoring in den USA. *Media Perspektiven, 11*, 730–736.
Schmidt, S. (2017). Hermann Budzislawski und die Leipziger journalistik. In M. Meyen & T. Wiedemann (Eds.), *Biografisches lexikon der kommunikationswissenschaft*. Herbert von Halem. Retrieved 15 June 2022, from http://blexkom.halemverlag.de/schmidt-budzislawski
Stiehler, H.-J. (1993). Einfach verhinderte verwissenschaftlichung. Theorie-Praxis-Beziehungen der DDR-Medienforschung vor der Wende. In G. Bentele & M. Rühl

(Eds.), *Theorien öffentlicher kommunikation* (p. 450–454). Ölschläger. (=DGPuK series of articles, vol. 19).

Stiehler, H.-J. (2008). Lenin, Vladímir, I. In L. L. Kaid & C. Holtz-Bacha (Eds.), *Encyclopedia of political communication* (p. 401–402). Sage.

Teichert, Will. (1972). Fernsehen als soziales Handeln. *Rundfunk und Fernsehen 20*, 421–439.

Zassoursky, Y. (2018). I tried to stop the Cold War mentality. In M. Meyen & T. Wiedemann (Eds.), *Biografisches lexikon der lommunikationswissenschaft*. Herbert von Halem. Retrieved 15 June 2022, from http://blexkom.halemverlag.de/iamcr-zassoursky

CHAPTER 12

IAMCR as Seen by the Secret Service from East Germany (GDR)

Jörg Becker

Introduction

That secret services the world over are interested in the work of communication scientists is a well-known fact and is well documented, for example, as regards the work of the West German Federal Intelligence Service (BND) in cooperating with journalists and broadcasting authorities (Schmidt-Eenboom, 2004). For another Western country too, namely the United States (US), it has, in the meantime, been shown that Dallas Smythe, an activist in IAMCR for many years, was observed by the Federal Bureau of Investigation (FBI) (Guback, 1994, p. 40). Either a secret service observes communication experts or it cooperates with them. We know therefore that since its foundation in 1947, the Central Intelligence Agency (CIA) has had numerous writers and journalists on its payroll, especially Trotskyites and homeless left-wingers. However, not only individual persons, but also whole institutions such as IAMCR can become objects of observation for a secret service. This has been demonstrated in the cases of the German Democratic Republic (GDR) and Romania (see also Chaps. 11 and 13).

This chapter deals with the involvement of communication and media scientists from the GDR in IAMCR between 1968 and 1988. It treats their role in IAMCR, the objectives they linked with their work in IAMCR, and their

J. Becker (✉)
University of Marburg, Marburg, Germany
e-mail: joerg.becker@komtech.org

© The Author(s), under exclusive license to Springer Nature Switzerland AG 2023

J. Becker, R. Mansell (eds.), *Reflections on the International Association for Media and Communication Research*,
https://doi.org/10.1007/978-3-031-16383-8_12

contacts with colleagues in Western countries, in particular, the Federal Republic of Germany (FRG).

The Secret Service of the GDR operated as a department of its own called Stasi within the Ministry for State Security (MfS). The Stasi files are disjointed and unsystematic with regard to their coverage of activities concerning IAMCR. The oldest document dates from 1968; the most recent is 1988. Other internal documentation that was secret, until it was located in the archives of the University of Leipzig, includes the administrative correspondence of Prof. Dr. Emil Dusiška (1914–2002) during the 1970s.[1]

Dusiška was a member of the Agitation Commission in the Politburo of the Central Committee of the Socialist Unity Party of Germany (SED) in 1966, and, as of 1969, he was Director of the Journalism Department at the Karl Marx University Leipzig and Secretary General of IAMCR (1972–1982). Both the Stasi files and those at the University of Leipzig, including files from the correspondence of Emil Dusiška, are accessible to academics and some files contain identical documents. The Stasi was a secretive organization and its files were never meant to be open to outsiders; internal documents are considered to be internal. Both sets of documents can be accessed today by academics when they can prove to be undertaking scholarly work. In order to obtain access to the secret Stasi files, the waiting time is approximately one and a half years.

In 1975 and 1978, Dusiška's agent handler at the Stasi indicated that he had assessed him positively. On the one hand: "D. is considered to be a comrade who is true to the party and reliable, and who champions the policy of our party and our government at any time. Prof. D. will always be a worthy representative of the GDR in the non-socialist economic area" (extract from Stasi assessment below, trans. by author). This handler did, however, criticize his weak leadership style and his scientific deficiencies (see Fig. 12.1).

The beginning of the first Stasi file on IAMCR reads like a bad crime story. The so-called object of scrutiny is IAMCR. It has the code name "Roof." In a document dating from late 1972, the object "Roof" is indicated as living at Rue du Petit Chêne 18bis in Lausanne and one individual, Jacques Bourquin, is described by a Stasi collaborator in great detail:

> Jacques E. Bourquin Dr. en droit [doctorate in law] represents about 15 largely international associations in Switzerland. Listed on his name plate are also [six associations] and the Association Internationale des Études et Recherche sur l'Information. I introduced myself as a German tourist in Switzerland who was

[1] Unless otherwise indicated, the quotations in this chapter are drawn from the following archival sources: The Federal Commissioner of the Federal Archive on the Secret Service of the former GDR: BVfS Leipzig. Abt. XV. 00378; ZMA BV Lpz. Abt. XX. 13478; MfS – HA II/13. 544; MfS / XV 5527/88 "Frieder"; MfS AP Nr. 74.150/92; MfS XV/1845/86 "Paul"; MfS XV/3600/80 "Gesandter"; MfS AIM 1630/91. Part I Volume 1 and Part II Volume 1; and Sektion_Journalistik_061, Sektion_Journalistik_063, Sektion_Journalistik_064, Sektion_Journalistik_065, Sektion_Journalistik_066 and PA_4837, both Leipzig University Archive (UAL).

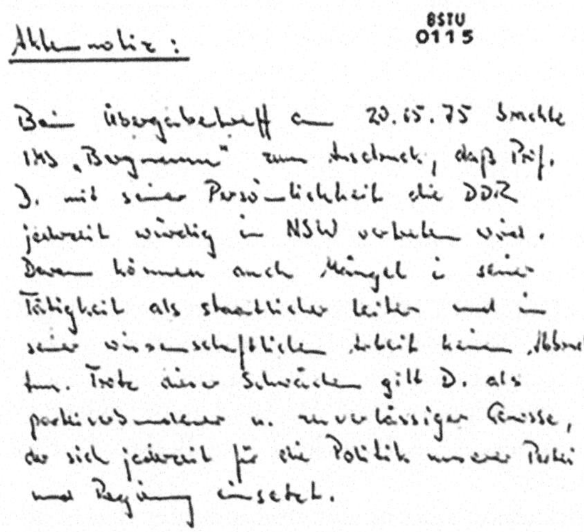
BStU
0115

Aktennotiz:

Beim Übergabetreff am 20.05.75 brachte IMS „Bergmann" zum Ausdruck, daß Prof. D. mit seiner Persönlichkeit die DDR jederzeit würdig im NSW vertreten wird. Dem können auch Mängel in seiner Tätigkeit als staatlicher Leiter und in seiner wissenschaftlichen Arbeit keinen Abbruch tun. Trotz einer Schwäche gilt D. als parteiverbundener u. zuverlässiger Genosse, der sich jederzeit für die Politik unserer Partei und Regierung einsetzt.

Fig. 12.1 Stasi Assessment of Emil Dusiška, 1975. Leipzig University Archive (UAL): ZMA BV Lpz. Abt. XX. 13478, p. 115. (Courtesy of Jörg Becker)

> doing a favour for his sociology friend and inquiring about work possibilities in Switzerland. Whereupon I was informed by the secretary about the character of the institution. The association has an annual budget of 1,500 dollars at its disposal, for which reason she worked as a secretary free of charge. The secretary (around 20, very attractive) was extremely pleasant and gave me the statues of the organisation. Relevant photographs of the building were taken.

In 1972, the Stasi was thinking about the benefits of having an individual GDR citizen within IAMCR with official membership. It was also considering whether the "installation of a conspiratorial and unofficial informer" in the management of IAMCR would be helpful. The Stasi expressed relief that, at this time, neither the BND of the FRG—West Germany—nor the US' CIA were known to be active in IAMCR. Most likely ignorant of this Stasi observation, Emil Dusiška participated in a session of the IAMCR Executive Committee in Barcelona in 1971. In an internal administrative report, he noted: "The flag of our Republic was hanging alongside the others during the whole week in the conference room of an old monastery," and "I was treated with respect." These sentences are indicative of the political aim of the GDR's membership in IAMCR: through membership in this international scientific association, the GDR was aiming to break free of its global political isolation so as to bring closer its diplomatic goal of gaining recognition as an equal sovereign state on an international level.

This goal was also the political aim of the IAMCR Conference in Leipzig in 1974. According to Emil Dusiška in a later internal administrative report, the conference "increased the renown of the GDR." The 126 participants from the socialist states accounted for more than half of the total of 251 conference participants and were thus able to successfully call the "western predominance in that scientific field" into question. In this context, it is worth recalling that the basic treaty between the FRG and the GDR, which *de facto* equated to recognition of the GDR, had been signed only in 1972. The United Nations (UN) accorded equal rights to the FRG and the GDR only in 1973 and the Helsinki Final Act laying down the inviolability of all the signatories' borders occurred in 1975.

The wording of internal GDR documents is instructive: the adjectives "progressive," "left," and "left-bourgeois" are used to characterize academics from capitalist foreign countries who the GDR's Stasi wanted to win over as potential allies who might support their Marxist-Leninist agenda. Those named included, among others, Cees Hamelink, Jörg Becker, Herbert Schiller, and Kaarle Nordenstreng.

In 1973, Emil Dusiška's documentation indicates that he formulated three objectives for the GDR's cooperation with IAMCR:

(1) To find out about new developments in capitalist countries
(2) To hamper IAMCR's influence in the Third World
(3) "In order to strengthen the influence of progressive and younger academics from the capitalist countries, attempts were to be made to integrate them into the different functions of the IAMCR in the coming years. This applies to the FRG, France, Switzerland, Finland, Spain, and overseas countries."

Emil Dusiška formulated these objectives in a way very similar to the expressed aim of the IAMCR Conference in Leipzig in 1974 which was stated as "giving young Marxist-Leninist or left-wing academics from Western Europe and non-European capitalist counties the opportunity to criticise the system."

During the 1974 Leipzig Conference, this meant, for example, attracting the interest of the Munich-based communications scholar, Horst Holzer, from West Germany. As a member of the German Communist Party (DKP), Horst Holzer is unlikely ever to have been invited to a conference in West Germany with a similar agenda to IAMCR's Leipzig Conference. Holzer was present in Leipzig, of course, but in West Germany, he was later barred from his profession in 1980, had to leave his university, and his books were removed from the university library.

Using negatively connotative adjectives "left-wing radical" or "ultra-left," Emil Dusiška's documents show that he distanced himself from IAMCR members like Roque Faraone from Uruguay and Dallas Smythe from Canada. This seems in keeping with the prevailing Leninist view of "left-wing radicalism" as being a typical childhood illness of Communism, that is, a conflict between old power pragmatics and young rebels seeking new approaches.

The internal Stasi documents indicate that Emil Dusiška's relations with then IAMCR President James Halloran were strained as they were inside the GDR itself with Lothar Bisky, a GDR scholar and IAMCR member. What is more, relations between Emil Dusiška and the Hungarian sociologist, Tamás Szecskö, who replaced Dusiška as Secretary General of IAMCR during the 1984 IAMCR Conference, were not particularly easy. Dusiška saw in Szecskö a "liberal," as seen from the perspective of the Eastern European countries, that is, an individual who was not a real socialist. This view may have been consistent with the fact that under Szecskö's direction, the Budapest Opinion Research Institute had oriented itself toward Western Europe. Dusiška's relations with the Slovenian journalist and another IAMCR member, Tomo Martelanc, also were not uncomplicated as indicated by the archival documentation.

Similarly, Emil Dusiška's attitude toward Elisabeth Noelle-Neumann, a member of IAMCR's International Council, was ambivalent. For example, in late January 1979, Dusiška was in Allensbach on Lake Constance in the FRG to take part in a session of the program committee for IAMCR's 1980 Conference in Caracas. Concerning the high cost of flights to Venezuela, he reported in his notes: "Mrs. Noelle-Neumann whispered to me in this connection that the GDR people were looking for a cheaper offer [than that offered by James Halloran], so as to enable the GDR people to fly there as well." In these times, one could really only whisper to someone sitting beside you in this kind of setting, and the opportunity arose because these two IAMCR heavyweight scholars from East and West Germany were seated side by side in Allensbach.

Noelle-Neumann's patronizing comment to Emil Dusiška concerning IAMCR's offer to support the cost of flights in 1979 is at odds with his earlier friendly treatment of her. Noelle-Neumann had traveled to Leipzig in 1973 for an IAMCR president's meeting. Emil Dusiška had put a driver and car at her disposal for a week so that she could come to know Leipzig and its environs. They had a common interest insofar as she had sought in the early 1970s to prevent the inauguration of a new IAMCR section focusing on Political Economy. Dusiška regarded the founding members of this section as mere "left wing radicals," while Noelle-Neumann had rejected them because she imputed a Marxist understanding of media and communications research to them. In this sense, both Emil Dusiška and Elisabeth Noelle-Neumann had an interest in seeking to ensure that their own positions within IAMCR would not be destabilized by new unpredictable forces.

A strange little detail helps to draw attention to another common interest of Emil Dusiška and Elisabeth Noelle-Neumann. Noelle-Neumann traveled from Mainz in a large Mercedes driven by a chauffeur to the IAMCR 1974 Conference in Leipzig with IAMCR President Jim Halloran in the back seat. At this conference, Dallas Smythe gave a lecture in the Working Group on Developing Countries. His oral delivery of the lecture included a critical observation on Noelle-Neumann's doctoral dissertation which had been completed in the Nazi era of 1940. Smythe seems likely to have included this intentionally, since his observation, in a footnote of the oral script, had nothing to do with the theme of his lecture on developing countries, and he could have avoided polemical comments concerning Noelle-Neumann. The footnote disappeared from Smythe's manuscript when it was prepared for publication and it was not present in the printed proceedings of the conference, edited by Emil Dusiška, but it can be found in Thomas Guback's *Counterclockwise* (1994). The question is, did Emil Dusiška want to protect Noelle-Neumann, or did she put pressure on Emil Dusiška regarding the inclusion of the footnote? What is clear is that Dallas Smythe and Elisabeth Noelle-Neumann were bound by a sincere mutual hostility.

Alongside the seemingly friendly dialog that occurred between Dusiška and Noelle-Neumann, quite the opposite was occurring in the background. In an internal working report held by Leipzig University on the above-mentioned President's preparatory meeting for Leipzig in 1973, Emil Dusiška stated retrospectively: "We succeeded in basically isolating the very active Prof. Noelle-Neumann, West-Germany, and the late-comer Prof. Roegele, West-Germany," both powerful conservative professors of communication research, she from Mainz University and he from Munich University. Reciprocally, the nature of the relationship of the anti-Communist Elisabeth Noelle-Neumann with the GDR was anything but friendly. Regarding the meeting of a preparatory group for the 1976 IAMCR Conference in Leicester which took place in Rostock in 1975, Noelle-Neumann reported that she had hidden behind a pillar in a hotel so as to listen unnoticed to conversations among GDR citizens. During her stay in Leipzig in 1973, on the occasion of a UNESCO conference, Noelle-Neumann would claim to have detected from their facial expression that the people she had observed in the GDR were unhappy. She called the face of the GDR citizens "the face of the Totalitarian," and it was on the basis of these facial observations that she later developed a test that she applied in her published empirical measurements of the expression of "happiness features."

Within the socialist state community of participants in IAMCR, they were active at regular meetings of deans of journalism faculties in the Council for Mutual Economic Assistance (COMECON) countries, the GDR, under Dusiška, played a prominent role, not the then USSR's Yassen Zassoursky. This at least is the impression conveyed by GDR files. Poland's and Czechoslovakia's representatives were aligned with the GDR, but interestingly the Polish representative played an increasingly independent role. In a 1983 document stamped "top secret," the Stasi warned against a colleague from Poland because he "represents positions that come close to those of the anti-socialist Solidarność." Some COMECON countries—Albania, Bulgaria, Hungary, Romania, and Cuba—seem to have played no role in IAMCR at all and they are scarcely mentioned in the GDR documents. However, it is important to be careful methodologically in ascribing influence based on the weight of participation of representatives of the socialist countries within IAMCR and, indeed, about the relations among the socialist countries themselves. It is not feasible to make general assumptions about their relative weight based on the unsystematic files available in the Leipzig University archive.

Finnish scholar Kaarle Nordenstreng, President in the early 1970s of the International Organization of Journalists (IOJ) located at the time in Prague, played a special role in the East-West dialog within IAMCR. He participated several times in informal meetings with IAMCR's leading figures such as Emil Dusiška and representatives from Poland and the Czechoslovak Socialist Republic (ČSSR), informally advising on staffing issues for the various official roles in IAMCR in the run-up to official IAMCR meetings. Through the good offices of Kaarle Nordenstreng, Emil Dusiška traveled to Finland on a lecture tour in December 1973. As Dusiška states, Nordenstreng presented himself as wanting to appear as a "representative of Marxist views." During his stay in Helsinki, Nordenstreng's wife, Ullamaja Kivikuru, took good care of Dusiška and provided interpretation for him.

Later, at the IAMCR 1976 Conference in Leicester, Nordenstreng sought to inaugurate a section called the "Materialist Theory of Mass Communication." At an informal preparatory meeting for this section, 27 IAMCR members participated, among them, Herbert Schiller, Robin Cheesman, Graham Murdock, Lothar Bisky, Yassen Zassoursky, Breda Pavlič, and András Szekfü. Roque Faraone from Uruguay wanted to name the new section "Marxist Communication Theory," but his proposal was rejected by Emil Dusiška on the grounds that the proposed section would endanger the unity of IAMCR.

The GDR participants at IAMCR conferences held in the capitalist world received travel directives that had to be processed through two GDR bureaucracies—the Agitation Department in the Central Committee of the SED and the Ministry of University and Technical Colleges. To take part in the 1976 Conference in Leicester, for example, the participants from the GDR were obliged to fight against "the myth of free information" and the myth of "pluralism of opinion" and to demonstrate through their participation the "class content of the imperialist mass media."

Two of the many IAMCR conference participants from the GDR were unofficial informers for the Ministry of State Security. One worked from 1951 to 1986 under the names "Gesandter" and "Paul," while the other worked under the name "Frieder." "Frieder" reported, among other things, that at the IAMCR 1984 Conference in Prague, he was approached by a Bundeswehr (West German armed forces officer) who (clearly) wanted to lure him over to the side of the Military Counterintelligence Service (MAD) in West Germany. Another explanation is that he may have wanted "Frieder" to recruit that West German officer for the Stasi in East Germany. The text we have by "Frieder" is open to both interpretations. Moreover, "Frieder" surmised in his notes that IAMCR member, Nabil Dajani, from Lebanon, was probably a "highly qualified agent of a secret service in Lebanon," and that a Danish colleague from the University of Copenhagen should be suspected of working for the Danish Secret Service. I know and like both "Paul" and "Frieder" personally, and for this reason, their identities are not revealed here.

At the IAMCR 1974 Conference, the participants were individually looked after by Leipzig University students. After the conference, they provided notes about their conversations with the West German conference participants. According to these notes, at 1:00 a.m., a West Berlin participant showed signs of having consumed too much alcohol and betrayed a frightful lack of knowledge of Karl Marx's *Das Kapital*, while another participant from the GRD was said to be clearly well-informed about West German post-war literature. I note again that because I know and like the Berliner and the colleague from the Ruhr district personally, I do not reveal their identities here.

It is difficult to draw general conclusions based upon these recorded observations. Drawing insight requires great care since the documentation is based on internal university office files that were designated as secret and they cover limited time periods. The snapshots provided in this chapter nevertheless suggest that in the middle of the Cold War, the main concern in the GDR was not so much to build a bridge between East and West, as to instrumentalize individuals from Western countries and the Third World for their own purposes. Perhaps, however, the actions reported here and the GDR policy should instead be interpreted simply as a reflection of a pragmatic interest-driven politics; a politics that would also have been present in the foreign relations actions of all countries.

The archived files do show that media and communications research in the GRD was subject to political framework conditions. Yet, to what country would this banal observation not apply? I am obliged to "also consider the social consequences of scientific insight" under the requirement of §1 of the Act of the University to which I am subject. It should also be noted that this chapter is written not from the "victor position" of a West German observer of the relations among West and East Germany academics or with the GDR itself. In the interests of transparency, it is important to note that I have productively studied the works of GDR computer scientists, Georg Klaus, a philosopher and cybernetician, and Klaus Fuchs-Kittowski, whose research concerned information technologies, information, and behavioral control. I am also preoccupied with media theories developed by the GDR author, Peter Hacks, with a focus on the antagonistic dramas of socialism. Furthermore, I collaborated with Lothar Bisky until his death in 2013.

The account I give in this chapter, based as it is on fragmentary documentation, is limited since it is difficult to interpret these fragments. What this chapter aims to do is to open up questions for future historians of IAMCR concerning the extent to which IAMCR engaged in a project of building friendly bridges between East and West during the Cold War, or whether its members became complicit in the GDR's own agenda.

References

Guback, T. (Ed.). (1994). *Counterclockwise: Perspectives on communication – Dallas Smythe*. Westview Press.

Schmidt-Eenboom, E. (2004). *Geheimdienst, politik und medien. Meinungsmache undercover*. Homilius Verlag.

CHAPTER 13

IAMCR Members under the Microscope of Romania's Securitate: A Preliminary Study

Ilinca Ungureanu-Burlan and Peter Gross

Introduction

This chapter is a preamble to the story of Romanian members of IAMCR who were targets of the Securitate (Department of State Security, Ministry of the Interior/Departamentul Securității Statului), the country's version of the Soviet KGB. It is a limited introduction to the topic, because the files of the four IAMCR members identified in July 2021 and obtained from Romania's National Council for the Study of the Securitate Archives/Consiliul Național Pentru Studierea Arhivelor Securității (CNSAS)[1] in October contain thousands

[1] The CNSAS was established in 2000, in accordance with Law nr. 187/1999, and houses Securitate files on individuals and informers. The process of obtaining the files included the submission of an application—with the names of the eight Romanian IAMCR members, their birth dates, and fields of activity—to the CNSAS board responsible for accrediting researchers. It took about four weeks for the board to consider the application and grant accreditation. Ms. Ungureanu-Burlan was notified on 30 June 2021 that our request for accreditation was granted and that she was scheduled to be admitted to the CNSAS archives on 29 July between 1:00 p.m. and 4 p.m. and again on 30 July between 9 a.m. and 1 p.m. She took notes and then requested copies of the files available for the four Romanian IAMCR members, which were delivered to us on disks on 17 October 2021.

I. Ungureanu-Burlan
University of Bucharest, București, Romania
e-mail: ilinca.ungureanu.burlan@amc.ro

P. Gross (✉)
University of Tennessee, Knoxville, TN, USA
e-mail: pgross@utk.edu

© The Author(s), under exclusive license to Springer Nature Switzerland AG 2023

J. Becker, R. Mansell (eds.), *Reflections on the International Association for Media and Communication Research*,
https://doi.org/10.1007/978-3-031-16383-8_13

of pages, which we have only partially examined at the time of writing in early 2022.[2]

Authoritarianism, state terror, and surveillance of citizens is a story that is to one degree or another shared among all Marxist-Leninist socialist republics in Eastern, Central, and Southeastern Europe. What differentiated one story from the other is the specific historical and cultural context in which the more or less similar interpretations and praxes of foundational Marxism-Leninism evolved. During Nicolae Ceaușescu's regime (1965–1989), Romania experienced a Stalinist version of the socialist ideology (Tismaneanu, 2003).

The Securitate

The "inescapable feature of life" in Romania during Ceaușescu's reign was the omnipresence of the Securitate (Deletant, 1995). Similar to its counterparts in other communist countries, the Securitate's ubiquity expressed itself in terror, first in the service of eliminating opponents of the Marxist-Leninist "revolution" (1945–1964) and secondly "to ensure compliance" once the communist regime was well entrenched (1965–1989).[3]

Arguing that the state terrorism of the early years of communism (1947–1964) was replaced by "selective violence," Stefano Bottoni (2017) agrees that it was another way of instilling fear meant to facilitate "policing the civil population." However, other scholars say it was more than that, and conclude that it constituted extensive "social control," turning the country into "an open prison *where arrest or torture were now hardly necessary to enforce obedience*" (emphasis added) (Barberá, 2019). Eventually, the violence of the "despotic power" bred an active "quasi-cooperative relationship between citizens and Communist authorities (infrastructural power)" during Ceaușescu's regime (Bottoni, 2017).

It is important to note, however, that the "obedience" and "quasi-cooperative relationship" arguments require an additional cultural explanation that rests on the effects of the very long history of foreign rule and of the Orthodox Church. Both have instilled a degree of inertia into the nation, inducing "a propensity to adopting a defensive stance rather than open revolt" (Vasile, 2009, p. 384). This is an exaggerated assertion, however. It is true that Romania did not have dissident groups or a long-running and effective

[2] This chapter is based on a preliminary analysis of the Securitate's seven volumes (over 7000 pages) of reports on Câmpeanu, code named "Pavo." This includes documents and ancillary materials such as intercepted correspondence with foreign colleagues, some related to IAMCR (I—file nr. I-0064759). An "I" designates an "Information" file. These documents are the source for quotes not included in the reference list.

[3] See footnote 1 for origins.

samizdat. Neither did it generate major, nation-wide anti-communist uprisings as East Germany (1956), Hungary (1956), Czechoslovakia (1968), and Poland (1981) experienced. However, we should remember that Romania's armed anti-communist resistance lasted well into the 1950s, longer than in any other Soviet Bloc country, and it had significant workers' strikes in 1986 and 1987.[4] Factoring in the regime's initial terror and subsequent "selective violence," the qualified historical-cultural context partially explains why intellectuals, academics, artists, and students "failed to contribute to the destabilization of the regime." In this regard, Romania resembled East Germany, both exemplifying sharp contrasts to Poland and Czechoslovakia (Vasile, 2009).

In addition to actual instances of "selective violence," and comparably to its secret police peers in the Socialist Bloc, some of whom they collaborated with, the Securitate deliberately fomented apprehension that all Romanians were continuously monitored, which was not strictly true.[5] Most foreigners who lived in or visited the country were indeed monitored. However, mostly, the state security agency was specifically attentive to Romanians who had contact with foreigners and were involved with international organizations (more on the Securitate in the next section).

This was the general political and cultural milieu and the reason—see next section—why four Romanian members of IAMCR were among those surveilled by the Securitate, according to files in the CNSAS. The agency sought to integrate at least two of them into its network of informers and perhaps succeeded with one of them.

The Securitate's most prominent target among the eight Romanians mentioned in IAMCR presidents' reports from the late-1960s to the mid-1980s, the list that served as a guide to requesting files from the CNSAS, was Pavel Câmpeanu. The others were George Ivașcu, Paul Caravia, and Ștefana Steriade, whose surveillance reports are folded into Câmpeanu's, for reasons outlined below. However, according to the CNSAS, Henri Dona, Elena Ionescu, Alexandru Dimitriu Păușesti, and Nestor Ignat, also mentioned in IAMCR presidents' letters to the membership as either members or contributors of papers and/or articles alongside the above-mentioned four colleagues, do not have Securitate files.

That said, we cannot assume that other files related to IAMCR's Romanian members, or to the possible surveillance of the association, did not or do not exist. There are instances in which some Securitate records were "seemingly lost, destroyed or ***never produced***" (emphasis added) after the fall of the communist regime in 1989 (Stan, 2005). We particularly question the purported absence of a file for Nestor Ignat, a hard-core Marxist-Leninist, at one time one of the editors of the communist newspaper *Scînteia*, and of the Central

[4] On the Romanian armed resistance, see Consiliul Național pentru Studierea Ahivelor Securității (2003), Miroiu (2010). For the workers' strikes, see Socor (1987).

[5] See examples of the Securitate's cooperation with other communist secret police, Herbstritt (2016), Bagieński (2020), and Nehring (2021).

Committee of the Romanian Communist Party's journal, *Class Struggle*, and Dean of the Faculty of Journalism at the party's ideological training center, the Ştefan Gheorghiu Academy. Despite being a staunch communist, he was nevertheless rejected in 1974 for membership on the Central Committee of the Communist Party, suggesting some degree of disfavor by or incompatibility with the Ceauşescu regime that ordinarily would have warranted the Securitate's attention.

The Securitate's Interest in IAMCR's Romanian Members

When Nicolae Ceauşescu ascended to Romania's leadership in 1965, he needed first and foremost to secure his power; increase the efficacy of his intelligence services, particularly the Securitate, to better track and suppress dissidents, instill fear among the population, and deal with the diaspora; and lastly, find a way to establish a unique identity for himself and the country within the Soviet camp and on the international scene.[6] The 1967 Middle East war; the 1968 Czechoslovak "Prague Spring" that led to a Soviet invasion; the 1968 Polish anti-communist protests—known as the Students' March—and later the 1981 Polish workers' strikes; the growing Soviet–Chinese rift that began in the 1950s and extended into the 1960s and 1970s; and changes in the leadership of the Soviet Union in the 1980s provided Ceauşescu with the opportunity to refashion his and Romania's image as a "maverick" in the communist world. Duplicitously as it turned out. The deception allowed Ceauşescu to set Romania up as a kind of Trojan horse that benefited both it and the Soviet Union in economic, political, technological, and conceivably other ways (Betea et al., 2009).

The obsessive need to protect unpopular authoritarian-totalitarian regimes was a more or less extensively shared state of mind among the regime leaders in all socialist republics. For Ceauşescu, it appears to have become more feverish after his 1971 visits to China and North Korea and his emulation of Mao Zedong's cultural revolution in China and embrace of the cult of personality (Roper, 2000; Mudde & Kaltwasser, 2017). This cult of personality required slavish obeisance to his wishes and the *de rigueur* use of descriptive monikers that included, among others, the "hero of the nation," "genius of the Carpathians," and "the exceptional personality of the contemporary world." It fed the megalomaniacal attention to all perceived anti-regime actions and pronouncements by Romanians.[7]

Any Romanian drew the Securitate's attention for however small his/her deviations from Marxist-Leninist self-righteousness and dissidence may have been or the form it may have taken. After all, the Securitate, whose 11,000 employees and 500,000 informers (in a country of 22 million citizens)—the third-largest such force among communist countries—was tasked with

[6] The Securitate's history is well described by Troncota (2003), Pelin (2003), Deletant (1995).

[7] This cult of personality extended to his wife, Elena Ceauşescu, who was barely literate, had a fake academic background, and was addressed as "academician," "doctor," "(chemical) engineer," and "world-renowned scientist," that is, when she was not called the "mother of the country."

guarding against any real, potential, and imaginary threats (Smith, 2006). Let's remember that the justification for the Securitate's establishment in August 1948 was the defense and securing of the People's Republic of Romania, that is, the Communist Party and its program, against internal and external enemies (Metaxioti, 2021).[8]

Therefore, the Securitate's scrutiny of Romania's IAMCR members is not surprising given the regime's paranoia with Romanians (a) having international connections, (b) potentially deviating from its ideological cant in general, and (c) constituting domestic opposition in particular, regardless of how it might have been expressed.[9] The adage "if you are not with us, you must be against us" served as the omnibus justification for what Romanian historian Adrian Cioflâncă called "the destruction of the classic distinction between the private and the public sphere, which in the Western world dates back from the Middle Ages" (Barberá, 2019, p. np).

The Securitate's direct attention to IAMCR's work is a possibility that is not, however, verified at this early stage of our examination of the thousands of pages of files of individuals who were its targets and/or informers. Aside from its penchant for monitoring citizens with international connections, the conceivable rationale for such tracking might have included self-protection from international scrutiny of the suppression of freedom of the press and speech, and/or furthering goals shared with sister communist regimes. For instance, did the Bucharest regime monitor Romanian members for their public stance regarding IAMCR's often stated calls for freedom of the press and speech, at times specifically naming a particular region of the world where it was suppressed, such as Latin America, but never mentioning the Soviet Bloc?[10] Were Romanian members and others from that bloc, together with their ideological cousins from Western countries, meant to assure the association's neutral stance regarding their own countries, which were some of the most egregious foes of both media and speech freedoms? Were these members also monitored to ascertain whether they ensured IAMCR's support for the New World Information and Communication Order (NWICO) that was of interest to the Communist Bloc and largely opposed by the United States (US) and its allies?[11]

[8] Legitimacy for its actions rested in the Romanian constitution of 1948 (modeled on the Soviet Union's constitution) and its two subsequent versions in 1952 and 1965. Romania's first communist constitution in 1948 (Article 29) specified that the freedoms provided for the country's citizens—speech, press, assembly, and demonstrations—could not be "exercised for purposes contrary to the socialist system and interests of employees." In the 1964 constitution, which announced that "socialism has won" and re-named the country a Socialist Republic, the wording was changed slightly to "against the socialist structure and the interests of those who work."

[9] Even jokes that were perceived as anti-regime/anti-communist could land you in jail. See Glăvan (2019).

[10] For example, see Halloran (1976).

[11] In the 1980s, a heated debate ensued in UNESCO over a NWICO proposed by the so-called non-aligned nations and supported by the communist states. The proposal focused on a more balanced approach to reporting on the so-called Third World and also curbing negative reports about these countries and their leaders. The US and others opposed the proposal on the grounds that it strongly hinted at control of the press/media and its contents and suppression of information that was critical of authoritarian/totalitarian regimes.

In line with the Securitate's modus operandi, Romanian academics who were contributors to and members of IAMCR were also among the targets of attempted and successful recruitment of informers.[12] Among their association colleagues were a large number of members from other communist countries. Their unchallenged primus inter pares during the 1960s–1980s was the Dean of the Faculty of Journalism at the Lomonosov Moscow State University, Yassen Zassoursky. An exceptional individual, highly educated, fluent in English, and apparently having carte blanche to travel all over the world—an unusual ability for Soviet citizens, even for academics—Zassoursky was also a long-serving Vice President of IAMCR. How many of the association's members from communist countries were their respective security services' agents or informers is unknown (see Chap. 19 in this volume). Joining them was a contingent of scholars from Western academic institutions, including true "fellow-travelers" from Western Europe and North America, some of whom were self-identified Marxists and may or may not have fully supported Soviet socialism.

What we have discovered to date about IAMCR's Romanian members mentioned above allows us only a preliminary glimpse into their activities and the reasons why the Securitate took an interest in them, and whether one or more were useful informers.

The Securitate's Targets

The four targets of interest to the Securitate had a mixed political background. Their interest in mass media and journalism had its roots in different disciplinary backgrounds, predominantly sociology. What they inevitably shared, given their involvement in an international organization and foreign contacts, was scrutiny by the Securitate.

Pavel Câmpeanu (1920–2003) and Ștefana Steriade (1924–)

Initially a Marxist who in the 1940s served a prison sentence for his activism in the same facility that also housed some of the most prominent future communist leaders of the country, Câmpeanu had distanced himself from the regime by the 1960s, becoming "an extremely important objective for the Securitate."[13] A sociologist and prolific author, he wrote a number of works on media, communication, and theater, and served as a pollster for the Office of Studies and Surveys of Romanian Television (Câmpeanu, 1972). He was the most active Romanian member of IAMCR, and the secret police paid special attention to this relationship. He was also an astute, uncompromising analyst of socialism and its Stalinist version in the manner of Yugoslavia's Milovan Djilas and

[12] For detailed expositions of the Securitate and its ubiquitous presence in the country, see Deletant (1995, 2001).

[13] See No Author (2009).

Poland's Leszek Kolakowski, both of them converts from communism whose seminal critiques of Marxism-Leninism continue to be relevant (Djilas, 1963, 1982; Kolakowski, 2005, 2008). Câmpeanu published a series of books in the US about Romanian communism.[14]

By the time the communist regime was overthrown in December 1989, the Securitate had amassed an impressive seven volumes (over 7000 pages) of reports on Câmpeanu, code named "Pavo," including documents and ancillary materials such as intercepted correspondence with foreign colleagues, some related to IAMCR (I—file nr. I-0064759). Consequently, the association is mentioned in Volumes 1, 2, and 4, which contain everything from informers' reports on Câmpeanu to copies of some of his correspondence with IAMCR presidents, for example with James D. Halloran (Folder nr. 215949 in Volume 2).

A "Plan of measures" against "Pavo," dated 30 June 1980, and drafted by the Ministry of Interior (Volume 1), was aimed at ascertaining whether he had made an agreement on behalf of Romanian Radio and Television to study public opinion in Romania with the then IAMCR President, James Halloran.[15] We found a subsequent letter (Volume 2) from Halloran written on 7 August 1980, congratulating Câmpeanu for having initiated an international research project under the flag of IAMCR and for "Pavo's" transmission of data regarding Romanian readers of the most important newspapers at that time (*Scînteia*, *România literară*, *Scînteia Tineretului*). In Câmpeanu's letter to Halloran, he mentions Nestor Ignat, Dean of the journalism faculty at the Ştefan Gheorghiu Academy and IAMCR member, being a "supporter" of a research project on news reporting about Ceauşescu's visits to several African countries.

The Securitate also intercepted another letter from Halloran to Câmpeanu, dated August 29, thanking him for information regarding the "study of images" that he, Halloran, handed over to Annabele Sreberny, who was to write a "first draft," presumably of an article or book chapter.[16] After Halloran informed "Pavo" of his election to the Executive Board (EB)/International Council (IC) of IAMCR in a 4 September 1980, letter, the latter responded on 26 September 1980, with a rather cryptic note that may or may not have increased the Securitate's interest in him and IAMCR:

> ... all of us work in different conditions to help our societies to not be dominatedby, but to dominate the flow of information, and in this way to use the modern techniques of communication not for the manipulation of, but for the democratic participation of every woman and man in the construction of better ways of life.

In Volume 4 (p. 274–276), a report on 2 June 1982, presents a transcript of a letter addressed to Câmpeanu by an "unidentified person in the Federal

[14] See Câmpeanu (1987, 1988).

[15] Câmpeanu worked at Romanian Radio and Television until 1980. We have not yet ascertained how and why he left.

[16] Sreberny was Professor Emeritus and former Director of the Centre for Media and Film Studies at the School of Oriental and African Studies, University of London.

Republic of Germany" in which IAMCR is obliquely mentioned: "I will ask Halloran [IAMCR president at that time] tomorrow to send you an official letter for the reunion in Paris ...." Another intercepted letter dated 18 August 1982 (Volume 4, p. 343), would have certainly caught the Securitate's interest. The letter to Câmpeanu from Ms. Beatrice Ernst (France) on behalf of the committee in charge of organizing the Mass-Media and Communications Congress in Paris from September 5 to 10, 1982, detailed the "reunion," and that:[17]

> The Congress will be presided by Mr. Francois Mitterand ... with the participation of the Minister of Communications, Culture and Research, as well as the Minister of Industry. Your reputation and your official position (within IAMCR) are very much appreciated by our international Forum. This is why we invite you to be in Paris on the 5th September. We also have the honor to announce ... you are invited as an elected representative of Romanian researchers.

As mentioned earlier, information about IAMCR member, Steriade, a sociologist and author of a number of articles and books, is included in Câmpeanu's file as she was his girlfriend, then wife, and one of his co-authors.[18] Moreover, they had relatives living in the US and Canada, and their daughter, Vera Câmpeanu, appears to have corresponded with unidentified individuals abroad and also facilitated her parents doing so via her connections in the Spanish Embassy in Bucharest. The embassy sent the Câmpeanus' correspondence in their diplomatic pouch (see Volume 6) and the couple is reported to have had foreign currency bank accounts, among other red flags that attracted the Securitate's attention. Details about what the Securitate compiled about Steriade and, specifically, if anything touched on her membership in IAMCR remain to be ascertained, as we have not read the entire contents of Câmpeanu's files.

Suffice it to say, "Pavo" and Steriade's involvement with IAMCR may have been the least of the Securitate's concerns, as it focused on a much more serious charge, in a report in Volume 3 of "Pavo's" file (p. 15, 2 February 1981). They were "suspected of espionage" for the US. In another 2 February 1981 (p. 18), entry, the Securitate reports on a meeting between Câmpeanu and French journalist Bernard Guetta, at which time he supposedly provided Guetta with information containing what the secret service considered denigrating aspects of the communist regime.

The same Volume 3 file lists "Pavo's" contacts, among them Professor F. Gerald Kline, Director of the School of Journalism at the University of Minnesota (US), and Jaques Rappaport, an attorney for the International Rescue Committee in New York, which the unnamed Securitate informer

[17] Câmpeanu had been elected the Romanian representative on IAMCR's Executive Board at the Caracas (Venezuela) Congress in August 1980.

[18] For example, see Steriade and Câmpeanu (1985).

considered to be a CIA cover and recruiter of Romanian immigrants in the US (9 February 1981, p. 15).

The Securitate informer who kept an eye on Câmpeanu was Gheorghe Magheru, code named "Ignat," according to the former's son, Gheorghe Câmpeanu.[19] Magheru joined the Ministry of Foreign Affairs in 1990 and had several prominent foreign postings. We have not yet found evidence of other informers directly focused on Câmpeanu, and it remains to be discovered whether IAMCR members George Ivaşcu and Paul Caravia acted in that role.

George Ivaşcu (1911–1988)

Ivaşcu has a two-volume Securitate file (I-258063). He was a Marxist journalist, literary critic, professor, and editor-in-chief of the most important Romanian literary magazine, *România Literară*. In addition, we found an R file (R-0001471) on him—an R file indicates that attempts were made to recruit him as an informer—focused on what the Securitate called "targets," but we have no evidence that he *officially* became a collaborator. From the Securitate's perspective, there was ample ammunition to closely monitor Ivaşcu's activities, doubt his "loyalty," and concurrently, to coerce him into collaborating. A report on 24 December 1972 (Volume 1), indicates that he met with the US cultural attaché at the time (p. 56) and US Ambassador Harry Barnes, Jr. (p. 58)—we assume he did so in his capacity as the editor of the prestigious *România Literară*—leading that particular Securitate report to conclude that Ivaşcu had "tendentious activity against the superior leadership of the [Romanian] state and the Communist Party."

Ivaşcu's past also made him suspect and gave the Securitate ample coercive powers over him. In the 1940s, he wrote for anti-Soviet newspapers, for example, *Soldatul*, *Santinela*, *Timpul*, and *Vremea*. According to an entry in his R file (R-0001471), Ivaşcu was asked to "rehabilitate himself" in the eyes of the Romanian Workers' Party/Partidul Muncitoresc Romîn (1948–1964), renamed in 1965 as the Romanian Communist Party.

The Securitate considered Ivaşcu an important potential recruit, listing a number of advantages that Ivaşcu had thanks to his connections abroad and how he "could become useful to our work," according to a third file labeled "External Information Service," a designation reserved for those who were followed specifically for their connections with foreigners in and outside Romania (File SIE 3874—microfilm, p. 39). Another entry in the same file (p. 28–29) indicates that the Securitate was planning to use a certain "Ionescu," presumably Ivaşcu, to help recruit one or two individuals to work in the Romanian section of the BBC. Whether he did so or not is unknown.

As yet, we have found no mention of Ivaşcu's contacts with IAMCR. Nonetheless, we do know that he was a member of the association, as

[19] See No Author (2009).

its President's (Jacques Bourquin) letter to the membership on 16 July 1970, indicates.[20]

Paul Caravia (1927–)

Paul Caravia had a history of fascist, Iron Guard, involvement in the 1940s and consequently, as his Securitate file (R-0243767) reports,

> In 1949, Mr. Caravia was condemned to 8 years in prison for fascist [Iron Guard] activity as part of the Youth Organization 'Axa' and afterwards as chief of the Legionnaire group from the Institute of Humanist Sciences in Bucharest … He regretted his actions and manifested the wish to rehabilitate.

Caravia also had a four-volume P file (P0015344), which is a "penal" or criminal file that we have not yet perused and may well be politically biased. His "rehabilitation" apparently reshaped him to become an informer and, subsequently, an agent of the Securitate, code named "Valentin Stănescu," as indicated by a notation in his file (R-0243767, p. 5), which signals a decision to "transfer the qualified informer 'Stănescu Valentin' to the category of Agents." In a letter to the Securitate on 5 November 1959, Caravia/Stănescu wrote that he wished to "repair my mistakes," presumably referring to his fascist past, and that he had decided "to continue working with Securitate organs" (R file, p. 16).

A sociologist and author of a number of books,[21] interested in the interdisciplinary study of communication, philosophy, and sociology, Caravia/Stănescu may, however, have been duplicitous, as a partial reading of his three-volume I file (I-R0243767) appears to suggest. He indeed may have been an informer/agent of the Securitate, or simply pretended to be. Concurrently, he may have been under surveillance until the end of the 1980s, given the implications of a 27 December 1985, entry in his file, penned by an informer or agent (it is not clear which), and noting,

> Caravia, scientific researcher, active member of this Commission [of Interdisciplinary Studies, Association of Scientists in Romania] has criticized the organization and the conduct of the scientific activity in our country but praised the Western society and especially the United States. He is thus offending the leadership of the Romanian Communist Party.

Whether Caravia informed on Câmpeanu or on any of the other Romanian IAMCR members, or the work of the association, is not substantiated by our limited exploration of his file.

[20] See Bourquin (1970).

[21] For example, Caravia (1999, 2000).

Conclusion

As we continue to read the thousands of pages in the files that we have identified, we take to heart Lavinia Stan's reminder that:

> the totality of repression in communist Romania was greater than the sum of individual cases the Securitate worked on ... Reading the Securitate files today cannot be done without contextualizing the information and remembering the wooden language the communist regimes used to give a veneer of legitimacy to their most atrocious human rights violations. (Stan, 2005)

The enormity of proof of these human rights violations leaves no doubt about the repressive authoritarian/totalitarian nature of the Marxist-Leninist regime. The examination to date of the three sets of files of Romanian IAMCR members demonstrates, at the very least, the Securitate's attention to their contributions, relationships, as well as potential usefulness to the secret police. By extension, IAMCR received considerable attention from the Securitate, at least in relation to Pavel Câmpeanu's involvement with the association.

This reminds us of the vulnerabilities of Romanian academics and intellectuals during the ever-present potential and real continuous scrutiny of their words, actions, and even thoughts, and also of their diverse value-driven responses to it during the communist regime. Their story—alongside those who collaborated, or feigned collaboration, with the Securitate—provides small suggestive glimpses into the psycho-social make-up of the nation's intellectuals and academics. In turn, this may explain, further contextualize, and add nuances to the thesis of the Romanians' "passivity" or "inertia" and their "quasi-cooperative relationship" with the communist regime, and to the occasional overt individual acts of resistance.

Other Securitate targets, and the informers who zeroed in on the association and its Romanian members, may also exist, and remain to be discovered. Moreover, still to be ascertained is if the Securitate had a direct interest in the association, seeking to influence its official position on certain matters of interest to Romania and/or to the Soviet Union or to the Soviet Bloc in general.

Completing the study will also necessitate reading the academic contributions made to IAMCR by its Romanian members to get a sense of their analysis of topics pertinent to the association and to the field of journalism/mass media; and, thus, also to those who might have attracted the attention of the Securitate, or contributed to meeting the exigencies of the Communist Party it served.

Finally, regardless of the nature and extent of the Securitate's attention to IAMCR members and possibly directly to the association, this is more than just a story about the actions of a communist secret service or the nature of socialist regimes, which is amply recorded and analyzed in myriads of studies. It is, above all else, a story about victims of communism, among them those who were coerced into being informers but never delivered on their "assignments."

Their story deserves to be told, as does the chronicle of the loyal informers and agents who were part of the oppressive machinery of Romania's Stalinist version of authoritarian Marxism-Leninism and its added cult of personality.

References

Bagieński, W. (2020). The Polish People's republic and the KGB intelligence cooperation after 1956. *Securitas Imperii, 37*(2), 70–84.

Barberá, M. G. (2019, December 25). Mikes, spies—How the Securitate stole Romania's privacy. *Balkan Insight*. Retrieved 15 June 2022, from https://balkaninsight.com/2019/12/25/keys-mikes-spies-how-the-securitate-stole-romanias-privacy/

Betea, L., Diac, C., Mihai, F.-R., & Tiu, I. (2009). *21 August 1968: Apoteoza lui Ceaușescu*. [Ceaușescu's Apotheosis]. Polirom.

Bottoni, S. (2017). Finding the enemy ethnicized state violence and population control in Ceausescu's Romania. *Journal of Cold War Studies, 19*(4), 113–136.

Bourquin, J. (1970, July 16). Letter to IAMCR members. Retrieved 15 June 2022, from https://iamcr.org/node/10510

Câmpeanu, P. (1972). *Radio, televiziune, public*. Editura Științifică.

Câmpeanu, P. (1987). *The origins of Stalinism. From Leninist revolution to Stalinism*. Routledge.

Câmpeanu, P. (1988). *The genesis of the Stalinist social order*. M. E. Sharpe.

Caravia, P. (1999). *Biserica Întemnițată: România, 1944–1989* [The Imprisoned Church: Romania, 1944–1989]. *Bucharest Institutul Național Pentru Studiul Totalitarismului*.

Caravia, P. (2000). *Gândirea interzisă; scrieri cenzurate, România, 1945—1989 [Forbidden thinking; censored writing, Romania, 1945–1989]*. Bucharest, Ed. Enciclopedică.

Consiliul Național pentru Studierea Ahivelor Securității. (2003). *Bande, bandiți și eroi. Grupurile de rezistență și Securitatea (1948–1968)*. Editura Enciclopedică.

Deletant, D. (1995). *Ceausescu and the securitate: Coercion and dissent in Romania, 1965–1989*. Routledge.

Deletant, D. (2001). *The securitate legacy in Romania: Security intelligence services in new democracies. Studies in Russia and East Europe*. Palgrave Macmillan.

Djilas, M. (1963). *Conversation with Stalin*. Harcourt Brace.

Djilas, M. (1982). *New class: Analysis of the communist system*. Mariner Books.

Glăvan, G. (2019). The life and times of Ceaușescu jokes. *Metacritic Journal for Comparative Studies and Theory, 5*(1), pp. 157–176. Retrieved 15 June 2022, from https://doi.org/10.24193/mjcst.2019.7.09.

Halloran, J. D. (1976, December). Letter to IAMCR members. Retrieved 15 June 2022, from https://iamcr.org/node/10510

Herbstritt, G. (2016). *Entzweite Freunde. Rumänien, die Securitate und die DDR Staatssicherheit 1950 bis 1989*. Vandenhoeck & Ruprecht.

Kolakowski, L. (2005). *My correct views on everything*. St. Augustine Press.

Kolakowski, L. (2008). *Main currents of Marxism: The founders—The golden age—The breakdown*. Norton & Company.

Metaxioti, J. (2021, February 4). The political status and policing: Ceaușescu's 'little spies'. *Balkans in-Site*. Retrieved 15 June 2022, from https://balkansinsite.pollsandpolitics.gr/the-political-status-and-policing-ceausescus-little-spies/

Miroiu, M. (2010). Wiping out 'the bandits': Romanian counterinsurgency strategies in the early communist period 1. *The Journal of Slavic Military Studies, 23*(4), 683–684.

Mudde, C., & Kaltwasser, C. R. (2017). *Populism: A very short introduction*. Oxford University Press.

Nehring, C. (2021). Active and sharp seizures: Cooperation between the soviet KGB and Bulgarian state security. *Journal of Cold War Studies, 23*(4), 3–33.

No Author. (2009, 9 June). Pavel Câmpeanu şi Securitatea. *Revista 22*. Retrieved 15 June 2022, from https://revista22.ro/dosar/pavel-campeanu-351i-securitatea

Pelin, M. (2003). *Un veac de spionaj, Contraspionaj Şi poliţie politica [A century of espionage, counterespionage and political police]*. Editura Elion.

Roper, S. D. (2000). *Romania: The unfinished revolution*. Routledge.

Smith, C. S. (2006, December 12). Eastern Europe struggles to purge security services. *The New York Times*. Retrieved 15 June 2022, from https://www.nytimes.com/2006/12/12/world/europe/12spooks.html

Socor, V. (1987, 4 December). *The workers' protest in Braşov: Assessment and aftermath* (p. 3–10). Romania Background Report 231, Radio Free Europe Research. Retrieved 15 June 2022, from https://www.europeana.eu/en/item/2022062/10891_osa_a6cd05be_b72b_425e_ad72_869a570e6d26

Stan, L. (2005, March 4). *Inside the securitate archives*. Wilson Center. Retrieved 15 June 2022, from https://www.wilsoncenter.org/article/inside-the-securitate-archives

Steriade, S., & Câmpeanu, P. (1985). *Oamenii și filmul. O privire sociologică asupra spectatorului de film*. Meridiane.

Tismaneanu, V. (2003). *Stalinism for all seasons: A political history of Romanian communism*. University of California Press.

Troncota, C. (2003). *Duplicitarii. O Istorie a Serviciilor de Informaţii Şi Securitate ale regimului communist din România/ The Dublicitous. A history of Communist Romanian intelligence*. Editura Elion.

Vasile, C. (2009). Propaganda and culture in Romania at the beginning of the communist regime. In V. Tismaneanu (Ed.), *Stalinism revisited. The establishment of communist regimes in east-Central Europe* (p. 367–385). Central European University Press.

CHAPTER 14

The MacBride Report: Critical Scholarship and the Report's Value to Future Generations

Andrew Calabrese and Robin Mansell

Introduction

The 1980 report of UNESCO's[1] International Commission for the Study of Communication Problems, *Many Voices, One World*, more commonly known as "The MacBride Report," was written in a much different global context than we witness today (MacBride, 1980).[2] At that time, the Cold War had a pronounced influence on geopolitical alliances, and the choice to be "non-aligned" was in reference to this great polarity. The aspiration of the authors of the report was to ensure that "communication," or what would come to be labeled the "information society," would develop in the interests of all the world's people. *Many Voices, One World* was the culmination of years of debate over the need to foster a new world information and communication

[1] United Nations Educational, Scientific and Cultural Organization.

[2] An earlier version of this statement was published by each of the authors of this chapter in *Quaderns del CAC*, Vol. 21, 2005, the journal of the Catalonian Broadcasting Council. For a contemporary review, see Nordenstreng and Somavia (2021). The authors thank Kaarle Nordenstreng for his earlier comments on this chapter.

A. Calabrese
University of Colorado, Boulder, CO, USA
e-mail: andrew.calabrese@colorado.edu

R. Mansell (✉)
London School of Economics and Political Science, London, UK
e-mail: r.e.mansell@lse.ac.uk

© The Author(s), under exclusive license to Springer Nature Switzerland AG 2023

J. Becker, R. Mansell (eds.), *Reflections on the International Association for Media and Communication Research*,
https://doi.org/10.1007/978-3-031-16383-8_14

order (NWICO) (Nordenstreng, 1994).[3] Contributions to the Commission's deliberations from 1977 to 1979 came from multiple scholars, including those affiliated with IAMCR. Francis Balle (International Council), James D. Halloran (President), Fernando Reyes Matta, and Yassen Zassoursky (Vice President) served as collaborating consultants. More than a dozen other IAMCR members, in addition to the consultants, contributed background papers, including Luis Ramiro Beltrán, Margaret Gallagher, Cees Hamelink, Ullamaija Kivikuru, Tomo Martelanc, Giuseppi Richeri, Herbert I. Schiller, and Tamàs Szecskö.[4]

Critical and Problem-Oriented Research

In his background paper, Halloran (1978, p. 1) emphasized that much media and communication research had generated unbalanced insight into processes and values: "we have more analyses and interpretations from certain value positions than from others." This led to invalid generalizations arising from "value free, positivistic, behaviouristic approaches" (p. 4), and he argued that this needed to be challenged. He called for a "critical, problem and policy-oriented" (p. 5) research approach that would treat communication as a contextualized social process structured in a wide variety of ways and conditioned by power relations that tend to "legitimate and reinforce the existing system and the established order" (p. 12). Halloran acknowledged the risks for researchers in proceeding in this way: "those who lifted the cloak with their research are now attacked by those who so obviously benefited from the silence" (p. 15).

Hamelink (1978, p. 2) noted in his background paper that establishing a NWICO would "demand a fundamental replacement of the stereotyped, alienating and discriminatory sets of ideas that current communications structures perpetuate." He stressed that the communication-industrial complex's control of financial capital, technology, and marketing would have to change and that this would require much more than attention to the flows of information. It would require "drastic changes" in the economic order, which, in turn, would necessitate respect for sovereignty and global interdependence based on equality, rather than on hierarchy.

[3] In 1968, UNESCO's General Assembly called for a work program "to promote and undertake studies and research on the role, and present state and effects of the media of mass communication in modern society" (quoted in Nordenstreng, 1994, p. 3). This led to a series of meetings of experts on mass communication which would involve Luis Beltrán, S. O. Biobaku, Nabil Dajani, James D. Halloran, Tomo Martelanc, Elisabeth Noelle-Neumann, Kaarle Nordenstreng, Walery Pisarek, and Dallas Smythe, among others active in IAMCR.

[4] MacBride Report Background papers are available at https://unesdoc.unesco.org/ark:/48223/pf0000375643?3=null&queryId=N-EXPLORE-f9c4e4b0-542c-4626-9fb2-ddbabd3aa7d0. Accessed June 15, 2022. An account of deliberations of the Commission is provided by Harley (1992).

Critical assessments by IAMCR scholars and others of the then prevailing media and communication order were echoed by Seán MacBride in his speeches prior to the finalization of the MacBride Report. In 1979, for example, he told the International Telecommunication Union's World Administrative Radio Conference that "the process of decolonization means that the distribution of resources and powers has to change" (p. 2), noting that "people are striving for more justice and aiming to strengthen their independence" (p. 2). He also cautioned that there was no unanimity as to which specific changes would be needed to give rise to a new world communication order.

In the MacBride Report itself, considerable emphasis was placed on the "communication process" as a means of diffusing power and reducing inequalities. The future information and communication environment was envisaged with considerable prescience when it was argued that—

> ... the basic decisions in order to forge a better future for men and women in communities everywhere, in developing as well as in developed nations, do not lie principally in the field of technological development: *they lie essentially in the answers each society gives to the conceptual and political foundations of development* (emphasis added). (p. 12–13)

Crucially, the report stressed the need to address deeper problems within the development process. In the language of the late 1970s, major problems and worrying trends included the potential for the spread of cultural domination, resulting from one-way or vertical flows of information and communication, the intensification of the "industrialization of communication," and the discriminatory outcomes of the dominance of markets by the private sector. It was acknowledged that "the subjects of imbalance and domination were among the most contentious in the early rounds of the world-wide debate on communications" (p. 164). To counter imbalances, the report acknowledged the "... need for the development of critical forms of education ... and the fostering of people's ability to choose more discriminatingly between the different products of the communication process" (p. 29). It was noted that a huge effort would be needed to counter imbalances. The MacBride Report identified numerous issues, among them finance. This was one of a triad of crucial issues that would need to be resolved to correct imbalances in the costs of access, when communication prices disadvantage poorer regions or countries and work against inclusivity. The report also noted inequity in the allocation of the radio frequency spectrum—a resource that it argued required fair treatment in order to foster participation in the communicative environment by all.

The NWICO was envisaged as "... an open-ended conceptual framework" which pre-supposed a new distribution of resources in line with the rights and needs of the poor. This was highlighted in the report's subtitle—"Towards a new, more just and more efficient world information and communication order." The report was prescient in writing about something akin to the internet: "… it is feasible to envisage … a web of communication networks, integrating autonomous or semi-autonomous, decentralized units" (p. 12). It observed that the development of new computerized networks would lead to the embedding of values of hierarchy, centralization, and increased control, and be accompanied by growing inequalities, unless steps were taken to avert this outcome. The MacBride Report's authors placed their hope in the mobilization of efforts to tackle and resist pressures coming from the United States (US) and other wealthy countries to do little or nothing to alleviate the inequalities and exclusions perpetuated by the development of a communication infrastructure that would reward some, but certainly not all.

Ideological Contestations

The MacBride Report, and the call for a NWICO that followed, precipitated the decision by the US government to withdraw its membership from UNESCO. In a letter dated 28 December 1983, from the Reagan administration Secretary of State George Schultz to UNESCO Director-General Amadou-Mahtar M'Bow, the reasons for the US withdrawal were given. Equal emphasis was placed on issues of mismanagement and "the injection of political goals beyond the scope of the cooperative enterprise" (Schultz, 1984, p. 84). What was clear to all involved was that the decision served big media and telecommunication industry interests in the US. Stating that the US government, "along with the American people generally" (p. 82), believe in UNESCO's constitution, Schultz wrote that "We plan to use the resources we presently devote to UNESCO to support such other means of cooperation" (p. 84). A key intended effect of withdrawal was to undermine the legitimacy of multilateral principles of global media governance and cultural policy that were not guided by market principles that serve big media interests.

The underlying ideological position of the US decision to withdraw from UNESCO was one that would be sustained for many years in both the government's domestic and foreign media and cultural policy. In a 1983 speech by Mark Fowler, Chairman of the Federal Communications Commission during the Reagan administration, he referred to television as "a toaster with pictures." Fowler's point was that culture in general, including the media, should be given no special consideration or treatment by governments in comparison with other areas of commerce (Mayer, 1983). The logic behind this view is that governments should play no role in the shaping or nurturing of culture, other than to enable profit-seeking global media corporations to thrive, and that is the premise of a "marketplace" approach to cultural policy. Of course, it is not true that a government that responds to big corporate interests is one that necessarily favors a free and competitive marketplace. The US withdrawal from UNESCO was the full expression of a government that actively aimed to shape markets in ways that favored its own media industry's interests.

Despite the resistance by many countries to submit cultural practices to the discipline of market or (neo)liberal trade and investment policies, the US has relentlessly pursued a foreign media policy that aims precisely at that outcome (Calabrese & Redal, 1995). And since the US government could not control the outcomes of UNESCO recommendations, it made sense to do as Secretary of State George Schultz stated, which was to pursue "other means of cooperation." Schultz may not have anticipated the exact ways in which such cooperation would be achieved, but US efforts to undermine the cultural influence of UNESCO and to elevate the economic influence of the World Trade Organization (WTO) are clear evidence of a single-minded trajectory in US foreign media policy since the time of the US withdrawal. That trajectory has aimed to destroy the effectiveness and legitimacy of multilateral agreements and institutions that the US cannot control.

The decision by the US to rejoin UNESCO in 2003 during the administration of George W. Bush was no surprise. After the US withdrawal in 1984, United Nations (UN) leaders worked assiduously to attract the US back into the fold, even to the point of turning away from the organization's own past. Thérèse Paquet-Sévigny, UN Under-Secretary-General for Information in 1990, clearly articulated an anti-NWICO position that was consistent with US policy and official ideology

> Over many years, the international debate on information and communication did not result in agreement on a common approach. I wish only to refer to some of the discussions, for instance, on concepts of a new world information order, which in the eyes of many actors in the field of communication have harmed international efforts to construct a world-wide information society. (Paquet-Sévigny, quoted in Roach, 1997, p. 116)

The path to "a world-wide information society" was not and is not something that has had to be constructed in a particular way, as this statement implies. Rather, UNESCO's leadership following M'Bow, under Director-General Federico Mayor Zaragoza (1987–1999), tended to subordinate that organization's past pretenses to moral leadership to a pattern of appeasement and conciliation and, in the process, they embraced the official US vision of what a global information society should look like.

For the US government, and for the governments of other affluent countries, the political task for the future became one of engineering the "creative destruction" of social-democratic welfare states and redirecting national policy efforts to build a neoliberal global information society (Calabrese, 1997, 1999). These efforts were based on an intellectual shift in economic thought from Keynes to Hayek during the Thatcher and Reagan eras. UNESCO conformed to that agenda by embracing, or at least not significantly opposing, a pro-WTO ideological framework as far as the idea of the global information society is concerned. Within this framework, and notwithstanding the touted Convention on Cultural Diversity that defied the WTO by affirming the idea of a "cultural exception," UNESCO lost much of its former relevance as a forum for democratic deliberation about global cultural policy (Calabrese, 2008).

Despite the overwhelming success enjoyed by US-based big media interests in neutralizing UNESCO's threat to neoliberal cultural norms, to the point that rejoining gave the US powerful insider status, the country again formally withdrew from the organization in January 2019, during the Presidency of Donald Trump. The 2019 withdrawal was in compliance with a US law that prohibits the country's membership in any UN agency that formally recognizes the sovereignty of a Palestinian state. However, it was in 2011, in response to UNESCO's formal recognition of Palestine, that the Obama administration ceased membership payments to UNESCO. In other words, Trump's decision to withdraw from UNESCO was not a contradiction of Obama's policy toward that organization, but rather it was consistent with the Obama administration's own refusal to recognize a Palestinian state (Calabrese & Barnes, in press). The history of the thorny US relationship with UNESCO since the Reagan era is intimately connected with the country's foreign policy toward Israel and Palestine, and cannot be explained solely as a matter of the pursuit of US media industry interests. Nevertheless, these dual agendas—US foreign policy with respect to Israel and Palestine, and the business interests of US-based media corporations—have complemented one another through the exercise of US soft power to defy the cultural policy interests of the majority of the countries of the world by asserting its ideological and economic hegemony.

Today, modern media and telecommunication infrastructures have made possible a new global market system and a new context for the spread of political, economic, and cultural ideas. Emerging with these new powers have come visions of how to eliminate global poverty and secure greater capacity for citizens of the world to bear witness to and fight against violations of human rights, wherever they may happen. This was evident in the UN General Assembly's "Millennium Development Goals," first announced in 2000, and in the efforts to pursue these goals through various international agencies and forums, including the World Summit on the Information Society (WSIS). With UNESCO no longer at the center of global cultural policy discourse, the WSIS became the site of noteworthy struggles to develop democratic principles of global media and cultural governance. The WSIS, which held its first phase in Geneva in 2003 and a second in Tunis in 2005, represented for many people throughout the world, particularly in the Global South, new hope for making important progress in articulating global norms and related policies in the area of communication rights (see also Chaps. 16 and 17). The 2003 WSIS produced a Declaration which began with a "Common Vision of the Information Society." This stressed information and knowledge rather than the communication process, but there were many echoes of the language of the MacBride Report:

> … common desire and commitment to build a people-centred, inclusive and development-oriented Information Society, where everyone can create, access, utilize and share information and knowledge, enabling individuals, communities and peoples to achieve their full potential in promoting their sustainable development and improving their quality of life, premised on the purposes and principles

of the Charter of the United Nations and respecting fully and upholding the Universal Declaration of Human Rights. (WSIS, 2003b, p. np)

The WSIS process enabled broadened participation and this was represented as the voice of "civil society"—that part of social life that is often distinguished from the state and the corporate sector—in the generation of a worldwide public discourse about the future of communication rights and the global policies that are needed to secure them. Of course, there are grounds for disagreement about how unified the voice of "civil society" was then or is now, given the broad range of issues that were brought to the WSIS under the banner of that idea (Calabrese, 2004). These issues included the communication rights of indigenous groups, workers, women, children, and persons with disabilities; intellectual property; community media; open source software; access to information and the means of communication; and global citizenship (WSIS, 2003a). Nevertheless, activism centered on the WSIS made it clear that there was considerable political will to establish and maintain an effective presence to represent "civil society" in a process that was ostensibly opened to multiple stakeholders. The grassroots activism that converged on the WSIS was a moment in which the progressive spirit of the MacBride Commission was made more democratic and multilateral.

Conclusion

Much has changed since the MacBride Report was published, not only in global politics, but also in the institutions and practices of global communication. A powerful challenge to the hopeful recommendations of that report and of the WSIS has come in the form of perilous uses of new means of communication by radical right-wing populist forces to violate the dignity and humanity of others by way of public deception, economic exploitation, political surveillance and repression, and other abuses of power. The litany of ways that social media are now used to undermine democratic institutions and principles, and to advance fascist tendencies, is all too familiar. In addition, just as the MacBride Report had called for measures to foster international cooperation, encourage partnerships for development, and put international mechanisms, including finance mechanisms, in place to achieve its goals, the WSIS called for a "digital solidarity agenda" which would include the establishment of financing mechanisms and the mobilization of funding to support efforts to reduce inequalities. Little progress was made insofar as the vast share of responsibility for major initiatives continues to default to countries and regions that are at risk of the greatest disadvantage. Challenges in the areas of finance and governance continue to be deeply rooted, and they persist in generating conflict between those seeking to profit from the means of communication and those seeking to promote world poverty reduction and a communication environment that fosters human dignity and respect.

Nevertheless, with all of its flaws, for which progressive communication activists (including the scholars who were active in IAMCR at the time) understandably have distanced themselves since the time of its publication (Hamelink, 1980; Mansell & Nordenstreng, 2006), the MacBride Report projects a spirit of hopefulness about how a better world is possible, about the continued importance of public institutions as means to ensure global justice at local, national, and transnational levels, and about the value of global communication as a means to generate knowledge, understanding, and mutual respect. Despite the report's flaws, its authors had the optimism of the will to advocate for a kind of globalization that values our common humanity. For these reasons, the historical significance of the MacBride Report should be reconsidered and perhaps even celebrated by current and future generations of communication activists.

References

Calabrese, A. (1997). Creative destruction? From the welfare state to the global information society. *Javnost—The Public, 4*(4), 7–24.

Calabrese, A. (1999). Communication and the end of sovereignty? *Info: The Journal of Policy, Regulation, and Strategy for Telecommunications, Information, and Media, 1*(4), 313–326.

Calabrese, A. (2004). The promise of civil society: A global movement for communication rights. *Continuum: Journal of Media and Cultural Studies, 18*(3), 317–329.

Calabrese, A. (2008). UNESCO. In W. Donsbach (Ed.), *International encyclopedia of communication* (p. np). Blackwell Reference Online, Blackwell Publishing.

Calabrese, A., & Barnes, C. (in press). UNESCO. Oxford Bibliographies Online.

Calabrese, A., & Redal, W. (1995). Is there a US foreign policy in telecommunications? Transatlantic trade policy as a case study. *Telematics & Informatics, 12*(1), 35–56.

Halloran, J. D. (1978). *The context of mass communication research*. MacBride Commission Working Paper No. 78. UNESCO.

Hamelink, C. (1978). *The new international economic order and the new international information order*. MacBride Commission Working Paper No. 34. UNESCO.

Hamelink, C. (Ed.). (1980). *Communication in the eighties: A reader on the "MacBride Report"*. IDOC International. Reprinted in Whitney, C., Wartella, E., & Windahl, S. (Eds.). (1982). *Mass Communication Review Yearbook, 3*, p. 241–249. Sage.

Harley, W. G. (1992). *Creative compromise: The MacBride Commission—A firsthand report and reflection on the workings of UNESCO's International Commission for the Study of Communication Problems*. University Press of America.

MacBride, S. (1979). *Shaping a new world information order (Address to the "Forum 1979")*. International Telecommunication Union, World Administrative Radio Conference.

MacBride, S., & Commissioners. (1980). *Communication and society today and tomorrow: Many voices, one world: Towards a new, more just, and more efficient world information and communication order*. Kogan Page, Unipub, UNESCO. (Reprinted by Kogan Page, 1981 and Rowman & Littlefield Publishers, 2004).

Mansell, R., & Nordenstreng, K. (2006). Great media and communications debates: WSIS and the MacBride report. *Information Technologies and International Development, 3*(4), 15–36.

Mayer, C. E. (1983, February 6). FCC chief's fears: Fowler sees threat in regulation. *Washington Post*, p. K1.

Nordenstreng, K. (1994). The UNESCO expert panel with the benefit of hindsight. In C. Hamelink & O. Linné (Eds.), *Mass communication research: On problems and policies—The art of asking the right questions—In honor of James D. Halloran* (p. 3–19). Ablex Publishing.

Nordenstreng, K., & Somavia, J. (2021). Revisiting 45 years of history in communication policies. *Media Development, 67*(2), 5–10.

Roach, C. (1997). The Western world and the NWICO. In P. Golding & P. Harris (Eds.), *Beyond cultural imperialism: Globalization, communication & the new international order* (p. 94–116). Sage.

Schultz, G. (1984). Letter from US Secretary of State George Schultz to UNESCO Director-General Amadou-Mahtar M'Bow, announcing the decision of the US government to withdraw its membership from UNESCO (1983, December 28). *Journal of Communication, 34*(4), 82, 84.

WSIS. (2003a, December 8). *Shaping information Societies for human needs. Civil society declaration to the World Summit on the Information Society* (Plenary). World Summit on the Information Society. Retrieved 15 June 2022, from https://www.itu.int/net/wsis/docs/geneva/civil-society-declaration.pdf

WSIS. (2003b, December 12). *Declaration of principles—Building the information society: A global challenge in the new millennium* (Report). World Summit on the Information Society. Retrieved 15 June 2022, from http://www.itu.int/dms_pub/itu-s/md/03/wsis/doc/S03-WSIS-DOC-0004!!PDF-E.pdf

CHAPTER 15

The MacBride Round Tables: In Pursuit of Equality, Plurality, and Diversity

Philip Lee

Introduction

The MacBride Round Tables were civil society's attempt to explore and develop the idea that a rights-based approach to global communications and mass media could challenge the hegemony of governments and corporate interests in a post-colonial world where political and economic structures favored the Global North over the Global South. This chapter records their progress and outlines their impact on subsequent debates in the field of communication rights.

After UNESCO was established in 1945 against a background of international politics reeling from the effects of wartime propaganda and the very beginnings of the Cold War, the role of mass communication in shaping public opinion was seen to be crucial to the pursuit of future peace and security. In this context, freedom of expression and information (soon to find its zenith in Article 19 of the Universal Declaration of Human Rights), international news flows, and the professional training of journalists began to receive the attention of media experts, newspaper editors, and publishers. "Accordingly, IAMCR grew out of a rapidly developing media field, particularly with respect to journalism, which created its own branch of institutional interests and a need for

P. Lee (✉)
World Association for Christian Communication, Toronto, ON, Canada
e-mail: PL@waccglobal.org

© The Author(s), under exclusive license to Springer Nature Switzerland AG 2023

J. Becker, R. Mansell (eds.), *Reflections on the International Association for Media and Communication Research*,
https://doi.org/10.1007/978-3-031-16383-8_15

professional education as well as for scientific research" (Hamelink & Nordenstreng, 2020, p. 16).

It was entirely fitting, therefore, that in 1976, barely 20 years after its foundation, IAMCR should take a keen interest when UNESCO's General Conference instructed its Director General, Amadou-Mahtar M'Bow, to undertake "a review of all the problems of communication in contemporary society seen against the background of technological progress and recent developments in international relations with due regard to their complexity and magnitude" (MacBride, 1980, p. xiv). One of IAMCR's early vice presidents and members of its Executive Committee, Bogdan Osolnik, served on what later became known as the MacBride Commission (see also Chap. 14).

M'Bow created what he called a "brains trust," an international commission of 15 prominent figures from 15 different countries and backgrounds under the presidency of the Irish statesman Seán MacBride. In the course of its work, they participated in numerous conferences, meetings, seminars, and discussion groups, and reviewed countless documents, codes of ethics, and papers on different aspects of communication. The outcome, published in 1980, was the report *Many Voices, One World*, whose slogan was "Towards a new more just and more efficient world information and communication order."

Seán MacBride was a keynote speaker at a consultation sponsored by the World Association for Christian Communication (WACC) held in London in October 1982 titled "A new Babel: The communication revolution." He underlined one of the conclusions of the UNESCO report, that they were "founded on the firm conviction that communication is a basic individual right, as well as a collective one required by all communities and nations. Freedom of information—and more specifically the right to seek, to receive and impart information—is a fundamental human right; indeed, a prerequisite for many others" (MacBride, 1980, p. 253).

Controversy and misunderstanding followed the publication of the MacBride Report, especially from powerful countries ideologically against democratization and empowerment. Robin Mansell and Kaarle Nordenstreng have pointed out that the report, which championed what became known as a New World Information and Communication Order (NWICO), was less a challenge to information ownership and control than to the political and economic hegemony of a few powerful countries

> The work of the MacBride commissioners was not primarily a scientific exercise to discover the worldwide state of media and communication; it was first and foremost designed to be a political stocktaking of the socioeconomic forces influencing the contemporary media and communication field... The MacBride Report, combined with recent work on the determinants of inequality in information societies, provides a foundation for essential future work on the politics of the media and communication globally, and on the prospects for equitable evolution of information societies. (Mansell & Nordenstreng, 2006, p. 21)

In a later article, Nordenstreng summarized—

> NWICO was attacked as a curb on media freedom, whereas in reality the concept was designed to widen and deepen the freedom of information by increasing its balance and diversity on a global scale. For its initiators, NWICO was an idealistic instrument of diplomacy, and Third World dictators did not need it as an excuse for suppressing media. The anti-NWICO campaign was an ideologically apologetic exercise by private media proprietors, and it became effective only because of the extraordinary power with which it was waged. (Nordenstreng, 2013, p. 350)

In retrospect, it is clear that the MacBride Report, the NWICO, and the MacBride Round Tables provided a framework for civil society organizations to coalesce around the notion of the right to communicate proposed by the French lawyer Jean D'Arcy in 1969 and itself submitted for consideration by the MacBride Commission (Dakroury et al., 2009, p. 21–41).

The Ten MacBride Round Tables (1989 to 1998)

Following the forcible removal of the MacBride Report from international agendas, civil society pursued the debate by establishing the MacBride Round Table on Communication, whose purpose according to its draft statute was—

> To promote the development of international communication towards a new world information and communication order, and to promote the acceptance of the Right to Communicate as a basic Human Right in society, and to promote a grass-roots campaign on behalf of the right to communicate. (personal records)

The Round Table met annually for ten years—Harare (1989), Prague (1990), Istanbul (1991), São Paulo (1992), Dublin (1993), Honolulu (1994), Tunis (1995), Seoul (1996), Boulder (1997), and Amman (1998). Thirty-three communication professionals and specialists from 14 countries and 18 non-governmental organizations (NGOs) participated in the first Round Table (1989), whose concluding statement underlined—

> the fact that ten years after its publication it is now clear that the debate over NWICO was not over one single issue but was indeed related to the entire structure of world communication resources. It included such vital areas as international law, telecommunications, international trade and tariffs, transnational data flow, intellectual and artistic property rights, and the individual's right to privacy. (Vincent et al., 1999, p. 316)

In addition, Zimbabwean participants made recommendations to encourage the free flow of information and news in what were then referred to as "Third World" countries. In addition, a United States (US) working group called for media monitoring and content analysis of news coverage, as well as direct access to world news from a non-US perspective, and issued three statements of concern respectively about Namibia, South Africa, and Palestine.

The second Round Table (1990) discussed current and future communication problems in the light of changes that had recently occurred in international relations and in the social lives of many individual countries. It was attended by 30 communication professionals and academics from 20 countries representing 19 international and regional organizations or institutions. Attendees recommended continued mobilization of public opinion about the negative effects of global imbalances in communication flows; the need for improvements in South–South communication; promotion of the right to communicate as one of the fundamental principles of a democratic order; and systematic monitoring of media coverage of events and issues relating to peace, development, and other global problems. Significantly, the Round Table also recognized the under-representation of women in the field of communications, whose "voices have not been sufficiently heard in the movement for a NWICO" (Vincent et al., 1999, p. 322).

The third Round Table (Istanbul, 1991) met at the end of a Conference on "News Media and International Conflict" convened by IAMCR and the Turkish Communication Research Association (ILAD), which commissioned a special issue of the international journal *Media Development* on "Reporting the Gulf War" (IAMCR & ILAD, 1991). The Round Table itself saw 30 participants from 14 different countries and 18 NGOs focus on growing concerns around the rapidly increasing concentration, homogenization, commercialization, and militarization of national and world cultures. The gathering called for the building of—

> new people's coalitions and constituencies that can help regain a significant measure of participation in cultural policy-making… [including]… a broad range of public groups, social movements, and organisations. They should enlist media professionals, citizen activists, consumer groups, women's minorities, religious, labour, environmental and other organisations in the new cultural struggle. (Vincent et al., 1999, p. 324)

The fourth Round Table (Guarujá, 1992) saw a larger group of 53 participants from 22 different countries representing 32 universities and 15 professional/media organizations. This was mainly because the Round Table took place in the context of the biennial conference of IAMCR and the then recent Earth Summit held in Rio de Janeiro. Participants focused on the state of public communication and the role policymakers and media workers could play in relation to peace and international understanding; the UNESCO-proclaimed Decade of Culture; civil society and social movements; imbalances in information technology and ways to harness information technology to the benefit of ordinary people; and women and communications. In the latter respect, the Round Table drew specific attention to—

> the possibility of gender discrimination built into the very conceptualisation, the hierarchical structure and binary logic of informatics, felt to be laden with gender-specific values, [and] a critique of information technology built upon a larger epistemological critique of the enlightenment notions of progress and rationality embodied in science and technology. (Vincent et al., 1999, p. 329)

The fifth Round Table (Dublin, 1993) was largely concerned with discussing what shape and direction future Round Tables should take. A keynote paper was presented by Associate Professor Colleen Roach titled "The MacBride Round Table as a Non-Governmental Organization? Questions /Concepts for Consideration." In it, she explored the continuing relevance of the NWICO/ MacBride Movement, the role of grassroots/new social movements and NGOs, and the MacBride movement's conceptual/practical challenges. The paper also focused on terminology, the diversity and scope of the MacBride agenda, and the issue of allies.

No statement was issued at Dublin, but the meeting did review draft statutes and a statement of intentions regarding establishing a permanent NGO "appropriately recognized by national and international bodies, and relating effectively to grassroots organizations around the world." In view of the later trajectory of the communication rights movement, it is worth noting that the draft statutes propose that—

> The principles of this NGO will be the right to communicate, democratization of communications, the empowerment of the world's peoples at the grass-roots, with particular emphasis on indigenous and native peoples, through communications and support for independent media which counter the growing transnational control of global communications. These principles place particular emphasis on the role and voice of women and other traditionally excluded groups. (personal records)

The sixth Round Table (Honolulu, 1994) was attended by over 100 people from some 20 countries, who addressed the empowerment of women and grassroots organizations; the rights of indigenous peoples and their cultures; the "information superhighway": efficiency versus equity in information flows; and the need to dialog with UNESCO, the International Telecommunication Union (ITU), and the General Agreement on Tariffs and Trade (GATT). The Round Table noted that the then developing information superhighways "will inevitably bypass poorer regions" and "widen the gap between the information rich and the information poor… to such an extent as to render it unbridgeable in the foreseeable future." It also emphasized that "No genuine civil society and no functioning public sphere are possible without the active participation of all marginalized groups" (Vincent et al., 1999, p. 333).

The seventh Round Table (Tunis, 1995) was attended by over 70 participants from 20 countries and chaired by Mustapha Masmoudi, one of the original MacBride Commissioners. The main themes of the meeting were Africa and the information superhighway, the role of women and grassroots organizations in the strengthening of democracy in Africa and elsewhere, and the danger faced by journalists in situations of violence and war. As the statement observed, it was—

> in many ways a journey home to Africa for a movement that owes a great debt to this region. It is to the Algiers Non-Aligned Summit in 1973 that many look for the origins of the struggle for a new and more equitable communication order. Tunisia also was one of the Non-Aligned countries to spearhead the struggle for a new international order in the fields of culture and communication. (Vincent et al., 1999, p. 335)

The eighth Round Table (Seoul, 1998) attracted more than 200 participants and took the theme "Communication and Culture: Identity, Plurality and Equality." George Gerbner, Dean of the Annenberg School for Communication at the University of Pennsylvania (1964–1989), gave the opening address. The Seoul Statement noted—

> a rising number of Declarations, Statements, Resolutions, Charters etc. issuing from conferences and other gatherings on the right to communicate, and on alternative and democratic media.... These statements are symptomatic of some very significant, and potentially far reaching, developments in the area of communications and media. (Vincent et al., 1999, p. 341)

> It also called for the international debate on democracy and equity in communication fully to explore and acknowledge significant variations within and between different regions of the world; for the promotion of democratic, alternative and developmentally-oriented media as a way of countering the process of globalisation and homogenisation of media and culture; and for democratising the process of devising and implementing mainstream media policy at national and international levels. (Vincent et al., 1999, p. 345–46)

The ninth Round Table (Boulder, 1997) was hosted by the University of Colorado College of Media, Communication and Information in association with the 12th colloquium of the European Institute for Communication and Culture. The theme was "Global Media and Global Responsibility: A Time to Choose." Over 50 participants attended, mainly from North American academia, who agreed on the need for—

> research to assess the real impact of alternative media, to explore the relevance of emerging technologies… the building of a broad-based social movement, self-reflective and self-critical and sustaining a common agenda [and] an international non-governmental platform to cover global regulatory agencies (ITU, WTO, etc.) and democratic forms of governance. (Vincent et al., 1999, p. 351)

The tenth and last Round Table (Amman, 1998) was held jointly with the Jordan Institute of Diplomacy and the Jemstone Media Network on the theme "The Right to Communicate: Culture and Communication in the Global Information Society." Over 150 people from more than 20 countries took part. No statement was issued, but participants affirmed the continuing and urgent need for promoting debate on the development of the media and communications, especially in the context of the global information society. They also underlined the need for a forum for media researchers, professional journalists, policymakers, and media and human rights activists to come together under the MacBride legacy and to discuss practical actions as well as theoretical questions in support of more just and equitable media and communication.

From the MacBride Round Tables to the Communication Rights Movement

In 2001, the UN General Assembly announced a World Summit on the Information Society (WSIS). That same year, the Platform for Communication Rights, a transnational group of NGOs and individuals involved in policy advocacy around global media and communication issues, initiated a campaign to promote Communication Rights in the Information Society (CRIS). It is fair to say that the platform itself emerged from and was in a very real sense a continuation of the MacBride Round Tables, and that the impact of the CRIS Campaign both on the WSIS debates and on the subsequent trajectory of the communication rights movement underlined and confirmed the importance of the work of the Round Tables.

This is evidenced in the objectives of the CRIS Campaign, which focused on areas that directly affect people's lives, such as:

- Strengthening the public domain, to ensure that information and knowledge are readily available for human development and not locked up in private hands;
- Ensuring affordable access to and effective use of electronic networks in a development context, for instance through innovative and robust regulation and public investment;
- Securing and extending the global commons for both broadcast and telecommunication, to ensure that this public resource is not sold for private ends;
- Instituting democratic and transparent governance of the information society from the local to the global level;
- Challenging information surveillance and censorship, government or commercial;
- Supporting community and people-centered media, traditional and new.

By the time WSIS in Geneva concluded in 2003, civil society organizations had distilled the key concerns of a decade of MacBride Round Tables (international law, telecommunications, international trade and tariffs, transnational data flow, intellectual and artistic property rights, and the individual's right to privacy; free flow of information and news; media monitoring and content analysis of news coverage; negative effects of global imbalances in communication flows; improvements in South–South communication; the right to communicate as one of the fundamental principles of a democratic order; under-representation of women in the field of communications; concentration, homogenization, commercialization, and militarization of national and world cultures; the positive role policymakers and media workers could play in relation to peace and international understanding; imbalances in information technology and ways to harness information technology to the benefit of ordinary people; the empowerment of women and grassroots organizations; the rights of indigenous peoples and their cultures; the need for alternative and democratic media; and the building of a broad-based social movement, self-reflective and self-critical and sustaining a common agenda into a comprehensive and detailed call (WSIS, 2003).

It identified communication as a fundamental social process, a basic human need, and the foundation of all social organizations. It went far beyond the right to freedom of expression and opinion to include the right to access public information and the public domain of knowledge, and many other rights of specific relevance to information and communication processes. This was the foundation of the communication rights movement, aided and abetted by many who had argued in public fora and academia for greater accessibility, affordability, diversity, and inclusion in global, national, and local communications.

Communication rights affirm that people have the right to be consulted and have a say in the decisions that affect them. Effective implementation of the principle of participation is a vital component of creating policies that are legitimate and aimed at overcoming social exclusion (see also Chap. 5 in this collection). The principles of communication rights determine who is participating (included or excluded) and which "voices" are listened to while decisions are being made.

Development practitioners soon took note. The World Congress on Communication for Development, Rome (25–27 October 2006), echoed the language of communication rights, noting that achieving progress toward sustainable development requires:

- The right and possibility for people to participate in the decision-making processes that affect their lives.
- Creating opportunities for the sharing of knowledge and skills.
- Ensuring that people have access to communication tools so that they can communicate within their communities and with people making decisions that affect them.
- The process of dialog, debate, and engagement that builds public policies that are relevant, helpful, and which have committed constituencies willing to implement them.

- Recognizing and harnessing the communication trends that are taking place at local, national, and international levels for improved development action.
- Adopting an approach that is contextualized within cultures.
- Related to all of the above, a priority to ensure that the people most affected by the development issues in their communities and countries have their say, voice their perspectives, and contribute and act on their ideas for improving their situation.

Conclusion

The MacBride Report and the dedicated work of the MacBride Round Tables led directly to the communication rights movement, largely energized by the CRIS Campaign and the WSIS. And yet, after 2006, there was a kind of falling away as political intransigence, transnational media conglomerates, deregulation, technological convergence, and the emergence of internet service providers and unregulated digital platforms began to seize the day. The kind of social progress implicitly envisioned by the MacBride Report and by the protagonists in the MacBride Round Tables took a back seat to globalization, neoliberalism, corporate greed, and eventually a politics of fear in the context of the return of right-wing politics and populism. That is not to say that the arguments of the MacBride Report, avidly debated in the meetings of the MacBride Round Tables, lacked validity or that its principles were misplaced. While the MacBride Report was not beyond criticism (Traber & Nordenstreng, 1992; Padovani & Nordenstreng, 2005), it still became the benchmark for that grander vision of societies in which communication rights are held to underpin democratic principles, sustainable development, and genuine social progress.

In a sense, this was all foreseen by the MacBride Report, whose first chapter—despite its unfortunately gendered language—notes:

> Communication maintains and animates life. It is also the motor and expression of social activity and civilisation; it leads people and peoples from instinct to inspiration, through variegated processes and systems of enquiry, command and control; it creates a common pool of ideas, strengthens the feeling of togetherness through exchange of messages and translates thought into action, reflecting every emotion and need from the humblest tasks of human survival to supreme manifestations of creativity—or destruction. Communication integrates knowledge, organisation of power and runs a thread linking the earliest memory of man to his noblest aspirations through constant striving for a better life. As the world has advanced, the task of communication has become ever more complex and subtle—to contribute to the liberation of mankind from want, oppression and fear and to unite it in community and communion, solidarity and understanding. However, unless some basic structural changes are introduced, the potential benefits of technological and communication development will hardly be put at the disposal of the majority of mankind. (MacBride, 1980, p. 3)

The vision of the MacBride Report and the MacBride Round Tables was one of equality, plurality, and diversity. There is still a long way to go.

Several IAMCR members were closely involved in organizing and participating in the MacBride Round Tables. In alphabetical order, the main actors were Alain Ambrosi, Jörg Becker, Farrell Corcoran, Awatef Abdel El-Rahman, George Gerbner, Cees J. Hamelink, Josiane Jouët, Wolfgang Kleinwächter, Eileen Mahoney, Vincent Mosco, Yvonne Mignot-Lefebvre, Mustapha Masmoudi, Hamid Mowlana, Kaarle Nordenstreng, Marc Raboy, Colleen Roach, Florangel Rosario-Braid, Rafael Roncagliolo, Seán O Siochrú, Slavko Splichal, Pradip N. Thomas, Michael Traber, and Richard C. Vincent.

References

Boulder Statement. (1997). In R. C. Vincent, K. Nordenstreng, & M. Traber (Eds.), (1999). *Towards equity in global communication: MacBride update*. Hampton Press.

Dakroury, A., Mahmoud, E., & Kamalipour, Y. R. (Eds.). (2009). *The right to communicate. Historical hopes, global debates, and future premises*. Hunt.

Hamelink, C. J., & Nordenstreng, K. (2020). *Basics of IAMCR history*. IAMCR. Retrieved 15 June 2022, from https://iamcr.org/sites/default/files/basics_of_iamcr_2nd_ed_rev2.pdf

Harare Statement. (1989). In R. C. Vincent, K. Nordenstreng, & M. Traber (Eds.), (1999). *Towards equity in global communication: MacBride update*. Hampton Press.

Honolulu Statement. (1994). In R. C. Vincent, K. Nordenstreng, & M. Traber (Eds.), (1999). *Towards equity in global communication: MacBride update*. Hampton Press.

IAMCR & ILAD (Turkish Communication Research Association). (1991, October). *Reporting the gulf war* [Special Issue]. *Media Development*. World Association for Christian Communication.

Istanbul Statement. (1991). In R. C. Vincent, K. Nordenstreng, & M. Traber (Eds.), (1999). *Towards equity in global communication: MacBride update*. Hampton Press.

MacBride, S. & Commissioners. (1980). *Communication and society today and tomorrow: Many voices, one world. Towards a new more just and more efficient world information and communication order*. Kogan Page,Unipub, UNESCO.

Mansell, R., & Nordenstreng, K. (2006). Great media and communication debates: WSIS and the MacBride report. *Information Technologies and International Development, 3*(4), 15–36.

Nordenstreng, K. (2013). How the new world order and imperialism challenge media studies. *TripleC: Communication, Capitalism & Critique, 11*(2), 348–358.

Padovani, C., & Nordenstreng, K. (2005). From NWICO to WSIS: Another world information and communication order? *Global Media and Communication, 1*(3), 264–272.

Prague Statement. (1990). In R. C. Vincent, K. Nordenstreng, & M. Traber (Eds.), (1999). *Towards equity in global communication: MacBride update*. Hampton Press.

Roach, C. (1993). *The MacBride round table as a non-governmental organization? Questions/concepts for consideration* [Keynote Paper]. Fifth MacBride Round Table, Dublin, Republic of Ireland.

Rome Consensus. (2006). *Communication for development: A major pillar for development and change*. World Congress on Communication for Development.

Seoul Statement. (1996). In R. C. Vincent, K. Nordenstreng, & M. Traber (Eds.), (1999). *Towards equity in global communication: MacBride update*. Hampton Press.
Traber, M., & Nordenstreng, K. (1992). *Few voices, many worlds: Towards a media reform movement*. World Association for Christian Communication (WACC).
Tunis Statement. (1995). In R. C. Vincent, K. Nordenstreng, & M. Traber (Eds.), (1999). *Towards equity in global communication: MacBride update*. Hampton Press.
Vincent, R. C., Nordenstreng, K., & Traber, M. (Eds.). (1999). *Towards equity in global communication: MacBride update*. Hampton Press.
WSIS. (2003, December 8). *Shaping information societies for human needs* (Civil Society Plenary). Civil Society Declaration to the World Summit on the Information Society. Geneva.

CHAPTER 16

IAMCR and the World Summit on the Information Society

Marc Raboy

Introduction

The decision to convene a United Nations World Summit on the Information Society (WSIS) originated with a resolution at a Plenipotentiary Conference of the International Telecommunication Union (ITU) in Minneapolis, Minnesota, in 1998. From this obscure and inauspicious beginning, the idea took shape over the next three years, culminating in the formal adoption of Resolution A/RES/56/183 of the United Nations (UN) General Assembly in December 2001. The UN delegated responsibility for leading the preparatory process of the WSIS to the ITU. For the first time, a UN summit would take place in two phases, separated by two years (2003 and 2005), and in two places, separated by a sea of history (Geneva and Tunis).[1]

The WSIS was the third attempt by the UN system to deal with information and communication issues on a global scale. In 1948, in the optimistic climate of the post-war era, the Universal Declaration of Human Rights spelled out,

[1] General background on the WSIS in this chapter is taken largely from previous writing by the author, including Raboy (2004a, 2004b), Raboy and Landry (2005), and Raboy et al. (2010).

M. Raboy (✉)
McGill University, Montreal, Canada
e-mail: marc.raboy@mcgill.ca

© The Author(s), under exclusive license to Springer Nature Switzerland AG 2023

J. Becker, R. Mansell (eds.), *Reflections on the International Association for Media and Communication Research*,
https://doi.org/10.1007/978-3-031-16383-8_16

for all, what the great revolutions of the eighteenth century had struggled to obtain for Europeans and Americans: that the capacity to seek, receive, and impart information is a basic human right. Three decades later, in the post-colonial climate of the Cold War, the non-aligned nations sparked a debate on a "new world information and communication order," (NWICO), drawing attention to such questions as the inequalities in North–South information flow, the cultural bias of technology, and the lack of communication infrastructure in the so-called Third World. The year 1948 was a moment of international consensus, but the debates of the 1970s were fraught with conflict. Media and communication researchers and scholars (including, in the 1970s, IAMCR members) were involved in both of these earlier moments, as experts. In the WSIS, however, many of them, including IAMCR as an association as well as dozens of individual members, aligned with a broad assortment of civil society organizations as *actors*.

IAMCR's involvement in the WSIS is indissociable from its wider connection to the shifts in international media and communication debates within the emerging global media and communication environment of the mid-1990s. Various IAMCR members were already involved, in this period, in initiatives seeking to influence the global media and communications policy environment, as well as in non-governmental organizations (NGOs) and civil society organizations active in this field. The backstory of these informal, non-institutional efforts to raise awareness and foster debate on media and communication *globally* was the crucial backdrop to both IAMCR's eventual institutional involvement and the rich texture of civil society investment in the WSIS. What follows is an admittedly personal, subjective view of this background.

Before WSIS

As outlined in Chap. 14 of this collection, IAMCR members had been critical academic actors in UNESCO's International Commission for the Study of Communication Problems, chaired by Seán MacBride, that resulted in the so-called MacBride Report of 1980 and the ensuing debate on a NWICO. In the wake of the collapse of the NWICO debate within UNESCO, a number of active IAMCR members created, in 1989, an informal discussion space known as the MacBride Round Table on Communication, "an international group of scholars, activists, journalists and other communication experts" devoted to pursuing discussion of the issues embodied in the MacBride Report, with a broad focus on addressing the question of communication equity worldwide. Round Table stalwarts included IAMCR members such as Kaarle Nordenstreng, Awatef Abdel El-Rahman, Wolfgang Kleinwächter, Slavko Splichal, Michael Traber, and Richard Vincent, as well as Mustapha Masmoudi, the former Tunisian ambassador to UNESCO and member of the original MacBride Commission (see Chap. 15 in this collection).

The MacBride Round Table was not the only activist initiative spearheaded by leading IAMCR figures in the 1990s. IAMCR past-President Cees Hamelink, through the Amsterdam-based Centre for Communication and Human Rights and along with the Malaysian-based NGO Third World Network, launched the People's Communication Charter, an international initiative intended to muster support for communication rights. One of the intellectual pillars of IAMCR, George Gerbner, was the founder and driving force of the US-based Cultural Environment Movement, which gathered grassroots community activists in a series of important conferences on democratizing global communications during the same decade.

At a meeting in London, United Kingdom, in November 1996, an array of these initiatives, allied with a cluster of international NGOs—such as the Association for Progressive Communication (APC), the World Association of Community Radio Broadcasters (AMARC), the international videographers' collective Vidéazimut, and the World Association for Christian Communication (WACC)—to launch a loose coalition called the London Platform for Democratic Communication. The London Platform would evolve three years later into the Platform for Communication Rights, which sponsored the campaign for Communication Rights in the Information Society (CRIS) that became the catalyst and organizational focus for much of the civil society activity at the WSIS.

In March 1999, this activity crystallized in the formation of *Voices 21*, "an informal association of media activists and concerned individuals ... [founded] with a view towards building a new social movement around media and communication issues." The *Voices 21* statement published at that time was signed by a 15-person interim organizing group, a majority of whom were leading IAMCR members such as George Gerbner, Cees Hamelink, Wolfgang Kleinwächter, Robert McChesney, Kaarle Nordenstreng, Marc Raboy, Pradip Thomas, and Richard Vincent, signing either in their own names or in affiliation with one or another of the aforementioned initiatives. (The other signatories were Alain Ambrosi and Karen Thorne of Vidéazimut, Michael Eisenmenger of Deep Dish TV, IAMCR's future Executive Director Bruce Girard, Cilla Lundström of APC, the future Coordinator of the CRIS campaign Seán Ó Siochrú, and Lynne Muthoni Waneki of EcoNews Africa.)

The Global Media Policy Working Group

The first formal involvement of IAMCR in this burgeoning social movement came with the creation of the association's Global Media Policy Working Group (WG) at the Glasgow Congress in 1998. The premise for the creation of the WG was that "the challenges of globalization demand new, transnational policy approaches aimed at enabling media and communication to better serve the global public interest." The embryonic WG held two sessions in Glasgow: the first focused on identifying issues, and the second on strategies for intervention. Beyond its academic objectives, the WG hoped to contribute to "building a constituency for worldwide popular mobilization in favour of global democratization of media, including a proposal to organize a World Congress on Media and Communication" (which happened to be one of the defining goals of *Voices 21*).

More than 70 people attended at least one of the WG sessions in Glasgow, on 28–29 July 1998, which led to the publication of an eight-article "symposium" in the journal *Javnost-The Public*, including Seán Ó Siochrú's presentation of the idea of a World Congress. As convenor of the WG, I made detailed notes which have never been published but which provide a time capsule for how we framed the issues and strategies at the time. One intervention I noted which stands out was George Gerbner's call for "doing something outrageous"; whatever the issue, the former Dean of the Annenberg School of Communication advised, "Don't be nice and make as much trouble as you can."[2]

The Global Media Policy WG convened two sessions at the 22nd IAMCR Congress in Singapore in 2000. The call specified:

> As scholars and as citizens, IAMCR members have a need, first, to understand the policy issues of the new global communication environment and, then, to put this knowledge to work with others in a broader effort to influence communication at the global level. The focus of the working group is therefore on finding ways to combine research and action.[3]

As in Glasgow, the sessions were structured so as to facilitate maximum discussion and exchange among participants, rather than formal papers. Sixty people attended one or both of the Global Media Policy sessions in Singapore. Our report published in the November 2000 issue of the *IAMCR Newsletter* stated:

> A strong and probably natural tension emerged at the interface of these two aspects of the group's work [research and action]. A wealth of new and reconfigured policy issues characterize the interests of communication policy scholars at the present time. There is, however, a wide range of views as to the best way to channel our research for maximum impact and public benefit.[4]

The second session began with a question: Is there a role for an epistemic community of media and communication researchers in influencing global media policy? And specifically, is there an institutional role for IAMCR in this regard, and if so, how to address it?

If there was, at this time, any awareness of what was brewing within the UN system regarding a WSIS, it still did not surface in Singapore.

[2] Marc Raboy personal archives.

[3] *IAMCR Newsletter 9*(2), April–May 2000, p. 24. All IAMCR Newsletters referred to in this chapter can be accessed at https://iamcr.org/node/10511. Accessed 15 June 2022.

[4] *IAMCR Newsletter 11*(1), November 2000, p. 34.

The Multi-Stakeholder Challenge

One of the innovative challenges of the WSIS was the institutional commitment of the UN (and personal commitment of its Secretary-General, Kofi Annan) that the Summit be organized as a multi-stakeholder partnership. This was much easier said than done. Civil society had for some time been included in various guises in UN summitry, but never as a full "partner." There was a difference between including some members of civil society in national government delegations, or allowing observer status, or providing space in the summit agenda and venue for civil society side events, and "partnership." For one thing, partnership had to mean having an equal say in the outcome.

Unexpectedly (from the perspective of the WSIS Secretariat in Geneva), civil society took the call to multi-stakeholderism literally. On 19–20 November 2001, the newly launched CRIS Campaign and a German foundation, the Friedrich Ebert Stiftung, organized a meeting of about 40 people (including at least a half dozen members of IAMCR) in Geneva, explicitly aimed at both the issues and the processes that would be relevant to civil society participation in the WSIS. On the second day, representatives from the ITU and UNESCO as well as the newly created "Civil Society Division" of the WSIS executive secretariat joined the meeting and a broad exchange took place regarding the range of possibilities for civil society involvement. For the first time, the meeting provided participants with a clear idea of what the WSIS would be about and how it would be structured. Importantly, both ITU and WSIS officials insisted that there would be significant civil society involvement and that this was seen as essential—despite the fact that a number of governments were hostile to the idea. Furthermore, it became clear that the agenda for the WSIS was at this point far from set.

This was the WSIS's first civil society consultation. But there was still no indication of what shape or form the contribution of civil society might take.

UNESCO, meanwhile, was organizing its own consultations in view of its eventual contribution to the summit. IAMCR formally took part in one of these UNESCO consultations in Leicester, United Kingdom, in December 2001, with the participation of President-elect Frank Morgan. In his report to the association, Frank Morgan noted that "nine of the 16 participants in the Leicester meeting were IAMCR members, from Africa, Asia, the Caribbean and Europe including a Past President, a Vice President and two International Councillors." The meeting encouraged UNESCO to resume research in media and communication "but recognised that the organisation is better placed to facilitate others than to undertake projects directly itself," Morgan later reported. One of the outcomes of the Leicester meeting was a commitment to hold three IAMCR-UNESCO round tables at the 2002 IAMCR Congress in Barcelona, one of them focused explicitly on the WSIS.[5]

[5] Frank Morgan, "UNESCO-IAMCR Round Table." *IAMCR Newsletter* 13(1), May–June 2002, p. 23.

The Global Media Policy WG, on its part, prepared to focus its Barcelona sessions on the WSIS preparations. The call referenced the global coalition of civil society organizations taking shape "with a view towards ensuring that issues broadly relevant to communication as a human right are prominently foregrounded on the Summit's agenda," and announced two goals: to highlight some of the issues of concern to the civil society coalition, and to try to generate some meaningful synergy between those concerns and research that was currently being done in the area of global media policy.[6]

The Road to Geneva

The 225 accredited civil society delegates who met in Geneva from 1–5 July 2002, in the first of three scheduled "PrepComs" that would lead up to the summit had no idea what to expect. Most of them had never met before and there was no clear sense of what the possible role of civil society could be. Some thought they might perhaps be allowed to observe governmental negotiations, while others sincerely believed they would have seats at the table and votes at the end of the day. All were in for a series of shocks.

The prepcom set the tone for a summit which would be focused on process at the expense of content. Government delegates debated for three days whether and to what extent non-government actors would be allowed to observe and under what circumstances they would be allowed to speak. Civil society, meanwhile, somewhat spontaneously organized itself into an open and inclusive "plenary," with a series of appended structures for coordination and development of content and themes which would endure through the end of the Geneva phase of the summit.

With only days to spare between the WSIS "prepcom" and IAMCR's Congress in Barcelona, I wrote to Frank Morgan, who was about to assume the presidency:

> Dear Frank, A number of IAMCR members present at the WSIS 'prepcom' in Geneva talked a bit informally about the role IAMCR might plan on playing in the lead-up to the 2003 Summit. We tossed around a few possibilities, ranging from a committee to monitor developments and suggest IAMCR interventions as appropriate, to developing a paper that could be a formal contribution to the debate, to adopting an official position regarding the politics surrounding the process. We thought we would try to find a moment to sit down with you and discuss this further in Barcelona, perhaps with a view towards presenting something to the general assembly Friday morning and/or the IC. What do you think? All the best, Marc.[7]

About 75 participants attended the two sessions of the Global Media Policy WG in Barcelona (2002). As announced, the sessions addressed issues related

[6] *IAMCR Newsletter 12*(2), November 2001, p. 35.
[7] Marc Raboy personal archives.

to the WSIS. An invited guest—IAMCR's future Executive Director Bruce Girard, then of the CRIS Campaign—presented an overview of the stakes at play and the outcome of the recent "prepcom" in Geneva. Since the agenda of the summit was far from finalized, the WG spent a good deal of its time brainstorming themes that it felt should be placed on the summit agenda and ways in which researchers and IAMCR could influence the summit process.[8]

In the event, the General Assembly (GA) voted in Barcelona to create a task force to facilitate and coordinate IAMCR involvement in the WSIS. The 12-member task force was then immediately set up by the International Council (IC). Chaired by President Frank Morgan, the task force included members Hopeton Dunn, Divina Frau-Meigs, Cees Hamelink, Wolfgang Kleinwächter, Claudia Padovani, Marc Raboy, Katharine Sarikakis, K.M. Shrivastava, Annabelle Sreberny, Pradip Thomas, and Daya Thussu.

In an article in the next issue of the *IAMCR Newsletter*, I laid out the stakes at play: "It is clear that the IAMCR task force will have to work actively between now and PrepCom 2 in order to influence the agenda of the Summit ...." I went on to provide a personal view of what I thought IAMCR's priorities should be in this regard (pending discussion within the task force, which had yet to meet in person or virtually):

> Our input ought to emphasize that 1) the WSIS should make an explicit statement about the right to communicate as a universal human right; and 2) the agenda should be broadened to include the importance of media and mass communication in any consideration of the so-called information society.[9]

The absence of a human rights perspective in the proposed WSIS guiding principles was also underscored by the Civil Society Coordination Group set up following PrepCom1. This was a major point of contention, as numerous government delegations had indicated—in both formal and informal declarations—that they were opposed to a discussion of human rights at a summit on the information society. In fact, much of the debate around procedure and the participation of civil society in the summit was being driven by this issue. "In addition to this fundamental point," I wrote—

> broadening the WSIS agenda is also a serious concern. There is a danger that the notion of the information society will be restricted to a focus on hardware and plumbing issues, particularly in light of the traditional approach of the ITU in this area. The input of UNESCO and other UN agencies will be important in this respect. But as an association of media and communication researchers, IAMCR should have something original to bring to the table. We could begin by developing our own notion of communication in the information society, and analysing the challenges of the new global mass media environment. Questions regarding

[8] *IAMCR Newsletter 13*(2), November 2002, p. 28.

[9] Marc Raboy, "IAMCR to invest in World Summit on the Information Society." *IAMCR Newsletter 13*(2), November 2002, p. 13, 16.

> the restructuring of media ownership, media regulation, public service and community media—among other things—all ought to be placed on the WSIS agenda ....[10]

All that said, IAMCR's *formal* activity at this stage of the WSIS preparatory process remained largely reactive. After attending the official WSIS meeting on "Content and Themes," in Geneva, in September 2002, Frank Morgan reported: "The preparation for the World Summit on the Information Society is fraught with complex difficulties. Yet it demonstrates the opportunities open to academic and industry researchers to contribute vital knowledge to the process ...."[11]

But some tension was beginning to appear between the President and the base of the membership. Frank Morgan saw IAMCR's role playing out by attaching itself to a larger agency like UNESCO, while most of the task force members were already contributing through their connections with civil society organizations, individual participation in the range of thematic civil society caucuses ranging from media to gender, and the CRIS campaign. "If IAMCR is to contribute effectively to the planning and outcomes of the Summit," he wrote—

> it is more likely to be through UN agencies such as UNESCO rather than through any of the activist factions that are forming around the event. This need not prevent individual members from contributing to those factions but it seriously limits their ability to invoke the Association's name in their cause.[12]

Indeed, the failure to bring these two approaches together effectively paralyzed IAMCR's institutional role in the first phase of the WSIS, where individual members were highly influential in a number of WSIS settings but the association itself was largely absent. The task force was never convened with a view toward developing a common IAMCR approach to the WSIS. It remained mainly a mailing list, an amalgam of individuals participating in varying degrees in the WSIS preparatory activities of "prepcoms," regional meetings, and content consultations as well as, importantly, through civil society caucuses and plenaries.

Frank Morgan acknowledged this reality in his report on Phase 1, which took place in Geneva from 10–12 December 2003:

> ... At WSIS, a number of members—including Cees Hamelink, Wolfgang Kleinwächter, Robin Mansell, Divina Frau Meigs, and Marc Raboy[13]—have made significant contributions. Nevertheless, for all its innovative attempt to bring the

[10] Marc Raboy, "IAMCR to invest in World Summit on the Information Society." *IAMCR Newsletter 13*(2), November 2002, p. 13, 16.

[11] Marc Raboy personal archives.

[12] Marc Raboy personal archives.

[13] ...and there were many others.

> private sector and civil society groups together with governments, to build a healthier, wealthier and more equitable world for all, the Summit has conspicuously neglected available, research-based information about the constitution and operation of information (or knowledge) societies. I have taken every available opportunity to remind the organisers of this gap and to assure them that we have the resources to help close it.[14]

In sum, for IAMCR, Phase 1 of the WSIS was more of a space where individual members shared information and brainstormed about possibilities for meaningful intervention, before going off to intervene in their own ways, without a strong institutional presence. This was fine, but while IAMCR was institutionally accredited and around a dozen members registered in Geneva in 2003 as IAMCR delegates, this meant little for IAMCR at the end of the day.

On the other hand, members' individual contributions were both important and generative, as reflected in six substantial articles in the IAMCR Newsletter of July 2004, assessing key aspects of Phase 1 (Cees Hamelink on human rights, Frank Morgan on cultural diversity, Wolfgang Kleinwächter on internet governance, Divina Frau-Meigs on the role of research, Annabelle Sreberny on gender, and Claudia Padovani on the multi-stakeholder approach).[15] IAMCR members were featured participants in WSIS side events such as the World Forum on Communication Rights and the World Electronic Media Forum, and in addition, contributed journal articles, book chapters, and monographs on various aspects of the WSIS that flooded the field in 2004 and 2005.

The official WSIS Declaration of Principles, despite its shortcomings, incorporated an important contribution of civil society. It was clear from the outset that the declaration would reaffirm the essence of Article 19 of the Universal Declaration of Human Rights ("Everyone has the right to freedom of opinion and expression; this right includes freedom to hold opinions without interference and to seek, receive and impart information and ideas through any media and regardless of frontiers.") but as a result of civil society lobbying, this assertion was expanded with the following corollary:

> Communication is a fundamental social process, a basic human need and the foundation of all social organization. It is central to the Information Society. Everyone, everywhere should have the opportunity to participate and no one should be excluded from the benefits the Information Society offers (WSIS, 2003b, para. 4).

This achievement was eclipsed, furthermore, by the civil society plenary's adoption of the exhaustive Civil Society Declaration on December 8, "Shaping Information Societies for Human Needs," which spelled out in great detail the core principles and challenges of "shaping a people-centred, inclusive and

[14] Frank Morgan, "A Year of 'Alarums and Excursions.'" *IAMCR Newsletter 14*(1), December 2003, p. 3.

[15] *IAMCR Newsletter 14*(2), July 2004, p. 34–42.

equitable concept of information and communication societies" (WSIS, 2003a, para. 1). The 23-page civil society declaration, unimaginable at the outset of the WSIS process two years earlier, is archived on the ITU's permanent WSIS website as an official outcome of the summit.[16]

The governmental summit, meanwhile, shifted its most important substantive issues to Phase 2: the questions of digital solidarity (in other words, how to fund the bridging of the global digital divide), and internet governance.

The Road to Tunis

The 2004 IAMCR Congress in Porto Alegre, Brazil, featured two plenaries and various section and WG sessions on the WSIS, as the association decided to up its game with regard to Phase 2. The GA formalized IAMCR involvement for Phase 2 in the following resolution re-incarnating the IAMCR-WSIS Task Force and giving it a clear mandate:

> In view of the active involvement of the IAMCR in the ongoing WSIS process, the General Assembly resolves to retain a taskforce on the WSIS, with the membership to be decided by the International Council. In the spirit of critical independent scholarship the task force is to have the following mandate:[17]

- to contribute to the sharing of relevant information and documentation about the WSIS process with the broader academic community,
- to facilitate the synthesizing of existing research on information society issues and feed this into the ongoing WSIS process,
- to assist in the clarification of crucial concepts (such as information society, communication, knowledge society, etc.),
- to assist in the development of effective and relevant alliances,
- to ensure effective representation of IAMCR in the WSIS process.

On the recommendation of newly-elected President Robin Mansell, the IC meeting following the congress in Porto Alegre elected Marc Raboy and Divina Frau-Meigs as Task Force Co-Chairs. The new Task Force members were Adilson Cabral, Andrew Calabrese, Bart Cammaerts, Hopeton Dunn, Cees Hamelink, Sophia Kaitatzi-Whitlock, Wolfgang Kleinwächter, Guillermo Mastrini, Frank Morgan, Claudia Padovani, Annabelle Sreberny, and Elena Vartanova, with Robin Mansell serving *ex-officio*.

IAMCR participation during Phase 2 was thus a bit more structured from the outset, but it was still mostly dependent on the interests and contributions of its most committed individuals. IAMCR members were extremely active in some areas but still not necessarily acting in the name of the association. Two

[16] See also WSIS (2005) Civil Society Statement: "Much more could have been achieved".

[17] Draft minutes, IAMCR General Assembly, Porto Alegre, July 30, 2004, item 11. IAMCR minutes are available at https://iamcr.org/node/10512. Accessed 15 June 2022.

members of the task force (Divina Frau-Meigs and Wolfgang Kleinwächter) were members of the WSIS Civil Society Bureau, representing particular WSIS caucuses, while Wolfgang Kleinwächter was also a civil society representative on the WSIS Working Group on Internet Governance (WGIG)—one of the few genuinely multi-stakeholder official WSIS structures.[18]

This took place in a general context where, paradoxically, the institutionalization of much of the civil society activity was accompanied by less intense involvement than in the first phase. This was in fact a leitmotif of Phase 2—the setting in of a kind of activist "WSIS fatigue," complicated by a sense of discomfort many felt about meeting in Tunisia, in light of the repressive nature of the Tunisian government in the early 2000s, marked by a poor record on human rights regarding freedom of expression, and a plethora of government-controlled civil society organizations.[19] In fact, the participatory civil society structures spontaneously created during the first phase of the WSIS were significantly undermined by Tunisian efforts to ensure that the politically fraught context would remain unchallenged. As a result, most NGOs, including IAMCR, focused on their own specific areas of interest in Phase 2 rather than on the broad questions of principle that had characterized civil society engagement in the first phase.

Ultimately the one area, exceptionally, where IAMCR made a unique contribution on its own account was in the drafting and promotion of an International Researchers' Charter, led by Divina Frau-Meigs, approved by the IC in Taipei in July 2005, and launched at an IAMCR standalone event in Tunis on 16 November 2005. The highlights of the Charter (as per Robin Mansell's presentation in Tunis) were as follows:

1. Researchers are entitled to seek, retrieve, receive and distribute information freely, regardless of geographical borders, ideologies and interests, and the medium used.
2. Working conditions must acknowledge that research is crucial to knowledge production and intellectual development.
3. Researchers are entitled to intellectual freedom and to transparent evaluation of their results.
4. The results of publicly funded research should remain in the public domain.
5. The universal free exchange among researchers of intellectual work should be regarded as being of critical importance to maintaining a democratic order.

[18] Marc Raboy and Divina Frau-Meigs, "Busy time ahead for IAMCR task force on WSIS." *IAMCR Newsletter 14*(3), October 2004, p. 10.

[19] Some, such as IAMCR past-President Cees Hamelink, declined to attend Phase 2 of the summit for this reason.

6. Culturally appropriate learning and research practices should be developed to foster community-based self-supporting systems of research.[20]

The Charter was circulated to universities, libraries, and academic associations throughout the world, and marked an important step for IAMCR as a world leader in the development of policy perspectives on behalf of media and communication researchers.

The Aftermath

Within days of the conclusion of the WSIS, Robin Mansell wrote to the task force co-chairs and members of the Executive Board regarding the future of IAMCR activity in media and communication policy:

> It is very clear that there is still a substantial contribution for IAMCR to make to issues addressed during the WSIS from governance of the Internet, to intellectual property rights, to the protection of human rights. Other issues are likely to continue to arise on the international stage and within the many regions and countries where IAMCR members are based.
>
> Now that the WSIS is over, it seems timely to reconstitute an IAMCR task-force with a mandate that is flexible and slightly broader to take up issues as they arise (including those still on the agenda) and in response to the interests of our membership.[21]

On 29 April 2006, Mansell wrote to the IC proposing the establishment of an IAMCR Task Force on Media and Communication Policy, as a standing committee of the association:

> The WSIS is now officially over, and the original mandate of the Task Force ended, but before disbanding, the Task Force members and the International Council have agreed to propose that IAMCR build on the model of the Task Force's achievement through the establishment of a standing task force to represent the association in the domain of media and communication policy.
>
> On behalf of IAMCR members, a standing Task Force on Media and Communication Policy would be established to maintain a global presence for IAMCR on important issues concerning media and communication policies, drawing on the interests and expertise of IAMCR members and reaching out to engage with the expertise of other individuals and organizations. The Task Force members will, in consultation with members at large, set a rolling agenda of issues

[20] For the full text of the Charter, see IAMCR, "Communication Research in the Information Age: Launching the International Researchers' Charter." WSIS Parallel Event, November 16, 2005, published in IAMCR (2005) International Researchers' Charter for Knowledge Societies. An IAMCR contribution to the WSIS. *IAMCR Newsletter, 15*(2), p. 18.

[21] Robin Mansell to IAMCR WSIS Task Force, e-mail, 8 December 2005.

> to be addressed, providing a focal point for debate and discussion within and beyond IAMCR ....[22]

The formal suggested text of the proposal closely mirrored that which created the WSIS Task Force two years earlier, with a few significant extensions (highlighted here in italic bold face type):

- In view of the active involvement of the IAMCR in the ongoing ***media and communication policy issues at international, regional and national levels***, the General Assembly resolves to establish a ***Standing Task Force on Media and Communication Policy***, with the membership to be decided by the International Council. In the spirit of critical independent scholarship the Task Force will:
- contribute to the sharing of relevant information and documentation about ***media and communication policy issues, as they arise***, with the broader academic community ***and civil society***;
- facilitate the synthesizing of existing research on information society issues and feed this into ***relevant international forums***;
- assist in the clarification of crucial ***policy-relevant concepts for the IAMCR membership***;
- assist in the development of effective and relevant alliances ***with other individuals and organisations concerned with key media and communication policy issues***; and
- ensure effective representation of IAMCR in ***selected forums (formal and informal) in line with IAMCR members' expressed interests***.[23]

The establishment of the IAMCR Standing Task Force on Media and Communication Policy was approved by the GA in Cairo in 2006.

The Legacy

So what can we take away from this frenetic experience? I tried to consider this question in an article for the *IAMCR Newsletter* of April 2006. The answer I think depends on one's level of expectations.

> O what a relief for most of those who tried to follow and take part in this process, from the first 'civil society' consultation in Geneva in November 2001 to the final plenary gavel in Tunis four years later. The WSIS will have been remarkable, mostly, for its process rather than its outcomes. Can we say that a global movement for communication democratization has emerged, in the spaces between and within the debates over financing the digital divide or controlling the dot in dot-com? Will WSIS be remembered as the Woodstock of the world's communication-for-democracy activists?

[22] Robin Mansell to International Council, e-mail, 29 April 2006.
[23] Robin Mansell to International Council, e-mail, 29 April 2006.

> IAMCR had ten official delegates in Geneva and thirteen in Tunis. Several more, including some of the most active, were there wearing other institutional hats. Our presidents (Frank Morgan in Phase I and Robin Mansell in Phase II) led the delegations on both occasions. IAMCR members were among the most actively involved in the CRIS campaign, the Civil Society Bureau, the Working Group on Internet Governance, the Civil Society Plenary, side events such as the World Electronic Media Forum and the World Forum on Communication Rights, and informal lobbying of numerous government delegations as well as the ITU and the UN itself at the highest levels.
>
> IAMCR also achieved a heightened public profile and scored a number of achievements in its own name, notably the launch of the International Researchers Charter. The task force ensured an IAMCR presence at key moments, the circulation of information back to the association and a network connecting IAMCR participants in the multitude of WSIS activities. In this respect it too was a success. In terms of coordination, sustained discussion (particularly with the general membership) and public visibility it could have done better.
>
> I think on balance the experience should be evaluated positively. It has shown that IAMCR and scholars more broadly have a role to play in international policy debates. The association will now decide what shape and form to give to this role in the future but clearly we should build on the WSIS experience. There will be more, not less, for us to do at the global policy level. The WSIS has signalled some of the issues (in some cases by failing to deal with them!): media governance writ large, intellectual property rights, ICT policies for development, protection of cultural diversity, freedom of expression, the role of communication in enhancing human rights .... We have a role to play with respect to these issues. As a community of researchers and as citizens.[24]

This is clearly still true, and even more so today. Looking back on the WSIS experience from the vantage point of 2021, I have two final takeaways: the WSIS process nourished a vast, substantial network of specialists, academics, and activists that have since been able to intervene in other related spheres (the UNESCO Convention on Cultural Diversity, the Internet Governance Forum, various WSIS+ implementation and follow-up activities), but it did *not* broaden the awareness of media and communication issues in other domains of research and global activism. Media and communication policy remains accessible almost exclusively to specialists despite its deep importance for the future of the planet, the future of democracy, and the future of struggles for social justice (as we are seeing at this time of writing with the soul-searching around the need to *do something* about the unbridled power of social media and big tech corporations ...). We still need to find ways and spaces to address these issues.

[24] Marc Raboy, "WSIS is over, long live WSIS?" *IAMCR Newsletter 16*(1), April 2006, p. 9, 21.

References

Raboy, M. (2004a). The World Summit on the Information Society and its legacy for global governance. *Gazette: The International Journal of Communication Studies, 66*(3–4), 225–232.

Raboy, M. (2004b). The WSIS as a political space in global media governance. *Continuum: Journal of Media and Cultural Studies, 18*(3), 347–361.

Raboy, M. (2006). WSIS is over, long live WSIS? *IAMCR Newsletter, 16*(1), 9, 21.

Raboy, M., & Frau-Meigs, D. (2004). Busy time ahead for IAMCR task force on WSIS. *IAMCR Newsletter, 14*(3), 10.

Raboy, M., & Landry, N. (2005). *Civil society, communication and global governance: Issues from the World Summit on the Information Society.* Peter Lang.

Raboy, M., Landry, N., & Shtern, J. (2010). *Digital solidarities, communication policy and multi-stakeholder global governance: The legacy of the World Summit on the Information Society.* Peter Lang.

WSIS. (World Summit on the Information Society). (2003a, December 8). Shaping Information Societies for Human Needs, *Civil Society Declaration to the World Summit on the Information Society* (Civil Society Plenary). Geneva. Retrieved 15 June 2022, from https://www.itu.int/net/wsis/docs/geneva/civil-society-declaration.pdf

WSIS. (World Summit on the Information Society). (2003b, December 12). *Declaration of principles.* Geneva. Retrieved 15 June 2022, from https://www.itu.int/net/wsis/docs/geneva/official/dop.html

WSIS. (World Summit on the Information Society). (2005, December 18). Much more could have been achieved. *Civil Society Statement on the World Summit on the Information Society* (Civil Society Plenary). Tunis. Retrieved 15 June 2022, from, https://www.itu.int/net/wsis/docs2/tunis/contributions/co13.pdf

CHAPTER 17

Lessons from the Non-Aligned Movement and NWICO for the Age of Data: Revisiting an Historical Struggle for Informational Sovereignty

Deepti Bharthur

Introduction

The evolution of global communication and media studies has been closely conjoined with the larger political and economic undercurrents of the time. In the post-war years, with more technological innovations breaking out, the proliferation of mass media, and a rapidly transforming societal context, communication began to emerge as an important question for social theory to engage with. This development was coterminous with the rise of communication and media studies as a dedicated field of study. By the 1960s, the field had broken away from its older parent traditions in the social sciences and established itself as an independent academic discipline. A global community of scholars had also by then emerged, primed to critically take on the communication challenges of the era. IAMCR's own journey from a small, mostly European academic community in the late 1950s to a key international voice within global communication debates has taken place within these larger developments (Wasko, 2013).

The academic milieu of the 1960s and the 1970s in communication and media studies can be said to have been defined by two critical trends. The first:

D. Bharthur (✉)
ITforChange, Bengaluru, India

© The Author(s), under exclusive license to Springer Nature Switzerland AG 2023

J. Becker, R. Mansell (eds.), *Reflections on the International Association for Media and Communication Research*,
https://doi.org/10.1007/978-3-031-16383-8_17

a large-scale expansion of the depth and breadth of the discipline, with more scholars entering the fray, and more programs and departments being set up around the world, thus internationalizing the field in a way that could not have happened before. The second: a broader ontological shift from the positivist tradition of research within the social sciences toward more critical bents of enquiry (Nordenstreng, 2011a). The IAMCR community of scholars, which was both shaped by and contributed to these developments, played a crucial role in furthering some of the key debates in communication and media studies of the 1960s and the 1970s. This was also the time when voices from outside the Global North from newly independent nations had begun to assert themselves on the world stage and were calling into question the many structural inequities prevalent in the communication and media landscape, the Non-Aligned Movement (NAM) being one such powerful global actor.

The NAM was one of the earliest geopolitical alliances to be established by the newly independent nations of Asia and Africa which emerged post–World War II. This alliance was formed with the intent to engage and advocate on the world stage in a voice independent of the dominant bipolar formations of the time—the Eastern Bloc led by the erstwhile Soviet Union and the United States (US)-led North Atlantic Treaty Organization (NATO). The origins of this movement were wrought in a complex set of historical conditions:

1. the birth of new countries in Asia and Africa, all of whom had waged hard-won battles for independence from European colonizers and suddenly found themselves as national entities in the global arena;
2. the sharp bipolar geopolitics of the Cold War between the US and the USSR; and
3. the emergence of a new multilateral system that was tasked with reshaping world relations.

One of the domains where NAM's policies, positions, and advocacy had a sizable impact was that of mass media and communication. In the period between the 1960s and the 1980s, NAM nations made concerted efforts to call out and challenge the dominant structures of media control and ownership, the skewed nature of informational flows and cultural imports from the Global North and also unequivocally to assert the right to communication and informational autonomy of the developing world. These decades of communication rights advocacy also saw the active involvement of the IAMCR fraternity, who made significant contributions to these debates through research and critical engagement (Nordenstreng, 2008, 2011a). Efforts made by the NAM as well as IAMCR scholars in this direction led to the broadening of UNESCO's mandate and the mass media declaration, the rise of the New World Information and Communication Order (NWICO), and the MacBride Commission report (see also Chaps. 14 and 16 in this collection).

This chapter traces the entwined histories of the NAM for communication equity over the decades of the 1960s and the 1970s and the growth of critical, internationalist perspectives in communication, and media studies scholarship that engaged with these questions, spearheaded by IAMCR. It discusses the impact of the articulation of anti-imperialist and anti-colonial communication paradigms and their success/impact in destabilizing the dominant narrative.

Beginning with a discussion of the NAM and its critical precursor, the Bandung Conference, the chapter discusses the heyday of NAM advocacy from the 1970s, including the demand for a NWICO, the transformation of UNESCO as a platform of advocacy on communication equity, and the setting up of the MacBride Commission. It analyzes the subsequent backlash to these efforts, the attempts to return to the status quo in the communication paradigm from the 1980s, and the impact of early globalization currents on the movement. Juxtaposing these developments with the important role played by IAMCR in complementing and bolstering these geopolitical negotiations around communication and media through academic work, research, and theorization, this chapter also traces how the political climate of the times shaped some of its enduring intellectual traditions and legacy. The chapter concludes by looking at the continued relevance of the NAM as an idea and as a powerful meta-narrative for the data economy and how the strategies it deployed in the Cold War period may serve the Global South today, revisiting within this discussion the role for actors such as IAMCR.

The Enduring Spirit of Bandung: A Pitstop on the Road to Non-Alignment

In 1955, the Asian-African Conference took place in Bandung, Indonesia, bringing together world leaders from 29 newly independent nations, mostly from Asia, but also a few from Africa. Little, if anything, united these countries politically, culturally, or economically, save one crucial aspect—a shared historical experience of colonialism. Emerging from the shadows of centuries of foreign rule, these disparate young nations banded together to assert forms of regionalism, nationalism, and leadership that were positioned explicitly against the waning age of empire. The Bandung Conference became the first global platform to articulate an anti-imperialist vision for political sovereignty and self-determination that was uniquely located outside the escalating ideological divide between the US and the USSR.

In public memory and diplomatic history, Bandung has become crystallized as a culmination point of the prevalent anti-status quo ideologies of its time—a call to forge international solidarities in opposition to capitalism, colonialism, and racialism. Its promise was no doubt significant. Prompted by the conference's purported objectives of discussing racialism and colonialism, prominent Black writers, including Richard Wright and James Baldwin, attended the conference. In his 1956 collection of essays on Indonesia which came from this visit, *The Color Curtain: A Report on the Bandung Conference,* Wright had observed this about the conference:

> The despised, the insulted, the hurt, the dispossessed—in short, the underdogs of the human race were meeting. Here were class and racial and religious

> consciousness on a global scale. Who had thought of organizing such a meeting? And what had these nations in common? Nothing, it seemed to me, but what their past relationship to the Western world had made them feel. This meeting of the rejected was in itself a kind of judgment upon that Western world! (Wright, 1956 as quoted in Nopper, 2015)

Scholarship on the conference has, as such, frequently attributed to Bandung many meanings—the earliest articulation of a political post-coloniality (Young, 2005), the idea of the third world, and a unity of the colonized (Menon, 2014), as well as the origins of the NAM. But the Bandung Conference did not manifest in some ahistorical fashion as a flash-point of anti-colonialist reckoning. Rather, it played out within a continuity of anti-colonial conscientization and realpolitik developments that both preceded and succeeded it (Van Dinh, 1976). Even as it performed an important political and symbolic function, there remained significant gaps between the promise of African-Asian solidarity and anti-colonialism contained within the Bandung moment and the realpolitik that was playing out at the time (Roberts & Foulcher, 2016). Vitalis (2013) argues that Bandung was erroneously classified as the birthplace of two broadly construed global identities, non-alignment and a post-colonial anti-racialism consciousness. However, these identities were always "distinct and ultimately competing" (p. 266).

To illustrate this better, there was very little African representation at Bandung, with the event remaining a largely Asian affair. Further, communiques and interactions regarding the conference within US diplomatic ranks seemed to highlight more than anything, concerns of a rising left-leaning pan-Asian nationalism that would find mutual fitment with the Soviet faction and sway with it the African nations' allegiance (Vitalis, 2013; Roberts & Foulcher, 2016).

While it played an important role in crystallizing the ideas that would drive the NAM and its agenda and its political positioning, Bandung was not the political origin of the NAM but rather its spiritual forebearer (Young, 2005). Key founding members of the alliance such as Marshall Tito and Kwame Nkrumah were absent from the Indonesian meeting as was any Latin American presence. It was not until six years after the Bandung Conference concluded that a founding summit in Belgrade established the NAM under the aegis of Indian Prime Minister Jawaharlal Nehru, Ghanaian President Kwame Nkrumah, Indonesian President Sukarno, Egyptian President Gamal Abdel Nasser, and Yugoslav President Josip Broz Tito.

Through the 1960s and the early 1970s, as more nations became independent, the NAM grew from a relatively smaller cluster of developing nations and made itself heard on the world stage on a range of issues. NAM nations, with occasional support from powerful consortia such as Organization of the Petroleum Exporting Countries (OPEC) as well as socialist powers, began to mount a spirited and coordinated challenge to the current international social, economic, and cultural order, putting Western powers in a defensive position

(Nordenstreng, 2010). Decolonization was by then firmly established as a guiding political framework for the NAM's activities within the international relations arena. With increasing recognition in the early 1970s of the structures of culture and communication imperialism—particularly, the global expansion of American capitalism and the development/deployment of satellite technologies—this lens began to be evoked in the communicative sphere (Schiller, 1978). As more scholars began to take a dedicated interest in issues of global political economy and international communication, these areas also grew to become the central focus of IAMCR. For instance, it was through widening engagements with the topic during this period that the International Communication Section of IAMCR, presently, one of the largest sections of the association, came into being. Similarly, the Political Economy Section, which has become a hallmark of IAMCR's theoretical engagement and is one of its most active sections, was officially formed in 1978 during the association's General Assembly meeting in Warsaw and was iteratively shaped through fairly contentious discussions and debates at meetings over the 1970s at Leicester and later in Paris (Wasko, 2013).

Challenging the Free Flow Doctrine

To understand the rising critique and challenges to the dominant paradigm of information and communication that coalesced over the decade into a demand for a NWICO, it is necessary to unpack the post-war context where a particular doctrine of the global communication order came to occupy supremacy—that of the "free flow" of information and communications (Boyd-Barrett, 2009).

The free flow of information and communications as an ideological doctrine became a cornerstone of American foreign policy in the 1940s and was widely evangelized in diplomacy efforts by the US with active support from influential American publications and media houses as well as the Associated Press (Schiller, 1975). Financial incentives through the Marshall Plan were made available to European countries who opened their markets to American cultural exports such as Hollywood. US funding for research and development into computer and satellite technologies also targeted making obsolete undersea cable communication and thereby the United Kingdom's (UK) dominance over the global information structure. As Nordenstreng (2011b) has observed, the free flow doctrine "has never been a neutral and ecumenical concept but rather a tactical argument in socioeconomic and ideological struggles" (p. 84). This is aptly demonstrated even today in the doctrine of free flows for data—where all data flows into corporate enclosures—mostly American, some Chinese.

The "free flow of information" entered international discourse toward the end of World War II through key documents such as the UNESCO constitution in 1945 and as part of the UN Declaration of Human Rights in 1948. For Western nations emerging from the harrowing experience of fascist regimes, a seemingly natural symbiosis between democracy and media was thought to be achieved through the principle of a free flow and exchange of information and communication (Boyd-Barrett, 2009). Thus, the idea continued to enjoy enduring intellectual engagement and political currency and was reaffirmed through instruments such as the 1972 General Conference of UNESCO's Declaration of Guiding Principles on the Use of Satellite Broadcasting for the Free Flow of Information, the Spread of Education, and Greater Cultural Exchange.

In the 1970s, NAM nations began to articulate a counterpoint to this communication and information paradigm, exposing chinks in the armor of this "given" wisdom. The principle of "free flow," when analyzed against disparate levels of technological and economic development among nations, highlighted sharp imbalances and, consequently, implications for nations' cultural and informational sovereignty (Schiller, 1978). This manifested in several ways; through transnational television broadcasting signals via satellite, which started in the 1960s through the Telstar Initiative, the deluge of Hollywood cinema in foreign markets, and the dominance of Western news agencies such as Associated Press (AP), Agence France Presse (AFP), and Reuters in controlling, not only news dissemination, but also news generation about the developing world.

Articulating a New World Information and Communication Order

Recognizing these issues, from mild, tentative statements issued at UNESCO meetings in the late 1960s to gradually launching into what has been described as a "decolonization offensive" (Nordenstreng, 2010), NAM nations embarked on a series of actions to articulate a NWICO. Several of these ideas were first discussed at the Conference of the Heads of State of the Non-Aligned Countries meeting in Algiers in 1973 (Van Dinh, 1976). A declaration was made to demand "concerted action in the fields of mass communication" as a part of the Action Programme for Economic Cooperation.

> It is an established fact that the activities of imperialism are not confined solely to the political and economic fields but also cover the cultural and social fields, thus imposing an alien ideological domination over the peoples of the developing world. The Heads of State or Government of Non-Aligned Countries accordingly stress the need to reaffirm national cultural identity and eliminate the harmful consequences of the colonial era, so that their national culture and tradition will be preserved. (The Economic Declaration of the Algiers Summit Meeting, 1973)

This was followed by the adoption of a special resolution on the "Cooperation in the Field of Diffusion of Information and Mass Communications Media" at the 1975 NAM Ministerial Conference in Lima, Peru, which reaffirmed the Algiers Programme of Action to reorganize the flow of global communication channels, foster capacity development and knowledge exchange among members, promote collective acquisition of communication satellites, and push for overall revision of international cable tariffs (Schiller, 1978). In later meetings, NAM also set up a self-financing news pool of press agencies of the non-aligned countries, through which developing nations hoped to compete against the major Western agencies and counter the highly skewed North-South international news flow as well as put forward a worldview that was more representative of the developing nations.

Several political breakthroughs toward the NWICO ideal were achieved in 1976. In March 1976, the Non-Aligned Symposium of Information was held in Tunis, which unequivocally laid down a political framework for a "new international order," giving rise to the concept. This was followed by a meeting in July 1976 in New Delhi where the New Delhi Declaration was issued. The declaration challenging the "libertarian theory of the press" argued that an abstract right to freedom of communication and information held little meaning without the material resources and means to realize it. It openly advocated for political action and pressure against "imperialist forces" that controlled information structures and flows. This declaration was later on adopted by the Fifth Conference of Heads of State or Government of the Non-Aligned Countries in Colombo, in August of the same year.

NAM's Efforts to Expand the UNESCO Mandate

In its early years (in the late 1940s and continuing through the 1950s) UNESCO's agenda largely followed the US-set free flow doctrine of the 1940s and served as an instrument of US foreign and cultural policy (Schiller, 1975, 1978). It was US influence, in fact, that led UNESCO to broaden its original mandate of furthering and promoting education, science, and cultural activities to the realm of media and communication. Its earliest resolutions were thus directed toward promoting tariff-free movement of media and cultural materials (Pohle, 2016).

Following USSR-led opposition to these efforts, UNESCO subsequently shifted focus to the operational aspects of communication and began to implement "Technical Assistance projects" to support communication infrastructure and enterprise development and professional capacity building in poorly resourced countries, initially in Europe and later in other parts of the world. But these overtures too were called out for the technical dependencies they were introducing into developing economies.

With a rapidly enlarging third-world constituency at the table, UNESCO's agenda began to undergo a gradual shift, focusing on the conditions determining communication and information exchange between nations (Schiller, 1975). UNESCO's transforming policy orientation provided organic opportunities for collaboration with IAMCR scholars who were pursuing similar research goals. In 1968, when the General Conference of UNESCO adopted a new strategy for promoting communication research and policy, it commissioned James Halloran to undertake a working paper on mass media and society for an expert meeting convened in Montreal in 1969. Halloran's close involvement in the conference brought in active IAMCR members including

Bourquin, Maletzke, Nordenstreng, and Smythe. The Montreal meeting and the report's publication (Halloran, 1970) were critical contributions to mass communication research.

In addition to deliberations and debates at its own forums, NAM nations continued to challenge the "free flow doctrine" and push for debates about a NWICO through the 1970s at various UNESCO-sponsored conferences. NAM nations exerted political pressure to broaden the mandate of the UN agency toward goals of communication equity; this led to UNESCO's central involvement in setting up and driving the MacBride Commission's work and its later role in the World Summit on the Information Society (WSIS) in 2003–2005 (Pohle, 2016).

The Eighteenth General Conference of UNESCO in 1974 established a problem area on "Communication between people and the exchange of information" for its six-year medium-term program 1977–1982. As part of this, a meeting of experts from UNESCO and Latin America was convened in Quito, Ecuador, in June 1975 to develop guidelines for policymakers on the development of news exchanges and national and regional news agencies (Schiller, 1978).

A significant victory for NAM nations was also the reframing of the language of free flows through UNESCO's 1978 "Declaration of Fundamental Principles Concerning the Contribution of the Mass Media to Strengthening Peace and International Understanding, the Promotion of Human Rights Information and to Countering Racialism, Apartheid and Incitement to War." In this critical document, the "free flow" principle was rephrased to "free and balanced flow of information."

In 1976 at UNESCO's General Conference in Nairobi, efforts to push forward the concept of a NWICO were made by then secretary-general M'Bow who acknowledged that "the distribution of communication media and the immense potential they represent reflects the uneven international distribution of economic power" (UNESCO, 1976, p. 22). The General Conference adopted a resolution reaffirming the critical role of communication globally, creating a mandate for UNESCO to support the development of communication systems that could liberate "developing countries from the state of dependence." It was this decision that later led the International Commission for the Study of Communication Problems, also known as the MacBride Commission, to closely examine global communication and its problems (see also Chap. 14 in this collection).

Scholarly enquiries on global media and journalism in the international sphere grew significantly in this period not least because of UNESCO's support for research in this area (Nordenstreng, 2008, 2011a). Nearly 100 papers were commissioned as part of the MacBride Commission's work, giving rise to a prolific body of scholarship addressing a broad spectrum of issues around communication and information, including dependencies and structural imbalances, NWICO, and the ethics and responsibility of journalists in global contexts. Key members of IAMCR, including then President James Halloran and Vice President Yassen Zassoursky, contributed to the Commission's background papers. IAMCR was also commissioned by UNESCO to carry out a study on foreign news. At IAMCR's Conference in August 1980 in Caracas, Venezuela, on "New Structures of International Communication," IAMCR activists also undertook a critical examination and engagement with the draft MacBride Report producing a collection of essays (Nordenstreng, 2008).

The most significant outcome of the NAM's influence on UNESCO was the MacBride Report—the culmination of deliberations and debates at conferences hosted by UNESCO and by NAM countries toward the articulation and development of a NWICO. The final report, *Many Voices, One World*, was presented to the next General Conference in 1980 (MacBride, 1980).

IAMCR's Role in NWICO

The political articulations from the NAM countries on structural inequities of the communicative landscape were complemented in large measure by an intellectual wave of thinking and theorization by key figures of the IAMCR fraternity. These contributions strengthened the decolonization perspective in the field of communication and media studies and are an important part of the story of NWICO, as well as the larger critical turn of the discipline as we know it today.

The recognition of power structures, once boxed up and set aside in the interest of objectivity, took center stage. Critical scholarship that explicitly committed to a progressive agenda became a defining feature of communication and media research in these two decades. Scholars from this tradition began to actively challenge American positivist notions, thus giving rise to powerful new perspectives and scholarship. This wave of research, articulation, and deliberation was helmed by notable scholars active within IAMCR, including Kaarle Nordenstreng, Jörg Becker, Dallas Smythe, Herbert Schiller, Cees Hamelink, James Halloran, Robin Cheesman, Nicholas Garnham, and Armand Mattelart.

IAMCR was also uniquely situated to contribute academically and professionally to the communication debates that were being raised in political circles. Unlike the other professional associations of the time, its membership spanned both the Cold War divide of the East and West, as well as the Global North and South. It thus had global reach and a base of institutions and individuals, including from Latin America, the Asia-Pacific, Africa, North America, and Western and Eastern Europe. This was reflected in IAMCR's 1966 Conference, organized in Herceg Novi, Yugoslavia, where over 70 participants from 17 countries came together to discuss mass media and national development.

The academic and research community forged and fostered over these two decades among IAMCR members was a project with a distinct political edge. It allowed the space for critical explorations of prevalent Cold War ideologies and the ideas associated with a NWICO. There was also a conscious effort of bridge building and collaborative association between critical researchers and academics from North America and Europe with political actors, activists, scholars, and media professionals in the developing nations. An example of this is the Latin American Association of Communication Researchers (ALAIC) which was started by Latin American intellectuals along with IAMCR members with support from UNESCO. ALAIC was very active in the 1970s on NWICO issues and mobilization.

The political negotiations of NAM nations working toward NWICO and the growth of critical scholarship (processes that were not necessarily mutually exclusive) that brought the lenses of dialectical materialism, political economy, and post-colonialism into communication research were parallel explorations of the same goal: that of how meaningful communicative equity is achieved. To that extent, their separate and sometimes entwined efforts were instrumental in forwarding key ideas that have left a lasting influence on the field, including the inseparable character of communication and power, the recognition of imbalances in the underlying communicative material structures in the world, and a normative tradition addressing structural and institutional reform toward realizing greater communicative agency and equity.

The explicit politicization of the field of communication, whereby critical scholarship and political activism became indistinguishable, is something Nordenstreng (2013, p. 355) has pointed out about this era.

> With such components central to both the political and intellectual tracks of the movement, each growing out of its own roots, it was natural that the two tracks at some point met and blended in a mix where it is difficult to tell where science ends and politics begins.

Post-80s and the Decline of NWICO

The MacBride Commission and its report's political impact itself was limited (Fuchs, 2015). While undoubtedly enriching the field of communication scholarship and jump-starting critical dialog on issues, the recommendations of the report did not find favor, especially with NATO powers, and thus did not see application as was hoped. Mattelart noted of the MacBride Report that,

> its greatest merit is the fact that it existed. It was the first time a document legitimized by a UN institution conferred viability on structural imbalances in the field of communications while also proposing a number of clues for solving them. (Mattelart, 2005, p. 53)

By the 1980s, global support for the NWICO agenda had chilled considerably (Kleinwachter, 1993). Both the NWICO and the MacBride Commission's efforts were heavily criticized by the US and the UK and encountered the strong counter-lobbying of Western media associations and groups through the coordinated actions of the World Press Freedom Committee (WPFC), who argued, without nuance, that the critique of the free flow doctrine was in effect an attack against free media altogether (Pickard, 2007). The eventual exit of the

US and the UK from the agency in 1984 and 1986 prompted changes within UNESCO's policies and outreach (given the serious dent to UNESCO's regular budget on account of the withdrawal of finances from these two major economic powers) and an eventual phasing out of its support for the ideas of the MacBride Commission and its report.

Viewed with hindsight, the US's withdrawal from UNESCO in 1984 had less to do with NWICO in and of itself and more to do with realignment of foreign policy priorities on account of other crucial factors such as the declining clout and eventual fall of the USSR, the advent of neoliberalism, and early globalization. NWICO's growing obsolesces in the "marketplace of ideas" and the shifting priorities of its fiercest advocate, the NAM nations, can also be connected to the subsequent realignment of world relations and power structures. In the 1990s, there was a visible shift from multilateralism toward bilateral relations and the rise of free trade regimes such as the North American Free Trade Agreement (NAFTA, now the United States-Mexico-Canada Agreement (USMCA)), and the World Trade Organization (WTO), which advocated for media deregulation as a prerequisite for inclusion in a new economic paradigm (Winseck, 1997; Boyd-Barrett, 2009). Unrestricted "trade in services," that is, media deregulation became a handy distortion of the original free flow doctrine, rapidly paving the way for an era of unprecedented media consolidation through transnational corporations (Thussu, 2005; Fuchs, 2015) and the transformation of the very structures of global communication into essential infrastructures of the economy (Schiller, 1999). Much of the decolonization ethos was lost in this paradigm shift as communication policy debates devolved into an ahistorical and depoliticized process (Pickard, 2007).

The structures of media and communication, consolidated in ownership through the process of globalization, went on to see a convergence on account of the digital. What played out in the decades since has been a rapid transmogrification of the internet from its early days as an interlinked, plural communicative, and information sphere to a sophisticated data-driven ecosystem of content, media, and news that is controlled by very large social platforms and driven by a targeted ad-model.

Redefining Non-Alignment for a New Data Order?

The NAM is often misread as a hasty post-colonial ideological reaction to the post-war/Cold War environment that lost traction in the ascendancy of globalization, and mixed opinions have prevailed on its long-term legacy and continued relevance. While the NAM's actions and positioning were indeed overtaken and reshaped by historical events, including a changing economic ideological context, the NAM's political-discursive contribution in providing a normative positioning and political critique of North-South relations was, and should still be seen as, a vital historical point. The NAM not only sought to be a critical avenue of self-determination for the developing world on the international stage, but also became a forum to further economic, social, political, and cultural agendas that were rooted in the continuities of the anti-colonialism and anti-imperialism struggles of its members. It also served as a vehicle to push and challenge the fledgling multilateral system of the UN whose mandate was yet nascent and being shaped by the post-war ethos of international cooperation. As such, the movement has had lasting normative influence in positioning and drawing attention to the skewed nature of North-South relations.

NWICO, which highlighted the skewed nature of the global information and communication landscape and asserted the need for redistribution of communication resources and the material means to shape one's cultural sovereignty, was perhaps "the most significant struggle over international communication policy in the Fordist era" as Chakravartty and Sarikakis (2006, p. 30) put it. It ultimately fell out of favor, succumbing to the seductive logic of neoliberalism.

NWICO's journey and the MacBride Commission's work point to how the realpolitik of the field ultimately overshadowed the critical scholarship that had found resonance with powerful actors in the international community. But it shows, without doubt, that critical media scholarship that applies itself to a public interest role can transform knowledge and intellectual paradigms and both feed into and learn from political discourse.

It was not as if a NWICO disappeared altogether from the world stage. Certainly, it did not fade away from the communication discipline where it continued to enjoy sustained engagement by scholars. The NWICO debates provided a defining framework for a lot of IAMCR's scholarly contributions and legacy from the decade of the 1960s and the 1970s.

Even as the rise of the internet presented a new information and technology architecture to contend with, the prescience and relevance of the key questions raised by NAM nations and the NWICO movement have continued to endure—how do we achieve a meaningful right to communication and realize informational sovereignty for the Global South in a context of ever-widening inequities in access and resources?

While the particular political context of the NAM itself stands radically changed today, we are yet again grappling with issues of technological and data concentration that ring as gravely and seriously as they did at the height of Cold War geopolitics. The global order is yet again cleaving into sharply escalating polarity between the US and China and a tenuous middle path is being chalked out in Europe (Oertel, 2020; Araya & Nieto-Gómez, 2020). On the one hand, the Chinese model promotes totalizing state control over communication and the informational platform ecosystem by allowing only domestic platforms to function within its borders; establishing strict control through blocks and filters of online content; and establishing rules for data localization (Puddephatt, 2020). Globally, China peddles influence through large tech companies such as Alibaba and Tencent as well as its global infrastructural roadmap, the Belt and Road Initiative (BRI). The US vision, in contrast, hinges on a global digital sphere run by private industry and is propped up by the Big Tech ecosystems of Silicon Valley, through the aegis of Amazon, Google, Microsoft, Facebook, and Google. Toward this, it has advocated for barriers against free flows of data as a cornerstone policy. Together, they have established disproportionate market dominance across countries and sectors and control over much of the world's data and digital assets.

The rapid growth of US tech companies and the lack of European innovation in the sector have also prompted the European Union (EU), which has traditionally aligned itself with the US, to rethink its policy pathways. Initially a purveyor of soft law within digital policy, the EU has sought to establish itself as a policy standard setter with more proactive and interventionist approaches through the General Data Protection Regulation (GDPR), and legislation such as the Data Governance Act and the Digital Markets Act. With its significant economic clout as a single market, the EU has been able to exercise authority over both companies that wish to do business in its territory as well as countries that comply with EU regulations and/or model their policies in line with the EU to be able to pursue economic opportunities with the bloc. The opt-out option provided to EU users with respect to WhatsApp's proposed privacy policy update in 2021 (ultimately scrapped), which would have allowed integration of data with the parent company of Facebook reflects the strategic concessions that the European market commands. Most developing nations today align themselves with either the Chinese or the US tech and information ecosystem and strive to achieve compliance with the EU's personal data policy standards.

Second, the free flow doctrine stands reinvented today and has cemented its unholy marriage with the free trade ideal, such as the Regional Comprehensive Economic Partnership (RCEP), the Comprehensive and Progressive Agreement for Trans-Pacific Partnership (CPTPP), and EU-Mercosur Free Trade Agreement, to perpetuate an uncritical discourse of free flows of data between and among nations. This simplistic maxim willfully disregards the staggering imbalances that exist in the global order, making such arrangements unidirectional and extractive, and ultimately advantageous to all but a limited group of nations and their industry behemoths.

The meta-narrative of sovereignty that emerges within this set of conditions, where the neoliberal state and the neoliberal market are givens, is in essence born acquiescent to the inherent power inequities within the global order that the NAM had worked so hard to highlight and bring into focus. This is even more so when this narrative is folded into a vision of "innovation" and tech-led economic progress that often prompts states to unquestioningly give a wide berth to tech corporations' activities within their markets. Even when overtures toward countering data extractivism are made—as has been attempted with the GDPR and other personal data protection frameworks that have emerged in recent years—these moves read as little more than an act of managing social morality for the sake of the market by preserving (an all too low) bottom line for citizen rights and welfare. To truly challenge the paradigm, as some developing nations have done through data localization measures or demanding accountability from tech corporations, is labeled as protectionist parochialism.

Lastly, the fundamental reconfiguration of the multilateral system of global governance—the very same that once afforded a key platform for the NAM and legitimized important discussions such as NWICO—into that of "multi-stakeholderism" has meant a further expansion of spheres of influence, voice, and power for private interests such as large technology corporations (Gleckman, 2019). Against this sobering reality, developing countries once again face an uphill battle to chart the course of their informational, technological, and data sovereignty.

The time may have come indeed for a newly redefined call to non-alignment for the data age. We need to deploy the prism of non-alignment, not merely as a political movement, but for seeking a strong ethos of solidarity and self-determination that goes beyond self-interest-based identitarian nationalism to examine the social resource of data's and society's relationalities as they play out among people and planet. Nations and communities must once again seek meaningful and mutually enriching "alignments" within a larger non-alignment that should seek to forge a new path. A new international order also needs to be reinvented for the new order that inspired the leaders who met under the NAM.

The Bandung Conference and its enduring "spirit" and the growth of the NAM as a powerful world actor demonstrated that strange bedfellows of nations could travel together in pursuit of a strong national and global post-colonial identity as well as common goals, irrespective of their own differences and without having to completely depend upon the aegis of a superpower to find their voice. Inspiring watershed exercises such as the MacBride Commission's work have shown that it is indeed possible to mobilize the multilateral system for galvanizing change and providing direction for systemic policy issues.

Indeed, the NAM's ascendancy on the global stage, IAMCR's growth into the association it is today, and the impact of both on the communication paradigm of its time hold valuable lessons for those who continue to remain invested in this objective. It indicates to us the value convergences that scholarship and activism can bring about, while, at the same time, highlighting their limitations and boundaries when pushing for policy-level change.

Over the decades, IAMCR's strong culture of critical research, which found its moorings in the NAM era and in the idea of centering questions of power and development, has gone from strength to strength. Scholars have drawn from the same to study and engage with key turning points in the global political economy of media and communication, including media consolidation and globalization, the rise of networks and, more recently, the platform economy. The association's notable engagement with the WSIS process can also be attributed to some extent to this larger legacy (Fig. 17.1).

Much as NAM leaders stressed the importance of democratizing the underlying material resources and infrastructure as key to true plurality and diversity in the world's communication and information landscape and their informational sovereignty, data as the means of production or the new knowledge capital, must allow plural visions of social flourishing and pathways to informational sovereignty for the Global South. A renewed imperative thus presents itself to counter the emergent forms of technological concentration, challenges to

Fig. 17.1 Experts Debate Global Trends in Freedom of Expression and Media Development, UNESCO Panel at IAMCR Conference, Eugene, 2018. (From left to right) **Olunifesi Adekunle Suraj**, University of Lagos; **Levi Obonyo**, Daystar University; **Manisha Pathak-Shelat**, MICA; **Aimée Vega Montiel**, National Autonomous University of Mexico; **Ramon Tuazon**, Asian Institute of Journalism and Communication; **Robin Mansell**, London School of Economics and Political Science. (Courtesy of IAMCR)

sovereignty, and communication rights as well as developing the autonomy of developing nations. There is a need for critical and informed agile scholarship that can grapple with these questions and actively shape normative rule-making in the public interest. IAMCR, with its reach, diversity, and range of foci is well placed to continue with its history of critical engagement toward this goal.

References

Araya, D., & Nieto-Gómez, R. (2020, November). *Renewing multilateral governance in the age of AI*. Modern Conflict and Artificial Intelligence-Essay Series. Centre for International Governance Innovation. Retrieved 15 June 2022, from https://www.cigionline.org/articles/renewing-multilateral-governance-age-ai/

Boyd-Barrett, O. (2009). Free flow of information. In C. H. Sterling (Ed.), *Encyclopedia of journalism*. Sage Publications.

Chakravartty, P., & Sarikakis, K. (2006). Revisiting the history of global communication and media policy. In *Media policy and globalization* (p. 24–48). Palgrave Macmillan.

Fuchs, C. (2015). The MacBride report in twenty-first-century capitalism, the age of social media and the BRICS countries. *Javnost-The Public*, *22*(3), 226–239. Retrieved 15 June 2022, from https://doi.org/10.1080/13183222.2015.1059626

Gleckman, H. (2019, September). They call it multistakeholderism. Where does that leave the UN? *PassBlue*. Retrieved 15 June 2022, from https://www.passblue.com/2019/09/02/they-call-it-multistakeholderism-where-does-that-leave-the-un/

Halloran, J. D. (1970). *Mass media in society: The need of research.* UNESCO. Retrieved 15 June 2022, from https://unesdoc.unesco.org/ark:/48223/pf0000003169

Kleinwächter, W. (1993). Three waves of the debate. In G. Gerbner, H. Mowlana, & K. Nordenstreng (Eds.), *The global media debate: Its rise, fall and renewal* (p. 13–34). Ablex.

MacBride, S. & Contributors. (1980). *Communication and society today and tomorrow: Many voices, one world: Towards a new, more just, and more efficient world information and communication order.* Kogan Page, Unipub, UNESCO.

Mattelart, A. (2005). The stammering discovery of the processes of internationalisation. *Quaderns del CAC, 21*(38), p. 53–54. Retrieved 15 June 2022, from https://www.cac.cat/sites/default/files/2019-05/Q21_mattelart_EN.pdf

Menon, D. M. (2014). Bandung is back: Afro-Asian affinities (Review of the book *Brown over black: Race and the politics of postcolonial citation*, by A. Burton). *Radical History Review*, *(119)*, 241–245. Retrieved 15 June 2022, from https://doi.org/10.1215/01636545-2402153

No Author. (1973, September 1–9). *The economic declaration of the Algiers Summit meeting.* 4th Summit Conference of Heads of State of Governments of the Non-Aligned Movement. Algiers.

Nopper, T. (2015, June 30). The illusion of Afro-Asian solidarity? Situating the 1955 Bandung conference. *Black Perspectives.* Retrieved 15 June 2022, from https://www.aaihs.org/the-illusion-of-afro-asian-solidarity-situating-the-1955-bandung-conference/

Nordenstreng, K. (2008). Institutional networking: The story of the International Association for Media and Communication Research (IAMCR). In D. Park & J. Pooley (Eds.), *The history of media and communication research. Contested memories* (p. 225–248). Peter Lang.

Nordenstreng, K. (2010). MacBride report as a culmination of NWICO. *Les enjeux de l'information et la communication, Supplement 2010-A.* Retrieved 15 June 2022, from https://www.researchgate.net/publication/265036640_MacBride_report_as_a_culmination_of_NWICO

Nordenstreng, K. (2011a). The New World Information and Communication Order: Testimony of an actor. *Widerworte: Philosophie-Politik-Kommunikation. Festschrift für Jörg Becker.* Retrieved 15 June 2022, from https://sites.tuni.fi/uploads/2019/12/08c5fb13-paris.pdf

Nordenstreng, K. (2011b). Free flow doctrine in global media policy. In R. Mansell & M. Raboy (Eds.), *The handbook of global media and communication policy* (p. 79–94). Wiley-Blackwell.

Nordenstreng, K. (2013). How the new world order and imperialism challenge media studies. *tripleC, 11*(2), 348–358.

Oertel, J. (2020). China: Trust, 5G, and the coronavirus factor. In C. Hobbs (Ed.), *Europe's digital sovereignty: From rulemaker to superpower in the age of US-China rivalry* (p. 24–32). European Council on Foreign Relations. Retrieved 15 June 2022, from https://ecfr.eu/publication/europe_digital_sovereignty_rulemaker_superpower_age_us_china_rivalry/

Pickard, V. (2007). Neoliberal visions and revisions in global communications policy from NWICO to WSIS. *Journal of Communication Inquiry, 31*(2), 118–139. Retrieved 15 June 2022, from https://journals.sagepub.com/doi/10.1177/0196859906298162

Pohle, J. (2016). *Information for all? The emergence of UNESCO's policy discourse on the information society (1990–2003).* Doctoral Thesis, ZBW. Retrieved 15 June 2022, from https://hdl.handle.net/10419/158025

Puddephatt, A. (2020). Governing the internet: The makings of an EU model. In C. Hobbs (Ed.), *Europe's digital sovereignty: From rulemaker to superpower in the age of US-China rivalry* (p. 13–24). European Council on Foreign Relations. Retrieved 15 June 2022, from https://ecfr.eu/publication/europe_digital_sovereignty_rulemaker_superpower_age_us_china_rivalry/.

Roberts, B. R., & Foulcher, K. (2016). Introduction: Richard Wright on the Bandung conference, modern Indonesia on Richard Wright. In B. R. Roberts & K. Foulcher (Eds.), *Indonesian notebook: A sourcebook on Richard Wright and the Bandung conference* (p. 1–31). Duke University Press.

Schiller, D. (1999). *Digital capitalism: Networking the global market system.* MIT Press.

Schiller, H. I. (1975). Communication and cultural domination. *International Journal of Politics*, *5*(4), 1–127. Retrieved 15 June 2022, from https://www.jstor.org/stable/27868829

Schiller, H. I. (1978). Decolonization of information: Efforts toward a new international order. *Latin American Perspectives*, *5*(1), 35–48. Retrieved 15 June 2022, from https://www.jstor.org/stable/2633338

Thussu, D. (2005). From MacBride to Murdoch: The marketisation of global communication. *Javnost—The Public*, *12*(3), 47–60. Retrieved 15 June 2022, from https://www.tandfonline.com/doi/abs/10.1080/13183222.2005.11008894

UNESCO. (1976). *Resolution 100.* 19th General Session of UNESCO, Nairobi.

UNESCO. (1978). *Declaration of fundamental principles concerning the contribution of the mass media to strengthening peace and international understanding, the promotion of human rights information and to countering racialism, Apartheid and incitement to war.* UNESCO, Paris.

Van Dinh, T. (1976). Non-alignment and cultural imperialism. *The Black Scholar*, *8*(3), 39–49. Retrieved 15 June 2022, from https://www.jstor.org/stable/41066081

Wasko, J. (2013). The IAMCR Political Economy Section: A retrospective. *The Political Economy of Communication*, *1*(1), p. 4–8. Retrieved June 15, 2022, from http://www.polecom.org/index.php/polecom/article/view/11/148

Winseck, D. (1997). Contradictions in the democratization of international communication. *Media, Culture & Society*, *19*(2), 219–246. Retrieved 15 June 2022, from https://journals.sagepub.com/doi/10.1177/016344397019002006

Vitalis, R. (2013). The midnight ride of Kwame Nkrumah and other fables of Bandung (Ban-doong). *Humanity: An International Journal of Human Rights, Humanitarianism, and Development*, *4*(2), 261–288. Retrieved 15 June 2022, from https://www.researchgate.net/publication/265725533_The_Midnight_Ride_of_Kwame_Nkrumah_and_Other_Fables_of_Bandung_Ban-doong

Young, R. J. C. (2005). Postcolonialism: From Bandung to the Tricontinental. *Historein*, *5*, 11–21. Retrieved 15 June 2022, from https://doi.org/10.12681/historein.70

CHAPTER 18

Cultural Diversity at UNESCO and ITU/WSIS: 50 Years of Milestones (1980–2020)

Divina Frau-Meigs

Introduction[1]

The debate on cultural diversity as a legal concept and binding instrument took place during the social turn of the internet from 2003 to 2006, with large-scale search engines and data-driven social media platforms (Facebook, YouTube, and Twitter) affecting the geopolitics of communication on an unprecedented scale, reminiscent of the 1980s' New World Information and Communication Order (NWICO). The social turn made it clear that the network of networks was a critical resource that impacted information and communication as well as audiences and communities worldwide. The debate went beyond post-Cold War and post-colonial issues, to recognize the growth of several regions of the world beyond Western countries (the BRICS—Brazil, Russia, India, China,

[1] The author was involved in both the Convention on the Protection and Promotion of the Diversity of Cultural Expressions (CDCE) and the World Summit on the Information Society (WSIS) as IAMCR's representative, first as Deputy Secretary General (1996–2004) and then as Vice President (2004–2008). She was a member of the NGO Liaison Committee at UNESCO and a member of the civil society bureau of the WSIS for IAMCR, representing the "education and research family," as well as a member of the cultural diversity caucus. She worked in close collaboration with IAMCR's Executive Committee led by successive IAMCR Presidents, Manuel Pares i Maicas, Frank Morgan, and Robin Mansell when it came to statements and contributions.

D. Frau-Meigs (✉)
Université Sorbonne Nouvelle, Paris, France

© The Author(s), under exclusive license to Springer Nature Switzerland AG 2023

J. Becker, R. Mansell (eds.), *Reflections on the International Association for Media and Communication Research*,
https://doi.org/10.1007/978-3-031-16383-8_18

South Africa), while acknowledging the dependence on the US for root servers and business services as global corporations such as Cisco, Apple, Microsoft, and Google redefined the field (Mattelart, 2005).

The debate on cultural diversity followed in the wake of NWICO and the MacBride Report in 1980, whose 25th anniversary was celebrated (Frau-Meigs et al., 2012). It shared with the NWICO the same basic issues, but it also brought some of its own because the digital dimension and neo-liberal globalization added a layer of complexity to the concert of nations (Giddens, 2001; Beck, 2003). The ideas that were carried over in the new millennium were no less controversial than in the late post-modern era, but they were clustered differently around key global issues of cyber-policy, cyber-security, and the digital divide in the World Summit on the Information Society (WSIS). They underwent both a dilution and a repurposing with an array of new notions and actors in a new era of "catalytic" diplomacy and legal innovation (Hocking in Melissen, 1999, p. 31–33).

The debate was carried on in two different arenas that were nonetheless interlocked: at UNESCO during the elaboration of the Convention for Cultural Diversity (2003–2005) and at the International Telecommunication Union (ITU) during the WSIS, between 2003 and 2005. These two elongated and multi-pronged processes that have continued since with yearly reporting and stocktaking confirmed the catalytic shift in global diplomacy since the 1990s. They were issue-oriented, relied on multiple stakeholders, and evolved according to an agile methodology, requiring several rounds of regional discussions and constant monitoring and adjusting, all the more so as they were aligned along the way with the United Nations' Sustainable Development Goals (SDGs), whose summit took place in 2015. They contributed to emerging third-generation human rights, also known as "solidarity rights," as they focus less on individuals and more on collectives, together with a right to a healthy environment, a right to communicate, etc. They were part of the new "soft law" approach to policy-making—empirical, bottom-up, and with no strong sanction mechanisms—leaving it to governance by multi-stakeholders to solve disputes.

The Convention and the Significance of Culture in Development

Cultural diversity lent itself ideally to this global and fluid catalytic process. The "Convention on the protection and promotion of the diversity of cultural expressions" (CDCE) created an *ad hoc* international instrument that was adopted in October 2005 (UNESCO, 2005). It focused on two major objectives: the recognition of the dual nature of cultural expressions as objects of trade and artifacts of cultural identity formation and the recognition of the sovereign right of governments to implement all measures they see fit to protect and promote their cultural diversity. To some extent, this was a regression compared to the "Universal Declaration on Cultural Diversity" (UNESCO, 2001) as the 2005 Declaration proposed an exception for media and information services, but it was a progression in that it encompassed all goods and services related to culture.

That Declaration followed from heated discussions of 1993, due to the Uruguay trade round, where the expression "cultural exception" was coined as the original rallying cry against the General Agreement on Tariffs and Trade (GATT). The purpose then was for the US and its allies to capitalize on the end of the Cold War and open all markets and all sectors to competition worldwide. But when the time came to treat media and information as services, France, followed by Canada, and a number of developing countries called for an "exception" to the trade agreements, considering that sector to be specific in that it cemented and strengthened social cohesion within multi-ethnic societies and, therefore, required state sovereignty in matters of aid and incentives for cultural goods (Frau-Meigs, 2002).

The "cultural exception" doctrine did not succeed entirely and was perceived as "anti-Americanism," but it terminated the GATT which was replaced by the World Trade Organization (WTO) with the adoption of the Marrakesh Agreement (1994). Cultural goods and services were not "excluded" from the WTO, but their liberalization was to be flexible and progressive, especially in the matter of audio-visual services such as the production, distribution, and broadcast of television programs and cinema films. The member states could decide on their commitments to market access and cultural policies. To consolidate this treatment, a new concept was called for and it emerged in 1999 during the run-up to the WTO Ministerial Conference in Seattle: "cultural diversity" regarding trade in audio-visual media. The new notion was conceptually neutral and could serve as a battle cry shared by the Global South. It presented the added advantage of referring to biology and ecology, where diverse ecosystems are more sustainable, differentiated, and resilient than deserts or monocultures.

The Convention debate shifted from protecting cultural expression to promoting it under a stricter enforcement of intellectual property (IP) laws (with developed countries fearing piracy) (Wagner, 2000). It also mitigated harms linked to enforcement of IP by strengthening the rights of indigenous people and traditional communities' ownership over their indigenous production. But it understated issues of access to knowledge, the public domain, and global cultural commons. These issues were actually carried over into the other arena, the WSIS, where indigenous people and linguistic issues were pushed both by the Cultural Diversity Caucus and by the Indigenous Caucus, as exemplified by their joint statement during PrepCom3 in September 2005.

The Convention brought to the fore, however, major issues that contributed to specifying what cultural diversity is about, without falling into the trap of essentialism: national identity, heritage transmission, media pluralism, and sustainable development. This discussion pleaded for maintaining policies such as state aids and tariffs in the face of free trade. To curtail the risk of cultural essentialism (pushed by theocratic member states), the preamble explicitly put cultural diversity under the umbrella of human rights and fundamental freedom standards (including freedom of expression and information), stating as its first guiding principle that "no one may invoke the provisions of this Convention in order to infringe human rights and fundamental freedoms" (Article 1). It placed the instrument as a contribution to, not a limitation on, freedom of expression and information, especially in the light of indigenous peoples and cultural minorities.

The CDCE provided a very pragmatic definition of cultural diversity, referring to "the manifold ways in which the cultures of groups and societies find expression" (Article 4). It focused on the empirical manifestations across cultures, such as the production, dissemination, and distribution of its expressions. It presented uniformization by market forces as an obstacle to be avoided. At the same time, it provided for a statistics-based approach to capture creative expressions and avoid reification and essentialism, thus also emphasizing that culture can be part of national wealth. And it ensured the sovereign right of governments to implement cultural policies and to adopt measures to protect and promote them, enshrining the dual value of media and expression as both trade and culture (Article 5).

Beyond the semantic discussions, the implementation debate was very heated and it would lead to political, legal, and economic consequences. The implementation discussion dealt with international coordination, funding, and the relationship to other instruments and entities such as the World Intellectual Property Organization (WIPO) and WTO. Issues of "rights of parties at the national level" (Article 6) and "relationship to other treaties" with "complementarity and non-subordination" (Article 20) were among the climactic moments of the Convention, as they risked being deleted under the pressure of the US that considered them as protectionist, distorting market laws, and violating citizens' rights to free expression and information. A series of commitments was nonetheless embedded to help developing countries adopt cultural policies and protect indigenous cultures, including preferential treatment for artists (Article 16), and provisions for an International Fund for Cultural Diversity (Article 18). The participation of civil society (Article 11) was also discussed when it emerged as a key actor in the multi-stakeholder process, especially reinforced in the WSIS (Drossou, 2005; Frau-Meigs & Kiyingou, 2012). The CDCE was finally adopted in October 2005 by 146 countries; the US and Japan pledging never to sign it.

IAMCR's Contribution

IAMCR engaged in the debate as an NGO with observer consultative status with UNESCO and was part of the *comité de liaison* (CLO) of non-governmental organizations (NGOs) of UNESCO that represented the voice of civil society (including researchers and NGOs, by UN standards). IAMCR members were present both at UNESCO and at the WSIS, which made it possible to coordinate issues and participate in large civil society alliances, as confirmed in the General Assembly of 2002 in Barcelona.[2] The main focus of IAMCR was twofold—process and content. On content, as shown in the extract below, IAMCR wanted to ensure that the narrow technological and legal discourse, typical of such venues, would be broadened to societal issues, and to warrant that, issues related to media and information governance as well as information and communication rights would be embedded in the agenda (See also Chaps. 14 and 16 in this collection). Consequently, IAMCR focused mostly on articles 4, 11, 13, 16, and 20 as they were among the most likely to ensure that civil society and local cultures would be represented.[3]

> Mr president, distinguished representatives of the member states
>
> Thank you for this opportunity of expressing the point of view of IAMCR, which represents an umbrella federation of research associations in the whole world, specialized on issues of media, communication and information research, in developed and developing countries. (...) We would like to contribute to the substance of the debate from our researchers' perspective, around two points: what research shows, what research recommends in terms of balance in diversity. (...)
>
> IAMCR wishes to express some concern about the future of the convention. We are concerned that the use of the term Intellectual Property subsumes different categories of rights and constituencies: artists, creators, producers, users, citizens... As it is currently understood and implemented, Intellectual Property only protects the rights holders, and so only one of the constituencies, not all the multi-stakeholders. By not taking into account this evolution, and other evolutions in the consumer and citizen uses of media and ICTs, the convention runs the risk of being out of synch with the evolution of cultural diversity itself.
>
> What research recommends:
>
> - the need for balance between openness of the markets and national cultural policies;
> - the need for balance between promotion of creativity and protection of patrimony;
> - the need for balance between developed countries' present offer and developing countries' fair access to the same historical public funding opportunities, mechanisms and processes as developed countries have benefited from in the past.
> - the need for balance in the vocabulary used in the official document between goods and services on the one hand, and, on the other hand, other non-proprietary and non-commercial forms of cultural exchange, like public domain, public services, creative commons, fair use, etc.

[2] See General Assembly report, 2002, https://iamcr.org/barcelona-minutes-of-the-23rd-iamcr-general-assembly. Accessed 15 June 2022.

[3] See Avant-Projet de convention, présentation des commentaires et amendements des ONG, UNESCO, CLT/CPD/2004/CONF.607/1 Part V décembre 2004 (in French and English) https://unesdoc.unesco.org/ark:/48223/pf0000140318. Accessed 15 June 2022.

> IAMCR wishes to express some hope about the future of the convention. We are hopeful that an open transparent process, that takes into account the contributions of all stakeholders will eventually lead to the drafting of a final document that will give its full meaning to the notion of diversity, that goes together with tolerance, respect, and pluralism, all for the benefit of cultures, worldwide.[4]

In the process, IAMCR tried to represent not only the community of researchers, but also a people-centered approach within a fledgling multi-stakeholder process. It participated in many preliminary draft meetings, with sessions of inter-governmental meetings of experts, as early as 2002 when PrepCom consultations were being held in UNESCO Paris and ITU Geneva, and particularly in early 2005, as both processes were gearing up to the end. It engaged in various initiatives by civil society groups, especially the Communication Rights in the Information Society (CRIS) campaign, Association for Progressive Communications (APC), and International Federation of Library Associations (IFLA), with converging interests. IAMCR was aware of the need to act within sites of global governance to address powers in communications, especially dealing with the "free trade" regimes of the WTO, Internet Corporation for Assigned Names and Numbers (ICANN), and ITU. UNESCO seemed a venue for counter-balancing these and other powerful agencies and the IAMCR Board decided to support it, while recognizing the flaws in the process. IAMCR participated in a number of thematic meetings that supported notions of "Cultural Diversity in Knowledge Societies" (vs. information society) as in the Saint-Petersburg thematic meeting, May 2005.[5]

Hence, the decision-shaping strategy used was sharing with policymakers, meeting with other sectors, both in the Convention and the WSIS arenas, bringing as much attention as possible to civil society, the media (freedom of expression, pluralism, and independence), and research (monitoring and independence). In fact, participating in both arenas, IAMCR supported issues in the WSIS that were understated in UNESCO, such as the rights of indigenous people and traditional communities' ownership over their indigenous production, and access to knowledge, the public domain, and the global cultural commons. Cooperating with the Cultural Diversity Caucus, IAMCR thus contributed to the WSIS Tunis Commitment in paragraphs 2, 5, 6, 7, and 11 as indicated below (ITU, 2005). Diversity became one of the key notions of Internet Governance (together with openness, interoperability, and security, together with multi-stakeholderism as the main process), pushed by the

[4] Extract, Contribution of IAMCR to the debate on the preliminary draft of the then-called "Convention on the protection of cultural contents and artistic expressions," February 2005.

[5] Reports and conclusions of the thematic meetings organized by UNESCO in preparation of the second meeting of the WSIS, UNESCO, CI-2005/WS/3 https://unesdoc.unesco.org/ark:/48223/pf0000140208. Accessed 15 June 2022.

Working Group on Internet Governance (WGIG) set up in 2004 to deal with the emerging issue of Internet Governance (Frau-Meigs, 2007).[6]

> The Cultural Diversity Working Group respectfully requests the following changes to the Political Chapeau/Tunis Commitment in paragraphs 2, 5, 6, 7, and 11 (…)
>
> 5. We reaffirm our resolution in the quest to ensure that everyone can benefit from the opportunities that ICTs can offer, by recalling that governments, as well as private sector, civil society and the United Nations and other international organizations, should work together to: [establish and] improve access to information [, knowledge] and communication infrastructure and technologies as well as to information and knowledge; build capacity; increase confidence and security in the use of ICTs; create an enabling environment at all levels; develop and widen ICT applications; [preserve, promote and protect] foster and respect cultural diversity; recognize the role of the media; address the ethical dimensions of the Information Society; and encourage international and regional cooperation.[7]

IAMCR approached both the CDCE and the WSIS as a golden opportunity for redefining its own vision and mission after NWICO and for renewing its consultative status with UNESCO. This proved fruitful as it led the association to redefine its research agenda with UNESCO and to revisit pressing and emerging research issues about cultural diversity, governance, and media and information literacy, among others (UNESCO, 2008; See Fig. 18.1).[8]

This implied a follow-up on developing key indicators for cultural diversity and helping to elaborate approaches to cultural economy statistics.[9] IAMCR also extended its international presence by joining the UN Economic and Social Council (ECOSOC) to oversee a UN system-wide follow-up to the WSIS, enabled by the catalytic logic of the agile process. IAMCR was thus involved in the follow-up to the WSIS Forum in Geneva. The WSIS Forum incorporated "cultural diversity" as action C8 and "media" as action C9, under UNESCO responsibility.[10] Both arenas co-joined efforts to support initiatives toward the SDGs with yearly reporting as of 2007 (See Fig. 18.2). IAMCR, thus, was invited to participate in the WSIS+10 stocktaking in 2015 in

[6] See WGIG final report, 2005 https://www.wgig.org/docs/WGIGREPORT.pdf. Accessed 15 June 2022.

[7] Extract: E-mail exchange on paragraph 5 of Tunis Commitment chapeau, culture@wsis-cs.org, 23 February 2005, see Mailman.gn.apc.or Mailing Lists, http://mailman.greennet.org.uk/mailman/listinfo/culture. Accessed 15 June 2022.

[8] See Communication and information: Towards a prospective research agenda, https://www.researchgate.net/publication/30524169_Communication_and_information_towards_a_prospective_research_agenda. Accessed 15 June 2022.

[9] See The Cultural Economy, UNESCO's Framework for Cultural Statistics, UNESCO Institute for Statistics, 2009, https://en.unesco.org/creativity/files/cultural-economy-unescos-framework-cultural-statistics. Accessed 15 June 2022.

[10] See WSIS Implementation by Action Line, https://www.itu.int/net/wsis/c8/index.html. Accessed 15 June 2022.

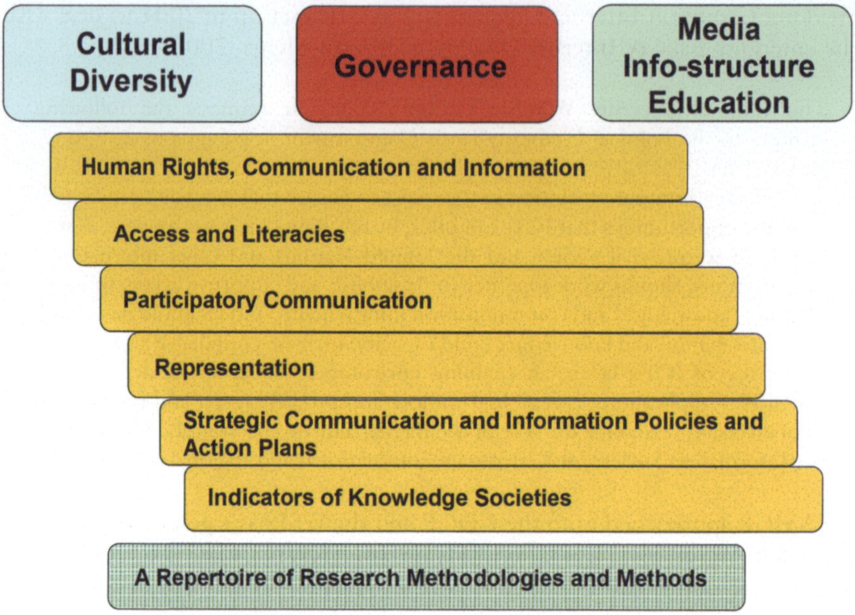

Fig. 18.1 IAMCR Contribution to UNESCO Research Agenda, *Communication and Information: Towards a Prospective Research Agenda. Report on an IAMCR/UNESCO Workshop to Elaborate a Policy-relevant Research Agenda*, IAMCR, 20–21 December 2007. (Courtesy of Robin Mansell)

New York.[11] UNESCO has been regularly invited to IAMCR annual world conferences that are part of the stocktaking process.[12]

The Ongoing Implementation: From a Rallying Cry to a Policy Tool in the Digital Era

The CDCE was implemented in March 2007 when the requested 30 states ratified it. As of 2020, 149 parties—148 States and 1 region, and the European Union (EU), had joined. Among the continuing and standing issues opened up by articles 13, 20, and 21, some provide valuable insights into the role of communication and information, as well as the media and information and communication technologies (ICTs) in culture. In this sense, the CDCE can be seen as a paradigmatic case of awareness-raising in relation to media's contribution to culture (Bernier, 2006; Vlassis, 2011).

[11] See recording, Divina Frau-Meigs, International Association Media & Communication Research, UN WSIS+10 consultation July 2015 https://www.youtube.com/watch?v=wTt1ArS7uvk. Accessed 15 June 2022.

[12] See WSIS-forum action lines report, 2019, Action C8 https://www.itu.int/net4/wsis/forum/2019/Files/Outcomes/DRAFT-WSISForum2019WSISActionLinesReport.pdf. Accessed 15 June 2022.

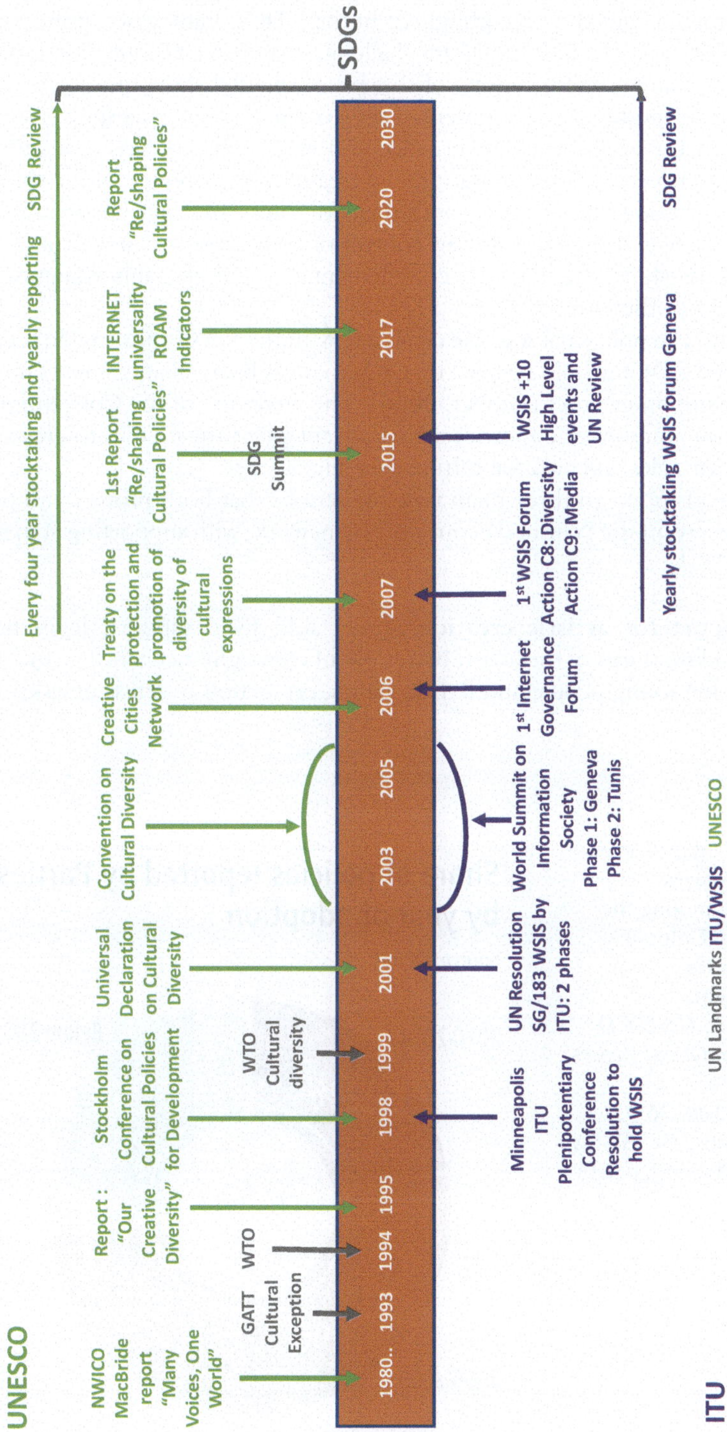

Fig. 18.2 Cultural Diversity at UNESCO and ITU/WSIS: 50 Years of Milestones, 1980–2020 (Created by Divina Frau-Meigs, 2022)

Three main issues can be highlighted in the CDCE framework: policymaking, creativity and IP, and digital era challenges to media and information. In these areas, there are illustrations of three fundamental shifts in implementation that have modified and augmented the notion of diversity: a shift in sovereignty, with the addition of governance and multi-stakeholderism; a shift in intellectual property, with the addition of creativity and literacy; and a shift in digital media goods and services, with the addition of Internet Universality to deal with increased digital platform control over information and data flows. Each of these shifts attests to the complementarity and non-subordination of the CDCE to other arenas.

In relation to policymaking, the challenge with the WTO consisted in seeing whether the CDCE would be used by states to resist bilateral agreements under pressure from other states (Graber, 2006). The direct use of the Convention is visible in the number of countries taking advantage of the CDCE to create or revamp their rules and aids for culture (See Fig. 18.3).

The trends point to three main types of actions that both protect and promote diversity, in the "cultural economy" framework, with supporting statistics (see Fig. 18.4):

- **Support for artistic creation**: direct aids, fiscal support, legislation, including status of the artist, better use of copyright mechanisms, incubators for young people and female artists, protection of artists at risk;

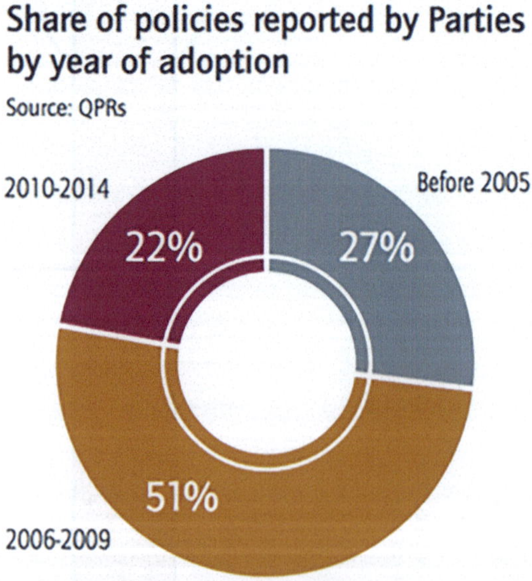

Fig. 18.3 Re/Shaping Cultural Policies: A Decade Promoting the Diversity of Cultural Expression for Development, 2005–2015, *UNESCO Convention Global Report 2015*, (ISBN: 978-92-3-100136-9, licensed under CC BY-SA 3.0 IGO [10558], p. 51)

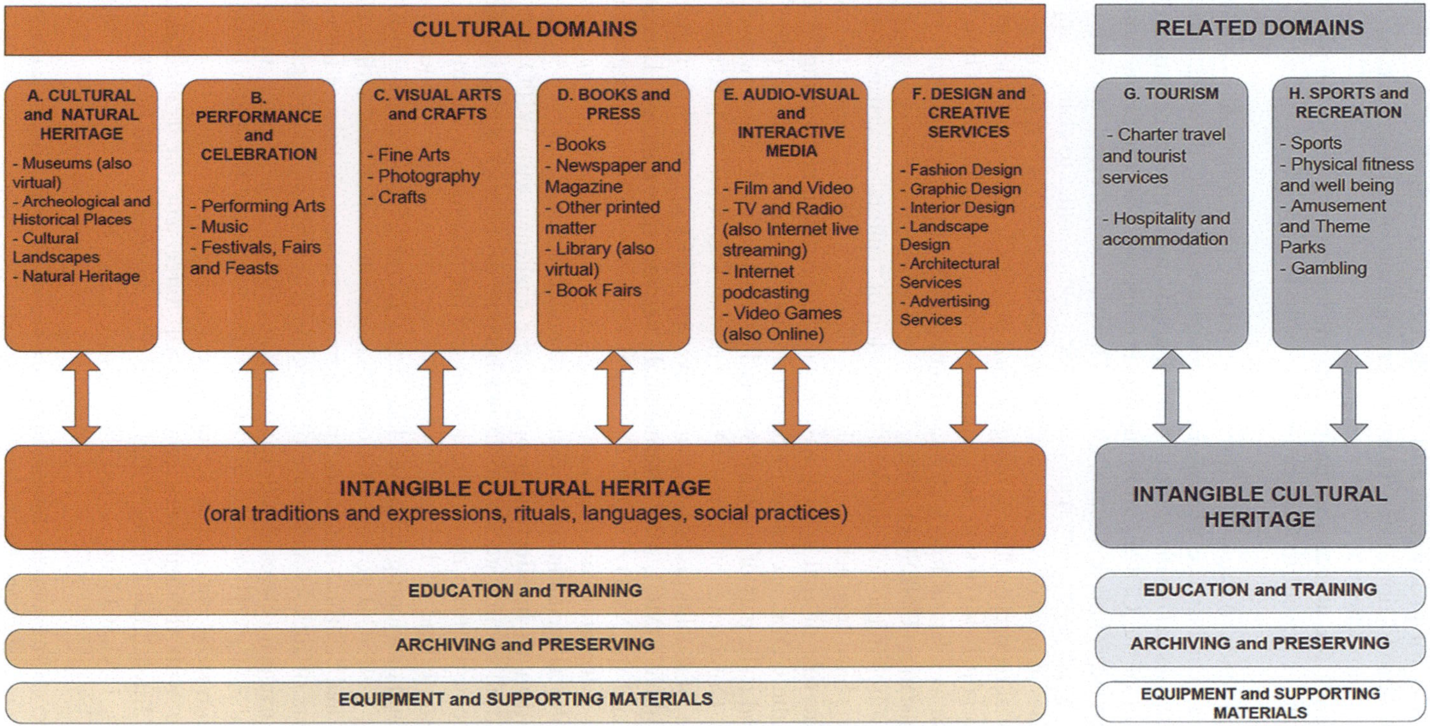

Fig. 18.4 The Cultural Economy, UNESCO Statistical Framework, *2009 UNESCO Framework for Cultural Statistics*, Paris (p. 24 at https://en.unesco.org/creativity/files/cultural-economy-unescos-framework-cultural-statistics)

- **Support for production and distribution**: direct funding of local creation, production infrastructure, promotion of market access, co-production schemes;
- **Support for access and participation**: for disadvantaged people and minorities, for cultural education, for media literacy.

Research tends to show that the impact of the CDCE on trade in cultural goods is not an instance of disguised protectionism since there have been greater increases in country trade in cultural goods, more than in countries that are not part of the CDCE, implying that it contributes to the promotion of cultural diversity (Jinji & Tanaka, 2020). There is also increased invocation of the CDEC as a legal basis by regional and local communities to claim or implement policies in favor of cultural diversity within the states (as is apparent in the recent global reports on "re/shaping cultural policies"), indicating a departure from the original idea of state sovereignty as a protection from threats by other states, such as bilateral free trade agreements (FTAs) under commercial pressure, for instance (UNESCO, 2015).

This resulted in the emergence of the notion of "cultural governance" as all stakeholders have been activated at all levels of power and contribution (Vlassis, 2015). The role of civil society has grown as organizations working in the sphere of the CDEC are asked to contribute to the signatory states' periodic reports, and to be part of the Civil Society Forum that is held every two years, prior to the Conference of Parties.[13] Among the most active are the International Federation of Coalitions for Cultural Diversity (IFCCD), the International Music Council (IMC), the International Network for Cultural Diversity (INCD), and the NGO/UNESCO Liaison Committee. This is a significant shift in the recognition of civil society actors, not just as beneficiaries or executants but also as agents in the early stages of policy design.

In relation to intellectual property, the challenge with WIPO was to ensure that all cultural goods would not become proprietary and disproportionately removed from the public domain and the information commons. To maintain some kind of balance between developed countries' monopolistic consortia and developing countries' local arts and crafts, one strategy consisted in creating UNESCO's own definition of "creative industries" and adding it to the traditional "cultural industries" paradigm to ensure a fair balance between the interests of authors and those of the general public for accessing knowledge, in particular (Caves, 2000; Cunningham, 2001). This addition aimed at counter-balancing WIPO's creation of a creative industries division in its small and medium-sized enterprises sector to retain them within the IP rules in accordance with the still very controversial Agreement on Trade-Related Aspects of Intellectual Property Rights (TRIPS), annexed to the WTO system since 1994. UNESCO supported the Creative Cities Network born in 2004,

[13] UNESCO Governing Bodies, Diversity of Cultural Expressions, https://en.unesco.org/creativity/governance/governing-bodies. Accessed 15 June 2022.

out of the Global Alliance for Cultural Diversity set up in 2002. The goal was to ensure international cooperation among cities and their regions and to bring together locally public, private, and associative partnerships. Such territorial entities would serve as umbrellas for individual artists, their training, and their safety, while contributing to the digital economy (Richieri Hanania, 2015).

The cities were labeled according to UNESCO's seven creative categories: literature, cinema, music, arts and crafts, design, media arts, and gastronomy.[14] As of 2019, 246 cities were part of the network in about 90 countries. From then on, the cultural and creative industries became the umbrella for work on issues of inclusion, translation, localization of goods and services, knowledge transmission, and education.

Media and Information Literacy was also promoted within UNESCO as a means to promote intercultural dialog. Consequently, as of 2006, it published its first handbook on Media Literacy and started building the Media and Information Literacy and Intercultural Dialogue (MILID) network of UNESCO chairs. By 2011, it had fostered the Global Alliance for Partnerships in Media and Information Literacy (GAPMIL, renamed MIL Alliance in 2020) to ensure the transfer of knowledge, protection of users' rights, and new literacies in the digital era. IAMCR reflected this engagement in its Media Education Section that was transformed into the Media Education Research Section to monitor policymaking, to share new pedagogical practices, and to help young people and adults alike to adjust to digital transformations (Frau-Meigs et al., 2020).

In relation to digital media goods and services, the challenge was to deal with the rise of a new international information order with the digital platforms establishing monopolistic control over information structures and data flows (Frau-Meigs et al., 2012). The need to upgrade the CDCE for the digital era, perceived during the WSIS, became increasingly urgent as UNESCO participated in the WSIS Forum. During NetMundial in 2014, convened as a means to deal with massive surveillance by governments, following on the Edward Snowden revelations on Wikileaks, it became clear to policymakers that the power of the digital platforms was threatening their sovereignty. The full weight of social media platforms added a layer of complexity that tested the robustness of the CDCE, especially its technical neutrality (as no specific media are ever mentioned, allowing for any innovation to be included). The focus changed with less attention to pluralism (due to the over-abundance of cheap media) and more on access, privacy, and identity formation.

After starting the process in 2013, UNESCO published its "guidelines on the implementation of the convention in the digital environment" in 2017.[15] They extended rights offline to offer the same protection online, "through any

[14] See The Creative Cities Network, https://en.unesco.org/creative-cities/home. Accessed 15 June 2022.

[15] See UNESCO Digital Guidelines https://fr.unesco.org/creativity/sites/creativity/files/digital_guidelines_en_full-3.pdf. Accessed 15 June 2022.

media of one's choice" (Article 8); they asked parties to strengthen systems of governance in the digital environment; they encouraged the support to cultural and creative industries; they refurbished the "preferential treatment provisions" (Article 16 of CDCE) to ensure more balanced flows of cultural goods and services from developing countries; and they reasserted the integration of culture in sustainable development frameworks and the role of civil society.

Together with these guidelines that do not modify the original CDCE text, UNESCO launched its Internet Universality initiative, acknowledging that the internet is an economic and social network of interactions that should be an enabler of human rights and should empower individuals and communities. The initiative was endorsed in 2015, with the states advocating policymaking necessities to foster inclusiveness, quality education, cultural diversity, and media pluralism. It implied enlarging cultural governance to embrace new actors such as the platforms, the access providers, and the cable operators. By 2017, UNESCO had consolidated the key principles underpinning Internet Universality and its empirical indicators, with the acronym ROAM: measuring its compliance with human Rights (R), evaluating its Openness (O) and Accessibility (A), and assessing the involvement of Multi-stakeholder actors (M) (Souter & Van der Spuy, 2019).[16]

Conclusion

The CDCE was supposed to fill a void due to the absence of cultural objectives in public international law and to counterbalance the WTO in potential conflicts between trade and culture. The Convention embedded a series of original notions and actions that have followed their course since, both in societal developments and in legal frameworks. It expanded the research field to issues and journals addressing cultural economics, international media law, media pluralism, and digital transformations, and is framed and featured in many interdisciplinary approaches.

As a third-generation right following a soft law logic, cultural diversity and its attendant CDCE are fragile in terms of enforcement and sanctions. However, the treaty can be seen as a reasonably successful attempt, especially when associated with the WSIS process and the SDGs' catalytic diplomacy. The Convention's empirical approach has made it possible for different states and socio-ethnic minorities to invoke it in arrangements that would have been rejected as external interventions or as colonial impositions had they been couched in hard law terms. Its adoption by regional systems, like the European Union or Latin America, has given it a geographic spread that is contagious and conducive to "sense-making" good practices through a horizontal inclusiveness that can only benefit individuals and communities worldwide. Having

[16] See UNESCO Internet Universality Indicators, https://en.unesco.org/internet-universality-indicators. Accessed 15 June 2022.

civil society participate in the practices in question and extending the dialog to other stakeholders contributes to the evolution of human rights as a whole.

References

Beck, U. (2003). *Power in the global age*. Polity.

Bernier, I. (with Hélène Ruiz Fabri). (2006). *La mise en œuvre et le suivi de l'UNESCO sur la protection et la promotion de la diversité des expressions culturelles: Perspectives d'action*. Gouvernement du Québec. Retrieved 15 June 2022, from https://www.unescodec.chaire.ulaval.ca/sites/unescodec.chaire.ulaval.ca/files/2006janvier.pdf

Caves, R. (2000). *Creative industries: Contracts between art and commerce*. Harvard University Press.

Cunningham, S. (2001). From cultural to creative industries; Theory, industry and policy implications. *Culturelink, 102*(1), 54–65.

Drossou, O. (Ed.). (2005). *Visions in process II: The World Summit on the Information Society and the road towards a sustainable knowledge society*. Boell Foundation.

Frau-Meigs, D. (2002). Cultural exception, national policies and globalisation: Imperatives in democratisation and promotion of contemporary culture. *Quaderns del CAC, 14*, 3–16.

Frau-Meigs, D. (2007). Convergence, internet governance, and cultural diversity. In T. Storsul & D. Stuedahl (Eds.), *Internet. The ambivalence of convergence* (p. 34–53). Nordicom.

Frau-Meigs, D., & Kiyingou, A. (Eds.). (2012). *Diversité culturelle à l'ère numérique: Glossaire critique*. La Documentation Française.

Frau-Meigs, D., Nicey, J., Palmer, M., Pohle, J., & Tupper, P. (2012). *From NWICO to WSIS: 30 years of communication geopolitics*. Intellect.

Frau-Meigs, D., Sirkku, K., Patek-Shellat, M., Hoeschann, M., & Pointz, S. (Eds.) (2020). *The handbook of media education research*. Wiley (IAMCR Series).

Giddens, A. (Ed.). (2001). *The global third way debate*. Routledge.

Graber, C. (2006). The new UNESCO convention on cultural diversity: A counterbalance to the WTO? *Journal of International Economic Law, 9*(3), 553–574.

ITU. (2005). *Tunis agenda for the information society*, Geneva. Retrieved 15 June 2022, from https://www.itu.int/net/wsis/docs2/tunis/off/6rev1.html

Jinji, N., & Tanaka, A. (2020). How does UNESCO's convention on cultural diversity affect trade in cultural goods? *Journal of Cultural Economics, 44*, 625–660. Retrieved 15 June 2022, from https://link.springer.com/article/10.1007/s10824-020-09380-6

Mattelart, A. (2005). *Diversité culturelle et globalisation*. La Découverte.

Melissen, J. (Ed.). (1999). *Innovation in diplomatic practice*. St-Martin's Press.

Richieri Hanania, L. (2015). The UNESCO convention on the diversity of cultural expressions as a coordination framework to promote regulatory coherence in the creative economy. *International Journal of Cultural Policy, 22*(4), 574–593.

Souter, D., & Van der Spuy, A. (2019). *UNESCO's internet universality indicators: A framework for assessing Internet development*. UNESCO.

UNESCO. (2001). *Universal declaration on cultural diversity*. Paris. Retrieved 15 June 2022, from http://portal.unesco.org/en/ev.php-URL_ID=13179&URL_DO=DO_TOPIC&URL_SECTION=201.html

UNESCO. (2005). *Convention on the protection and promotion of the diversity of cultural expressions.* Paris. Retrieved 15 June 2022, from https://en.unesco.org/creativity/convention

UNESCO. (2008). *Communication and information: Towards a prospective research Agenda.* UNESCO/IAMCR Report, Paris, 20–21 December 2007. Retrieved 15 June 2022, from http://eprints.lse.ac.uk/4265/1/Communication_and_information-towards_a_prospective_research_agenda_%28LSERO%29.pdf

UNESCO. (2015). *Re/Shaping cultural policies: A decade promoting the diversity of cultural expression for development, 2005–2015: Convention Global Report.* Paris. Retrieved 15 June 2022, from http://diversidadaudiovisual.org/wp-content/uploads/2016/04/reshaping.pdf

Vlassis, A. (2011). La mise en œuvre de la convention sur la diversité des expressions culturelles: Portée et enjeux pour l'interface 'commerce-culture'. *Études internationales, 42*(4), 493–510.

Vlassis, A. (2015). *Gouvernance mondiale et culture: De l'exception à la diversité.* Presses universitaires de Liège.

Wagner, D. R. (2000). The keepers of the gates: Intellectual property, antitrust, and the regulatory implications of systems technology. *Hastings Law Review, 51*, 1073–1076.

PART III

IAMCR and National and Regional Scholarship

CHAPTER 19

IAMCR and Russia

Kaarle Nordenstreng

Introduction

This chapter addresses the IAMCR in Russia[1]—the biggest country in Europe both geographically and in population size, although a large part of it is located in Asia. For over half of the history of IAMCR (1957–1991), the country was known as the Soviet Union (USSR)—the second superpower leading the "Socialist East" (in contrast to the "Capitalist West" led by the United States (US)) and included several republics in Eastern Europe and Central Asia, which later became independent. Since 1991, it has been Russia—capitalist in principle but different in many respects from the Western countries. Its longer history goes back to the Czarist period of imperial Russia, which was abolished in the Socialist revolution of 1917.

The chapter begins with a brief historical review of relevant research traditions in Russia-USSR from the nineteenth to the mid-twentieth century—as background to Russia in IAMCR which has a marked presence in this country, especially in its first few decades. The emphasis is on factual details about the

[1] This chapter is based on documents in the IAMCR history archives, on interviews with Yassen Zassoursky in 2014–2015, on materials received from Elena Vartanova, Ivan Zassoursky, and Oleg Manaev in 2021, as well as on the author's personal experience since 1966.

K. Nordenstreng (✉)
Tampere University, Tampere, Finland
e-mail: kaarle.nordenstreng@tuni.fi

© The Author(s), under exclusive license to Springer Nature Switzerland AG 2023

J. Becker, R. Mansell (eds.), *Reflections on the International Association for Media and Communication Research*,
https://doi.org/10.1007/978-3-031-16383-8_19

participation of Russian scholars in IAMCR conferences and governing bodies, mainly during the Soviet period. The impact of international contacts on individual scholars is shown by one case from Byelorussia, while a more profound analysis of international exchanges—both the influence of IAMCR on Russian scholars and vice versa—is left to later research.

Deep Roots in Russian History

Russia has a long and rich history of media and journalism. Czarist Russia was one of the cradles of European culture in the eighteenth and nineteenth centuries, with literature and journalism flourishing in St. Petersburg as in other metropolises such as Vienna, Berlin, Paris, and London. Early views of the role of media in society—in Russia as well as elsewhere—typically grew out of the tension between the press and the state and church authorities. In Russia, this manifested in official censorship introduced by Empress Catherine the Great in 1796—after her regime had initially promoted education and intellectual freedom but then resorted to curtailing press freedom in order to keep the European revolutionary movements at bay. As pointed out by Gennady Zhirkov (2011, p. 178): "The confrontation between authorities and opposition was the engine of understanding the problems of journalism and its theorizing."

Zhirkov's useful overview in the *Russian Journal of Communication* shows how the paradigmatic thinking about media in society was determined throughout the Czarist era by the classic power relationship between state and journalists, in practice enshrined in legal documents and imperial decrees. The same more or less open conflict continued after the Great October Revolution of 1917 until the collapse of the Soviet Union in 1991 and it still persists in contemporary neo-authoritarian Russia.

However, the conflict between authorities and journalists has not produced notable advances in theories of journalism and press freedom. Instead, Russia became a significant environment for promoting literacy and audience research (Zhirkov, 2011). This development began in the last quarter of the nineteenth century with initiatives such as the people's publishing house of Leo Tolstoy along with readership studies carried out by statisticians. The results were published as books, beginning with "What people read?" in 1884 (see Zhirkov, 2011). The first analyses of press content followed at the turn of the century, for example, a quantitative breakdown of 30 years of the journal *Niva*. Individual papers carried out studies of their audiences, conducted by means of questionnaires, summarized by Russkie Vedomosti in its 50th anniversary issue in 1913.

Reviewing the audience research of the pre-revolutionary period, bibliographer Nicholas Rubakin (1919) concluded that "the experimental study of the readership started here, in Russia, much earlier than abroad." Zhirkov (2011, p. 193) notes that the Russian intelligentsia entered the revolutionary period with skills and a tradition for studying audiences, and this was permitted to continue as the new authorities were seeking interaction with the people.

Indeed, the roots of mass communication research were promising until the 1920s, as was the state of sociology in general. However, the political development of the Soviet Union then turned hostile to these avenues of social science for decades—until after Stalin's death in 1953 and a thaw in the Cold War in the mid-1950s.

Although press history did not create major research traditions, one name needs to be noted here: Professor Nikolay Yakovlevich Novombergsky (1871–1949). As an ingenious and polymath scholar, he studied the Russian legislature of the seventeenth century, the history of Russian medicine, as well as issues of press freedom. He delivered lectures at the Russian Higher School of Social Sciences in Paris in late 1904 and early 1905, focusing on the history of journalism. While Czarist authoritarianism seemed impregnable, his lectures analyzed the processes of press liberation in France, Germany, and England compared to Russia, where the course of events reaffirmed his belief that the development of society is impossible without press freedom. This caused him to conclude:

> In effect, the press has been freed from the age-old practice of slavery. It is now only a matter of legal liberation, which will bring emancipation of life in Russia to its successful close. Scattered, multitribal, multireligious but free Russia has a very bright future. (Novombergsky, 2001, p. 4)

Another name not to be missed in the Russian communication research tradition is Vladimir Ivanovich Vernadsky (1863–1945), a mineralogist, geochemist, and geologist, widely known as one of the scholars who developed the concept of biosphere (Vernadsky, 1926). Less known is his parallel concept of noosphere, which he introduced as the third stage in the earth's development, after the lifeless geosphere and the biological biosphere (Vernadsky, 1945). He positioned the noosphere as the superior stage of evolution on earth and envisioned it as the space for human life and culture, the next layer of life on top of the biosphere. This can be seen as a fundamental idea underlying the popular concept of the public sphere, but its potential has not been fully exploited in communication theories. Recently, however, it has been discovered as a source of inspiration for a Russian movement advocating total openness in publishing (I. Zassoursky, 2015). The pioneering champion of public domain and open-access publishing is nowadays seen to be Leo Tolstoy (1828–1910), who made most of his works available for everyone to read and publish free of charge.

Main Gate at Moscow State University

The founding of IAMCR in 1957 was facilitated by a relaxation of Cold War tension in the second half of the 1950s, and it was natural for the Soviets to be involved in its inception. The Soviet Union is among the 29 countries under which individual members were listed at the time of the inaugural conference in December 1957.[2] The list includes only one name from the USSR, while notably the US and France have long lists of members. The USSR is totally absent from the list of institutional members in 17 countries. No Soviets appear among the participants from the 15 countries at the founding conference. It seems that officially the USSR was still not fully engaged.

The Soviet on the list was Evgeny Lazarevich Khoudiakoff,[3] who was eminently well-suited to be the number one representative of the USSR: Professor and Dean of the Faculty of Journalism at Moscow State University (MSU)—the leading academic institution in the country. Although not present at the actual conference, he participated, with a junior colleague from the faculty serving as translator, in preparation of the conference in October 1957. This coincided with the opening course of the International Centre for Higher Education in Journalism established in Strasbourg under the auspices of UNESCO.[4]

Khoudiakoff was succeeded by his Deputy Dean, Yassen Nikolajevich Zassoursky,[5] as the Soviet representative in IAMCR relations in 1961, at the time of the third conference in Vevey on Lake Geneva. Zassoursky intended to attend that conference but could not make it, and likewise missed the fourth conference in Vienna in 1964; no other Soviets attended these events, either. Finally, in 1966, Zassoursky was present in Herceg-Novi, where he was elected to the Executive Committee. In the next conference in Pamplona in 1968, although absent due to being denied a visa to Franco's Spain, he was elected one of four vice presidents. He held this position (one among 5–12 vice presidents) for 20 years through the presidential terms of Jacques Bourquin and James Halloran. After 1988, Zassoursky continued in the Professional

[2] See documents of the founding conference at https://iamcr.org/node/10512. Accessed 15 June 2022.

[3] Khoudiakoff, born in 1906, was educated at the Moscow Communist Institute of Journalism and in the Higher Party School. He worked as a journalist first in his native East Kazakhstan region, and after 1933, in the central press, moving in 1948 to the newspaper *Izvestia* becoming its Deputy Editor-in-Chief in 1950. In 1952, he was sent to the newly established Faculty of Journalism at Moscow State University, becoming its first Dean. As Professor, he headed the Department of History, Theory and Practice of the Soviet Press. In the early 1960s, his health deteriorated, and in 1963, he asked to be relieved of his duties as Dean; he died in 1964. More on his biography in the Russian Wikipedia at Худяков, Евгений Лазаревич—Википедия Accessed 15 June 2022.

[4] See report of Hifzi Topuz at https://iamcr.org/node/2945. Accessed 15 June 2022.

[5] Zassoursky, (1929–2021), was educated at the Moscow State Pedagogical Institute of Foreign Languages, from where he graduated in 1948, and in 1951, defended his PhD thesis ("Theodore Dreiser's Path to Communism"). From 1951 to 1953, he worked as an Editor at the Foreign Literature Publishing House. In 1953, he began to work at the new Faculty of Journalism of Moscow State University, becoming Head of the Department of Foreign Journalism and Literature. In 1956, he was appointed Deputy to Dean Yevgeny Khoudiakoff, and in 1964, he became the Dean, holding that position until 2007, when he was appointed President of the Faculty. More on his biography in the Russian Wikipedia at Засурский, Ясен Николаевич—Википедия. Accessed 15 June 2022. See also an interview with Zassoursky by Michael Meyen (2018a).

Education Section, and after 2004, in the Working Group (WG) on Post-Socialist Media initiated by him.

UNESCO was the channel which brought the Soviets (Khoudiakoff) to the founding stage of IAMCR as it had done with most other national circles of mass communication research. UNESCO was also instrumental in supporting Zassoursky to become personally acquainted with European centers in the field. This happened in 1956 on a UNESCO fellowship for three months, facilitating visits to France, Germany, and the United Kingdom (UK). The invitation came through the Soviet National Commission for UNESCO, whereby Zassoursky was an official representative. In his interviews with me, Yassen recalled with enthusiasm these visits and contacts, beginning with Hifzi Topuz and Jacques Leauté, who invited him to join the Council of the International Centre for Higher Education in Journalism, enabling visits to Strasbourg at least once a year.

With 22 years as Vice President and another two decades in the section and WG operations, Zassoursky was one of the longest-serving individuals in IAMCR history. He was the dominant voice from USSR-Russia in IAMCR from the late 1960s until the early 2010s—for almost 50 years—serving as a gatekeeper for his compatriots' participation in IAMCR and also as an authority among IAMCR members in other Central-East European socialist countries.

Both the national and regional roles were natural and Yassen Nikolajevich performed them not only for political but mainly for organizational interests—not as a dictator safeguarding the Soviet "party line" but rather as a godfather speaking with the unquestioned authority of the leading power in Eastern Europe. After all, in the Cold War era, the USSR was accepted in this region as a self-evident big brother in all areas of life—the clandestine activities of dissidents notwithstanding. However, in the particular field of communication research, the Soviet Union was less prominent than were Poland, Czechoslovakia, and the then East Germany (German Democratic Republic, GDR), as became clear in the IAMCR founding conference.[6]

Yassen was occasionally viewed—especially among those in the West with anti-Soviet attitudes—as a hard-liner pursuing political rather than scholarly objectives. Such a reputation was fed by clashes at some plenary sessions with Cold Warriors such as the Polish emigré in France, George Mond, who in

[6] Among the participants of the founding conference were Mieczyslaw Kafel, Director of the Scientific Institute of the Press in Warsaw, Vladimir Klimes, Director of the Section of Journalism at the Charles University in Prague, and Hermann Budzislavski, Journalism Professor of Karl Marx University in Leipzig. Klimes was elected to the Executive Committee as the only member from Eastern Europe. There are no mentions of Soviets in the conference minutes, except in the list of members immediately thereafter (see https://iamcr.org/node/10512 Accessed 15 June 2022). Meanwhile, one of the six international organizations represented at the conference was the International Organization of Journalists (IOJ) which, at that time, was under the control of the Soviet Union. Thus, one may say that the Soviet presence at the founding conference was maintained indirectly through the IOJ, represented by its French President Jean-Maurice Hermann, who according to the minutes, was quite active at the conference.

Konstanz in 1970 was elected to the Executive Committee, and paradoxically, was co-chairing the Section for International Understanding from 1972 to 1978. I also remember the debate in Leicester in 1976 after Stuart Hall's paper in the plenary session on the structures and contexts of media production (chaired by Yassen and me), where Yassen challenged Hall with sharp remarks on cultural studies.

In general, Yassen had a fairly positive approach to young Western "new left" scholars such as Robin Cheesman (Denmark), Jan Ekecrantz (Sweden), and Armand Mattelart (Belgium). He also got along well with conservatives such as Elisabeth Noelle-Neumann and Martin Löffler from West Germany. He had excellent relations with North American colleagues, both mainstream, such as Raymond Nixon and Ramona Rush, and "progressives" such as George Gerbner and Herbert I. Schiller. Naturally, he had smooth relations with colleagues from the so-called fraternal countries in Eastern Europe. Nor did he have any problems with younger and potentially dissident-minded scholars from these countries either; for example, Wolfgang Kleinwächter (East Germany) and Tamas Szecskö (Hungary).

Over the years, Yassen gained the reputation across geopolitical regions and generations as a jovial and knowledgeable IAMCR colleague. He was known as an ecumenical figure with a legendary memory and incredible networks—a promoter rather than a controller. Admittedly, not everyone was profoundly impressed; some had doubts about the motives of this extraordinary man. My Finnish colleagues and I never entertained such doubts as our experience with him was entirely positive. The same experience was testified to by Janet Wasko in her interview with Michael Meyen (2018b), who asked her: "From an Eastern perspective, you must have been seen as a fellow from the heart of the capitalist world. Did you ever fear to be misused by socialist countries' concerns?" She replied:

> Many of us were just excited to be able to engage with and get to know people from socialist and third world countries. The value of IAMCR was bringing people together from all of those different countries. Of course, there were the politics going on, but I never felt misused. Maybe we were in various ways, but I did not feel it. In fact, many of us made connections with people in Eastern Europe. I remember the conference in Prague in 1984 where we had an informal meeting with Yassen Zassoursky, who was always there representing the Soviet Union, and with some of the critical US people. In a way, just to have this discussion was one of the attractions. (Meyen, 2018b)

After 1985, Yassen was a vocal advocate of *perestroika* and *glasnost*. He was a personal friend of Mikhail Gorbachev, as demonstrated in the book ***Russian Media Challenge***, which we edited with his Deputy Dean Elena Vartanova (2001). In the 1990s, Yassen helped to enlarge the circle of Russian scholars attending IAMCR conferences. As an embodiment of Gorbachevian liberal values and a global worldview, he continuously built up international networks bridging the gap between teachers and researchers from Russia and the rest of the world for decades. Moreover, he always wanted to hold an IAMCR conference in Moscow but never managed to do so.

Yassen was not only an administrator and networker but also a scholar, whose publications speak for themselves. They were mostly in Russian, for example "Temptation to freedom. Russian journalism: 1900–2007" (2007) as well as edited volumes, "To a mobile society: utopias and reality" (2009) and "Mass media in Russia" (2011). Among his English publications, in addition to the above-mentioned *Russian Media Challenge*, is an anthology *Beyond the Cold War: Soviet and American Media Images*, edited with Everette Denis and George Gerbner (1991). Regarding his publications in Russian, Yassen clearly supported the above-mentioned idea of noosphere by wanting to transfer all his writing to the public domain to be published in open access under the terms of open licenses.

Yassen's impressive legacy as an educator of Soviet journalists from the mid-1950s to the end of the 1980s, and thereafter of journalists of the Russian Federation from the 1990s onward, became duly appreciated after his death in August 2021. This is aptly acknowledged in his obituary by Andrei Richter (2021) pointing out that Yassen not only protected students but also provided sanctuary in his faculty to critical intellectuals and sociologists such as Boris Grushin.[7] There is no doubt that the faculty made an important contribution to a new intellectual climate in the last years of the Soviet Union and the first decade of post-Soviet Russia—supported by a worldwide network with IAMCR as a central catalyst.

Soviet Attendance at Conferences

Yassen Zassoursky attended most of the biennial IAMCR conferences in the 1970–1980s, and most other Soviets in their lists of attendees were from his MSU Faculty. The Konstanz Conference in 1970 had only Zassoursky from the USSR; and the Buenos Aires Conference 1972, when James Halloran started his 20-year-long presidency, did not have a single Soviet participant. Subsequent conferences during the 1970–1980s have the following records (See Figure 19.1 for Zassoursky with other 1976 Conference participants).

- Leipzig 1974 had the theme "The contribution of the mass media to the development of consciousness in a changing world." There were seven participants from MSU, including Zassoursky and Professor Yury Sherkovin. The latter presented a keynote paper on "Mass information processes and problems of personality socialization."[8] Other Soviet participants were the Dean of the Faculty of Journalism, Leningrad University,

[7] A Soviet and Russian philosopher, sociologist, and historian who pioneered public opinion polling, see https://en.wikipedia.org/wiki/Boris_Grushin Accessed 15 June 2022.

[8] Included in the first conference report and bibliography produced by IAMCR with the support of UNESCO, see Sherkovin (1976).

Fig. 19.1 IAMCR Conference 1976, Leicester. (From left to right) **Yassen Zassoursky** IAMCR Executive Committee 1966–1968, IAMCR Vice President 1968–1988, International Council 1988–1992, Section Head—Professional Training/ Education 1978–1988; **Walery Pisarek**—IAMCR Bureau 1972–1976, IAMCR Vice President 1976–1986, Section Head—Bibliography 1970–1990; **Alice Bunzlova**—International Council 1976–1986; **Emil Dusiška**—IAMCR Executive Committee 1970–1972, IAMCR Secretary General 1972–1982, Section Head—Technology/and Satellites 1968–1978. (Courtesy of IAMCR)

and two teachers from the Soviet Communist Party School in Moscow. The conference was attended by 250 participants from 31 countries, the largest number, 75, from the GDR as the host country and the host Karl Marx University, followed by West Germany with 20, Sweden with 13, US and Hungary both with 11, and the USSR with 10 participants. Most European countries from the East and the West had about half a dozen participants.

- Leicester 1976, with the theme "Mass media and man's view of society," was attended by over 300 participants from 40 countries. Only three came from the USSR: Zassoursky and Sherkovin from MSU and Professor N. Mansurov from the Soviet Academy of Sciences. Mansurov presented one of the three main papers in the session devoted to different approaches to the study of media audiences, with the title "Studies into information media and cultural institutions in the USSR."[9]

- Warsaw 1978 on "Mass media and national cultures" had nearly 500 participants from 38 countries, among them nine from the USSR—Zassoursky, Sherkovin, five others listed under MSU, and two under the Soviet Academy of Sciences. One of these was Dr. Boris Firsov, Head of the Mass Media Research Unit of the Institute of Sociology located in Leningrad, delivering one of the three main papers in a session on mass media and national culture with the title "Socio-cultural characteristics of the development of the mass communication media in the USSR: Mass communication as a social phenomenon."[10] Firsov had been introduced to IAMCR during a three-month fellowship at UNESCO in Paris a couple of years earlier.
- Caracas 1980 on "New structures of international communication – the role of research" was attended by some 300 participants from 40 countries. As in Buenos Aires eight years earlier, no Soviets had come to this distant Latin American location. Most European countries, including France, had just a handful of participants.
- Paris 1982 on "Communication and democracy: Directions in research" attracted about 400 participants from 37 countries. As many as 55 of them were from the US, while about 30 were listed under the host country France, the same as for West Germany, the Netherlands, Spain, and Sweden; Norway and the UK had over 20. Three participants came from Hungary and Poland; two from East Germany and Czechoslovakia. The USSR had only one participant: Zassoursky. He had two roles in the program: as a speaker in a semi-plenary reviewing research and as the Head of the Professional Education Section, which had two sessions.
- Prague 1984 on "Social communication and global problems" was attended by 440 participants from 44 countries. Nearly 90 of them were from the host country and 17 from the USSR (half of them from the Soviet National Council of IAMCR). The program had only opening and closing plenaries, and most of the time was devoted to meetings of the Sections and WGs. Zassoursky's Professional Education Section had three sessions and a two-day workshop on promoting textbooks in journalism education. The pre-conference was hosted by the IOJ in its conference center, and it produced an application for UNESCO's International Programme for the Development of Communication (IPDC) funding, later leading to a decade-long "textbook project" funded by FINNIDA.
- New Delhi 1986, highlighted by the UN International Year of Peace, was attended by 360 participants from 40 countries, 123 from India alone. The largest number of participants outside India came from the US, Denmark, Sweden, and Finland, with a record number of Third World

[9] The main papers were not printed but only summarized in the second conference report, see McCron (1978).

[10] The main papers were likewise summarized in the third conference report, see Pickering (1980).

countries represented by at least one scholar. Three were listed under USSR. Zassoursky and a colleague from MSU, plus an officer from the USSR National Commission for UNESCO. Zassoursky chaired two sessions of the Professional Education Section, one of them jointly with the Communication Technology Section. The third session, devoted to peace and ethics in journalism education, was a panel including Zassoursky and colleagues from the US, India, and Colombia.

- Barcelona 1988 with the theme "Mass communication and cultural identity" was another record conference. Its program, including plenaries as well as section and WG sessions, included no other Soviet names than Zassoursky chairing one session of his Professional Education Section. There were several other East Europeans among the over 500 names listed in the program.
- Bled 1990 on "Developments of communications and democracy" followed the same pattern, whereby Soviets were few, while a number of participants came from Central and Eastern Europe, particularly from the host country, Slovenia. However, there was one participant from the USSR: Oleg Manaev from the Byelorussian Soviet Socialist Republic, who presented a paper on media audience research in the USSR and effectively seized the opportunity for new contacts and networking (more on him below).

After the collapse of the USSR at the end of 1991, it was replaced by Russian Federation and several independent states. At this stage, Russian attendance was relatively modest, mainly from the MSU Faculty of Journalism. Zassoursky continued to attend conferences, and after the mid-1990s, he brought with him junior faculty members, including Andrei Richter, Elena Vartanova, and Ivan Zassoursky (his grandson).

While reviewing Soviet attendance at IAMCR conferences, it should be noted that Soviets also hosted conferences in journalism and media studies—mostly organized in Moscow with Yassen Zassoursky as the mastermind. Accordingly, Soviets were not only recipients in international exchanges but also provided platforms for colleagues from abroad—first and foremost from the "fraternal socialist countries" but increasingly also from the Western and developing countries. And IAMCR members were among the standard participants at these meetings. An ample example is the "International conference on the scientific and technological revolution and journalism" held at the MSU in 1973. It was attended by scholars and journalists from most socialist countries, and the US, Canada, Finland (Herbert I. Schiller, Dallas W. Smythe, Kaarle Nordenstreng), Ecuador, India, Nigeria, as well as representatives of UNESCO, IAMCR, and the IOJ.[11]

[11] A summary report of the conference is provided in *The Democratic Journalist* (monthly journal of the IOJ), see Yamskoi (1973).

Soviets and Post-Soviets in Governing Bodies

Yassen Zassoursky has a long record in IAMCR leading positions: first as a member of the Executive Board (1966–1968), then as Vice President (1968–1988), as well as Head of the Section for Professional Education (1978–1990). He attended not only most conferences, but also practically all International Council (IC) and Executive Board meetings. He was the predominant Soviet voice in IAMCR until the 1990s. In 2006, Yassen initiated a WG on Post-Socialist and Post-Authoritarian Media, serving as its head until 2012, when it was taken over by Anastasia Grusha from his Faculty (together with German and Finnish co-heads).

In addition to Zassoursky, the first Soviet to assume a position in IAMCR leading bodies was Aleksandr Fedoseevich Berezhnoy, Dean of the Faculty of Journalism at Leningrad State University, the second largest institution of journalism education and research in the USSR. He was elected a member of the Executive Committee in 1968 at the Pamplona Conference, while Zassoursky became one of the Vice Presidents. Neither he nor Zassoursky attended the conference, but President Bourquin had obviously made a deal whereby both Moscow and Leningrad were prominently represented in the leadership. Berezhnoy continued on the Executive Committee until 1976, when the new statutes replaced this body by the IC. He attended few meetings and was more of a formal representative.

Alexei Burmistenko, an associate of both the MSU Faculty of Journalism and the Soviet Union of Journalists, became a member of the IC in 1984, serving for one four-year term.

Andrei Richter, who built a media law center at the MSU Faculty of Journalism in the 1990s, attended IAMCR conferences after the mid-1990s and was immediately elected member of the IC in 1996. In 1998, he followed Wolfgang Kleiwächter as Head of the Law Section and in this capacity was also a member of the Council. He held this position until 2010, arranging a section meeting at every annual conference—as the only Russian involved in this niche section.

Elena Vartanova, Deputy Dean of the MSU Faculty of Journalism, attended IAMCR conferences as of 1995, mainly the Sections of International Communication and Professional Education. She was elected to the IC in 2000, retaining that position for two four-year terms. In 2004, she headed a new WG on the Digital Divide, in 2012, passing its leadership to Olga Smirnova from her Faculty, later followed by Anna Gladkova (together with a British co-head).

Oleg Manaev, a sociologist at the Belarusian State University in Minsk, became an IAMCR member in the late 1980s, and was elected to the IC from an independent Belarus in 1992 for a four-year term. His recent reminiscence of IAMCR is impressive:

> I'll never forget those shiny times of the late 1980s and early 1990s, when IAMCR and its enthusiasts opened to me not only the world of mass communication research but the World and the new Vision of it. I think I would not have become what I have become—both as a professional and as a person—without this unique experience.[12]

A Case in Point

Oleg Manaev[13] and his stories are worth highlighting as an exemplary case of how international contacts were spreading, especially in the border zones such as Central-Eastern Europe in times of political transitions. Manaev's process started in April 1988 while visiting colleagues and friends, Marju Lauristin and Peeter Vihalemm in Tartu (Estonia). From them, he learned that the *European Journal of Communication (EJC)* was going to publish a special issue introducing research in countries within the Soviet orbit and got the address of its editor Karol Jakubowicz (1989). The special issue came to include Manaev's (1989) article "A Vicious Circle in Soviet Media-Audience Relations" and Jakubowicz took him to a meeting in Piran (Slovenian Republic of Yugoslavia), hosted by Slavko Splichal from the University of Ljubljana in September 1989.

At the Piran meeting, Oleg "met incredible people," who, in addition to Jakubowicz and Splichal, included Colin Sparks (UK), Marc Raboy (Canada), Peter Bruck (Austria), Alex Edelstein and Peter Gross (US), and Francois-Xavier Hutin (France). Hutin invited Oleg to attend the Annual Conference of the French Society of Information and Communication Sciences in 1990 and to give lectures in several French universities. These experiences, with the special issue of the *EJC*, meant that "the dream of my life began to come true: the entry into the big World began."

Then Oleg was invited to visit the US, Canada, and the United Kingdom (UK). As he reports:

> The World not only began to open, but everything also suddenly spun right away as in a kaleidoscope. I met and had unforgettable discussions with such famous media and communication scholars as Armand Mattelart, Jose Delofeu, Michael Palmer, Bernard Miège, Régis Debray in France; James Halloran, Olga Linné, Denis McQuail, Annabelle Sreberny-Mohammadi, John Keane in the UK; George Gerbner, Ben Bagdikian, Kurt Lang and Gladys Lang, Hamid Mowlana, David Paletz in the USA; G.J. Robinson and Serge Proulx in Canada, and many others.[14]

At the IAMCR Conference in Bled 1990, Peter Lewis (UK) invited Oleg to join a UNESCO project on "alternative media linking global and local."

[12] Personal communication with the author, Manaev providing a document used as the source below.

[13] See https://www.manaevoleg.org for his publications, conferences, and photos. Accessed 15 June 2022.

[14] See footnote 12.

Moreover, George Gerbner and Marsha Siefert invited him to contribute in 1991 to the *Journal of Communication* special issue on contemporary developments in the USSR with an article "The influence of Western Radio on the Democratization of Soviet Youth" (Manaev, 1991). Oleg goes on:

> Inspired by such a genuine interest of IAMCR in the research on media and communication "behind the Iron Curtain", I decided to organize an international colloquium "Interaction of Mass Media, Public and Power Institutions in Democratization Process" in Minsk in late 1991. I cannot express in words the feelings of pride and delight that I felt when meeting my friends in snowy Belarus just ten days before the collapse of the USSR! In 1993 the most important concepts as discussed at that colloquium, as well as impressive research data were published in the book *Media in Transition: From Totalitarianism to Democracy* (Manaev & Pryliuk, 1993) with a Preface by IAMCR President Cees Hamelink.
>
> But after mid-1990s the political process in my country went backwards and I had to concentrate more and more on researching our internal problems. However, the cold political winds did not sweep away the traces of the IAMCR scientific heritage in Belarus. For a quarter of a century, the Department of Social Communication, the first of its kind in the former USSR, has been operating at Belarusian State University, which we created with the active participation of our French, British and Spanish colleagues within the TEMPUS project.[15]

I asked Oleg if Moscow had any role in his story. He replied that Yassen/MSU had no role in making the contact and his way to IAMCR, although they had known each other since the early 1980s.

Postscript

In general, IAMCR proceeded in the Soviet Union and Russia through individuals who were attracted by their personal interests and guided by their institutional powers and resources. The level of Soviet-Russian participation, as measured in the number of registered IAMCR members, was never as high as was the US, the UK, or German participation. However, IAMCR membership of USSR-Russia continued throughout its history at a level which justifies calling them faithful partners.

References

Denis, E., Gerbner, G., & Zassoursky, Y. (Eds.). (1991). *Beyond the cold war: Soviet and American images*. Sage.

Jakubowicz, K. (1989). Introduction to a special issue on mass communication research east of the Elbe—Coming out from under the shadow. *European Journal of Communication*, *4*(3), 243–245. Retrieved 15 June 2022, from https://doi.org/10.1177/0267323189004003001

[15] See footnote 12.

Manaev, O. (1989). A vicious circle in Soviet media-audience relations. *European Journal of Communication*, *4*(3), 287–305. Retrieved 15 June 2022, from https://doi.org/10.1177/0267323189004003005

Manaev, O. (1991). The influence of Western radio on the democratization of Soviet youth. *Journal of Communication*, *41*(2), 72–91. Retrieved 15 June 2022, from https://doi.org/10.1111/j.1460-2466.1991.tb02310.x

Manaev, O., & Pryliuk, Y. (Eds.). (1993). *Media in transition: From authoritarianism to democracy*. Abris, BSU, IISEPS.

McCron, R. (1978). Different approaches to the study of mass media audiences. Report of the 3rd session of the IAMCR conference 1976. In *Mass media and man's view of society*. A Conference report and international bibliography (p. 55–70). Adams Bros. & Shardlow Ltd.

Meyen, M. (2018a). Yassen Zassoursky: I tried to stop the Cold War mentality. In M. Meyen & T. Wiedemann (Eds.), *Biografisches Lexikon der Kommunikationswissenschaft* (p. np). Köln, Herbert von Halem. Retrieved 15 June 2022, from http://blexkom.halemverlag.de/iamcr-zassoursky/

Meyen, M. (2018b). Janet Wasko: I really do have a lot of questions. In M. Meyen & T. Wiedemann (Eds.), *Biografisches Lexikon der Kommunikationswissenschaft* (p. np). Köln, Herbert von Halem. Retrieved 15 June 2022, from http://blexkom.halemverlag.de/iamcr-wasko/

Nordenstreng, K., Vartanova, E., & Zassoursky, Y. (Eds). (2001). *Russian media challenge*. Prologue by Mikhail Gorbachev. Aleksanteri Institute.

Novombergsky, N. Y. (2001). Liberation of press in France, Germany, England and Russia (in Russian). In *Istorija pechati. Antologija* [Press history. Anthology] (p. 197–419). Aspect Press.

Pickering, M. (1980). Mass media and national culture: Structure, content, values, impact. In *Mass media and national cultures*. Report on the 2nd Session of the IAMCR Conference 1978. In *Mass media and national cultures*. A conference report and international bibliography (p. 24–38). Adams Bros. & Shardlow Ltd.

Richter, A. (2021, August 11). 'He protected us' Remembering Yassen Zassoursky, the journalism scholar who midwifed Russia's post-Soviet free press (E. Tolley, Trans.). *Meduza*. Retrieved 15 June 2022, from https://meduza.io/en/feature/2021/08/11/he-protected-us

Rubakin, N. A. (1919). *Etudypo psihologii chitatel'stva* [Studies on psychology of reading]. St. Petersburg.

Sherkovin, Y. (1976). Mass information processes and problems of personality socialization (Paper). In J. Halloran (Ed.), *Mass media and socialization. International bibliography and perspectives by International Association for Mass Communication Research* (p. 45–56). J. A. Kavanagh & Sons. IAMCR-UNESCO.

Vernadsky, V. I. (1926). *Biosfera* [Biosphere]. Reprinted in *Biosfera I Noosfera* [Biosphere and Noosphere]. Moscow, Nauka, 1989. Retrieved 15 June 2022, from https://noosphere.ru/pubs/731365

Vernadsky, V. I. (1945). The biosphere and the noösphere. *American Scientist*, *33*(1), p. 1–12. Retrieved 15 June 2022, from https://www.jstor.org/stable/27826043

Yamskoi, N. (1973). Mass media and the scientific and technological revolution. *The Democratic Journalist*, *31*(11), 5–8.

Zassoursky, I. (2015, December 28). Infrastructure of the noosphere: Federal Reserve System and the open banks of knowledge (in Russian). *Chastny Korrespondent*

[Private Correspondent]. Retrieved 15 June 2022, from https://monoskop.org/images/a/a0/Vernadsky_Vladimir_Biosfera_i_noosfera_1989.pdf
Zassoursky, Y. N. (2007). *Iskushenie svobodoj. Rossijskaja zhurnalistika: 1900–2007* [Temptation to freedom. Russian journalism: 1900–2007]. Moscow State University Press.
Zassoursky, Y. N. (Ed.). (2009). *K mobil'nomu obshchestvu: Utopii i real'nost'* [To a mobile society: Utopias and reality]. Moscow State University Press.
Zassoursky, Y. N. (Ed.). (2011). *Sredstva massovoy informatsii Rossii* [Mass media in Russia]. Aspect Press.
Zhirkov, G. V. (2011). Journalism and journalism theory in Russia: A historical overview from the 18th to the early 20th century. *Russian Journal of Communication*, *4*(3–4), 177–197. Retrieved 15 June 2022, from https://doi.org/10.1080/19409419.2011.10756804

CHAPTER 20

IAMCR and the Development of Communication and Media Research in China

Deqiang Ji and Franziska Scholz

Introduction

As one of the leading international academic associations in journalism, media, and communication studies, though based in Europe for most of its history, IAMCR offers a unique platform for scholars from all around the world to present their research, exchange ideas, and build networks on a regular basis. The generic features of IAMCR, since its foundation in 1957, including diversity, inclusiveness, and global justice, drew special attention and active participation from Third World countries during the Cold War, and later, the developing world, in an accelerated globalization process. Among others, China has been involved increasingly in the internationalization of IAMCR through multiple and continuous avenues such as Chinese scholars presenting conference papers, serving on the administration bodies, and participating in collaborative research projects, with Chinese institutions and individuals registering as IAMCR members. In the greater China region, Taiwan hosted the 2005 Conference and Beijing hosted the 2022 Conference (online). The locality of the conference matters for attracting regional scholars and a greater Chinese participation was seen at the 2022 Conference—this is likely to continue in future years.

D. Ji (✉) • F. Scholz
Communication University of China, Beijing, China
e-mail: jideqiang@cuc.edu.cn

© The Author(s), under exclusive license to Springer Nature Switzerland AG 2023

J. Becker, R. Mansell (eds.), *Reflections on the International Association for Media and Communication Research*,
https://doi.org/10.1007/978-3-031-16383-8_20

The influence of IAMCR in China is surging while the involvement of China in IAMCR is enlarging. Besides the above-mentioned physical involvement of Chinese scholars and institutions in IAMCR, the geopolitical implications of IAMCR as a non-Western-centric network highlight the contribution by non-Western scholars and the diversity of the international academy which also resonates with China's pursuit of indigenous theories, "transcending the Euro-American biases of the field" (Zhao, 2011, p. 559), and its growing presence in the international academic community. Furthermore, alongside state-driven projects of building world leading universities and disciplines, IAMCR offers a comparatively easier way for Chinese scholars and their affiliated institutions to build genuine international connections that can be counted among the achievements of internationalization or globalization.

IAMCR's Encounters with China: An Historical Summary

It is not easy to detect China's presence in the early years of IAMCR. Thanks to IAMCR's digital archives, we examined the newsletters of IAMCR from 1965 to 2008. Based on this text-based research, encounters between IAMCR and China have been classified into the following three aspects: membership, service position, and conference participation—all extracted from these well-compiled newsletters by generations of IAMCR's leadership.

Membership

Before the 1980s, the membership structure of IAMCR was similar to the organizational principle of hosting IAMCR conferences which, according to *News Items*[1] in February 1984, was a three-cornered approach, that is, a Western country, a Socialist country, a Third World country, though this arrangement was considered too difficult to maintain in the future. However, China did not appear in the Socialist country category until 1985. In the July 1985 edition of *News Items*, it was noted that—

> for the first time the Association is able to welcome new members from the People's Republic of China. The President visited Beijing, returning an earlier visit to headquarters by a delegation from the Republic. He gave several lectures in different institutions, and found a great interest in the Association.

In the June 1994 edition, Cees J. Hamelink mentioned that the most recent new Associate Member was the Chinese Communication Association (CCA), which was a US-based association organized by diaspora Chinese communication scholars. It appears that the number of members from China itself grew

[1] All IAMCR News Items referred to in this chapter can be accessed at https://iamcr.org/taxonomy/term/184. Accessed 15 June 2022.

quite slowly. The newsletter of November 2005[2] reports only six members in China with four located in Hong Kong. In specific IAMCR sections, members from China were also mentioned. In the May–June 2002 edition of the newsletter, the Junior Scholars Network warmly welcomed members from China. In recent years, with the growing popularity of IAMCR in China, and particularly the necessity of becoming a formal member to attend its annual conference, more and more Chinese universities, scholars, and students have registered institutional and individual memberships in IAMCR.

Service Position

Throughout the history of IAMCR, very few Chinese names were found in the administrative bodies of IAMCR, including the International Council (IC), sections, and working groups (WGs). According to the archives, Yufu Huang was the first Chinese scholar to be elected to the IC in Sydney in 1996, completing her term in 2000. She was a Research Fellow with the Document and Information Center of the Chinese Academy of Social Sciences when her service started. She wrote a retrospective article in Chinese to summarize the election result and key themes in the 1996 Conference. She proudly emphasized that "this is the first time a representative from China was elected to the international council who is also the only representative from Asian countries out of the 30 members" (Huang, 1997). After Huang, Georgette Wang from Taiwan ran for election to the IC in 2004 and served at least until 2008 when the digital archive ends. In 2020, Changfeng Chen from Tsinghua University in Beijing was elected to the IC and was the only representative from China at the time of writing. Besides membership in the IC, several Chinese scholars have served the association as heads of sections and WGs, especially in recent years. Deqiang Ji from the Communication University of China has served as Vice Chair of the International Communication Section since 2016. Yik-Chan Chin with the Hong Kong Baptist University (now with Beijing Normal University) was also elected in 2016 to be the Co-Chair of the Public Service Media Policies WG. Sibo Chen, with Ryerson University (now Toronto Metropolitan University), has served as Co-Chair of the Emerging Scholars Network since December 2018. At the Madrid Conference in 2019, Yu Hong from Zhejiang University was elected Vice Chair of the Political Economy Section, while Weiyu Zhang, with the National University of Singapore, was elected Vice Chair of the Communication Policy & Technology Section. Compared to the twentieth century, it is expected that an increasing number of Chinese scholars, located either in China or beyond, will play more important roles in the organization and further the internationalization of IAMCR in the twenty-first century.

[2] All IAMCR Newsletters referred to in this chapter can be accessed at https://iamcr.org/node/10511. Accessed 15 June 2022.

Diaspora Chinese scholars who are working in the critical political economy tradition and identifying with IAMCR's positionality in promoting a more balanced world communication order have an extensive engagement with IAMCR. Specifically, their roles can be understood on two dimensions: as active participants in IAMCR's scholarly activities and governance and as bridges between IAMCR and domestic Chinese scholars. In this regard, Yuezhi Zhao, a mainland Chinese originating scholar who has done extensive research on Chinese and global communication from a transcultural political economy perspective, has been a key figure. She not only participated in many IAMCR conferences, but also served as a member of IAMCR's Scholarly Review Committee, the Adjudication Committee for the Dallas W. Smythe Best Paper Award, and the ICT Policy Task Force of IAMCR. During the 2005 World Summit on Information Society (WSIS) (Tunis Phase), Yuezhi Zhao also actively participated as an IAMCR member in the deliberations leading to the production of the Summit's Civil Society Declaration. From her close engagement with one of IAMCR's founding members, Dallas W. Smythe, on China's developmental path during her graduate studies at Simon Fraser University to her more recent major undertaking to translate IAMCR's *Handbook of Political Economy of Communications* into Chinese, Yuezhi Zhao has been an active figure in promoting substantive scholarly exchanges between IAMCR, its core members, and China.

Conference Participation

Much earlier than the aforementioned IC memberships, as noted in the June 1987 edition of *News Items*, one Occasional Paper written by a Chinese scholar is documented. Anxiang Ming presented a paper on "China's Mass Communication: For the Two Civilizations," published by IAMCR Secretary General's office. Anxiang Ming is a renowned communication scholar with the Institute of Journalism and Communication of the Chinese Academy of Social Sciences. He is representative of the first generation of communication scholars in the Post-Cultural Revolution era. He directed the Center of Communication Studies at the Institute and contributed enormously to the introduction of Western mass communication theories and research on the information highway and mass communication. Among his important contributions, two landmarks in the history of communication studies in China deserve special attention. At the end of 1982, he initiated the first national symposium on communication studies and co-authored with Li Zhang and other colleagues the first introductory book on communication studies in the Chinese mainland, published as *A Brief Introduction to Communication Studies* (*chuanboxue jianjie*) (Ming & Sun, 1983). IAMCR was recognized by Ming and other early explorers he represented as an important platform to connect with the international academic community in a two-fold historical process of introducing Western communication theories into China and presenting communication studies from China to the international academy.

Since Ming's ice-breaking connection with IAMCR, Chinese scholars were increasingly active in IAMCR's academic activities. For example, the 2000 Conference of IAMCR focused specifically on Asia. Chinese scholars such as Jonathan Zhu and Georgette Wang based in Hong Kong, Taiwan, and the United States (US) participated in several sessions. Several Chinese scholars were invited to speak in the plenary session of IAMCR's annual conference. According to the Newsletter of November 2002, Yuan Feng, Assistant to the Chief Editor for *China Women's News* and coordinator of the Media Monitor Network for Women, Beijing, was invited to join the plenary session on Women and Communication Scholarship at the IAMCR 2002 Conference in Barcelona. "She spoke eloquently about the situation of women journalists in China who attempt to foreground issues of concern to women in their work," as Karen Ross and Katharine Sarikakis summarized, "she elaborated on the impact of the Beijing Conferences on the position of women workers in media industries, but also spoke about the increasing recognition of gender in social and cultural life." The Beijing Conference referred to and which Feng Yuan highlighted was the United Nations World Conference on Women held in Beijing in 1995. Interestingly, the November 1995 edition of the newsletter indicates that IAMCR participated in this conference with Margaret Gallagher as IAMCR's representative. In a summary article of his attendance and observation of the 2002 Barcelona Conference, Guanshi Jie, a pioneer international and intercultural communication scholar based at Peking University, also documented Yuan Feng's participation and emphasized that the 2002 Conference witnessed the largest number of participants from the Chinese mainland in IAMCR's 45-year history, which is three, together with some scholars from Hong Kong, Taiwan, and overseas (Guan, 2002, p. 12). Different from Huang's introductory review of IAMCR, Guan showed a stronger intellectual involvement in the 2002 Conference because the conference theme of 2002 was of great relevance to him as a key founding figure of international communication research in China.

This interaction demonstrates an historical linkage between IAMCR and China, and it laid a foundation for closer exchanges. In the following years, several leading Chinese communication and media scholars were invited to speak at IAMCR plenary sessions which attracted rising attention among IAMCR members to the changing dynamics of the media system in China and how Chinese scholars were presenting their indigenous research on a global stage. In Dublin in 2013, Zhengrong Hu from the Communication University of China delivered a plenary speech on "Lost in Global Capitalism? Economic Vulnerability, Value Crisis, and the Shift of Soft Power in China." As a well-established authority on the political economy of Chinese communication, Yuezhi Zhao from Simon Fraser University was a plenary speaker at the 2008 IAMCR Congress in Stockholm and at the 2020 IAMCR Congress (online). Deqiang Ji from the Communication University of China spoke at the closing plenary session at the IAMCR 2017 Conference in Cartagena, which was also a celebration event for the 60th anniversary of IAMCR. Contributions by

Chinese scholars were also recognized by IAMCR prizes. Chloris Qiaolei Jiang, who was a doctoral student at the Chinese University of Hong Kong, won the 2011 Herbert Schiller Award for a paper entitled "Techno-Nationalism and Creative Industries: The Development of the Chinese Online Game Industry in a Globalized Economy."

In terms of paper submission and acceptance, we selected the 2010, 2015, and 2020 conferences as examples to calculate the most popular sections or WGs for Chinese scholars and students. The top five are International Communication (INC), Audience (AUD), Journalism Research and Education (JRE), Gender and Communication (GEN), and Mediated Communication, Public Opinion & Society (MPS).

In order to interpret how Chinese scholars articulate their research scope into IAMCR, we choose the top three sections as examples. It is not surprising that the International Communication Section ranks number one. For most Chinese scholars and students, if their research topic only focuses on China or has no clear connection with the remaining specific fields of research, submission to INC is a reasonable option. Presentations over the years by Chinese scholars generally have focused on the macro-level, looking at East-West and North-South dimensions and pertinent developments, including opportunities for and media frames of Asian regions, specifically China. Meanwhile, it also has enlarged the imaginary scope for Chinese scholars to join the internationalization of academia underpinned by the growing involvement from China. This has also reinforced the confidence of Chinese scholars in the international academic community. Alongside a changing focus of research from media as a tool for political mobilization to media as a market to serve consumers, the importance of audience, simply defined as the receiver of information or as a consumer of an information commodity, experienced an unprecedented surge. This historical change also drove Chinese scholars' involvement in audience studies within the framework of IAMCR. Since the 1982 Beijing Survey (Rogers et al., 1985), audience studies emerged in the context of reintroducing a market mechanism into China's media system. Meanwhile, the audience was considered as a central concern by media practitioners and researchers mainly because of the centrality of the attention economy in media operations, and this led to a segmented view of the communication process. The third of the most popular IAMCR sections amongst Chinese scholars addresses the topic of Journalism Research and Education. Interest in this field has seen a slower, but relatively stable and constant rise throughout the last decade. Since the 1920s, journalism education in China has evolved into its own hybridized model, transforming through various stages over the past 100 years. In the 1920s when modern newspapers and universities emerged and expanded in the big cities such as Beijing and Shanghai, journalistic education was based on the US journalism education tradition, specifically the Missouri School of Journalism (Guo & Chen, 2017). By 1949, the US model was no longer adequate. The Soviet model was embraced and journalism theories were influenced by the Marxist-Leninist schools of thought, on the one hand, and enriched by and articulated with the Chinese Communist Party-led revolutionary journalistic practices, on the other. In the 1960s, after divergence from the Soviet Union, the journalistic education system was transformed once more. It was Deng Xiaoping's reform and opening-up policy in the late 1970s that augmented and brought about significant changes in every sector, including social changes which stimulated media development significantly, especially demonstrable in the television industry (Guo & Chen, 2017). With the official recognition of the fields of Journalism and Communication as a first-tier discipline in the social sciences by the Ministry of Education in 1998, academic education and research in this field was further advanced. A hybrid paradigm underpinning journalism has developed, which includes both imported Western liberal journalism and domestic revolutionary journalism theories. The latter is encapsulated in the terminology of Marxist journalism. A concern among journalism educators in China today is the gap between academics and professionals (Long & Zeng, 2016) in the industry, with education being regarded as being overly theory-focused. In the IAMCR JRE Section, Chinese scholars have predominantly analyzed journalism practice in China, the profession of journalism in Chinese media overall, and critically researched the predicament of Chinese journalists in the digital age. Many papers were collaborative efforts, which are strongly encouraged by the JRE Section. These collaborations endeavor to bridge gaps in paradigms that developed out of a Western-dominated discourse. These paradigms no longer depict transitional media systems around the world. As the JRE Section strives to approach journalism research and education from a truly global perspective, the contributions by Chinese scholars to IAMCR's annual conferences have successfully probed obsolete paradigms and contributed to reducing the gap in China between journalism academics and professionals in the industry.

In addition to the above-mentioned individual participation and thematic grouping of contributions, Chinese scholars and institutions also organized academic activities within the framework of IAMCR. For example, in collaboration with Universidad Complutense de Madrid, the local host of the IAMCR 2019 Conference, The National Centre for Communication Innovation Studies of the Communication University of China organized a pre-conference themed "Communicating China with the World: New Dynamics in International Communication," which gathered a large number of Chinese and international scholars. In an effort to boost the participation of young scholars from mainland China and address IAMCR's lack of attention to rural communication and cultural issues, Yuezhi Zhao led a special effort to organize two coordinated panels on rural communication and culture (one for the Political Economy Section and one for the International Communication Section) at the 2018 IAMCR Congress at the University of Oregon. Together, these two panels featured as many as six junior mainland Chinese scholars and doctoral candidates as paper writers and presenters.

The subject of participation in IAMCR by China arguably has shifted from individuals to groups and institutions. Perhaps because of intensified exchanges between IAMCR and China, academic events held in China were included in and promoted by IAMCR's newsletters. For example, a conference on "Media and Communication Research in the Age of Globalization" to be held in Guangzhou, China, in 2001 was mentioned by Naren Chitty in his report about the under-represented areas network, The Global Communication Research Association (GCRA). The November 2005 edition of the newsletter mentioned both the Asia Media and Information Center (AMIC) annual conference held at the Communication University of China and a conference in Guangzhou on ICT and Sustainable Development. Earlier that year, the calls for participation in both conferences were included in the April edition of the newsletter, which was good for the promotion of the China-based academic events among IAMCR members. The April 2005 edition also contained an announcement that the new open-access journal, *Westminster Papers in Communication and Culture*, would publish a future issue on media in China.

Sometimes IAMCR's newsletters contain information about academic publications by its members and others. Several Chinese scholars were mentioned with their books or articles, including Chin-Chuan Lee, Johnathan Zhu, and Tsan-Kuo Chang. Regarding the contribution by Chinese mainland scholars, the March Newsletter noted a publication titled "The Global Journalist—News People around the World" (Weaver, 1998). Chapter authors included several Chinese scholars, among them Chongshan Chen from the Chinese Academy of Social Sciences. Chen is a female scholar and an important figure in the adoption of survey-based empirical methods to study audiences in China. The Beijing Survey designed and led by her is widely considered a landmark in the history of audience analysis in China.

Chinese Scholars "Going Out" and the Positionality of IAMCR

In the past four decades, China has experienced a series of significant changes in many areas, including in academia, and more so, in the broadly defined field of media and communication studies. Those changes can be classified on two dimensions. On the one hand, imported Western theories were organically, in a Gramscian sense, articulated with the dynamic practices within China's transitional media policy and information environment by different generations of scholars. In other words, under the influence of those selected Western theories, specifically the post-positivist paradigm underpinned by the Columbia tradition associated with the work of Paul Lazarsfeld and his colleagues, a number of Chinese scholars grew to become professional media experts and communication scholars who had a strong awareness of belonging to a global academic community, despite a series of obvious contextual difficulties in the process of simply reducing China's historical and societal complexities to meet the interpretive requirements intrinsic to those theories. However, those difficulties or disintegrations reserved possibilities for Chinese scholars to draw alternative intellectual resources from both domestic and international environments. On the other hand, an increasing number of domestic scholars have realized their globalized identification and pursued international recognition by participating in academic events organized by leading international and regional associations and through multiple forms of publications. Jonathan Zhu (2002, p. 157) once highlighted the internationalization of communication studies in/from China, while most Chinese scholars concentrated on the domestication of communication studies from the West. Central to this collective behavior, regardless of generational differences, is the motivation to build the legitimacy of media and communication studies in China as a newcomer in the academy and to enhance connections with international academic circles which, to a large extent, are dominated by Western scholars. There are two primary reasons for legitimacy building with regard to both domestic and international contexts. Domestically, the major challenge is to institutionalize media and communication research as an independent discipline that differs from its previous direct subordination to political settings and responds to the emerging market-oriented media reform. Internationally, any effort to *jie gui* (reconnect) with American- or Western-oriented global paradigms or approaches is encouraged. This motivation gradually has been institutionalized within the globalization processes of China's higher educational system, crystallized in the *shuang yi liu* (double world-class project).

Against this historical background, several international academic associations in addition to IAMCR—International Communication Association (ICA), National Communication Association (NCA), Association for Education in Journalism and Mass Communication (AEJMC), and AMIC—captured the attention of Chinese scholars. ICA and IAMCR are the most popular in the eyes of Chinese scholars and students. ICA is recognized widely as the most "international" mainly because of its American origins and stronger competition in the selection of annual conference papers in comparison to IAMCR. The perception of IAMCR is complex. Born in the framework of UNESCO, IAMCR is intrinsically more international than other associations and is underpinned by the organizational principles of justice and diversity in international academic research and exchange. In China, the impression of IAMCR is two-faceted. First, IAMCR is indeed an international association due to its geographically Western origin in the lens of epistemological orientalism and modernism. Second, IAMCR is different from a "pure" Western association because it embodies the richness and complexity of the concept of the West, through, for instance, its three working languages and its wide engagement with the developing world exemplified by the aforementioned membership structure. After attending the 2002 Conference in Barcelona, Shijie Guan (2002, p. 12) highlighted that IAMCR differs from ICA due to its greater internationality. For example, IAMCR attracted more members from Third World countries. Besides, on a surface level, the changing and diverse host cities for annual conferences, particularly in the developing world, such as Cartagena, Nairobi, and Beijing, also matters for Chinese scholars to build a truly global imagination of IAMCR.

The selection of host cities provides an opportunity for scholars and students from a host country and region to build close connections and understand the relevance of IAMCR for their academic careers. In order to maintain the diversity of the association, the acceptance rate for papers for IAMCR annual conferences is comparatively higher than ICA's, making it easier to get submissions accepted from countries like China. As a result, in recent years, the number of submissions, accepted submissions, and final presentations from China at IAMCR has increased enormously. The dilemma is evident. A higher acceptance rate offers a great opportunity for Chinese scholars and students to participate in such a long-standing and large-scale international academic fiesta, but this high rate reduces the competitiveness and lowers the evaluation of the research outputs. It might be argued that diversity cannot co-exist with quality, particularly on the operational level, but the IAMCR conference itself is not only an exhibition of research papers. It is a dynamic space for thought exchanges and network building. A number of IAMCR members also have memberships with other associations and there is a large overlap among leading international associations. In this sense, IAMCR offers a perfect gateway for Chinese scholars and students to experience a sense of being international in their going-out journeys. It is also comparatively easier for China-based researchers to be acknowledged within the organizational structure of IAMCR since it is characterized by diversity, justice, and inclusiveness.

Two Visits and the Changing Paradigms in Media and Communication Studies in China

Considering the connectivity between China and IAMCR should go hand-in-hand with a summary of the changing paradigms in media and communication studies in China, particularly over the past four decades during which China shifted its focus from political struggle and an ideological-oriented movement to an arguably de-politicized developmental path underpinned by economic reform, an opening-up policy, and reconnection with the global capitalist system.

Before the start of this new period, however, we may recall two very critical moments in the history of China's encounters with Western media and communication scholars. There are two scholars who presented a sharp comparison in terms of their interaction with China and their intellectual legacies appropriated by Chinese scholars of different generations. The early one is Canadian scholar Dallas W. Smythe. He visited China twice in the 1970s, before the widely recognized ice-breaking visit by Wilbur Schramm in 1982. According to Wang et al. (2014), with the financial support of the Canada Council, Smythe visited China for the first time. During this visit, he tried to find the possibility of an alternative technical roadmap in China to counterbalance the dominant model of American modernization, which by its nature, served capitalist consumerism. Based on his reading of Mao's works and examination of the democratic communication practices during the Cultural Revolution, Smythe explained to Chinese government officials and scholars who he interviewed that the Western modern one-dimensional television system was serving consumerism and authoritarianism.

As a solution, Smythe suggested to Chinese government officials and experts that they create an interactive television system to serve mass democracy. The response he received from his Chinese interviewees was pessimistic. He found that Chinese experts and bureaucracies were inclined to perceive technology as a neutral tool with its nature defined by the system in which it is used. Smythe sincerely expected that China could focus on the provision of public goods and collective consumption instead of following the capitalist old path of individual consumerism. These ideas were encapsulated in his famous article "After Bicycles, What?" in 1973. Six years later, he visited China again and found that China had walked the road of consumerist capitalism. As Wang et al. (2014) concluded, despite some misleading impacts of the ideological narratives of the Cultural Revolution, Smythe incorporated the two-line struggle logic in understanding technological processes and tried to imagine China as an alternative and socialist model, at least on the normative level. His intellectual legacy is still of great relevance and importance for Chinese scholars today as we constantly reflect on whether we are walking away from the socialist nature of an ever-changing media and communication system. Smythe's influence is found mostly in the community of critical scholars.

In contrast, the American scholar, Wilbur Schramm, brought a scientific approach and a seemingly value-free but intensively de-politicized knowledge system to China, which resonated with the historical background in which Dallas W. Smythe had found China's great turn or transformation toward consumerist capitalism. Since then, Chinese media and communication scholars have massively moved to study a series of new topics such as media markets, media economics, media management, media policy, audience analysis, and media effects. Media and information technology are considered only as a kind of communication instrument that deserves financial investment and scientific use. Alongside the marketization process, media and communication studies were developed to analyze and predict these newly emerged media and communication industries and to further legitimize their existence and prosperity, amid the changing relationship between media and politics. To serve the consumer or market, rather than the people or society in a political discourse, became the most important organizational principle of those market-oriented media organizations. In this sense, Wilbur Schramm and his groundbreaking visit to the Chinese mainland demonstrated a relationship of mutual need between his missionary international popularization of media and communication as a scientific and administrative discipline and a large number of Chinese scholars' search for a substitution for previously political and ideological-laden press theories. This historical encounter was both accidental and inevitable. Forty years later, Schramm's legacy is still influential, while his Cold War mindset has been gradually recognized. Chinese scholars sometimes still rely on his work to define the legitimacy of media and communication studies as a subject at universities and as a well-established discipline in China's higher education system.

The work of these scholars emphasized different traditions and perspectives on the normative implications of their work. Smythe's critical orientation to research and politics, developed through his political economy of communication, made him a subject of interest to the Federal Bureau of Investigation (FBI), when he was appointed in 1948 to the Institute of Communications at the University of Illinois Urbana-Champaign. The Institute was directed by Wilbur Schramm, who Smythe believed was the FBI's informant on him during his tenure at the university (Babe, 2000, p. 115). This comparison implies an intertwined logic in contemporary Chinese history. On the one hand, a reforming China quickly adopted a capitalist logic in restructuring its media industry and the corresponding educational and intellectual system. On the other hand, the question about a socialist developmental path, in either theory or practice, is not well discussed and is even overshadowed. To a large extent, this dilemma, which is deeply rooted in the mindset of Chinese media and communication scholars, drives them to build wide and close connections with international academia to confirm or change what they have in mind regarding the relations between media and society in a globalizing context. IAMCR, with its inclusiveness and diversity, provides an excellent platform for Chinese scholars to take on this adventure.

After 40 years, alongside the importation and appropriation of additional theories from the outside world, Chinese media and communication scholars have accumulated more options for formulating creative theoretical frameworks to interpret the changing media landscape and its integration within an informationized and mediated society. It is easy to find that any newly emerged and mostly interdisciplinary field of research in the international academy has its response in China. For example, Chinese media and scholars are increasingly keen to conduct research and build dialog and collaborations with international scholars in interdisciplinary arenas, including research on digital platforms, digital labor, computational communication, fandom, feminism, participatory culture, media materiality, and so on. In a word, the connection between China and the world, in terms of media and communication scholarship, has been multi-sided and systematic.

However, as Dallas Smythe's work reminds us, the socialist or capitalist struggle within China's modern information and communication system still deserves critical scholarship. The current formulation and consolidation of digital capitalism or platform imperialism has engendered more and more reflections on the concentration of communication power with digital platforms and the regulatory challenges the government is facing. Furthermore, this reflective and critical scholarship is merging with a similar trend toward critiques in international academia which target a new round of media conglomeration, but on a different scope and scale. The reason is simple. China has played a crucial role in driving the growth and spread of digital capitalism while the socialist state is still adjusting its policies and strengthening its capacities to further contain the creative destruction of capitalism in the digital age. We can possibly expect a more plural, hybrid, and contradictory future for media and communication research in China. This may resonate well with the differentiated international academic community that IAMCR attempts to represent and embrace.

Concluding Remarks: After 40 Years, What?

This review of contributions by Chinese scholars to IAMCR and specifically to its conferences, as well as the opportunities offered by IAMCR for Chinese scholarship to go abroad, provides insight into the interests and trends of Chinese media and communication research. Driven by an increasingly clear aim of constantly and deeply internationalizing Chinese media and communication scholarship, the involvement of Chinese scholars in IAMCR is likely to grow significantly in the coming years. In addition to growth in the number and diversity of papers, two new trends mark a substantial change in collaboration between IAMCR and the Chinese academy. First, Chinese scholars are actively serving in the IC, sections, and WGs as elected leaders and, second, there is more institutional cooperation between IAMCR and Chinese universities in co-organizing academic activities and co-publishing academic journals and books. Compared with other international academic associations in the field of media and communication, IAMCR is likely to maintain its high popularity in the future. Meanwhile, universities in China, especially those located in first-tier cities that have more financial and human resources and greater motivations to go global, will continuously explore opportunities to build partnerships with other associations, and this might reverse the influence of IAMCR in China.

Zhengrong Hu et al. (2013) have emphasized the shifting paradigms in communication studies in China over past decades against the background of China's opening-up and reform policy in a neoliberal globalization process. Chinese scholars have realized the difficulty of simply employing Western theories in Chinese contexts (Hu et al., 2013, p. 155). The contributions to IAMCR's Sections and WGs have accentuated this transcendence from unipolar to multipolar, hybridized communication and media research. The active involvement of Chinese scholarship in IAMCR has had a two-fold impact. On the one hand, it has strengthened the connection and interaction with Western theories and helped Chinese scholars to realize the diversity within and beyond Western academia due to encounters with IAMCR members with diverse academic and cultural backgrounds. On the other hand, it has drawn the attention of Chinese scholars to rethink their identity on the international stage and reevaluate one of the key challenges they face. This is the question about what the genuine theoretical contribution to media and communication research is from a Chinese perspective and how Chinese theories and practices can be effectively and creatively communicated with Western and other non-Western theories.

Last, but not least, it is crucial to consider whether and how the growing involvement of China in IAMCR has changed the association in terms of the membership structure, elements of the conference program, and the diversity of scholarship. Chinese topics are appearing more often at the annual conferences and Chinese perspectives are attracting increasing attention from international scholars. We can imagine that both practice and theory from China in a fast-changing media and communication environment will have an enduring impact on the international scholars' recognition of Chinese media and society through Chinese scholars' participation in IAMCR. These Chinese elements will not only contribute to the building of diversity as the spirit of IAMCR, but also provide an opportunity for scholars from other countries to be reflective about their impressions of China and its complex media and social system and to rethink the components and ethics of international communication in the twenty-first century.

The year 2022 marked the 40th anniversary of Wilbur Schramm's visit to China. Though earlier histories were already found and are increasingly discussed, the contribution of Wilbur Schramm and his "post-positivist" approach in line with the Columbia tradition helping with the establishment of communication studies in the Chinese mainland, is still central to the collective memory of contemporary Chinese scholars. However, alongside the rising demand for multiple intellectual resources across the globe in developing communication studies in China, the intellectual legacies derived from the long and rich history of IAMCR is of great importance. Resonating with Dallas Smythe's questioning of China's developmental path during his historic visits, it might be timely to propose a similar question: after 40 years, what? It is argued that the future of media and communication studies in and from China will be based on closer and deeper interactions with international academic associations as represented by IAMCR that offer such a long-standing critical tradition toward the relationship between knowledge and power in a truly global view.

References

Babe, R. E. (2000). *Canadian communication thought: Ten foundational writers.* Toronto University Press.

Guan, S. (2002). A summary of the 23rd Conference and Convention of the International Association for Media and Communication Research. *Chinese Journal of Journalism & Communication,* 5, 12–16.

Guo, K., & Chen, P. (2017). The changing landscape of journalism education in China. *Journalism & Mass Communication Educator, 72*(3), 297–305.

Hu, Z. (2013). *Lost in global capitalism? Economic vulnerability, value crisis, and the shift of soft power in China* (Plenary Speech). IAMCR Conference, Dublin, Ireland.

Hu, Z., Zhang, L., & Ji, D. (2013). Globalization, social reform and the shifting paradigms of communication studies in China. *Media, Culture & Society, 35*(1), 147–155. Retrieved 15 June 2022, from https://doi.org/10.1177/0163443712464569

Huang, Y. (1997). Developing countries on the information highway: Notes on the 20th Conference of IAMCR. *Social Sciences Abroad, 1*, 76–78.

Jiang, C. Q. (2011). Techno-nationalism and creative industries: The development of the Chinese online game industry in a globalized economy (Paper). IAMCR Conference, Istanbul, Turkey.

Long, Y., & Zeng, X. (2016). Journalism education in China: The reality and challenges in the digital era. *Journal of Applied Journalism & Media Studies, 5*(1), 117–137. Retrieved 15 June 2022, from https://doi.org/10.1386/ajms.5.1.117_1

Ming, A. X. (1987). *China's mass communication: For the two civilizations: Some aspects of the transformation of the mass communication system in China*. Mass Communication Research Centre.

Ming, A., & Sun, L. (Eds.). (1983). *A brief introduction to communication studies.* People's Daily Press.

Rogers, E., Zhao, X., Pan, Z., & Chen, M. (1985). The Beijing audience study. *Communication Research, 12*(2), 179–208.

Smythe, D. W. (1973/1994). After bicycles, what? In T. Gubeck (Ed.), *Counterclockwise: Perspectives on communication* (p. 230–244). Westview Press.

Wang, H., Zhao, Y., & Qiu, L. (2014). After bicycle, what? The politics and ideology of technology. *Open Times, 4*, 95–96.

Weaver, D. (Ed.). (1998). *The global journalist: News people around the world.* Hampton Press.

Zhao, Y. (2011). The challenge of China: Contribution to a transcultural political economy of communication for the twenty-first century. In J. Wasko, G. Murdock, & H. Sousa (Eds.), *The handbook of political economy of communications* (p. 558–582). Routledge.

Zhu, J. (2002). International experiences in the internationalization of Communication Studies: Impacts from individual academic training and institutional reward and punishment system. In G. Zhang & Z. Huang (Eds.), *Communication studies in China: Retrospection and prospect* (p. 157–170). Fudan University Press.

CHAPTER 21

India and IAMCR: A Perspective

Sanjay Bharthur

Introduction

> The creation of IAMCR (1957) was a result of UNESCO's efforts to bring the scientific and cultural community of the East and West closer to each other. This was happening at the same time as mass media of communication were entering the new era of electronic media. With electronic media becoming more prevalent and many newly independent nations attempting to build the first infrastructure of communication, there was a period of growth of news agencies, broadcasting systems, and private and governmental telecommunication structures. The period of 1950s is also very important since a fundamental change was taking place in international affairs. The rise of the so-called third world was leading to the strengthening of alliances within less industrialized countries, as exhibited by the non-aligned movement under the leadership of India, Indonesia and other countries following the Bandung Conference (1954) … The fourth group of participants, and the smallest, represented the third world which often played a marginal role in the leadership of IAMCR, and due to a variety of economic and political reasons, their membership remained low. (Mowlana, 1997, p. np)

Since the spotlight is on IAMCR in this chapter, the umbrella of the association's influence on respective scholars' works and the kinds of questions they have raised is undoubtedly interesting but quite ambitious to capture at the individual level. Focusing on India with its subcontinental size also presents a complex challenge and may not capture its diversity regarding language, religion, and demographic profile, not to say its struggle to promote equity.

S. Bharthur (✉)
Manipal Institute of Communication, Manipal, Karnataka, India

© The Author(s), under exclusive license to Springer Nature Switzerland AG 2023

J. Becker, R. Mansell (eds.), *Reflections on the International Association for Media and Communication Research*,
https://doi.org/10.1007/978-3-031-16383-8_21

IAMCR and the "Third World"

In the preface to its history, then IAMCR President Robin Mansell (2007) notes that it "connects in many ways to the political-economic and cultural developments in the world since the second world war. It brings to life the great narratives in the social sciences and humanities within which the phenomenal growth in mass communication has taken place and continues to flourish" (Hamelink & Nordenstreng, 2007). This seems to be the guiding philosophy that a small IAMCR leadership initiated and nurtured, so that the association has grown into a significant forum for academic activities in the media and communication field.

Many phases of IAMCR can be identified, including its conscious concern for "Third World" countries and their media development. An examination of presidential communications reveals an incremental approach to such concerns, including the symbolic gesture of holding conferences in these countries. Since IAMCR enjoys class "A" consultative status with UNESCO, its close linkages with ideas and thoughts in the media and communication field are synergistic. While the entire range of scholars' interventions cannot be presented here, influential scholars who consistently maintained a specific and general interest in "Third World" countries from a global or comparative perspective and have been active in IAMCR are recognized.

No claim that India represents the whole gamut of "Third World" countries can be made or is intended. However, on mass media-related issues, a significant context such as India with its diversity and multiple problems in many social sectors, enabled researchers to offer very substantial comparative analytical insight, and two IAMCR conferences were held in India (1986 and 2014).

Contextual Reflections and India's Experience

Notwithstanding a very long period of colonization that impacted the Indian subcontinent, it is essential to recognize civilizational patterns in society. Research in communication and media studies has focused on non-Western perspectives, recognizing the crucial influences of Hinduism, Buddhism, and Islam in communication patterns (Adhikary, 2010; Dissanayake & Wang, 1984; Mowlana, 2007). A syncretic assessment is provided by Jayaweera of the complexities of the subcontinent and the simplistic development paradigms and research highlighted in Western strands of theory and research. Alternatively, he emphasized the need to focus, for example, on political debates surrounding demand for a new world information and communication order (NWICO), the application of new information and communication technologies (ICTs) and their consequences, especially for the integrity and survival of local cultures, the need to look at communication education, and the overall relationship between communication and development (Jayaweera, 1985).

The naïve perception of information as being available for consumption if only media structures were to become available was challenged through the development of economic theories, insisting that information needs to be understood as both product and commodity (Melody, 1981) and by addressing the larger question of who owns and controls information dissemination through the media. The corporatization of the media and the military-industrial complex that underlies such ownership was flagged quite early by Dallas Smythe, Nicholas Garnham, and others (Smythe, 1981; Garnham, 1979). Schiller emphasized a cultural factor in such patterns in the imperialistic and corporate designs carried through mass media, especially television (Schiller, 1981). The MacBride Commission, while discussing the dimensions of the cultural industry in the context of media, also noted:

> The cultural industry is not a mere ideological apparatus, if we understand this to mean an apparatus, as described by Poulantzas, that does not create ideology but is limited to promoting and disseminating it. The cultural industry does also create ideology. (MacBride, 1980, p. 51)

Much later, these issues would be formally addressed in trade-related matters where the audiovisual services form an important communication component.

Development, the Politics of Tied Aid, and Mass Communication

Its initial heavy reliance on aid guided India's approach to development. The politics of aid and its relationship to development in many developing countries is a subject of many discourses in the general development studies literature. Adopting a centralized planning institutional mechanism in India gave rise to considerable tensions between the various states and the central government in the federal structure. Although perceived as necessary, communications, particularly radio and telephony, were not a priority as there were more pressing needs such as food, education, and so on. Therefore, the broadcasting sector had to argue its case, and it came mainly from the UNESCO platform that had incorporated mass media development as one of its goals.

In India, when television was introduced apparently for development purposes and later expanded through a nationwide satellite, there were concerns about how it was slipping away from social sector applications and its appropriation by and for commercial purposes by providing a medium with a larger appetite for entertainment content, backed by advertising revenue rather than development-related content.

This was the backdrop against which the government appointed a committee to examine the software dimension of television in India. The report, in two parts, raised a perceptive query—"Television for Whom and for What?" in part one and charted a path toward a developmental television medium, setting out how the India of our dreams could be built in part two (Joshi, 1985). Within the report, sections dealt with culture and women as the neglected half. It argued for a communication revolution, and endorsed what Mahatma Gandhi had said.

> I refuse to be dazzled by the seeming triumph of machinery. What I object to is the craze of machinery, not machinery as such…Today machinery helps a few to ride on the backs of millions. The impetus behind it is not philanthropy but greed. (Cited in Joshi, 1985, p. 20)

Cultural imperialism via reruns of the United States' (US) syndicated television programs was also flagged in the report. However, in terms of development support that the media could lend, it upheld the Nehru-Sarabhai framework, an approach that visualized the media's transformative power. The Nehruvian approach to communication policies reflected Nehru's strong belief in science and technology and centralized planning (Bharthur, 2006).

Within IAMCR scholarship, there were arguments about the need for cultural autonomy in planning (Hamelink, 1977) and cultural screens in Dallas Smythe's work (Melody, 1992). Both suggested a conscious effort to recognize a nation's independent approach and strengths to negotiate content's dominant and one-way flow.

A Colonial Factor

India's long colonial experience has been debated and analyzed and is subject to intense academic scrutiny. The country's struggle for independence in 1947 was a movement spearheaded by many leaders who communicated utilizing existing systems of communication embedded in multiple languages, cultures, and religions. The arrival of the printing press in Goa, India, in 1556 (historians claim it to be the first in Asia), was unintended as it was headed to Ethiopia, whose king had requested Portugal to send a printing press since it would help in missionary activity. But the press stayed in Goa as relations between Portugal and Ethiopia had soured (Priolkar, 1958; Ranganathan, 2020). We cannot explain the role of the printing press during the European colonial era in India in the same way as in Europe (Eisenstein, 1979). Cultural historians, however, have explained its relationship to the then manuscript writers (Venkatachalapathy, 2012) and, much later, to newspapers (Barns, 1940; Kesavan, 1997; Otis, 2018). There are exciting explanations about why the art of transferring knowledge beyond manuscripts did not develop to the extent it should have, and a Western view would observe this as a case of the manuscript writers seeking to retain a monopoly of knowledge (Turco, 2013). A large body of Indian scholarship agrees with this view to explain the unequal caste system.

The evolution of newspapers in colonial India, their relationship to social reforms, and later nationalist struggles were highlighted by Indian researchers. Despite low literacy levels, nationalist leaders such as Tilak, Gandhi, and Nehru (to name a few) considered newspapers as practical tools to reach the people. Gandhi's 150th birth anniversary (2019) was an occasion for hundreds of articles touching upon his thoughts on the economy, communal harmony, and analyzing his communication practices. Gandhian Studies is incorporated in many academic circles to understand his economic philosophy. Some authors have proposed a framework that helps us understand the role of newspapers in the colonial, nationalist, and post-independence phases (Ram, 2011).

Mass Media and National Development

Among the many formative areas that IAMCR focused on, the relationship between mass media and national development was significant (Chu & Schramm, 1968; Schramm, 1964). Without claiming to recall all the literature in this area, the influence of Rogers (diffusion), Lerner (modernization and leapfrogging), and Lucian Pye (politics) was very significant. These were crucial influencers who had a significant impact on many nations in Africa, Asia, and Latin America that had gone through periods of colonization. However, there were specific responses to their mass media deficit in the national development argument. A few scholars examined the relevance and strategies of iconic national leaders such as Mahatma Gandhi in India or Mao in China, who led their nations to liberation without any access to the media, as we understand it today. Kusum Singh posits a mass line argument to stress the efficacy of their strategies. Mass line theory provides the foundation for both Gandhi's and Mao's efforts to narrow the difference between the leaders and the led. They sought ways for the elite to be more concerned about the masses and their problems.

> India and China raise the question of obvious connections between two different kinds of national movements...Gandhi sought independence from the British and took the form of social and moral reform while Mao sought socialist and radical restructuring of the system. (K. J. Singh, 1979, p. 96)

While highlighting the links between interpersonal and mediated communication, the MacBride Commission points out that events in the political and social life of many "developing countries such as the long march of the Gandhian movement in India, the liberation movements in Africa, the successive mass political campaigns in China and the overthrow of the monarchy in Iran" (MacBride, 1980, p. II–28). In the Indian context, journalism and the production of newspapers to promote independence was a common practice. Gandhi advocated journalism without advertising support and communicating in regional languages (Guha, 2003).

Jawaharlal Nehru, the first Prime Minister, recognized the need to address communications infrastructure and the role of a free press. The Indian National Congress set up various committees to examine sectors and communications was one of them. The approach was to recognize the inadequacy of infrastructure and incorporate its development into India's planning philosophy which was centralist and socialist (K. T. Shah, 1948). Nehru's belief in the freedom of the press and democracy ensured an enabling provision in the Constitution to protect it. As far as broadcasting is concerned, he believed in the BBC model, although the licensing fee for broadcast receivers was inadequate for sustaining a public broadcasting system's operation in India. Therefore, governmental support nurtured its growth, and the question of the government's relationship to broadcasting has rankled many committees. There has been no change in perception of the government's intention to retain control over broadcasting, despite cosmetic changes in the institutional setup under the public service broadcaster, Prasar Bharati. A minister, when asked, had mentioned that they maintain an arm's length relationship with "Prasar Bharati and that steps suggested by an expert committee for further autonomy were under consideration" (PTI, 2014).

Mass Media as a Variable in International Assistance

India accepted the importance ascribed to the mass media by UNESCO to achieve the minimum mass media facilities needed for development:

> UNESCO has suggested that each country should aim to provide for every 100 of its inhabitants at least ten copies of daily newspapers, five radio receivers, two cinema seats, and two television receivers. (UNESCO, 1961, p. 63)

An assessment of the technical needs for mass media in India by UNESCO in July 1948, less than a year after its independence, noted that there was no national news agency covering the entire nation and the only one that covered the nation was a subsidiary of Reuters. Its assessment of the status of the press noted the dominance of English both in terms of circulation and revenue across the significant publication hubs in India, with the Hindi and Urdu press having a distant second and third position. Technology that better supported the production of English newspapers was also a factor, since English newspapers in India accounted for 55 percent of newspaper circulation, with three to four copies of newspapers available for every 1000 of its population. Radio, transferred as a state subject to the government of India (GoI), was limited in access and reach. One radio set for every 1500 persons was estimated. The lack of foreign exchange to facilitate the purchase of radio receivers, including limited manufacturing capacity, were cited as hurdles in extending the medium. By the late 1940s, the film industry had developed an indigenous base for producing and distributing films. The film industry, with its commercial dynamics and newspapers, treated as sacrosanct based on claims about respect for freedom of the press, was not involved in discussions about the transformative role of the media as much as, for example, broadcasting. It was transferred to the government by the British, and its expansion and development were an option for government policy. Colonial histories of broadcasting implicate the motives of the British in keeping its growth minimal along with control (Chatterji, 1987; Lionel, 1960). Accounts of the long histories of the railways and telegraph in

India attribute their development to colonial intent (Headrick, 2010), for example, by invoking the classical Marxian framework (Marx, 1853).

This chapter focuses on the contribution by Indian and other scholars in the core and peripheral IAMCR network to the analysis of the development of broadcasting and, later, media, with less attention to print and film, notwithstanding their many tangible contributions. The norms of these mass media were to provide a basis for international assistance to developing countries. Thus, when the Director-General of UNESCO proposed to the GoI that it would help organize rural radio forums (Bhat & Krishnamurthy, 1965), this was accepted. At the time, support for radio forums was suggested and recommended to other developing countries based on the Indian experience. The forum idea was also based on a—

> considerable amount of research including Kurt Lewin's wartime experiments in changing social attitudes and behaviours, which demonstrated that a critical attitude change is often easier to achieve in a group than in individuals and that when a decision for behavioural change is taken in such a group, it is more likely to be carried out than if it does not originate in a group; moreover, several experiments of which some of Carl Hovland's may be cited as examples, on the effectiveness of a prestigious communicator (such as radio can provide for the forum); and finally the long tradition in communication research concerning the effectiveness of two-way communication (such as occurs when the radio station broadcasts to the forum, and the forum's questions and decisions are reported back to the station. (Schramm & Coombs, 1987, p. 109)

State Control of Broadcasting

A related argument for state control of broadcasting was to fulfill the state's social sector obligations. The narrative of broadcasting (radio and television) for development has been a consistent theme in policy articulations. The rural radio forums of the late 1950s, the Delhi School Television project, and the Satellite Instructional Television Experiment (SITE) attest to this. An international parallel argument focused on mass media as a missing link in development, with an extensive paradigmatic literature suggesting that the spread of the transmission of the mass media would fill an information void. Much later, when the emphasis shifted to telecommunications, similar information gap articulations were also evident in the Maitland Commission. The Commission did not authorize any study as it felt that the role of information and telecommunications infrastructure in developing countries (its focus) had been studied and therefore was informed by the research (Maitland, 1984, p. 1)

Mass media centricity in development thinking and government policy choices completely ignores the communication patterns of societies such as India. One of the many background documents prepared for the MacBride Commission was the role of the traditional media. They were treated not as media of the past but as important functionally and culturally (Ranganath HK, 1978) in India and other countries such as Egypt and the African continent.

Even if the growth of the mass media overtook earlier communication patterns, it did not obliterate traditional media. Assessing the contribution of traditional media in terms of their continuity and relevance is beyond the scope of this chapter. However, it is important to stress that the Nehruvian approach to promoting the idea of planning and seeking people's civic participation meant that folk and other traditional media featured prominently in policy in the absence of a mass media infrastructure commensurate with the requirements of the Indian nation (Vidyalankar, 1963).

An extensive network of field-based communication units with song and drama and various forms of puppetry was supported by the Ministry of Information and Broadcasting. With changing times and the digital push, these units were merged into one unit as the Bureau of Outreach and Communication (BOC) in December 2017. The three units operating at the field level are intended for "Branding of the Government as a prime facilitator of people's empowerment and positioning of messages through Print, Audio-Visual, Outdoor, Digital Media to realize the same, is BOC's mandate." The policy guidelines have been adapted in sync with emerging media scenarios to maximize the reach of information dissemination (P. Mitra, 2018).

In the context of the SITE experiment, a comprehensive review of its evaluations also emphasized the importance of traditional media as part of the personal dimension of communication:

> Probably most Third World nations now use some traditional media forms to promote rural development. But the oldest form of traditional communication-face-to-face interaction between persons who respect each other, remains the most potent form of message transmission. Electric media inherently suffer from a loss of immediacy and personal adaptation found most compellingly indirect talk. The SITE experience supports the conviction of many humanists of the information age- that media technology will never replace the personal dimension of human communication. (Starosta & Merriam, 1986, p. 39–45)

Institutional Dimensions of SITE

There was considerable discussion and debate among scholars about research traditions captured effectively in a special issue of the *Journal of Communication* (Vol 33, no. 3, 1983) on "ferment in the field" pointing to differences between administrative and critical research. The retirement of James Halloran as President of IAMCR was an occasion to recognize his contribution. Cees Hamelink and his colleague edited a book *Mass Communication Research: On Problems and Policies* (Hamelink & Linné, 1994), asking the right question within the framework of communication research on problems and policies. A few scholars from the "Third World" were also critical of approaches and policies regarding communication. In the context of this essay, the late Prof. K. E. Eapen, a long-standing member of IAMCR and former Vice President, has reflected on many issues related to education, training, and research. In the book edited by Hamelink and Linné mentioned above, Eapen stated:

> From hindsight, at the dawn of the 1990s, it is intriguing that the visible holes in the Dominant paradigm of the Communication-Development concept were not perceived and articulated earlier than they were. The myopic vision was perhaps sustained because the nations surrounding it originated within the U.S.A. and were applied elsewhere. The intended target was especially the so-called underdeveloped world, made up of the poorer nations of Africa, Asia, and South America. (Eapen, 1994, p. 277) (Fig. 21.1)

Many "Third World" countries and scholars focused their attention on the SITE. A year-long experiment in India (1975–1976) demonstrated the use of communication satellites over a large area of a country that National Aeronautics and Space Administration (NASA) was interested in, and television for instruction in the rural areas by the GoI. This arrangement was not merely an experiment but involved many significant aspects of the geopolitics of technology transfer. The dominant mass media literature favored the benefits of exogenous information in instruction concerning crucial practices in agriculture and health and assumed a transformative process from a traditional and transitional to a modern society. Discussions among "Third World" scholars, in contrast,

Fig. 21.1 Eapen K. Eapen (1923–2010). Member IAMCR International Council 1980–88; Vice President 1988–1994, member Professional Education Section (Courtesy of Ranji Cherian)

questioned these transformative approaches because they ignore structural, contextual, and cultural factors (Beltrán, 1975; Eapen, 2006).

Key IAMCR Scholars and Their Influence on Certain Aspects of SITE

As a graduate student at Simon Fraser University, Canada, my focus on Indian media and communications began with coursework that grappled with contemporary approaches to cultural studies and communication and development frameworks beyond the dominant paradigm, and I was interested in policies. India had become a textbook case of satellite technology for communication through the SITE (Frutkin, 2015), and its evaluation revealed mixed outcomes (Agrawal, 1981; Chander & Karnik, 1976).

SITE was novel because it skipped the introduction of television in urban areas first and took it directly to some 2400 Indian villages. The experiment placed television at the center of the narrative, but this medium had already gone through its initiation with the launch of a television service in 1959, and with UNESCO's assistance and showcasing of television equipment at the Delhi Industrial Fair (N. Kumar & Chandiram, 1987). In 1965, the incremental expansion of the medium had been proposed by All India Radio, and this was contrary to the space organization's plan of opting to use the communication satellite as the basis of nationwide television. The policy processes leading to the decision to emphasize broadcasting reflected the complexity of India's decision-making and the push it received from influential scientist-administrators. Vikram Sarabhai, who led these efforts, was suitably honored during his birth centenary in 2019. His views on development within the mass media television framework of using television were consistent with an emphasis on radio broadcasting and were captured by various scholars writing about communication and media in India (A. Shah, 2016; Chowdhry, 2004; Sarabhai, 1969).

SITE, or mass media for national development, was a dominant discourse in international forums, including IAMCR, which focused on this theme. This experiment also reflected the then articulated view of minimum mass media norms for developing countries. Due to its size, the scale of poverty, and other factors, India's experience was viewed as a framework for other developing countries, be it radio or television.

The experiment and its planning reflected a host of NASA and the US government policy decisions that, in the era of heightened geopolitics, was uncomfortable with India's Non-Aligned approach and its ambitions regarding the atomic energy program. Sarabhai inherited Homi Bhabha's mantle as chairman of the program and was the leading force in conceiving and developing the Indian space program, within which SITE occupied a minor role but had implications for the development of India's satellite launch capability. Sarabhai's vision was, "I have a dream, a fantasy may be, that we can leapfrog our way to development" (Shah, 2019). It may be relevant to point out that Daniel Lerner was a consultant to Sarabhai.

> An Applications Technology Satellite (ATS-6) developed by the NASA leads directly into the next decade because it is already stationed over India for a challenging series of educational experiments (both educational and instructional television). For several years I was a consultant to the director of the Indian experiment-the late Dr Vikram Sarabhai. Under his direction, unfortunately, cut short by his premature death, the Indian experiment was a brilliant example of a leapfrogging process which communication technology makes possible. Given the problems raised by India's acceleration of history and its instant mobilisation of the periphery, this leapfrogging over the long western experience is what India needs most. (Lerner & Nelson, 1977, p. 162)

NASA's enthusiasm for parking the Applications Technology Satellite (ATS) with orbital coverage of India was not matched by the US State Department's assessment. Among many reasons for the State Department's reluctance was the fact that while India had agreed initially to allow the setting up of a Voice of America (VoA) transmitter in Kolkata for a token sum of one rupee in exchange for specified hours of transmission, it aimed at combating China's transmission in the region. In 1963, India had a border debacle with China, and among the many reasons identified was the lack of radio's reach to explain the situation to the people. VoA's powerful transmitter was offered to allow India to reach out to them, leading to a stormy discussion in the Indian Parliament, and the deal was canceled. The foreign policy aspect of this deal had rankled the Americans (Brecher, 1974) and was cited by the State Department's official representative to NASA as an instance of the undependable nature of India.

The more significant interests in expanding VoA in the Middle East in the late 1950s and the murky beginning of the modernization paradigm and the role of the Bureau of Applied Social Science led to the publication of Lerner's *Passing of the Traditional Society* (Samarajiwa, 1984). In addition, the State Department wanted India to buy a commercial satellite rather than engage in a loan that NASA had agreed. The harsh conditions placed in the agreement for SITE that restricted the loan of ATS for one year only also indirectly meant that India had to buy the satellite, which it did from Ford Aerospace and Communications Corporation (FACC), for its subsequent use. It is relevant to note that US foundations, including the Ford Foundation, were active think tanks in India's development planning (Rosen, 1985). Thus, the relationships that gave rise to the SITE were complex within the US where the technology was developed, and in India where it was deployed.

Both William Melody and Dallas W. Smythe, who formed the doctoral committee for my dissertation, were active scholars in the IAMCR network. The argument that communication technology is not neutral but shaped by political and institutional factors was central to their work and formed the axis of my study of the SITE. SITE did not benefit from social science input until near the start of the experiment, and its evaluation was confined to the field level over the one-year duration of the experiment. This much-needed evaluation component was criticized as indicative of the inadequacy of the SITE process (Agrawal, 1981; Eapen, 2006; Starosta & Merriam, 1986). Nevertheless, the science and technology establishment's enthusiasm placed a high premium on this experiment. An oblique but essential aspect was that Mrs Gandhi, Prime Minister at that time, decided to approve the Indian National Satellite System (INSAT) as a hub for television and telecommunications in India within months of the start of SITE before a comprehensive evaluation had been completed (Sanjay, 1991). Further, the nation was placed under an internal emergency regime (1975–77) with all liberties suspended, including the press, while broadcasting remained under the control of the government (GOI, 1977; I. B. Singh, 1980). The SITE project was conducted during the internal emergency of India.

A one-year SITE project was too short to conclude that television had changed people's attitudes or behaviors. However, the implications were significant because SITE demonstrated the viability of adopting a communication satellite as the central transmission hub in India for broadcasting and telecommunications. My academic training led to the germination of a shift toward examining technology transfer in my research. Around 1983, UNESCO had initiated work in this direction (Hancock, 1984); the politics of the adoption of television broadcasting standards had also been examined, and Smythe, whose work on the audience as a commodity to be sold to advertisers (Smythe, 1981), had advocated for an IAMCR section on Communication Satellites, with the best paper award instituted in his honor reflecting his contribution to critical thinking in the media and communication field (Melody, 1992).

Despite these critical assessments of the politics of technology, the expansion of television continued, although some development enthusiasts lamented shifting goals in content that required advertising revenue and structural reforms following liberalization in 1991 that led to the mushrooming of private television channels in India (Gupta, 2005; Naregal, 2000). Information revolution analysis in the 1980s in India emphasized the genre of pro-development soap operas inspired by México's telenovelas (Rogers & Singhal, 1988). The telecasting of Indian epics, the *Ramayana* and *Mahabharata* by the state broadcaster through a sponsorship arrangement with reputed filmmakers, echoed political interests and the rise of Hindu nationalism in India (Chandar, 2019; A. Mitra, 1993; Rajagopal, 2001). Interestingly, the present polity, the Bharatiya Janata Party (BJP) that governs the country, was not in sight of coming to power at that time, nor did it have access to the state-run television network, Doordarshan, for telecasting the Hindu epics to garner support for its electoral ambitions.

Journalism and Mass Communication Education

The World Journalism Education Council (WJEC), collaborating with UNESCO, hosted its meeting in India in August 2021 and focused on many challenges and issues. This meeting also marked the centenary of Indian journalism education. Many Indian scholars have reflected on its status and issues (Bharthur, 2012; Mira, 2017; Raman, 2015), highlighting gaps between journalism education and employment opportunities, the scope of training, and the need for multidisciplinary research approaches.

Kaarle Nordenstreng, a long-standing member of IAMCR, was chairing the association's then Professional Education Section, now rechristened as the Journalism and Research Education Section. One of the projects he initiated was promoting critical scholarship textbooks for different regions building on the results of a field study in South Asia, showing there was a domination of mainstream textbooks from North America and fewer from Europe (Eapen et al., 1991). While textbooks are undoubtedly crucial in shaping the understanding of students and scholars, it is also essential to understand how the journalism education curriculum was shaped, including the launching of Journalism and Media and Communication (J&MC) programs in India. Many of the leading educators in J&MC were trained formally in US universities and carried that approach into shaping the programs. There is also a considerable outflow of students pursuing higher degrees in the US, with Australia and the United Kingdom (UK) as other destinations. Within the Association for Education in Journalism and Mass Communication (AEJMC), the diaspora South Asian scholars opened a separate section called the South Asian Communication Association (SACA).

Prof. P. P. Singh launched the first formal journalism program in Lahore in 1942. He also compiled one of the first status reports on Journalism Education in Southeast Asia for UNESCO in 1959. Nehru invited him to be the editor of his paper, *National Herald*, but by the time Singh was available to take up the assignment, another person had been appointed. Singh was an alumnus of the Missouri School of Journalism 1937–1938 and a contemporary of Elisabeth Noelle-Neumann with whom, as a university newspaper reports, he engaged in a debate on developments in Germany, specifically on the brand of Nazi nationalism which she defended while P. P. Singh criticized how inequities were being addressed (1937). Ms Noelle-Neumann was one of the first women to be inducted into IAMCR's top planning circle.

The missionary-oriented launch of journalism programs in Hislop's College, Nagpur, brought the US approach to India (Beltzer, 1952). The US model, modified by a contextual sensitivity launched by the Indian pioneers, set the pattern (Wolseley, 1953) for further Indian journalism programs. A standoff between journalism editors/professionals about the relevance of a university education endured until the media houses realized an additional revenue stream could be generated by launching media schools as an extension of their business, and many media-backed journalism schools continue to function.

A recommendation by a study team on mass communication, sponsored by the Ford Foundation, was the setting up of a national institute for training in mass communication (MIB, 1963), and the Indian Institute of Mass Communication (IIMC) was established in 1965. Apart from its forays into formal diploma programs in J&MC, for which it is well-known, its significance is also felt by journalists and media professionals in more than 100 developing countries who have been trained with assistance from the GoI. It also heralded the formalization of a development journalism program in India. However, its goal of leading a research program in the subject has yet to reach fruition.

IAMCR Research Traditions and Impact on India

The research trajectory of J&MC in India can be viewed through the lens of resident and diaspora scholars mainly attached to US universities. However, James Halloran's (President of IAMCR from 1972 to 1990) interest in "Third World" studies encouraged a few Indian scholars to pursue their studies at the University of Leicester, and a Development Studies Program at The Hague offered some opportunities.

The issue is not where Indian students studied, or Indian scholars pursued their research, but the criteria used to establish the rigor needed in research, including where they publish. This is a gray area in India, and the current institutional push is toward research for its own sake and publication in a basket of indexed international journals. In the face of this trend, IAMCR, to some extent, provides an annual opportunity for many students and middle-level scholars to participate in a conference that has a peer-review mechanism.

The questions plaguing many scholars in India are the research processes and plans regarding research questions and methodology. The allusion here is not so much to earlier much-castigated studies in the dominant paradigm of media extension and/or health communication where, for example, diffusion research traditions ruled. The politics and economics of research have undoubtedly varied, but the scholarly output about and from India increased significantly with independent and collaborative scholarly contributions. Srinivas Melkote, Arvind Singhal, Pradip Thomas, Radhika Parmeshwaran, Sundeep Muppadi, and Daya Thussu, to name a few, sustained their studies in India and drew comparisons with other contexts. As Section Head of Political Economy in IAMCR, Pradip Thomas reflected on technology, education, and India's caste and class factors in developing India's media and communication system (Thomas, 2010).

Paradigm Passes

The dominant paradigm in media and communication research has passed at least in some areas of scholarship in India, emphasizing more relevant research such as participatory and communitarian approaches in India. Of significance is a focus on community radio (K. Kumar, 2003; Sinha & Malik, 2018) and recognition of this medium by UNESCO by instituting a Chair in Community Radio at the University of Hyderabad. The rapid growth of television access and content through the public service broadcasting structure has been analyzed, for example, for its implications for the Indian polity (Rajagopal, 2001). Communitarian, participatory, and the audience as active negotiators, including ethnographic approaches, have developed.

The formal launch of Digital India in 2015 as a flagship program has antecedents in the boost that the SITE gave to television and telecommunications and subsequent developments in information/knowledge societies. This program is both a celebration of enhanced access and an expression of concerns about inequities. India affords the scale of an economy that potentially ensures a mobile phone-intensive user base, but the divides are about the control of and differential access to networks. With welfare scheme registration linked to mobile phone access and use, welfare beneficiaries have a stake in facilitating devices for communication.

Emerging realities include significant issues around mergers and acquisitions in the telecommunication sector, the rise of dominant Over-the-Top (OTT) players such as Netflix and Amazon, and jurisdictional conflicts about the rules governing microblogging sites such as Twitter (Chikermane, 2021) in the wake of the government's proclamation of a digital code of ethics. These developments ring a bell about concerns raised earlier about trans-border information flows (Sauvant, 1983) and indicate that issues about transnational media control apply to digital platforms. In the current context, there is considerable faith among the proponents of the Digital India program in how digital networking enables people to raise issues, whether these concern the protection of safety for women or the expression of discontent by farmers' movements.

Castells' framework of a network society underpins such confidence, even though corporations and states have the resources to sustain challenges to their power structure. In his keynote at IAMCR's Conference in Hyderabad, he referred to the internet as a network of hope and outrage (Castells, 2014). Many in India believe that the mainstream media has capitulated to state and commercial pressures to promote the idea that social media use supports both hope and dissent. Although farmers and other groups' long-standing campaigns and movements have resorted to social media, the regulation of such media contemplated in India and other countries seems likely to hinder the full potential of social media along the lines of the Castellan framework.

The first IAMCR conference to be held in India was in 1986 in New Delhi and this resulted from a long negotiation and persuasion by the critical Indian organizers.

Box 21.1 IAMCR IN SOUTH ASIA: THE CONFERENCE IN NEW DELHI

The idea of organizing an IAMCR conference in India germinated in the early 1970s. Dr Binod Agrawal contacted then IAMCR President Prof. James D. Halloran at the University of Leicester to initiate discussion about hosting the conference in India.[1] Dr Agrawal worked as a Rural Sociologist at the Indian Agriculture Research Institute in New Delhi and the Space Applications Centre (ISRO), in Ahmedabad, on the social evaluation of the Satellite Instructional Television Experiment (SITE) project. Encouraged by Prof. K. E. Eapen of Bangalore University, Dr R. K. Mukerjee of Banaras Hindu University, and Dr Agrawal, Prof. Halloran invited Dr Agrawal to attend IAMCR 1976 in Leicester, UK. Following the IAMCR Paris 1982 Conference, India submitted a formal request to host IAMCR 1986 in New Delhi. During the IAMCR 1984 Conference in Prague, Indian delegates lobbied hard for the conference proposal against other contenders. Many conference attendees, including Prof. Halloran, were not in favor. It was thanks to Prof. Eapen and Dr Agrawal's efforts at the 1984 General Assembly that the decision went in favor of New Delhi. Prof. William H. Melody (Simon Fraser University, Canada) and others also supported the Indian proposal and the decision was taken against a majority of US and European votes (Fig. 21.2).

Fig. 21.2 Binod C. Agrawal. Member IAMCR International Council 1988–1992. (Courtesy of Padma Rani)

[1] Box text contributed by the late Binod C. Agrawal and Padma Rani.

(continued)

Box 21.1 (continued)

A National Organizing Committee was formed with Dr D. P. Pattannayak as Chair and Dr Agrawal as Organizing Secretary, with the Mass Communication and Research Centre—now Anwar Jamal Kidwal Media Resource Centre (AJK MRC)—of Jamia Millia Islamia University, New Delhi, as the official host. The conference theme was "Communication Technology, Development, and the Third World" and it was attended by over 450 participants from more than 40 countries. Prof. K. E. Eapen was elected as Honorary Life Member of IAMCR for his contributions to the association and Prof. Halloran's initial apprehensions about India as a conference venue were significantly reduced. Prof. Olga Linné, Vice President of IAMCR (1992–2000), recalled that the IAMCR General Assembly was applauding and shouting "Peggy, Peggy, Peggy" at the end of the conference.

Indian scholars have increased their participation in IAMCR, encouraged by the University Grants Commission, travel funding from the Indian Council of Social Science Research, and by increasing academic requirements to publish internationally. Another active member of IAMCR, Prof. Dipak De, Department of Extension Education, Institute of Agricultural Sciences, Banaras Hindu University, Varanasi, received the Distinguished Contribution Award at IAMCR 2015 in Montreal, having served as a member of the International Council and supported the Finance Committee for many years. Prof. K. M. Shrivastava, Indian Institute of Mass Communication (IIMC) in New Delhi, also participated actively. Dr. Agrawal, was Professor at the Manipal Academy of Higher Education and Chair of the IAMCR Religion and Communication Working Group. IAMCR returned to India for the 2014 Conference, led by Prof. Usha Raman, Department of Communication, University of Hyderabad, and was jointly organized by the University of Hyderabad and the School of Media and Communication, English & Foreign Languages University, Hyderabad.

The Indian Space Research Organization that had played a vital role in SITE was a significant source of support. Yash Pal, a contemporary of Vikram Sarabhai, delivered the keynote address at the IAMCR 1986 Conference, and he and many other space scientists firmly believed in the potential of technology. Yash Pal became the Director of the Space Applications Centre (SAC) in 1972 and was responsible for hastening the implementation of SITE that was delayed for various reasons (Sharif, 2018; D. C. Sharma, 2017). By 1986, INSAT, a natural sequel to SITE, had become the hub of the communications infrastructure in India, giving a fillip to the spread of broadcasting, including the institutionalization of television in education and telecommunications that accelerated the spread of telephony from a privilege to a need.

IAMCR Concerns about Media Resonate in India as Well

Issues around media ownership are an essential consideration in India, and this stems from a strong belief in the media's democratizing potential. Concerns since independence include the relatively recent assessment by the Telecom Regulatory Authority of India (TRAI) on how the media ownership structure in India is leading to a shrinking public sphere (in the Habermasian tradition) and how this is shaping political debate (Malla, 2019; Diwakar et al., 1965; TRAI, 2014). As part of IAMCR's 60th anniversary, supported by UNESCO, this issue was examined with a concentration of media ownership being identified as a problem. The most significant are the threats concentration poses to freedom of expression and democracy.

> Active citizenship, upon which democracy depends, requires the presence of many voices and perspectives in public debate and undue concentration of media ownership threatens this, given the central role of the media in providing the forums in which public debates take place. (Mendel et al., 2017, p. 11)

Other areas have engaged IAMCR's attention and focused on Indian scholars' research, including pre- and post-MacBride Commission Report implications. B. G. Verghese was an Indian member of the commission. A leading journalist, he served as press advisor to Mrs Gandhi and chaired a Committee on Broadcasting that recommended a trust framework for public broadcasting in India. As editor of one of the most significant English language newspapers, he had launched a development journalism publication called *Our Village, Chhatera* in 1969 and sustained it for seven years (Aggarwal, 1978; Verghese, 1976).

A robust framework in which India took the lead and sustained the argument was produced concerning news agency cartels, formulating the news agency pool idea, and infrastructure. This was based on the principles of the Non-Aligned Movement (NAM) that developed mainly in response to the geopolitics of the then polarized superpowers (news agencies and pool efforts are discussed in Chap. 17). Keval J. Kumar, a senior IAMCR member, recalling the contributions of Indian journalists such as D. R. Mankekar, argues that in the context of the MacBride call for a NWICO (including news agency structure), there could be greater control by states over dangerous information flows (K. J. Kumar & Biernatzki, 1988). The arguments, contradictions, and pressures of the collective efforts of the Non-Aligned, and many regional attempts to promote a more equitable world order, are reflective of their aspirations and development plans. It also demonstrates a mosaic of resistance and a willingness to produce and promote content. More recent collective efforts such as the BRICS countries (Brazil, Russia, India, China, and South Africa) have not explicitly factored media into their discourses but are keen on negotiating with multilateral mechanisms (Bharthur, 2016). Kaarle Nordenstreng has published an ambitious media system study (Nordenstreng, 2020) that highlights similarities in country and regional approaches, but emphasizes their differences in legacy and new media.

Recent India-Focused Studies by IAMCR Active Members

The distinctive character of India's media system has been researched by Daya Thussu, a prolific scholar in media and communication studies. He developed and translated soft power in the Indian context by examining its communication landscape and film industry (Thussu, 2013). His work on how the media participate in communicating India's soft power acknowledges the role of Buddhism and its spread from India. His argument is as follows

> That India could build a counter-narrative was essentially based on the idea that India has a different version of Islam, and it has a lot of Muslims living within the country. Even before Modi came to power, I don't think our governments and policymakers really took this particularly seriously. Think of Buddhism, for instance. Think of what the Chinese Government is doing. China has the largest population of Buddhists in the world. You go to Shanghai or Beijing and look at their museums. How wonderfully they have kept all the amazing Buddhist art, paintings, etc. All this in a country where it was seriously undermined for many decades. Even today, religion is not something they celebrate, but they've used Buddhism as part of their public diplomacy in Central, East, and Southeast Asia. I have to say to Modi's credit that he did promote Buddhism. ((A. Sharma & Arora, 2016) interviewing Thussu)

The reasons for incorporating Buddhist principles into India's foreign policy also have been examined:

> It is within this context that one can understand the efforts of the Indian Government at incorporating Buddhist heritage to form a basis for further diplomatic, economic, cultural, and strategic associations within its foreign policy. The established transnational network for Buddhism, and the important role of the faith in the lives of millions across the world, allow it to possess the potential for Indian foreign policy. (Kishwar, 2018)

This approach also adds to India's tourism potential, and there is now a special train package called the Buddhist Circuit. In the *Mahaparinirvana Sutra*, the Buddha tells his followers that they can attain merit and a noble rebirth by going on a pilgrimage to where he gained enlightenment. He gained enlightenment in Bodh Gaya, he first taught at Sarnath, and he attained Nirvana in Kushinagar. The Indian railways have developed a package tour connecting these centers. Lumbini, where he was born, is in present-day Nepal, for which the package tour provides a convenient link.

Conclusion: IAMCR-India Networking and Opportunities

A focus on Indian scholarship draws attention to scholars who have enriched the media and communication field due to their critical questions about intent, motivation, and the factors influencing the evolution and consolidation of the country's communication structures. These concerns were also present in IAMCR's contributions to understanding the relationships between culture, development, technology, and professional education. The discussion of SITE as a landmark policy decision provides an additional focus on institutional relations, the colonial background, the post-independence stance to the NAM, and its echoes in the formation of the news agencies pool (Tiffen, 1976) to counter the monopoly of the "globals" (as the MacBride Commission refers to them). Consistent with a critical approach to these issues, Indian journalism and mass communication educators such as Prof. Eapen offered critical notes on the SITE project (Eapen, 1988, 2006), refuting the use of dangling metaphors for communication satellites such as "a teacher in the sky."

The shaping of India's approach to media and communication recounted in this chapter culminated in the current media ecosystem, which has changed drastically over time. More than 900 television channels, hundreds of radio stations, including nearly 50 community stations, and a resilient hard copy newspaper culture with Indian language newspaper circulation that is far ahead of their English counterparts. The digital media space boasts millions of mobile phones and digital devices with a nearly 40 percent internet penetration rate. Universal concerns about the changes in the media ecology and its regulation are reflected distinctively in India-specific concerns about the fragile social fabric and the spread of institutional and user-generated content, about negotiating neighborly relations and contending with ideological conflicts and volatile reactions by different sections of society.

Recent IAMCR conferences have seen a significantly increasing participation by Indian researchers, with papers focusing on the themes highlighted in this chapter. IAMCR's differential membership fees that apply to India have also helped sustain membership and active participation, as did the recent election of Prof. Usha Raman as Vice President of IAMCR. Prof. Eapen was elected Vice President of IAMCR in the late 1980s.[2]

The fault lines in India's social structure and multi-religious fabric are recurring issues that often inflect its development narrative, including its competitive position as a significant economic power, notwithstanding a significant gap with China. The correlation between media and development in the context of rapid media development and new media access is not reflected in the Sustainable Development Goals (SDG) Index, where India is placed at 120, with other countries in South Asia faring better except for Pakistan (Sachs, 2021). The well-intentioned call for an SDG 18—communication for all—goal

[2] See https://iamcr.org/eapen. Accessed 15 June 2022.

by Jan Servaes has reiterated the gap in expectations for the role of media and communication in development and may offer new initiatives (Center for Intercultural Dialogue, 2021) to make communication for and in development a more prominent theme. For example, many Indian scholars, including Melkote, have done considerable work in this area (Melkote & Steeves, 2015), and critical perspectives are emerging.

To mark the 50th anniversary of IAMCR in 2008, UNESCO's historical assessment of the field of communication and development invoked Amartya Sen's approach to welfare economics and poverty alleviation. Media is highlighted as a tool, but more critical questions and challenges are identified, such as the absence of unified policy frameworks on ICTs and their roles in development; rising commercialism in public and community media; misunderstandings about what communication for/and development entails; the dangers of equating media practice with public relations or publicity; and the problems of inadequate training opportunities (UNESCO, 2008).

It is helpful to recall what Prof. Eapen had to say about IAMCR, of which he was a member for almost four decades:

> IAMCR, nonetheless was by and large a European scholarship bank with some input from academics of the Americas. There were hardly any members from Asia or Africa. Another drawback is its propped up annual membership that few from the Third World could afford to pay-hard currency almost equivalent to a month's salary of a professor or media professional outside the industrialised nations. I felt that the IAMCR needed diversity in its membership that included a truly international milieu. This was partly reflected in the Delhi Assembly with some African presence and the first ever Chinese and Cuban attendees...to see an Iranian American, Hamid Mowlana as IAMCR President was no less heartening. Mass has given over media in the organisation and the issue of high membership fees for members from developing countries has been addressed. (Eapen, 2001, p. 48)

IAMCR today, with its network and membership across multiple countries, including the traditional "Third World," annual conferences, and publication initiatives, can be expected to play a significant role in addressing these challenges, especially with the participation of Indian scholars and students. The enlargement of the membership base in India is likely to get a boost from the recently appointed ambassadors and their enthusiasm to further energize media and communication scholarship.

References

Adhikary, N. M. (2010). An introduction to Sadharanikaran model of communication. *Bodhi: An Interdisciplinary Journal, 3*(1), 69–91.

Aggarwal, N. (1978, July). The newspaper as an agent of development. *Idrc Features, 5.* https://idl-bnc-idrc.dspacedirect.org/bitstream/handle/10625/56129/IDL-56129.pdf?sequence=1 Accessed 15 June 2022

Agrawal, B. C. (1981). *SITE social evaluation: Results, experiences and implications.* Space Applications Centre.

Barns, M. (1940). *The Indian press; A history of the growth of public opinion in India*. Allen & Unwin Ltd.
Beltran, L. R. (1975). Research ideologies in conflict. *Journal of Communication, 25*(2), 187–193.
Beltzer, L. (1952). Challenge of India lures Professor Wolseley. *The Journal of Education, 135*(1), 11–23.
Bharthur, S. (2006, January 27). Communication policies in the Nehru era. *The Hoot*. http://asu.thehoot.org/story_popup/communication-policies-in-the-nehru-era-1927 Accessed 15 June 2022.
Bharthur, S. (2012). Journalism and mass communication education: An assessment. *Asia Pacific Media Educator, 22*(1), 115–126.
Bharthur, S. (2016, October 10). *The missing media discourse at BRICS. The Hoot*. http://asu.thehoot.org/research/research-studies/the-missing-media-discourse-at-brics-9714 Accessed 15 June 2022.
Bhat, B., & Krishnamurthy, P. (1965). Radio rural forums spread through India. In *No 48 Radio Broadcasting Serves Rural Development* (p. 51). UNESCO.
Brecher, M. (1974). India's decisions on the voice of America: A study in irresolution. *Asian Survey, 14*(7), 637–650.
Castells, M. (2014, July 16). Networks of outrage and hope. Social movements in the internet age. *UoH (University of Hyderbad) Herald*. http://herald.uohyd.ac.in/networks-of-outrage-and-hope-social-movements-in-the-internet-age/ Accessed 15 June 2022.
Center for Intercultural Dialogue. (2021, May 26). CFP sustainable development goals SDG18 communication for all. https://centerforinterculturaldialogue.org/2021/05/26/cfp-sustainable-development-goals-sdg18-communication-for-all/ Accessed 15 June 2022.
Chandar, S. (2019, September 11). How a 1980s TV soap did the spadework for Hindu nationalism. *Quartz India*. https://qz.com/india/1744726/doordarshans-ramayan-serial-was-hindu-nationalisms-second-rath/ Accessed 15 June 2022.
Chander, R., & Karnik, K. (1976). *Planning for satellite broadcasting: The Indian instructional television experiment*. UNESCO.
Chatterji, P. C. (1987). *Broadcasting in India*. Sage Publications.
Chikermane, G. (2021, May 23). The 'government' of Twitter has to follow the government of India, period. *ORF*. https://www.orfonline.org/expert-speak/the-government-of-twitter-has-to-follow-the-government-of-india-period/ Accessed 15 June 2022.
Chowdhry, K. (2004). *Science policy and national development*. Indian Council of Social Science Research and Vikram Sarabhai Foundation.
Chu, G., & Schramm, W. (1968). *Learning from TV what the research says*. National Association of Educational Broadcasters, United States.
Dissanayake, W., & Wang, G. (1984). *Continuity and change in communication systems: An Asian perspective*. Ablex Publishing.
Diwakar, R. R., Mani, A. D., Bhat, A. R., Alva, J., Mukerjee, H., Chaturvedi, B. D., Indernarayen, P., Durga Da, Ansari, H. U., Singh, N., & Dehlvi, Y. (1965). *Report of the enquiry committee on small newspapers, 1965*. New Delhi, Ministry of Information and Broadcasting. http://archive.org/details/dli.csl.590 Accessed 15 June 2022.
Eapen, K. E. (1988, March 9). *Conference on the constraints of nation building, development and communication*. Constraints on Nation Building, Mysore.

Eapen, K. E. (1994). Communication and development the contribution of research. In C. Hamelink & O. Linné (Eds.), *Mass communication research: On problems and policies: The art of asking the right questions: In honor of James D. Halloran* (p. 277–290). Greenwood Publishing Group.

Eapen, K. E. (2001). Reflections on journalism/communication education and research in India and abroad. In S. R. Melkote & S. Rao (Eds.), *Critical issues in communication looking inwards for answers essays in honor of K. E. Eapen* (p. 35–51). Sage Publications.

Eapen, K. E. (2006). The cultural component of SITE. *Journal of Communication, 29*(4), 106–113.

Eapen, K. E., Thakur, B. S., & Sanjay, B. P. (1991). *Journalism education and textbooks in SAARC countries (Report)*. IAMCR.

Eisenstein, E. (1979). *The printing press as an agent of social change*. Cambridge University Press.

Frutkin, A. W. (2015). Genesis of SITE. In P. M. Rao & B. Suresh (Eds.), *From fishing hamlet to red planet India's space journey* (p. 953–963). HarperCollins and ISRO.

Garnham, N. (1979). Contributions to a political economy of mass communication. *Media, Culture & Society, 1*, 123–146.

GOI. (1977, August). White paper on the misuse of mass media. Government of India. https://publicarchives.files.wordpress.com/2014/09/white-paper-on-the-misues-of-mass-media-during-the-internal-emer.pdf Accessed 15 June 2022.

Guha, R. (2003, August 6). Gandhi the journalist, The Hindu. *ramachandraguha*. http://ramachandraguha.in/archives/gandhi-the-journalist-the-hindu.html Accessed 15 June 2022.

Gupta, S. (2005). Post-liberalisation India: How free is the media? *South Asia: Journal of South Asian Studies, 28*(2), 283–300.

Hamelink, C. (1977). *Cultural autonomy in global communications. Planning national information policy*. Longman.

Hamelink, C., & Linné, O. (Eds.). (1994). *Mass communication research on problems and policies: The art of asking the right questions - in honor of James D. Halloran*. Ablex.

Hamelink, C., & Nordenstreng, K. (2007). *IAMCR in retrospect 1957-2007: In Memoriam: James D. Halloran*. IAMCR. https://iamcr.org/sites/default/files/iamcr_in_retrospect_0.pdf Accessed 15 June 2022.

Hancock, A. (Ed.). (1984). *Technology transfer*. UNESCO.

Headrick, D. (2010). A double-edged sword: Communications and imperial control in British India. *Historical Social Research / Historische Sozialforschung, 35*(1(131)), 51–65.

Jayaweera, N. (1985, November 21-22). *The communication challenge in Asia*. AMIC-BERNAMA-WACC Seminar on Communication Challenges in Asia: Kuala Lumpur [Keynote]. https://dr.ntu.edu.sg/bitstream/10220/1172/1/AMIC_1985_11_06.pdf Accessed 15 June 2022.

Joshi, P. C. (1985). *An Indian personality for television, Volume 1*. Report of the Working Group on Software for Doordarshan. Ministry of Information and Broadcasting, India.

Kesavan, B. S. (1997). *History of printing and publishing in India*. National Book Trust.

Kishwar, S. (2018, February 23). *The rising role of Buddhism in India's soft power strategy*. Issue No. 228. Observer Research Foundation, New Delhi. https://www.orfonline.org/research/the-rising-role-of-buddhism-in-indias-soft-power-strategy/ Accessed 15 June 2022.

Kumar, K. (2003). Mixed signals: Radio broadcasting policy in India. *Economic and Political Weekly, 38*(22), 2173–2182.
Kumar, K. J., & Biernatzki, W. E. (1988). International news flows. *Communication Research Trends Centre for Study of Communication and Culture, 9*(3), 1–16.
Kumar, N., & Chandiram, J. (1987). *Educational television in India*. Arya Book Depot.
Lerner, D., & Nelson, L. M. (1977). *Communication research—A half-century appraisal*. University Press of Hawaii.
Lionel, F. (1960). *The natural bent*. Andrew Deutsch.
MacBride, S., & Contributors. (1980). *Communication and society today and tomorrow: Many voices, one world: Towards a new more just and more efficient world information and communication order*. Kogan Page, Unipub, UNESCO.
Maitland, D. (1984). *The missing link*. International Telecommunication Union, Geneva. https://www.itu.int/osg/spu/sfo/missinglink/The_Missing_Ling_A4-E.pdf Accessed 15 June 2022.
Malla, V. (2019, March 18). The politics of Indian media houses—By ownership. *Medium*. https://medium.com/@vikrammalla/the-politics-of-indian-media-houses-by-ownership-82ecbe2dafab Accessed 15 June 2022.
Marx, K. (1853, July 22). *The future results of British rule in India*. https://marxists.architexturez.net/archive/marx/works/1853/07/22.htm Accessed 15 June 2022.
Melkote, S. R., & Steeves, H. L. (2015). *Communication for development in the third world: Theory and practice for empowerment* (3rd ed.). Sage Publications.
Melody, W. H. (1981). *The economics of information as resource and product*. In Wedemeyer, D. J. (Ed.), Pacific Telecommunications Conference. Papers and Proceedings of a Conference, p. C7-5-9. January 12–14, Honolulu, Hawaii. Pacific Telecommunications Council.
Melody, W. H. (1992). Dallas Smythe: A lifetime at the frontier of communications. *Canadian Journal of Communication, 17*(4), 99.
Mendel, T., Garcia, A., & Gomez, G. (2017). *Concentration of media ownership and freedom of expression: Global standards and implications for the Americas—UNESCO Digital Library*. UNESCO.
MIB. (1963). *Report of the mass communication study team*. Indian Ministry of Information and Broadcasting. Ford Foundation.
Mira, D. (2017). Journalism education in India: Maze or mosaic. In S. R. Goodman & E. Steyne (Eds.), *Global journalism education in the 21st century challenges and innovations* (p. 113–136). Knight Center for Journalism in the Americas.
Mitra, A. (1993). *Television and popular culture in India: A study of the Mahabharat*. Sage Publications.
Mitra, P. (2018, March 16). *MIB consolidates three media units under new Bureau of Outreach Communication*. QRIUS. https://qrius.com/mib-consolidates-three-media-units-under-new-bureau-of-outreach-communication/ Accessed 15 June 2022.
Mowlana, H. (1997). IAMCR: A historical perspective [Address to 40th Anniversary Conference, Oaxaca]. https://iamcr.org/hist-perspective?msclkid=af84dc7dab8f11ec9e281c01e0b88be8 Accessed 15 June 2022.
Mowlana, H. (2007). Theoretical perspectives on Islam and communication. *China Media Research, 3*(4), 23–33.
Naregal, V. (2000). Media reform and regulation since liberalisation. *Economic and Political Weekly, 35*(21/22), 1817–1821.

Nordenstreng K. (2020). *Data – Media systems in flux: The challenge of the BRICS countries.* https://research.uta.fi/brics/data/ Accessed 15 June 2022.
Otis, A. (2018). *Hicky's Bengal Gazette: The untold story of India's first newspaper.* Westland.
Priolkar, A. K. (1958). *The printing press in India, its beginnings and early development, being a quatercentenary commemoration study of the advent of printing in India in 1556.* Marathi Samshodhana Mandala.
Press Trust of India (PTI). (2014, May 3). Govt maintains arm's length with Prasar Bharati: Manish Tewari. *The Indian Express.* https://indianexpress.com/article/india/politics/govt-maintains-arms-length-with-prasar-bharati-manish-tewari/ Accessed 15 June 2022.
Rajagopal, A. (2001). Hindu nationalism and the cultural forms of Indian politics. In *Politics after Television: Hindu Nationalism and the reshaping of the public in India* (p. 30–71). Cambridge University Press.
Ram, N. (2011). Sectional President's Address: The changing role of the news media in contemporary India. *Proceedings of the Indian History Congress, 72*, 1289–1310. https://www.jstor.org/stable/44145741 Accessed 15 June 2022
Raman, U. (2015, December 1). Failure of communication: India must face up to the rift between its newsrooms and classrooms. *The Caravan.* https://caravanmagazine.in/perspectives/failure-of-communication-rift-between-india-newsrooms-clasrooms Accessed 15 June 2022.
Ranganath, H. K. (1978). Not a thing of the past: Functional and cultural status of traditional media in India—UNESCO Digital Library (No. 92; p. 10). UNESCO. https://unesdoc.unesco.org/ark:/48223/pf0000034652 Accessed 15 June 2022.
Ranganathan, M. (2020, July). Print history: Anant Kakba Priolkar- A fetish for print anniversaries. *PrintWeek.* https://www.printweek.in/features/print-history-anant-kakba-priolkar-a-fetish-for-print-anniversaries-43453 Accessed 15 June 2022.
Rogers, E., & Singhal, A. (1988). Television soap operas for development. *Gazette, 41*, 109–126.
Rosen, G. (1985). *Western economists and Eastern societies: Agents of change in South Asia, 1950-1970.* Johns Hopkins University Press.
Sachs, J. (2021). *Sustainable development report 2020: The sustainable development goals and Covid-19: Includes the SDG Index and Dashboards.* Cambridge University Press.
Samarajiwa, R. (1984). The murky beginnings of the communication and development field: Voice of America and the passing of traditional society. In N. Jayaweera & S. Amunugama (Eds.), *Rethinking development communication* (p. 3–19). Asian Mass Communication Research and Information Centre.
Sanjay, B. P. (1991). *The role of institutional relationships in communication technology transfer: A case study of the Indian National Satellite System (INSAT).* National Library of Canada. https://core.ac.uk/download/pdf/56367765.pdf Accessed 15 June 2022.
Sarabhai, V. A. (1969). *Television for development.* Rajratan Press.
Sauvant, K. P. (1983, December). The work of the UNCTC on transnational corporations and transborder data flows. *Transborder data flows: Proceedings of an OECD conference* (p. 165-169). North-Holland.
Schiller, H. I. (1981). *Information in the age of Fortune 500.* Praeger Publishers.
Schramm, W. (1964). *Mass media and national development: The role of information in the developing countries.* Stanford University Press.

Schramm, W., & Coombs, P. (1987). *New educational media in action: Case studies for planners-1*. International Institute for Educational Planning.
Shah, A. (2016). *Vikram Sarabhai - A life*. Penguin.
Shah, A. (2019, May 18). Vikram Sarabhai and India's space odyssey. *Live History India*. https://livehistoryindia.webdunia.info/wp-content/uploads/2019/05/pic2.jpg Accessed 15 June 2022.
Shah, K. T. (1948). *National planning committee series: Communications*. Vora & Co. Publishers Ltd.
Sharif, A. (2018, July 24). Remembering Yash Pal, The people's scientist who left an indelible mark on India! *The Better India*. https://www.thebetterindia.com/152205/yash-pal-peoples-scientist-india/ Accessed 15 June 2022.
Sharma, A., & Arora, V. (2016, June 10). Interview: India's soft power: An interview with professor Daya Kishan Thussu. *The Diplomat*. https://thediplomat.com/2016/06/interview-indias-soft-power/ Accessed 15 June 2022.
Sharma, D. C. (2017, July 25). Professor Yash Pal, An unconventional icon of Indian science. *The Quint*. https://www.thequint.com/voices/opinion/yash-pal-passes-away-2 Accessed 15 June 2022.
Singh, I. B. (1980). The Indian mass media system: Before, during and after the national emergency. *Canadian Journal of Communication, 7*(2), 38–49.
Singh, K. J. (1979). Gandhi and Mao as mass communicators. *Journal of Communication, 29*(3), 94–101.
Singh, P. P. (1937, November 24). Two foreign visitors write of Nazi rule. *The Columbia Missourian*. https://www.noelle-neumann-leaks.net/columbia%20missourian.html Accessed 15 June 2022.
Sinha, A., & Malik, K. K. (2018). Reimagining community media – a rhizomatic analysis of Khabar Lahariya in central India. *Media Asia, 45*(3–4), 102–113.
Smythe, D. W. (1981). *Dependency Road: Communications, capitalism, consciousness and Canada*. Ablex.
Starosta, W. J., & Merriam, A. H. (1986). The impact of media technology in peasant societies: The case of SITE. *Educational Communication and Technology, 34*(1), 39–45.
Thomas, P. N. (2010). *Political economy of communications in India: The good, the bad and the ugly*. Sage Publications.
Thussu, D. K. (2013). *Communicating India's soft power: Buddha to Bollywood*. Palgrave Macmillan.
Tiffen, R. (1976). A new information order? International agencies and the flow of news. *Southeast Asian Journal of Social Science, 4*(2), 65–76.
TRAI. (2014). *Recommendations on issues relating to media ownership*. Telecom Regulatory Authority of India. https://trai.gov.in/sites/default/files/Recommendations_on_Media_Ownership.pdf Accessed 15 June 2022.
Turco, B. L. (2013). Propagation of written culture in Brahmanical India. *Scripta, 6*, 85–93.
UNESCO. (1961). *Mass Media in Developing Countries*, No. 33. UNESCO.
UNESCO. (2008). *Reports prepared for UNESCO on the occasion of the International Association of Media and Communication Research (IAMCR) 50th Anniversary Conference 2007: Media, communication, information: Celebrating 50 years of theories and practice*. UNESCO.

Venkatachalapathy, A. R. (2012). *The province of the book*. Permanent Black.
Verghese, B. G. (1976). Project Chhatera –An experiment in development journalism. *Media Asia, 3*(1), 5–12.
Vidyalankar, C. A. N. (1963). *Report of the study team on five year plan publicity*. Ministry of Information and Broadcasting. http://archive.org/details/dli.csl.193 Accessed 15 June 2022.
Wolseley, R. (1953). *Journalism in modern India*. Asia Publication House.

CHAPTER 22

IAMCR and Pakistan

Wajiha Raza Rizvi

Introduction

Pakistan and IAMCR's relationship began with the association's founding conference in Paris in 1957.[1] Professor Abdus Salam Khurshid, Department of Journalism, University of the Punjab, Pakistan, joined as a member of the Executive Committee, was re-elected at the first General Assembly (GA) in Milan in 1959, and had a lifelong relationship with the association as a permanent member of the EC. Khurshid served IAMCR under Raymond B. Nixon, President (1959–1964) during IAMCR's consolidation period (1964–1972), under Jacques Bourquin, President (1964–1969), and others, despite Pakistan's

[1] IAMCR archives including bulletins, newsletters, and abstract books were the basis for the analysis in this chapter. All those cited as academic authors were involved in IAMCR. The full titles and abstracts of all papers discussed are available in the IAMCR archives. You may also contact the author at wajiharaza@fulbrightmail.org for specific references and online links.

W. R. Rizvi (✉)
Beaconhouse National University, Lahore, Pakistan

Film Museum Society, Lahore, Pakistan

© The Author(s), under exclusive license to Springer Nature Switzerland AG 2023

J. Becker, R. Mansell (eds.), *Reflections on the International Association for Media and Communication Research*,
https://doi.org/10.1007/978-3-031-16383-8_22

1965 and 1971 wars[2] with India.[3] His contributions coincided with the Major General Sahibzada Sayyid Iskander Ali Mirza (1956–1958) and Field Martial Muhammad Ayub Khan (1958–1969) eras in Pakistan.

This chapter draws on IAMCR archival materials from 1957 onwards to present a profile of how scholarship about Pakistani film and print and other media evolved, citing both Pakistani scholars and others whose work helped to shape scholarly discussion and who were active in IAMCR. Papers presented at IAMCR conferences by both Pakistani and other scholars were surveyed to provide a meta-analysis of the themes and issues that have been addressed. The analysis shows that while much scholarship addressed political debates in Pakistani print media, research also focused on film, television, and radio, as well as on politics, ethics, education, and the media's role in interfaith dialog, the war on terror, and other geopolitical struggles.

Building the Pakistan-IAMCR Relationship

The context for Pakistani scholarship in the late 1950s and early 1960–70s was that Khan had established the Pakistan Television Corporation in 1964 (with four stations in Lahore, Dhaka, Rawalpindi, and Islamabad). He had also established the Pakistan Writer's Guild and the National Press Trust though writers and journalists strongly condemned his interventions in their content and ethical practice, and he supported networking of media academics and professionals abroad. In 1959, Khurshid had cooperated with Martin L. John, University of Florida, on an examination of the function of the press and the philosophy of news in major countries of the world and the reason for differences. He sought to set up a National Council in Pakistan with support from the General Secretary of IAMCR, Fernand Terrou, and then IAMCR President, Jacques Bourquin, both of whom were involved in drafting Article 19 during the United Nations (UN) Conference on Freedom of Information. It looked

[2] Pakistan (comprising distantly located east and west wings) partitioned from India on the basis of the two-nation theory that distinguished Muslims from Hindus on the ground of religion in 1947. Its founder, Muhammad Ali Jinnah, aimed at providing a separate homeland to "a happy and contended" Muslim nation (1948), that he claimed to have saved from the oppression of the politically dominant Hindu majority. Jinnah's two-nation theory failed in 1971, as the Muslims of East Pakistan announced liberation from Pakistan, forming Bangladesh, the land of Bengali-speaking people. Since the Fall of Dhaka, various political parties have expressed separatist ideas and mottos of independence in Pakistan-held Kashmir, Sindh, and Balochistan. Pakistan has always heavily censored media coverage of its turbulent political history, which is characterized by sectarianism, 32 years of martial law, and inept leadership that sought better relations with the far-off countries of the first world than with its immediate second or third world neighboring countries or powers. In doing so, Pakistan played a significant role in the wars that the first world fought against the second or third world for peace. These collaborations with the allies usually improved the economic condition of Pakistan, a country whose societal edifice is intensely and expansively parochial, ultra-conformist, and resistant to democratic ideals.

[3] Jinnah, M. A. (1 July 1948) 'Quaid-i-Azam's Speech.' Online. http://www.sbp.org.pk/about/history/h_moments.htm. Accessed 15 June 2022.

like a timely approach, as India and Pakistan also had jointly hosted the conference held by the Commonwealth (formerly Empire) Press Union in South Asia in 1961, giving the impression of a shared journalistic ethos that transcended the momentous de-colonization transition that had begun a decade or more earlier.

Khurshid elaborated on Pakistan's media scene and ethical issues in his department's quarterly professional research journal devoted to press, film, radio, television, and public relations. He presented Pakistan's position at the IAMCR 5th GA in 1966, emphasizing the media's role in Pakistan's national development, a theme that coincided with the goals of an IAMCR working session on national development through mass media. At the association's 6th GA, Bourquin reported that Khurshid had sent IAMCR the program of a seminar on the Ethics of Journalism held in Lahore under the presidency of the Minister of Information in 1968 with numerous journalists attending, thanking Khurshid for his efforts, and encouraging similar efforts in other countries.

Throughout the 1960s, as indicated in then President Bourquin's newsletter,[4] IAMCR encouraged its members to publish academic work and establish personal contacts to achieve a better human and scientific understanding as a necessary condition to international cooperation. Khurshid emphasized the production of knowledge and critical debate on important socio-political and international issues. Bourquin highlighted Khurshid's work *Journalism in Pakistan, 1st phase 1845-1867* (1971), and Pakistan consistently appeared in presidential letters throughout the association's first decade. Khurshid shared his department's *Journalism* quarterly with IAMCR which appeared in English, Arabic, and Urdu, reflecting IAMCR's interest in scholarly publications in multiple languages.

East Pakistan had become Bangladesh on 21 December 1971, when India arrested 92,000 soldiers of Pakistan. The situation was resolved when Pakistan's President Zulfiqar Ali Bhutto signed the *Simla Agreement* with India's Prime Minister Indira Gandhi on 2 July 1972. Ever since, India has stressed the *Simla Agreement* to avoid the United Nations' (UN) intervention in Pakistan-India controversies, insisting the two countries' need to mutually resolve their issues. While arguments continue, Pakistan's role in international war and peace issues has escalated, revealing it as an ally of the US and the UN. Field Martial Khan's early support for research encouraged scholars to discuss political and communication aspects of these issues at IAMCR conferences and to publish actively, for example, during the Dhaka crisis in 1971, Khurshid published *Mass Communication Media in Pakistan*.

The key role that Khurshid had played in connecting Pakistani professors to IAMCR was strengthened during IAMCR's Iranian-American Hamid Mowlana's Presidency (1994–1998). Mugheesuddin Sheikh, Dean/Director of the Institute of Communication Studies, University of the Punjab, was highly supportive of Mowlana's approach to mass media and culture as

[4] See https://iamcr.org/node/10511. Accessed 15 June 2022.

indicated in his IAMCR newsletter contributions quoted here. He played a key role in streamlining a well-functioning Press Council in Pakistan. Sheikh emphasized what Mowlana called, “the spectacular shift in superpower relations and the explosion of communication technologies” that “have altered the landscape of international relations and blurred nation-state boundaries.”[5] Mowlana emphasized “the Islamic code of ethics for journalists,” the communication revolution in the Arab world and Iran during two media conferences in Iran and the United Arab Emirates (UAE), and recruited IAMCR institutional and individual members from the Arab world, France, Africa, and Pakistan.[6] He was concerned that “Africa, and Mo’s [Mowlana] native Pakistan which he loved and which loved him” were “too often ignored by a western media that can only portray peace and routine politics and economics close to home.”[7]

While IAMCR had always been attentive to scholarship from the Muslim world, Mowlana boosted the relationship and this was the basis for setting up the Working Group (WG) on Islam and Media. Bushra Hameedur Rahman and Abida Ashraf [Eijaz], Institute of Communication Studies, University of the Punjab in Pakistan, along with Fatma Elzahraa Elsayed, Faculty of Mass Communication, Cairo University, Egypt, further developed the WG as Chair and Vice Chair. They also encouraged the participation of women scholars from Pakistan at IAMCR’s annual conferences.

Media and Peace

Mowlana emphasized facilitating Asian media in promoting a culture of peace. Scholars who were active in IAMCR were also present at affiliated IAMCR member conferences and this work was highlighted in IAMCR newsletters. For example, the Asian Media Information and Communication Centre (AMIC) reported that 20 “communication researchers, media practitioners, religion representatives belonging to Hinduism, Islam, Christianity and Buddhism” from Pakistan as well as India, Indonesia, Japan, Malaysia, Philippines, Singapore, and Sri Lanka had presented a report on media and a culture of peace at a symposium in Manila in 2000. The symposium focused on practical problems faced in promoting peace by religious groups and the media’s role in promoting a culture of peace, enhancing inter-faith understanding, and resolving conflict. This led to an Asia Peace Network (“PeaceNet Asia”) and a directory of media persons and institutions that could work to improve dialog, exposure, and understanding and reporting on peace and conflict issues through meetings, training, and research.

[5] See Hamid Mowlana (1995) Newsletter *5*(1) https://iamcr.org/node/10511. Accessed 15 June 2022.

[6] See IAMCR Newsletter 1997, p. 3. https://iamcr.org/node/10511. Accessed 15 June 2022.

[7] See IAMCR Newsletter 1997, p. 32. https://iamcr.org/node/10511. Accessed 15 June 2022.

This agenda underpinned Pakistani researchers' work on media education and training, the media's role in war, conflict, interfaith dialog, coverage of human rights and gender conditions, media policy and freedom of information, as indicated by papers presented at IAMCR conferences. For example, Shazia Saeed (2012) emphasized that journalists can manage conflict between the North and South through gatekeeping and consensus strategies. Ahsan Akhtar Naz and this writer examined interfaith dialog, analyzing its coverage in *Time* and *Newsweek*, acknowledging the role of Pope John Paul in promoting peace during his tours of the Muslim world (Naz & Rizvi, 2014). When IAMCR was emphasizing communication policy, freedom of expression, and journalism across the world, the Danish (2005) and Charlie Hebdo (2012) cartoon controversies resulted in inter-faith controversies, which were examined in papers presented at IAMCR, as were representations of Pakistan in the Western media during the war on terror (Rahman, 2010; Eijaz, 2010).

Elisabeth Eide, a long-time member of IAMCR, was conducting post-doctoral research and teaching a course at the University of the Punjab, funded by the Oslo-Metropolitan University (then Oslo Akershus University College) flagship project to study press representations of "the West" during the cartoon/caricature crisis. In 2008, she also compared transnational journalism practices focusing on the history of freedom of expression in Pakistan, comparing Orientalism with mediated Occidentalism in the Pakistani press during the Danish caricature crisis (Eide, 2008a, 2008b). The Chair of the Media and Islam WG, Rahman (2016), identified how academics used a libertarian perspective in discourses around freedom of expression and mass media ethics during the cartoon controversies.

Naveed Iqbal [Chaudhry] (2011) emphasized Pakistan's geopolitical position in his work, based on in-depth interviews with the cartoonists and examined comic journalism art caricatures of the United States (US) Kerry-Lugar Bill of 2009 (Enhanced Partnership with Pakistan Act). He argued that the Bill was essentially treated as a non-military aid package for Pakistan due to its weak economy and its involvement in a "war on terror" as a front line American ally (Iqbal, 2011). The theme of Pakistan's participation in the war on terror was well-represented at IAMCR conferences. Another IAMCR member, Phyza Jameel, compared the framing of 9/11 news in the elite American, French, Italian, and Pakistani newspapers (Jameel, 2012). Savera Shami examined how Pakistani print media portrayed the domination of the US in Pakistan's internal affairs after the US Navy SEALs killed Bin Laden in Abbottabad in 2011 (Shami, 2012). In a paper titled "Malala versus drones," Firasat Jabeen argued that Orientalism perpetuated itself like a prophecy, based on the coverage of (un)worthy victims in US and Pakistani newspapers (Jabeen, 2019). Shaista Malik analyzed the role of media in creating a relationship between Pakistani religious extremism and the perception of Islam and Muslims in the minds of non-Muslims from the West (Malik, 2010). Naeem Sheikh studied coverage of inter-state and intra-state conflicts in the *Dawn* (English) and *Jang* (Urdu) newspapers, emphasizing the media's role in fostering the reconciliatory behavior among Pakistani social groups in the regional peace process (Sheikh, 2008).

Pakistan's geopolitical position gave rise to IAMCR scholars' studies of governmental changes in the country before and after 9/11. Amna Ashraf and Naveed Chaudhry (2012b) studied the frames of political cartoons in Pakistan's Urdu press (*Jang* and *Nawa-i-Waqt*) during the 2008 General Elections, emphasizing how the public forced General Pervez Musharraf to leave government and give way to democratically elected political parties. John A. Lent (2011), an active IAMCR member and Chair of the Comic Art WG, observed that Pakistani "women were not vicious enough to be political cartoonists." Sobia Abid and Zahid Bilal (2012) focused on the mimicry of politicians in comic programs on television news channels in Pakistan by examining the influence of mimicry on audience awareness of democracy, politics, political parties, and development issues. They found that Pakistani cartoons addressed issues in a monotonous way and that the legacy of the print media elite was visible in the electronic media of Pakistan. Various scholars affiliated with IAMCR have demonstrated great interest in studying the legacy and growth of professional journalism practices in Pakistan with respect to the public interest and the media's obligations toward society since 2001.[8]

Communication Policy, Ethics, Safety, and Digital Colonization

Media, Society and State

Daya Kishan Thussu (2016), an Indian scholar, drew Pakistani scholars' attention to the impact of increasing concentrations of media power on the practice of journalism, the purchase of media outlets by politicians, and the problems created by corporations whose core businesses were located elsewhere. Muhammad Shaikh (2010) from Sindh Madressatul Islam University elaborated issues of transparency and freedom of information, while Mohammad Ullah (2010) from Chittagong University discussed how Pakistan had used law enforcement agencies and the state of emergency to withhold fundamental rights so as to legally and violently intimidate media practitioners and to overcome political stand off on many occasions. Venkat Iyer (2001) conducted a survey addressing the state of freedom of information against the backdrop of the political and legal realities in Pakistan, noting the difficulties, while Brian Shoesmith and Shameem Mahmud (2007) observed that in Pakistan, it is impossible to address all the communication policy initiatives because they have lingered for so long.

[8] See AMIC 2001 in Members' new work. IAMCR Newsletter, *12*(2), p. 42. https://iamcr.org/node/10511. Accessed 15 June 2022.

Journalism Practice, Ethics, and Safety

Jyotika Ramaparasad (2012) studied the ethics and values of Pakistani journalists, finding that "both situation and absolutist ethics are present." Sadia Jamil (2015) found that social, political, or legal structures and the national ideology constrained Pakistani journalists while undertaking their work and that they often performed as passive actors. Jamil (2016) also emphasized the training and safety of Pakistani journalists, while Irfan Ashraf (2015) examined the symbiotic relationship between the Western construct of objectivity and the interests of the state and opposing militants in the context of dangers in reporting from Pakistan's northwest Pashtun tribal belt, highlighting some of the limitations of the objectivity model of journalism. My research presented with Anila Saleem showed, for example, that Radio Pakistan catered to socioeconomic development (Saleem & Rizvi, 2021). I also pioneered examinations of gender representations in Pakistani fims, sparking debate on the gaze and censorship at IAMCR conferences (Rizvi, 2014, 2016) and pointing to the decline of the family film in Pakistan. M. J. R. David (2007) noted an irreversible trend in South Asian community radio such that the lobby for editorially independent community radio was strong in Pakistan as early as 2007, with most community radio stations being digitally enabled at the start of the new millennium. These research contributions to IAMCR emphasized that journalism performance, ethics, and the safety of journalists are tied together.

Digital Colonization

Abida Eijaz (2010) attended to the implications of digital colonialism in the context of the US-Afghan and US-Iraq conflicts, and Hina Ayaz (2012) examined divergence between foreign news and domestic news coverage. Lubna Shaheen (2015) considered how the dependence of Pakistani newspapers on foreign news agencies leads to the replication of verbatim stories and to delays in the process of building an anti-terrorism narrative by the state. Azmat Rasul and colleagues studied textual and visual morality frames of friendly attacks by the North Atlantic Treaty Organization (NATO) forces in Pakistan in the elite English press in the US and Pakistan (Rasul, 2012; Rasul, et al., 2012), finding that euphemistic language helps to build favorable public opinion towards war by dehumanizing those who are victimized. These studies contributed insights into the way social media challenges the traditional paradigm of crisis communication and has a strong influence on attitudes, opinions, and behaviors, creating a space for critical examination of the issues.

Media and Religion

Media and religion have also been common themes in research contributions by Pakistani scholars. Tazeen Javed (2008) addressed women's participation and the rise of religious television programming in Pakistan since 2000, supported by the Aga Khan Foundation. Focusing on televangelism and talk shows targeting children with the general public participating by phone, email, and text messages, she showed that more women than men seek the approval of the religious clerics for socio-economic reasons. Her findings were endorsed by Johannes Ehrat, Chair of IAMCR's Religion and Communication WG in 2008, who commented on her insights into new messiahs, postmodernity, and the impact of "socialized religion" and "marginal phenomena."[9] My own work also found a parallel between the marginalization of Pakistani Hindu minorities and aboriginal Australians who struggle to appropriate their identities in reference to their shared social experience of local media (Rizvi, 2012).

Other research pointed to a trope in Pakistani media focusing on minority and blasphemy issues. For example, Hina Ayaz (2011) analyzed coverage of Christian-Muslim riots, indicating how mainstream print media constructed stereotypes and identities of non-Muslims through reports of desecration of the Quran in Gojra in 2009. Focusing on the effect of representations on university students, Eijaz [Ashraf] (2011) explained how *Jang* and *Dawn* constructed social meanings of blasphemy laws after Governor Salman Taseer's murder. She also examined digital media, addressing the coverage of the Asia Bibi blasphemy case in religious and non-religious e-newspapers, while Cherian George's (2012) paper emphasized hate spin as a common political strategy to suppress progressive voices in Pakistan. Nikhil Moro (2012) emphasized that the Constitution of Pakistan does not define minorities but devotes text to the protection of "minorities." IAMCR scholarship emphasized that Pakistan must improve its law enforcement for its own stability and public safety, and the breadth and depth of scholarship have contributed to planning for a better future for Pakistan's public.

Media Training and Education

IAMCR scholars contributed studies on media training and education in Pakistan. Turo Uskali and colleagues studied the Innovation Journalism Fellowship Program 2004–2008, indicating how 26 mid-career journalists from Sweden, Finland, and Pakistan had responded to debate on innovation processes and ecosystems, highlighting the relevance of "innovation journalism" for economic development and competitiveness (Uskali et al., 2008); and in their paper, Turo Uskali and Maria Lassila-Merisalo (2010) showed that this connection was benefitting advanced journalism practice in the country. David Nordfors and others (2010) pointed to Pakistan's contribution to a journalism reform program, while Ashraf and Chaudhry (2012a) focused on the curricula, facilities, and practices in public sector universities.

This research demonstrated that academia was struggling to support the rapidly growing electronic media industry in Pakistan. IAMCR collaborated

[9] Ehrat, Johannes Ehrat. Media, Religion and Culture. *IAMCR Newsletter*, *18*(1), 2008, p. 31. https://iamcr.org/node/10511. Accessed 15 June 2022.

with Pakistani researchers to offer co-sponsored training opportunities for researchers. Rahman, President of the Association of Media and Communication Academic Professionals (AMCAP, Pakistan), organized a Doctoral Spring School for scholars and faculty at the University of the Punjab, Lahore, in 2020, and another at the Fatima Jinnah Women University, Rawalpindi, in 2021, co-sponsored by the Punjab Higher Education Commission (PHEC), Pakistan, and the European Communication Research and Education Association (ECREA). These brought together prominent academics to support young Asian scholars,[10] with IAMCR President, Nico Carpentier, to examine media and communication policy, values, ethics, and research in the country annually at least until 2023.

Crises and Development Issues

IAMCR scholars have shown solidarity with Pakistan in times of national crises and public discontent. Sveltana Kulikova, Emily Metzgar, and Steven Stuglin (2010) analyzed stories about Benazir Bhutto's 2007 assassination in world newspapers, finding that 15 percent of Indian stories "equated Bhutto's death with the death of Pakistan," 52 percent adopted a pessimistic tone about Pakistan's future, and seven percent suggested that "the assassination may give the country a new impetus for democratic developments." Azmat Rasul et al. (2015) examined thematic versus episodic coverage, issue versus image, and source frames in relation to journalistic objectivity during a national crisis/tragedy (Benazir Bhutto's murder), finding that journalists applied predetermined frames, apparently caring little for balanced coverage of this tragic event. In this context, scholars emphasized the need for greater journalistic objectivity in Pakistan.

Issues of governmental support and/or suppression of non-governmental organizations (NGOs) in supposed civil societies informed Pakistani scholarship and were emphasized at IAMCR conferences. For example, Paula Chakravartty and Katharine Sarikakis (2006) pointed to opposition to NGO activities by the authoritarian regime in Pakistan which did not accredit NGOs, raising concerns about human rights at the World Summit on the Information Society (WSIS) in Geneva and Tunis. Zarqa Ali (2012) examined gender and climate change awareness in Pakistan's print media. Mariam Shaikh (2012) studied media skepticism about climate change, comparing the monsoon floods in Pakistan, and floods caused by hurricanes and tropical storms in the US, finding that the American media reported uncertainty, while the Pakistani media offered informed choices. Ali (2011) had found that Pakistani media victimized women as helpless in their visual representations of flood coverage to generate sympathy among readers and donors who might provide moral and material help. Farah Azhar (2016) analyzed profiles of young women on matrimonial websites, finding that users objectified them, while Zarqa Shahen

[10] IAMCR 2021. AMCAP Spring School 2021. https://iamcr.org/. Accessed 15 June 2022.

(2008) highlighted taboo-breaking gendered online interactions in Pakistan some years earlier. Rahman (2010) analyzed the framing of Pakistani Muslim women in *Time* and *Newsweek* from 1979 to 2002 to see if women were seeking change in the Islamic framework or emancipating under foreign influence after Zia's Islamization (1977–1988) and Musharraf's modernization (2001–2008).

Conclusion

Pakistani and non-Pakistani researchers have discussed Pakistani media topics throughout IAMCR's history. They have raised concerns about issues in Pakistan and representations of Pakistan in foreign media. They also stressed the importance of building personal contacts and resources, training opportunities, and archiving. Pakistani research collaborations with IAMCR scholars drew attention to differences in the function of the press among countries around the world. IAMCR distributed information about Pakistani literature in English/Urdu through its bulletins, newsletters, and conference abstract books, contributing to a two-way transfer of knowledge. It collaborated with Pakistani scholars, who played a significant role in setting up a Press Council, and worked toward improving media ethics, media education, and research in the country. IAMCR researchers have emphasized solidarity with Pakistan and this has contributed to media and communication planning and progress in the country. Research by those such as Chandrika Kaul (2008) presented on the Partition and the mediation of Pakistani independence, as covered by the Indian press, has been useful to Pakistan for understanding how it is represented in foreign press and in planning future relations. Similarly, studies by Habtamu T. Dugo (2008) and Elisabeth Eide (2008b) and by Lisa Leung (2010) have been valuable in understanding media experiences and complex diasporic identities of Pakistanis. This research has been of great assistance to support Pakistan's case when comparing Orientalism with Occidentalism in Western and Pakistani media, respectively, and in challenging libertarian perspectives on freedom of expression. These and other studies presented over the years at IAMCR have identified areas that Pakistan can consider for planning and achieving redress in media and communication where there is a need for recommendations for improvement.

References

Abid, S., & Bilal, Z. (2012). Mimicry of politicians and audience perception: Analysis of political comic programs of TV news channels in Pakistan (Conference Paper). Durban. *IAMCR Book of Abstracts*. Retrieved 15 June 2022, from https://iamcr.org/sites/default/files/IAMCR_2012_Abstracts.pdf.

Ali, Z. (2011). Role of ICTs in connectivity of Pakistani youth. (Conference Paper). Istanbul. *IAMCR Book of Abstracts*. Retrieved 15 June 2022, from https://iamcr.org/sites/default/files/Istanbul2011-programme.pdf.

Ali, Z. (2012). Gender and climate change in the print media of Pakistan and New Zealand. (Conference Paper). Durban. *IAMCR Book of Abstracts*. Retrieved 15 June 2022, from https://iamcr.org/sites/default/files/IAMCR_2012_Abstracts.pdf.

Ashraf, I. (2015). Conflict, objectivity and gatekeeping: Challenges in Pakistan's tribal belt (Conference Paper). Montreal. *IAMCR Book of Abstracts*. Retrieved 15 June 2022, from https://iamcr.org/sites/default/files/Community%20Communication%20Section.pdf.

Ashraf, A., & Chaudhry, N. (2012a). Media education in Pakistan; Curricula, facilities and practices in public sector universities (Conference Paper). Durban. *IAMCR Book of Abstracts*. Retrieved 15 June 2022, from https://iamcr.org/sites/default/files/IAMCR_2012_Abstracts.pdf.

Ashraf, A., & Chaudhry, N. (2012b). Political cartoons: Urdu press during general elections 2008 in Pakistan (Conference Paper). Durban. *IAMCR Book of Abstracts*. Retrieved 15 June 2022, from https://iamcr.org/sites/default/files/IAMCR_2012_Abstracts.pdf.

Ayaz, H. (2011). Portrayal of non-Muslims in Islamic media: An analysis of Christian-Muslim riots in mainstream print media of Pakistan (Conference Paper). Istanbul. *IAMCR Book of Abstracts*. Retrieved 15 June 2022, from https://iamcr.org/sites/default/files/Istanbul2011-programme.pdf.

Ayaz, H. (2012). Historical research on foreigner and Pakistani correspondents reporting from tribal or northern parts of Pakistan (Conference Paper). Durban. *IAMCR Book of Abstracts*. Retrieved 15 June 2022, from https://iamcr.org/sites/default/files/IAMCR_2012_Abstracts.pdf.

Azhar, F. (2016). Object of affection-Online matrimonial websites in Pakistan (Conference Paper). Leicester. *IAMCR Book of Abstracts*. Retrieved 15 June 2022, from https://iamcr.org/sites/default/files/GEC-abstracts-2016.pdf.

Chakravartty, P., & Sarikakis, K. (2006). Reflections on an acronym: Re-distribution and recognition in global policy. *IAMCR Newsletter, 16*(1), 6. https://iamcr.org/node/10511. Accessed 15 June 2022.

David, M. J. R. (2007). Changing landscape of South Asian community radio: Moving towards the Telradio model (Conference Paper). Paris. *IAMCR Book of Abstracts*. Retrieved 15 June 2022, from https://iamcr.org/sites/default/files/iamcr_paris_2007_abstracts.pdf.

Dugo, H. T. (2008). Oromo diaspora, quest for democracy, and bitsphere/new media. (Conference Paper). Stockholm. *IAMCR Book of Abstracts*. Retrieved 15 June 2022, from https://iamcr.org/sites/default/files/iamcr_2008_abstracts.pdf.

Eide, E. (2008a). Exploring mediated Occidentalism: Press representations of 'the west' during the caricature crisis (Conference Paper). Stockholm. *IAMCR Abstract Book Stockholm*. Retrieved 15 June 2022, from https://iamcr.org/sites/default/files/iamcr_2008_abstracts.pdf.

Eide, E. (2008b). Out of the immigrant closet: Complex identities and media experiences (Conference Paper). Stockholm. *IAMCR Book of Abstracts*. Retrieved 15 June 2022, from https://iamcr.org/sites/default/files/iamcr_2008_abstracts.pdf.

Eijaz [Ashraf], A. (2010). Electronic colonialism: Outsourcing as discontent of globalization (Conference Paper). Braga. *IAMCR Book of Abstracts*. Retrieved 15 June 2022, from https://iamcr.org/sites/default/files/International%20Communication%20S.pdf.

Eijaz [Ashraf], A. (2011). Media representations and social meanings of blasphemy laws in Pakistan (Conference Paper). Istanbul. *IAMCR Book of Abstracts.* Retrieved 15 June 2022, from https://iamcr.org/sites/default/files/Istanbul2011-programme.pdf.

George, C. (2012). Hate spin: Taking offence as a political strategy (Conference Paper). Beijing. *IAMCR Book of Abstracts.* Retrieved 15 June 2022, from https://iamcr.org/sites/default/files/IAMCR_2012_Abstracts.pdf.

Iqbal [Chaudhry], N. (2011). Comic journalism art of Pakistan covering Karry Lugar Bill 2009 (Conference Paper). Istanbul. *IAMCR Book of Abstracts.* Retrieved 15 June 2022, from https://iamcr.org/sites/default/files/Istanbul2011-programme.pdf.

Kaul, C. (2008). 'At the stroke of the midnight hour': Lord Mountbatten, British media and the Indian independence 1947 (Conference Paper). Stockholm. *IAMCR Book of Abstracts.* Retrieved 15 June 2022, from https://iamcr.org/sites/default/files/iamcr_2008_abstracts.pdf.

Khurshid, A. S. (1971, September 5-29). *Mass communication media in Pakistan* (Seminar). AMIC Traveling Seminar: Asian Mass Communication Research & Information Centre, Singapore.

Iyer, V. (Ed.). (2001). *Freedom of information: An Asian survey.* Asian Mass Communication Research & Information Centre (AMIC).

Jabeen, F. (2019). Malala versus drones: The perpetuation of Orientalism through a case study of worthy and unworthy victims in Pakistan (Conference Paper). Cartagena. *IAMCR Book of Abstracts.*

Jameel, P. (2012). Mobile technologies changing lives of female rural teachers in Pakistan (Conference Paper). Durban. *IAMCR Book of Abstracts.* Retrieved June 15, 2022, from https://iamcr.org/sites/default/files/IAMCR_2012_Abstracts.pdf.

Jamil, S. (2015). Freedom of expression & press freedom: An ethnographic account of challenges and constraints faced by the Pakistani journalists (Conference Paper). Montreal. *IAMCR Book of Abstracts.* Retrieved June 15, 2022, from https://iamcr.org/sites/default/files/Journalism%20Research%20and%20Education.pdf.

Jamil, S. (2016). Journalism in danger: Threats to journalists' safety in Pakistan (Conference Paper). Leicester. *IAMCR Book of Abstracts.* Retrieved June 15, 2022, from https://iamcr.org/sites/default/files/JRE-abstracts-2016.pdf.

Javed, T. (2008). The rise of religious television programming in Pakistan and women's participation (Conference Paper). Stockholm. *IAMCR Book of Abstracts.* Retrieved June 15, 2022, from https://iamcr.org/sites/default/files/iamcr_2008_abstracts.pdf.

Kulikova, S., Metzgar, E., & Stuglin, S. (2010). Five days that shook the world: Coverage of Bhutto's assassination by the world newspapers (Conference Paper). Braga. *IAMCR Book of Abstracts.* Retrieved June 15, 2022, from https://iamcr.org/sites/default/files/Emerging%20Scholars%20Network%20S.pdf.

Lent, J. A. (2011). Gleanings from interviews with women cartoonists worldwide (Conference Paper). Istanbul. *IAMCR Book of Abstracts.* Retrieved June 15, 2022, from https://iamcr.org/sites/default/files/Istanbul2011-programme.pdf.

Leung, L. (2010). Negotiating (diasporic) identities: South Asians' pro/consumption of TV dramas on the internet in Hong Kong (Conference Paper). Braga. *IAMCR Book of Abstracts.* Retrieved June 15, 2022, from https://iamcr.org/sites/default/files/Mediated%20Communication%20Public%20Opinion%20and%20Society%20S.pdf.

Malik, S. (2010). Journalists for democracy and human rights, Pakistan. Western media amid growing religious extremism in Pakistan: Non-Muslim perspective' in United States of America, Germany, Australia and United Kingdom about Islam and Muslims. (Conference Paper). Braga. *IAMCR Book of Abstracts*. Retrieved June 15, 2022, from https://iamcr.org/sites/default/files/Islam%20and%20Media%20WG.pdf.

Moro, N. (2012). Becoming minority: How news coverage has produced and un-produced minorities in South Asia (Conference Paper). Durban. *IAMCR Book of Abstracts*. Retrieved June 15, 2022, from https://iamcr.org/sites/default/files/IAMCR_2012_Abstracts.pdf.

Naz, A. A., & Rizvi, W. R. (2014). The role of global elite media in interfaith dialog. (Conference Paper). Hyderabad. *IAMCR Book of Abstracts*. Retrieved June 15, 2022, from https://iamcr.org/sites/default/files/IAMCR-2014-Programme_opt.pdf.

Nordfors, D., & Uskali, T., with additional authors from InJo Initiatives Around the World US. (2010). The evolution of a journalism reform programme: The lessons of international innovation journalism initiatives (Conference Paper). Braga. *IAMCR Book of Abstracts*. Retrieved June 15, 2022, from https://iamcr.org/sites/default/files/Journalism%20Research%20and%20Education%20S.pdf.

Rahman, B. H. (2010). Framing of Pakistani Muslim women in international media: Muslim feminist's perspective (Conference Paper). Braga. *IAMCR Book of Abstracts*. Retrieved June 15, 2022, from https://iamcr.org/sites/default/files/IAMCR_2012_Abstracts.pdf.

Rahman, B. H. (2016). Ethics and freedom in mass media: A systematic review of literature from libertarian and communitarian perspectives with reference to cartoon controversy (Conference Paper). Leicester. *IAMCR Book of Abstracts*. Retrieved June 15, 2022, from https://iamcr.org/leicester2016/abstract-books.

Ramaparasad, J. (2012). Pakistani journalists: Ethics and value (Conference Paper). Istanbul. *IAMCR Book of Abstracts*. Retrieved June 15, 2022, from https://iamcr.org/sites/default/files/Istanbul2011-programme.pdf.

Rasul, A. (2012). One world, two voices: Framing of friendly attacks in the elite English press of the United States and Pakistan (Conference Paper). Durban. *IAMCR Book of Abstracts*. Retrieved June 15, 2022, from https://iamcr.org/sites/default/files/IAMCR_2012_Abstracts.pdf.

Rasul, A., McDowell, S., & Robinson, B. (2012). Assassinating objectivity: Framing of the political murders in the elite press (Conference Paper). Durban. *IAMCR Book of Abstracts*. Retrieved June 15, 2022, from https://iamcr.org/sites/default/files/IAMCR_2012_Abstracts.pdf.

Rasul, A., McDowell, S., Robinson, B., & Bilir, D. (2015). Moral disengagement and war on terror: A qualitative content analysis of drone strikes in the US elite press (Conference Paper). Montreal. *IAMCR Book of Abstracts*. Retrieved June 15, 2022, from https://iamcr.org/sites/default/files/Journalism%20Research%20and%20Education.pdf.

Rizvi, W. R. (2012). BeDevil: Colonialism and the children of miscegenation (Conference Paper). Durban. *IAMCR Book of Abstracts*. Retrieved June 15, 2022, from https://iamcr.org/sites/default/files/IAMCR_2012_Abstracts.pdf.

Rizvi, W. R. (2014). Visual pleasure in Pakistani cinema (Conference Paper). Hyderabad. *IAMCR Book of Abstracts*.

Rizvi, W. R. (2016). The censorship of visual pleasure in Pakistani cinema (Conference Paper). Leicester. *IAMCR Book of Abstracts*. Retrieved June 15, 2022, from https://iamcr.org/sites/default/files/GEC-abstracts-2016.pdf.

Saeed, S. (2012). Role of journalists in managing conflict between the North & South: A case of representing each other as 'other' (Conference Paper). Durban. *IAMCR Book of Abstracts*. Retrieved June 15, 2022, from https://iamcr.org/sites/default/files/IAMCR_2012_Abstracts.pdf.

Saleem, A., & Rizvi, W. R. (2021). The role of radio Pakistan in socioeconomic development in Central Punjab (Conference Paper). Nairobi. *IAMCR Book of Abstracts*. Retrieved June 15, 2022, from https://iamcr.org/nairobi2021/abstract-books.

Shaheen, L. (2015). Are the news priorities of Pakistani press set by international news wires' A critical analysis of international pages of three English newspapers of Pakistan (Conference Paper). Montreal. *IAMCR Book of Abstracts*. Retrieved June 15, 2022, from https://iamcr.org/sites/default/files/International%20Communication.pdf.

Shahen, Z. (2008). Internet usage patterns among Pakistani youth: A gender perspective (Conference Paper). Stockholm. *IAMCR Book of Abstracts*. Retrieved June 15, 2022, from https://iamcr.org/sites/default/files/iamcr_2008_abstracts.pdf.

Shaikh, M. (2010). Transparency and freedom of information in the Muslim world (Conference Paper). Braga. *IAMCR Book of Abstracts*. Retrieved June 15, 2022, from https://iamcr.org/sites/default/files/Law%20S.pdf.

Shaikh, M. (2012). The media and skepticism of climate-change science: A comparative study of approaches by environmental journalists in the United States and Pakistan covering extreme weather events (Conference Paper). Durban. *IAMCR Book of Abstracts*. Retrieved June 15, 2022, from https://iamcr.org/sites/default/files/IAMCR_2012_Abstracts.pdf.

Shami, S. (2012). Portrayal of US in Pakistani print media after Osama Bin Laden killing (Conference Paper). Durban. *IAMCR Book of Abstracts*. Retrieved June 15, 2022, from https://iamcr.org/sites/default/files/IAMCR_2012_Abstracts.pdf.

Sheikh, N. (2008). Role of media in reconciliatory behavior of Pakistani social groups during Pakistan India peace process (Conference Paper). Stockholm. *IAMCR Abstract Book*. Retrieved June 15, 2022, from https://iamcr.org/sites/default/files/iamcr_2008_abstracts.pdf.

Shoesmith, B., & Mahmud, S. (2007). Communication and media policy in a postmodern state: Bangladesh and its accommodation of the new technologies (Conference Paper). Paris. *IAMCR Book of Abstracts*. Retrieved June 15, 2022, from https://iamcr.org/sites/default/files/iamcr_paris_2007_abstracts.pdf.

Thussu, D. K. (2016). Emerging trends in journalism in South Asia (Panel). Leicester. *IAMCR Book of Abstracts*. Retrieved June 15, 2022, from https://iamcr.org/sites/default/files/JRE-abstracts-2016.pdf.

Ullah, M. (2010). Professional journalism and media freedom under the state of emergency in the South Asian nations (Conference Paper). Braga. *IAMCR Book of Abstracts*. Retrieved June 15, 2022, from https://iamcr.org/sites/default/files/Law%20S.pdf.

Uskali, T., & Lassila-Merisalo, M. (2010). How to educate innovation journalists? Experiences of the innovation journalism education in Finland 2004–2010 (Conference Paper). Braga. *IAMCR Book of Abstracts*. Retrieved June 15, 2022,

from https://iamcr.org/sites/default/files/Journalism%20Research%20and%20Education%20S.pdf.
Uskali, T., Nordfors, D., & Sandred, J. (2008). The experience of the Innovation Journalism Fellowship Program 2004–2008 (Conference Paper). Stockholm. *IAMCR Book of Abstracts*. Retrieved June 15, 2022, from https://iamcr.org/sites/default/files/iamcr_2008_abstracts.pdf.

CHAPTER 23

IAMCR and the Caribbean Region: Rethinking our Thinking—Understanding the Epistemic Effects of Colonialism in Higher Education

Marjan de Bruin

Introduction

> "The cultural and intellectual richness of the Caribbean makes it necessary that this region will be covered," I was told without any hesitation by the lead editor of this book. "And don't forget all your great intellectuals and poets, like Césaire and others," he added. I should share with the audience some of the critical Caribbean Communication and Media Theories and, of course, he continued, all Caribbean countries would need to be included in this chapter. For my editor, and many others, the Caribbean seemed to be one string of countries, with a variety of English-, Spanish-, French-, or Dutch-speaking residents, surrounded by the Caribbean Sea. His ways of seeing suggested high expectations about a fascinating region, but it also made me think of John Berger's statement that "the relationship between what we see and what we know is never settled." (Berger, 1972, p. 7)

How could I do justice to such diverse countries, I asked myself. Where are the critical Caribbean communication and media theories? I have seen original media and communication work that focused on the region; it pointed at the region's uniqueness or identified the gaps when common theories would not apply. I recently saw the beginning of new theories, on their way to becoming

M. de Bruin (✉)
University of the West Indies, Kingston, Jamaica
e-mail: marjan.debruin@uwimona.edu.jm

© The Author(s), under exclusive license to Springer Nature Switzerland AG 2023

J. Becker, R. Mansell (eds.), *Reflections on the International Association for Media and Communication Research*,
https://doi.org/10.1007/978-3-031-16383-8_23

great, with similarities to the Caribbean—but most of these "theories" were still in a stage of development.

I had the feeling I would disappoint my editor in his belief that the string of countries in the Caribbean—from Commonwealth of The Bahamas near the United States (US) to Trinidad and Tobago, including countries on the Latin-American continent bordering the Caribbean Sea, such as, Suriname, Guyana, Republic of Colombia—needed to be seen as one region, regardless of academics' confrontation with serious language barriers.

Indeed, across the countries, the Caribbean region did produce great minds, for instance, Aimé Césaire, from Martinique—famous for having coined the word "négritude" in French; or Édouard Glissant from Guadeloupe—one of the most influential figures in Caribbean thought and cultural commentary; not to forget Sylvia Wynter, born in Cuba and renowned Jamaican writer, who launched the "sociogenic principle" and developed a "critical race theory" to explain "how the European man came to be considered the epitome of humanity" (Wynter, 1999).[1] But also, Walter Rodney from Guyana, with his groundbreaking book in 1972 on *How Europe Underdeveloped Africa* (Rodney suffered a politically motivated assassination in 1980); or, Gabriel García Márquez, born in Cartagena, Colombia—the same Cartagena where IAMCR in 2017 celebrated its 60th anniversary. Márquez, who left law school wanting to be a journalist, became a globally famous storyteller/novelist, receiving the Nobel Prize for Literature in 1982; and, of Jamaican origin, Stuart Hall, one of the founding fathers of Cultural Studies. New generations from the Caribbean would follow these writing heroes, too many to whom homage can be paid.

IAMCR has had very few members across the Caribbean. From the late 1980s until the time of writing, a growing concentration of IAMCR members is living in Jamaica; a smaller section resides in Trinidad and Tobago, and sometimes, members from Cuba, Haiti, or Puerto Rico have been seen and met at conferences.[2] The Caribbean diaspora, mostly located in the United Kingdom, the US, and Canada, is not included in the description above.

Countries in the Caribbean region have vast differences. For outsiders, these differences may seem negligible; they may see the commonality in the region's richness in natural resources, its diversity of art and cultures, and perhaps also its priorities in life.

I had been one of these outsiders. I came to the Caribbean as a white, Dutch woman, who at the time knew little about the region, other than what the tourist gaze would offer. Coming from The Netherlands I had never been part of a white minority; I did not know the underlying race and ethnicity boundaries of the countries in the Caribbean and was not used to the sharp dividing lines between social classes—sharper in one country than in another one. "Eurocentrism" was

[1] See https://en.wikipedia.org/wiki/Sylvia_Wynter for quote. Accessed 15 June 2022.

[2] Sources: IAMCR current records and personal meetings during IAMCR conferences.

not at the top of my vocabulary. It did not take long, however, to feel the privilege of these new encounters.

The change from The Netherlands to the Caribbean had opened my eyes, not only to the challenges in the region that needed attention, but also to the narrowness of my own "knowledge base." The Caribbean's historical connection with Europe was known to me, but I had never been aware of the possible future implications of the pervasive subliminal colonial socialization of the formerly enslaved African people as inferior to Europeans.

As a newcomer to the region, I could not differentiate the similarities or differences between the Caribbean countries, until I learned more and understood that the real, or certainly most important, historically speaking similarity across Caribbean countries started in their past.

Similarities across Caribbean Countries

It was in their past—more than 400 years ago—when Caribbean countries experienced the ordeal of Spanish, English, French, and Dutch rivalries that were building up centuries of European colonization—from cruel native genocide, exploitation, and the unimaginable transatlantic slave trade between Africa and the West Indies to setting up of European property through a racialized system of chattel slavery (CARICOM Reparations Justice Program, 2021). The repercussions of this enslavement go beyond the descriptions in history books about the effects of plantations and the forced labor that enslaved people in most Caribbean countries had to go through.

European colonizers were solely focused on maintaining the extractive states, ruled by an elite class extracting wealth, as well as extractive institutional arrangements which served and benefitted planters. "The main purpose of extractive states was to transfer wealth from the colony to the colonizer" (Beuermann & Schwartz, 2018, p. 152). Improving these extractive institutions was out of the question, even after the Abolition and Emancipation Acts. There was no incentive for the colonial elite to go after any change as long as the entrenched racially stratified plantation societal order was maintained. "The prevailing values and demands of those who ruled the society" (Lamming, 2004, p. 5) would persist "long after the colonial regime ended" (Beuermann & Schwartz, 2018, p. 47). A horrible perspective, even while bearing in mind that countries with broad similarities may have continued on different development pathways, which perhaps could lead to different performances.

The reality of the imperial reason being able to reduce human beings to a sub-human (Ndlovu-Gatsheni, 2018; de Santos, 2014), or even, as was the case in the Caribbean, to a chattel category, with no knowledge and no understanding, was frightening and would create a deep gap in the later society. A case in point is the passing in the British Parliament of the post-emancipation *Negro Education Grant 1835–1845* with its explicit precepts of religious indoctrination, conformity, and rote learning "to maintain the tranquility" of the colony (Gordon, 1958, p. 140). The implication of this lack of genuine support for the development of Caribbean people was an education system, which by design and practice, always supplied a ready and abundant number of illiterate and/or poorly educated persons to be absorbed as cheap labor agricultural workers.

Homegrown Higher Education—Hold Back by Colonizers

To identify some of the major factors which play a substantial role in the colonizers' holding back of Caribbean education—including media and communication in higher education—requires another brief dive into history: when the British colonizers across the world began to prepare their colonies for "self-government." The British Colonial Office had proposed a range of subjects and structures in the Caribbean for new institutions of study and teaching, reflecting the British motherland, spelling out what was needed, and defining which fields of inquiry were most necessary—a "residential university on the pattern of Oxford and Cambridge" (Braithwaite, 1965, p. 79).

Other colonizers in the region had started higher education in their colonies much earlier: the Spanish founded the Universidad de La Habana in 1728 as well as the University of Puerto Rico, which was founded in 1903. France, with Guadeloupe and Martinique as two of its provinces, instituted the Université des Antilles in the mid-1850s, while Haiti's State University started in 1820. These countries started their university education programs when the English-speaking Caribbean was still struggling with British colonization.

The overriding mission of the Colonial Office had been "to ensure that their promotion of higher education was met … without sacrificing continuing British interest and influence" (Cobley, 2000, p. 13). British staff, and early Caribbean nationalists who had been educated abroad and absorbed Eurocentric cultural and education models, came over from Europe to teach the "best of the British abroad" (Braithwaite, 1965, p. 79).

Finally, in 1948, the British Colonial Office located the University College of the West Indies (UCWI) in Kingston, Jamaica. The UCWI was in principle an "extraneous model," practically waiting for its removal that would come when Jamaica had its independence in 1962.

Although presumably liberating, the British colonizers were still building and expanding their imperialism, this time under the education umbrella. What should have been a necessary mission for setting up higher education turned out to have been a colonial impact. Before this "real" university in 1962 would be ready for its launch, some of the region's well-known academics—Eric Williams and C. L. R James—had questioned "the essentialism of the traditional historiography and the master narrative imposed on former colonised peoples" (Shepherd, 2007, p. 6). While the Colonial Office in the Caribbean was carefully managing the UCWI throughout the 1950s, mirroring the British at home, the European continent preparations by UNESCO were taking place to work toward an IAMCR founding conference to be held in December 1957—five years before, in 1962, the University of the West Indies (UWI) would become a university of the Caribbean people.

Destabilizing the Hegemonic European Knowledge Paradigms and Discourses

The "indigenous" UWI was essentially an adaptation of an educational system "as a country moves from the status of a colonial dependence to that of an independent country" (Braithwaite, 1965, p. 1). The expectations for this homegrown university were high—the region was elated and the nationalists had been active since the 1920s. However, the pressures and forces of earlier years were not immediately dissolved. The hidden factor that had been running underneath the stream of political changes was the terror of the old colonial empire: a "breeding ground for every uncertain self ... together with lack of cultural confidence"—explaining the daily exercise in self-mutilation, the "terror of the mind." There were contradictory feelings of "being at once independent and neo-colonial, struggling through new definitions of itself to abandon the protection of being a frontier created by nature" and "struggling to the status of being a region for itself, with the sovereign right to define its own reality and order its own priorities" (Lamming, 2004, p. 9).

In spite of this underground struggling, the UWI became an important platform for Caribbean scholars and philosophers "to destabilize the hegemonic European knowledge paradigms and discourses, and produce knowledge about the region that is designed to anchor its citizens to a more empowering past" (Shepherd, 2011, p. 4). But destabilizing knowledge paradigms and discourses would take time.

Even almost 40 years after independence, the higher educational systems within the Anglophone Caribbean were still characterized as continuing to reflect "the academic traditions of their former colonizer" (Cobley, 2000), with British traditions still "as an integral part of the education system in the English-speaking Caribbean" (Peters, 2001).

The start of the UWI in 1962, in Kingston, Jamaica, had not included a media and communication department. This would only be launched in 1974, just after IAMCR had had its first conference in Buenos Aires in 1972. This conference had signaled a new beginning of cooperating with UNESCO. It was the same UNESCO that helped and supported the setting up of CARIMAC, which during its first years was named the Caribbean Institute of Mass Communication (currently named Caribbean School of Media and Communication).

The emphasis of this chapter, thus far, has been on the historical pressures, gaps, beatings, and barricading of people in the Caribbean. However, the hegemonic European knowledge in paradigms or in discourses did not only occur in academic knowledge production. Epistemological hierarchy is continuously reproduced when Western knowledges are presented as being relevant and valuable, while non-Western and indigenous knowledges are "either patronisingly celebrated as local or native culture, commodified or appropriated for Western gain, or else not recognised as knowledge at all" (Stein & Andreotti, 2016, p. 2).

As Director of CARIMAC after Brown's start with a deanship, I had many times experienced this patronizing. Often when I sat in meetings and negotiations with international funding agencies, I had felt the subtlety of power of some of the Northern universities' colleagues about where, even in "collaborative" projects, the actual finances should go; who would best know what was needed in certain projects; and who were the actual decision makers—regardless of any indigenous knowledge. I still remember my suppressed anger when it was clear that projects with a pre-set output—prepared by the funding agency outside the Caribbean—and oftentimes not fulfilling the needs of local communities and NGOs, still had to be fulfilled without any changes, because the funding agency could not be changed anymore. I recall the subtle dominance of the visitor, who "knows best." I also know of scholars coming from outside the region, who "functioned as 'hunter-gatherers' of raw data, as well as 'native informants'" (Ndlovu-Gatsheni, 2018, *p. 8) whereby countries outside of the Caribbean "remained sites of processing of raw data into concepts and theories" (Ndlovu-Gatsheni,* 2018, *p. 8).*

Many South universities have experienced the "highly uneven accumulated social, economic and epistemic effects of colonialism and slavery for populations around the globe" (Ndlovu-Gatsheni, 2018, p. 8). Sites of interaction of North-South relations show specific hierarchies in which "international" (Northern) knowledge coming from the stakeholders in the North would be at the top, and "local" (Southern) knowledge from the stakeholders in the South at the bottom"—"a sign of re-colonization" (Girvan, 2007, p. 3).

CARIMAC's Development and IAMCR's Support

UNESCO, which had been of substantial support for IAMCR, also played an important role in CARIMAC's establishment in 1974. In the earlier colonial dispensation in the region, broadcast media and newspapers had been the important media houses with either government ownership and control, or British ownership and control (Brown, 1990) and much de-colonization work was to be done. For example, the setting up of the Caribbean News Agency (CANA) in 1976 "enabled the region to break the almost total dependence on foreign news agencies and define some of its own news–read: reality" (de Bruin, 2002, p. 2).

When Aggrey Brown took the helm of CARIMAC, between 1979 and 2002, he identified the remains of colonization without having labeled them as such. He pointed at the informal censorship—absence of diversity in viewpoints and interests represented in the media (Brown & Sanatan, 1987). UNESCO drew attention to other challenges—state ownership in many Caribbean countries and divestment/privatization of media (Wilson,

1989)—as well as the need for alternative communication to break through the boundaries of upper-class traditions, cultural penetration, ownership and control, and training and professionalism.

A few years after Brown's start as Director of CARIMAC, IAMCR and CARIMAC seem to have discovered each other for further collaboration—Cees Hamelink (at the time at the Institute of Social Studies in The Hague) and Aggrey Brown (The UWI Institute of Mass Communication, CARIMAC in Kingston, Jamaica) organized a joint workshop on *Telecommunication Policy in the Caribbean Region* in the midst of the Jamaican Blue Mountains.

Knowing that "re-thinking thinking" was going to be crucial for the Caribbean, Brown made his institutional team diverse, as long as the team members would believe, know, and communicate "that research in the Caribbean must begin to take the Caribbean side" (Brown & Sanatan, 1987, p. 10). Brown knew that earlier—referring to the early 1980s meeting—"the challenges of citizenship and sovereignty in the contemporary Caribbean" had failed and warned against the perception that "our views need to be validated from outside" and that "we must begin from within the Caribbean" (Brown & Sanatan, 1987, p. 10). Even stronger was Nettleford's statement who referred to "the collective intellect and imagination of a region which is still in the process of de-colonization as part of its post-colonial formation" (Nettleford, 1987, p. 1).

CARIMAC's de-colonial thinking at that time can be found in very practical works which perhaps would fall under decoloniality as Walsh (2018) describes: "not in a static condition, an individual attribute, or a lineal point of arrival or enlightenment" (p. 17), but making "visible, open up, and advance radically distinct perspectives and positionalities that displace Western rationality as the only framework."

It was still a time in the Caribbean—the late 1980s, with no homegrown educational material on journalism and communication—a gap, which a few years earlier in the mid-1980s, had become one of Brown's many pet-topics, together with Nordenstreng and supported by UNESCO and IAMCR. Dunn joined the duo in the mid-1990s. Working with IAMCR's Professional Education Section, it became clear that "in regions with Anglophone or Francophone histories books were dominated by literature from Europe and North America, first and foremost the USA." What may seem to be "just" a bibliographic survey of textbooks only can be seen from a different perspective and becomes a "decolonial move that requires the cultivation of a decolonial attitude in knowledge production" (Ndlovu-Gatsheni, 2018, p. 24).

Aggrey Brown, Hopeton Dunn, and I had become passionate members of the association and encouraged other members of staff to join. For each of us, engagement with IAMCR members, who were coming from all corners of the globe and demonstrating a genuine interest in the development of media and communication in the Caribbean, was always encouraging. Perhaps it was also the critical mass that worked well—meeting large audiences, while being used to sharing with a relatively small number of colleagues, and discovering a greater diversity of challenges and solutions. It was the diversity across regions which inspired us, as if the growing networks coming out of these connections provoked the exchange that was needed to challenge ourselves even more.

Several faculty members of CARIMAC became leaders of IAMCR working groups and sections, others participated in the association's committees, or became members of the Executive Board.[3] It was not always only positive what we experienced. We would meet the odd member who had no idea of the Caribbean's current position and history. It could be painful sometimes, when colleagues lacked any knowledge about the centuries of Europe's imprisoning of human beings through the Transatlantic Slave Trade–Eurocentrism "as an epistemology of ignorance" (Alcoff, 2017, p. 397).

Critical Caribbean Media and Communication Theories

So far, I have not touched upon the cardinal question this book's editor had put on the table—What about the critical Caribbean media and communication theories?—a question I can only respond to as far as the English-speaking Caribbean is concerned.

Professionals and academics in media and communication in the Caribbean region only recently started with critical reflections on communication and media works. The historical background of colonization, de-colonization, and perhaps also re-colonization plays a crucial role in this inception. With a young UWI—founded in 1962—and departments relevant to critical theories on communication and media, only established in 1974—media and communication researchers in the Anglophone Caribbean had a late start compared to many other universities elsewhere in the field. Here, too, the connection between IAMCR and media and communication departments, for example, CARIMAC in the Caribbean, played a key role in the development of this new field of inquiry.

Over the years, CARIMAC's growing relationship with IAMCR had become an important feeding source for Caribbean members who were able to project outside the region, forcing, in their relationships with other continents, to be explicit about their challenges and thinking.

A good example of encouraging beginnings is Dunn who warns against "too uncritical adoption of externally generated theoretical constructs and media content" and emphasizes insight "must come from all parts of the world and not just from the privileged North" (Dunn et al., 2021, p. 6). Others in the region underscore the need to embrace inclusive new paradigms and approaches from previously peripheral spaces (Gordon-Bell, 2021); or describe how "international policies and systems of governance are adopted wholesale by many developing countries, creating a hegemony that fosters deeper relations of dependency and inequity in the global media economy" (Obika, 2019,

[3] Hopeton Dunn as Secretary General, starting in 2012, and myself, Marjan de Bruin, as one of the Vice Presidents, elected in 2000.

p. 217). Prendergast tries explicitly to come to a Critical Caribbean Media Theory and praxis through "empowerment communication and media, located in the community as philosophically dynamic, politically revolutionary, and educationally transformational people-owned, operating in social justice systems" (Prendergast, email interview, 2 January 2022). It is the deconstruction of traditional hegemony, Prendergast underscores, which is needed to allow "new ways for people to redefine, control, manage and defend their own experiences and resources, providing us with a window for further development of Critical Media Theory and Praxis, unique to the Caribbean" (Prendergast, email interview, 2 January 2022).

Interesting approaches on a variety of levels, but Livingston A. White, currently Head of CARIMAC, finds too many questions remaining under the surface and suggests that Caribbean researchers reflect on their work on various levels: philosophically, theoretically, methodologically, educationally, and practically (White, 2015, p. 15). For instance, from a philosophical perspective, researchers must be able to understand communication in Caribbean contexts and interrogate the bodies of "knowledge of communication" they created. Theoretically, White emphasizes that we need to investigate the systems of explanation which we have "applied to our research in communication" (2015, p. 15). Methodologically, researchers may want to know how Caribbean cultural nuances have affected how we choose to collect data; and educationally, the question could be—Why have we focused on some aspects of communication and ignored others? "Let us keep the conversation going, grapple with the issues and aim to achieve the recognition and respect that the communication discipline in the Caribbean deserves," White argues. But "a strong Caribbean philosophy for media and communication research has yet to emerge" (White, email interview, 4 January 2022).

The Invisible Connections Between the Past and the Present

From an academic point of view, there is still much to be contemplated, to be criticized, or not to be taken for granted. Challenges will be deep and difficult, apart from having had a late institutional start compared with other higher education institutions. The region's history is in need of self-reflection, searching for connections with de-colonial praxis, and the politics of knowledge building. The concepts of epistemic injustice or epistemic responsibility and the coloniality of knowledge seem, also in other continents, to have come to the surface, questioning the remaining colonial and de-colonial structures.

This interrogation recently seems to have come to the surface more openly, with encouraging beginnings and efforts to continue new thinking and working toward a solid foundation which could help to build further.

References

Alcoff, L. M. (2017). Philosophy and philosophical practice: Eurocentrism as an epistemology of ignorance. In I. A. James, J. Medina, & G. Pohlhaus (Eds.), *The Routledge handbook of epistemic injustice* (p. 397–408). Routledge.

Berger, J. (1972). *Ways of seeing*. British Broadcasting Corporation and Penguin Books.

Beuermann, D. W., & Schwartz, M. (Eds.). (2018). *Nurturing institutions for a resilient Caribbean* (p. 47–152). Inter-American Development Bank (IADB): Country Department Caribbean Group.

Braithwaite, L. E. (1965). The role of the university in the developing society of the West Indies. *Social and Economic Studies, 14*(1), 76–87. [Selected papers on Education presented at the VIIth Latin-American Congress of Sociology, (March 1964)]. Sir Arthur Lewis Institute of Social and Economic Studies, Mona, Kingston.

Brown, A. (1990, May 22–27). *Caribbean cultures and mass communication in the 21st century* [Round Table discussion]. Caribbean Studies Association Conference, Port of Spain, Trinidad.

Brown, A., & Sanatan, R. (1987). *Talking with whom? A report on the state of the media in the Caribbean* (p. 1–10). CARIMAC UWI.

CARICOM Reparations Justice Program. (2021). *Ten point reparation plan*. Retrieved 15 June 2022, from https://caricom.org/caricom-ten-point-plan-for-reparatory-justice/

Cobley, A. (2000). The historical development of higher education in the Anglophone Caribbean. In G. D. Howe (Ed.), *Higher education in the Caribbean: Past, present, and future directions* (p. 1–23). UWI Press.

de Bruin, M. (2002, December). *Professional training in media and communication–CARIMAC graduates. CARIMAC occasional paper no. 5*. Caribbean Institute of Media and Communication, University of the West Indies, Mona.

de Santos, B. S. (2014). *Epistemologies of the south. Justice against epistemicide*. Routledge.

Dunn, H. S., Moyo, D., Lesitaokana, W. O., & Barnabas, S. B. (2021). Releasing the psychic inheritance. In H. S. Dunn, D. Moyo, W. O. Lesitaokana, & S. B. Barnabas (Eds.), *Re-imagining communication in Africa and the Caribbean—Global South issues in media, culture and technology* (pp. 1–14). Palgrave Macmillan.

Girvan, N. P. (2007). *Power imbalances and development knowledge*. Paper for the project Southern Perspectives on Reform of the International Development Architecture. The North-South Institute/L'Institut Nord-Sud.

Gordon, S. (1958). Negro education grant 1835–1845: Its application in Jamaica. *British Journal of Educational Studies, 6*(2), 140–150.

Gordon-Bell, N. (2021). Towards an integrating Caribbean paradigm in communication thought: Confronting academic dependence in media research. In H. S. Dunn, D. Moyo, W. O. Lesitaokana, & S. B. Barnabas (Eds.), *Re-imagining communication in Africa and the Caribbean—Global South issues in media, culture and technology* (pp. 51–73). Palgrave Macmillan.

Lamming, G. (2004). *The sovereignty of the imagination*. Arawak Publications.

Ndlovu-Gatsheni, S. J. (2018). *Epistemic freedom in Africa. Deprovincialization and decolonization*. Routledge.

Nettleford, R. (1987). *Talking with whom. A report on the state of the media in the Caribbean* (Foreword), p. 1. CARIMAC UWI.

Obika, A. (2019). *Communications policy reforms in the Caribbean: Media governance strategies in Jamaica and Trinidad and Tobago.* Unpublished doctoral dissertation. The University of the West Indies, Mona Campus.

Peters, B. (2001). Tertiary education development in small states: Constraints and future prospects. *Caribbean Quarterly, 47*(2 & 3), 44–57.

Rodney, W. (1972) *How Europe underdeveloped Africa* (Revised edition). Howard University Press.

Shepherd, V. (2007). *'I want to disturb my neighbour': Lectures on slavery, emancipation and postcolonial Jamaica.* Ian Randle Publishers.

Shepherd, V. (2011). *Obstacles to the Creation of Afrocentric Societies in the Commonwealth Caribbean.* Presentation made to the WGPAD's 10th Session, during the International Year for People of African Descent, 28 March-1 April.

Stein, S., & Andreotti, V. D. O. (2016). Decolonization and higher education. In Peters, M. (Ed.), *Encyclopedia of educational philosophy and theory* (pp. 1–6). Springer Science+Business Media. Retrieved 15 June 2022, from https://link.springer.com/referenceworkentry/10.1007/978-981-287-532-7_479-1

Walsh, C. (2018). The decolonial *for:* Resurgences, shifts, and movements. In W. D. Mignolo & C. Walsh (Eds.), *On decoloniality, concepts, analytics, praxis* (pp. 15–32). Duke University Press.

White, L. A. (2015). Charting the course of communication studies in the English-speaking Caribbean: Disciplines, developments and future directions. *The Journal of Human Communication Studies in the Caribbean, 1*(1), 7–17.

Wilson, G. (1989). *Attitudes of Caribbean media professionals to mass media in the region.* UNESCO.

Wynter, S. (1999). Towards the Sociogenic principle: Fanon, identity, the puzzle of conscious experience and what it is like to be 'Black'. In M. Durán-Cogan & A. Gómez-Moriana (Eds.), *National identity and sociopolitical change: Latin America between marginizalization and integration* (pp. 30–66). University of Minnesota Press.

CHAPTER 24

Brazil in History and in the Present: IAMCR and the Participation of Brazilians

Fernando Oliveira Paulino

Introduction

The objective of this chapter is to systematize information on the participation of Brazilians in the history of IAMCR from the association's foundation to the present. For this, bibliographic research was carried out and there was an analysis of data requested from the IAMCR Secretariat. From the information presented in this paper, it is possible to discern a mutual strengthening of both the association and the field of communication in Brazil as a result of the participation of Brazilians in events organized by IAMCR.

The main challenges identified are the need to maintain and expand the participation of Brazilians in IAMCR's conferences and in its positions of coordination and direction. Brazil has a significant number of learning, research, and outreach activities (Rebouças, 2012). Above all, there is a need to propose and ensure that Brazilian researchers can count on having a greater number of representatives in the association and greater visibility at events, such as opening round tables and plenary sessions.

F. O. Paulino (✉)
University of Brasilia, Brasília, Brazil

Latin American Communication Researchers Association (ALAIC), Caracas, Venezuela
e-mail: paulino@unb.br

© The Author(s), under exclusive license to Springer Nature Switzerland AG 2023
J. Becker, R. Mansell (eds.), *Reflections on the International Association for Media and Communication Research*,
https://doi.org/10.1007/978-3-031-16383-8_24

Early Years

The participation of Brazilian researchers in the activities of IAMCR follows its history since its foundation. In 1957, stimulated by the creation of other scientific organizations, a group of professors and researchers of communication joined IAMCR. Among them was a Brazilian, Danton Jobim Marques de Melo (Marques de Melo, 2005), at the time, editor of the newspaper *Diário Carioca* and a professor teaching the journalism course at the then University of Brazil, in Rio de Janeiro.

The invitation for Jobim to participate in the foundation of IAMCR had been made by Jacques Kayser and took account of the fact that Brazilians moved between the market and the academy. It was also made because Jobim had taught, some years earlier, a course at the Sorbonne University, publishing the lectures in book form with the title *Introduction au Journalisme Contemporain* (1954a).

Before this, in 1953, he had served as Visiting Professor at the University of Texas, being responsible for a course on Latin American Journalism. As a result of this experience at the University of Texas, he was the first Brazilian academic to publish an article in *Journalism Quarterly*, "French and U.S. Influences upon the Latin American Press" (Jobim, 1954b).

In 1954, Jobim received the Maria Moors Cabot Prize, awarded annually by Columbia University to Latin American journalists who stand out in the struggle to defend press freedom. Four years later, being an important bridge between academic production inside and outside Brazil, Jobim participated in the preparatory meeting for the creation of the International Center for Superior Studies in Journalism for Latin America (CIESPAL). In 1960, he published the book, *Espírito do Jornalismo*, containing a translation of his Parisian lectures and other essays.[1]

Restrictions with the Dictatorship and Resumption with Democratization

During the military dictatorship from 1964 to 1985, the prospects for cooperation between Brazilian researchers and researchers from other countries were restricted, affecting their participation in IAMCR conferences. During the 1970s and early 1980s (Gobbi, 2018), researchers such as Fernando Perrone, exiled in Paris, and Nelly de Camargo, participated with a paper dedicated to communication and culture, and Ingrid Sarti, with very important contributions to reflections on the world order of information and communication.

With the beginning of the democratization process in Brazil, driven by the creation of scientific organizations (in which Intercom, the Brazilian Society

[1] Later, Danton Jobim became more directly involved with party politics, having been elected (1970) and re-elected Senator for the state of Guanabara. Researchers attribute both the deaths of Danton (1978) and his brother, diplomat José Jobim (in 1979), to the military dictatorship.

for Interdisciplinary Studies in Communication, stands out nationally in 1977, and regionally ALAIC, the Latin American Communication Researchers Association, in 1978, both entities associated with IAMCR), the promulgation of the 1988 Constitution, the regular offer of research event notifications, and the creation of State Research Support Foundations, there were improved conditions for the participation of Brazilian researchers in IAMCR conferences.

A person who stands out in this period is Professor José Marques de Melo, elected to the IAMCR International Council (IC) in 1988 and serving until 1992. In this year, he was elected Vice President and served until 1994. In 1990, Marques de Melo was also Chair of the Science Journalism in the World Working Group (WG) and Co-Chair of the WG on Regional Media & Cultural Diversity in 1994.

The growth of Brazilian participation in IAMCR (Paulino, 2013) contributed to the fact that, in August 1992, researchers from 50 countries met in the city of Guarujá in the state of São Paulo to discuss mass media and their role in the configuration of a fully globalized cultural environment. At this conference, the Brazilian delegation ranked second for the total number of accepted papers with 42. The country with the highest number of presentations was the US with 95.

From then on, there was a notable presence of Brazilians in the following conferences: Seoul 1992 and Sidney 1994, and an even greater number in 1996. At the Glasgow 1998 Conference, there was an acceptance of 52 scientific papers produced by Brazilians, a number lower only than the contribution by colleagues from the US, who had 115 scientific papers accepted (Marques de Melo, 2000).

The continuous participation of Brazilian researchers in the events of IAMCR and other international entities, the technological transformations, and the economic and political stabilization of Brazil, all contributed to a greater degree of circulation and an internationalization of information in teaching, research, and extension activities in the country.[2]

This environment was favorable for Pontifícia Universidade Católica do Rio Grande do Sul (PUCRS), a traditional academic institution in the country, to host IAMCR's conference in July 2004 with the theme "Communication between the peoples of the world."

Jacques Wainberg, Professor and Chair of the local organizing committee, noted during a meeting of IAMCR's Executive Board (EB) that the conference would be attended by more than 550 participants, of whom approximately 50 percent would come from abroad. As pointed out by Professor Neuza Demartini Gomes (2004), a member of the organizing committee, there were

[2] At the time of writing in early 2022, there were 57 postgraduate programs in Brazil (https://compos.org.br/programas/ accessed 15 June 2022) offering master's and/or doctoral training in communication. The total number of communication researchers in the country is in the thousands. A detailed review 12 years ago found that these included "1,410 doctors, 722 women (51%) and 688 men (49%) and 3,769 masters, with 2,210 women (59%) and 1,559 men, representing 41%."

Table 24.1 Countries hosting two or more IAMCR conferences

3 Times	France: Paris, 1957, 1982, and 2007
	Spain: Pamplona, 1968; Barcelona, 1998; Madrid, 2009
	Germany: Konstanz, 1970; Leipzig, 1974 and 1999
2 Times	Brazil: Guarujá, 1992; Porto Alegre, 2004
	India: New Delhi, 1986; Hyderabad, 2014
	United Kingdom: Leicester, 1976 and 2016
	México: Oaxaca, 1997; Mexico City, 2009
	Ireland: Dublin, 1993 and 2013
	Turkey: Istanbul, 1991 and 2011

Table 24.2 Conferences, participants, and Brazilian participation

Conference	*Total no. of participants*	*Participants from Brazil*	*Percentage of Brazilians in relation to total number of participants in the conference*
2005 Taipei	277	3	1.1%
2010 Braga	1230	106	8.6%
2012 Durban	683	25	3.7%
2014 Hyderabad	664	24	3.6%
2015 Montreal	1270	58	4.6%
2016 Leicester	1978	56	2.8%
2017 Cartagena	1387	157	11.3%
2018 Eugene	869	35	4.0%
2019 Madrid	1780	66	3.7%
Total	10,138	530	5.2%

105 selected papers from Brazil, the country with the highest number of presentations, surpassing the US, which came second with 91.

Hosting the 1992 and 2004 IAMCR conferences placed Brazil in a select group of nine countries that have hosted the main IAMCR conference at least twice, as can be seen in Table 24.1.

Twenty-First Century and Permanent Participation by Brazilians in IAMCR Conferences

After the Porto Alegre 2004 Conference, Brazilians maintained continuous participation and this typically expanded when the conferences were held in countries with direct flights to and from Brazil.

Table 24.2 shows, for example, a significantly greater participation in the conferences held in Portugal (Braga, 2010) and Colombia (Cartagena, 2017).

In addition to the quantitative aspect, it is worth mentioning the continued participation of Brazilians in the coordination of sections or WGs, among them Claudia Lago, Adilson Cabral, Denize Araujo, and Fernando Oliveira Paulino, and the participation of colleagues such as César Bolaño (former treasurer and member of the IC) and Andrea Medrado (Vice President at the time of writing, elected in 2020) in activities of the IC and also in the association's EB.

Another aspect that deserves mention is the presentation and holding of special sessions that sought to promote dialog and greater exchange between Brazilian researchers and those from other countries. For this purpose, Intercom organized sessions with the participation of colleagues such as Sonia Virgínia Moreira and Edgard Rebouças, and Brazilians also participated in sessions organized on an ongoing basis by ALAIC (Latin American Communication Research Association) since Istanbul 2011, when Nico Carpentier ECREA (European Communication Research and Education Association) and César Bolaño and Fernando Oliveira Paulino started this initiative.

Likewise, with the objective of contributing to the circulation of knowledge and greater visibility for research carried out in Brazil and other Latin American countries, there have been publications and launches of books with the aim of systematically collating research carried out in Brazil with perspectives discussed on cooperation. Among these works are the books *Research Traditions in Dialogue—Communication Studies in Latin America and Europe,* edited in 2020 by Fernando Oliveira Paulino, Gabriel Kaplún, Miguel Vicente Mariño, and Leonardo Custodio (Paulino et al., 2020), after a shared process of defining themes, shared talks and release talks, and the book *New Concepts and Territories in Latin America* (2017), edited by Adilson Cabral, César Bolaño, Denize Araujo, Fernando Andacht, and Fernando Oliveira Paulino, with 33 chapters discussing issues from nine Latin American countries (Argentina, Brazil, Chile, Colombia, Cuba, México, Paraguay, Uruguay, and Venezuela).

Table 24.3 demonstrates the importance of efforts to hold special sessions, panels, and publications which contribute to greater diversification in the programming of IAMCR conferences. Such efforts can and should be carried out in partnership with Latin American colleagues and with those from other

Table 24.3 Plenaries, opening ceremonies, and Brazilian participation

Conference	*No. of plenary and opening ceremony members*	*No. of Brazilians as opening ceremony and plenary members*	*Percentage of Brazilians in opening ceremonies and plenaries*
2007 Paris	16	0	0.0%
2009 México	30	1	3.3%
2010 Braga	22	3	13.6%
2011 Istanbul	15	1	6.7%
2012 Durban	17	0	0.0%
2013 Dublin	18	0	0.0%
2014 Hyderabad	22	1	4.6%
2015 Montreal	10	0	0.0%
2016 Leicester	9	0	0.0%
2017 Cartagena	15	1	6.67%
2018 Eugene	14	0	0.0%
2019 Madrid	10	0	0.0%
Total	198	7	3.5%

Note: Table prepared based on data provided by Bruce Girard whom we thank for information

so-called Global South regions that do not have a regular and continuous seat during the main moments of IAMCR conferences as indicated by a sample of the events. As can be seen, the proportion of Brazilians participating in plenary and opening events (3.5%) is significantly lower than the proportion of Brazilians participating in the conferences (5.2%) (see Tables 24.2 and 24.3).

Conclusion

This chapter has sought to demonstrate the historical involvement of Brazilian researchers within IAMCR which was accentuated with the country's democratization process after the military dictatorship, with financial resources becoming available for travel, and with the possibilities for connection that digital technology offers.

If the structural conditions to support research in communication are maintained or expanded, there may be an even greater tendency for Brazilians to attend and participate in publications, events, and other activities related to IAMCR/ALAIC, and other international organizations. For this to happen, it will be essential to defend and promote democracy in Brazil in the face of autocratic and authoritarian measures.

Future work is needed to verify the reality of the development of the field of communication in Brazil and the conditions influencing the absorption of the significant contingent of doctoral and master's students who graduate each year. In future, it may also be possible to assess the extent of Brazilian contributions to global scientific production and the possibilities for Brazilians and other researchers from the so-called Global South to influence the production and circulation of knowledge.

In addition to difficulties related to the (lack of) command of English, the predominant language in international scientific events, there are still many difficulties to overcome the prevailing practice of exporting data and information by the poorest countries in exchange for "industrialized goods," that is, articles and books produced by more structured publishers with high prices in relation to the conditions of access to works by researchers from the South.

The two books noted above (*Research Traditions in Dialogue—Communication Studies in Latin America and Europe* and *New concepts and territories in Latin America*), for example, as well as other works produced by WGs and task forces with the participation of researchers from the South, are published openly and free of charge. The traditional way of publishing sometimes generates noise and difficulties in accessing works produced in the Global North, whereas open access brings greater possibilities of resources and higher visibility in international conferences.

To transform the current reality and promote diversity that is positive for North, South, East, and West, a dialog between peers as well as quantitative and qualitative analysis are essential. There is still a significant way to go with many challenges and possibilities.

References

Cabral, A., Bolaño, C., Araujo, D., Andacht, F., & Paulino, F. O., Eds. (2017). *New concepts and territories in Latin America. Página 42*. Retrieved 15 June 2022, from https://www.academia.edu/33891287/New_Concepts_and_Territories_in_Latin_America_Nuevos_Conceptos_y_Territorios_en_Am%C3%A9rica_Latina_Eds_Adilson_Cabral_C%C3%A9sar_Bola%C3%B1o_Denize_Araujo_Fernando_Andacht_Fernando_Paulino

Gobbi, M. C. (2018). José Marques de Melo e o pensamento comunicacional Brasileiro. Proposta de uma cartografia nacional. *Teresina, Revista Brasileira de História da Mídia*, *7*(2), 44–68. Retrieved 15 June 2022, from https://revistas.ufpi.br/index.php/rbhm/article/view/7681/4964

Gomes, N. D. (2004). XXIV Conferência da IAMCR: A comunicação entre os povos do mundo. São Bernardo do Campo, Brasil. *Comunicação e Sociedade*, *43*, 233–236. Retrieved 15 June 2022, from https://www.metodista.br/revistas/revistas-ims/index.php/CSO/article/viewFile/3988/3873

Jobim, D. (1954a). *Introduction au journalisme contemporain*. Librairie Nizet.

Jobim, D. (1954b). French and U. S. influences upon the Latin American Press. *Journalism Quarterly*, *30*(1), 61–66. Retrieved 15 June 2022, from https://journals.sagepub.com/doi/abs/10.1177/107769905403100106

Jobim, D. (1960). *Espírito do jornalismo*. Livraria São José.

Marques de Melo, J. (2000). A produção acadêmica Brasileira em comunicação: perspectivas dos novos tempos. *Revista FAMECOS, Rio Grande do Sul*, *11*, 7–26. Retrieved 15 June 2022, from https://revistaseletronicas.pucrs.br/ojs/index.php/revistafamecos/article/view/3048

Marques de Melo, J. (2005). O pioneirismo de Danton Jobim na pesquisa jornalística Brasileira. *Niterói: Revista Contracampo*, *12*, 12–22. Retrieved 15 June 2022, from https://periodicos.uff.br/contracampo/article/view/17383

Paulino, F. O. (2013). A participacão Brasileira no congresso da IAMCR em Dublin, África do Sul. In J. C. G. R. Lima & J. Marques de Melo (Eds.), *Panorama da comunicação e das telecomunicações no Brasil: 2012/2013* (p. 39–46). Ipea. Retrieved 15 June 2022, from https://www.ipea.gov.br/portal/images/stories/PDFs/livros/livros/livro_panoramadacomunicacao2012_2013_vol03.pdf

Paulino, F. O., Kaplún, G., Mariño, M. V., & Custodio, L., Eds. (2020). *Research traditions in dialogue—Communication Studies in Latin. America and Europe*. Publishing Media XXI. Retrieved 15 June 2022, from https://www.alaic.org/site/wp-content/uploads/2020/12/Research-Traditions-in-Dialogue.pdf

Rebouças, E. (2012). Boston, ICA. In D. Castro & J. Marques de Melo (Org.), *Panorama das comunicações e das telecomunicações no Brasil 2011/2012—Volume 2—Flagrantes* (vol. 2, p. 17–26). Ipea. Retrieved 15 June 2022, from https://www.ipea.gov.br/portal/images/stories/PDFs/livros/livros/livro_panoramadacomunicacao_volume02_2012.pdf

CHAPTER 25

IAMCR and the Middle East and North Africa: Questions of Place, People, and Paradigms

Naomi Sakr

Introduction

Names of scholars from the Middle East and North Africa (MENA) who were prominent in IAMCR from its creation in 1957 to the present day are so few that people familiar with the organization's history tend to recall them readily. Yet, reasons for their small number are not offered so promptly. Hamid Mowlana, the Iranian-born, US-employed academic who held the IAMCR Presidency from 1994 to 1998, seemed to lay the blame on the association itself when reflecting on issues of representation and participation at an IAMCR meeting in Oaxaca, México, in 1997. He cited a long delay in holding IAMCR conferences in the Global South, specifically the Asia Pacific region and Latin America. Once these events took place, he said, they "evoked some response from amongst scholars in the regions and we were able to recruit some members." He also implicated what he saw as a blind spot in the association's focus in terms of research questions and paradigms. "I must say," he added, "at least one geographic and cultural area was not concerned specifically in terms of the questions asked—and here I point to the Islamic world" (Mowlana, 1997).

This chapter tests the validity of Mowlana's suggested threefold explanation for limitations in IAMCR-MENA networking, even while accepting its logic that events in different parts of the globe could act as catalysts for wider

N. Sakr (✉)
University of Westminster, London, UK
e-mail: N.Sakr01@westminster.ac.uk

© The Author(s), under exclusive license to Springer Nature Switzerland AG 2023
J. Becker, R. Mansell (eds.), *Reflections on the International Association for Media and Communication Research*,
https://doi.org/10.1007/978-3-031-16383-8_25

membership but that differences of vision could stand in the way. This chapter therefore reviews IAMCR-MENA relationships in terms of meeting venues ("place"), influential scholars ("people"), and the approaches to media and communication research ("paradigms"), bearing in mind that each of these three dimensions evokes contested narratives in which developments both inside and outside IAMCR are seen to play a part. In the matter of conference locations, for example, the choice of Argentina in 1972 may have met a geographical criterion without meeting a political one, since the country was in the dying days of a military dictatorship that took power in 1966. As for people, Kaarle Nordenstreng, whose involvement with IAMCR began in 1966 and whose Finnish background gave him an advantage in terms of East-West diplomacy (Nordenstreng, 2013a), believed representation to be relatively wide. He lists Brazil, Egypt, India, Indonesia, Israel, Peru, and Uruguay among countries whose scholars were involved in establishing the association as a body with a "broad—even global—base, with institutions and individuals from all continents affiliated with it" (Nordenstreng, 2008, p. 229). With regard to the notion espoused by Mowlana, of an "Islamic community" paradigm not only distinct from but standing in opposition to so-called Western epistemologies (Schlesinger & Mowlana, 1993, p. 6), its implicit assumption of a "unified and ahistorical West as well as a singular East" has been challenged (Khiabany, 2006, p. 7). Mowlana has been critiqued for assuming that a "global fault line" exists vertically "between civilizations" instead of horizontally "between social groups in massively polarized societies" (Khiabany, 2006, p. 19).

It may be important to recall that individuals from MENA countries—Tunisia, Algeria, and Egypt—were definitely present in diplomatic maneuvers and intellectual debates behind IAMCR's relationship with UNESCO and associated calls for a New World Information and Communication Order (NWICO), linked in turn to ideas about a New International Economic Order (Pavlič & Hamelink, 1985). Those ideas prized autonomy and self-reliance for parts of the world affected by imperialism and colonization, as reflected in declarations issued at conferences of the Non-Aligned Movement (NAM) and the Group of 77 during the 1970s (Pavlič & Hamelink, 1985, p. 25). MENA involvement in foundational debates continued through the saga of UNESCO's 1980 MacBride Report, *Many Voices, One World*, drafted under scrutiny from "several IAMCR activists" (Nordenstreng, 2008, p. 240). What happened to those institutional, personal, and intellectual links with IAMCR thereafter? Relying on IAMCR archives and the anonymized recollections of both European and MENA veterans of the association, gathered in the latter part of 2020, this chapter retraces IAMCR-MENA relationships from the 1970s to the present day, bearing in mind that repression after uprisings in Iran in 2009 and Arab countries in 2010–2011, plus the rise of so-called Islamic State (IS) after 2013, has hindered international exchange in the most recent decade. It begins by exploring efforts to hold IAMCR meetings in the MENA region, goes on to consider the role of MENA scholars in the association, and then reviews the extent to which there has been a meeting of minds. Drawing on this evidence, it proposes reasons for the limited nature of IAMCR-MENA interactions.

Conference Bridge-Building and Safety Concerns

Because IAMCR conferences were held only biennially until 1990, the number of such events from the founding conference in Paris in 1957 to the virtual one in Nairobi in 2021 totaled 48. Of these, just three took place in the MENA region: in Istanbul in 1991 and in 2011, and in Cairo in 2006. Behind these events and others that failed to materialize is a revealing story of bridge-building efforts thwarted by military invasion and conflict.

The 1991 Conference is emblematic for having very nearly been postponed. Writing in the association's first official newsletter, rushed out in June 1990 in time for that year's conference in the Slovenian resort of Bled in August, Mowlana, then IAMCR Vice President, announced that an invitation from the Turkish Communication Research Association to host an IAMCR conference in Istanbul the following summer would be discussed in Bled (Mowlana, 1990, p. 8). However, the first days of August saw the forces of Iraqi dictator Saddam Hussein, for long supported by Western and Arab governments as a counterweight to the spread of Iranian influence, invade Kuwait, triggering a war in which a US-led coalition moved in January 1991 to reverse the invasion. In the next newsletter, dated February 1991, Cees Hamelink, IAMCR President at the time, announced a decision to "postpone the conference for the time being" because of uncertainty among members about traveling to Turkey (Hamelink, 1991, p. 3). Even so, the Istanbul gathering went ahead. Most of the 100 attendees were from Turkey, but IAMCR International Council (IC) members also convened for a swiftly organized reflection on media performance in the war that had just taken place (McKercher, 1991, p. 1). Twenty years later, Istanbul again hosted an IAMCR conference, at Kadir Has Üniversitesi, which coincided with uprisings across the MENA region. Thereafter, following a failed coup in 2016, Turkey entered a period of repression, triggering an IAMCR statement in support of Turkish academics who had been arrested and harassed, making an official IAMCR return to the country unlikely any time soon.

As Hamelink mulled alternatives to Istanbul in 1991, he mentioned that the IAMCR IC might meet in 1993 "in the Arab region," in combination with a "major scientific congress jointly convened by Arab colleagues and the IAMCR" (Hamelink, 1991, p. 3). Although the 1993 Conference eventually took place in Dublin, Cairo did host two IAMCR-affiliated events with an Africa focus in October 1992, one dealing with journalism training and another assessing implications of the African Charter on Human and Peoples' Rights. Behind these was the Kenya-based African Council for Communication Education, which also chose Cairo as the venue for a conference it organized in October 1993. But it took another missed opportunity in 2000 before a full-scale IAMCR conference eventually convened in Cairo in 2006. Mowlana (1997, p. 4), looking forward in his newsletter column to conferences in Glasgow in 1998, Leipzig in 1999, and Singapore in 2000, noted that Cairo had been "recommended in principle for the year 2000" but this had been "postponed at the request of the host country, pending further notification."

Plans for a conference in Tel Aviv in July 2001 were also called off and moved to Budapest instead. The word "canceled," pasted over a page announcing the event in a 2000 newsletter (IAMCR 2000, p. 41), obliterated a significant amount of hopeful preparation. This had been going on ever since the International Communication Association (ICA) met in west Jerusalem in 1998, prompting the Second Chair of the Israeli Communication Association, formed in 1995, to work toward hosting IAMCR in Tel Aviv. In the face of skepticism within IAMCR, the aspiring Israeli hosts urged the IC meeting in Leipzig in 1999 to respond proactively to what were seen at the time as improving prospects for Israeli-Palestinian peace. The Council's condition, that Palestinians should be actively involved, inspired elaborate arrangements, made through intermediaries, to bus up to a dozen coachloads of participants from their hotels on the Tel Aviv seafront to Ramallah on the West Bank, where Palestinians would host them for half a day. The conference plan survived renewed resistance from two Egyptians, including one on the IC, expressed at the IAMCR Conference in Singapore in 2000. But it did not survive the start of the second Palestinian uprising in September that year. Frank Morgan, writing as President-elect a year later, said Tel Aviv had been deemed "not safe." Without mentioning either the uprising or the shooting of Palestinian protestors that had triggered it, he referred to the killing of a "crowd of kids outside a nightclub, near the proposed conference venue" (Morgan, 2001, p. 4)—an incident that took place in June 2001, long after the Tel Aviv Conference had already been called off. A suicide bomber at the Dolphinarium nightclub killed 21 people, including 16 teenagers.

Safety was again a major concern for many IAMCR members when the association's conference took place in Cairo in 2006. The event began two weeks after fighting between Hezbollah and Israeli forces unleashed what Annabelle Sreberny-Mohammadi, then IAMCR Vice President, called "terrible violence" over "Lebanese and Israeli towns and villages" (Sreberny-Mohammadi, 2006, p. 1). Other reasons members had given for staying away included bird flu, heat, and a "renewed threat of terrorism" (Sreberny-Mohammadi, 2006, p. 1). Here the threat arose from bombings at the Sinai tourism resorts of Taba, Sharm el-Sheikh, and Dahab as well as Cairo, in the two years immediately before the conference, which had killed scores of people and injured many more, most recently in April 2006 (BBC News, 2006). There were also visa problems in Cairo, recorded in an IAMCR General Assembly (GA) motion denouncing the Egyptian government for not issuing visas to participants from several countries, including Iran and Nigeria (Prehn, 2006, p. 11). However, in contrast to the alarming macro environment, conference preparations had involved ground-breaking contacts at the micro level between the host institution, the American University in Cairo (AUC), and media departments at other Egyptian universities, including the Cairo University Media Faculty. These contacts were significant in the light of differences between US-oriented scholars at AUC and those prominent members of Cairo University Media Faculty staff, led by Awatef Abdel El-Rahman, who were known for attacking the alleged distortion of Arab culture and undermining of pan-Arabism as a political ideology by "anti-Arab imperialists" (Ayish, 2016, p. 479). Having sought to block the Tel Aviv Conference in 2000, Abdel El-Rahman, who had a place on the IAMCR IC for eight years from 1992, disagreed in principle with welcoming Israelis to the AUC campus, despite the Egypt-Israel Peace Treaty signed in 1979.

As noted earlier in relation to the conference in Argentina in 1972, MENA venues for IAMCR conferences were not the only controversial ones. The association met in Spain under General Franco in 1968 and in East European cities under repressive regimes. Its 2015 meeting in Montreal was the first-ever hosted in North America in nearly 60 years of the organization's existence, and the 2018 Conference in Eugene was held while a US ban on travelers from seven Muslim-majority countries was in place. Controversy also marked the second World Summit on the Information Society (WSIS), held in Tunisia, a MENA country, in 2005. Although not an IAMCR conference, WSIS was an important event in the IAMCR calendar, offering a platform to present its International Researchers' Charter for Knowledge Societies (see also Chaps. 16 and 18 in this collection). Ironically, although the kind of safety concerns experienced in Istanbul, Tel Aviv, and Cairo did not appear to preoccupy delegates in Tunis, safety to report freely from the summit was not guaranteed. The Rome-based news agency Inter Press Service reported an end-of-summit appeal to the United Nations (UN) Secretary General on behalf of the International Freedom of Expression Exchange (IFEX), calling for a formal investigation into the treatment of journalists by the Tunisian authorities, while the US delegation expressed "disappointment" over a lack of freedom of expression and assembly in Tunis (IPS, 2005). As a succession of reports on human rights and free speech across the Middle East testified at the time, similar situations would have arisen had WSIS 2005 been held in most other parts of the region.

"High costs" and "Dubious Benefits" for MENA Participants

IAMCR representatives have regularly reviewed the challenge of recruiting members in the Global South since the start of the 1990s, and efforts to redress international imbalances, at least in terms of nationality if not gender, date back before that. A numerically unsatisfactory situation with regard to Middle East members was revealed in March 1997, when Gertrude Robinson showed

(1997, p. 8), as part of a wider membership analysis, that there were just 27 individual Middle Eastern members out of a total of 605 for the association as a whole, and only ten associated with institutions out of 926. Ten years later, despite the 2006 Conference having taken place in Cairo, the ratios had worsened, with the Membership Committee counting only 15 individual paid-up Middle Eastern members of the association and no institutional members at all (Kivikuru, 2007, p. 21). Possible reasons for the low number were offered in a report by a ten-person Review Committee in 2000, which attributed a "lack" of members from "smaller geographic regions such as the Caribbean, the Middle East and Oceania" to several interrelated factors. First, development of both media and communication systems was lagging in those areas, along with media and communication research. Secondly, the "relatively high costs of membership and participation" were set against an estimation that "the benefits of membership for people from these regions" were "dubious" (IAMCR Committee of Review, 2000, p. 14). Costs may be prohibitive even in rich MENA countries, because membership subscriptions and conference registration fees are linked to research activity that may be inconvenient to authoritarian regimes and have consequently "never been a priority for supervisory authorities" (Ferjani, 2012, p. 104–105). Individuals may seek to achieve international recognition for research in humanities and social sciences but without institutional support (Ferjani, 2012, p. 105–106).

The impact of high costs and dubious benefits can be seen in the stories of MENA members who had places on the IAMCR IC between 1972 and 2004. It is widely accepted that the few dozen participants at early IAMCR meetings were "mainly from Western Europe" (Meyen, 2016, p. 96). From the early 1970s, however, that situation changed, partly driven by the shared desire of members from Eastern and Western Europe to internationalize, with Eastern Europeans reportedly keen to win colleagues from Asia, Africa, and Latin America over to "socialist ideas on how to educate journalists" (Meyen, 2016, p. 97) (See Chaps. 11, 12 and 13 in this collection). Nordenstreng (2008, p. 236) recalls that the Leipzig Conference in 1974 was attended by several prominent communication researchers from "as far afield as Colombia and Singapore, Canada and Lebanon," whose travel expenses were covered because they were on a UNESCO panel that was due to meet before the conference. The Lebanese researcher traveling to Leipzig was Nabil Dajani, thought to be the first graduate from the Arab region to earn a PhD in mass communication, obtained from the University of Iowa in 1968 (Ayish, 2016, p. 489). Dajani gained international visibility in the early 1970s through articles published in the journals now called *International Communication Gazette* (founded in 1955) and *Journalism and Mass Communication Quarterly* (founded in 1924). He served in UNESCO's International Panel of Experts on Communication Research from 1971 to 1975 and IAMCR's IC from 1972 to 1984, during which time he was close to James D. Halloran of the University of Leicester in the United Kingdom, Kaarle Nordenstreng, and Herbert I. Schiller of the US, who were elected President and Vice President, respectively, in 1972 and held these positions into the 1980s.

Dajani's involvement was affected and eventually curtailed by the Lebanese civil war, which erupted in 1975 and continued to 1990, and its impact on the American University in Beirut, where he worked. He was followed on the IC by a Cairo University Media Faculty academic named Ragia Kandil. Her nomination may also be attributable to UNESCO-IAMCR networking, through UNESCO's link to her cousin, a renowned Egyptian journalist. Hamdy Kandil, who started his career in the Egyptian press before it was nationalized by President Nasser in 1960, worked with UNESCO from 1974 to 1986, contributing to a UNESCO study on *Development of Communication in Arab States: Needs and Priorities*, published in 1985. When Ragia Kandil took her place on IAMCR's 28-seat IC in 1984, she was the only person from her region, even though Brazil, Kenya, and India had two representatives each. On secondment in Qatar at the time, she had an opportunity to contribute toward broadening IAMCR leadership but seems, from the records, for whatever reason, not to have taken it. She was elected to a five-member Nomination Committee formed at the June 1991 IAMCR meeting in Istanbul with the specific aim of implementing "IAMCR's desire ... to make its leadership more gender-balanced as well as geographically representative" (Méar, 1991, p. 19). Kandil was one of two women in the Nomination Committee, the other being its Canadian Chair, Annie Méar. When it finalized its slate the following year, the Nomination Committee revealed (Méar, 1992, p. 1) that Kandil "could not be reached for comments" during its meetings in May and June 1992, leaving the report to be prepared by just four members, of whom only Roque Faraone from Uruguay was from the Global South.

In contrast, Kandil's successor on the IC Awatef Abdel El-Rahman was a prominent presence at IAMCR events, which required lots of expensive travel to venues like Guarujá, Brazil, in 1992, Sydney, Australia, in 1996, Oaxaca, México, in 1997, and Singapore in 2000, where she contributed papers to Gender and Communication Section panels. Some observers assumed, given the limited budgets believed to be available to Cairo University staff, that Abdel El-Rahman was mainly self-funded. This may or may not have been the case, as EGYPTAIR and Cairo University, both at the time directly linked to government budgets, may have had transfer pricing arrangements that would offset the cost of fares for a university staff member of sufficient rank with the right connections. On the other hand, self-funding for conference attendance was reportedly not unusual among IAMCR members from outside Europe in that period, including for those in the US. Whether self-financed or not, Abdel El-Rahman's participation brought a level of international exposure for Cairo University media scholarship that has been rare since then. Most of her work, including a trenchant critique of so-called Zionist penetration of minds and political boundaries still quoted in anglophone references (Hudson & Iskander, 2014, p. 9), was published in Arabic. Nevertheless, for IAMCR purposes, she operated in English. She reported on textbook production and the source of educational materials for communication studies in the Arab world for an overview published in 1991 by the University of Tampere (Nordenstreng & Brown, 1998, p. 82, 89), and in 1993 was on the steering committee of a project established within IAMCR Professional Education Section to look at new perspectives in journalism training in Europe, Africa, and the Caribbean and Pacific areas. Abdel El-Rahman's presence at the IAMCR Conference in Brazil in 1992 is indicated by her contribution to the 4th MacBride Round Table which took place at the same venue immediately afterwards, where she spoke on NWICO-related issues, including "ethnocentric" reporting of the 1991 Gulf War and the failure of the NWICO framework and original MacBride Report to engage with issues of women and media (Roach, 1993, p. 13). It may be noted that Abdel El-Rahman's tenure on the IC coincided with that of Israeli scholar Dov Shinar, then based at Ben-Gurion University of the Negev.

When a new 29-person IC was elected in 2000, its two Middle Easterners were Magda Amer, another Egyptian from Cairo University, and Alina Bernstein of the College of Management Academic Studies in Israel. But, only four years later, elections to an IC slimmed down to half its previous size resulted in overwhelming representation from Europe, North America, and Australia, accounting for 12 out of 15 members. None of the other three was from the Middle East and nor, at the time of writing, had anyone from the region been elected from then on.

However, any account of IAMCR-MENA relationships over the decades would be incomplete without noting the Iranian background and identity of Hamid Mowlana, who held office at various levels through the 1990s. IAMCR records Mowlana's nationality as American. He arrived in the US in 1958, returned to Iran after completing a PhD at Northwestern University in 1963, and spent a short period editing the Iranian daily *Kayhan* but returned to the US in 1964, working at the University of Tennessee before moving to the American University in Washington in 1968 where he stayed until his retirement in 2007. Despite his location, perceptions of Mowlana among other IAMCR members were colored by his close association with Iran, reflected in his contacts and academic writing. Mowlana's chapter in *Triumph of the Image*, a collection he edited with George Gerbner and Herbert Schiller immediately after the US-led war on Iraq in 1991, is written from an Iranian nationalist standpoint: in it he declares that, were it not for the military and economic aid received by Iraq, "the Iranians would have been completely capable of not only overthrowing Saddam Hussein but also marching into the streets of Baghdad" (Mowlana, 1992, p. 34). Mowlana's name did not appear on the list of IAMCR signatories to a March 1994 statement against the *fatwa* issued by Ayatollah Khomeini of Iran in 1979 "encouraging the assassination" of the Indian-born British novelist Salman Rushdie (Carlsson et al., 1994, p. 9). Nor did it appear when the statement was reissued with more signatures three months later (Bakke et al., 1994, p. 7). Had he signed, Mowlana might have been less welcome in Iran when he attended the annual Press Festival in Tehran in 1995.

Contradictions between his view of IAMCR's mission and achievements under his presidency and those of veterans of the association surfaced in 1999 when he described an assessment presented by Nordenstreng in the same edition of the newsletter as "inaccurate and misleading" (Mowlana, 1999, p. 9). Such discord would hardly have helped to promote IAMCR membership among Middle Easterners, doubtful about the benefits of taking part.

Disparate Definitions of "Third World Perspectives"

IAMCR soul-searching at the end of the 1990s led to the formation of the Review Committee mentioned above. The soul-searching reflected differences and divergences in ways of thinking that may, alongside the logistical and membership issues this chapter has already addressed, help to put MENA representation in the association into perspective. The divergences can be considered in terms of political ideology and resulting differences of approach to the study of media and communication. Starting with ideology means reviewing the political outlook of key figures in the association in its early days, especially the two radical political economists, Herbert I. Schiller and Dallas W. Smythe, and their familiarity with conditions and scholarship in the MENA region.

Scrutinizing the work of Schiller, an American, and Smythe, a Canadian, who worked for a time in the US, undermines Mowlana's assertion (1997) that "other schools of thought, especially from the third world and non-western perspectives" found no place in an intense debate that got underway within IAMCR in the 1970s, between predominantly American "positivist, empirical, behavioral science oriented schools of communication" and "critical and interpretive sociological perspectives" rooted in Europe. There is, in fact, a strong coincidence of vision in the World Systems Theory espoused by Schiller, and that set out by the Egyptian Marxist and activist Samir Amin, widely seen as a pioneer of Dependency Theory (Kvangraven, 2019, p. 633–634) for works such as his 1976 book, *Unequal Development*. Amin identified so strongly with the "third world," that in 1973, he founded the Third World Forum (Kvangraven, 2019, p. 635). Born and raised in Port Said, he completed his PhD in Paris but returned to Egypt to work at the Egyptian Institute for Economic Management until he was forced into exile by Egypt's President Nasser because of his Communist Party membership (Kvangraven, 2019, p. 634). As prominent IAMCR member Ulla Carlsson has noted (2005, p. 207–208), some of Amin's later work expressly referred to media and communications monopolies. Even in the 1970s, however, Smythe (1977, p. 21) drew attention to Amin by name, linking Amin's theory of "accumulation on a world scale" with "Herbert Schiller's work on the relation of the mass media to the American empire." Schiller himself, meanwhile, argued that "cultural imperialism today" has to be understood in the context of a "world system within which there is a single market" whose "terms and character are determined in the core and radiate outwards" (Murdock, 2006, p. 222).

There are several reasons to believe that Schiller and Smythe and several of their IAMCR colleagues were attuned to Third World perspectives on world affairs. According to IAMCR's own notes on the prize it awards in Smythe's name, he—like Amin—had to leave his workplace because of resistance to his views. According to Graham Murdock (2006, p. 213), the "Third World was never simply an abstract concept" for Schiller because he had been posted to North Africa for military service in 1943, where, "after brief periods in Algeria and Tunisia, he spent two years in Casablanca," glimpsing destitution far beyond anything "he had seen in Depression America." As a result, Schiller came to realize that the poverty of the "dispossessed paid for the 'advanced' world's affluence," this being "the pivot of the imperial project" (Murdock, 2006, 2013). Nordenstreng (2010, p. 2) notes how growing manifestations of power by developing countries in the early 1970s worked "against the vested interests of the Western world order" and suggests that "polarization of the Arab-Israeli conflict" was a corollary to the "offensive of the 'underdog' against the West." A participant in several IAMCR conferences recalls that Schiller questioned Israeli occupation of Palestinian territory following the 1967 war and that the association held a vote on recognizing the Palestinian Liberation Organization (PLO) after the Arab League recognized it as the sole legitimate representative of the Palestinian people in 1976. This led to a PLO representative from Beirut being invited to the IAMCR Conference in Caracas, Venezuela, in 1980. Further investigation indicates that the invitation was accepted but without this cementing any lasting Palestinian-IAMCR connection.

It can be argued that 1980, the year of UNESCO's MacBride Report, *Many Voices, One World*, marks an endpoint for institutionalized MENA input into the NWICO project of reorganizing "existing communication channels" to "initiate a new international order of information"—to use the words adopted at the 1973 Non-Aligned Summit in Algiers and a 1976 symposium in Tunis (quoted in Hamelink, 1994, p. 198). Algerian presidents in the 1960s and the 1970s pursued a militant anti-imperialist policy of solidarity with other newly independent Third World countries, inspired by thinkers such as Frantz Fanon of Martinique who practiced psychology in Algeria and the Algerian jurist and diplomat Mohammed Bedjaoui. In Tunis, a key figure at the 1976 symposium was the Minister of Information, Mustapha Masmoudi, former head of the Tunisian Press Agency and a member of the MacBride Commission. The Commission also included Egyptian lawyer and deputy parliamentary speaker Gamal El-Oteifi. IAMCR activists pursued the MacBride Commission agenda of promoting a "more just and effective world information order" (Hamelink, 1994, p. 200) but the agenda was rejected by the US, which withdrew from UNESCO in protest, and by governments of US client states or those that saw effective information flows as a threat to regime survival. The fact that the old order suited some in the Second and Third Worlds as much as the First, affected efforts to change it in both IAMCR and the wider world. In the former case, resistance to creating a Political Economy Section came in part from representatives of Eastern European states who "did not want western leftists to challenge their monopoly" (quoted in Wasko, 2013, p. 5). In the latter, "national collaborators" in the Third World were to blame, alongside imperialists, for working against a NWICO by not "do[ing] anything at home, even if a lot could be done" (quoted in Nordenstreng, 2013b, p. 349).

The syndrome of blaming imperialists while not doing "anything at home" is seen in the way communication programs developed in the MENA region after the NWICO project petered out. According to one account of this development, the three decades from the mid-1980s to the mid-2010s "witnessed a dramatic rise in media education programs, scholarly outlets, professional bodies and international connections" but without this being "matched by genuine intellectual contributions" to global communication studies or "reflecting critical cultural features that define [the region's] unique identity" (Ayish, 2016, p. 488, 475). Some might say the emergence of an Islam and the Media Working Group in IAMCR in 2008 did provide an "indigenous alternative to Western-centric communication theories and concepts" suited to MENA scholars (Ayish, 2016, p. 480). However, a tendency by some of these scholars to conflate "Arab" culture with Islam in phrases such as "Arab-Islamic ethics and morality" or "Arab-Islamic traditions" (Ayish, 2016, p. 480) overlooks Iranian-Islamic traditions as well as those of other large Muslim-majority countries such as Indonesia, Nigeria, and Pakistan, which are outside the MENA region. It is also unclear how far self-professed exponents of an "Islamic" communication perspective have been prepared to push "political and moral issues relating to communication as a human right" (Ayish, 2016, p. 489) up the Arab or Iranian communication studies agendas. Mowlana, who sees Islamic community cohesion, based not on concepts of nation, political community, or free will, but on "divine rights" and the "will of Allah" (1994, p. 223–224), was challenged on his record vis-à-vis human rights at the IAMCR Conference in Montreal in 2015. Attendees were made aware of his post as official advisor to, and grantee of, the former Iranian President Mahmoud Ahmadinejad, at a time when the latter clamped down on all forms of expression and forcefully crushed Iran's 2009 Green Movement Revolt.

Conclusion

Close analysis of factors constraining IAMCR-MENA relationships shows how many of them operate beyond the reach of IAMCR itself or scholars in the MENA region. Even setting aside mounting geopolitical obstacles in the past 10 years, the previous decades saw repeated crises deterring attempts to hold international conferences in capitals with suitable host institutions. Two US-led wars against Iraq had serious long-lasting consequences for regional security, as did flare-ups of violence between Israel and its Palestinian and Lebanese neighbors, as well as suicide bombs and car bombs across the region. As for constraints on membership, these certainly included factors under IAMCR control, such as high costs and uncertain benefits. But the low priority attached to research by MENA academic institutions proved a wider structural issue impeding membership, arising from the authoritarian political systems in which MENA scholars work. When it comes to approaches to media and communication research, the authoritarian backdrop is also key. There was a time in the 1970s when both IAMCR and MENA thinkers and officials campaigned for a NWICO. That this campaign ended has more to do with changes at the level of political leadership in the US and MENA states dependent on US financial support than with any fault line said to exist between "western epistemologies" (Schlesinger & Mowlana, 1993, p. 6) and "Islamic," "Third World," or Global South perspectives. In the face of exogenous and structural obstacles, individual efforts to promote MENA representation in IAMCR have been an uphill struggle.

References

Ayish, M. I. (2016). Communication studies in the Arab world. In P. Simonson & D. W. Park (Eds.), *The international history of communication study* (p. 474–493). Routledge.

Bakke, M., et al. (1994). This is not just about Rushdie! *IAMCR Newsletter, 4*(2), 7.

BBC News. (2006, April 25). Triple blast rocks Egypt resort. *BBC News.* Retrieved 15 June 2022, from http://news.bbc.co.uk/1/hi/world/middle_east/4940506.stm

Carlsson, U. (2005). From NWICO to global governance of the information society. In O. Hemer & T. Tufte (Eds.), *Media and glocal change: Rethinking communication for development* (p. 193–214). CLASCO.

Carlsson, U., et al. (1994). This is not just about Rushdie! *IAMCR Newsletter, 4*(1), 9.

Ferjani, R. (2012). In search of the great absence: Cultural studies in Arab universities. In T. Sabry (Ed.), *Arab cultural studies: Mapping the field* (p. 101–122). I B Tauris.

Hamelink, C. (1991). President's column. *IAMCR Newsletter, 1*(2), 1–3.

Hamelink, C. (1994). *The politics of world communication.* Sage.

Hudson, L., & Iskander, A. (2014). Introduction: Publics, imaginaries, soft power, and epistemologies on the eve of the Arab uprisings. In L. Hudson, A. Iskander, & M. Kirk (Eds.), *Media evolution on the eve of the Arab Spring* (p. 1–12). Palgrave Macmillan.

IAMCR. (2000). Tel Aviv 2001. *IAMCR Newsletter, 10*(1), 41.

IAMCR Committee of Review. (2000). Proposals for statutory change. *IAMCR Newsletter, 9*(2), 10–15, 26–30.

IPS. (2005, November 18). WSIS: Private sector advances in public space. *Inter Press Service.* Retrieved 15 June 2022, from http://www.ipsnews.net/2005/11/wsis-private-sector-advances-in-public-space/

Khiabany, G. (2006). Religion and media in Iran: The imperative of the market and the straightjacket of Islamism. *Westminster Papers in Communication and Culture, 3*(2), 3–21.

Kivikuru, U. (2007). Membership committee report. *IAMCR Newsletter, 17*(2), 20–23.

Kvangraven, I. H. (2019). Samir Amin: A pioneering Marxist and Third World activist. *Development and Change, 51*(2), 631–649. https://doi.org/10.1111/dech.12562

McKercher, C. (1991). News media and international conflict. *IAMCR Newsletter, 1*(3), 1–3.

Méar, A. (1991). Call for nominations. *IAMCR Newsletter, 1991*(2), 19.

Méar, A. (1992). Nomination committee report. *IAMCR Newsletter, 1992*(2), 1–3.

Meyen, M. (2016). The IAMCR story. Communication and media research in a global perspective. In P. Simonson & D. W. Park (Eds.), *The international history of communication study* (p. 90–106). Routledge.

Morgan, F. (2001). Reflections in the murk. *IAMCR Newsletter, 12*(2), 4–5.

Mowlana, H. (1990). Putting IAMCR still more firmly on the map. *IAMCR Newsletter, 1*(1), 7–8.

Mowlana, H. (1992). Roots of war: The long road of intervention. In H. Mowlana, G. Gerbner, & H. I. Schiller (Eds.), *Triumph of the image: The media's war in the Persian Gulf, a global perspective* (p. 30–50). Westview Press.

Mowlana, H. (1994). Civil society, information society, and Islamic society: A comparative perspective. In S. Splichal, A. Calabrese, & C. Sparks (Eds.), *Information society and civil society: Contemporary perspective on the changing world order* (p. 208–232). Purdue University Press.

Mowlana, H. (1997). *IAMCR: A historical perspective* (Speech at IAMCR's 40th anniversary meeting). IAMCR Conference, Oaxaca, Mexico. Retrieved 15 June 2022, from https://iamcr.org/hist-perspective

Mowlana, H. (1999). UNESCO: High point in relations with IAMCR. *IAMCR Newsletter, 9*(1), 9.

Murdock, G. (2006). Notes from the number one country: Herbert Schiller on culture, commerce and American power. *International Journal of Cultural Policy, 12*(2), 209–227. https://doi.org/10.1080/10286630600813727

Murdock, G. (2013). Communication in common. *International Journal of Communication, 7*, 154–172.

Nordenstreng, K. (2008). Institutional networking: The story of the International Association for Media and Communication Research (IAMCR). In D. Park & J. Pooley (Eds.), *The history of media and communication research: Contested memories* (p. 225–248). Peter Lang.

Nordenstreng, K. (2010, November 19). *The New World Information and Communication Order: Testimony of an actor* (Speech). Colloquium on 30 Years of Communication Geopolitics, Paris, France.

Nordenstreng, K. (2013a). Promoting democracy and equality: Interview with Michael Meyen. In *Biografisches Lexikon der Kommunikationswissenschaft*, June 21. Retrieved 15 June 2022, from http://blexkom.halemverlag.de/promoting-democracy-and-equality/

Nordenstreng, K. (2013b). How the new world order and imperialism challenge media studies. *tripleC, 11*(2), 348–358.

Nordenstreng, K., & Brown, A. (1998). Inventory of textbooks in communication studies around the world. *Javnost – The Public, 5*(1), 79–89. https://doi.org/10.1080/13183222.1998.11008669

Pavlič, B., & Hamelink, C. (1985). *The new international economic order: Links between economics and communications.* UNESCO. Retrieved 15 June 2022, from https://digitallibrary.un.org/record/901?ln=en

Prehn, O. (2006). Report on IAMCR General Assembly. *IAMCR Newsletter, 16*(2), 10–11.

Roach, C. (1993). Report of 4th MacBride Round Table. *IAMCR Newsletter, 3*(1), 12–14.

Robinson, G. (1997). Treasurer's report. *IAMCR Newsletter, 7*(2), 6–8.

Schlesinger, P., & Mowlana, H. (1993). Editorial. *Media, Culture and Society, 15*(1), 5–8.

Smythe, D. W. (1977). Communications: Blindspot of Western Marxism. *Canadian Journal of Political and Social Theory, 1*(3), 1–27.

Sreberny-Mohammadi, A. (2006). Global jaw-jaw. *IAMCR Newsletter, 16*(1), 1.

Wasko, J. (2013). The IAMCR political economy section: A retrospective. *Political Economy of Communication, 1*(1), 4–8.

CHAPTER 26

IAMCR and Africa: Harmonizing Discourses of History, Hegemony, and Hope

Bruce Mutsvairo, Ylva Rodny-Gumede, and Colin Chasi

Introduction

An IAMCR study based on a 1986 to 1995 project that sought to unpack the regional relevance of locally produced communication textbooks concluded that there was an overwhelmingly Western-centric dominance of books that were used at African institutions of communication education, particularly those with a Francophone orientation (Nordenstreng & Brown, 1998). This domination was felt in other disciplines as well, with historian Alois Mlambo (2006, p. 19) claiming that this massively helped marginalize Africa "in terms of economic development" and that Western domination limited the continent's "capacity to participate fully in the global knowledge community." How has the long-standing dominance of Western scholarship fared over the years, particularly in media and communication studies? What role has IAMCR played in helping advance and preserve African media and communication scholarship over the years? These are the intricate, yet important questions we seek to uncover in this chapter.

B. Mutsvairo (✉)
Utrecht University, Utrecht, The Netherlands

Y. Rodny-Gumede
University of Johannesburg, Johannesburg, South Africa
e-mail: yrodny-gumede@uj.ac.za

C. Chasi
University of the Free State, Bloemfontein, South Africa
e-mail: chasict@ufs.ac.za

© The Author(s), under exclusive license to Springer Nature Switzerland AG 2023

J. Becker, R. Mansell (eds.), *Reflections on the International Association for Media and Communication Research*,
https://doi.org/10.1007/978-3-031-16383-8_26

The chapter does not present the history of African media and communication studies. This is *not* because the authors (who between them have well over 40 years of experience in this field) cannot attest to the paucity of work that historically locates the field in Africa. Indeed, we lament that this paucity is partially responsible for the absence of work that conceptualizes key concepts such as "communication" and "media" with a consideration for African experiences, perspectives, histories, and traditions. In this context, lamentably, Africans normally still have to "suspend disbelief" in response to the questionable relevance of the variously hidden or conspicuously present Western histories that form the diet of media and communication scholarship. With this as background, respectfully, our view is that it is impossible to do justice to the practices and allied *histories* (national, regional, continental, diasporic, institutional, biographical, epistemic, etc.) of African media and communication studies that need to be presented. We resolve instead merely to put forward observations—historiographic in nature—that bear on these histories in order to assert the need to read and write African media and communication histories. We assert that doing so can and should further the goal of humanizing the discipline.

Explicitly or not, deliberately or not, the received history of the field of media and communication studies (which is largely "legitimated as" having a Western provenance) is normally at work in all spheres of teaching, learning, and research. This has a bearing on how a discipline is institutionalized (Pooley & Park, 2012, p. 76). We note that a historiographic understanding—where histories of disciplines reveal knowledge-power relations—merits the attention of scholars in media and communication studies. We write from an *a priori* position which assumes that how human beings understand the world around them is in some part informed by how they understand the historical context in which they find themselves. This is also to say that the words and meanings that people use in their sense-making endeavors are informed by the histories they accept. For this reason, when peoples assume colonial histories (with their cultures, traditions, and norms), the epistemicide that this entails produces dynamics that vitiate such peoples' abilities to use disciplinary processes to meet their own needs (cf. wa Thiong'o, 2009).

It is important to acknowledge that we do not assume it is obvious who or what is referred to when one speaks of Africa, and/or of Africans (cf. Mudimbe, 1988, 1994). Similarly, when one speaks of an African scholarship, it is not clear who or what one is including (Janz, 2009; Appiah, 1992; Hountondji, 1983). When we speak of African media and communication scholarship, we accept ambiguity insofar as we are referencing scholarship about African practices (which may be written by people who are not themselves Africans), relating to the continent of Africa (which may include diasporic contributions), and so on. In dealing with this complex matter, we do not think it is useful to present an oversimplifying definition and, instead, we think it preferable to challenge the reader to imagine and question who and what Africans are, and what African scholarship entails. We do, however, take as our fundamental gripe and reason for writing the observation that there is a need to speak about how historically informed perspectives continue to "other" Africans in ways that ensure that universities' knowledge work replicates and perpetuates African marginalizations (cf. Ndlovu-Gatsheni, 2017).

We first reflect on the African context of media and communication studies and how IAMCR plays into the dynamics through which Africans are marginalized. Second, we look toward a reimagining of IAMCR-Africa relations. With reference to the African moral philosophy of *ubuntu*, we posit that there are humanizing possibilities for thinking about the contributions that Africans can and must be enabled to make to the field of media and communication studies and to IAMCR.

Attempting to capture the full extent of African media and communication scholarship and the more important trends and historical lines of thoughts in and from an African perspective in a single chapter is extremely difficult. To address the African context adequately would require an account of the history of the continent, including a discussion about how Africa and Africans have been influenced by centuries of slavery and colonialism and their influences on the politics, economics, and social fabrics of the peoples, practices, and artifacts of the continent. It would also be necessary to consider socio-cultural factors manifested in the linguistic diversity of the continent and to avoid eliding the colonialism that delineates African academic practices along Anglophone, Francophone, and Lusophone planes.

We hope, nevertheless, that the chapter will be read, not as an effort to essentialize Africans as "others" who are marked by purported differences from Westerners (Appiah, 1992), but in the spirit of insisting that African historical experiences can be generative of novel solutions to particular problems in ways that the whole world can benefit from, including those involved in media and communication studies at IAMCR. Indeed, to write about Africa as a country or even one region would involve falling back upon well-established tropes and stereotypes that are unhelpful for the purposes of furthering the field in ways that respect and honor African experiences, values, and interests. Where this chapter approaches African histories, this is so only to the extent needed to buttress our argument that more work needs to be done to embrace African experiences and to address African needs in media and communication studies.

The Field of Media and Communication Studies

Subject associations such as IAMCR seek to advance a discipline. For this reason, they are fundamentally tied to notions of what the discipline is. More to the point, they are bound up in their struggles for legitimacy and in the ways in which disciplinary centers of power are socially, economically, and politically constructed. When they call themselves international, this historically entails "a process of submitting institutions of the rest of the world" to sets of practices that center the West and marginalize the rest (Ndlovu-Gatsheni, 2021, p. 85). From this vantage point, even where such an association—as is the case with

IAMCR—expressly ties itself to notions of solidarity with marginalized communities, it finds itself invariably and ironically producing and reproducing global patterns of advantage and disadvantage. As an example, IAMCR was first hosted in Durban, South Africa, in July 2012—more than 50 years after the formation of IAMCR. The choice of Durban ironically perpetuated the colonially established dominance of South Africa as a "gateway to Africa." To add to and simultaneously vitiate the irony, for some Africans traveling to South Africa would have been more expensive than flying to some European metropoles. We are not interested, here, in further developing this particular example though we hope other scholars will develop, celebrate, and critically complicate our understanding of such events as the Durban Conference in the light of critical de-colonial considerations. Instead, we will discuss how IAMCR invariably perpetuates colonial patterns with reference to the relations that African media and communication scholarship has with IAMCR. In so doing, we argue for an ubuntu-centered approach (the concept is discussed below) to building a truly international media and communication association.

Studying communications and the media involves engaging with "real-world" phenomena, conceptually and often in reference to specific interests. For this reason, which is foundational to arguments for making the field a basis for a new form of humanities scholarship (cf. Miller, 2012), studies in this area are always (and at least) inter or transdisciplinary since "real world concerns" always escape the narrow confines of disciplinary praxis.

Addressing "real-world" relational and other considerations, it is to be expected that across different geographical or cultural contexts, there will be great variations and weights given to a variety of traditions of scholarship and their founding influences. Put differently, the real-world phenomena that media and communication scholars concern themselves with are necessarily approached from multiple perspectives by different people with a variety of interests. For this reason, the field of media and communication studies cannot, for example, have a singular history. Yet some scholars have postulated that the history of media and communication studies is almost exclusively North American and Western European (Pooley & Park, 2012; Demeter, 2018), despite it long being known that colonial legacies mark media and communication practices. This further reinforces our claim that there cannot be one history of the field of media and communication studies because of the diversity and multiplicity of colonial experiences among and within Anglophone, Lusophone, and Francophone countries in Africa.

When media and communication scholars are socialized into the discipline, the history and language of the concepts and ideas they imbibe are Western. It is in recognition of this that Ngũgĩ wa Thiong'o (1996), for example, becomes an undervalued conceptualizer of an African root of media and communication scholarship when he argues for African use of mother tongues as a way of re-centering Africans and their concerns. However, even the languages of media and communication studies reflect how Africans are embodied in colonial structures that deny the relevance of historical and other contextual factors

(Tomaselli & Shepperson, 2003, p. 136; Tomaselli, 2004, p. 218). This results in a situation in which the practice of media and communication studies, as with the general practice of science in post-colonial settings, must be regarded as racist (cf. Dubow, 1995). In this context, African scholars continue to grapple with the challenge, for example, of beginning to provide "a basis for placing indigenous communication systems at the center of oral polity within the global south" (Manyozo, 2018, p. 15.).

To recognize the systematic ways in which the field of media and communication studies excludes African experiences and concerns, we can consider how the field of health communication, with its plethora of theories (Melkote and Steeves, 2015), fails to recognize an African theory in response to the HIV/AIDS pandemic which inordinately affects Blacks in the Sub-Saharan region (Chasi, 2016). The significance of this failure is brought into sharp relief by the COVID-19 crisis which has rendered Africans unable to draw on contextually relevant theories to help shape their responses. This is the result of long-held ideas which view disciplines as constructs mainly of the Anglo-Saxon world, making Africa and indeed the rest of the Global South, a testing ground for Eurocentric theories, and thoughtless undermining and marginalizing of conceptual contributions from non-Western societies (Mutsvairo, 2018).

Epistemological Marginalization

When Africans are negated, denied, or othered by dominant scholarship which centers on the West, this also occurs in contexts of international academic and research associations that are established to overcome legacies of unjust marginalization. How academics and researchers participate in such associations, without this necessarily being the intention, often merely plugs Africans into global circuits of knowledge-power. There is an unequal balance in knowledge exchange not only between scholars but also in research when scholarship in and from Africa is often treated merely as area studies without the generalizability of European and North American scholarship. Thus, even where global media and communication studies scholars meet at an association such as IAMCR, Africans remain purveyors, or conveyors, or objects of Western knowledge, schema, and practices. Something of this is in evidence when one considers the dominant ways in which scholars in the field map and give standing to media and communication studies as a discipline and academic field of research. This is evident, for example, in discussions dating back to the 1983 *Journal of Communication* first special issue on the "Ferment in the Field" that did not concern itself with Africa. This is not to deny that African scholarship and contributions are sporadically recognized in such debates. For example, in the first issue, Wilbur Schramm (1983) pointed to the late appearance of communication studies in Africa, and Cees Hamelink (1983) averred that Western scholars are enculturated to study the world in ways that do not free them to envisage new points of departure.

Hamelink (1983) lamented how Western thought colonized others so that they fail to make contributions that reflect their unique experiences and needs. Building on this, one can agree with Ngũgĩ wa Thiong'o (2009, p. x) when he says, "Africa is headed by Wrong Heads"! Saying so foregrounds how even "senior African scholars" who engage with IAMCR and other similar international forums normally are led by Western others—even as regards facts, issues, and cultural and material concerns that relate to them and the African places from which they come. The point is that associations such as IAMCR should encourage and enable scholars to address new departures.

To speak of African scholarship is fundamentally to invoke a set of practices that is dismembered from everyday needs, experiences, and practices of Africans. As Mbembe (2001, p. 11), among others, recognizes, the knowledge of Africans that universities produce serves only to entrench the gross marginalization of Africans. Often without necessarily intending to do so, many Africans become hosts and purveyors of Western knowledge. However, African media and communication scholars must not see themselves only as victims because their contributions to the field are being widely acknowledged. Western universities are seeking partnerships with many African institutions, including those outside South Africa. Collaborations between African and non-African scholars, including diasporic Africans, are on a rise while European universities are beginning to teach courses that acknowledge Africa as a key player in the field. The London School of Economics and Political Science's postgraduate program collaboration with the University of Cape Town is a good example. The establishment of a new Chair in Media, Politics and the Global South at Utrecht University in April 2022 further underscores recognition of non-Western scholarship in media and communication studies in Europe. Media and communication scholars focusing on the Global South have also teamed up to raise epistemological concerns about the failure to acknowledge African contributions to the development of the field (cf. Mutsvairo et al., 2021).

Yet colonial injustices have not fully faded. Thinking about the state of dismemberment that characterizes African thinking and living, wa Thiong'o (2009, p. 3–5) avers that the burial alive of Waiyaki, a Kenyan chief who fought against colonial rule, powerfully symbolizes how colonial rule involves imbricating arrangements that simultaneously dispossess Africans and makes them disappear as people who have agency, dignity, and worth. It reflects how Western colonial rule systematically denies the presence and merits of the colonized by declaring, for example, that the lands taken are empty at the point of conquest.

If the above is correct, African scholars and researchers may find that attending IAMCR is tantamount to approaching a small-scale replication of the global relations of peripheries and centers. The common experience is of Africans submitting abstracts, being involved in communities of scholarship, and attending conferences without participating as equals. This is best illustrated through the lack of conference opportunities and hosting on the continent, the lack of African scholars in executive positions within the association, as well as the lack of African speakers and keynote addresses. For this reason, it is extremely difficult for many to look up toward their own world of needs. This realization may be understood if one recalls that a main motivating thought behind the Black Consciousness Movement in South Africa is to help Black people to "manage to hold their heads high" (Biko, 1987, p. 48) amid forces that work to make African thought marginal even for Africans themselves.

The burial alive of Waiyaki in land that was appropriated by colonialists symbolizes how land comes to serve colonial ends and to metaphorically bury the agency, needs, and worth of native communities. So too, immersion in Western streams of thought and concerns means Africans are dislocated from their own bodies of everyday interest—even when this happens in forums that explicitly aim to promote African culture and civilizations. Even critical scholarship that is offered up at forums such as IAMCR is penned in words and forms that come with colonialism and ends up being authored in ways authorized and produced according to the possibilities of colonialism and apartheid.

Associations such as IAMCR also offer possibilities for participation in global networks of thought that may otherwise be unlikely to materialize for individual African scholars. These possibilities are associated with the elaboration of the freedom with which African scholars and researchers can enable their communities to work democratically. For example, the authors of this chapter met through IAMCR and have become lifelong friends. This is not only anecdotal evidence of how IAMCR has impacted individuals, but an indication of how IAMCR has influenced the careers of Africans and of people who work in Africa, and of how it has become a meeting point for scholars. However, it is not cheap to access IAMCR. Despite paying a conference fee considerably smaller than that paid by their American and European colleagues, African scholars do not always have institutional support and most have to pay from their meager salaries, which is why many African media scholars have not heard of IAMCR.

We contend that participation in IAMCR networks is marked by ideal cultural production norms insofar as the most marginalized and oppressed (which typically includes Africans) are enabled to draw on resources, rules, and symbolic forms to make the most of human choices and values, thereby enabling individuals to become the most they can be. Africans therefore arrive at IAMCR for perpetual tutelage, and this ensures that Africans are presented as though they are unworthy to be trusted to make use of their own understandings, using their own methods, making their own theories—to act in ways that speak to their lived needs.

Summing up, Africans are DDIS'D peoples, even at IAMCR. This is to say that they are:

- Dislocated, marginalized, and alienated from their concerns and from the broader community of humanity that should build with them the conceptual grounds upon which better worlds can be imagined and enacted.

- Denied recognition as persons whose being is found in the world as "nothing else than a series of undertakings, that [are] the sum, the organization, the ensemble of relationships which make up that undertaking" (Sartre, 1985 p. 33). This is evident in the ways that the roles, agency, and histories of Africans are erased from how the field is theorized.
- Illegitimated as perpetual "others," who must always make cases for the relevance of their experiences, needs, frames, perspectives, methods, and theories, amid practices that consistently other them. It is in this context that Chasi and Rodny-Gumede (2016, p. 3) have felt compelled to contend that "if communication scholars are to break through the policed and disciplined insularity of present communication studies, they will have to act out known movements by which smash-and-grab burglars extract valuables from heretofore secure orders." In addition, Chasi and Rodny-Gumede (2020, 2021) have argued that innovation in communication and media studies requires the opening of the field to views and concerns that de-colonially center Africans alongside others.
- Silenced by all the epistemicidal norms through which disciplinary common conceptual grounds exclude African insights, methods, terminologies, and other schemas. Silence involves "a person who either feels unable to talk about certain subjects or emotions or is unaware of certain aspects of his or her history," and such silence can be seen as "a result of prohibition and policing" (Morrell, 2003, p. 44). The silencing of African scholars speaks to how their voices arise outside the boundaries of what is uttered and utterable in mainly Western scholarly languages, publications, and platforms—that include IAMCR. To speak of the silencing of African scholarship is to refer "to the absence of something which should be present" (Sifianou, 1997 p. 64). It is to recognize how even when Africans are present, their silence is, nevertheless, socially constructed by ongoing colonial modes of coding that backgrounds their expressions while foregrounding Western matter(s).
- De-throned, or simply denied sovereignty, by practices that insist that they may only have standing when they are negatively (re)presented as having the image of what the West is not. The coinage of "de-throning" as the denial of sovereignty helps to elaborate how African scholars may always experience insecurity and powerlessness vis-à-vis the apparent indomitableness of colonial regimentations that stand in the way of the possibility that their speech may be granted the dignity and worth that others are accorded. To lament how Africans are de-throned is to speak against how they are made instruments of systems of meaning that violently produce and sustain their otherness, even in contexts such as IAMCR.

The Era of De-colonization

Banda (2001) sets the history of the media in Africa across three major epochs, namely, the era of colonialism, the post-colonial era, and the era of globalization. We add a fourth which we call the "age of de-colonization" marked by the promotion and recognition of local solutions to challenges, be they local or global. For media and communication studies, this era has been dominated by calls for the promotion of local scholarship and pedagogies as evidenced by the ubiquitous wave of de-colonization in the Global South. Trying to understand how media and communication scholarship has developed and how it concerns itself with African realities is an imposing task. Partly, this is because globally, the discipline is comparatively young. It is also partly because the challenge for scholars is acute in relation to African scholarship which has largely been issued from Western programs (cf. Tomaselli, Mboti & Rønning, 2013). This has led to multiple calls for the de-colonization of African scholarship as illustrated by handbooks on the topic, for example—*Palgrave Handbook on Media and Communication Research in Africa: Reframing Ontologies* (Mutsvairo, 2018), *Decolonising Political Communication in Africa* (Karam & Mutsvairo, 2021), *Decolonizing Journalism Education in South Africa* (Rodny-Gumede, et al., 2021), and *Routledge Handbook of African Media and Communication* (Mano & milton, 2021), among others. The presence of these volumes strengthens a call for dialog between Western and non-Western scholarship which can no longer be ignored. Such a dialog can chart the way toward the discipline interrogating its received schema, facts, and concerns so that it works to grant justice and equity with dignity and worth in all aspects of research and pedagogy.

Calls for de-colonization are reverberating from epicenters in Africa and the Global South, and they are altering the research agenda substantially with a renewed emphasis on deeper and more substantial transformative scholarship. The de-colonization debate is also re-energizing discussions around inequities in the global knowledge economy. These debates are not entirely new since a scholarly "consensus on the need to internationalize media studies…in an era characterized by an acceleration of globalization processes" (Ndlela, 2007, p. 324; 2009) has existed for some time. However, just what "global" or "international" scholarship entails is unclear, and these internationalization notions rarely refer to theories of global or universal origin, diversity, inclusivity, or significance (Rodny-Gumede & Chasi, 2021), and instead, tend to refer to theory from the Global North. Rather than understanding the Global South on its own terms and despite calls to "'dewesternize', 'decolonize', or 'internationalize'" the field of media and communication studies, the Global South continues to be theorized from the vantage point of the Global North (Willems, 2014, p. 8). The result is that scholarship of the North, as well as the South, has "failed to acknowledge the agency of the Global South in the production, consumption, and circulation of a much richer spectrum of media culture that is not a priori defined in opposition to or in conjunction with media from the Global North" (Willems, 2014, p. 7). As Moyo and Mutsvairo (2018, p. 29) argue, the de-colonization of higher education and knowledge production is intimately linked to false claims of universality of Western knowledge and the inherent Western geo- and body politics of knowledge production. The point is that, as Chasi and Rodny-Gumede (2016, p. 695) state,

> deliberately or otherwise, the dominant Western scholarship of communication reflects Northern histories as though the rest either do not exist or only exist to the extent that this either aids or does not interfere with Northern doctrinal theorization, denying our common humanity, shared history, and future.

Marked Rise in African Media and Communication Scholarship

As for the history of media and communications research in Africa, the discipline has seen significant growth over the last three decades which is echoed in enrolments in journalism and media and communication programs in tertiary education institutions, albeit with enormous variations in the level of facilitation or distribution of resources among these institutions. The pattern generally follows the relative wealth of countries which, in turn, influences research productivity in the media and communication discipline as in all areas of the academy (cf. Lugalambi, 2009).

The growth of the discipline in Africa is also reflected through an increase in the number of scholarly journals in the field, albeit mostly based in South Africa—*Communicatio: South African Journal for Communication Theory and Research* (1974); *Ecquid Novi: African Journalism Studies* (1979); *Critical Arts: A Journal of South-North Cultural and Media Studies* (1980); *Communicare: Journal for Communication Sciences in Southern Africa* (1981); *African Media Review* (1986); *Communitas: Journal for Community Communication and Information Impact* (1995); *African Communication Research* (1997); and *Journal of African Media Studies* (2009) (Mano & Milton, 2021, p. 3). Preceding and parallel to the establishment of these journals, publications in the field have grown substantially. Whereas earlier research on the media in Africa was often written by scholars outside the continent with a heavy slant toward Anglo-American as well as French theories and methodologies that influenced the discipline in and from Africa to this day, there are more signs of indigenous theorization and insights (Mano and Milton, 2021, p. 5). In his discussion of media and communications studies in Africa and how it is taught on the continent, Tomaselli (2009, p. 13) concluded that the discipline is highly influenced by "where and when African academics have studied, and as many African scholars have obtained their degrees abroad, the African influences on scholarship have been minor." According to Tomaselli (2009, p. 14), those scholars who studied in the United States have been steeped in a largely positivist approach and, in contrast, those who studied in the then Soviet Union brought back an equally positivist approach steeped in Stalinist

Marxism, while scholars who study in the United Kingdom have tended toward "British" cultural studies.

African-born media and communication scholars from countries such as Cameroon, Ghana, Kenya, Uganda, Zimbabwe, and many others have made inroads over the last 30 years. Collaborations with scholars in European countries such as Norway, for example, helped Zimbabwe groom its first Black media and communication scholars, most of whom studied at the University of Oslo under Professor Helge Rønning and his colleagues (cf. Tomaselli, Mboti & Rønning, 2013). Since the 1990s, African media and communication studies has developed into a multifaceted and disciplinarily diverse field, which, while still dominated by Anglophone traditions and the English language, is disproportionately well represented by scholarly work from South Africa and Nigeria (Fair, 2014).

Given the histories of authoritarian rule and the fight against colonial rule, and for some of the newly independent states in Africa, the ushering in of former liberation movements into government and the restructuring of society, media and communication studies in the 1970s and 1980s tended toward the normative and toward research on media for development in the interest of promoting educational programming through public broadcasting, particularly, through radio (Fair, 2014). Parallel to this, critical studies focused on authoritarian government control of the media and on cultural imperialism through imported media content (Fair, 2014).

This is important research, but it has tended toward "area studies" and, importantly, studies in and from Africa should not be treated as such. As Waisbord (2015, p. 180) contends, a focus on a wider swathe of international contexts should not lead to the Balkanization of the field. Instead, as he says, a true internationalization and de-Westernization of the field will come from the "de-centralization" of theories and research agendas in ways that foreground globalized perspectives on questions from a multitude of media and political systems. From an African perspective, achieving this will necessitate a rethinking of current IAMCR-Africa relations.

Rethinking IAMCR-Africa Relations

From the foregoing, it may appear that we contest the notion of IAMCR and any other socio-sphere that involves conceptualizing some people in decontextualized and universal terms. Further, and indeed, we contend that local and grounded perspectives matter. In taking this position, we envisage IAMCR as a multiversal space in which no one is provincialized by confining particularisms and neither is anyone disembodied by impossible universalisms (Césaire, 2000, p. 84). We imagine IAMCR as a forum where all particularisms are placed in conversation with each other in a communicatively achieved democratic "flatland" marked by "the immediacy of interaction-mediated-by-(typically)-talk, in all its circumstantial situatedness" (Taylor & Van Every, 2000, p. 209). Importantly, we do so from the vantage point of the quintessentially African moral thought system of ubuntu which does not constrain "people's individuality and personhood" (LenkaBula, 2008, p. 383).

To not draw upon the experiences, knowledges, cultures, and innovations of Africans when thinking about how to reimagine IAMCR and the scholarship of its members is to miss the possibility of gaining vital insights from Africans. This is pitiable because Africans have developed systems of thought that are capacious enough to be of interest to those who would rehumanize global and local societies. For example, while grappling with the question of how to recover a humanity "dismembered, distorted, disoriented, [and] oppressed" (Ndebele, 2017, p. x, 2013) by conditions of apartheid and colonialism, Steven Bantu Biko founded the Black Consciousness Movement, which sought to counter the dehumanization of all of humanity (cf. Biko in Arnold, 2017, p. 55–56).

The African moral philosophy of ubuntu offers important insights into how peoples may enact ways of internationally communing as communities of researchers. This includes communing in spaces such as those constituted by IAMCR to enable each individual to become the most that they can be. In this regard, the African moral philosophy of ubuntu can be a valuable resource because of how it uniquely,

> recognises the rights and the responsibilities of all people, whether individual or collective. It promotes social and individual wellbeing and wholeness. It is a concept which attempts to describe the relationship of a person as being-with-others. It sets the limits or recommendations of what being with others entails or requires. It encourages persons to open themselves to others, to learn of others as they learn about themselves too. (LenkaBula, 2008, p. 379)

In other words, ubuntu anticipates, conceptualizes, enacts, and supports ways of communing through which people can learn to excel and generally produce relationships that enable individual and collective growth.

With the de-colonization debate emanating from epicenters in Africa and southern Africa and South Africa, African scholarship has emerged more prominently alongside a Global South emphasis, and equity and inequities in the global knowledge economy are being foregrounded. This, hopefully, will go some way toward countering the Western insularity that dominates the discipline and to, as Chasi and Rodny-Gumede (2016, p. 696) contend, recognizing that experiences of media development in the post-colony and the Global South are not only equal to, but also necessary for, the advancement of media and communication scholarship as a whole. Such a re-centering will take courage and will require IAMCR to listen to a wider array of voices and to be prepared to question some of its underlying assumptions about diversity and being international. This is a project that goes beyond the geographical locations of conferences and meetings and language diversification and translations.

As indicated above, subject associations such as IAMCR seek to advance a discipline, and they do so by engaging with scholars and through scholarship within a particular discipline. Apart from scholarly engagements through the annual conference held in different locations selected by an open "bid" to host it among members and their universities, IAMCR also provides a platform for collaborative research and a range of publishing opportunities through book series and the circulation of a "Call for Papers" in the field. Being an international body, the association is explicit in emphasizing that its strength is garnered from "the strong academic and professional experience of its members and their diverse geographical and cultural origins."[1] IAMCR boasts members from more than 100 countries across all continents. It also maintains links with other media and communication associations around the globe and seeks to advance global research collaborations.

African membership is comparatively low as reflected in data on conference attendance since 2007, with South African scholars and scholarship dominating. And as for the rotation of conference locations, the conference has only been hosted on the African continent twice, once in Durban in 2012 and once in Kenya in 2021 (albeit online due to the COVID-19 pandemic). Worse still, for the most part, conference attendance appears to be largely dominated by Anglophone scholars. The late Belgian scholar Marie-Soleil Frère, a long-standing IAMCR member, devoted much of her career to documenting the marginalization of Francophone Africa in continental media and communication research outputs. Her influential books, *The Media and Conflicts in Central Africa* (2007) and *Elections and the Media in Post-conflict Africa: Votes and Voices for Peace* (2011), bore testimony to this scholarly neglect. IAMCR, as a bridge-builder, has played a pivotal role in bringing African media and communication scholars to the world. Yet, IAMCR could do more to market Francophone African scholarship. There are many ways this can be done, including by encouraging non-Anglophone membership, by hosting the next "African" edition of IAMCR in a country such as Cape Verde or Mauritius (two countries with media environments that are free from repression), or by spotlighting research from non-Anglophone African countries.

As for local media and communication associations on the African continent and IAMCR, discussions have been limited. For example, the Southern African Communications Association (SACOMM) has not featured prominently as a partner for IAMCR. While the International Communication Association (ICA) has begun a process of engaging through regional hubs and conferences, such as the ICA Africa Conference held in cooperation with the East African Communication Association (EACA) in Ghana in 2018, IAMCR has not engaged in similar activities. In this context, it must be noted that more cooperation is needed between the African media associations such as SACOMM and EACA, which on a few occasions have held their annual conferences on overlapping dates, making it impossible for members to attend both conferences.

[1] https://iamcr.org/iamcr-profile Accessed 15 June 2022.

Importantly, we need to make sure that collaborations and the internationalization project within (as well as outside) the association entail a wider Global South interaction to create opportunities that contribute to wider debates on de-colonizing knowledge production in the field. This can be done by using the association as a platform and vehicle for building alliances with scholars in other parts of the world who are making similar arguments around inequities in knowledge production.

All in all, the approach taken by the authors of this chapter is not to pathologize IAMCR or any of its members. To do so would be unjust and it is important to show that the de-colonial imperative is not *only* directed at those that are deemed fit "to be corrected." From our positions on the margin, we do not speak of the de-colonial imperative being directed at those who are deemed "abnormal," for we know that we are those who have been marked "abnormal." Our view of embracing practices, including those marked by ubuntu, which dialogically builds more just societies, is a radically inclusive stance.

IAMCR mirrors and mimics global and other patterns of domination and marginalization. This may be observed in how Africans interact within and with IAMCR, even though the association gives voice to inclusivity and to aspirations for a world in which human rights and human dignity are granted to all. This irony is precisely why it is important for scholars to think carefully about and attend diligently to the de-colonizing of this bastion of scholarship. Many African scholars recognize the impact this organization has had on us, and IAMCR's importance, especially to early career scholars, cannot be underestimated. It provides a platform to interact and for dialog which is an important role, particularly when we consider the fact that being in the academy can be quite lonely.

The foundations are laid and IAMCR has made strides toward greater engagement with the Global South. It is interesting and important to recall that, as already noted, the authors of this chapter met through IAMCR and that their membership with IAMCR has fostered a close research relationship and friendship. IAMCR has also provided a platform for interaction among many African scholars and, recently, through the "IAMCR African Team" WhatsApp group created during IAMCR's conference in Madrid in 2019 which, at the time of writing, consisted of 50 members from across the African continent and beyond.

References

Appiah, K. A. (1992). *In my father's house: Africa in the philosophy of culture*. Oxford University Press.

Arnold, M. W. (Ed.). (2017). *The testimony of Steve Biko*. Picador Africa.

Banda, F. (2001). The media in Africa. In P. J. Fourie (Ed.), *Media studies: Media history, media and society* (pp. 60–89). Juta.

Biko, S. (1987). *I write what I like*. Heinemann.

Césaire, A. (2000). *Discourse on colonialism*. Monthly Review Press.

Chasi, C. (2016). Can HIV/AIDS communication theory make Rhodes fall? In B. Ngcaweni (Ed.), *Sizonqoba! Outliving AIDS in Southern Africa* (p. 157–168). Africa Institute of South Africa.

Chasi, C., & Rodny-Gumede, Y. (2016). Smash and grab, truth and dare…. *International Communication Gazette, 78*(7), 694–700. https://doi.org/10.1177/1748048516655731

Chasi, C., & Rodny-Gumede, Y. (2020). Innovation in media and communication studies: Reflections from South African academics. *Communicatio: South African Journal for Communication Theory and Research, 46*(2), 107–125. https://doi.org/10.1080/02500167.2020.1796728

Chasi, C., & Rodny-Gumede, Y. (2021). Towards a research agenda for African media and communication studies: Pathfinders must first know where they are. In Y. Rodny-Gumede, C. Chasi, Z. Jaffer, & M. Ponono (Eds.), *Decolonising journalism education in South Africa: Critical perspectives* (p. 73–85). UNISA Press.

Demeter, M. (2018). Theorizing international inequalities in communication and media studies: A field theory approach. *KOME – An International Journal of Pure Communication Inquiry, 6*(2), 92–110. http://komejournal.com/files/KOME_DemeterM2018.pdf Accessed 15 June 2022.

Dubow, S. (1995). *Scientific racism in modern South Africa.* Witwatersrand University Press.

Fair, J. E. (2014). Media and journalism - African studies. *Oxford Bibliographies.* https://www.oxfordbibliographies.com/view/document/obo-9780199846733/obo-9780199846733-0149.xml Accessed 15 June 2022.

Frère, M.-S. (2007). *The media and conflicts in Central Africa.* Lynne Rienner Publishers.

Frère, M.-S. (2011). *Elections and the media in post-conflict Africa: Votes and voices for peace?* Zed Books.

Hamelink, C. J. (1983). Emancipation or domestication: Toward a utopian science of communication. *Journal of Communication, 33*(3), 74–79. https://doi.org/10.1111/j.1460-2466.1983.tb02408.x

Hountondji, P. J. (1983). *African philosophy: myth and reality* (E. Henri & R. Jonathan, Trans). Indiana University Press.

Janz, B. B. (2009). *Philosophy in an African place.* Lexington Books.

Karam, B., & Mutsvairo, B. (2021). *Decolonising political communication in Africa reframing ontologies.* Routledge.

LenkaBula, P. (2008). Beyond anthropocentricity – Botho/Ubuntu and the quest for economic and ecological justice in Africa. *Religion and Theology, 15*(3-4), 375–394.

Lugalambi, G. (2009). Building an agenda for media and communication research in Africa. *Nordicom Review, 30*, 209–216.

Mano, W., & Milton, V. C. (Eds.). (2021). *Routledge handbook of African media and communication studies.* Routledge. https://www.routledge.com/Routledge-Handbook-of-African-Media-and-Communication-Studies/Mano-Milton/p/book/9781138574779 Accessed 15 June 2022.

Manyozo, L. (2018). The context is the message: Theory of indigenous knowledge communication systems. *Javnost-The Public, 25*(4), 393–409. https://doi.org/10.1080/13183222.2018.1463351

Mbembe, J. A. (2001). *On the postcolony.* University of California Press.

Melkote, S. R., & Steeves, H. L. (2015). *Communication for development: Theory and practice for empowerment and social justice* (third edition). Sage. https://us.sagepub.

com/en-us/nam/communication-for-development/book246160#contents Accessed 15 June 2022.
Miller, T. (2012). *Blow up the humanities.* Temple University Press.
Mlambo, A. S. (2006). Western social sciences and Africa: The domination and marginalisation of a continent. *African Sociological Review, 10*(1), 161–179. https://www.academia.edu/23254753/Western_Social_Sciences1_and_Africa_The_Domination_and_Marginalisation_of_a_Continent Accessed 15 June 2022.
Morrell, R. (2003). Silence, sexuality and HIV/AIDS in South African schools. *The Australian Educational Researcher, 30*, 41–62. https://link.springer.com/article/10.1007/BF03216780 Accessed 15 June 2022.
Moyo, L., & Mutsvairo, B. (2018). Can the subaltern think? The decolonial turn in communication research in Africa. In B. Mutsvairo (Ed.), *Palgrave handbook on media and communication research in Africa* (p. 19–40). Palgrave.
Mudimbe, V. Y. (1988). *The invention of Africa.* Indiana University Press.
Mudimbe, V. Y. (1994). *The idea of Africa.* Indiana University Press.
Mutsvairo, B. (Ed.). (2018). *Palgrave handbook on media and communication research in Africa.* Palgrave.
Mutsvairo, B., Borges-Rey, E., Bebawi, S., Márquez-Ramírez, M., Mellado, C., Mabweazara, H. M., Demeter, M., Glowacki, M., Badr, H., & Thussu, D. (2021). Ontologies of journalism in the Global South. *Journalism and Mass Communication Quarterly, 98*(4), 996–1016. https://doi.org/10.1177/10776990211048883
Ndebele, N. S. (2013). *The cry of Winnie Mandela.* Picador Africa.
Ndebele, N. S. (2017). The envisioned self (Foreword). In S. Biko (Ed.), *I write what I like* (p. vii–xiv). Picador Africa.
Ndlela, N. (2007). Reflections on the global public sphere: Challenges to internationalizing media studies. *Global Media and Communication, 3*(3), 324–329. https://doi.org/10.1177/17427665070030030402
Ndlela, N. (2009). African media research in the era of globalization. *Journal of African Media Studies, 1*(1), 55–68. https://doi.org/10.1386/jams.1.1.55_1
Ndlovu-Gatsheni, S. J. (2017). The emergence and trajectories of struggles for an 'African university': The case of unfinished business of African epistemic decolonisation. *Kronos, 43*(1), 51–77. http://www.scielo.org.za/scielo.php?script=sci_arttext&pid=S0259-01902017000100004&lng=en&nrm=iso&tlng=en Accessed 15 June 2022
Ndlovu-Gatsheni, S. J. (2021). Internationalisation of higher education for pluriversity: A decolonial reflection. *Journal of the British Academy, 9*(1), 77–98. https://doi.org/10.5871/jba/009s1.077
Nordenstreng, K., & Brown, A. (1998). Inventory of textbooks in communication studies around the world. *Javnost - The Public, 5*(1), 79–89. https://doi.org/10.1080/13183222.1998.11008669
Pooley, J. D., & Park, D. W. (2012). Communication research. In P. Simonson, J. Peck, R. T. Craig, & J. Jackson (Eds.), *The handbook of communication history* (p. 76–90). Routledge. https://www.jeffpooley.com/pubs/PooleyPark2012.pdf Accessed 15 June 2022.
Rodny-Gumede, Y., & Chasi, C. (2021). Decolonising media and communication studies: An exploratory survey on global curricula transformation debates. In W. Mano & v. c. Milton (Eds.), *Routledge handbook of African media and communication* (p. 107–125). Routledge.
Rodny-Gumede, Y., Chasi, C., Jaffer, Z., & Ponono, M. (Eds.). (2021). *Decolonising journalism education in South Africa: Critical perspectives.* UNISA Press.

Sartre, J-P. (1985). *Existentialism and human emotions* (Frechtman, B., & Barnes, H. E., Trans). Kensington Publishers.

Schramm, W. (1983). The unique perspective of communication: A retrospective view. *Journal of Communication, 33*(3), 6–17. https://doi.org/10.1111/j.1460-2466.1983.tb02401.x

Sifianou, M. (1997). Silence and politeness. In A. Jaworski (Ed.), *Silence: Interdisciplinary perspectives* (p. 63–84). Mouton de Gruyter.

Taylor, J. R., & Van Every, E. J. (2000). *The emergent organisation: Communication as its site and surface*. Lawrence Erlbaum Associates Publishers.

Tomaselli, K. G. (2004). First and third person encounters: Ecquid Novi, theoretical lances and research methodology. *Ecquid Novi: African Journalism Studies, 25*(2), 210–234. https://doi.org/10.1080/02560054.2004.9653295

Tomaselli, K. G. (2009). Repositioning African media studies: Thoughts and provocations. *Journal of African Media Studies, 1*(1), 9–21. https://doi.org/10.1386/jams.1.1.9_1

Tomaselli, K., Mboti, N., & Rønning, H. (2013). South-North perspectives: The development of cultural and media studies in Southern Africa. *Media, Culture & Society, 35*(1), 36–43. https://doi.org/10.1177/0163443712464556

Tomaselli, K. G., & Shepperson, A. (2003). State of the discipline: South African communication studies in the 1990s. *Communicare, 22*(1), 131–158. https://www.researchgate.net/publication/340845063_State_of_the_discipline_South_African_Communication_Studies_in_the_1990s Accessed 15 June 2022.

Waisbord, S. (2015). De-Westernization and cosmopolitan media studies. In C.-C. Lee (Ed.), *Internationalizing "International Communication"* (p. 178–200). University of Michigan Press.

wa Thiong'o, N. (1996). The allegory of the cave: Language, democracy and a new world order!: Lecture III of the Clarendon Lectures in English, Oxford, May 15, 1996. *Black Renaissance/Renaissance Noire, 1*(3). https://www.proquest.com/docview/215524534 Accessed 15 June 2022.

wa Thiong'o, N. (2009). *Something torn and new: An African renaissance*. Basic Civitas Books.

Willems, W. (2014). Beyond normative dewesternization: Examining media culture from the vantage point of the Global South. *The Global South, 8*(1), 7–23. https://doi.org/10.2979/globalsouth.8.1.7

CHAPTER 27

France: Complex Relations with IAMCR Marked by Significant Changes from the Mid-1960s

Armand Mattelart and Bernard Miège

Introduction

Reflecting on the relationship between French academics and IAMCR (then called the AIERI) more than 50 years after its birth and into its development requires an approach that must not limit itself to the organization's accounts of its own history and our own *bons souvenirs*.[1] This history will only become fully fleshed out if we do not restrict our historiography to what is immediate and, at the same time, work to broaden its scope:

- *Temporally*, by positioning it in the long term (which to us appears to be a period of 25 years or so, covering the middle of the 1960s until the early

[1] The English language version of this text was revised by Jeremy Shtern and his graduate student, Danielle Rudnicka-Lavoie. An initial review of the original French text was done by Norman Landry.

A. Mattelart
Paris 8 Université Vincennes-Saint-Denis, Saint-Denis, France

B. Miège (✉)
Université Grenoble Alpes, Grenoble, France

© The Author(s), under exclusive license to Springer Nature Switzerland AG 2023

J. Becker, R. Mansell (eds.), *Reflections on the International Association for Media and Communication Research*,
https://doi.org/10.1007/978-3-031-16383-8_27

1990s). In so doing, it is important to keep in mind that this approach unfortunately sets aside the first ten years of the association's existence. Though IAMCR was founded in Paris and its first President Fernand Terrou was French, during this period, it was almost exclusively devoted, at least from the French point of view, to teaching journalism and just a bit of mass media; and

- *(Inter-) disciplinarily*, by going well beyond the press or *mediatique* frameworks adopted at the time of IAMCR's creation in favor of a more inclusive approach that takes into account information and communication phenomena and their technological dimensions.[2]

This choice of adopting this broader vision is due to the fact that *a posteriori* we consider this period (let us say, from 1965 to 1990) to be essential and foundational. In any case, it set up what came next, the period that began prior to the turn of the century that is still ongoing. Thus, we do not see how we could explain current relations between the international association and academics in France without starting at this point of departure, in particular, given that so many French academics were, and increasingly are, specialists in the sorts of questions and issues that IAMCR began taking into account during that period (with a few significant differences which will be noted later).

But what characterizes the initial period prior to 1965? How are we justified in distinguishing it so clearly from the one we are about to deal with? It seems to us that we have to go back to the founding of UNESCO, and in particular to the United Nations (UN) Conference on Freedom of Information in March–April 1948, and to the claims made by information professionals at the time (most of them newspaper publishers) about the inadequacy of their governments' information programs and the advisability of inserting new programs of action into the perspectives emerging within the UN and UNESCO. In his PhD thesis, defended at the University of Bordeaux in 1991, Jean-Louis Santoro opportunely points out that,

> …they (the information professionals) will succeed in bringing five major approaches to fruition:
>
> 1. An agreement on the importation of educational, scientific, or cultural objects;
> 2. Creation of the International Press Institute;
> 3. The reopening of the IFP (the French Press Institute);
> 4. The creation of the Strasbourg International Centre for Higher Education in Journalism;
> 5. The creation of the IAMCR-AEIRI effective in 1957. (Santoro, 1991)

[2] For additional background, see Mattelart and Mattelart (1992, 1998) and Miège (1995, 1989a, 1989b).

This framework would remain in place throughout the 1940s and the 1950s. But in our view, these priorities were supplanted by other perspectives by the 1960s. We place these perspectives at the center of our contribution. However, we do not do this without some difficulty, as both of us—in our own ways and sometimes on the front lines—have been actively involved in this over the course of this period (with the exception of its beginning). This obviously does not guarantee us sufficient methodological distance. But this trait is certainly shared by other authors of this book; and it does not prevent us from making our case through the articulation of a series of questions to which we provide the beginnings of answers.

Such issues are best declared upfront; they are the result of the interplay of a series of elements which seem to us to interact to shed light on what the relationships were like, from the French perspective, between IAMCR and potentially interested academics. We will first mention these elements, and then see how they intervened and how they played a more or less decisive role:

- The proximity, not only geographical, to UNESCO headquarters;
- The proposal of intellectual productions and theories related to the field, whose diffusion has been more or less globalized;
- The restructuring of French universities after the events of May–June 1968;
- The pronounced bipolarization of the French political scene;
- Interest in (and/or strong opposition to) the issues envisaged in the framework of New World Information and Communication Order (NWICO); and
- Finally, the emergence and growth of significant innovation in information and communication technologies.

The role played by eminent French administrative and intellectual personalities in the creation of UNESCO and their role in the first years of IAMCR's operation, the location of its headquarters in Paris, as well as the close links forged with the organization since its founding in Paris in 1957, all suggest what could be described as a privileged relationship between UNESCO and France. Traces of this vision can still be found in diplomatic circles and it is present among many foreign colleagues who observe that French people, whether as managers or civil servants, are still quite recognizable among the staff. But this vision is deceptive and even illusory. For example, despite successive relaunches and attempts to boost French participation, the French Commission for UNESCO has never succeeded in federating French participation across the various fields of competence of the international organization and in ensuring that the stakeholders on the ground are aware of and engaged in UNESCO monitoring and programming.

In other words, French academics specializing in information and communication (and this is also the case in other fields) are largely unaware of UNESCO's activities, even though the organization is located in Paris and

French people are involved in its management and administration. This disconnect seems to have only increased over time. It does, however, help to explain why relations with AIERI-IAMCR did not develop much, despite the fact, as we shall discuss below, that they were in close proximity on two separate (if difficult to compare) occasions: in the period up until 1965, during the debates over freedom of information (essentially, of the press) and in the 1970s during the debates on the NWICO.

Intellectual and Theoretical Proposals

When UNESCO was founded in 1946, the French delegation refused to adopt the terms "communication" and "means of communication" introduced by the US delegation. The French government of the time felt that the meaning of these terms was in sharp contrast to the legal, cultural, and political traditions of France and that this language was a reflection of the mass dissemination practices of a society with a high level of technological development. The conception of the State, public service, culture, and national identity was what separated the French tradition from that of the United States (US). For more than 20 years, until the 1970s, French representatives instructed UNESCO interpreters to use the terms "information" and "means of information" instead of communicational vocabulary. The word "communication," they felt, implies a dialogical and reciprocal process. "Information," on the other hand, implies the "one-way vertical delivery of an undiversified message, produced by few to anonymous recipients rather than exchange with them" (d'Arcy, 1983).

This terminological dispute explains why the same non-governmental research organization authorized in 1957 to be represented at UNESCO still bears different names—for French speakers: *Association Internationale des Etudes et Recherches sur l'Information* (AIERI); for English speakers: *International Association for Mass Communication Research* (IAMCR); since 1996, *International Association for Media and Communication Research* and, for Spanish speakers: *Asociación Internacional de Estudios en Comunicación Social* (AIECS).

In reality, this battle of words (and necessarily of the concepts that they underlie) already had a precedent. When radio and cinema began to flourish at the end of the 1920s, the term "mass communication" had become a problem in continental Europe, to the point that researchers preferred the term "public communication," justifying the use in this way:

> This term implied more than merely the activities of the mass media. Because public communication is public in the sense of excluding no one from its messages, it follows that any number of people can become receivers; such a group of people may or may not be call a 'mass', depending on the circumstances. (Stappers, 1983, p. 142)

In 1974, Raymond Williams, in turn, tried to move away from the systematic use of "mass communications": "It is a term which seems to have got into every language and into the most diverse schools, which describes and too often predicts departments and research programs and conferences, and which it is time to bury" (Williams, 1974, p. 22).

The journey of information and communication sciences toward institutional recognition has been long and chaotic. Initially, there was only the Centre d'Etudes Scientifiques de la Presse, created in 1937, and attached to the University of Paris. It closed during World War II and resumed its activities in 1947, and then was renamed the Institut Français de Presse (IFP) in 1951. In 1957, it became a research and teaching institute. At that time, its Director Fernand Terrou (1905–1976) was elected President of IAMCR for two years. As of 1962, as an information lawyer, he had rejected the Anglo-Saxon term "mass communications," in a small, dense book entitled *L'Information*, (Terrou, 1962). Later, when he penned *Histoire de la Presse* with Pierre Albert, he introduced himself as "Director of the French Institute of Press and *Information Sciences*" (Terrou & Albert, 1970–1974).

In November 1945, the first Congress of the National Federation of the French Press used the term "Instruments of culture" to summarize the function of "the various means of information, the press, the cinema and sound and visual broadcasting." During the long journey toward legitimization, collective representations of the field of communication and information have often found themselves torn between a technological tradition and a dominance of aesthetics of culture and the weight of literary tradition. This is one of the features of the specificity of French social training, which is both its strength and its weakness. Its strength: in the 1990s, France argued in favor of a policy based on the "cultural exception" of "products of the mind" as a principle of public regulation of market logic, in the words of President François Mitterrand. Its weakness: by giving priority to the cultural dimension, gaps became wider. The French tradition has been slow to recognize and identify the challenges of a culture that is increasingly linked to technology, industry, and the market, all of which are logically linked to the supranational framework. The delay in the development of the audiovisual system is also not unrelated to the precedence of the education system as a place of socialization and construction of the general will (Institut national de l'audiovisuel, 1999). Thus, in 1962, when 82 percent of British households were equipped with a television set, France was at the bottom of the rankings of European Union countries with 27 percent, far behind the Netherlands (50 percent) and Federal Germany (41 percent). The same deliberate pace of implementation can also be seen in terms of telephone equipment. For a long time, the national administration considered telecommunications to be a non-priority sector (Lauraire, 1987). It was not until the beginning of the 1980s that the gap was closed. The lack of studies on the media at that time contrasts with the number of studies on education as a reproducer of social relations (Bourdieu, 1979; Bourdieu & Passeron, 1963, 1970; Baudelot & Establet, 1971).

The research is quantitatively insufficient and focuses on reductive aspects of the field of knowledge on communication, largely inspired by linguistic, psycho-sociological, or cybernetic approaches. Research on the press is dominated by a professional communications perspective which has dodged any question on citizens' freedom of expression and democracy in the media, escaping to a problematic exclusively centered on the freedom for professionals to do their job well. This type of research, therefore, does not question the status of journalistic techniques but rather endorses the conception of journalism, not as a social practice, but as a transparent vehicle. In addition to this professional communications perspective that is in symbiosis with the dominant mode of media operation, there is a lack of research on the economy and the management of communication systems made difficult by the lack of transparency of information in the world of information.

The absence of the transnational dimension and the historical perspective has long been a recurrent feature of communication approaches. This is highlighted in the report *Technology, Culture and Communication* commissioned by the Minister of Research and Industry (Mattelart & Stourdzé, 1985; Carey, 1975). However, this deficiency does not only concern the field of communication, as is shown by the observations made in other reviews on the state of the humanities and social sciences in France carried out in 1981 under the chairmanship of the anthropologist, Maurice Godelier. Thus, in the sociological section of the latter report, Jean-Claude Passeron spoke of the "hexagonalism of French sociology" and pointed out the characteristic "hole" in knowledge about "cultural areas." According to the sociologist of culture, the most striking lack being in the areas of the North American, the Muslim and/or Arab world, and Northern Europe (Passeron, 1982, p. 202). In the section devoted to historical disciplines, the historian Michel Vovelle insisted on the "great misery of non-European histories, whether in the United States or in the Third World, despite brilliant exceptions." He also pointed out that "certain sectors of historical science have been the subject of the same acknowledged abandonment, such as the history of science" (Vovelle, 1982, p. 258).

However, French research had made an early start in taking into account the global dimension of communication. At the dawn of the twentieth century, at a time when the notions of "globalism" (worldism) and "internationalization" applied to communication flows were already emerging historically, Gabriel Tarde (1843–1904), the precursor of social psychology, had already studied the formation of "international audiences," thanks to the accelerated circulation of major newspapers such as *Times* and *Le Figaro* (Tarde, 1901). This experience had even inspired the research of the Chicago School, in particular, that of Robert Ezra Park (1864–1944) on journalism, crowds, and audiences (1938, 1955).

Jacques Kayser, a founding member of IAMCR and deputy to Fernand Terrou since 1957, undertook one of the rare analyses on the international circulation of information in the early 1950s. The most famous study by this Director of Research at IFP, who died in 1963, is the comparative analysis he carried out for UNESCO on the treatment by 17 daily newspapers with large circulation in different countries of a week's worth of news about foreign countries, published under the title *Une semaine dans le monde* (A Week in the World) (1953). This study then served as a model for research. The *Centro internacional de estudios superiores de periodismo en América Latina* (CIESPAL), set up in Quito in 1959 by UNESCO to promote the development of research work on "journalism," played a central role in disseminating the method (Kayser, 1953, 1963).

In 1960, the *Centre d'Etudes des Communications de Masse* (CECMAS) was created within the *Ecole Pratique des Hautes Etudes, VIe section: Sciences économiques et sociale.* The following year, the Centre acquired a journal: *Communications.* This Centre represents the first serious attempt in France to create a research environment and a research problem in communication. The sociological approach is represented by Edgar Morin (1962) and Georges Friedmann (1966), Director of the Centre. The socio-semiological analysis was led by Roland Barthes and, for cinema analysis, Christian Metz (1968–1972). It was at this time that the European Critical Project was being built both by the founders of the Centre of Contemporary Cultural Studies (CCCS) at the University of Birmingham and by the pioneers of socio-semiotics at the University of Bologna, where Umberto Eco and Paolo Fabbri taught (Mancini & Wolf, 1990). Structural linguistics played a leading role around CECMAS, where Jean Baudrillard (1972), Algirdas Julien Greimas, Julia Kristeva, Violette Morin, Tzvetan Todorov, and the Argentinian, Eliseo Verón, among others, gravitated. It all began in 1950 when the anthropologist Claude Lévi-Strauss became acquainted with the theories of Roman Jakobson during his forced exile in the US during World War II and presented the new science of language as the unifying and interdisciplinary paradigm of a "science of communication." "By associating itself more and more closely with linguistics, to constitute one day with it a vast science of communication," he proposed, "social anthropology can hope to benefit from the immense perspectives open to linguistics itself, through the application of mathematical reasoning to the study of communication phenomena" (Lévi-Strauss, 1950, translated, p. 36–37). This project (a multidisciplinary perspective) was certainly received with skepticism by the historian Fernand Braudel, who objected that it had forgotten the long term in favor of a "race to the present" (Braudel, 1958). But in the 1960s, structural linguistics became common sense and established itself as the dominant science until the end of the 1970s. It gave rise to the first analyses of media texts. Semiologists devoted themselves to "messages," isolating themselves in the text (the "corpus") by ignoring the user subject and the context of transmission and reception. It was believed that power was housed in the structure of the text. This first-generation of semiology tracked down latent contents, second meanings, connotations, in short, ideology or "mythologies," according to the title of one of Roland Barthes' seminal books. At the time, the concept of ideology had been underpinned by the theories of power formulated mainly by the sociologist Pierre Bourdieu on the reproduction of social inequalities through the school apparatus and cultural practices (e.g., photography) and by the philosopher Louis Althusser on the ideological apparatus of the state, of which the media were one component.

The influence of CECMAS, and more particularly, the work of Roland Barthes' team, has reached far beyond the borders of France. On the other hand, while there were many exports of "French theory," there were very few imports at the time. Thus, while *Cultural Studies* and the journal *Screen* were replete with the many sources of this theory, the reverse was not true (Robins, 1979). This one-way flow of internationalization explains why the major works of Raymond Williams, a major figure in Cultural Studies, took longer to be translated into French. Only one excerpt from *The Country and the City* was published in 1977 in the journal *Actes des sciences sociales* (Williams, 1977), edited by Pierre Bourdieu. In a collection he directed, the French sociologist published *The Uses of Literacy*, a classic by Richard Hoggart (1957), another founding member of the Birmingham Centre 13 years after the original edition. Between 1960 and 1980, when Roland Barthes died, CECMAS changed its title twice—in 1974, it became the Centre for Transdisciplinary Studies: Sociology, Anthropology, Semiology (CETSAS); in 1979, the word "Semiology" was deleted and the term "Politics" was substituted (CETSAP). In 1975, the French Commission of UNESCO invited Georges Friedmann to join the *Groupe de réflexion sur le concept de droit à l'information*, a working group composed of Fernand Terrou, Hubert Beuve-Méry, Director of the newspaper *Le Monde*, and Claude Bellanger, President of the International Federation of Newspaper Publishers. On 15 November 1977, George Friedmann died suddenly in Paris.

We cannot fail to point out the contributions of other researchers, outside the academic world, who are beginning to reflect on the new technological environment. Thus, as early as 1954, Jacques Ellul (1912–1994), in *La Technique ou l'enjeu du siècle* (1954), foresaw the importance of the technical myth. He explored it in greater depth in 1977, in his work *Le Système technicien*. In 1962, he tackled the commonly accepted assertion that one can easily distinguish between information and propaganda, considering information as the condition for the existence of propaganda. He shows that propaganda is not limited to psychological warfare but encompasses public relations, advertising, and communication (Vitalis, 2006). He insists on the fact that technology, which has gone from the status of tool to one of creator of an artificial environment, has now become a "system" through the inter-technical connection made possible by computers. According to him, the imperative was to reflect on the function of social regulation that it now assumed. In this way, he converged with Henri Lefebvre (1901–1991), who never ceased to refute the link between information technology and the construction of a society managed by a "new species" that wanted to be and considers itself global and which reduced what it touched, and above all, the contradictions—the "cybernanthrope," no doubt the "last of men" announced by Nietzsche (Lefebvre, 1967). As Henri Lefebvre noted in 1978, according to the "formidable ideology of communication" coming directly from the US and indirectly from the world technocracy, communication, information, and knowledge would merge to the point of convergence.

Régis Debray's ambitious project, which was actually little recognized within the universities, laid the foundations of a new science, "general mediology," a product of another generation. He announced this in *Le Pouvoir intellectuel en France* (1979) and developed it in his *Cours de médiologie générale* (1991). His analysis of the intellectual considering their own function of *transmission* and their function as an officiant of the apparatuses of transmission was the starting point for this global theory of mediology which sought to establish a—

> systematic correlation between symbolic activities on the one hand: ideology, politics, culture on the one hand, and the organisational forms and systems of authority induced by this or that mode of production, archiving and transmission of information on the other.

By taking up the intuitions of Marshall McLuhan, Régis Debray contributed to breaking a postulate inherited from the culture of the "typographic man"—the priority of content over form—by insisting that the medium itself determines the character of what is communicated and leads to a new type of civilization. Refraining from exalting technical determinism, the mediologist wanted, above all, to bring out "the objective determinations of the apparatuses of thought," as demonstrated by his *Cours de médiologie générale* (1991, p. 77).

It was not until the mid-1970s that communication sciences really began to enter the university curriculum (De la Haye & Miège, 1978). The creation of the Committee for Information and Communication Sciences, which organized several meetings and colloquia, and especially which founded the 52nd section of the University Advisory Committee in 1975, are signs of a slow emergence (Boure, 2002).

The French university system is certainly original; among the characteristics that still clearly differentiate it from the systems of many other countries, we highlight:

- The national character of the vast majority of degrees;
- Recruitment of teacher-researchers according to common rules and their remuneration within the framework of the state civil service; and
- The financing from the State Budget of a part, still significant but in reduction, of operating and investment expenses.

Over the last few decades, these and other aspects have often undergone profound changes, particularly with regard to the management autonomy of institutions and their own initiatives in the provision of training, which has led to a rather unequal structuring of institutions. However, the most significant changes are already long-standing, dating back to the 1960s and 1970s. And some of them are of direct concern to us: the organization of teaching of course, the activities of the various categories of teacher-researchers, and their collaboration as well as the internal workings of institutions, but also the range of courses on offer and the organization of subjects, which vary greatly from one subject to another, with some undergoing profound changes and even innovations, while others continue as before.

Some disciplines have therefore undergone major changes and have even been the site of real advancement: this is particularly the case for information and communication. While there were only a few disciplines before the protest movement of May–June 1968, essentially in undergraduate technology studies (journalism, documentation, book studies, etc.), they steadily multiplied in the following two decades despite the lack of resources allocated to them and the open reticence of representatives of long-"established" disciplines. Gradually, they were instituted in more than half of the universities, starting with the most recognized ones, which included the majority of students. And quite quickly, they have taken in far more students than the traditional disciplines, while at the same time, they have managed to avoid being overwhelmed by the strong, and sometimes very strong, demand for these programs from new students. And if we look at the number of tenured professors, information and communication are now among the top disciplines in the humanities and social sciences, even though they continue to be under-resourced and rely on the services of non-tenured and qualified professionals (for teaching in connection with professional specialties).

It is fundamental to note that in spite of proven reluctance and resistance and the acknowledged lack of resources, the discipline of information and communication has succeeded in being implemented in French universities, while offering a very varied range of training courses from undergraduate to postgraduate studies, without the need for national regulations, and therefore made extensive use of specific initiatives taken by the institutions. This history is quite particular, at least in the human and social sciences, and it has even given rise to some research work that is little or poorly known by many current teacher-researchers. And the discipline of Information and Communication Sciences (*Sciences de l'information et de la communication*, SIC), which has gradually emerged as a discipline after having been an interdisciplinary grouping, has always had, and still has, detractors and opponents (who, for example, are now advocates of the "digital humanities").

What do the above considerations have to do with the relations that French academics have, or do not have, with IAMCR-AIERI? In our opinion, three distinct aspects can be deduced from this and merit being highlighted:

- The emergence (as mentioned above) of the new discipline *sciences de l'information et de la communication* (SIC), and its progressive structuring, as well as the weight of its specialties and professional courses at the undergraduate and graduate levels in this structuring, which constitutes a strong mark of what French university courses in information and communication have been and still are. Not only does this clearly differentiate them from those that preceded them (essentially of a legal-political nature), but it also distinguishes them from generalist courses of cultural or theoretical training, based on communication theories;

- The autonomy of the information and communication sciences (in France: SIC) has been built at the cost of significant efforts in the field of research and doctoral training, in order to convince both the host universities and the national evaluation bodies of the solidity of the foundations of the SCIs;
- Finally, the fact that the careers of teacher-researchers in France are the responsibility of the State civil service, in terms of both entrance examinations and career development, despite the growing role of institutions, has probably had the effect of diverting both young PhDs and experienced teacher-researchers from participating in the activities of an international "generalist" association such as IAMCR-AIERI. In building up a reputation, priority is given to journals and books disseminated within the national framework, even though during this period international exchanges have multiplied and the knowledge of foreign theories, themes, and methodologies has actually increased, as have publications in English.

Throughout the period that interests us, these three aspects have played a strong role but cannot be put on the same level. Clearly, participation in the activities of IAMCR-AIERI being little recognized in the advancement of careers of teacher-researchers working in French universities has never been a determining factor. For some, their interest was mainly limited to the activity of one section, corresponding to their political-scientific interests, but in this respect their practice differed little from following the activities of many sectoral "groupings," for example, linked to journals. This explains why only a few, often advanced researchers, were attentive to the international association's offer of intellectual exchange and debate. Finally, another element to be considered is that it was not until the turn of the century that publications in languages other than French began to be taken into consideration—slowly. In research in the human and social sciences, and especially in the humanities, the French language has long maintained a clear primacy.

Political Bipolarization

Political changes directly or indirectly influence the functioning of universities and research programs—this trait is regularly verified, especially in democratic regimes. And its effects can be felt even more in a country like France where higher education and research are overwhelmingly organized within the framework of the civil service of the State. However, it is not enough to make this observation; we must also add that the reference period we have chosen is one in which the political cleavages were particularly active.

We must recall that the 5th Republic, which was established in 1958 to match General de Gaulle's return to power, put an end to the colonial wars while also establishing a rather authoritarian mode of government that was divisive, in that it regularly pitted the majorities and strongly constituted minorities against each other on issues. At a time of strong economic growth, this did not favor the social-cultural modernization of the country, and above all, the consideration of the demands of newly emerging populations. This rigidity was not for nothing in the explosion of May–June 1968, when the requirements and demands of a large part of the youth and the working classes were asserted with determination. In the two decades that followed (in fact until 1986), the cleavages between right and left were at the heart of French political life on the political scene and were expressed vigorously, especially during the presidential and legislative elections, even though aspirations and sensitivities were more complex and uncomfortable with this binary pattern.

It should be borne in mind that this characterization of French political life, which has a strong influence on the functioning of public services including universities, can be observed in tandem with the progress of information and communication in French society, as well as the way in which they were handled in university courses. The theme of freedom of information which was designed to accompany and report on the functioning of the print media was no longer operative on its own at the time of the rise in power of mass generalist television. Currently, the explosion of the new post-television and post-telephony audiovisual media has already begun, but also the left/right political divide retains all its power of differentiation, generating irreconcilable oppositions as it appears from the examination of the following facts:

- The first 15 years (at least) of existence of the SCIs (in France SIC) were not easy. On the contrary, they gave rise to open or hidden opposition, particularly in the bodies where appointments or promotions of teacher-researchers were decided. Scientific issues were often relegated to the background and the difficulties were great when it came to establishing the frameworks of the discipline, all the more so as the new members brought with them their past perceptions, which were influenced by the disciplines or themes from which they came. In this context, also marked by the confrontation of partisan political positions and the influence of state authorities, clarification could only come about over time, and therefore, with the arrival of a new generation and the affirmation of work carried out in new research teams. It is therefore conceivable that active participation in international scientific associations or events was not a priority. Initiatives were only taken at the end of the 1970s and during the 1980s.
- The interest in the NWICO and the debates it generated ultimately concerned only a small minority of academics in the discipline. In a general climate still largely marked by the "Cold War," a majority of them were only partially interested and concerned, as their anti-imperialist positions (expressed in an explicit critique of American theories of communication, especially the empirical-functionalist conceptions) complemented by a primarily Third-Worldist vision, and showed little appetite for the "Second

World." This fact should be noted all the more since a significant part of the political left, to which they belonged, remained attached to the Soviet Union. But since the events of May–June 1968, a notable part of the intellectuals and youth rejected both North American economic and political liberalism and East European state communism. This period was undoubtedly one of those in which the commitment of these social categories was most resolute.

- This political polarization was equally true for those with a left-wing sensibility (in its great diversity) and those with a right-wing sensibility. During the preparation of an IAMCR-AIERI Conference held in Paris in July 1982, we recall witnessing the attempts of those who followed in the footsteps of the first French founding members to defeat this conference, since, according to them, freedom of information would no longer be guaranteed with the rise to power of a united left government.

Around the NWICO

Since the 1940s, the US has made the doctrine of "freedom of information" and the "free flow of information," a key element of its foreign policy. This is precisely what the non-aligned movement wanted to change by calling for a NWICO. This question was the focus of a debate at UNESCO in Paris from 1975 to when the US withdrew at the end of December 1984. In 1977, the International Commission for the Study of Communication Problems was set up under the chairmanship of Seán MacBride of Ireland. It was an opportunity to raise awareness of the inequality of exchanges and power relations between North and South. "Decolonising Information" became the watchword (Bourges, 1978). Numerous researchers of all nationalities came together at the conferences and meetings organized by IAMCR-AIERI in Leicester (1976), Paris (1977), and Warsaw (1978), which led to the foundation of the Section on Political Economy (Wasko, 2013). In September 1982, at the IAMCR-AIERI Conference held in Paris on the theme "Communication and Democracy," it was noted that few French researchers spoke in the plenary sessions or in the section workshops (Screberny-Mohammadi, 1983). The same was true 25 years later, in July 2007, at the Conference on "Media, Communication and Information: Celebrating 50 years of theory and practice," also organized by IAMCR and held in the French capital.

In fact, it is, above all, the contributions published by researchers in press organs such as *Le Monde diplomatique* that testify to the commitment translated into action in academic circles. They are all the more interesting in that articles published in the major French daily press are rare or accuse UNESCO of being "too politicised" (Roach, 1981). The issues dealt with in *Le Monde diplomatique* are many and varied: from the data war in November 1979 to computer science in the Third World in April 1982, and, five years later, the "Art of Deformation: the Lies that Undermine Democracy," by the director of the monthly, Claude Julien (1987). In January 1982, the German Jörg Becker, an author of several articles in the monthly, published "Europe and the Third World in the Information Battle" (Becker, 1982). In December 1974, Herbert I. Schiller (1919–2000), a Professor at the University of California, wrote an article on "The Mechanisms of International Dominance" in a dossier centered on "Cultural Imperialism" (Schiller, 1974b), a paper on "The Genesis of the Principles of the Free Flow of Information" (Schiller, 1975, see also Schiller, 1974a), and another article in March 1978, with the title "The United States Seeks to Maintain its Domination," this time in a dossier on "The right to Information in the Face of Scientific Progress: the Conditioning of Citizens" (Schiller, 1978). During the academic year 1982–1983, Herbert Schiller, who was a long-time active member of IAMCR and its Vice President, held a seminar at the Department of Anglo-American Studies of the University of Paris VIII. In 1983 and 1987, he was Lecturer in Communications at the University of Grenoble III, one of the first three (along with Bordeaux III and Strasbourg) to obtain a master's degree in this field.

Technical Changes in Progress or Announced

The period 1965–1990 cannot be understood without taking into account a whole series of technical changes that have lastingly and profoundly modified the very framework of actions that must now be considered as info-communicational. The news press was largely competing for access to daily information, as mass generalist television was at its peak in most countries, developed or not. However, major innovations were already announced, from the computer sector, particularly microcomputing, telephony (and first of all, telematics which precedes mobile telephony), and video, as well as the networking of all these components which will give rise to the internet as well as the computerization of information retrieval.

So, this period has nothing in common with the one that preceded it, where the press competed with radio and gradually with television but continued on its way and retained a sort of monopoly of informational thought, for example, in the international debates that took place within UNESCO or about its supporters. Whether the innovations mentioned had come about or were still awaited, the context had profoundly changed, as witnessed by the often highly conflicting debates in the MacBride Commission, on the subject of telecommunications satellites as well as on television broadcasting satellites.

However, this change of context should not be seen as solely under the pressure and dependence of technical changes. Indeed, these changes are accompanied by new practices; hence, the boom in companies as well as in public or local authorities and initiatives in the field of communication, which hindered the monopoly of the press and advertising agencies and opened the way to new professions with specific skills, justifying the launch of new university training courses.

At the end of the day, the use of these six elements (all of which are explanatory factors), which are obviously inter-related, seems to us to shed more light on the relations between French academics and IAMCR-AIERI during this key period. In fact, the differences with the previous period are striking and the openings toward the future, some of which are already underway but which will take several decades to be realized, are at work, both in the policies implemented, in the organizational methods, and in the representations of the different categories of the population.

References

Althusser, L. (1970). Ideology and ideological state apparatuses. In *Essays on Ideology* (p. 1–60). Verso (original language French).

Barthes, R. (1972). *Mythologies.* (Lavers, A., Trans.). Vintage Books, 2000. First published in the UK by Jonathan Cape, 1972. Original work published by *Edition du Seuil*, 1957.

Baudelot, D., & Establet, R. (1971). *L'Ecole capitaliste en France.* Maspero.

Baudrillard, J. (1972). *Pour une critique de l'économie du signe.* Gallimard. (Levin, C., Trans.). *For a critique of the political economy of the sign.* Telos Press (1981).

Becker, J. (1982, January). L'Europe et le tiers-monde dans la bataille de l'information. *Le Monde Diplomatique.* Retrieved 15 June 2022, from https://www.monde-diplomatique.fr/1982/01/

Bourdieu, P. (1979). *La distinction. Critique sociale du jugement.* Editions de Minuit.

Bourdieu, P., & Passeron, J.-C. (1963, December). Sociologues des mythologies et mythologies des sociologues: les mass-médiologues. *Les Temps modernes*, p. 998–1021.

Bourdieu, P., & Passeron, J.-C. (1970). *La reproduction* (Trans. *Reproduction in Education, Society and Culture*, Sage, 1990). Editions de Minuit.

Boure, R. (2002). *Les origines des sciences de l'information et de la communication—Regards croisés* (Coordinated). Editions du Septentrion.

Bourges, H. (1978). *Décoloniser l'information,.* Editions CANA.

Braudel, F. (1958). Histoire et sciences sociales: La longue durée. *Annales Economies, Sociétés, Civilisations, 13*(4), 725–753.

Carey, J. W. (1975). Review essay: Communication and Culture. *Communication Research, 2*(2), 173–191.

d'Arcy, J. (1983). Les médias modernes, moyens de communication. In A. Lichnerowicz, F. Perroux, & G. Gadoffre (Eds.), *Information et communication: Séminaires interdisciplinaires du Collège de France: I* (p. 223–242). Maloine S. A. Editeur.

De la Haye, Y., & Miège, B. (1978). Les sciences de la Communication: Un phénomène de dépendance culturelle. *Communication Information, 2*(3), 7–23.

Debray, R. (1979). *Le Pouvoir intellectuel en France.* Ramsay.

Debray, R. (1991). *Cours de médiologie générale.* Gallimard.

Ellul, J. (1954). *La technique ou l'enjeu du siècle.* A. Colin.

Ellul, J. (1977). *Le système technicien.* Calmann-Lévy.

Friedmann, G. (1966). La sociologie des communications de masse. In G. Le Bras (Ed.). *Aspects de la sociologie française* (p. 79–88). Editions ouvrières.

Hoggart, R. (1957). *The uses of literacy: Aspects of working-class life.* Chatto & Windus.

Institut national de l'audiovisuel (INA). (1999, May–June). La recherche en information et communication. *Les Dossiers de l'audiovisuel, No. 85.* In F. Clairval (Ed.), Un bilan provisoire: La recherche en information et communication, *Communication & Languages* (Vol. 122, p. 122–123).

Julien, C. (1987, May). L'art de la déformation. *Le Monde Diplomatique*. Retrieved 15 June 2022, from https://www.monde-diplomatique.fr/1987/05/JULIEN/12263
Kayser, J. (1953). *Une semaine dans le monde. Étude comparée de 17 grands quotidiens pendant sept jours*. (Trans. One-week's news: Comparative study of 17 major dailies for a seven-day period, Paris, UNESCO, 1953). UNESCO.
Kayser, J. (1963). *Le quotidien français*. A. Colin.
Lauraire, R. (1987). *Le téléphone des ménages français. Genèse et fonctions d'un espage socal immatériel*. La Documentation française.
Lefebvre, H. (1967, 1971). *Vers le Cybernanthrope*. Denoêl-Gonthier.
Lefebvre, H. (1978). *De l'Etat.4. Les contradictions de l'Etat moderne*. Union générale d'éditions.
Lévi-Strauss, C. (1950). *Introduction a l'oeuvre de Marcel Mauss*. Presses universitaires de France.
Mancini, P., & Wolf, M. (1990). Mass media research in Italy: Culture and politics. *European Journal of Communication, 5*(2), 187–205.
Mattelart, A., & Mattelart, M. (1992). *Rethinking media theory. Signposts and new directions* (French Edition 1986). University of Minnesota Press.
Mattelart, A., & Mattelart, M. (1998). *Theories of communication. An introduction* (French Edition 1995). Sage.
Mattelart, A., & Stourdzé, Y. (1985). *Technology, culture and communication. A report to the French Minister of Research and Industry* (French ed. 1982). Elsevier.
Metz, C. (1968–1972). *Essai sur la signification du cinéma* (Vol. 1–2). Klincksiek.
Miège, B. (1989a). *The capitalization of cultural production*. International General Editions.
Miège, B. (1989b). *La Société conquise par la communication*. Presses Universitaires de Grenoble.
Miège, B. (1995). *La Pensée communicationnelle*. Presses Universitaire de Grenoble.
Morin, E. (1962). *L'Esprit du temps*. Grasset.
Park, R. E. (1938, September). Reflections on communication and culture. *The American Journal of Sociology, 44*(2), 187–205.
Park, R. E. (1955). The natural history of the newspaper. Reprinted in Hughes, E. C. (Ed.), *Society, collective behaviour, news and opinion, sociology and modern society, 1918–1942, Collected papers of Robert Ezra Park, Volume 3*, (p. 89–104). Free Press.
Passeron, J.-C. (1982). Sociologie: bilans et perspectives. In M. Godelier (Ed.), *Rapport sur l'état des sciences de l'homme et de la société en France* (p. 183–220). La Documentation française.
Roach, C. (1981). French press coverage of the Belgrade UNESCO conference. *Journal of Communication, 31*(4), 175–187.
Robins, K. (1979). Althusserian Marxism and media studies. The case of *Screen*. *Media, Culture & Society, 1*(4), 355–370.
Santoro, J.-L. (1991). *La liberté de l'information, logiques institutionnelles et logiques professionnelles au plan international (1947–1972)* [Doctoral thesis, University of Bordeaux III].
Schiller, H. I. (1974a, December). Les mécanismes de domination internationale. *Le monde diplomatique*. Retrieved 15 June 2022, from https://www.monde-diplomatique.fr/1974/12/SCHILLER/32784
Schiller, H. I. (1974b). Freedom from the 'free flow'. *Journal of Communication, 24*(1), 110–117.

Schiller, H. I. (1975). Genesis of the free flow of information principle. *Instant Research on Peace and Violence*, 2. Tampere.

Schiller, H. I. (1978, March). Les Etats-Unis cherchent à conserver leur domination. *Le monde diplomatique*. Retrieved 15 June 2022, from https://www.monde-diplomatique.fr/1978/03/SCHILLER/34655

Screberny-Mohammadi, A. (1983) *Communication and democracy: Directions in research, A report on a conference by Annabelle Sreberny-Mohammadi*, IAMCR, Leicester.

Stappers, J. G. (1983). Mass communication as public communication. *Journal of Communication, 33*(3), 141–145.

Tarde, G. (1901). *L'opinion et la foule*. PUF, Paris, 1990. Translated as *Gabriel Tarde On Communication and Social Influence. Selected Papers*, Clark, T. N. (Ed.). Chicago University Press, 1969.

Terrou, F. (1962). *L'Information*. Presses Universitaires de France.

Terrou, F., & Albert, P. (1970–1974). *Histoire de la presse*. Presses Universitaires de France.

Vitalis, A. (2006). Propagandes d'hier et d'aujourd'hui. In Troude-P. Chastenet (Ed.), *Cahiers Jacques Ellul N° 4,* (p. 81–91). L'esprit du temps.

Vovelle, M. (1982). Rapport sur les disciplines historiques. In M. Godelier (Ed.), *Rapport sur l'état des sciences de l'homme et de la société* (p. 258). La Documentation française.

Wasko, J. (2013). *The IAMCR: political economy section: A restrospective, 1*(1), 4–8.

Williams, R. (1974). Communications as cultural science. *Journal of Communication, 24*(3), 17–25.

Williams, R. (1977). Plaisantes perspectives. *Actes de la recherche en sciences sociales, 17–18*, 29–36.

CHAPTER 28

IAMCR, My Affable Companion in Slovenia's Journey from Yugoslavia to Europe

Slavko Splichal

The Charm of the First Encounter with IAMCR

My first "live" encounter with IAMCR was the 1974 Conference at Karl Marx University in Leipzig, in which I participated as an aspiring research assistant with a paper on international radio propaganda. For a number of reasons, attending the Leipzig Conference remained indelibly in my memory. I could not forget the publication of my paper presenting results of comprehensive content analysis of foreign radio propaganda programs for Yugoslavia, in the conference proceedings *Der Anteil der Massenmedien bei der Herausbildung des Bewusstseins in der sich wandelnden Welt* (AIERI, 1974) as this was my first paper published outside Yugoslavia. Moreover, regardless of the conference, my paper was related to IAMCR because it was based on the project "External Radio Broadcasting and International Understanding: Broadcasting in Yugoslavia," funded by UNESCO's program for international communication research, to the design and implementation of which IAMCR also made an important contribution.

By then, I had already visited a number of East European countries, including Hungary, Czechoslovakia, and the Soviet Union, but the visit to the German Democratic Republic (GDR) dramatically worsened my experience with the "really existing socialism." I traveled to the conference with my colleagues from Ljubljana by car through Austria and Czechoslovakia. When we

S. Splichal (✉)
University of Ljubljana, Ljubljana, Slovenia
e-mail: slavko.splichal@guest.arnes.si

© The Author(s), under exclusive license to Springer Nature Switzerland AG 2023

J. Becker, R. Mansell (eds.), *Reflections on the International Association for Media and Communication Research*,
https://doi.org/10.1007/978-3-031-16383-8_28

arrived at the GDR border in the evening, the Germans detained us for several hours and carefully inspected our documents, the car, and all the materials we had with us (newspapers and copies of our conference papers) before letting us go. For Yugoslav citizens, especially for Slovenes, who at the time were free to cross the border with Italy and Austria and did not need visas for most of the countries around the world, it was a real adventure. When, despite rather strict controls, we were able one day to evade the conference protocol and go for a private dinner and conversation at the home of one of the professors at the university, I became impressively aware of the material and intellectual hardships of the people in the GDR.

Finally, prior to the conference, my international experience was modest, but very inspiring. As an undergraduate, I had the opportunity to listen to lectures by foreign visiting professors, including Dallas Smythe, and I assisted Professor Alex Edelstein in conducting surveys on interpersonal communication and decision making in Ljubljana. At the very beginning of my employment at the university in July 1971, I participated in the International Summer School on International Journalism on the Croatian island, Dugi Otok, in the Adriatic Sea, where most of the approximately 20 participants were from the United States (US), and one of the lecturers was Jim Halloran. Generally, I could say that I was brought up with a very liberal attitude towards "capitalist science." I developed my critical-Marxist orientation only after completing my master's degree in 1974, when I started writing my doctoral dissertation on mass communication, human freedom, and alienation, defended in 1979, and published in Slovene in 1981 (Splichal, 1981, 2020).

After all my "liberal" experiences of the early 1970s, listening to the ideologically orchestrated debates in Leipzig made me quite frustrated. On the other hand, it was refreshing to listen to prominent critical scholars such as Dallas Smythe and Herb Schiller "defeating" representatives of conservative/administrative empirical research represented by Elisabeth Noelle-Neumann in an open-stage dialog.

The Seeds of 1968

I knew about the association before, but that was rather superficial. As a sophomore, I was not involved in the preparations for the International Conference on Mass Communication and International Understanding, organized by the School of Sociology, Political Science and Journalism (later transformed into the Faculty of Social Sciences at the University of Ljubljana) in Ljubljana in September 1968—a week after the Soviet invasion of Czechoslovakia—under the auspices of IAMCR and UNESCO. Yet from today's perspective, I can say that this conference, which was attended by some 120 participants from 25 countries, was an extremely important stimulus for the development of media and communication research in Slovenia, and thus for my own career as well.

The main organizers of this event, the first of its kind in former Yugoslavia, were Bogdan Osolnik, France Vreg, and Tomo Martelanc, all of whom made an important contribution to the development of journalism and communication studies at the School of Sociology, Political Science and Journalism in Ljubljana. It was just two years after the IAMCR Conference in 1966 in Herceg Novi, which Bogdan Osolnik helped organize. Bogdan Osolnik and Tomo Martelanc played an important role in the earliest period of the formation of IAMCR. Osolnik was later also a member of the famed UNESCO International Commission for the Study of Communication Problems (The MacBride Commission) and co-author of its report *Many Voices, One World*, more commonly known as "The MacBride Report." (MacBride & Commissioners, 1980). France Vreg, on the other hand, was the main "liaison" with the International Sociological Association (ISA) and its RC14—Research Committee for Communication, Knowledge and Culture.

France Vreg was one of the founders and head of the journalism department at the School of Sociology, Political Science and Journalism (later also Dean of the faculty), which became the major institutional framework for journalism education as well as communication and media theory and research in Slovenia. Although the school was a public educational institution established by the Communist Party, it enjoyed a decent degree of autonomy—with occasional authoritarian interventions, to which Vreg was also exposed in the mid-1970s because of his book *Družbeno komuniciranje* (Social Communication, 1973) blamed for promoting "bourgeois science." As the formation of the journalism department in Ljubljana was mostly inspired, in organizational terms at least, by American schools of journalism which Vreg had visited in the 1960s, his book (defended as a doctoral thesis in sociology in 1972) was largely based on his study of American literature.

Ideological Classifications and (Dis)qualifications

Under the auspices of the University of Ljubljana, in the summer of 1968, just before the Soviet invasion of Czechoslovakia, the Department of Journalism organized the symposium "Mass Media and International Understanding," which was attended by more than a hundred Western European and American participants. The book *Mass Media and International Understanding* (Vreg, 1969) with 50 papers presented at the symposium, which France Vreg had edited before he began writing his doctoral dissertation, reflected his and Bogdan Osolnik's efforts to go beyond ideological divisions, which at that time dominated the international media research community and restrained communication research in Yugoslavia. The participants in the 1968 symposium in Ljubljana included a number of eminent persons from different intellectual paths and parts of the world, including Jean Schwoebel (from French *Le Monde*), Juan Beneyto from Spain, Elisabeth Noelle-Neumann from Germany, Herbert Schiller from the US, Gertrude Robinson from Canada, Dinker Rao Mankekar (renowned editor from India), Dallas W. Smythe from Canada, Yassen Zassoursky from Russia, and Kaarle Nordenstreng from Finland. Such openness, promoted by the symposium in Ljubljana, became a thorn in the side of the Slovenian Communist Party's hardliners in the 1970s, the effects of which Vreg felt after the publication of his own book in 1973.

It was not appreciated in the mainstream academic circles either. In his review of the book, Stanley Smith (1982) from Arizona State University suggested that, as any other volume composed of all the papers presented at a single symposium, the book was -

> destined to diversity in subject, quality and philosophy. ... In addition to diversity, one might anticipate, under these circumstances, certain other tendencies: (1) a heavy emphasis upon Third World concerns over the fact that the industrialized nations dominated world communication at that time (1968); (2) an ideological imbalance toward the left because of the political orientation of the host country and the reputation of the IAMCR of being subject to Marxist influence; and (3) an over-representation of material from the host country. (Smith, 1982, p. 116)

At the time of the dominance of the "four theories of the press" in international communication research, such an assessment was, of course, not unexpected. This was a period of strict ideological classifications and (dis) qualifications. The reviewer's assessment of the "ideological imbalance against the left due to the political orientation of the host country" was soon "balanced" with the assessments of the Slovenian political authorities that Vreg's book was "unbalanced" against Marxism.

In a way, IAMCR was forced to follow these qualifications by alternately organizing conferences in three ideological-political "camps" if it wanted to reduce the dominance of the "liberal world." On the other hand, paradigmatic differences in approaches to communication phenomena in IAMCR did not play such an important role. "The IAMCR's reputation for being subject to Marxist influence" was one of the typical Western ideological constructs and prejudices of the time, in which Communism was criminalized, especially in the US but also in Western Germany, and Marxism was not considered a scientific theory but equated with Soviet ideology.

This is not to say that there were no different political groups within IAMCR—both among representatives of the West and the East and the non-aligned countries, as probably in every international scientific organization. Naturally, there were—as there are today—different scientific paradigms which manifested as differences between sections more than within sections. I remember that in the 1980s, I analyzed, together with my colleagues, the conceptual structure of sessions of ISA research committees at several congresses, and the analysis showed significant differences and similarities, among them (Splichal et al., 1989). Similar results would probably be found for IAMCR as well. Due to the limited "popularity" of communication research in the "Eastern Bloc" and its lower representation at IAMCR conferences, the diversity of approaches that (may) have been applied in these countries was also less obvious at the conferences.

In Yugoslavia, the development of the new discipline was largely marked by "productive inclusivism" or eclecticism, a kind of "cohabitation" of different communication schools and theoretical paradigms that contributed to its definition, development, and institutionalization at universities. I analyzed, with a group of my students, 32 Yugoslav social science journals for the period between 1964 and 1986 and found out that only 18.7 percent of 311 articles related to (mass) communication, which had been published by 181 authors and had an empirical character; an additional 7.7 percent were both theoretical and empirical, but only 7.1 percent of them included statistical data analysis (Splichal, 1994a). The first media-related empirical studies in Yugoslavia were published as late as 1969 and they dominated the scene during the short period of democratization until 1974 (particularly reporting social survey and audience research results), but after 1975 they almost disappeared for some time.

During the last decade of socialism, in the 1980s, when communication and journalism education and research programs became a regular component at many universities in all republics of the former Yugoslavia, Marxist/critical communication scholarship has gradually been marginalized in favor of more eclectic "mainstream" approaches. Paradoxically, the more socialism was influenced by the model of capitalism and followed it, the less communication theory and research was inspired by a Marxist critique of capital and class relations, alienation of work and communication, and domination of political and economic elites (Džinić et al., 1984).

Of course, these features of communication research in Yugoslavia cannot be generalized to other socialist countries, nor can participants in IAMCR conferences be considered genuine representatives of "national" media research landscapes. This is probably even less so for the most prominent national representatives in IAMCR bodies. From the socialist countries, Dusiška from GDR, Pisarek from Poland, Zassoursky from the Soviet Union and Szecskö from Hungary played an important role in them, and there were certainly significant differences among them in terms of scientific research orientations and achievements (not to speak of their more dogmatic or liberal political orientations), but I could not say that they represented some kinds of dominant research currents or even paradigms in their respective countries. In any case, such a thing could certainly not be attributed to any "representative" of Yugoslavia in IAMCR bodies, be it Osolnik, Martelanc, or myself, and even less, of course, to the "representatives" of Western countries.

IAMCR, UNESCO, and Media Research in Slovenia

At the time of the 1968 Ljubljana symposium, Bogdan Osolnik worked at the Yugoslav Ministry of Information; as a former career diplomat, he established excellent international connections, particularly with UNESCO. As one of the first members of IAMCR, he was much attached to the association because of his interest in communications, mass media, and public opinion, and particularly because IAMCR had members from both political blocs as well as the non-aligned countries. According to his memoirs, he decided to organize a conference in Herceg Novi (largely subsidized by the Yugoslav authorities) to support the openness of the organization, but also to promote the Yugoslav socialist self-management system, at the time when IAMCR was in financial difficulties and under pressure to align itself with one of the blocs (Brlek et al., 2017). Nevertheless, he never tried—nor did his Slovenian colleagues—to use the association for political purposes, unless we consider the pursuit of peace, international understanding, and cooperation to be a political project beyond scientific ethics. As a vice president of IAMCR, he was very much involved in the organization of the conferences in Switzerland and Spain, and, particularly, in promoting the association in Yugoslavia along with the emerging communication-related activities of UNESCO, which he actively encouraged.

Osolnik invited Breda Pavlič to help the organizing committee in preparing the 1968 symposium, which turned out to be decisive for her career, starting with her assistantship (1970) at the Faculty of Social Sciences, after completing her master's degree in Regina, Canada, under the supervision of Dallas Smythe. For ten years, from 1970 until 1980, I shared an office with her at the faculty.

At that time, Tomo Martelanc, a former journalist and Director of Slovenian Television, served as the Secretary for Education and Culture in the then Government of Slovenia (from 1965 to 1969). When he joined the faculty in 1970 as senior lecturer in the journalism department, he was member of the UNESCO Advisory Panel for International Mass Communication Research and Chair of the Information Committee of the Yugoslav UNESCO Commission. Being very internationally active, he managed to obtain significant external research funding, including the UNESCO grant for the study of "External radio broadcasting and international understanding: Broadcasting to Yugoslavia" that would be completed in 1977. In 1971, UNESCO adopted an international program for communication research. Within that program, "research into international communication structures" was one of the most important themes, which could best be coordinated by international organizations such as IAMCR. The first three-year project of this program (1973–1976) was conducted in Slovenia, and I was in charge of a research design to analyze 15 news programs of foreign radio stations from 14 countries that broadcast in Yugoslav languages to different national audiences in socialist Yugoslavia, aiming at identifying common features and differences in radio propaganda. The study was completed and published as a monograph *External Radio Broadcasting and International Understanding: Broadcasting to Yugoslavia* in the series, Reports and Papers in Mass Communication (Martelanc et al., 1977), following the first publication arising from the study, *Television Traffic: A One-way Street* by Kaarle Nordenstreng and Tapio Varis (1974), and preceding studies on the operation of international news agencies and on the effects of the transnational corporations on the conduct of international communication.

Despite the use of "functionalist research methods" of content analysis of radio programs and computer-assisted multivariate statistical analysis (in 1974 already!), revealing conflicting ideologies in foreign radio news programs broadcast to Yugoslavia, the broadcasting study was not considered ideologically controversial by political "reviewers." Moreover, the successful completion of the internationally praised project finally gave the green light to establish the Social Communication Research Centre at the Faculty of Social Sciences, which was previously prevented by objections that communication research should not be a separate field of research and that the research group did not have enough qualified researchers. However, the next research project on the Yugoslav press agency Tanjug and the Non-Aligned News Agencies Pool (NANAP, established in 1975), also funded by UNESCO as part of its international communication research program, triggered ideological attacks from Belgrade. We were accused of providing (ideological) enemies with confidential information about the work of Tanjug and other non-aligned news agencies.

In the 1970s, similarly to other socialist countries, the political bureaucracies in Slovenia and Yugoslavia were still very reluctant to support empirical social research. For decades, sociology was considered a "bourgeois science" and restrictively included in academic life, in contrast to the ideologically preferred political science. Later, this anti-Marxist "class character" was attributed mainly and selectively to empirical research, particularly surveys. It should come as no surprise, therefore, that not only books but also the vast majority of communication-related journal articles published in that period did not emerge from empirical research. Yet in fact, empirical research in the former socialist societies often acted as a critical impulse against ideologized abstract social sciences, formalism, and simplified generalizations, and was aimed at investigating differences in interests and social contradictions in the processes of the development of socialism. Media research was no exception: journalism education and communication research became the target of ideological criticism for "the lack of Marxist foundations," which was part of a more general conflict between party-state bureaucracy and "liberal intellectuals." Fortunately, this political intervention was short-lived. By the 1980s, communication and journalism education and research programs became a regular component of universities in all the republics of the former Yugoslavia.

After completing the analysis of foreign propaganda for Yugoslavia, I participated in a series of international empirical studies that were initiated, in one way or another, within IAMCR. The first was the "Foreign Images" study undertaken for UNESCO by IAMCR between 1978 and 1982. It was carried out by 13 national teams, covering 29 different countries, and fully reported in *Foreign News in the Media: International Reporting in 29 Countries* published by UNESCO in 1985 (Sreberny-Mohammadi et al., 1985). Probably under the impression of the success of this international project, I suggested to Colin Sparks to design and conduct a collaborative international survey on the attitudes of journalism students towards the journalistic profession. During the ISA and IAMCR congresses in New Delhi, in August 1986, the core of the international research team was established. National surveys in 22 countries were administered from May 1987 to January 1988, but the final report *Journalists for the 21st Century: Tendencies of Professionalization Among*

First-Year Students in 22 Countries did not appear until 1994 (Splichal & Sparks, 1994).

Tomo Martelanc, Bogdan Osolnik, and Breda Pavlič—all particularly active in the International Communication Section of IAMCR—were "guilty" of my active involvement in the association. On the other hand, France Vreg was more inclined towards participation in the ISA and its Research Committee for Communication, Knowledge and Culture, chaired by José Vidal-Beneyto. In the 1970s and 1980s, members of the board of this research committee included France Vreg, Tamás Szecskö, Elihu Katz, Kurt Lang, Denis McQuail, Lothar Bisky, Valery Korobeinikov, and Peter Dahlgren among others. In 1985, an international meeting on "Communication and Life Styles" initiated by the committee was organized in Ljubljana, by the Section for Communication and Public Opinion of the Yugoslav Sociological Association together with the Faculty of Social Sciences, which Vreg and I coordinated.

After being elected a member of IAMCR International Council in Prague in 1984, I also became an active member of ISA. When at the 1990 Congress of ISA in Madrid, Paul Beaud was elected President of the board of the Research Committee for Communication, Knowledge and Culture (RC14) to replace Beneyto, I became member of the board (together with Nick Garnham, Richard Sennett, and Jesús Martín Barbero, among others). Prior to the congress in Madrid, the Slovenian Sociological Association organized a meeting of the ISA Research Council in September 1988 in Ljubljana, at which it was agreed to establish an International Sociological Institute and a graduate school at the Faculty of Social Sciences in Ljubljana under the auspices of ISA. Both institutions were formally established the following year and promoted at the 12th congress of ISA in Madrid in July 1990. In the role of the newly appointed Director of the institute, I organized the IAMCR Conference in Bled in 1990, but after organizational and conceptual frictions at the faculty, I was soon relieved of my duties and the institute lost its initial momentum. Despite the important creative connections the institute established, it was closed down after the breakup of Yugoslavia, while the postgraduate school never started working at all.

NWICO, Media Democratization, and the Fall of the Iron Curtain

Nevertheless, during the preparations for the 1990 IAMCR Conference in Bled, the broader context of global economic and political changes was more important than these administrative and internal "political" issues. The decade of the 1980s proved once again the close but controversial relationship between communication and democracy. On the one hand, for example, the new challenges were reflected in UNESCO's departure from the doctrine of the New World Information and Communication Order (NWICO), the abandonment of the MacBride Commission's approach, and the adoption of neoliberal solutions to the problems of (international) communication. The idea of organizing NWICO round tables to promote "new order" ideas that UNESCO initiated in the early 1980s was completely abandoned by its new leadership. Facing a "new order" in international communication which was even far less congruent with the genuine ideas of NWICO than the dominant forms of international communication by the end of the 1970s discussed in the MacBride Report, led some "alternative" NGOs—Federation of Southern African Journalists, International Organization of Journalists (IOJ), and the Media Foundation of the Non-Aligned—to organize an "alternative" MacBride round table in Harare, Zimbabwe. The three-day discussions were summed up in the "Harare Statement of the MacBride Round Table on Communication" (Harare Statement, 1989) and a number of additional documents, including the agreement on follow-up actions. Although the Harare meeting revealed that the interest in NWICO was still very much alive, it was also clear that the idea was dead within UNESCO (See also Chap. 15 in this collection).

On the other hand, in the late 1980s, the socialist countries of Central and Eastern Europe and the Soviet Union began the imitative process of adopting neoliberal solutions to change the entire social structure and political and economic system, including the transformation of the media. After the late 1970s, in a number of socialist countries the party-state media monopoly was broken, although a significant part of the new and independent media remained illegal or semi-legal. During the late 1980s, the endeavors aimed at social liberalization (seemed to) have succeeded: peaceful (r)evolutions in the region introduced radical political, and partly economic, changes. As in all modern democratic revolutions, the media were of vital importance in the wake of popular movements, which may not have succeeded without them. Democratic elections and emerging freedom of the press marked impressive political changes in these countries. Thus, the theme of communication and democracy was certainly the timeliest theme for the 1990 Conference of IAMCR in Slovenia, which at the time of the Bled Conference was still part of the Socialist Federal Republic of Yugoslavia, but just a few months later, it declared its independence as the Republic of Slovenia.

The organization of the 1990 IAMCR Conference in Bled was also a natural consequence of the efforts to systematically address the processes of democratic change, which Hanno Hardt and I initiated two years after the ISA RC14 meeting in Ljubljana. In 1987, we organized a conference on "The Role of the Media in the Cultural, Sociopolitical, and Economic Frames of Democratic Industrial Societies" in Dubrovnik, Croatia, sponsored by the German Volkswagenstiftung. The meeting turned out to be the first in a series of colloquia we organized under the Euricom "brand" in the decades that followed. In 1989, the second colloquium organized in Piran, Slovenia, was devoted to "Democratization and the Media," where we analyzed the prospects for democratic change in Eastern Europe on the eve of revolutions. These collaborative initiatives were key to our decision to organize an IAMCR conference in Slovenia.

The Slovenian authorities greatly appreciated the decision of IAMCR to entrust the organization of its 1990 Conference to Slovenia in the critical period of the independence process. This appreciation was best demonstrated by the high state decoration presented to the President of IAMCR, Jim Halloran, on that occasion by the President of the Republic of Slovenia, Mr. Milan Kučan. Paradoxically, it was a Yugoslav decoration, as Slovenia did not have its own state decorations before independence.

With the 1990 IAMCR Conference in Bled, Slovenia, critical communication research was given a major impetus and a new venue for international cooperation. After the IAMCR Conference in Bled, together with Janet Wasko, I edited the book *Communication and Democracy*, consisting of a selection of papers presented at the conference, which was published in the Ablex Communication and Information Science Series in 1993. In the face of the impending decline of socialism and the breakup of Yugoslavia, critical communication thought in Slovenia (re)gained its place in the international Colloquia on Communication and Culture. Following the Bled Conference, the organization of "Communication and Culture Colloquia" continued even more systematically, especially after the European Institute for Communication and Culture (EURICOM) was officially established in 1992 and the decision was made to start publishing an independent journal *Javnost—The Public* in 1994. Similar to the IAMCR vision to bridge the East-West divide, EURICOM was founded with the purpose of bridging the two parts of formerly divided Europe by promoting research and publication in the areas of media and communication research. To enable a more systematic and continuous publication of ideas discussed at the colloquia and beyond, the colloquia were soon followed by the launch of the EURICOM journal *Javnost—The Public*. The decision to set up a new journal was based on the realization that with the intensification of EURICOM colloquia, the publication of papers presented at colloquia became an increasing problem, as negotiations for publication of papers in edited books or special journal issues implied years of delays. The decision to start publishing our own journal turned out to be the right one, as the new journal soon gained a wide range of readers and entered the circle of journals indexed in the Social Sciences Citation Index (SSCI).

In 1994, EURICOM assisted the World Association for Christian Communication (WACC) in organizing a colloquium devoted to "Ethno-Religious Nationalist Conflicts and the Media." When IAMCR then "lost" the promised organizer for the 2005 off-year conference, we decided to help organize the IAMCR conference in addition to organizing our 1995 EURICOM colloquium devoted to "virtual democracy." Together with the Faculty of Social Sciences, EURICOM was the main organizer of the 1995 IAMCR "Communication Beyond the Nation-State" Conference in Portorož, Slovenia. The theme of the 1995 IAMCR Conference came naturally to mind when looking at various initiatives that "undermined" national and cultural identities in Europe and elsewhere since the early 1970s, in contrast to the previous period of stability, reinforced by two world wars, which seemed very much resistant to change. On the occasion of the conference, seven papers presented at the conference were published in a special issue of *Javnost—The Public* (1995).

If I mention wars, let me recall my long conversation with George Gerbner during the conference about the short period of his life spent in Slovenia with partisans during World War II. He told me that at the beginning of the war, he had been trained as a paratrooper, and as such, he joined the Secret Intelligence group of the US Strategic Command in Italy. In January 1945, he parachuted into the occupied territory of northern Slovenia along the Austrian border to operate with the Slovene partisans until the end of the war and victory over the occupying forces and their local collaborators. Our lives are often much more intertwined than we think they are.

Unfulfilled Utopias, Missed Opportunities, New Challenges

In the 1990s, I spent most of my energy managing EURICOM and its regular colloquia, and in particular, publishing the journal *Javnost—The Public*, while for a short period (1991–1993), I was also the Dean of the Faculty of Social Sciences. During that time, and especially in the new millennium, media and communication research has grown tremendously in terms of publications, scholars, and students. Within the European Science Foundation (ESF), we have tried to contribute to a more systematic development of the discipline (or field) during this period, but with limited success. An ESF instrument—the Forward Look—Media studies: new media and new literacies—was designed to develop medium- to long-term views and analyses of future developments with the aim of defining research agendas and priorities at national and European level in four broad areas of critical issues: political engagement, digital divides, the creative economy, and identity formation. Based on a two-year series of workshops of the scientific committee chaired by Peter Golding and myself, we produced the report *Media in Europe: New Questions for Research and Policy* (Alvares et al., 2013) and a special issue of *Javnost—The Public* (Golding & Splichal, 2013), which summarized conclusions and recommendations of the workshops to draw up a strategic research and science policy agenda for media studies in Europe for the next five to 10 years. Unfortunately, the implementation of the proposals did not take place, as the ESF was "reformed" (in fact, abolished) in 2016 after 43 years of promoting European research through its networking, funding, and coordination activities.

IAMCR was one of the important frameworks for discussions on the future of media research in Europe. The Forward Look was lengthily discussed at the 2011 IAMCR Conference in Istanbul, our conclusions and recommendations were presented at the 2013 Conference in Dublin, and further actions were discussed in Leicester during the 2016 Conference.

I believe that the ideas on the future of media and communication research generated within the ESF Forward Look are not only important for Europe but for other parts of the world as well. They are fully in line with the aims of IAMCR as a global professional association of media and communication researchers promoting "media and communication research throughout the world, addressing socio-political, technological, policy and cultural processes." Today, critical approaches in theory and empirical research—whether they are called "Marxist" or otherwise—are especially important because we are facing dramatic changes that can be characterized in terms of globalization, mediatization, internetization, commodification, growing populism, and authoritarianism, often resulting in a decline in the democratic potential of communication, either "old" or "new." By strengthening its core commitments, IAMCR can make today, as it has in the past, an important contribution to the democratization of communication, which has been at the heart of its efforts since its early beginnings.

In my 1994 book, *Media Beyond Socialism* (Splichal, 1994b), I challenged the view that the burial of authoritarian practices in socialist countries was followed by a smooth transition to democracy. Instead, I argued that the media imitated Western economic and political practices often subjected to the negative influences of authoritarianism, commercialism, and nationalism. I claimed that countries suffered greatly not only from a lack of civilian participation and control, but also from the erosion of the intellectual foundations of social transformation that were lost after the sudden takeover of political and economic power. Although political changes have significantly broadened the horizons of human freedom, today I unfortunately find not only that my assessment of new threats was fairly accurate at the time, but also that the situation in many countries has worsened. This, in particular, deepens my belief in the need to promote critical media and communication research, which should be recognized by IAMCR.

References

AIERI (Association Internationale des Etudes et Recherches sur l'Information et la communication). (1974, September). Der Anteil der Massenmedien bei der Herausbildung des Bewusstseins in der sich wandelnden Welt, Internationale wissenschaftliche Konferenz, Sektion Journalistik, VDJ der DDR, AIERI IX. Generalversammlung der AIERI Leipzig, DDR, Volume 2, 17–21.

Alvares, C., Cardoso, G., Dahlgren, P., Erstad, O., Fornäs, J., Golding, P., Nieminen, H., Sparks, C., Splichal, S., & Xinaris, C. (2013). *Forward look: Media in Europe: New questions for research and policy*. European Science Foundation.

Brlek, S. S., Prodnik, J. A., & Osolnik, B. (2017). The intention was to democratise the sphere of communication: An interview with Bogdan Osolnik. *tripleC, 15*(1), 231–250.

Džinić, F., Mirčev, D., Slavko, S., Stanojević, M., & Novosel, P. (1984). *Towards democratic communication: Mass communication research in Yugoslavia*. Yugoslav Center for Theory and Practice of Self-Management Edvard Kardelj.

Golding, P., & Splichal, S. (2013). New media, new research challenges: An introduction. *Javnost—The Public, 20*(2), 5–10.

Harare Statement (1989). In R. C. Vincent, K. Nordenstreng, & M. Traber (Eds.), *Towards Equity in Global Communnication: MacBride Update 1999.* Hampton Press.

Javnost—The Public. (1995). Special Issue on Communication beyond the nation-state, *2*(2).

MacBride, S., & Commissioners. (1980). *Communication and society today and tomorrow: Many voices one world. Towards a new more just and more efficient world information and communication order.* Kogan Page, Unipub, UNESCO.

Martelanc, T., Slavko, S., Pavlič, B., Ferligoj, A., Batagelj, V., & Murko, M. D. (1977). *External radio broadcasting and international understanding: Broadcasting to Yugoslavia.* Reports and Papers in Mass Communication No. 81. UNESCO.

Nordenstreng, K., & Vario, T. (1974). *Television traffic: A one-way street? A survey and analysis of the international flow of television programme material.* Reports and Papers on Mass Communication No. 70. UNESCO.

Smith, S. (1982). Review of *Mass media and international understanding,* by France Vreg. In N. C. J. Jain (Ed.), *International and intercultural communication annual, 6* (p. 116–119). US Speech Communication Association.

Splichal, S. (1981). *Množično komuniciranje med svobodo in odtujitvijo* (Mass communication between freedom and alienation). Obzorja.

Splichal, S. (1994a). Indigenisation vs. ideologisation: Communication science on the periphery. *European Journal of Communication, 4*(3), 329–359.

Splichal, S. (1994b). *Media beyond socialism.* Westview.

Splichal, S. (2020). A Marxist approach to communication freedom. *tripleC, 18*(1), 337–349 [Abridged version of *Množično komuniciranje med svobodo in odtujitvijo* [*Mass Communication between Freedom and Alienation]*, 1981 published in Slovene, p. 123–138].

Splichal, S., & Sparks, C. (1994). *Journalists for the 21st century: Tendencies of professionalization among first-year students in 22 countries (Communication and information science).* Ablex Publishers Inc..

Splichal, S., & Wasko, J. (Eds.). (1993). *Communication and democracy.* Ablex.

Splichal, S., Ferligoj, A., & Mlinar, Z. (1989). Integration and differentiation in international sociology: Clustering of ISA research committees. *BMS. Bulletin Méthodologie Sociologique. 21*, 24–32.

Sreberny-Mohammadi, A., Nordenstreng, K., Stevenson, R., & Ugboajah, F. O. (1985). *Foreign news in the media: International reporting in 29 Countries.* Reports and Papers on Mass Communication No. 93. UNESCO.

Vreg, F. (Ed.). (1969). *Mass media and international understanding.* Ljubljana University, Department of Journalism at the School of Sociology, Political Science and Journalism.

Vreg, F. (Ed.). (1973). *Družbeno komuniciranje* (Social communication). Obzorja.

PART IV

Reflections on People

CHAPTER 29

George Gerbner and the Anti-Fascist Tradition of Communication Research

Victor Pickard

Introduction

George Gerbner was one of the most politically engaged and public-facing communication scholars for nearly half a century, remaining active well into the 2000s. His work continues to hold profound relevance for many of the media-related challenges facing us today. This chapter provides an overview of his academic career, specifically connecting it to the history of IAMCR, an international body of which Gerbner was a key member. To bring this context to light, I draw from the extant biographical and archival records, including mentions of Gerbner in presidential addresses, newsletters, and bulletins from IAMCR's digital archives.[1] Together, these materials offer a compelling view of Gerbner's engagement as a public scholar in general and his involvement with IAMCR in particular (Fig. 29.1).

Sketching key themes from this historical narrative, this chapter is a preliminary analysis of what I hope will become a much longer treatment of Gerbner's research tradition within a broader critical intellectual history of the field of

[1] Archives are available at https://iamcr.org/digital-archive. Accessed 15 June 2022.

V. Pickard (✉)
University of Pennsylvania, Philadelphia, PA, USA
e-mail: victor.pickard@asc.upenn.edu

© The Author(s), under exclusive license to Springer Nature Switzerland AG 2023

J. Becker, R. Mansell (eds.), *Reflections on the International Association for Media and Communication Research*,
https://doi.org/10.1007/978-3-031-16383-8_29

Fig. 29.1 George Gerbner (1919–2005). Member IAMCR International Council 1970–1978, Vice President 1984–1986. (Courtesy of Dan Schiller)

communication. There is a tendency to obscure these more radical traditions—theoretical frameworks that denaturalize the dominant forms and institutions of communication—and therefore it is imperative for critical scholars to rescue these threads from the margins to reassert them within mainstream communication research where they belong.

Biography

George Gerbner's pioneering career in the field of communication was preceded by an adventurous early life.[2] Born in 1919 in Budapest, Hungary, Gerbner's intellectual interests initially focused on folklore and poetry.[3] In 1938, he entered the University of Budapest after winning the top prize in a national high school competition in Hungarian literature. After a year of studying folklore at the university, this early success was derailed when he fled the country in 1939 to avoid being conscripted into the military by the pro-Nazi Hungarian government. After a circuitous route that took him through stays in Italy, France, Cuba, and Mexico, Gerbner eventually emigrated to the United

[2] I thank Jörg Becker for his helpful research assistance in writing this chapter and for generously providing useful context, especially for the IAMCR History Section.

[3] This chapter draws from some of the extensive archival materials located online as part of the George Gerbner Archive at the University of Pennsylvania: https://web.asc.upenn.edu/Gerbner/Archive.aspx. Accessed 15 June 2022.

States (US). He hitchhiked to California and enrolled at University of California, Los Angeles (UCLA), but later transferred to Berkeley where he finished an undergraduate journalism degree. He then worked for the *San Francisco Chronicle* as a reporter and editor.

In 1943, he became a US citizen and promptly enlisted in the military to fight in World War II. First trained as a paratrooper, he was recruited by the Office of Strategic Services (the OSS, predecessor to the CIA) and sent on a mission in which he was to parachute behind enemy lines in Austria. However, the pilot mistakenly dropped him in Slovenia where he and another soldier on his mission joined a partisan brigade to fight and report on German troops in retreat from Greece. During the armistice, Gerbner was reassigned in Austria to help arrest Hungarian soldiers and politicians who had aided the fascists during the war, including the former Hungarian Prime Minister, Dome Sztojay, who was later executed for war crimes. While in Hungary, Gerbner met Ilona Kutas, a famous actress who also taught theater, and they married in 1946. After six more months working as an editor for the US Information Service in Vienna, Gerbner returned to California with Ilona to start a family, with the intention of beginning a long career in journalism.

In California, Gerbner initially struggled to find gainful employment, but by happy accident, he was given the opportunity to work as a journalism instructor at John Muir Junior College in Pasadena after the person who held the position abruptly quit. From that point onward, Gerbner remained in academia. In need of teaching credentials, he began his graduate work at the University of Southern California's (USC) School of Education. He wrote his master's thesis on education and television and then stayed on to author an award-winning dissertation on general theories and models of communication. Gerbner became increasingly interested in the social aspects of mass communication, and while still a graduate student at USC, he worked with Theodor Adorno on the psychodynamics and implicit cultural assumptions embedded in television drama.

Also at this time, Gerbner became politically involved with the Independent Progressive Party, which was aligned with Henry Wallace's 1948 presidential campaign, and he volunteered as an editor for their newspaper. Gerbner's leftist activism during the anti-Communist hysteria of the McCarthy era led to him being called up to testify in front of California's House Un-American Committee (HUAC). Although he was considered "small fry" at the time, he was interrogated for 45 minutes over whether he was a communist and whether he taught subversive materials in his classroom. While this red-baiting likely led to him losing his part-time teaching job at the journalism school in Pasadena, he fortunately was able to then procure a better job as a research assistant at the USC Cinema Department.

It was at USC that in 1956 Gerbner fortuitously met Dallas Smythe, the founder of the North American political economy research tradition, who was visiting USC for a summer teaching position. Smythe recruited Gerbner to teach at his home institution, the Institute of Communications Research at the

University of Illinois, Urbana-Champaign. Gerbner taught there for eight years before moving to the University of Pennsylvania, where he became the longest-serving dean of what was then called the Annenberg School of Communication from 1964 to 1989. During his long tenure, Gerbner built up a top graduate program within what was still a new field of communication. In addition to spearheading many research projects over the years, Gerbner edited the field's preeminent journal, the *Journal of Communication*, from 1974 to 1991. After retiring from the deanship, he taught for a few more years on the faculty until he retired from Penn in 1994. In 1997, he joined the faculty of Temple University as the Bell Atlantic Professor of Telecommunications, where he continued to focus on teaching and activism until his death in December 2005.

George Gerbner's Contributions to Critical Communication Research

Even as he devoted himself to full-time administrative duties at the University of Pennsylvania's Annenberg School, Gerbner maintained an active research agenda. His most significant media effects research focused on television violence and developed into his Cultural Indicators Project. Formally launched in 1968, the project tabulated and critically analyzed television portrayals of women, people of color, aging, gender stereotypes, news coverage of health issues, portrayals of science, and many other subjects. Over the years, the Cultural Indicators Project compiled a massive database of several thousand television programs and tracked how television imagery and storylines influenced Americans' view of society. This research led Gerbner to develop "cultivation theory" (1970) and to formulate what he referred to as the "Mean World Syndrome": the more media audiences were exposed to violence on television, the more dangerous they believed their society to be.

Gerbner's "cultivation analysis" of commercial television's long-term effects has potentially significant, but largely under-studied implications for social media today. As he explained in an interview with John Lent, "The theory of cultivation is different from effects as a kind of short-term change" (Lent, 1995, p. 96). Gerbner argued that, while administrative, market-oriented communication research concludes that media are not very effective, they overlook the importance of everyday cultivation of a consistent cultural orientation—one that is so strong, it cannot be easily changed. According to Gerbner, this tells you that "you're up against a daily long-term cultivation of stable tendencies that large communities absorb over long periods of time and that are not easily changed, unless there is societal change" (Lent, 1995, p. 96). Therefore, Gerbner maintained, "the theory of cultivation has as its target the making of social policy" and it recognizes "the difficulty of changing opinion and policy without structural change in society" (Lent, 1995, p. 96). With such policy interventions as their ultimate objective, he and his fellow researchers published annual reports on the depiction of violence and on how key subjects were covered in the media. Armed with this data, Gerbner became a common figure at congressional hearings focused on scrutinizing popular media (Ledger, 1984). For Gerbner, the stakes could not be higher when considering the detrimental effects of corrosive media content. Democracy itself was threatened by a media system saturated in violent imagery and dangerous stereotypes.

More broadly, Gerbner centered a structural critique in his analysis of how commercial media consistently fail to serve the democratic needs of society. He emphasized that profit imperatives in the commercial media system placed major constraints on what was covered and what ultimately constricted our social imaginary for what we could and should do toward confronting political problems. He argued, "who tells the stories of a culture really governs human behavior" (Oliver, 2005, p. n.p.). He perceived a troubling and dangerous shift in who controls such cultural narratives: "It used to be the parent, the school, the church, the community. Now it's a handful of global conglomerates that have nothing to tell, but a great deal to sell" (Oliver, 2005, p. n.p.).

Gerbner also played an important role in advancing critical scholarship within the field. Although it is difficult to imagine it happening today, as the *Journal of Communication* editor, Gerbner often featured radical analysis and media criticism from a wide range of methodological and theoretical frameworks. Gerbner regularly invited critical commentaries from public intellectuals outside the field to contribute essays and reviews. He also sought to internationalize the field and invited notable scholars such as Stuart Hall to join the editorial board.

In trying to make sense of how Gerbner remained committed to leftist activism while holding positions of academic power during the Cold War, it is quite probable that he often was forced to keep his cards close to his chest. Gerbner himself readily acknowledged that he downplayed his political convictions and tried not to seem too polemical while serving as Dean at the Annenberg School: "As Dean for a whole faculty and school, I had to be fairly prudent in expressing personal points of view" (Lent, 1995, p. 94–95). Instead of engaging in overt polemics, he tried to advance radical critique via substantive empirical research, a strategy he found to be quite effective: "If you can support your arguments and your conclusions with publicly credible, repeatable evidence, you assume an authority that otherwise cannot be gained" (Lent, 1995, p. 95). While he felt that this kind of critical work led to "a certain degree of isolation," he was comfortable for "being known as an analyst and a critic of the mainstream, rather than a part of the mainstream." It is, he observed, a "price that I would consider well worth paying" (Lent, 1995, p. 95).

Gerbner became even more activist during his "retirement" years when he launched the Cultural Environment Movement (CEM). As his former student and frequent collaborator, Michael Morgan noted, the development of the CEM was a more explicitly political project, based on the assumption that "existing media structures in the United States are beyond the reach of democratic policy making" (Morgan, 1995, p. 113; see also Morgan, 2012). Through the CEM, Gerbner sought to create a social movement whose focus was to radically reform our media system—a model that would later inspire subsequent media reformers such as Robert McChesney.

George Gerbner and IAMCR

It is instructive to situate George Gerbner's career within the history of IAMCR.[4] Gerbner first became an IAMCR member in 1967, and in 1970, he became Head of IAMCR's Publication Section. Through the 1970s, he became increasingly involved with IAMCR, though he did not become a core active member until the 1980s and the 1990s. He frequently circulated announcements about new publications and tried to facilitate communication and collaboration between international and US-based scholarship. When he became editor of the *Journal of Communication* in 1974, Gerbner publicized the journal to IAMCR membership, encouraging closer ties. In 1978, he was a plenary speaker at the Warsaw Conference. In 1987, at the ICA annual meeting in Montreal, he helped organize a joint session of the International Communication Section of IAMCR and the ICA, featuring the topic "International Communication as a Field of Study: The State of the Art." The session reportedly was attended by 310 researchers from around the world, some of whom presented work, including Gerbner, who presented on the theme of "International Research Collaboration."[5]

By the 1990s, Gerbner had become a key figure within IAMCR, serving as the Head of the Research/Policy Committee (1991–1993), holding a seat on IAMCR's International Council from about 1991 to 2000, and closely cooperating with Herbert Schiller and Hamid Mowlana (Gerbner, et al., 1993, 1996). Gerbner took part on a closing panel at the 1991 IAMCR meeting in Istanbul to criticize how the news media covered the Gulf War. The 1992 *IAMCR Newsletter* announced the publication of Gerbner's co-edited book with Mowlana et al. (1992), *Triumph of the Image: The Media's War in the Persian Gulf—A Global Perspective*. According to the description, the book—

> contains studies assembled from many countries throughout Europe, Asia, and the Middle East ... [with] contributions from thirty-five authors in eighteen countries ... explor[ing] the social, economic, and political context of media coverage in their countries, the domination of one image in most of them, and the struggle for alternative perspectives.[6]

[4] This section benefited from personal correspondence with Jörg Becker.

[5] Some of these efforts, as well-meaning as they were, may have generated a degree of skepticism among younger, left-leaning IAMCR scholars who saw the Annenberg School, financed by a US media magnate, as epitomizing the established power structure. Given that Gerbner sometimes acted as a kind of bridge-builder between IAMCR and the ICA—which was often seen as a core fixture of the US-dominated academic establishment—also may have fed suspicions.

[6] See https://www.amazon.co.uk/Triumph-Image-Perspective-communication-industries--ebook/dp/B079NNR4F8/ref=tmm_kin_swatch_0?_encoding=UTF8&qid=&sr=. Accessed 15 June 2022.

Gerbner continued to engage with the IAMCR community in the late 1990s and the early 2000s, for example, announcing the launch of the CEM in 1995. At the 1997 Oaxaca Conference, Gerbner, along with Herbert Schiller, were given honorary awards by the IAMCR General Assembly in recognition of their outstanding and long-time contribution to the association and the profession. With Hamid Mowlana in 2000, Gerbner co-authored an eloquent eulogy for the *IAMCR Newsletter* memorializing Herbert Schiller's passing. Much of what they wrote about Schiller also could have easily applied to Gerbner himself: "he strived for a just and fair society."[7]

Conclusion: Implications for Today

The field of communication has much to recover from its intellectual history, particularly critical traditions that have been pushed to the margins (Pickard, 2016, 2021). When we tell stories about our field, we make implicit value judgments. Choices regarding how the field narrates its own history are inherently political; such narratives reflect implicit assumptions about discursive parameters and what qualifies as legitimate scholarship. Dominant historical narratives typically emphasize specific subfields and research traditions while ignoring others. The neglected historical thread represented by George Gerbner's work brings into focus a reformist and policy-focused research tradition that was both deeply empirical and unremittingly critical of the commercial status quo in our core media systems. Recovering such critical traditions of politically engaged policy research could both enrich the field of communication and benefit democratic society writ large. In recovering these erasures, we may consider what factors contribute to elevating some historical narratives about the field of communication over others. And we might envision how different the field could look today were it defined by such critical scholarship.

Gerbner's critical research and the example he set forth as a public-facing scholar holds many important implications for the media and communication-related challenges facing democratic societies today. A major theme that emerges from all of Gerbner's work is his commitment to anti-fascism and his understanding that media are a critical site of struggle for this contestation. As one profile in *The Atlantic* (Stossel, 1997) noted, "Fascism is the specter that looms, tenebrous, over all of Gerbner's life and work." The author of the piece, after much skepticism, concluded, "The more one contemplates the pervasiveness of stereotypical patterns in television, the more one perceives the inaccurate picture of reality it cultivates in viewers—and the more one inclines toward a charitable understanding of Gerbner's fears about fascism."

Today, with the rise of right-wing populism, Gerbner's concerns seem not only prescient but prophetic. Fascistic tendencies are again ascendant in many

[7] *IAMCR Newsletter*, *9*(2), April-May, 2000, p. 8. https://iamcr.org/node/1051. Accessed 15 June 2022.

democratic countries around the world as societies face increasing pressures from right-wing populism, authoritarianism, and various forms of "democratic backsliding" in increasingly illiberal democracies (Bermeo, 2016). Gerbner's work shows us how empirical research can be deployed toward useful analysis that exposes fascistic tendencies in our media system, penetrating to the structural roots, and opening the door toward policy interventions that can promote democracy. Gerbner's anti-fascism holds a natural affinity with the subfield of political economy, which explicitly saw a commitment to anti-fascist activism as a central normative aim animating its scholarship since its origins (Schiller, 1999), and long has maintained a strong tradition within IAMCR (Wasko, 2013).

The communication field has an important but as yet unrealized role to play in fighting back fascism and promoting global democracy. As a scholar-activist, Gerbner pointed the way for how communication scholars can engage with the policy process to help create a more democratic media system. In articulating how we should choose our research trajectory, Gerbner recommended the following criteria: "Is it right? Does it make any real difference? Would the world be any different if I didn't do it?" (Lent, 1995, p. 98). Confronting such questions, we could do much worse than to take inspiration from Gerbner's activism and scholarship.

References

Bermeo, N. (2016). On democratic backsliding. *Journal of Democracy, 27*(1), 5–19.

Gerbner, G. (1970, March 1). Cultural indicators: The case of violence in television drama. *The Annals of the American Academy of Political and Social Science, 338*(1), 69–81.

Gerbner, G., Mowlana, H., & Nordenstreng, K. (1993). *The global media debate: Its rise, fall and renewal.* Ablex.

Gerbner, G., Mowlana, H., & Schiller, H. I. (1996). *Invisible crises: What conglomerate control of media means for America and the world.* Routledge.

Ledger, M. (1984). The dean of communications. *The Pennsylvania Gazette*, 14–20. Retrieved 15 June 2022, from https://web.asc.upenn.edu/gerbner/Asset.aspx?assetID=2760

Lent, J. A. (Ed.). (1995). *A different road taken: Profiles in critical communication.* Westview Press.

Morgan, M. (1995). Critical contribution of George Gerbner. In J. A. Lent (Ed.), *A different road taken: Profiles in critical communication* (pp. 99–117). Westview Press.

Morgan, M. (2012). *George Gerbner: A critical introduction to media and communication theory.* Peter Lang.

Mowlana, H., Gerbner, G., & Schiller, H. I. (Eds.). (1992). *Triumph of the image: The media's war in the Persian Gulf, A global perspective.* Routledge.

Oliver, M. (2005, December 29). George Gerbner, 86; Educator researched the influence of TV viewing on perceptions. *Los Angeles Times.* Retrieved 15 June 2022, from https://www.latimes.com/archives/la-xpm-2005-dec-29-me-gerbner29-story.html

Pickard, V. (2016). Communication's forgotten narratives: The lost history of Charles Siepmann and critical policy research. *Critical Studies in Media Communication, 33*(4), 337–351.

Pickard, V. (2021). Unseeing propaganda: How communication scholars learned to love commercial media. *Harvard Kennedy School (HKS) Misinformation Review, 2*(2), 1–9.

Schiller, D. (1999). The legacy of Robert A. Brady: Antifascist origins of the political economy of communications. *Journal of Media Economics, 12*(2), 89–101.

Stossel, S. (1997, May). The man who counts the killings. *The Atlantic*. Retrieved 15 June 2022, from https://www.theatlantic.com/magazine/archive/1997/05/the-man-who-counts-the-killings/376850/

Wasko, J. (2013). The IAMCR political economy section: A retrospective. *The Political Economy of Communication, 1*(1), 4–8.

CHAPTER 30

Dallas W. Smythe and Détente at IAMCR

Gregory Taylor

Introduction

Dallas W. Smythe is a highly-regarded figure in the history of IAMCR. An annual prize in his name recognizes "the critical, innovative and engaged spirit that characterised Smythe's contribution to media/communications analysis" (IAMCR, 2020). Smythe's early contributions were foundational to the establishment of the political economy of communication as a recognized section within IAMCR in 1978 (Wasko, 2013) and he played a central role in the growth of the association in the 1960s and 1970s. However, his connection to IAMCR was not without its periods of turbulence, and in the later years of his life, he was less connected to the association. A true iconoclast, Smythe's fiercely critical orientation, a stand which made him the subject of an ongoing Federal Bureau of Investigation (FBI) inquiry when he worked in the United States (US), could often place him at odds with even his own colleagues within the burgeoning critical school of communication studies of the late 1960s and early 1970s. Dallas Smythe was, and remains, a controversial scholar, who challenged much of the academic orthodoxy of his day. To explore Smythe's relationship with IAMCR is to understand his strong streak of independence, even while he offered key collaborative contributions to the growth and impact of the organization (Fig. 30.1).

A clear case study to appreciate the mercurial nature of Dallas Smythe's relationship with IAMCR can be found in his association with the Panel of Experts convened by UNESCO and IAMCR at the end of the 1960s and

G. Taylor (✉)
University of Calgary, Calgary, AB, Canada
e-mail: gregory.taylor2@ucalgary.ca

© The Author(s), under exclusive license to Springer Nature Switzerland AG 2023

J. Becker, R. Mansell (eds.), *Reflections on the International Association for Media and Communication Research*,
https://doi.org/10.1007/978-3-031-16383-8_30

Fig. 30.1 Dallas W. Smythe (1907–1992), Member IAMCR Bureau 1970–1976, Section Head—Satellites (and Technology) 1970–1980. Dallas Smythe Prize awarded from 2008 for his contributions to political economy of communication and national and international communication policy. (Courtesy of IAMCR Archive)

the early 1970s. UNESCO has been connected to IAMCR since its founding in 1957, and the idea of the organization had been discussed at UNESCO for a decade prior (Wasko, 2013). Smythe's connection with UNESCO begins and ends at the IAMCR conference. This relatively brief period, between 1968 and 1972, set in motion a series of events that resulted in a significant collaborative scholarship but also left a strain between Smythe and IAMCR that continued for the remainder of this foundational political economist's career. This period of Smythe's work is a window not only into the changing face of IAMCR and Communication Studies in the late 1960s–early 1970s, but also a reflection of the greater global power dynamics at play during the era. Kaarle Nordenstreng justifiably refers to this period as "a new chapter … in the world history of communication research" (Nordenstreng, 1994, p. 3). It is a chapter where, despite his numerous contributions, Smythe would largely find himself written out of the story.

This chapter offers fresh insight into these key years by combining accounts from Smythe himself, written reflections from colleagues, as well as illuminations provided by materials in the Dallas Smythe Archive at Simon Fraser University. The picture it reveals is one of a rapidly developing field of study reflecting the shifting international political landscapes of the late 1960s–early 1970s, and interpersonal tensions between key people in the field. Kaarle Nordenstreng has written on the IAMCR-UNESCO relationship during this period (Nordenstreng, 1994; Wasko et al., 1993), and as a key member of the UNESCO panel, he certainly had a front row seat for much of the drama which unfolded. What is missing from these accounts is the voices of other actors, including Smythe himself.

Smythe's experience reflects a period when being a critical scholar was a radical act worthy of government notice. Prior to his academic career, Smythe was interviewed by the FBI in 1942 while he was a US federal employee, and though he was cleared of any wrongdoing, the FBI kept an active file on Smythe during his years as a professor at the University of Illinois, aided by unnamed but much speculated upon campus informants.[1]

Though born in Saskatchewan, Smythe left Canada when he was quite young, became an American citizen in 1932, and much of his intellectual growth took place in the US both as a scholar and in his many years as a public servant. He established an impressive early career trajectory that included stints as the Chief Economist for the Federal Communications Commission (FCC) and, when he turned to academia, he founded the study of the political economy of communications at the University of Illinois in 1948. Smythe returned to Canada and became a Canadian citizen in 1965. Though Canadian communications scholars often cite Smythe as key in critical Canadian scholarship, Smythe was, of course, unafraid to bite the hand of his re-adopted country, and turned his critical gaze to Canadian communications history and challenged highly regarded Canadian scholars in the field such as Harold A. Innis, whom Smythe saw as technologically determinist (Babe, 2000, p. 135). It was while Smythe was employed at the University of Regina in Saskatchewan that he experienced some of his greatest achievements and most profound rejections within IAMCR.

The Early Association with UNESCO

At IAMCR 1968 in Ljubljana, in what was then Yugoslavia, Smythe, Herbert I. Schiller, Kaarle Nordenstreng, and James D. Halloran in Smythe's words "formed a natural little group" (Smythe & Guback, 1994, p. 213) based upon a common understanding of an international information order which recognized, among other things, autonomy for developing nations. Using contacts Nordenstreng and Halloran had established with UNESCO, this "little group" sought a formal meeting with UNESCO representatives which led to a key gathering in Montreal in June 1969. The UNESCO Secretariat liaised with Halloran about who should be in attendance and a group of 30 was convened.

[1] The author would like to thank Benjamin J. Birkinbine of the Reynolds School of Journalism & Center for Advanced Media Studies at the University of Nevada for generously allowing access to the 195-page Smythe FBI file he accessed via a FOIA request.

The setting was a pre-MacBride Report UNESCO still coming to terms with the power of the rapidly expanding global media. This meeting produced "Mass Media in Society: The Need of Research" (UNESCO, 1970). The stated purpose of the panel might seem obvious in hindsight but was bold for the time: "the relevance and importance of mass media to society have not as yet been as widely recognized and appreciated as would seem to be necessary" (UNESCO, 1970, p. 2). The brief eight-page report set the stage for further work in clear areas such as the need for research, recognizing the one-way flow of global information systems, the specific media requirements of developing nations, and media policy cooperation between countries.

Smythe claims to have had a strong influence in the wording of this document (Smythe & Guback, 1994, p. 214). In a handwritten note attached to a copy of the Montreal report in the Dallas Smythe Archive, Smythe writes of the Montreal meeting, "It was a direct consequence of the 1968 Ljubljana meeting of IAMCR" (Dallas Smythe Archive. F-16-8-1-0-7). The report's recommendations were approved by the 16th General Conference of UNESCO in 1970 and resulted in a continued relationship between IAMCR and UNESCO which lasted for a decade.

The success of Montreal meant that this little group now had solid institutional support and the next meeting was held in Paris in 1971 with largely the same people in attendance. The product of this meeting was a 30-page document that Kaarle Nordenstreng refers to as "UNESCO's classic in the field of communication research" (Nordenstreng, 1994, p. 7), *Proposals for an International Programme of Communication Research* (UNESCO. Panel of Consultants on Communication Research, 1971). The report bore a striking resemblance to its Montreal predecessor but received far wider recognition and acceptance. In a later reflection, Nordenstreng praises the strong ties between the scholars and the UNESCO Secretariat, which he describes as a "perfect understanding" where no restrictions were placed upon the scholars involved (Nordenstreng, 1994, p. 9).

Indeed, UNESCO had become very supportive of the group that had germinated at IAMCR in 1968. In July 1972, eleven members of IAMCR who had been part of the 1971 Paris Report received notice from IAMCR President Jacques Bourquin inviting them to Buenos Aires for the IAMCR conference and noting that "Your travel and accommodation expenses will be paid for by UNESCO" (Bourquin, 1972b). This would have been welcome news for many academics who struggled to find funding to attend the first IAMCR conference to be held outside Europe.

Despite the façade of political support and academic comradery, this seemingly ideal partnership between critical academics and a prominent global political institution proved short-lived, and Dallas Smythe once again found himself pushed (or pushed himself) to the political margins.

The Split in Buenos Aires

As Thomas Guback notes, Smythe's connections to UNESCO "came to a screeching halt" after he presented "Reflections on Proposals for an International Programme of Communications Research" at IAMCR in Buenos Aires in 1972 (Smythe & Guback, 1994, p. 213). In this controversial paper, Smythe expounded upon his theory of "cultural screenings" to serve as a potential check on the inherent imperial implications of Western-based communication technologies, in particular, areas of popular culture provided by Western cultural industries. More significantly, it publicly called upon the very UNESCO Panel he had been central in creating to do more. In the opening paragraph he writes, "now I want to make some critical analysis of our work in the light of later experience" (Smythe in Smythe & Guback, 1994, p. 216). The paper was a gauntlet, thrown before his colleagues and the very organization that had sponsored the participation of himself and several others in attendance. Reflecting on this paper more than a decade later, Smythe noted, "That's the one that got me terminated in UNESCO" (Smythe & Guback, 1994, p. 215).

To understand Dallas Smythe's contributions in Buenos Aires, one must first understand a journey Smythe had taken earlier that year to the People's Republic of China (PRC). Between the Paris UNESCO meeting of 1971 and the Buenos Aires Conference of 1972, Smythe had spent a month in China (PRC) and it had a profound effect. He met with important scholars and government officials in China to discuss the growing influence of communications technology.

This was the "later experience" that caused him to re-evaluate elements of the 1971 Report. Smythe saw first-hand the difficulty in developing a mass media that was outside the Western paradigm. He also saw much of the technology of the West as an ideological Trojan horse. Smythe was a strong supporter of the Chinese cultural revolution. When he returned from his visit to the PRC in 1972, he stopped in Budapest and visited with IAMCR member András Szekfü. Dallas was dressed in blue Mao-jeans and Mao-jacket and wore a Mao-cap with a red star. While this political fashion statement was apparently done for comical effect, it was clear Smythe had been deeply affected by his journey to China and it had an immediate impact on his scholarship.

In his 1972 IAMCR talk, Smythe openly challenged the points he himself had contributed to less than two years previously. Among the points raised in "Reflections on Proposals for an International Program of Communications Research":

> The case which can be made for cultural screening there seems to be little doubt that the burden of proof rests with those who would introduce foreign technology to justify its intrusion. (Smythe in Smythe & Guback, 1994, p. 222)

> If the developing nation accepts the consumer goods which it wants from the western imperialist system, it inevitably accepts the values of that system. (p. 219)

> To endorse the 'international marketing system' function of selling western imperialist technology in the communications area and to invite developing nations to accept such technology *without the caveat of prior cultural screening* (his italics) is to do the gravest disservice to the need of developing nations to determine their own future technology. (p. 223)

Along with his deliberately provocative presentation, Smythe arrived at IAMCR in Buenos Aires with printed copies of an unpublished paper he had written entitled "After bicycles, what?" (1973/1994). He also sent this paper to the Chinese government "as a piece of friendly criticism and advice from a concerned 'family' member within the international socialist movement" (Zhao, 2007, p. 94). This paper became an academic underground classic and was one of Smythe's most well-known essays, though it was never formally published until two decades later. In it, Smythe elaborates on his theory of cultural screens, the inherent ideology in technologies, and the future of Chinese socialism. The paper further burnished Smythe's already impeccable radical credentials. Among his points:

> (The Chinese Cultural Revolution) has...demonstrated to its people's satisfaction that the process works. Food, clothing, housing, (and) health services are available equitably and adequately to the whole population. (Smythe & Guback, 1994, p. 230)

> ...consumer goods, which embody capitalist values such as style and planned obsolescence, are a trap which capitalism presents to new socialist systems—a trap which the masses of Chinese peasants, workers and PLA soldiers should beware. (p. 241)

> And the United States' communication and cultural diplomacy since 1945 in favour of the 'free flow of information' is blood brother to its world-wide imperial policy of economic expansion. (p. 244)

With "Bicycles," coupled with the conference paper critiquing his own very successful UNESCO Panel, Smythe substantially rocked the apple cart that he himself had helped build.

The IAMCR president's letter sent a few months after Buenos Aires does not explicitly call out Smythe when discussing IAMCR's relationship with the UNESCO project, but Smythe's work was clearly in conflict:

> The research we are going to carry out will contribute to widen our knowledge, but they must allow, eventually, to determine a policy protecting the information freedom the liberty of seeking information or opinions of transmitting them, of publishing or broadcasting them, of distributing or expressing them and, finally, of receiving them and the institutional liberty of the press, radio and television, that is the rights and duties of mass media in view of their importance in today's society. (Bourquin, 1972a)

All this rhetoric of broadcasting and distribution freedom runs contrary to the very notion of cultural screens advocated by Smythe. "After Bicycles, What?" explicitly outlined a correlation between information flows and imperialist expansion. The IAMCR organization clearly took great pride in its strong association with UNESCO, which proved increasingly difficult to reconcile with Smythe's emphatic position.

The Sacking of Smythe

By the time of the next report of the UNESCO Panel in 1972, Dallas Smythe was no longer part of the Expert Committee. A copy of the 1972 UNESCO Report in the Dallas Smythe Archive contains a handwritten note from him which succinctly states, "This is the next link in the chain (after Buenos Aires). I'm out. But communications policy is very much in I'm happy to say" (UNESCO, 1972).

Though Smythe was no longer a part of the panel, the foundational 1971 UNESCO Report in which he had been a key voice still reverberated across both academic and political organizations. The 1972 Report notes that "The International Panel of Consultants on Communication Research which advised UNESCO in 1971 on its mass communication research programme, ... prepared the way for the meeting reflected in this report" (UNESCO, 1972, p. 18).[2] Despite the presence of some panel members such as Nordenstreng, the 1972 Report was not nearly as provocative. It contains passages Smythe would have clearly found technologically deterministic such as:

> The introduction of communication technology into the traditional forms of communication through the country may cause shifts of power and influence among social classes and may change the leadership structures. The innovation and spread of ideas, values and practices can be directly affected by the presence of new communication systems. (UNESCO, 1972, p. 10)

Nordenstreng referred to the dropping of Smythe from the UNESCO Panel in 1973 as "anti-intellectual repression" (Wasko et al., 1993, p. 253) that can happen in unconventional partnerships between academia and political organizations. Reflecting on the UNESCO Panel, Nordenstreng sees the conflict as largely inevitable, saying he believes it is misleading "to suggest that a truly scientific study ever could be free from political implications" and vaguely mentions, "political forces may directly interfere in the intellectual inquiry through institutional moves..." In the same paper, he notes, "Schiller, Smythe, and most critical scholars made their observations from an academic ivory tower" (p. 256), implying they do not fully grasp the give-and-take of actual

[2] The quote is from a handwritten note attached to the report sourced from the Dallas Smythe Archive, Simon Fraser University.

policymaking. Certainly, for Smythe, this accusation seems curious if not flat-out wrong, given his many years as a federal civil servant.

In his account of the change in Panel membership, Nordenstreng obliquely notes in passing that while some changes in membership were expected and normal "in Smythe's case, it is arguable that the replacement was politically motivated" (Nordenstreng, 1994, p. 9). In Smythe's view, it was politically motivated; there was no argument. His removal from the UNESCO Panel was shortly followed by similar bad news from IAMCR (Fig. 30.2).

In 1976, Smythe received a letter from IAMCR President James D. Halloran, informing him that elections had been held at the 1976 IAMCR Conference in Leicester and that Smythe was no longer a member of the Permanent Board of IAMCR. Halloran wrote a polite send-off:

> I would like to take this opportunity of thanking you most sincerely for the work you have done for the Association whilst serving as a member of the Permanent Bureau and until recently as President of the Satellite Section. I would also like to think I can count on your active involvement in our affairs for many years to come. (Halloran, 1976)

The news did not come as a shock to Smythe. He was already aware of his removal and had received a letter in October of that year from Georges H. Mond of the Institut Francais de Presse et des Sciences de l'information, who claimed the dropping of Smythe was purposeful, yet Mond could not understand the rationale for excluding a scholar of Smythe's caliber: "As you probably know, you and myself were excluded of the new executive body of IAMCR; as for me I know very well why. But you?" (Mond, 1976).

Kaarle Nordenstreng later described his own role in the vote which removed Smythe from the executive of IAMCR. In his view, Smythe was removed to facilitate a more inclusive membership in the board, although the process seems hastily conceived:

> ...the slate for elections was adopted by the general assembly, as proposed by Halloran. His proposal was prepared behind the scenes during the conference itself, by Nordenstreng, who tried to achieve a balanced representation not only in terms of geopolitics but also of scholarly generations as well as gender. Accordingly, Nordenstreng brought to the list seven women, including Nelly de Camargo of Brazil, Anita Werner of Norway, and Gertrude Robinson of Canada. Robinson's entry pushed out Dallas Smythe, who had been a bureau member since 1970. (Nordenstreng in Park & Pooley, 2008, p. 239)

In an October 1976 letter to Nordenstreng, Smythe is far more blunt about why he believes he was removed not just from the UNESCO Panel but the IAMCR Executive Committee. He conveys that he has been informed by Herbert Schiller that, "I had been dumped from the IAMCR executive committee in what (quoting Schiller) 'was practically a personal decision as far as I can make out'" (Smythe, 1976). Clearly, in Smythe's mind, his dismissal from

Fig. 30.2 Kaarle Nordenstreng, Dallas W. Smythe, and Herbert I. Schiller at a Meeting on Information Technology in Moscow, 1973. (From left to right) **Nordenstreng**—IAMCR Executive 1970–1972, Vice President 1972–1986, International Council 2004–2006, Section Head—Developing Countries 1972–1974, Section Head—Professional Education 1990–1996, Chair Section/Scholarly Review Committee 1996–2010; **Smythe** (1907–1992), IAMCR Bureau 1970–1976, Section Head—Satellites (and Technology) 1970–1980; **Schiller** (1919–2000) IAMCR International Council 1970–1972, 1988–1990, Vice President 1972–1986. (Courtesy of Dan Schiller)

the UNESCO Panel and the IAMCR Executive Committee (EC) were related. In the letter, Smythe sketches what he sees as the likely scenario which unfolded in Buenos Aires in 1972:

> ... my outspoken Marxist views irritated the West Germans and Americans in UNESCO. They dumped me from the UNESCO panel...Why? ...The Chinese are about to take an active role in IAMCR. By dropping me the executive of IAMCR is unalloyedly committed to détente (for it is no secret that my theoretical writings put me in the position of being critical of the East European regimes).

> In political terms, the dumping of me "tidies up" the IAMCR executive: now no one in it is disposed to criticize détente; the Chinese, if they come in, will be alone in doing so. (Smythe, 1976)[3]

In Smythe's eyes, his removal from the UNESCO Panel and the IAMCR EC were not just the product of inter-personal conflict and organizational upheaval, though both played a role; Smythe believed his pro-China, anti-American stance was too radical for a period characterized by a thaw in US-Soviet relations, known as *détente*, and increased tensions between the USSR and China. In 1970, Mao had decided that the USSR was a more important enemy than the US, which had opened the door to Nixon's visit to China in 1972. Smythe clearly had a positive attitude towards China which made him vulnerable inside IAMCR, as many influential IAMCR officers supported the foreign policy of the USSR. He believed his pro-China stand placed him clearly on the periphery of IAMCR and UNESCO during the period of détente.

Until the 1976 Leicester Conference, which Smythe did not attend, he had been a member of IAMCR's Permanent Bureau and the President of the Communication Satellite Section. He lost both these positions at the Leicester Conference. In 1978, Dallas tried to re-incarnate his old section at IAMCR under the name "Communication Satellite and Technology Section," serving as the Section Head and developing a background for the 1978 IAMCR Conference in Warsaw. But Smythe's days in high-ranking IAMCR positions were over.

By 1980, the UNESCO-IAMCR relationship that had begun with such a promise at IAMCR in 1968 was essentially done. The loss of Smythe seemed to coincide with the wind being knocked out of the sails of the Panel. As Nordenstreng observed in 1993:

> The Panel, with its more or less critical orientation, lost momentum at the very point (1975–1976) when its message was picked up by the most determining forces of the international community, notably, the Non-Aligned Movement (NAM) sponsoring a New World Information and Communication Order (NWICO), along with the East-West constellation sponsoring the Helsinki Accords. (Nordenstreng in Wasko et al., 1993, p. 252)

Nordenstreng later further described the gradual unraveling:

> By this time (1980), the UNESCO panel of consultants on communication research had ended its term and could no longer meet parallel to IAMCR, thus ending UNESCO's indirect subsidy. UNESCO's support to thematic publica-

[3] In this letter, Smythe also names fellow IAMCR members he believed were instrumental in him "being dumped" from the UNESCO Panel. Since I have no way to confirm these accusations, I have left them out of this chapter.

tions was also discontinued, … This was due to changing priorities in UNESCO's communication program … (Nordenstreng in Park & Pooley, 2008, p. 240)

The "little group" of 1969 was officially over, though it seems any pretense of vitality had been gone for some time. As a punctuation mark on the fall of the organization during this era, in 1985, the US officially withdrew from UNESCO, something it had threatened to do since 1978.

Conclusion

Despite the substantial bumps along the way, IAMCR remained central to Smythe's international academic community. The collection *Illuminating the Blindspots: Essays Honoring Dallas W Smythe* was initially presented at a Special Session of IAMCR in Chicago in 1991, the year before Smythe died (Wasko et al., 1993). The conclusion of that book envisages that "The life and work of Dallas Smythe will inform us for a long time to come" (p. 409). Revisiting his scholarship and activism in 2021, it seems clear this prediction has held true.

The related examples of Smythe being removed from both the UNESCO Panel and, subsequently, the IAMCR EC, clearly demonstrate that notwithstanding all the accolades, Smythe was not always an easy fit in the wider academic community. Whether Smythe was the victim of the politicization of the organizational process, interpersonal tensions, or his own iconoclastic nature, his relationship with IAMCR was never to be as close as it had been in the 1960s and early 1970s. However, in no way was he finished as a scholar of consequence as he drifted away from IAMCR; his most recognized works, the 1977 article "Communications: Blindspot of Western Marxism" (Smythe, 1977), and the book *Dependency Road* (Smythe, 1981) were still to come.

Despite his sense of being "dumped" at IAMCR, Smythe lost none of his scholarly impact. Again, the durability of these works is routinely recognized by many in the field. "Blindspot for Western Marxism" and the ensuing written debates with Graham Murdock remain essential reading for critical communication scholars (Murdock, 1978; Smythe, 1978) that still spark arguments decades after publication (Meehan in Wasko et al., 1993; Fuchs, 2012). Likewise, in his foreword to *Dependency Road*, Smythe's "grand work of synthesis" (Babe, 2000, p. 117), Herbert Schiller foresees "the book will not lose its relevancy" (Schiller in Smythe, 1981, p. xxii). The foreword, like the book, has proven prescient. These contributions continue to reverberate in critical communication scholarship.

In his 1995 book, *A Different Road Taken*, John Lent notes the difficulty in arriving at a consensus definition of what exactly we mean by "critical communication" (Lent, 1995). By just about any way you want to define it, Smythe remains a critical scholar who continually and vigorously challenged the political and academic orthodoxy of his era, sometimes to his personal detriment. There was never a détente between Smythe and the systemic power imbalances he viewed as embedded in our communication order. In the US, he was a federal employee who argued against the American hegemony of the time to the extent that it triggered an FBI investigation into his life; at the University of Illinois, he challenged his field by introducing the first political economy of communications course; when he moved to Canada, Smythe published many works questioning the direction of Canada's media, while also providing research for the Canadian government.

It should have been no surprise that he was willing to turn his sharp critical gaze to organizations such as UNESCO or IAMCR. Dallas Smythe remained fiercely independent, no matter who was paying his expenses.

References

Babe, R. E. (2000). *Canadian communication thought: Ten foundational writers*. University of Toronto Press.

Bourquin, J. (1972a, December). *26th presidential letter*. IAMCR. Retrieved 15 June 2022, from https://iamcr.org/fr/node/10510

Bourquin, J. (1972b, July 14). [Dear colleagues,]. F-16-8-1-0-6. Dallas Smythe Archive. Simon Fraser University.

Fuchs, C. (2012). Dallas Smythe Today—The audience commodity, the digital labour debate, Marxist political economy and critical theory. *tripleC: Communication, Capitalism and Critique*, *10*(2), 692–740. Retrieved 15 June 2022, from https://www.triple-c.at/index.php/tripleC/article/view/443

Halloran, J. D. (1976, December 3). [Dear Dallas]. F-16-8-1-0-10. Dallas Smythe Archive. Simon Fraser University.

IAMCR. (2020). 2020 Smythe award winner. Retrieved 15 June 2022, from https://iamcr.org/awards/smythe-2020-winner

Lent, J. A. (1995). *A different road taken: Profiles in critical communication*. Westview Press.

Mond, G. H. (1976, October 12). [Dear Professor Smythe,]. F-16-8-1-0-10. Dallas Smythe Archive. Simon Fraser University.

Murdock, G. (1978). Blindspots about Western Marxism: A reply to Dallas Smythe. *Canadian Journal of Political and Social Theory/Revue canadienne de théorie politique et sociale*, *2*(2), 109–115. Retrieved 15 June 2022, from https://journals.uvic.ca/index.php/ctheory/article/view/13744

Nordenstreng, K. (1994). The Unesco expert panel with the benefit of hindsight. In C. J. Hamelink, O. Linné, & J. D. Halloran (Eds.), *Mass communication research: On problems and policies: The art of asking the right questions: In honor of James D. Halloran* (p. 3–19). Ablex Publishing Corporation.

Park, D. W., & Pooley, J. (2008). *The history of media and communication research: Contested memories*. Peter Lang.

Smythe, D. W. (1973/1994). After bicycles, what? In Gubeck, T. (Ed.), *Counterclockwise: Perspectives on communication* (pp. 230–244). Westview Press and F-16-6-1-0-178. Dallas Smythe Archive. Simon Fraser University. Retrieved 15 June 2022, from https://atom.archives.sfu.ca/f-16-6-1-0-178

Smythe, D. W. (1976, October 23). [Dear Kaarle,]. F-16-8-1-0-10. Dallas Smythe Archive. Simon Fraser University.

Smythe, D. W. (1977). Communications: Blindspot of Western Marxism. *Canadian Journal of Political and Social Theory/Revue canadienne de theorie politique et sociale, 1*(3), 1–27. Retrieved 15 June 2022, from https://journals.uvic.ca/index.php/ctheory/article/view/13715

Smythe, D. W. (1978). Rejoinder to Graham Murdock. *Canadian Journal of Political and Social Theory/Revue canadienne de théorie politique et sociale, 2*(2), 120–127. Retrieved 15 June 2022, from https://journals.uvic.ca/index.php/ctheory/article/view/13745

Smythe, D. W. (1981). *Dependency road: Communications, capitalism, consciousness, and Canada*. Ablex Publishing.

Smythe, D. W., & Guback, T. H. (1994). *Counterclockwise: Perspectives on communication*. Westview Press.

UNESCO. (1970). *Mass media in society: The need of research*. UNESCO.

UNESCO. (1971). *Proposals for an international programme of communication research* (Panel of Consultants on Communication Research). Dallas Smythe Archive. Simon Fraser University.

UNESCO. (1972, July). *Report of the meeting of experts on communication policies and planning*. Dallas Smythe Archive. Simon Fraser University.

Wasko, J. (2013). The IAMCR political economy section: A retrospective. *The Political Economy of Communication, 1*(1), 4–8. Retrieved 15 June 2022, from http://www.polecom.org/index.php/polecom/article/view/11/149

Wasko, J., Mosco, V., & Pendakur, M. (1993). *Illuminating the blindspots: Essays honoring Dallas W. Smythe*. Ablex Publishing.

Zhao, Y. (2007). After mobile phones, what? Re-embedding the social in China's 'Digital Revolution'. *International Journal of Communication, 1*(1), 92–120. Retrieved 15 June 2022, from https://ijoc.org/index.php/ijoc/article/view/5

CHAPTER 31

Herbert I. Schiller

Cees J. Hamelink

Introduction

Herbert Schiller and I met in 1973 when he was a guest professor in Amsterdam and participated in a workshop on media research for which he wrote "Mass Communication Research on the Power Structures of Society." From that moment on we shared a long history of walking dialogs, visits to jazz clubs (he introduced me to Julian Cannonball Adderley), joint travel to destinations such as the Soviet Union (not easy because Herb was a nervous traveler), working with Armand Mattelart on the "The Corporate Village," (Hamelink, 1977) meetings with ex-CIA operative Philip Agee and intense conversations about our common interests. This continued until three days before his death in 2000 (Fig. 31.1).

When Jörg Becker invited me to write a chapter on Herb, I was not sure whether to accept. What was there left to write about after all the obituaries that others and I had written, the splendid biography by Richard Maxwell (2003), or the lucid analysis of his work by Graham Murdock in the *International Journal of Cultural Policy* (2006). Moreover, it is always a daunting challenge to write about close friends without falling into the trap of producing a hagiography.

Upon some reflection, it seemed to me that the best way to contribute to a book that would form part of writing IAMCR's history would be an attempt to understand what the significance of Herb Schiller has been for the association. He inspired and supported the idea of a section on Political Economy and was for several years, one of the Vice Presidents of the association. However,

C. J. Hamelink (✉)
University of Amsterdam, Amsterdam, Netherlands

© The Author(s), under exclusive license to Springer Nature Switzerland AG 2023

J. Becker, R. Mansell (eds.), *Reflections on the International Association for Media and Communication Research*,
https://doi.org/10.1007/978-3-031-16383-8_31

Fig. 31.1 Herbert I. Schiller (1919–2000), Member IAMCR International Council 1970–72, 1988–90, Vice President 1972–86. Herbert Schiller Prize awarded from 2008 for his work challenging accepted orthodoxies and centers of power. (Courtesy of Dan Schiller)

Herb was not an administrator, manager, or policymaker and he never aspired to such a position. He also was not an activist in the sense of an "on the barricades rebel," but he was an activist as a public intellectual. His persuasive and captivating public speaking must have motivated many among his young audiences to take some form of action. But when I tried to get him involved in movements such as the People's Communication Charter or the Cultural Environment Movement, he preferred to do what he did best: analyze the global informational/cultural environment and its management by big business.

Early Contributions

IAMCR was, certainly in the first years after its constitution in 1957, a forum for conventional media research on legal, social, and historical themes. Its research interests were firmly embedded in the UNESCO framework of the free flow of information doctrine. There was more administrative than critical research. Herb Schiller brought a different perspective when he headed the Working Group (WG) on Economy and Structure of the Mass Media in Leipzig during the 1974 Conference. The sessions heard papers on the monopolistic organization of news agencies and the effects on news contents, the strengths and limitations of world-wide news agencies, the structure of bias in mass media research, the economic and political aspects of the American film industry, the interaction between the economy and policy in the mass media, the expansion of international media enterprises and the consequences for international relations, elites, and national media systems in the Middle East, direct satellite broadcasting and international research, the connection between media monopolies and manipulation in France, and the relationship between socialist and capitalist journalism and the masses of people. This gave a real international perspective to the intellectual agenda of the association. As Graham Murdock wrote, "He was one of the first to grasp that the locus of global power in the postwar era was moving from the appropriation of territory to the annexation of imagination" (2006, p. 210).

Herb Schiller also contributed to breaking up the unproductive distinction between quantitative and qualitative research. Most of his work was descriptive but his narrative style was supported by large quantities of empirical data. He used numbers not to quantify the obvious but to support critical arguments. He argued that however much science may claim to be objective, in the end, it is always guided by subjective preferences in its presuppositions. He showed how one could go beyond the descriptive and take normative positions. For someone like myself, who always believed that the social sciences should not only analyze how society is managed but also guide the pathway to thinking about how society should be, Herb's normative approach to the issue of power was enormously inspiring.

Herb Schiller was, for many of us in the association, a good example of how to function as a public intellectual through his lectures, but also through his "Herb Schiller reads the New York Times" for Paper Tiger Television.[1] His reading of this newspaper was both intellectually enlightening and good entertainment. He demonstrated the role of the public intellectual in a 1980 Caracas IAMCR dialog with Ithiel de Sola Pool (See Chap. 32). This exchange that I had the privilege to moderate was a meeting of two very different mindsets—fundamentally disagreeing, but mutually respecting. This was intellectual dialog at its best and it showed where the association could make a difference. Herb also stimulated the association to take public stands on such issues as the New International Information Order (NIIO).

As Time Went By

It is important to realize that despite a good deal of acclaim, Herb Schiller's position remained a minority one in the global community of communication scholars. And as time went by, the pressure on academics to use terms such as "critical" and "independent" as mere window-dressing increased, and the spaces for fundamental critical reflection diminished. The successful global proliferation of a formula that subjects an expanding range of social services to calculability, predictability, and rationality has also begun to affect universities around the globe. The model for the world of higher learning consists of a competitive, neurotic anxiety about quantifiable methods of assessment, and funding mechanisms that are ill-equipped to deal with interdisciplinary,

[1] See https://www.youtube.com/watch?v=3bbLHY847F0. Accessed 15 June 2022.

innovative, and "out of the box" research. Just as the industry that was so eloquently criticized by Schiller has become the driving force behind the knowledge economy, so also, the academy has become more industrialized.

Universities have begun to produce more and more knowledge under intellectual property rights arrangements. The industrialization of intellectual work implies that knowledge is increasingly recognized only if published in scholarly journals that are managed by the global publishing industries that control the rights to scientific/intellectual content. Academic employment has adopted the post-Fordist forms of part-time, short-time, or flexible-time contracts across the globe. The uncertainty of these arrangements clashes with openness to the independent critical academic mindset. Academic work has become a form of intellectual embedding. Like the phenomenon of embeddedness in journalism, the notion can apply equally to intellectuals and communication scholars. Their embeddedness occurs through institutional and funding practices and constraints (in academia, private think tanks, or public policy centers) leading to research that best serves dominant administrative and commercial interests.

In this context, a special concern is also that in communication research, younger generation scholars who are following up the critical political economy approach of such colleagues such as Peter Golding, Robin Mansell, Vincent Mosco, Graham Murdock, Janet Wasko, the late Dallas Smythe, or the late Herbert Schiller, continue to be a minority. Yet, critical studies to understand how processes of neoliberal economic globalization affect socio-political communicative relations are urgently needed. They must address questions such as how can one realistically expect global digital solidarity in an economic system that promotes inequality and competitive strife? Do such essential conditions for genuine public communication as availability of public space and time collide with the driving forces of globalization? These are the kinds of essential existential questions of morality and sense-making that Schiller raised in his inquiries when he proposed that academics should take responsibility for the social environment they investigate.

Herb Schiller's proposal in the 1973 workshop on Mass Media Research that I referred to above was to study the control mechanisms in media systems, how they organize, package, and export their messages and how the informational/entertainment component of the cultural sphere contributes to the deterioration of our living spaces. This is still valid!

This is certainly so in the time of COVID-19, in which the consciousness industry spends much energy in framing the pandemic and its messianic solution through global vaccination programs. The early twenty-first century is witness to a major exercise in mind management steered by big business (pharma, finance, and high-tech industries) and sanctioned by autocratic governments, opportunistic political parties, establishment mainstream media, semi-scientific celebrities in virology and epidemiology, and frightened electorates. Advances in information/communication technology as crucial tools in data manipulation, surveillance applications, algorithms that remind us to stay connected, censorship by social media platforms such as Facebook and Twitter, are welcomed massively and with remarkably little, if any, critical reflection. This should remind us of how Schiller raised, with a regularity that bordered on the obstinate, the issue of technology's neutrality. For Schiller, technology was not a self-generating process, but a social construct defined by existing relations of power. He thought that basing the value of technology on the mode of its utilization obscures the fact that behind the generation of technology, there are intentions that respond to a hierarchy of societal goals. Following the dominance of industrial needs, most technology is based upon the interest to "master" it and is operative in nature. This mechanistic technology is incapable of solving the critical problems the planet faces. Schiller argued that this type of technology was at the basis of mind management and cultural domination and served poorly human ambitions of liberation and conscientization. In his writing and talking about advances in communication/information technologies, Schiller was a master at demystifying and de-expertizing, so that discussion could be brought back to issues of control and domination.

Honoring his heritage, as an international association, we should, in addition to the Schiller Award, focus in our meetings and research projects on the essential themes of the manipulation of consciousness, the corporate control of the public sphere, the deceptive promises of the information society, and the appropriation of new information/communication technologies by the leading "Frightful Five" high-tech companies. And most importantly of all, we should engage in a global dialog about Schiller's most elementary question: "What kind of society do we want to live in?" We should undertake this with the academic discipline and humanitarian commitment that characterized Herb Schiller's contribution to IAMCR.

Selected Authored, Co-authored, and Co-edited Books by Herbert I. Schiller

Mass communication and American empire. New York: Augustus M. Kelley. 1969.

Super-state: Readings in the military-industrial complex. With Philipps, J. D. University of Illinois Press. 1970.

The mind managers. Beacon Press. 1973.

Communication and cultural domination. International Arts and Sciences Press. 1976.

National sovereignty and international communication. Edited with Nordenstreng, K. Ablex. 1979.

Who knows: Information in the age of the Fortune 500. Ablex. 1981.

Information and the crisis economy. Ablex. 1984.

Culture Inc: The corporate takeover of public expression. Oxford University Press. 1989.

Hope and folly: The U.S. and UNESCO, 1949–1985. With Hermann, E & Preston, W. Jr. University of Minneapolis Press. 1989.
The Ideology of international communication. With Alexandre, L., Anderson, R., Mahoney, E., Preston, W. Jr. & Roach, C. Edited by Alexandre, L. New York Institute of Media Analysis. 1992.
Triumph of the image: The media's war in the Persian Gulf—A global perspective. Edited with Gerbner, G. & Mowlana, H. Westview Press. 1992.
Beyond national sovereignty: International communication in the 1990s. Edited with Nordenstreng, K. Ablex. 1993.
Information inequality: The deepening social crisis in America. Routledge. 1996.
Invisible crisis: What conglomerate control of media means for America and the world. Edited with Gerbner, G. & Mowlana, H. Westview Press. 1996.
Living in the number one country: Reflections from a critic of American empire. Seven Stories Press. 2000.

References

Hamelink, C. J. (1977). *The corporate village: The role of transnational corporations in international communication.* IDOC International.
Maxwell, R. (2003). *Herbert Schiller.* Rowman & Littlefield Publishers.
Murdock, G. (2006). Notes from the number one country. Herbert Schiller on culture, commerce and American power. *International Journal of Cultural Policy, 12*(2), 209–227.
Schiller, H. I. (1973). Mass communication research on the power structures of society: A proposal. In C. J. Hamelink (Ed.), *Mass communication research* (p. 43–45). Lutheran World Federation.

CHAPTER 32

Perspectives on Communications Research: An Exchange

Ithiel de Sola Pool, Herbert Schiller, and Cees J. Hamelink

The 1980 General Assembly of the International Association for Mass Communication Research took place in Caracas, Venezuela. After one session in which Ithiel de Sola Pool delivered a paper on communication research and Herbert Schiller was discussant, some members took the initiative to arrange a direct exchange of views addressed to questions posed through moderator Cees Hamelink.[1] *This session resulted in what we believe to be a scholarly exchange of*

[1] Ithiel de Sola Pool was Sloan Professor of Political Science and Director of the Research Program on Communications Policy at the Massachusetts Institute of Technology. Herbert I. Schiller was Professor of Communications at the University of California at San Diego. Moderator Cees Hamelink at the time of first publication was a Senior Lecturer in International Communications at The Institute of Social Studies, The Hague, The Netherlands. This chapter was first published in 1981 in the *Journal of Communication*, *31*(3), p. 15–23. It is republished here with the permission of Oxford University Press.

I. de Sola Pool (Deceased)
Massachusetts Institute of Technology, Cambridge, MA, USA

H. Schiller (Deceased)
University of California at San Diego, La Jolla, CA, USA

C. J. Hamelink (✉)
University of Amsterdam, Amsterdam, Netherlands

© The Author(s), under exclusive license to Springer Nature Switzerland AG 2023

J. Becker, R. Mansell (eds.), *Reflections on the International Association for Media and Communication Research*,
https://doi.org/10.1007/978-3-031-16383-8_32

perspectives and beliefs governing the thinking and work of two productive and principled scholars who joined forces on one level and joined issues on another—The Editors of *Journal of Communication.*

Hamelink: What are the fundamental assumptions that each of you makes in your activities as communications scholars? What are the basic assumptions that lead you to do the kinds of research that you do, and to make the kinds of statements that you do, to take the kinds of positions that you take?

Pool: What led me into the field of communications and has continued to maintain my interest in it is that communications is a way of looking at all human behavior. I'm not particularly interested in studying just the institutions that are organized to disseminate mass media information. I'm interested in the totality of human behavior.

There are various ways of studying that; economists study it in terms of exchange relationships, trade-offs, and values. Sociologists study it from the point of view of role-relations. Some people, such as Herb Schiller, study it with a focus on class. To me, communications is interesting because it is an effective way of looking at human behavior.

Unlike some other people who believe that their approach is the one right one, and that other approaches are less fundamental or less important, I am merely saying that for me, this is an interesting approach. It enables one to look at virtually any aspect of human activity.

Schiller: I'll be as personal as I think this question demands. I have a very strong belief in the possibility of human fraternity, in the possibility of community, in the sense in which human beings can treat each other in a way in which respect and dignity are offered. I found communications as one means, a means which permits me to try to understand why we fall so far short of that possibility, and how we might make it a little more likely that we could take at least a few modest steps in that direction.

Hamelink: There is a related question asked as to the kinds of research the particular assumptions that you have would lead you to engage in. This goes, I think, necessarily to the one or the other kinds of research that you would deem to be important and would deem to be aligned with your assumptions.

Pool: The statement I made just before would not help answer that question because I was suggesting that communications is a way of coping with almost any social research problem; it is an approach.

In selecting one's specific research problems, one selects them by many criteria, including value issues such as those that Herb Schiller just mentioned, and about which I don't see any real disagreement between us. Also, one is guided by scientific criteria: some investigations are likely to pay off, to produce valid findings; others are likely to fail.

In terms of value assumptions, my personal interests focus very largely on questions of political participation: political participation in advanced countries, political participation in developing countries, and political participation through the use of new media. I doubt that we are likely to differ much at this fundamental level. Obviously, if one goes to a more concrete level of how to implement participation, one would find wide differences.

Schiller: Well, building on what I just said, along with the assumption of the belief in community, I would add also that I don't believe that human beings are in any way human if they are not social. I feel that it is absolutely essential and imperative to understand the total social nature of human existence, and of one human being. Consequently, the notion that a person can be totally free as an individual, to me, is a senseless proposition. And therefore, when it comes to selecting areas for study or research, I go back to these basic notions and ask what it is at any social time, in any social period, that prevents the recognition of the social factor in the development of humanness. This leads, it seems to me, to a materialist analysis because I reject a genetic explanation. I reject any type of hereditary explanation, so we are left only with social institutional explanations.

Then one is forced, at least in my judgment, to examine the social institutions in any period that condition behavior and condition individual outlooks.

Hamelink: Now from this rather general introduction, it seems we can go along systematically into more particular areas. Something Karl Marx has said is that philosophers should not only explain the world, but they should help change the world. How does that go for communications research?

Pool: Marx said that in the context of a very special set of philosophical views and theories. In agreeing that Marx's proverb is true, I don't necessarily accept all that context, all that baggage that goes with it.

What qualifications would I add to the rather banal truism of the proverb? One qualification concerns how a philosopher, as a philosopher, goes about changing the world. He can do it as a citizen, which he is. But, as a citizen, he is not necessarily reflecting his quality as a philosopher. In fact, most of the philosophers I know are rather poor political activists. The traits of philosophers and effective activists, more often than not, do not go together. So that, as a philosopher, he may best change the world primarily through the process of increasing understanding, creating a better way of analyzing things, arriving at a closer approximation to the truth.

Insofar as Marx's statement is taken by some people in the Marxist tradition to mean that one somehow has an obligation to confuse one's analysis with political biases, I simply don't accept it. One does have obligations to act as a citizen, whether one is a philosopher or not, and whether or not one's actions follow from one's philosophical specialty. But if one is a philosopher, one does have an obligation to clarify whatever one is working on, not to confuse it by one's political preferences. By one's contribution to understanding, one will help to change the world.

Schiller: First of all, if you don't believe your task is to change the world, then you have to believe your task is to maintain the world. And that leaves, it seems to me, no room for further discussion. So I don't think there's any question of where that choice comes down. Then the matter is when you opt for change, does that necessarily mean that you opt for illogicality, for some type of emotionality which is not well-founded on rational analysis, or even as I believe, Ithiel Pool is suggesting (maybe I misunderstand him), automatically relating critical analysis with political activism. I think almost all of us here, because we are a highly academic group, can attest to the incredible amount of pointless work that is undertaken. I'm not making judgments on quality, but on the pointlessness of work. One thinks, for example, in the United States, and probably in most Western industrially advanced societies, of the number of incredibly talented people doing absolutely pointless things—maybe even injurious things. What I am suggesting in this response is, if one is lucky enough to have a position in which you are entitled to select, or at least have some small maneuverability in selecting, an area for your analysis and inquiry, it would seem to me that you would try to have pointedness, relevance, which would contribute to change.

Hamelink: Now the next question asks that since mass communications some fifty years from now will be so totally different from what it is today, is much of what we discuss here irrelevant?

Schiller: Let me begin with an analogy. I teach at the University of California, San Diego, which is located approximately 80 miles south of Disneyland. Many of my students grew up, literally grew up in Disneyland. Often they are very upset when that venture in commercial entertainment is questioned. I was there once—was taken there by two students. I noticed a fascinating exhibit. If I'm not mistaken, it was the General Electric Corporation's exhibit. It presented, among other things, the history of washing—actual laundering. And in that exhibit, you find constructions and replications of ancient times; in one scene, women are pounding wet wash on rocks; in a later period, they are using some other kind of elementary materials; in a still later period, but already into the industrial era, a very primitive wringer is in use. Finally, in our time, there appears a washing machine with so many buttons it looks like the control panel of a Boeing 747. But in every period, one thing remained constant, and you all know what it was. The women were doing the washing. This brings me back to the question.

I'm sure we'll have dazzling types of technology. We already have many examples. In fact, there's nothing like being taken to some new plant or some new studio where some of this equipment is already installed, to be dazzled. And I'm prepared to believe that this instrumentation may accomplish many wonderful things and have many kinds of unforeseen yet attractive results. The options are there and not beyond the realm of possibility. Yet, all this new equipment does not, of itself, fundamentally necessitate changed social relations. It may, but unless there is anticipation, unless there is some sort of direction, very often the new technologies are used for the same practices that have prevailed over very long historical periods. Today we have television, but television is by no means the type of instrument that it was suggested it would be when it first came into our homes. Video cassettes are the future; cable TV is the future, actually it is already here; direct broadcasting from satellites is already here; all of these developments are here and will be refined and extended. But unless we make very, very careful preparations and, in my judgment, very fundamental social changes, I don't believe any of this equipment will necessarily be used to human advantage. It may very well be used to human disadvantage.

Pool: There's something wrong with the questions that have been asked so far. Somebody ought to ask the question **if** Professor Pool and Professor Schiller agree so much, why are they viewed as being on opposite poles in some respects. Certainly, nothing that's been asked so far has really drawn any polarization between us. I would agree with everything Professor Schiller just said.

Fifty years is not a long time. I've just been writing something on the 1927 Radio Act in the United States. The thing that has surprised me and shocked me is that every one of the issues that we now debate about broadcast policy came up—was not solved, was not really understood—but came up in discussion in the US Congress and in related institutions in discussing the Radio Act of 1927. The question of public ownership, private ownership, pluralism, the advantages of few channels versus many channels, the question of advertising—all these questions were there. Nobody in 1927 anticipated video cassettes or videodiscs or computers. You can't say that of television. The predictions about television go back long before that, to around 1910 or 1912. Some of the forecasts are very good and some of them very bad.

Any attempt to understand processes that go on for half a century, or a century, or two centuries, is by no means useless just because the forecasts are bound to be wrong and increasingly wrong, as we look further into the future. Even if our forecasts can't be infallible, we will do better as planners if we attempt to understand the ongoing process and look as far as we can into the future.

Schiller: I'd like to respond to that. I think you may be correct in saying that all of these questions were considered in 1927 when the Radio Act was being enacted or before the Act was enacted. But the question that we as researchers and communications scholars are concerned about is, could one have made a reasonable prediction *then* of what might occur, if we were analyzing how the institutions were organized at that time? It's my belief you could have. In the same way, you could have made a prediction about television in 1950, when it became a mass medium in the United States. Given the social structure in existence, it was inevitable that TV would become a national disaster, which I think it is.

Equally predictable were developments in Europe, beginning with the adoption of commercial television in Britain in 1954, largely with the connivance and promotion of the American advertising agency, J. Walter Thompson.

We see this continuous movement to commercialization of broadcasting across Europe, each country with its own specific conditions and situations. Yet, France goes commercial. Italy is going commercial. Germany is going commercial. These developments can be explained. We can explain what's happening and what's going to happen in these societies. There are a few valiant hold outs in Scandinavia but the satellite will be beamed down on them and they'll eventually go commercial too. We can predict these changes because we know what the social system is that is bringing this about and what the dynamic forces are behind it. We are not, therefore, sitting here without any capacity of understanding these developments.

Hamelink: I was a bit worried when I attended a conference of computer experts a while ago and one of the world's leading computer experts said that he believed it was highly necessary that we would use the advanced computer technology to come to more pre-programmed decisions, since the overload of information is such that managers and politicians can't deal with it any more, and that we have to leave more and more to pre-programmed decisions. It was Herbert Simon, as you probably well know, who said this. That may well be true, but that may also worry some of us and may lead to some of the ethical questions. If that is all technologically possible, how do we go about our autonomous capability of dealing with all that information? Since most of us are basically information illiterates, since most of us do not really know how to cope with information, how are we going to cope with all the information if it's exponentially increased in the next decade? That's a question not only of a technological nature, but also of a moral nature.

Pool: That's a very interesting question. A Japanese study has attempted to do a census of all the different kinds of flows of information in their society—mails, radio, TV, newspapers, telephone calls, just about everything one could think of. They found that the number of words produced in Japanese society was growing at about 10 percent per annum. The number of words consumed was growing at about three percent per annum. Now what does that mean?

To measure the number of words that people are consuming, they measured people's time budgets—how much are they viewing TV, listening to radio, and so on, how many hours a day. But if you double the number of channels broadcasting, then you are putting out twice as many words—but if the listening habits remain the same, the consumption remains constant.

If the material being put out is growing three times as fast as the material consumed, people need better instruments under their own control to peruse it, to process it, and to find what they want in it. Take the most naive kind of example: if you have a million-book library, that's lovely. But if it's not catalogued, or if it's badly catalogued, it's hopeless. So any device, computerization of the catalogue, or any other such device, that will enable you to more speedily pore through this material and select what you want as an individual, is positive to handling the information overload.

Computers can be that type of instrument that helps people to handle the growing volume of information better. To talk of "pre-programmed decisions" is misleading because it suggests that somehow, the computer is going to be programmed to force you to do something you don't want to do. Obviously this can be done. This is a social decision, and certain kinds of authoritarian societies might make that kind of choice. But it is equally possible to use better devices to give people more power to handle what would otherwise be an unmanageable overload.

Schiller: I disagree on every point. First of all, I don't think there is any information overload. I think there's an anti-information overload. I would say that we are inundated with increasing amounts of garbage information. I would also say that—and I can speak only for my own society, although I've noticed similar trends in other places—we deliberately nourish the institutions which are the major culprits in the production of this anti-information. What are some of these institutions? The entire advertising system is one culprit. If one picks up a Sunday newspaper, one has to feel a twinge of regret for the tree that was cut down to produce a Sunday edition that is 99 percent instantly disposable. Now this is characteristic of our entire system. It is true not only in the most obvious examples of commercialization. It is true also in the proliferation of—and here I use a very difficult word to be precise about, but I think we all can come at least to some kind of recognition of what I'm saying—the proliferation of totally nonproductive types of enterprise. Throughout our society, the institutions that are most closely associated with property, with property protection, with property sale, and with property management—all these areas—are the producers of incredible amounts of anti-information.

This conclusion could apply just as well to academic enterprise. A vast amount of the academic enterprise is non-informational, maybe anti-informational. Why? Because the poor victims, at the bottom and also at the top of the academic ladder, are under pressure to show that they're "productive." This is only a secondary case, but one, I think, that's close to many hearts.

Over fifty years ago—and I'm quoting someone I wouldn't ordinarily quote—Ortega y Gasset said that one of the greatest contributions librarians could make would be to protect their readers against a rising tide of worthless material. Now Ithiel says we have to develop new electronic means of retrieval—for what? To retrieve one pearl in ten truckloads of garbage? I say get rid of the garbage before you start worrying about pearls. Electronic instrumentation won't help the more basic problem of institutional production of enormous amounts of unessential information.

Pool: We have now identified the most fundamental difference between Herb and myself. The difference is not whether most of the material produced is garbage or not—I think we can agree on that; it inevitably is. Nor would we always differ on which items are garbage. I think Herb and I probably share very similar tastes in TV programs. The question is, who is to decide? I do not accept Ortega y Gasset's preference that some librarian or censor decides for me, or you, or anyone else, what is the garbage to be excluded. My answer is to find devices that enable every person to decide this for himself.

Schiller: I don't want to be hung up with Ortega y Gasset. I want to insist that we, in our kind of advanced, industrial societies are encouraging, promoting, and emphasizing the production of material that we sometimes call information but that is not information.

Hamelink: It seems to me that the debate between North American social scientists monitored by a Dutchman is sort of the worst example of cultural imposition when you have a meeting in a Third World country, and in order to make this even worse I'm going to conclude with a last question that is not exactly put on paper but that many people have been asking—the question of the application of all that we have been talking about to Third World countries.

Pool: Clearly, there are value issues here. What is development? Everybody who talks about development repeats the correct, obvious, statement that it is an ambiguous concept and different people mean different things by it. So when I give my answer to Hamelink, it is partly a statement of what I mean by development. When I talk about development, I'm talking about giving control over their lives to millions of people who are now deprived of any influence in their society, deprived of the ability to be effective. They are deprived by lack of food, by lack of money, by lack of education, and by lack of political freedom. By development, I am talking about moving toward a participant society. And so, the particular communications developments that are important for the Third World countries, important by this criterion, are those that give voice to those people who do not now have a voice.

Certainly, governments need means of communication; they need to be able to broadcast patriotic national messages. But what I value more than that is the ability to give peasants the opportunity to be heard, to express themselves—not just on political matters, though on those too. They also have to be able to be more effective in marketing their commodities, to be able to be more effective in demanding better medical care, or whatever it is they need. Means of communication of that sort go from the bottom up.

What is useful for such bottom-up communication is not necessarily just the old technologies; obviously, traditional technologies play a role. The old technologies of word-of-mouth, of conversation, of writing things down and distributing them are important. But there are also new technologies that have a great deal to contribute to participant communication. There are ways of providing voice to a village that it never had before—through a different structure, perhaps by a telephone system, perhaps by simplified printing such as xerography, perhaps by a different way of producing audio material such as cassettes. In this respect, studying the technology of modern communication can have a very important role in promoting development in the Third World.

Schiller: I take a completely different view. It's not easy to say what Third World countries can get out of our discussions, but I would hope that two central themes might emerge. One would be a very clearheaded and accurate understanding of what is the model of development that has been held out to the developing world for several decades for emulation. This means the Third World countries should understand what that model is actually about, how it operates, what are its costs and what are its effects on the societies that have adopted it.

Once that is understood, the next step is to recognize that all of these kinds of new communication technology may have—though I doubt it—in their present forms, some hopeful potentials of the character Ithiel Pool speaks about. But at this moment, given the existing distribution of power, given existing arrangements of control, and given the dynamics of how the Western model operates to extend its influence, in my judgment, the new electronic technology serves exclusively as a conduit for pumping into the developing world all of the various messages and all of the values which, in the long run, inflict the kinds of damage to people that I have heard my colleague here say he deplores.

He wants people to have a voice. He wants people to have opportunities to live more decent lives. Well, with electronic technology, as it is presently structured and operating, what people will be receiving will be marketing messages. They will be hearing and seeing messages that tell them about the glories of automobile transportation, for instance. I'm not going to argue here the merit of such claims. But in countries which have essential needs, which have absolutely urgent priorities for food and medical care and similar basic wants, to promote a consumer society of the kind we have—and even the words "consumer society" don't actually describe what goes on in our types of societies—with electronic instrumentation acting as a vehicle to introduce and to inculcate it in the people of these countries, in my estimation, would be a very sorrowful development.

Hamelink: Our time is up. Thank you, Professor Schiller. Thank you, Professor Pool.

CHAPTER 33

Stuart Hall and IAMCR

Usha Raman and Aditya Deshbandhu

Introduction

At a plenary session during the IAMCR 2014 Conference in Hyderabad, India, a diverse group of scholars recalled the influence of Stuart Hall on their individual intellectual journeys, a prelude to the announcement of an award in his memory. Hall had passed away earlier that year, at the age of 82. While this was a formal acknowledgment of Hall's contribution to the kind of critical scholarship in media and communication studies that the association has been home to, it also formed a neat complement to the two existing memorial awards in recognition of Dallas W. Smythe and Herbert I. Schiller. Unlike these scholars, however, Hall's relationship with IAMCR was less defined, and not as closely tied to the association's establishment and early development. Yet his influence can be seen in the many strands of work that run through the sections and working groups (WGs), and in IAMCR's core principles of inclusion and diversity. Hall's approach to media studies and cultural analysis stands along with Smythe's and Schiller's political economy approach as an important way to critically and thoughtfully resist what had, in the 1970s and early 1980s, become an overwhelmingly positivist discipline of communication studies (Fig. 33.1).

U. Raman (✉)
University of Hyderabad, Hyderabad, India
e-mail: usharaman@uohyd.ac.in

A. Deshbandhu
University of Exeter, Exeter, UK

© The Author(s), under exclusive license to Springer Nature Switzerland AG 2023

J. Becker, R. Mansell (eds.), *Reflections on the International Association for Media and Communication Research*,
https://doi.org/10.1007/978-3-031-16383-8_33

Fig. 33.1 Stuart Hall (1932–2014). IAMCR Stuart Hall Prize awarded from 2014 to celebrate Hall's lasting contribution to scholarship in communication and culture. (Courtesy of Open University, UK)

Stuart Hall: The Early Years

Stuart Hall achieved considerable renown during his lifetime, and has been profiled both in the popular and academic press, where his activism, political beliefs, and scholarship were often woven together. It, therefore, may suffice to outline his life and career very briefly here. Hall was born in Kingston, Jamaica, into a family he once characterized in an interview as "colonial romance" (Adams, 2007). He moved to England in 1951 at the age of 19 to study at Oxford as a Rhodes Scholar and an "anti-colonial student" (MacCabe, 2008, p. 14). During his time at Oxford, Hall grappled with questions of identity and his relationship with Jamaica and Jamaican culture. His engagement with his own diasporic positioning in his newfound settings and his observation of the arrival of a colonial workforce in post-war Britain on ships like *The Windrush* caused him to raise a series of questions that marked his foray into cultural studies-

> What are they doing there? How long are they going to be here? How are they going to fit in? How could they live? Who will they become? (MacCabe, 2008, p. 33)

Hall was an editor at the *Universities and Left Review* and the *New Left Review* (MacCabe, 2008, p. 12) before he joined Richard Hoggart and

Raymond Williams in 1964 at the University of Birmingham to start the first cultural studies program at a British University. With time, the Centre for Contemporary Culture Studies (CCCS) and its distinct way of thought with regard to the intertwining of culture and society came to be informally referred to as the "Birmingham School" by students of communication the world over. Hall's view of cultural studies combined the cultural and the political as he saw the two as inseparable in the context of late capitalism and its effect on the working class and its culture. He and his contemporaries at CCCS viewed media forms like television as ambivalent sites to study the inseparable connections that were being forged between the cultural, the economic, and the political, by corporate power. This grew to be an approach that gained relevance with the growing presence of media in all spheres of life, and particularly in recent times, when dissemination technologies and content converge, and in many ways, *become* culture. Hall's exhortation to look at media texts within the broader contexts of production, circulation, and consumption opened the door for many situated, nuanced studies that found their way into the presentations and discussions at IAMCR conferences.

The Leicester Conference

Nordenstreng (2008) and then Hamelink and Nordenstreng (2016) note Hall's presence at the IAMCR conference that was organized in Leicester in late August and early September 1976. Both scholars observe its importance in their accounts of the history of IAMCR, which was undergoing a significant transformation, following the General Assembly two years earlier (1974) in Leipzig, Germany (Nordenstreng, 2008; Hamelink & Nordenstreng, 2016, p. 8). The Leicester Conference, attended by over 300 scholars from 40 countries, is documented as the best attended IAMCR meeting up to that point, and had a program with four broad themes. Hall (identified as a scholar from both Jamaica and the United Kingdom (UK)) addressed the theme, "structures and contexts of media production," along with Michael Tracey and John Pollock. Other notable communication scholars who addressed the 1976 Leicester Conference included George Gerbner, Lothar Bisky, Peter Golding, Elisabeth Noelle-Neumann, Albert L. Hester, Luis Ramiro Beltrán, and Phil Harris. Discussants across sessions included names like Cees Hamelink and Elihu Katz. Most of these scholars continued to engage closely with the association, some taking on significant leadership roles.

Hall's address at the symposium (as he called it) was titled "Broadcasting, Politics and The State: The Independence/Impartiality Couplet," where he builds the key argument that drives his framework of encoding and decoding (Hall, 1980). This is often erroneously cited as "presented at the AMCR conference in Leicester in 1976" in the numerous versions of the document that are available to download as PDFs from online repositories today. However, the Stuart Hall Archive at the University of Birmingham's Cadbury Research Library notes the presence of a typed copy of "Broadcasting, Politics and The

State: The Independence/Impartiality Couplet" by Stuart Hall, delivered at the IAMCR Conference 1976 (Stuart Hall Archive, US 121, n.d.). The curious case of the missing "I" (from AMCR Conference) is also addressed in a Finnish translation of encoding and decoding where the scanned version of the photocopied document indicates the missing "I" in its references. We wish to note this error and point out that the archives indicate the role played by IAMCR's Leicester Conference in helping Hall frame his best known idea.

Over the years, several scholars and IAMCR members have mentioned the efforts and contributions of Stuart Hall in helping IAMCR in its various roles and functions along with guiding and mentoring early researchers and scholars at the conferences he was a part of. Hopeton Dunn, one of the principal voices for the establishment of the Stuart Hall Award after his passing in 2014, notes:

> Hall's work formed the theoretical foundation for numerous papers that were presented at IAMCR's annual conferences over the years, and he himself was an active member of the Association during important stages of his academic life. His work was widely acclaimed globally, and embraced by both established and emerging scholars across continents. (Personal communication, January 2, 2022)

Similarly, Janet Wasko, in her interview with Lent and Amazeen (2015a), refers to Hall along with Frederic Jameson as one of the "hot scholars of the time" (p. 108), pointing to the need to link political economy with culture to examine the various dynamics and tensions that she explores in her work. Graham Murdock, too, in his interview with Lent and Amazeen (2015b) notes the support he received from Hall when he wished to apply to lead the newly formed Political Economy Section at IAMCR in 1978, or when Hall served as a referee along with Schiller and Giddens to support his promotion at Leicester (p. 155). Murdock also credits the role played by Hall and Nicholas Garnham during the surge of left scholarship in Britain in the 1970s and 1980s as their media analyses ensured that he (Murdock) was not alone when he tried to interpret communication and culture communication from a Marxist standpoint. The IAMCR Conference returned to Leicester four decades later, in 2016, with an opening plenary theme that reflected the preoccupations of Hall: Communication and Crises.

Political Economy and Cultural Studies at IAMCR

Stuart Hall's imprint on the association is also felt in the ethos, guidelines, and principles of the various WGs and their contributions to global communications scholarship. The Popular Culture WG, for example, has always exemplified the spirit of inquiry that Stuart Hall championed and fostered, not only in the application of a critical perspective to examine media forms and practices, but also in providing presenters and participants a safe space to initiate dialog, shape new ideas, and further a collaborative understanding of global media practices and trends while grappling with the essential question of what makes something popular. With scholars like Garry Whannel (a former colleague and collaborator of Hall at the CCCS) having served as a Convenor for several years, the WG has not just carried on Hall's commitment to understanding the nature of the popular but also attempted to nurture Hall's commitment to working in groups and trusting collaborations to understand and unlock prevalent social problems. (See also Chap. 4 in this collection). Similarly, many of the questions that the Digital Divide WG attempts to answer as it negotiates with varied understandings of identity, access, and disconnectedness in a networked world, are informed by Hall's commitment to multiculturalism.

Of the various sections at IAMCR, the Community Communication and Alternative Media Section, extends Hall's idea of a democratic multicultural society by highlighting "media that originates, circulates and resonates from the sphere of civil society" (IAMCR, 2022a), while they also emphasize issues of "media access, participation and reception; media projects undertaken by marginalized and underrepresented groups and development and support of community-based media institutions and infrastructures" (IAMCR, 2022a). The Section also channels Hall's flair for activism by documenting communication practices of social movements and studying innovative forms of media activism. Many of the members of this group span the academic-activist divide, drawing on their scholarship to inform social movement work. Similarly, the Political Economy Section examines a defining characteristic of Hall's work when it looks at the role of power in the production, distribution, and exchange of mediated communication (IAMCR, 2022b). As members of the section study social relations in their totality and consider how they have developed over time, the section also situates its academic work in socio-cultural contexts when it evaluates events "according to standards of social justice, and intervene to bring about a more just and democratic world…" (IAMCR, 2022b). The Political Economy Section also examines the idea of political insecurity while being concerned with issues of democracy, and the limited financial resources and opportunities available to alternative media outlets (see also Chap. 3 in this collection).

In the decades since Hall first articulated the approach to media and communication analysis that came to be known as cultural studies, much has changed in the media landscape, with digital technology and networked modes of information creation and dissemination becoming dominant. Scholarship represented in the Communication Policy & Technology Section of IAMCR too has drawn on Hall's work to critically examine the changing contexts of production and consumption and the implications for media regulation.

Clearly, Hall is one of those theorists in media and communication, particularly those who challenged the dominant view at the time, whose work has found relevance across the areas represented by the various sections and WGs of IAMCR. Perhaps this quote from Katherine Sender and Peter Decherney in a 2016 issue of *Critical Studies in Media Communication* sums it up best:

> Elegantly integrating a broad view of structure and ideology with nuanced attention to particular cultural forms, Hall made connections between thinkers in

different fields, traditions, and national contexts, and, at the same time, he never lost sign of the specificity of applying theory. (Sender & Decherney, 2016, p. 381)

The Stuart Hall Award

The Stuart Hall Award was constituted at the 2014 IAMCR Conference organized in Hyderabad, India, and is awarded once every three years, as it cycles between the Dallas Smythe and the Herbert Schiller prizes. The Stuart Hall Award is given "to a paper devoted to the critical study of culture" as observed by Janet Wasko, the then President of IAMCR (Wasko, 2014). In his recollection of the constitution of the award in 2014, Hopeton Dunn observes:

> The case for an IAMCR memorial award in honour of Stuart Hall was an easy one to make to the association. Many scholars operating from IAMCR's sections and working groups, and those in its leadership, were fully aware of the phenomenal scholarly impact that Hall had made in the fields of Cultural Studies and Communications Studies globally. It was not difficult therefore for the IAMCR Executive Committee, under the presidency of Professor Janet Wasko, to endorse the establishment of the Stuart Hall Award, and support the convening of a conference plenary session in Hall's honour at the IAMCR Hyderabad Conference, India, in July 2014. (Personal communication, January 2, 2022)

At the plenary session that Dunn mentions in his recollection, a panel of five speakers, namely: Garry Whannel, Susie Tharu, Colin Sparks, and Sandra Ristovska were led by Dunn himself to pay tribute to Hall's illustrious academic life. By leading the plenary, Dunn first read out the tribute paid by Graham Murdock who could not attend the Hyderabad Conference. Murdock's remarks credited Hall for his indispensable contribution to cultural studies and for his role in establishing it as a key theoretical and methodological tradition in media studies and communication. Murdock, who had worked closely with Hall during his years in Birmingham, noted

> It is no exaggeration to say that without his work Cultural Studies would not have developed in the way that it has or established itself quite so firmly as an indispensable current of thought and analysis within the study of media and communication. (Murdock, 2014)

Murdock went on to note that Hall's influence went beyond the academy, or perhaps more correctly, moved generations of students to seek connections between their study of media and the culture they were all a part of. Continuing in the same vein, Dunn observed:

> His contribution is regarded as one of an interventionist and a polemicist. Someone who didn't write books for writing books sake, but who intervened on topics and issues because he felt it was important, he intervened because he wanted to correct or to enhance an argument and he intervened because he

wanted to make a difference. Given his view that scholarship and the academy is meant to serve and not just to exist. (Dunn, 2014)

Dunn was followed by Indian feminist scholar, Susie Tharu, who credited Hall for shaping her research and urged scholars to observe in Hall's work his ability to write and unpack complex concepts by rooting them in specific settings. In her 13-minute tribute, Tharu quipped that Hall was, notably, "not a French theorist," distinguishing him from the Eurocentric philosophies that were the flavor of the times while also pointing to what we might today call his "Otherness" (Tharu, 2014).

Garry Whannel, in his address, spoke not just of Hall's ability to shape thinking but also his characteristic chuckle as he recalled what it meant to work at the CCCS in Birmingham. Like Dunn, Whannel also noted how Hall was not concerned with writing dense theoretical monographs, but instead was committed to making scholarship a collective endeavor as he focused on co-writing and mentoring, and inspiring and collaborating (Whannel, 2014). Colin Sparks, in his tribute, spoke of his experience of meeting Hall at the CCCS, when Hall presided over its "heroic phase" (Sparks, 2014). He praised Hall for unshackling culture studies from English literature and his willingness to work with a range of ideas from other disciplines, an approach that transformed culture studies into a world view and transcended its narrow British limitations (Sparks, 2014). Lastly, Sandra Ristovska, at the time a doctoral candidate, observed how Hall's work continues to remain a source of inspiration for students of communication worldwide and is relatable to them on several levels, particularly to those who were not from the established centers of academic power. As Ristovska put it, Hall's work, encountered by chance in a university bookstore, opened up for her, a graduate student from a Balkan state, ways of thinking about "questions of power, truth and knowledge in representation" and affirming that "theory should not be divorced from cultural practice" (Ristovska, 2014).

The Stuart Hall Award was given for the first time in 2015 at the Montreal Conference, with Hopeton Dunn serving as the first Chair of the award committee. Since then, the award has been conferred twice more, in 2018 (Eugene, USA) and 2021 (Nairobi, Kenya). The list of the awardees is as shown in Table 33.1.

Conclusion

Towards the conclusion of the documentary *The Stuart Hall Project* (John Akomfrah, 2013), we see Hall reflecting on the state of the world in the late 2000s and early 2010s. He admits that for the first time in his life, he feels both out of place and part of a time that has no more room for him. As the music turns melancholic, one cannot help but wonder if he sufficiently equipped his students, collaborators, and all those who engage with his work with the necessary tools to not merely survive in such a space and time, but to initiate and

Table 33.1 IAMCR Stuart Hall Awards

Year of award and location of annual conference	*Name of the recipient(s)*	*Title of paper and section/ Working group submitted to*	*About recipient(s)*
2015, Montreal, PQ, Canada	Faith Kibere	*The Politics of Representation in Kibera Slum, Kenya*—submitted to the Audience Section	Faith Njeri Kibere was a fourth year Media and Communication PhD candidate at the University of Leicester, UK. Her research interests were appropriation of new media technologies in Sub-Saharan Africa and how media and communication intersect with development.
2018, Eugene, Oregon, US	Toussaint Nothias and David Cheruiyot	*A 'Hotbed' of Digital Empowerment? Media Criticism in Kenya: Between Playful Engagement and Co-option*—submitted to the International Communication Section	Toussaint Nothias was a Lecturer at the Center for African Studies at Stanford University. With a PhD from the University of Leeds, Toussaint focused on the impact of colonial power relations on contemporary journalistic practices, and on representations of Africa in global media. David Cheruiyot was a PhD candidate at the Department of Geography, Media and Communication, Karlstad University, Sweden. His research interests included media accountability, media representation, blogging and citizen journalism, data journalism, as well as communication for social change.
2021, Nairobi, Kenya[a]	Hanna E. Morris[b]	*Constructing 'Rights' and 'Wrongs' in Climate Media Discourse Through the Prism of American Exceptionalism*—submitted to the Environment, Science and Risk Communication Working Group	Hanna E. Morris is an interdisciplinary scholar of media, culture, and the climate crisis. She was a PhD candidate at the Annenberg School for Communication, University of Pennsylvania.

Notes: [a]The 2021 Conference, hosted in Nairobi, was organized and facilitated as a virtual conference due to the COVID-19 pandemic. [b]The 2021 Award included an honorable mention for Wunpini Fatimata Mohammed's paper "Why we Need Intersectionality in Ghanaian Feminist Politics and Discourse," submitted to the Gender and Communication Section

engage in meaningful discussions on the many issues of social justice that we are faced with today. Hall's direct engagement with IAMCR may have been limited to the 1976 Conference, but his work has influenced many scholars, young and seasoned, who are part of the association. The values of inclusion and diversity that drive IAMCR, the determined focus on creating bridges between peoples, ideas, and cultures, an unerring commitment across its many units, to examining the interplay of power, capital, and media forms at multiple levels, all in some way, recall the philosophy that characterized Hall's scholarship.

References

Adams, T. (2007, September 23). Cultural hallmark. *The Guardian*. Retrieved 15 June 2022, from https://www.theguardian.com/society/2007/sep/23/communities.politicsphilosophyandsociety

Akomfrah, J. (Writer & Director). (2013). *The Stuart Hall project* [Documentary]. Smoking Dogs Films; Lina Gopaul.

Dunn, H. (2014, July 15–19). The Tribute to Stuart Hall, conference plenary session IAMCR 2014, Hyderabad, India. *YouTube*. Retrieved 15 June 2022, from https://www.youtube.com/watch?v=-AyyYG4XOYw

Hall, S. (1980). Encoding and decoding. In S. Hall, D. Hobson, A. Lowe, & P. Willis (Eds.), *Culture, media, language* (p. 51–61). Hutchinson.

Hamelink, C., & Nordenstreng, K. (2016). Estudiando la historia a través de la Asociación Internacional para el Estudio de la Comunicación Social (IAMCR). *Anuario Electrónico De Estudios En Comunicación Social 'Disertaciones'*, *9*(2), 46–67. Retrieved 15 June 2022, from https://doi.org/10.12804/disertaciones.09.02.2016.03

IAMCR. (2022a). Community communication and alternative media section, IAMCR. Retrieved 15 June 2022, from https://iamcr.org/s-wg/section/cam

IAMCR. (2022b). Political economy section, IAMCR. Retrieved 15 June 2022, from https://iamcr.org/s-wg/section/poe

Lent, J. A., & Amazeen M. A. (2015a). Janet Wasko. In J. A. Lent & M. A. Amazeen (Eds.), *Key thinkers in critical communication scholarship* (p. 205–223). Palgrave Global Media Policy and Business. Palgrave Macmillan. Retrieved 15 June 2022, from https://doi.org/10.1057/9781137463418_11

Lent, J. A., & Amazeen M. A. (2015b). Graham Murdock. In J. A. Lent & M. A. Amazeen (Eds.), *Key thinkers in critical communication scholarship* (p. 146–165). Palgrave Macmillan. Retrieved 15 June 2022, from https://doi.org/10.1057/9781137463418_8

MacCabe, C. (2008). An interview with Stuart Hall, December 2007. *Critical Quarterly, 50*(1–2), 12–42.

Murdock, G. (2014, July 15–19). *A tribute shared by Hopeton Dunn at the IAMCR conference in Hyderabad, India*. From the personal archive of Hopeton Dunn, used with permission.

Nordenstreng, K. (2008). Institutional networking: The story of the International Association for Media and Communication Research. In D. W. Park & J. Pooley (Eds.), *The history of media and communication research: Contested memories* (p. 225–250). Peter Lang.

Ristovska, S. (2014, July 15–19). The tribute to Stuart Hall (Conference plenary session). IAMCR 2014, Hyderabad, India. *YouTube*. Retrieved 15 June 2022, from https://www.youtube.com/watch?v=skumWELz-5I

Sender, K., & Decherney, P. (2016). Stuart Hall lives: Cultural studies in an age of digital media. *Critical Studies in Media Communication*, *33*(5), 381–384. Retrieved 15 June 2022, from https://www.tandfonline.com/doi/full/10.1080/15295036.2016.1244725

Sparks, C. (2014, July 15–19). The tribute to Stuart Hall (Conference plenary session). IAMCR 2014, Hyderabad, India. *YouTube*. Retrieved 15 June 2022, from https://www.youtube.com/watch?v=vaQvd74j1To

Stuart Hall Archive US 121. (n.d.). University of Birmingham Cadbury Research Library: Special Collections. Retrieved 15 June 2022, from https://calmview.bham.ac.uk/GetDocument.ashx?db=Catalog&fname=US121+Stuart+Hall+Archive+finding+aid.pdf

Tharu, S. (2014, July 15–19). The tribute to Stuart Hall (Conference plenary session). IAMCR 2014, Hyderabad, India. *YouTube*. Retrieved 15 June 2022, from https://www.youtube.com/watch?v=tr6KABAm93A

Wasko, J. (2014, July 15–19). The announcement of the Stuart Hall Award in the tribute to Stuart Hall (Conference plenary session). IAMCR 2014, Hyderabad, India. *YouTube*. Retrieved 15 June 2022, from https://www.youtube.com/watch?v=-AyyYG4XOYw

Whannel, G. (2014, July 15–19). The tribute to Stuart Hall (Conference plenary session). IAMCR 2014, Hyderabad, India. *YouTube*. Retrieved 15 June 2022, from https://www.youtube.com/watch?v=U2toVFa-3Qo

CHAPTER 34

My Work with James Halloran

Peggy Gray

Introduction

IAMCR was established in Paris in 1957 by experts from 15 countries in association with UNESCO. Its purpose was to promote research into problems related to the press, radio, television, and film throughout the world. In 1970, James (Jim) Halloran, who, in 1966, had established at Leicester University, the first Centre for Mass Communication Research (CMCR) in Britain, became a vice president. Two years later, in 1972, at the meeting in Buenos Aires, he became president of the association. Jim had published his book, *Control or Consent* (Halloran, 1963) and I met him at an education conference in London in 1968, just before he began research into the press handling of a demonstration in London against the Vietnam War, which led to the publication of the book, *Demonstrations and Communication* (Halloran et al., 1970). I offered to help with the research and was hired at Leicester to work on the project on a casual basis. That was the beginning of a long working relationship lasting more than 25 years (Fig. 34.1).

In 1974, Jim asked me to accompany him as Administrative Assistant to IAMCR's Leipzig Conference, his first as president of the association. This was very exciting for me as it was the first time I had crossed the Iron Curtain, which we did with Elisabeth Noelle-Neumann from Mainz University in her Mercedes (my return alone and by rail was quite an adventure!). In Leipzig, Jim introduced me to many interesting people, including Nabil Dajani, Emil Dusiška, Cees Hamelink, Alan Hancock, Kaarle Nordenstreng, Bogdan

P. Gray (✉)
Glasgow, UK

© The Author(s), under exclusive license to Springer Nature Switzerland AG 2023

J. Becker, R. Mansell (eds.), *Reflections on the International Association for Media and Communication Research*,
https://doi.org/10.1007/978-3-031-16383-8_34

Fig. 34.1 James Halloran (1927–2007), Cees J. Hamelink and Peggy Gray at IAMCR Conference 1990, Bled. (From left to right) **Halloran**—IAMCR Vice President 1970–72, President 1972–90; **Hamelink**, International Council 1976–80, Vice President 1980–88, President 1988–94, Section Head—Law 1988–2000, Chair—Legal Committee 1990–94, 1996–2000, Chair—Elections Committee 2002–06, Chair—Future IAMCR Scenarios 2012; **Gray**—Administrative Assistant to President James Halloran 1974–90. (Courtesy of IAMCR)

Osolnik, Walery Pisarek, and Yassen Zassoursky. I learned a lot about IAMCR, life in Eastern Europe, and Jim's determination to build bridges between East and West. I also discovered what members wanted from their membership of the association and its bi-annual conferences. Some of the people I met in Leipzig became good friends.

This was the beginning of my years of working closely with Jim to expand and promote the association, 18 of them, as its Voluntary Administrative Assistant and Conference Organizer.

Conferencing around the World

The 1976 Conference was in Leicester and its theme, "Mass Media and Socialisation," is recalled in the post-conference publication, *Mass Media and Man's View of Society* (Halloran et al., 1978). I was responsible for the organization of the conference, including provision of accommodation in the University Halls of Residence, and the provision of meeting rooms and facilities which I negotiated with the university, the organization of a reception for participants given by the Lord Mayor of the City, registration, and care of participants.

I prepared to welcome people from Eastern and Western Europe, the United States (US) and Canada, Latin America and the Caribbean, Africa, and Asia; indeed more than 300 people from some 40 countries. I was assisted in the welcome and care of participants by colleagues from CMCR, my husband Martin and two young daughters, and Jim's children. We all worked hard to make everyone feel at home, genuinely cared for, and able to explore the area and move around wherever they chose to, with information and transport provided.

During that conference, many international friendships were made. New people came on board as officers, the statutes were revised, and the International Council (IC) was formed with careful planning to make it representative of worldwide geopolitics, the wide range of specialist interests, and for the first time, a gender balance in the governance of the association. Jim worked closely with UNESCO, which made a grant to the association providing funds to enable young scholars and people from what was then designated as the Third World to attend the conference. UNESCO also funded the post-conference publication already mentioned, which included an extensive international bibliography for each of the four conference sessions covering diverse approaches across the various institutions in different political regimes around the world (including Eastern and Western Europe, North America, and other regions) with different educational and media regimes.

After the Leicester Conference, I worked, in addition to my full-time research post at the CMCR until 1990, as the main contact for IAMCR members, old and new, and as the pivotal person for all future conferences. I provided the bridge to Jim Halloran who, in addition to heading the CMCR, was in regular communication with UNESCO and university research centers and their leaders around the world who were concerned with communication studies and international understanding. He traveled a great deal to attend meetings, give lectures, and to further international understanding and cooperation.

In this period, a high priority was East-West relations and understanding. This was high on our agenda, so the next conference was in Warsaw in 1978 with the theme, "Mass Media and National Cultures." George Oledzki was responsible for that conference and we were very happy to work closely with him and welcome him to Leicester. Life in communist Poland in the 1970s was very different from that in Western Europe, and I recall these differences being reflected in discussions in the conference hall. We also held Program Committee meetings in Warsaw and Kraków where Walery Pisarek was our host. By now, membership of the association (22 in 1972) had reached approximately 1000, almost half of whom attended the conference, representing 38 countries, figures not exceeded until the Prague Conference in 1984 when participants came from 46 countries. As it had done for Leicester, UNESCO funded a post-conference report entitled *Mass Media and National Cultures* (IAMCR, 1980), including an international bibliography. Again, many new friendships were formed, leading to more interaction between East and West.

Jim continued to work with international organizations and institutions and to develop research at the Leicester center, regularly writing presidential letters to members to keep them up to date with membership information. We also wrote reports on IC and Executive Committee meetings and decisions, on conferences and plans for future conferences, the development of sections and working groups (WGs), issues the organization should address, and relationships with related organizations concerned with media and communications. Jim was always pleased to receive feedback and members and officers of the association were very welcome in Leicester.

I, too, was busily engaged, keeping in contact with members, welcoming new members and planning the next conference, as well as attending many international meetings with Jim as his Administrative Assistant and Conference Organizer. We learned a great deal about media and communications in the countries we visited, their influence and impact on communities, and how ways of life differed among countries governed by distinct types of political regimes. All this encouraged a desire to organize international comparative research and dialog, such as the "Foreign Images Study" (Sreberny-Mohammadi et al., 1985), which looked at press portrayal of development in a number of countries, including Hungary, India, Malaysia and Netherlands. Meanwhile, IAMCR special interest WGs were growing in number, and new sections were developing and being added for those concerned with Political Economy and Professional Education.

The next conference was in Venezuela, a country that neither Jim nor I knew at all, in 1980, with the theme, "New Structures of International Communication: the Role of Research." We met the local group in Caracas, responsible for conference planning, to familiarize ourselves with the location and to enable us to work together in the planning process in the run-up to the conference. We were warmly welcomed and we came to know the people with whom we would be planning and organizing the conference and also the layout of the conference center and accommodation. We learned a great deal about the venue, the culture, and the people of Venezuela, this interesting city, and the conditions in which people lived. We were well-prepared to advise participants, almost 300 in number, in our pre-conference information on suitable behavior and any precautions needed to keep safe in Caracas.

The General Assembly (GA) met and the elections for Executive Board (EB) and IC produced some new faces, including Gertrude Robinson (Canada) as Deputy Secretary General and Nelly de Camargo (Brazil) as one of the nine vice presidents. Unfortunately, the financial support from UNESCO was not sufficient to provide for a post-conference publication. WGs and sections met and kept in touch with their members, as we continued to do from IAMCR's headquarters in Leicester while planning for the 25th anniversary conference to be held in Paris in 1982 with the theme, "Social Communication and Global Problems." François-Xavier Hutin led the Planning Committee and worked exceedingly hard to organize the conference on the ground. The hosts also paid for the post-conference publication.

We were honored to be given a reception at the Élysée Palace, where we were regally entertained and welcomed by the Mayor, Jacques Chirac. Members were able to fully enjoy the 25th anniversary celebrations and to advance their knowledge, international friendships, and research relationships.

Jim was of course busy, not only with IAMCR, but also with progressing research into broadcasting and the development of new communications media and the influence of all the new developments on various sectors and groups within society in Britain and around the world. Many new projects were being pursued by staff and research students at CMCR and some had international comparisons. Some were funded by British broadcasting institutions and others by a variety of organizations and companies as well as by Prix Jeunesse International and British government departments and institutions with whom Jim had contacts. I was involved with some of these projects and, at the same time, I was teaching research methods to our students, keeping in touch with IAMCR members and planning for the next conference to be held in Prague in 1984.

Jim worked with various broadcasting authorities in Britain to understand the influence of television, radio, and print media on various sections of society. Under his direction, members of staff and research students at the Leicester center undertook a wide range of studies, including the portrayal of alcohol, sport, the family, young people, and ethnic minorities and the impact and implications of the development of new technologies and media for these groups. Among others, I worked on projects looking at mass media and sport; international understanding; the portrayal of alcohol on prime-time television and accompanying behavior and its influence on sections of society; the images of the industry and the implications for the family, education, and leisure pursuits; and other activities concerning the development of new technologies. Jim also worked with other colleagues on studies including those concerned with ethnic minorities and television; mass media and education; and mass media and health education. He undertook a number of comparative research studies involving other countries, including journalism and journalists in Britain and West Germany, and media and development for which research was undertaken in three regions of India to examine the impact of various forms of communication on rural development and the lives and cultural values of the people. I undertook research on communication and new technologies.

Reference to reports on these and other studies with which Jim and/or I were involved at this time can be found in the "Register of Current and Recently Completed British Research on Mass Media and Mass Communication" (Gray, 1983) that I compiled and which was published by Leicester University.

Planning for the 1984 Prague Conference on "Communication and Democracy: Directions in Research" was ongoing, and I was in close touch with Alice Bunzlova and her team in Prague and with the Program Committee, while Jim continued to keep members informed through presidential letters. There were meetings of the EB in Hungary, where our host was Tamás Szecskö, and in May 1984 in Tampere hosted by Kaarle Nordenstreng, as well as in Prague where Alice Bunzlova was our main point of contact. All of these people became my good friends and, indeed, friends of my family. I worked closely with Alice Bunzlova's team and the very successful conference was attended by 440 people from 46 countries. The number of sections and WG meetings was increasing with each conference, and social events were always important, as were post-conference tours. I remember with great pleasure the Wagner Opera in the splendid Prague Opera House and the beauty of the city.

The Prague hosts paid for the post-conference monograph. In the elections, Tamás Szecskö became Secretary General and Olof Hultén (Sweden), Treasurer. There were some new faces among the 11 vice presidents. It was agreed that the 1986 Conference would be in New Delhi, the first on the Indian subcontinent. Jim and I went to New Delhi to meet those who would be responsible for planning and organization on the ground and to become familiar with the city, the venue, and the likely places for members to visit. The conference theme was "Communication Technology, Development and the Third World." Key people involved in the conference planning and organization were Binod C. Agrawal and K. E. Eapen. Some 360 members representing 42 countries attended the conference. (See also Chap. 21 in this collection).

Many of us, who had not previously visited India and were not familiar with life in the country, had an opportunity to form impressions en route from the airport to New Delhi's city center. The conference venue was a lovely hotel, close to very affluent areas, but with many people from different backgrounds close by. One of the most memorable things that happened to me was early one morning as I walked along the hotel underground corridor. I felt an amazing presence as a man bowed as he passed by and I then realized that I had encountered the Dalai Lama. Later in the morning as I was leaving to go to a meeting, I found the lobby lined with people waiting to see him pass through. The conference was a success academically and socially and, as usual, the post-conference publication carried the conference theme as its title. After New Delhi, the next meeting was to be in 1988 in Barcelona, when many changes were planned.

The membership was increasing and, from our headquarters, we continued to keep members informed through presidential letters, and section and WG leaders kept their members up to date. We were very much aware that members would like an IAMCR journal, but costs and logistics did not allow this. At this time, regional associations in the media and communications field were being set up and there were rumblings of the need for change. By now, Jim had been president for almost 16 years and there was pressure to modernize, both through changes in leadership and revision of the association's statutes. As we were preparing for the conference to be held in Barcelona, addressing "Mass

Communication and Cultural Identity," it was agreed that at that GA, the statutes would be revised. The Barcelona Conference was a great success with 614 participants from 46 countries. As usual, there was a good social life accompanying the academic discussions. I had to deal with members having things stolen as they enjoyed themselves in the Ramblas even though I had warned everyone to be careful. As I was slumbering the morning after the conference had ended, I received a call from the airport from someone whose passport had been stolen, asking for help and advice.

At the IC meeting in Barcelona, the position of president-elect was established and filled by Cees J. Hamelink. It was laid down that the president could, in future, serve only for one four-year term after two years as President-elect, and then a further two years as past-President. Jim, therefore, ceased to be President at the Bled Conference in 1990, and I ceased to be Administrative Officer of the organization and Conference Organizer. The iron curtain had been broken and Europe was changing dramatically at this time. Slovenia was in the process of separating from Yugoslavia and we hoped all would be peaceful for the conference, the theme of which was very relevant to the situation, "Developments in Communication and Democracy." I already knew Tomo Martelanc and Bogdan Osolnik, who was a friend of Jim's, and I enjoyed working with Slavko Splichal of Ljubljana University, who was a very important member of the team that organized the conference. The venue was on the beautiful Lake Bled and a good time was had by all.

In the 18 years during which Jim had been President, membership had grown from 22 paid-up members to 1850 and they now came from 60 countries. The farewells to Jim and myself were so generous and kind, leaving me with particularly fond memories of that conference. My farewell gift from the Hungarian members was a lovely glass bowl on which was engraved the words "Peggy's Secret; organisation by friendship," which still has pride of place in my home today. Jim served as past-President until 1992 when the conference was at Guarujá in Brazil, and then became an honorary president.

I, too, had given up my work as main contact for members and conference organizers, but I happily assisted Cees J. Hamelink in the preparation and organization of the Brazil Conference. I had become a member of the IC in 1988, and Jim and I continued to be very active in the organization, attending conferences after 1990: Guarujá, but also Dublin in 1993, and Seoul in 1994. I did not get to the 1996 Sydney Conference, although I had done some preparatory exploring there, because my daughter was about to have her first child and wanted me around!

The 40th anniversary of the founding of IAMCR was in 1997 and a special conference was planned to take place at Oaxaca in Mexico. Clearly, both Jim and I planned to go and I was excited about visiting Mexico City because, since a small child, I had been fascinated by the volcano called Popocatépetl. My husband Martin and I set off to spend a few days there before flying to Oaxaca for the conference. The evening we arrived, we were eating in the rooftop restaurant of our hotel in the city square, when we felt dust/ash dropping around us; the waiters quickly moved us inside, and the next morning we learned that we had been the last plane to land before the airport was closed due to an eruption! A couple of days later, we flew out of the airport and the view of the erupting volcano was spectacular. The conference in Oaxaca was splendid. Jim met us there and we were warmly welcomed by our hosts and we enjoyed an amazing celebration of the Ruby Anniversary. I value and have on show the commemorative locally made pottery dish that I was given.

The conference in 1998 was in Glasgow and it was easy for us to be there, especially as my daughter and her new family lived there, and so my husband and I, now both fully retired, as was Jim, enjoyed the reunion with many IAMCR friends.

We were all set to go to Paris in 2007 for the 50th anniversary celebration of the association, but sadly, Jim, who had been ill for some time, died. Nevertheless, Martin and I went and enjoyed being in one of our favorite cities and celebrating along with old IAMCR friends. We fondly recall the visit to the Eiffel Tower and catching up with Yassen Zassoursky as we traveled in the lift with him and his wife.

The following year at the conference in Stockholm, Martin and I were accompanied by most of Jim's children, and we were able to pay tribute to Jim and all that he had contributed to IAMCR and to international cooperation and research in the fields of mass communication, mass media, and new technologies, as well as to international friendships and understanding. At the main session, Cees J. Hamelink gave a wonderful tribute to Jim, including some beautiful music. The president and other colleagues and friends also gave addresses. Stockholm was a very happy occasion for us all.

Conclusion

I thought that would be my last IAMCR meeting but was delighted to receive an invitation from Janet Wasko to attend the conference to be held in Leicester in 2016. By then, we were in our 80s and I had had a heart attack and quadruple heart bypass surgery. We had left Leicester and moved to Stone in Staffordshire to be closer to one of our daughters, Penny, who had assisted at both the 1976 Leicester and 1982 Paris Conferences. I was thrilled at the idea of attending another conference and meeting with old friends and colleagues again. At the event, I was very surprised and honored to be presented with an IAMCR Distinguished Contribution Award. The plaque is proudly displayed on the wall of our new home in Glasgow to which we moved at the end of 2018 after Penny had gone to live and work on the island of Guernsey, so we moved to join her sister Julia, who as a youngster, had helped at the first Leicester Conference.

Jim was the longest-serving President of IAMCR. He devoted himself to raising money for research and to enable international meetings; keeping people around the world well-informed; championing international friendships and understanding; developing a university center that welcomed students from all over the world to undertake research on mass communication and developments in communication technology, many of whom returned to their countries to teach and continue research; and employing researchers and teachers who were to become leaders of other institutions studying and teaching about developments in the field. He welcomed researchers, educators, students, and all IAMCR members to the Leicester center and into his own home, and assisted many who suffered from political and economic discrimination in their own countries or institutions. Under his 18-year leadership, the organization's membership grew almost hundredfold and friendships developed across the world.

I am proud to have assisted Jim in this and to have had the opportunity to meet so many people and learn so much about not only the subjects we studied, but also about differing cultures and political systems and the importance of tolerance and international understanding. Also, of course, I greatly appreciate the many long-standing friendships I was able to develop in the association. Some of those lovely people are sadly no longer with us but are fondly remembered. I value contact with friends in IAMCR and hope that all newer and younger members will enjoy similar experiences and value their opportunities for learning and sharing academic findings and exploration, as well as the support of the organization and friendships made across the world through IAMCR.

References

Gray, P. (1983). *Register of current and recently completed British research on mass media and mass communication*. Leicester University.

Halloran, J. D. (1963). *Control or consent*. Sheed and Ward.

Halloran, J. D., Elliott, P., & Murdock, G. (1970). *Demonstrations and communications: A case study*. Penguin Books.

Halloran, J. D., Gray, P., McCron, R., & Harris, P. (1978). *Mass media and man's view of society*. Adams Bros & Shardlow Ltd.

IAMCR. (1980). *Mass media and national cultures: A conference report and international bibliography*. IAMCR.

Sreberny-Mohammadi, A., Nordenstreng, K., Stevenson, R., & Ugboajah, F. (1985). *Foreign news in the media: International reporting in 29 countries* (Final report of the "Foreign Images" Study Undertaken for UNESCO by IAMCR, Reports and Papers on Mass Communication). UNESCO.

Appendix A: IAMCR Leadership 1957–2020

This appendix lists persons elected to serve in various leadership positions from the founding of IAMCR in 1957 until 2020. The leadership was elected at the biennial General Assembly (GA) held during conferences, initially convened every two years and, since 1990, annually. The first years of foundation and consolidation until the mid-1960s were dominated by leading academics from Europe, both West and East, and North America. The first two presidents in the 1950s were from France and the United States (US), while the members of the Bureau and the Executive Committee came from Belgium, Canada, Czechoslovakia, Italy, Poland, Switzerland and the United Kingdom (UK). In addition, the first executive committees in 1957–1959 also had representatives from Brazil and Pakistan. The geographical coverage was gradually extended by the mid-1970s to include colleagues from Argentina, Ecuador, India, Indonesia, Japan, Lebanon, Nigeria, and Philippines.

From Leicester 1976 onwards, the statutory aim of achieving fair and balanced geographical distribution in the International Council (IC) was achieved to a degree, although the composition was still predominantly (West) European and North American, with a few names from Asia, Africa, the Arab world, and Latin America. The number of colleagues from the developing countries increased gradually from seven in 1976 to 13 in 1996, but it never reached half of the seats, obviously reflecting the size of the research communities. In 2004, when the number of elected seats on the IC was 15, only three were held by colleagues from developing countries; in 2020 their number was still five. The section heads as additional IC members made the balance somewhat better.

The president, vice presidents and other Executive Board (EB) members typically came from among those who had served in the larger Executive Committee/IC. Notable exceptions who went straight to EB positions were the following: James D. Halloran (Vice President, 1970; President, 1972), Louis

© The Author(s), under exclusive license to Springer Nature Switzerland AG 2023

J. Becker, R. Mansell (eds.), *Reflections on the International Association for Media and Communication Research*,
https://doi.org/10.1007/978-3-031-16383-8

Beltrán (Vice President, 1974), Frank Ugboajah (Vice President, 1984), Naren Chitty (Secretary General, 1996), Ole Prehn (Deputy Secretary General, 1996), Elizabeth Fox, Carmen Gómes Mont, Michael Palmer, John Sinclair (Vice Presidents, 1996), Frank Morgan (President-Elect, 2000), Marjan de Bruin, Eddie Kuo, Tawana Kupe, Katharine Sarikakis, Jan Servaes (Vice Presidents, 2000), César Bolaño (Treasurer, 2004), Hopeton Dunn (Secretary General, 2008), Beate Josephi (Treasurer, 2008), Aimée Vega Montiel (Vice President, 2012), Maria Michalis (Secretary General, 2012), Nico Carpentier (Treasurer, 2012), Gerard Goggin (Secretary General, 2016), Elske van de Fliert (Treasurer, 2018) and Andrea Medrado and Usha Raman (Vice Presidents, 2020)—albeit Prehn, Morgan, Josephi and Carpentier after serving as section heads. Apppendices A and B are based on IAMCR documents, most of which are available at https://iamcr.org/digital-archive. They were compiled by Kaarle Nordenstreng and, for the years since 2010, with the assistance of the IAMCR Secretariat. Every effort has been made to achieve accuracy. Any errors should be reported to the editors of this collection.

Note: Nationality is in brackets when first listed in any category, but not repeated thereafter.

General Assembly	*President*	*Vice Presidents*	*Secretary General (SG)*	*Treasurer*	*Bureau*	*Executive Committee*
1st 1957 Paris (France)	Fernand Terrou (France); Deputy President, Jacques Kayser (France)	Jacques Bourquin (Switzerland), Mieczyslaw Kafel (Poland), Raymond B. Nixon (US)		Jacques Bourquin	Claude Bellanger (France), Marcel Stijns (Belgium)	Roger Clausse (Belgium), Francesco Fattorello (Italy), Domenico de Gregorio (Italy), Danton Jobim (Brazil), Abdus Salam Khurshid (Pakistan), Vladimir Klimes (Czechoslovakia), Neil Morrison (Canada), Oscar Riegel (US), Robert Silvey (UK), E. B. Simpson (UK), Jean Tardieu (France)
2nd 1959 Milan (Italy)	Raymond B. Nixon	Jacques Bourquin, Mieczyslaw Kafel	Fernand Terrou; Deputy SG, Jacques Kaiser	Same as above	Claude Bellanger, Francesco Fattorello, Giuliano Gaeta (Italy), Martin Löffler (FRG), Marcel Stijns + Section Heads	R. Clausse, D. Gregorio, D. Jobim, A. S. Khurshid, V. Klimes, N. Morrison, O. Riegel, R. Silvey, E. B. Simpson, J. Tardieu
3rd 1961 Vevey (Switzerland)	Raymond B. Nixon; Honorary President, Fernand Terrou	Jacques Bourquin, Mieczyslaw Kafel, Jacques Kaiser	Maarten Rooy (Netherlands)	Same as above	Claude Bellanger, Francesco Fattorello, Vladimir Klimes, Martin Löffler, Marcel Stijns + Section Heads and Coordinators	Hermann Budzislawski (GDR), R. Clausse, J. Fernandez (Ecuador), D. Gregorio, D. Jobim, A. S. Khurshid, Haruo Kondo (Japan), Paul F. Lazarsfeld (US), J. Marinovitch (Yugoslavia), J. W. Mole (Canada), N. Morrison, O. Riegel, Wilbur Schramm (US), E. B. Simpson, J. Tardieu
4th 1964 Vienna (Austria)	Jacques Bourquin; Past President, Raymond B. Nixon; Honorary President, Fernand Terrou	Francesco Fattorello, Mieczyslaw Kafel, Haruo Kondo	Vladimir Klimes; Deputy SG, E B Simpson	Mieczyslaw Kafel	Claude Bellanger, Marcel Stijns + Section Heads and Coordinators	Juan Beneyto (Spain), H. Budzislawski, J Fernandez, D. Gregorio, D. Jobim, A. S. Khurshid, P. F. Lazarsfeld, J. Marinovic, J. W. Mole, O. Riegel, J. Tardieu

(*continued*)

(continued)

General Assembly	*President*	*Vice Presidents*	*Secretary General (SG)*	*Treasurer*	*Bureau*	*Executive Committee*
5th 1966 Herceg Novi (Yugoslavia)	Jacques Bourquin; Honorary President, Fernand Terrou	Same as above	Same as above	Same as above	Claude Bellanger, Jovan Marinovic + Section Heads and Coordinators	J. Adams (US), A. Bay (Indonesia), J. Beneyto, H. Budzislawski, R. Clausse, J. Fernandez, D. Gregorio, I. Iman (AUR), D Jobim, A. S. Khurshid, P. F. Lazarsfeld, G. Maletzke (FRG), J. W. Mole, B. Oslonik (Yugoslavia), O. Riegel, P. Roy (India), J. Tardieu, I. Tetelowska (Poland), R. Vehmas (Finland), Y. Zassoursky (USSR)
6th 1968 Pamplona (Spain)	Jacques Bourquin; Honorary President, Fernand Terrou	Francesco Fattorello, Mieczyslaw Kafel, Haruo Kondo, Yassen Zassoursky	Vladimir Klimes; Deputy SG, Otto Roegele (FRG)	Francesco Fattorello	Claude Bellanger, Jovan Marinovic + Section Heads and Coordinators	J. Adams, A. Benito (Spain), A. F. Bereznoi (USSR), B. Blin (France), H. Budzislawski, R. Clausse, J. Fernandez, P. Gabor (Hungary), J. Garcia Morejon (Brazil), J-L Hébarre (France), M. Kasagi (Japan), A. S. Khurshid, M. S. Kirloskar (India), P. F. Lazarsfeld, G. Maletzke, J. W. Mole, B. Osolnik, O. Riegel, M. Rooy, I. Tetelowska, R. Vehmas
7th 1970 Konstanz (FRG)	Same as above	Francesco Fattorello, James D. Halloran (UK), Mieczyslaw Kafel, Bogdan Osolnik, Yassen Zassoursky	Same as above	Juan Beneyto	Claude Bellanger, Alex Edelstein (US), Francisco Manrique (Argentina), Jovan Marinovic, Dallas W. Smythe (Canada) + Section Heads	A. Benito, A. F. Bereznoi, E. Dusiška (GDR), V. Escardo (Argentina), J. Fernandez, P. Gabor, A. Garbarino (Italy), J. Garcia Morejon (Brazil), G. Gerbner (US), J-L Hébarre, O. Hultén (Sweden), F. Kempers (Netherlands), P. Levy (Belgium), G. Maletzke, S. Marjanovic (Yugoslavia), G. Mond (France), E. Noelle-Neumann (FRG), K. Nordenstreng (Finland), D. W. Riegel, H. I. Schiller (US), Y. Uchikawa (Japan)

8th 1972 Buenos Aires (Argentina)	James D. Halloran; Past President, Jacques Bourquin; Honorary President, Fernand Terrou	Francesco Fattorello, Vladimir Klimes, Kaarle Nordenstreng, Bogdan Osolnik, Herbert I. Schiller, Yassen Zassoursky	Emil Dusiška; Deputy SG, Otto Roegele	Same as above	Claude Bellanger, Alex Edelstein, Francisco Manrique, Jovan Marinovic, Dallas W. Smythe, Walery Pisarek (Poland) + Section Heads	A. Benito, A. F. Bereznoi, N. Dajani (Lebanon), V. Escardo, M. Eydalin (Italy), G. Feliciano (Philippines), J. Fernandez, P. Gabor, A. Garbarino (Italy), J. Garcia Morejon, G. Gerbner, O. Hultén (Sweden), F. Kempers, Levy, G. Maletzke, S. Marjanovic, E. Noelle-Neumann, R. Noseda (Argentine), A. Opubor (Nigeria), O. Riegel, J-L Seurin (France), Y. Uchikawa
9th 1974 Leipzig (GDR)	James D. Halloran; Honorary President, Fernand Terrou and Jacques Bourquin (Honorary Presidents not listed after this)	Same as above	Same as above	Same as above	Claude Bellanger, Alex Edelstein, Francisco Manrique, Jovan Marinovic, Dallas W. Smythe, Walery Pisarek + Section Heads	A. Benito, A. F. Bereznoi, N. Dajani, V. Escardo, M. Eudalin, G. Feliciano, J. Fernandez, P. Gabor, A. Garbarino, J. Garcia Morejon, G. Gerbner, O. Hultén, F. Kempers, P. Levy, G. Maletzke, S. Marjanovic, G. Mond, E. Noelle-Neumann, A. Opubor, O. Riegel, J-L Seurin, Y. Uchikawa
10th 1976 Leicester (UK)	James D. Halloran	Luis Beltrán (Colombia), Francisco Fattorello, Kaarle Nordenstreng, Alfred Opubor, Bogdan Osolnik, Walery Pisarek, Herbert I. Schiller, Yassen Zassoursky	Same as above	Same as above	**International Council** A. M. Auda (Egypt), C. Bellanger, A. Bunzlova (Czechoslovakia), N. de Camargo (Brazil), P. Campeanu (Romania), R. Cheesman (Denmark), N. Dajani, M. Eydalin, H-H Fabris (Austria), G. Feliciano, G. Gerbner, B. Golebiowski (Poland), C. J. Hamelink (Netherlands), O. Hultén, F. Kempers, O. Linné (Denmark), T. Martelanc (Yugoslavia), H. Mowlana (Iran), E. Noelle-Neumann, A. Pasquali (Venezuela), B. Pavlič (Yugoslavia), G. Robinson (Canada), L. Rao (India), P. Sepstrup (Denmark), A. Suffert (France), T. Szecskö (Hungary), Y. Uchikawa, A. Werner (Norway) + Section Heads	

(*continued*)

(continued)

General Assembly	*President*	*Vice Presidents*	*Secretary General (SG)*	*Treasurer*	*Bureau*	*Executive Committee*
11th 1978 Warsaw (Poland)	Same as above	Same as above	Same as above	Same as above		Same as above except Bellanger replaced by F. Balle (France) and Pasquali replaced by O. Capriles (Venezuela)
12th 1980 Caracas (Venezuela)	Same as above	Luis Beltrán, Nelly de Camargo, Cees J. Hamelink, Tomo Martelanc, Kaarle Nordenstreng, Alfred Opubor, Walery Pisarek, Herbert I. Schiller, Yassen Zassoursky	Emil Dusiška; Deputy SG, Gertrude Robinson	Same as above		B. Bhatia (Malaysia), F. Balle, A. Bunzlova, N. de Camargo, P. Campeanu, O. Caprilles, R. Cole (US), N. Dajani, M. Djordjevic (Yugoslavia), K. E. Eapen (India), A. Edelstein, M. Eydalin, H-H Fabris, F. Fleck (Switzerland), B. Golka (Poland), S. Gunaratne (Australia), O. Hultén, F. Kempers, E. Noelle-Neumann, R. Roncagliolo (Peru), R. Salinas (Chile), C. Sarkar (India), P. Sepstrup, A. Suffert, T. Szecskö, Y. Uchikawa, A. Werner + Section Heads
13th 1982 Paris (France)	Same as above	Same as above	Acting SG, Gertrude Robinson	Same as above		Same as above
14th 1984 Prague (Czechoslovakia)	Same as above	B. Bhatia, Nelly de Camargo, Richard Cole, George Gerbner, Cees J. Hamelink, Tomo Martelanc, Kaarle Nordenstreng, Walery Pisarek, Rafael Roncagliolo, Herbert I. Schiller, Frank Ugboajah (Nigeria), Yassen Zassoursky	Tamás Szecskö; Deputy SG, Gertrude Robinson	Olof Hultén		P. Anzola (Columbia), A. Barros-Lemez (Uruguay), J. Becker (FRG), K. Boafo (Ghana), A. Burmistenko (USSR), A. Bunzlova, M. Chenouffi (Tunisia), M. Guthberg (Jamaica), N. Dajani, K. E. Eapen, A. El-Rahman (Egypt), F. Fleck, B. Golka, F-X Hutin (France), F. Kempers, V. Lowe (Malaysia), A. Mattelart (France), A. Méar (Canada), E. Nordahl Svendsen (Denmark), M. Parés i Maicas (Spain), F. Reyes Matta (Chile), G. Richeri (Italy), R. Salinas, B. Signitzer (Austria), S. Splichal (Yugoslavia), I. Tyson (Australia), Y. Uchikawa, H. Uekermann (FRG), J. Wasko (US), C. Wilhoit (US) + Section Heads
15th 1986 New Delhi (India)	Same as above	Same as above	Same as above	Same as above		Same as above

16th 1988 Barcelona (Spain)	James D. Halloran; President-Elect, Cees J. Hamelink	K E. Eapen Hamid Mowlana (US)	Tamás Szecskö; Deputy SG, Annie Méar	Same as above	M. Adnan (Malaysia), B. Agrawal (India), J. Becker, K. Boafo, A. Brown (Jamaica), N. de Camargo, U. Carlsson (Sweden), R. Cheesman, B. Dervin (US), M. Egbon (Nigeria), R. Faraone (Uruguay), N. Garnham (UK), G. Gerbner, P. Gray, F-X Hutin, Y. Ito (Japan), K. Jakubowicz (Poland), J. Jouët (France), R. Kandil (Qatar), J. Marques de Melo (Brazil), J. Mbindyo (Kenya), G. Murdock (UK), M. Parés i Maicas (Spain), L. Rao, G. Robinson, H. I. Schiller, S. Splichal (Yugoslavia), J. Wasko (US), R. White (UK), Y. Zassoursky + Section Heads
17th 1990 Bled (Slovenia)	Cees J. Hamelink; Past President, James D. Halloran	Same as above	Same as above	Same as above	Same as above
18th 1992 Guarujá (Brazil)	Cees J. Hamelink; President-Elect, Hamid Mowlana (US)	Kwame Boafo, Francois-Xavier Hutin, Olga Linné, K. E. Eapen, José Marques de Melo, Annie Méar	Robin Cheesman; Deputy SG, Slavko Splichal	Gertrude Robinson	A. Brown (Jamaica), N. de Camargo, U. Carlsson, F. Corcoran (Ireland), B. Dervin, A. El-Rahman (Egypt), A. Fadul (Brazil), R. Faraone, M. Gallagher (France), O. Gandy (US), G. Gerbner, P. Gray, Y. Ito, K. Jakubowicz, J. Jouët, C-W Kim (South Korea), K. Lundby (Norway), O. Manaev (Byelorussia), D McQuail (UK), G. Mont (Mexico), M. Parés i Maicas, F. Perrone (Brazil), L. Rao, R. Roncagliolo, J. Sanchez (Colombia), T. Syvertsen (Norway), L. U. Uche (Nigeria), J. Wasko, L. van Zoonen (Netherlands) + Section Heads
19th 1994 Seoul (South Korea)	Hamid Mowlana; Past President, Cees J. Hamelink	Francois-Xavier Hutin, Olga Linné, José Marques de Melo, Annie Méar	Same as above	Same as above	Same as above
20th 1996 Sydney (Australia)	Hamid Mowlana; President-Elect, Manuel Parés i Maicas	Elizabeth Fox (US), Carmen Gómez Mont (Mexico), Olga Linné, Michael Palmer (France), John Sinclair (Australia)	Naren Chitty (Australia); Deputy SG, Ole Prehn (Denmark)	Same as above	A. Brown, M. Burkle (Mexico), G. Daza Hernandez (Colombia), E. De Bens (Belgium), B. Dervin, J. Downing (US), A. El-Rahman, D Frau-Meigs, C-W Kim, U-M Kivikuru (Finland), I. Kovats (Hungary), M. Krohling Kunsch (Brazil), T. Lavender (UK), K. Lundby, P. Maarek (France), U. Maier-Rabler (Austria), T. Masilela (South Africa), V. Nightingale (Australia), S-A Nohrstedt (Sweden), J. Protzel (Peru), L. Rao, A. Richter (Russia), D. Shinar (Israel), K. M. Shrivastava (India), A. Sreberny-Mohammadi (UK), T. Syvertsen (Norway), S. Venturelli (US), J. Wainberg (Brazil), F. Wete (Cameroon), H. Yufu (China) + Section Heads

(*continued*)

(continued)

General Assembly	*President*	*Vice Presidents*	*Secretary General (SG)*	*Treasurer*	*Bureau*	*Executive Committee*
21st 1998 Glasgow (Scotland)	Manuel Parés i Maicas; Past President, Hamid Mowlana	Elizabeth Fox, Carmen Gómez Mont, Olga Linné, John Sinclair	Same as above	Annie Méar		Same as above
22nd 2000 Singapore	Manuel Parés i Maicas; President-Elect, Frank Morgan (Australia)	Marjan de Bruin (Jamaica), Eddie Kuo (Singapore), Tawana Kupe (South Africa), Katharine Sarikakis (UK), Jan Servaes (Belgium)	Ole Prehn; Deputy SG, Divina Frau-Meigs	Same as above		M. Amer (Egypt), J. Bardoel (Netherlands), A. de Beer (South Africa), A. Bernstein (Israel), G. Cimadevilla (Argentina), J. Downing, H. Dunn (Jamaica), S. Fasal (UK), O. Gandy, L. N. Gomes (Mexico), A. Goonasekera (Singapore), M. Hagerup-Lyngvaer (Australia), A-M Jönsson (Sweden), U-M Kivikuru, W. Kleiwächter, P. Maarek, M. de Moragas Spa (Spain), M. Raboy (Canada), G. F. Setareh (France), K. M. Shrivastava, J. Sinclair, A. Sreberny, P. N. Thomas (UK), D. K. Thussu (UK), R. Teer-Tomaselli (South Africa), S. Vaidyanattan (India), E. Vartanova (Russia), G. Wang (Taiwan), J. Wilke (Germany) + Section Heads
23rd 2002 Barcelona (Spain)	Frank Morgan; Past President, Manuel Parés i Maicas	Marjan de Bruin, Eddie Kuo, Katharine Sarikakis, Jan Servaes, Ruth Teer-Tomaselli	Same as above	Same as above		Same as above except Bernstein, Dunn, Goonasekera and Kivikuru who did not continue
24th 2004 Porto Alegre (Brazil)	Frank Morgan; President-Elect, Robin Mansell; Past President, Frank Morgan	Divina Frau-Meigs, Annebelle Sreberny	Ole Prehn	César Bolaño (Brazil)		M. de Bruin, A. Calabrese (US), D. De (India), J. Downing, S. Kaitazi-Whitlock (Greece), V. Nightingale, K. Nordenstreng, C. Padovani (Italy), M. Raboy, J. Sinclair, D. K. Thussu, T. Tufte (Denmark), E. Vartanova, G. Wang, J. Wilke + Section Heads
25th 2006 Cairo (Egypt)	Robin Mansell	Same as above	Same as above	Same as above		Same as above

26th 2008 Stockholm (Sweden)	Robin Mansell, President-Elect, Annabelle Sreberny Past President, Robin Mansell	John Downing, Ruth Teer-Tomaselli	Hopeton Dunn (Jamaica)	Beate Josephi (Australia)	S-G Baek (Korea), A. Calabrese, H. Joshi (India), S. Kaitatzi-Whitlock, G. Kaplun (Uruguay), W. Kleinwächter, C. Padovani, M. Raboy, K. Sarikakis, J. Sinclair, P. N. Thomas, D. K. Thussu, T. Tufte, E. Vartanova, E. Väliverronen (Finland) + Section Heads
27th 2010 Braga (Portugal)	Annabelle Sreberny	Same as above	Same as above	Same as above	Same as above
28th 2012 Durban (South Africa)	Annabelle Sreberny, President-Elect, Janet Wasko; Past President, Annabelle Screberny	Pradip N. Thomas Aimée Vega Montiel (Mexico)	Maria Michalis (UK)	Nico Carpentier	E. Akpabio (Namibia), D. Araujo (Brazil), S-G Baek (Korea), G. Hadl (Japan), B. Hamada (Qatar), T. Jacobson (US), B. Josephi, F. Krotz (Germany), P. Maarek, S. Milan (Netherlands), C. Paterson (UK), M. Pinto (Portugal), E. Pollack (Sweden), K. Sarikakis (Austria), R. Teer-Tomaselli + Section Heads
29th 2014 Hyderabad (India)	Same as above	Same as above	Same as above	Same as above	Same as above
30th 2016 Leicester (England)	Same as above	Graham Murdock Aimée Vega Montiel	Gerard Goggin (Australia)	Anthony Moretti (post not taken up)	E. Akpabio, C. Anyanwu (Australia), D. Araujo, A. Bernstein, C. Bolaño, F. Krotz (Germany), P. Maarek, G. Mastrini (Argentina), R. Maxwell (US), K. Mendes (Canada), C. Padovani, J. Pierson (Netherlands), S. Ristovska (US), H. Sousa (Portugal), T. Watanabe (Japan) + Section Heads
31st 2018 Eugene, Oregon (US)	Same as above	Same as above	Same as above	Elske van de Fliert (Australia)	Same as above
32nd 2020 Tampere (online) (Finland)	Janet Wasko, President-Elect, Nico Carpentier; Past President, Janet Wasko	Andrea Medrado (Brazil) Usha Raman	Same as above	Same as above	E. Akpabio, L. Albornoz (Spain), C. Anyanwu, D. Araujo, S. Chen (China), A. Gladkova (Russia), T. Jacobson (US), T. Kupe, C. Lago (Brazil), F. Martin (Australia), S. Milan, C. Padovani, S. Ristovska, H. Sousa, K. Torkkola (Finland) + Section Heads

Appendix B: IAMCR Sections, Working Groups and Commissions 1959–2021

This appendix lists the sections and other operative bodies with the persons leading them to 2021. *Sections* are listed in the chronological order of their foundation, repeating the list for each General Assembly (GA) year with current titles and heads. In the case of the International Communication Section, it is listed in 1978 Warsaw as successor to the former International Understanding Section, which was discontinued at that time. For example, the Communication Satellites and Technology Section is listed in 1978 as a new section, later renamed Communication Technology (1980-) and Communication Technology Policy (1990-), although it also might have been listed as a successor to the earlier Technology Section (1966-) with its roots in the combined Section for Economy and Technology, which was one of the four original sections founded in 1959.

Working Groups (WGs) for emerging topics are listed, first in Leicester 1976, then in Paris 1982 and, later, whenever new WGs were established and when their name or chair was changed. They are not repeated for each GA year and their eventual discontinuation is not recorded.

Committees for administrative tasks are listed, first in Bled 1990, in alphabetical order and repeated for each biennial GA year if there was a change.

© The Author(s), under exclusive license to Springer Nature Switzerland AG 2023

J. Becker, R. Mansell (eds.), *Reflections on the International Association for Media and Communication Research*,
https://doi.org/10.1007/978-3-031-16383-8

(continued)

Established/ Confirmed by General Assembly	*Sections and Other Bodies* *Sections in order of founding year, others in alphabetical order*	*Heads and Conveners* *Nationality in brackets when first listed*
1959 Milan	**Section:**	
	Historical Studies	Giuliano Gaeta (Italy)
	Juridical and Political Science Studies	Fernand Terrou (France)
	Psycho-Sociological Studies	Wilbur Schramm (US)
	Economical and Technical Studies	Marcel Stijns (Belgium)
	Coordination:	
	Bibliography	Wilbur Schramm
1964 Vienna	**Section:**	
	History	Vladimir Klimes (Czechoslovakia)
	Legal Matters	Martin Löffler (FRG)
	Psycho-Sociological Matters	Wilbur Schramm and Alex Edelstein (US)
	Economy and Technology	Marcel Stijns
	Professional Training	Francesco Fattorello (Italy)
	Marketing and Advertising	Leo Bogart (US)
	Terminology and Methodology	Mieczyslaw Kafel (Poland)
	Coordination:	
	Publications	Maarten Rooy (Netherlands)
	Studies and Research	Fernand Terrou
1966 Herceg Novi	**Section:**	
	History	Vladimir Klimes
	Legal Matters	Martin Löffler
	Psycho-Sociological Matters	Wilbur Schramm and Alex Edelstein
	Economy	Marcel Stijns
	Technology	Charles Minassian (France)
	Professional Training	Francesco Fattorello
	Marketing and Advertising	Leo Bogart
	Terminology and Methodology	Mieczyslav Kafel
	Coordination:	
	Publications	Maarten Rooy
	Studies and Research	Fernand Terrou
1968 Pamplona	**Section:**	
	History	Vladimir Klimes
	Legal Matters	Martin Löffler
	Psycho-Sociological Matters	Alex Edelstein
	Technology	Charles Minassian and Emil Dusiška (GDR)
	Professional Training	Francesco Fattorello
	Marketing and Advertising	Leo Bogart
	Terminology	Bernard Voyenne (France)
	Methodology	Wilbur Schramm
	Bibliography	Irena Tetelowska (Poland)
	International Understanding	Bogdan Osolnik (Yugoslavia)
	Coordination:	
	Studies and Research	Fernand Terrou (France)

(*continued*)

(continued)

Established/ Confirmed by General Assembly	*Sections and Other Bodies* *Sections in order of founding year, others in alphabetical order*	*Heads and Conveners* *Nationality in brackets when first listed*
1970 Constance	**Section:**	
	History	Günter Heidorn (GDR)
	Legal Matters	Martin Löffler
	Socio-Psychological Matters	Alex Edelstein
	Technology	Emil Dusiška and Charles Minassian
	Professional Training	Francesco Fattorello and Tomo Martelanc (Yugoslavia)
	Terminology	Bernard Voyenne
	Bibliography	Walery Pisarek (Poland)
	International Understanding	Bogdan Osolnik
	Satellites	Dallas W. Smythe (Canada)
	Economics	Florian Fleck (Switzerland)
	Publications	George Gerbner (US) and Frans Kempers (Netherlands)
1972 Buenos Aires	**Section:**	
	History	Günter Heidorn
	Legal Matters	Martin Löffler
	Socio-Psychological Matters	Alex Edelstein
	Technology	Emil Dusiška and Charles Minassian
	Professional Training	Francesco Fattorello and Tomo Martelanc
	Terminology	Bernard Voyenne
	Bibliography	Walery Pisarek
	International Understanding	Bogdan Osolnik and George Mond (France)
	Satellites	Dallas W. Smythe
	Developing Countries	Kaarle Nordenstreng (Finland) and Alfred Opubor (Nigeria)
	Publications	George Gerbner and Frans Kempers
	Television	Annette Suffert (France)
1974 Leipzig	**Section:**	
	History	Günter Heidorn
	Legal Matters	Martin Löffler
	Social Psychology	Alex Edelstein
	Technology	Emil Dusiška and Charles Minassian
	Professional Training	Francesco Fattorello
	Terminology	Bernard Voyenne
	Bibliography	Walery Pisarek
	International Understanding	Bogdan Osolnik and George Mond
	Satellites	Dallas W. Smythe
	Developing Countries	Alfred Opubor
	Publications	George Gerbner and Frans Kempers
	Television	Annette Suffert
1976 Leicester	**Section:**	
	History	Günter Heidorn
	Law	Martin Löffler
	Social Science	Alex Edelstein

(*continued*)

(continued)

Established/ Confirmed by General Assembly	***Sections and Other Bodies*** *Sections in order of founding year, others in alphabetical order*	***Heads and Conveners*** *Nationality in brackets when first listed*
	Technology and Satellites	Emil Dusiška
	Professional Training	Francesco Fattorello
	Bibliography	Walery Pisarek
	International Understanding	Bogdan Osolnik and George Mond
	Developing Countries	Alfred Opubor
	Television	Annette Suffert
	Working Group:	
	Materialist Theory	Robin Cheesman (Denmark)
1978 Warsaw	**Section:**	
	History	Günter Heidorn
	Law	Martin Löffler
	Social Psychology	Annette Suffert and Olga Linné (Denmark)
	Professional Training	Francesco Fattorello and Yassen Zassoursky (USSR)
	Bibliography	Walery Pisarek
	International Communication	Breda Pavlič (Yugoslavia)
	Developing Countries	Alfred Opubor
	Communication Satellites and Technology	Dallas W. Smythe
	Political Economy	Robin Cheesman and Tamás Szecskö (Hungary)
1980 Caracas	**Section:**	
	History	Günter Heidorn
	Law	Martin Löffler
	Social Psychology	Olga Linné
	Professional Education	Yassen Zassoursky
	Bibliography	Walery Pisarek
	International Communication	Breda Pavlič and Hamid Mowlana (US)
	Communication Technology	William Melody (Canada)
	Political Economy	Robin Cheesman and Tamás Szecskö
1982 Paris	**Section:**	
	History	Günter Heidorn
	Law	Martin Löffler
	Sociology and Social Psychology	Olga Linné
	Professional Education	Yassen Zassoursky
	Bibliography	Walery Pisarek
	International Communication	Breda Pavlič and Hamid Mowlana
	Communication Technology	William Melody (Canada)
	Political Economy	Robin Cheesman
	Working Group:	
	Community Radio and Television	Ole Prehn (Denmark)
	Gender and Communication	Madeleine Kleberg (Sweden)

(*continued*)

(continued)

Established/ Confirmed by General Assembly	*Sections and Other Bodies* *Sections in order of founding year, others in alphabetical order*	*Heads and Conveners* *Nationality in brackets when first listed*
1984 Prague	**Section:**	
	History	Günter Heidorn
	Law	Martin Löffler
	Sociology and Social Psychology	Olga Linné
	Professional Education	Yassen Zassoursky
	Bibliography	Walery Pisarek
	International Communication	Hamid Mowlana
	Communication Technology	William Melody
	Political Economy	Robin Cheesman
	Working Group:	
	Comic Art	John Lent (US)
	Media Education	Birgitte Tufte (Denmark)
1986 New Delhi	**Section:**	
	History	Günter Heidorn
	Law	Martin Löffler
	Sociology and Social Psychology	Olga Linné
	Professional Education	Yassen Zassoursky
	Bibliography	Walery Pisarek
	International Communication	Hamid Mowlana
	Communication Technology	William Melody
	Political Economy	Zoltan Jakáb (Hungary)
	Working Group (Only new and revised Working Groups are listed in 1986 and onwards):	
	New Directions in Intercultural Communication Scholarship	Anantha Babbili (US)
1988 Barcelona	**Section:**	
	History	Günter Heidorn
	Law	Cees J. Hamelink
	Sociology and Social Psychology	Olga Linné
	Professional Education	Yassen Zassoursky
	Bibliography	Walery Pisarek
	International Communication	Hamid Mowlana and Colleen Roach (US)
	Communication Technology	William Melody
	Political Economy	Zoltan Jakáb
	Working Group:	
	Environmental Issues and the Mass Media	Anders Hansen (UK)
	Network on Qualitative Audience Research (NECTAR)	Klaus Bruhn Jensen (Denmark)
1990 Bled	**Section:**	
	History	Gertrude Robinson (Canada)
	Law	Wolfgang Kleiwächter (GDR)
	Sociology and Social Psychology	Olga Linné

(*continued*)

(continued)

Established/ Confirmed by General Assembly	*Sections and Other Bodies* *Sections in order of founding year, others in alphabetical order*	*Heads and Conveners* *Nationality in brackets when first listed*
	Professional Education	Kaarle Nordenstreng
	Bibliography	Robin Cheesman
	International Communication	Howard Frederick (US)
	Communication Technology Policy	Robin Mansell (UK)
	Political Economy	Vincent Mosco (Canada)
	Political Communication Research	David Paletz (US)
	Gender and Communication	Madeleine Kleberg
	Working Group:	
	Assessment of Quality in Broadcast Programming	Sakae Ishikawa (Japan)
	Communication, Myth and Ritual	Steward Hoover (US)
	Contemporary Popular Culture: Brazilian Perspective	James Lull (US)
	Current Issues in Development Support Communication	Srivinas Melkote (US)
	Ethnicity, Racism and the Media	Charles Husband (UK)
	International Theater of Consumption: Cross Cultural Analysis of Advertising	Sut Jhally (US)
	Joint IAMCR/WAPOR Sessions on Mass Media and Public Opinion	Wolfgang Donsbach (FRG)
	Joint Law Section and IPSA Research Committee on Political Communication	Philippe Maarek (France)
	Mass Media and Popular Fiction	Peter Larsen (Norway)
	Media and Cultural Policy in Small European Countries	Jean-Claude Burgelman (Belgium)
	Media and Tourism	K. M. Shrivastava (India)
	Media Systems in Transition	Slavko Splichal (Slovenia)
	Multimedia	Nelly de Camargo (Brazil)
	Online Academic Community	Tom Jacobson (US)
	Participatory Communication Research Network	Jan Servaes (Belgium) and Tom Jacobson
	Racism and Media	Teun van Dijk (The Netherlands)
	Science Journalism in the World	José Marques de Melo (Brazil) and Pierre Fayard (France)
	South-South Cooperation in Communication	Rafael Roncagliolo (Peru)
	Third World Communications	Gerald J. Sussman (US)
	Committee:	
	Fundraising and Finance	Olof Hultén
	Legal	Cees J. Hamelink

(*continued*)

(continued)

Established/ Confirmed by General Assembly	*Sections and Other Bodies* Sections in order of founding year, others in alphabetical order	*Heads and Conveners* Nationality in brackets when first listed
	Membership	Kwame Boafo (Ghana)
	Publications	Brenda Dervin (US)
	Research Policy	George Gerbner
	Section Review	Karol Jakubowicz (Poland)
1992 Guarujá	**Section:**	
	History	Mary Mander (US)
	Law	Wolfgang Kleiwächter
	Sociology and Social Psychology	Wolfgang Donsbach (Germany)
	Professional Education	Kaarle Nordenstreng
	Documentation and Information Systems	Yvonne Mignot-Lefebvre (France)
	International Communication	Howard Frederick
	Communication Technology Policy	Robin Mansell
	Political Economy	Vincent Mosco
	Political Communication Research	David Paletz
	Gender and Communication	Madelene Kleberg
	Local Radio and Television	Ole Prehn
	Media Education Research	Birgitte Tufte
	Working Group:	
	Alternative Directions in Communication Scholarship	Anantha Babbili
	Communication and Popular Issues	Kwame Boafo (Ghana) and Silvie Cohen (US)
	Popular Culture	Ib Bondeberg (Denmark)
	Committee:	
	Fundraising and Finance	Gertrude Robinson
	Legal	Cees J. Hamelink
	Membership	Kwame Boafo
	Publications	Robert White (UK)
	Research Policy Review	Manuel Parés I Maicas (Spain)
	Section Review	Karol Jakubowicz
1994 Seoul	**Section:**	
	History	Mary Mander
	Law	Wolfgang Kleinwächter
	Sociology and Social Psychology	Wolfgang Donsbach
	Professional Education	Kaarle Nordenstreng
	Documentation and Information Systems	Yvonne Mignot-Lefebvre
	International Communication	Abbas Malek (US)
	Communication Technology Policy	Rohan Samarajiva (US)
	Political Economy	Manjunath Pendakur (US)
	Political Communication Research	David Paletz

(continued)

(continued)

Established/ Confirmed by General Assembly	*Sections and Other Bodies* *Sections in order of founding year, others in alphabetical order*	*Heads and Conveners* *Nationality in brackets when first listed*
	Gender and Communication	Liesbet van Zoonen (Netherlands)
	Local Radio and Television	Ole Prehn
	Media Education Research	Birgitte Tufte
	Participatory Communication Research	Jan Servaes
	Working Group:	
	Regional Media and Cultural Diversity	José Marques de Melo and Carmen G. Mont (Mexico)
	Committee:	
	Fundraising and Finance	Gertrude Robinson
	Human Rights	Shalina Venturelli (US)
	IAMCR in the Twenty-First Century	Aggrey Brown (Jamaica)
	Legal	Hamid Mowlana
	Membership	Francois-Xavier Hutin (France)
	Publications	Robert White
	Research Policy Review	Manuel Parés i Maicas
	Section Review	Karol Jakubowicz
1996 Sydney	**Section:**	
	History	Jürgen Wilke (Germany)
	Law	Wolfgang Kleinwächer
	Sociology and Social Psychology	Wolfgang Donsbach
	Professional Education	Frank Morgan (Australia)
	Documentation and Information Systems	Yvonne Mignot-Lefebvre
	International Communication	Abbas Malek
	Communication Technology Policy	Rohan Samarajiva
	Political Economy	Majunath Pendakur
	Political Communication Research	David Paletz
	Gender and Communication	Liesbet Van Zoonen
	Local Radio and Television	Nicholas Jankowski (Netherlands)
	Media Education Research	Birgitte Tufte
	Participatory Communication Research	Jan Servaes
	Committee:	
	Fundraising and Finance	Gertrude Robinson
	Human Rights	Shalina Venturelli
	IAMCR in the Twenty-First Century	Aggrey Brown
	Legal	Cees J. Hamelink
	Membership	Francois-Xavier Hutin
	Publications	Robert White
	Research Policy Review	Manuel Parés i Maicas
	Section Review	Kaarle Nordenstreng

(*continued*)

(continued)

Established/ Confirmed by General Assembly	*Sections and Other Bodies* *Sections in order of founding year, others in alphabetical order*	*Heads and Conveners* *Nationality in brackets when first listed*
1998 Glasgow	**Section:**	
	History	Jürgen Wilke
	Law	Andrei Richter (Russia)
	Sociology and Social Psychology	Wolfgang Donsbach
	Professional Education	Frank Morgan
	Documentation and Information Systems	Yvonne Mignot-Lefebvre
	International Communication	Abbas Malek
	Communication Technology and Policy	Ursula Maier-Rabler (Austria)
	Political Economy	Graham Murdock (UK)
	Political Communication Research	David Paletz
	Gender and Communication	Marjan de Bruin (Netherlands)
	Local Radio and Television	Nicholas Jankowski
	Media Education Research	Keval J. Kumar (India)
	Participatory Communication Research	Tom Jacobson (US)
	Working Group:	
	Islam and Media	Mohammad A. Siddiqi (US)
	Junior Scholars Network	Katharine Sarikakis (UK)
	Media Production Analysis	Chris Paterson (UK) and Knut Helland (Norway)
	Committee:	
	Fundraising and Finance	Annie Méar (Canada)
	Human Rights	Shalina Venturelli
	Legal	Cees J. Hamelink
	Membership	Francois-Xavier Hutin
	Publications	Annabelle Sreberny
	Research Policy Review	Jan Servaes
	Section Review	Kaarle Nordenstreng
2000 Singapore	**Section:**	
	History	Terhi Rantanen (Finland)
	Law	Andrei Richter
	Psychology and Public Opinion	Wolfgang Donsbach
	Professional Education	Mohd Safar Hasim (Malaysia) and George Thottam (US)
	Documentation and Information Systems	Yvonne Mignot-Lefebvre
	International Communication	Abbas Malek
	Communication Technology and Policy	Ursula Maier-Rabler
	Political Economy	Graham Murdock
	Political Communication Research	David Paletz
	Gender and Communication	Karen Ross (UK) and Gita Bamezai (India)

(*continued*)

(continued)

Established/ Confirmed by General Assembly	***Sections and Other Bodies*** *Sections in order of founding year, others in alphabetical order*	***Heads and Conveners*** *Nationality in brackets when first listed*
	Community Communication (earlier Local Radio and TV)	Nicholas Jankowski and Per Jauert (Denmark)
	Media Education Research	Keval J. Kumar
	Participatory Communication Research	Thomas Jacobson
	Audience and Reception Studies	Klaus Bruhn Jensen
	Junior Scholars Network	John Sullivan (US)
	Working Group:	
	Ethics of Society and Ethics of Communication	Manuel Parés i Maicas
	European Broadcasting Policies	Jo Bardoel (Netherlands)
	Global Media Policy	Marc Raboy (Canada)
	Intercultural Communication	Miquel Rodrigo (Spain)
	Media, Religion and Culture	Jose Martinez de Toda (Italy)
	Media and Sport	Alina Bernstein (Israel)
	Popular Culture	Garry Whannel (UK)
	Committee:	
	Fundraising and Development	Divina Frau-Meigs (France)
	Human Rights	Shalini Venturelli
	Legal	Philippe Maarek
	Membership	Francois-Xavier Hutin
	Publications	Annabelle Sreberny
	Section Review	Kaarle Nordenstreng
2002 Barcelona	**Section:**	
	History	Terhi Rantanen
	Law	Andrei Richter
	Psychology and Public Opinion	Friedrich Krotz (FRG) and Hillel Nossek (Israel)
	Professional Education	Beate Josephi (Australia)
	International Communication	Arnold de Beer (South Africa)
	Communication Technology and Policy	Hopeton Dunn (Jamaica) and Pascal Verhoerst (Belgium)
	Political Economy	Janet Wasko (US)
	Political Communication Research	Philippe Maarek
	Gender and Communication	Karen Ross (UK) and Gita Bamezai (India)
	Community Communication	Laura Stein (US)
	Media Education Research	Keval J. Kumar
	Participatory Communication Research	Ullamaija Kivikuru (Finland)
	Audience and Reception Studies	Tony Wilson (Australia) and Umi Khattab (Australia)
	Junior Scholars Network	Rosa Leslie Mikeal (US) and Sandor Vegh (US)
	Media and Sport	Alina Bernstein

(*continued*)

(continued)

Established/ Confirmed by General Assembly	*Sections and Other Bodies* *Sections in order of founding year, others in alphabetical order*	*Heads and Conveners* *Nationality in brackets when first listed*
	Working Group:	
	Environmental Issues, Science and Risk Communication	Anders Hansen
	Health, Technologies and Communication	Milton Campos (Canada)
	HIV/AIDS and Communication	Marjan de Bruin (Jamaica) and Thomas Tufte (Denmark)
	Media, Religion and Culture	Johannes Ehrat (Italy)
	Committee:	
	Conference Policy	Katharine Sarikakis
	Development	Eddie Kuo (Singapore)
	Elections	Cees J. Hamelink
	Fundraising	Divina Frau-Meigs
	Legal	Philippe Maarek
	Membership and Participation	Ruth Teer-Tomaselli
	Newsletter	Marjan de Bruin
	Publications	Jan Servaes
	Section Review	Kaarle Nordenstreng
	Task Force on WSIS	Marc Raboy
2004 Porto Alegre	**Section:**	
	History	Peter Putnis (Australia)
	Law	Andrei Richter
	Psychology and Public Opinion	Friedrich Krotz and Hillel Nossek
	Professional Education	Beate Josephi
	International Communication	Allen Palmer (US)
	Communication Technology and Policy	Hopeton Dunn and Pascal Verhoerst
	Political Economy	Janet Wasko
	Political Communication Research	Philippe Maarek
	Gender and Communication	Todd Holden (Japan)
	Community Communication	Laura Stein
	Media Education Research	Keval J. Kumar
	Participatory Communication Research	Ullamaija Kivikuru and Rico Lie (Netherlands)
	Audience and Reception Studies	Tony Wilson (Australia) and Umi Khattab (Australia)
	Junior Scholars Network	Rosa Leslie Mikeal and Sandor Vegh (US)
	Media and Sport	Alina Bernstein
	Working Group:	
	Alternative Directions in Communication Scholarship	Anantha Babbili
	Diaspora and Media	Shehina Fazal (UK)
	Digital Divide	Elena Vartanova (Russia)
	Ethics of Society and Ethics of Communication	Manuel Parés i Maicas (Spain)
	Post-Socialist Media	Yassen Zassoursky

(*continued*)

(continued)

Established/ Confirmed by General Assembly	***Sections and Other Bodies*** *Sections in order of founding year, others in alphabetical order*	***Heads and Conveners*** *Nationality in brackets when first listed*
	Committee:	
	Budget	César Bolaño (Brazil)
	Conference	Ole Prehn
	Elections	Janet Wasko and Cees J. Hamelink
	Fundraising	Annie Méar
	Legal	Philippe Maarek
	Membership and Participation	Ullamaija Kivikuru
	Publications	Annabelle Sreberny
	Scholarly Review	Robin Mansell and Kaarle Nordenstreng
	Task Force on WSIS	Divina Frau-Meigs and Marc Raboy
2006 Cairo	**Section:**	
	History	Peter Putnis and Carlos Barrera (Spain)
	Law	Andrei Richter and Wolfgang Kleinwächter
	Psychology and Public Opinion	Friedrich Krotz and Hillel Nossek
	Professional Education	Beate Josephi and Ibrahim Saleh (Egypt)
	International Communication	Allen Palmer
	Communication Technology Policy	Hopeton Dunn and Pascal Verhoest
	Political Economy	Janet Wasko and Helena Sousa (Portugal)
	Political Communication Research	Philippe Maarek and Dominic Wring (UK)
	Gender and Communication	Todd Holden
	Community Communication	Laura Stein
	Media Education Research	Joseph Borg (Malta) and Tania Ribeiro (Brazil)
	Participatory Communication Research	Rico Lie and Pradip N. Thomas (Australia)
	Audience and Reception Studies	Virginia Nightingale (Australia) and Brian O'Neill (Ireland)
	Emerging Scholars Network	Rosa Mikeal Martey
	Media and Sport	Alina Bernstein
	Working Group:	
	Chinese Communication Association	Bonnie Peng (Taiwan)
	Post-Socialist and Post-Authoritarian Media	Yassen Zassoursky
	Committee:	
	Elections	Janet Wasko
	Legal	Philippe Maarek
	Membership and Participation	Ullamaija Kivikuru
	Publications	Annabelle Sreberny
	Scholarly Review	Robin Mansell and Kaarle Nordenstreng
	Task Force on Media and Communication Policy	Andrew Calabrese (US)

(*continued*)

(continued)

Established/ Confirmed by General Assembly	*Sections and Other Bodies* *Sections in order of founding year, others in alphabetical order*	*Heads and Conveners* *Nationality in brackets when first listed*
2008 Stockholm	**Section:**	
	History	Peter Putnis and Carlos Barrera
	Law	Andrei Richter and Wolfgang Kleinwächter
	Psychology and Public Opinion	Friedrich Krotz and Hillel Nossek
	Journalism Research and Education	Beate Josephi and Ibrahim Saleh
	International Communication	Sujatha Sosale (US) and Tania Cantrell (US)
	Communication Policy and Technology	Hopeton Dunn and Jo Pierson (Belgium)
	Political Economy	Janet Wasko and Helena Sousa
	Political Communication Research	Philippe Maarek and Dominic Wring
	Gender and Communication	Todd Holden (Japan) and Ellen Riordan (US)
	Community Communication	Per Jauert and Elinor Rennie (Australia)
	Media Education Research	Joseph Borg and Tania Ribeiro
	Participatory Communication Research	Rico Lie and Pradip N. Thomas
	Audience and Reception Studies	Virginia Nightingale and Brian O'Neill
	Emerging Scholars Network	Rosa Mikeal Martey
	Media and Sport	Alina Bernstein
	Working Group:	
	Health Communication and Change	Marjan de Bruin and Thomas Tufte (Denmark)
	Committee:	
	Legal	Philippe Maarek
	Membership and Regionalisation	César Bolaño and Daya Kishan Thussu (UK)
	Scholarly Review	Robin Mansell and Kaarle Nordenstreng
	Task Force on Media and Communication Policy	Andrew Calabrese (US)
2010 Braga	**Section:**	
	History	Carlos Barrera
	Law	Sandra Braman (US)
	Mediated Communication, Public Opinion & Society	Friedrich Krotz and Hillel Nossek
	Journalism Research and Education	Beate Josephi and Ibrahim Saleh
	International Communication	Sujatha Sosale
	Communication Policy and Technology	Jo Pierson
	Political Economy	Helena Sousa
	Political Communication Research	Philippe Maarek

(*continued*)

(continued)

Established/ Confirmed by General Assembly	*Sections and Other Bodies* *Sections in order of founding year, others in alphabetical order*	*Heads and Conveners* *Nationality in brackets when first listed*
	Gender and Communication	Todd Holden
	Community Communication	Gabi Hadl
	Media Education Research	Divina Frau-Meigs and Manuel Pinto (Portugal)
	Participatory Communication Research	Rico Lie
	Audience	Nico Carpentier
	Emerging Scholars Network	Stefania Milan and Sara Bannerman (Canada)
	Working Group:	
	Public Service Media Policies	Leen D'Haenens (Belgium) and Jo Bardoel
	Visual Culture	Sunny Yoon (Korea)
2012 Durban	**Section:**	
	History	Chandrika Kaul (UK) and Epp Lauk (Estonia)
	Law	Sandra Braman
	Mediated Communication, Public Opinion & Society	Hillel Nossek and Corinna Lüthje
	Journalism Research and Education	Ibrahim Saleh
	International Communication	Herman Wasserman (South Africa)
	Communication Policy and Technology	Jo Pierson
	Political Economy	Helena Sousa
	Political Communication Research	Christina Holtz-Bacha (Germany)
	Gender and Communication	Aimée Vega Montiel (Mexico) and Margaretha Geertsema-Sligh (SA)
	Community Communication	Arne Hintz (UK)
	Media Education Research	Divina Frau-Meigs and Manuel Pinto
	Participatory Communication Research	Pradip N. Thomas
	Audience	Brian O'Neill
	Emerging Scholars Network	Francesca Musiani (France) and Sandra Ristovska (US)
	Media and Sport	Alina Bernstein
	Working Group:	
	Crisis Communication	Ester Pollack (Sweden)
	Committee:	
	Some detail missing	
	Budget renamed Finance	Nico Carpentier (Belgium)
	Conference	Maria Michalis (UK)
	Environment	Gabi Hadl
	Fundraising	Janet Wasko
	Future IAMCR Scenarios	Cees J. Hamelink
	Legal	Philippe Maarek
	Paper Promotion	Ruth Teer-Tomaselli

(*continued*)

(continued)

Established/ Confirmed by General Assembly	*Sections and Other Bodies* *Sections in order of founding year, others in alphabetical order*	*Heads and Conveners* *Nationality in brackets when first listed*
	Publications	Claudia Padovani (Italy) and Marjan de Bruin
	Regionalisation and Membership	Ibrahim Saleh (South Africa)
	Scholarly Review	Tom Jacobson
	Task Force on Changes in Academia and the Future of IAMCR	Friedrich Krotz
	Task Force on Ethics	Vacant
	Task Force on Media Policy renamed Committee on Policy Intervention	Jeremy Shtern (Canada) and Stefania Milan (Netherlands)
2014 Hyderabad	**Section:**	
	History	Epp Lauk and Chandrika Kaul
	Law	Sandra Braman
	Mediated Communication, Public Opinion and Society	Hillel Nossek
	Journalism Research and Education	Ibrahim Saleh
	International Communication	Herman Wasserman
	Communication Policy and Technology	Jo Pierson
	Political Economy	Rodrigo Gómez (Mexico)
	Political Communication Research	Christina Holtz-Bacha and Maria-Jose Canel (Spain)
	Gender and Communication	Kaitlynn Mendes (Canada) and Margaretha Geertsema-Sligh
	Community Communication	Arne Hintz
	Media Education Research	Divina Frau-Meigs and Manuel Pinto
	Participatory Communication Research	Satarupa Dasgupta (US)
	Audience	Peter Lunt (UK)
	Emerging Scholars Network	Francesca Musiani and Sandra Ristovska
	Media and Sport	Alina Bernstein
2016 Leicester	**Section:**	
	History	Nelson Costa Ribeiro (Portugal)
	Law	Loreto Corredoira (Spain)
	Mediated Communication, Public Opinion and Society	Corinna Lüethje (FRG)
	Journalism Research and Education	Cláudia Lago (Brazil)
	International Communication	Karen Arriaza Ibarra (Spain)
	Communication Policy and Technology	Aphra Kerr (Ireland) and Francesca Musiani
	Political Economy	Rodrigo Gómez
	Political Communication Research	Christina Holtz-Bacha and María José Canel

(*continued*)

(continued)

Established/ Confirmed by General Assembly	*Sections and Other Bodies* *Sections in order of founding year, others in alphabetical order*	*Heads and Conveners* *Nationality in brackets when first listed*
	Gender and Communication	Wajiha Raza Rizvi (Pakistan) and Mehita Iqani (South Africa)
	Community Communication and Alternative Media	Salvatore Scifo (UK) and Andrea Medrado (UK)
	Media Education Research	Sirkku Kotilainen (Finland)
	Participatory Communication Research	Nico Carpentier
	Audience	Peter Lunt
	Emerging Scholars Network	Sylvia Blake (Canada) and Ksenia Ermoshina (France)
	Media, Communication & Sport	Alina Bernstein and Deirdre Hynes (UK)
2018 Eugene	**Section:**	
	History	Nelson Costa Ribeiro (Portugal)
	Law	Loreto Corredoira (Spain)
	Mediated Communication, Public Opinion and Society	Corinna Lüethje (Germany)
	Journalism Research and Education	Cláudia Lago (Brazil)
	International Communication	Karen Arriaza Ibarra (Spain)
	Communication Policy and Technology	Aphra Kerr
	Political Economy	Rodrigo Gómez
	Political Communication Research	Christina Holtz-Bacha and María José Canel
	Gender and Communication	Wajiha Raza Rizvi and Mehita Iqani
	Community Communication and Alternative Media	Salvatore Scifo and Andrea Medrado
	Media Education Research	Sirkku Kotilainen
	Participatory Communication Research	Nico Carpentier
	Audience	Peter Lunt and Annette Hill (UK)
	Emerging Scholars Network	Sylvia Blake (Canada)/Sibo Chen (Canada) and Ksenia Ermoshina
	Media, Communication & Sport	Alina Bernstein and Xavier Ramón (Spain)
	Working Group:	
	Crisis, Security and Conflict Communication	Rikke Bjerg Jensen (UK)
	Media Sector Development	Nicholas Benequista (US) and Susan Abbott (UK)
	Religion and Communication	Yoel Cohen (Israel)
	Rural Communication	Sarah Cardey (UK) and Rico Lie
2020 Tampere	**Section:**	
	History	Nelson Costa Ribeiro
	Law	Loreto Corredoira (Spain) and Rodrigo Cetina Presuel (US)
	Mediated Communication, Public Opinion and Society	Corinna Lüethje

(*continued*)

(continued)

Established/ Confirmed by General Assembly	***Sections and Other Bodies*** *Sections in order of founding year, others in alphabetical order*	***Heads and Conveners*** *Nationality in brackets when first listed*
	Journalism Research and Education	Sadia Jamil (UAE)
	International Communication	Karen Arriaza Ibarra
	Communication Policy and Technology	Francesca Musiani and Julia Pohle (Germany)
	Political Economy	Rodrigo Gómez
	Political Communication Research	Marie Grusell (Sweden)
	Gender and Communication	Carolina Matos (UK) and Wajiha Raza Rizvi
	Community Communication and Alternative Media	Amparo Cadavid (Colombia) and Vinod Pavarala (India)
	Media Education Research	Sara Pereira (Portugal), Ruchi Jaggi (India), Michael Hoechsmann (Canada), and Leena Ripatti-Torniainen (Finland)
	Participatory Communication Research	Ana Duarte Melo (Portugal) and Dorismilda Flores-Márquez (Mexcio)
	Audience	Peter Lunt and Annette Hill
	Emerging Scholars Network	Sibo Chen and Ksenia Emoshina (Russia)
	Media, Communication and Sport	Alina Bernstein and Xavier Ramón
	Working Group:	
	Communication in Post- and Neo-Authoritarian Societies	Katja Lehtisaari (Finland)
	Health Communication	M Gavaravarapu Subba Rao (India) and Yolanda Paul (Jamaica)
	Music, Audio, Radio and Sound	Ignacio Gallego (Spain) and Mia Lindgren (Australia)
	Committee:	
	Clearinghouse for Public Statements	Robin Mansell
	Commission on IAMCR History	Jörg Becker (Germany)
	Committee for the Improvement of Academic Life	Chika Anyanwu (Australia)
	Conference	Gerard Goggin (Singapore)
	Elections	Beate Josephi
	Environment Impact	Graham Murdock
	Evaluation Committee for the Section/Working Group and Committee/Task Force Fund	Elske van de Fliert (Australia)
	Finance	Elske van de Fliert
	Fundraising Commission	Vacant
	Legal	Philippe Maarek
	Membership	Helena Sousa
	Publications	Maria Michalis
	Scholarly Review	Tom Jacobson

(*continued*)

(continued)

Established/ Confirmed by General Assembly	*Sections and Other Bodies* *Sections in order of founding year, others in alphabetical order*	*Heads and Conveners* *Nationality in brackets when first listed*
	Task Force on the Global Alliance for Media and Gender (GAMAG)	Aimée Vega Montiel (Mexico)
	Task Force on the Global Alliance for Social and Behavioral Change (GASBC)	Tom Jacobson
Nairobi 2021 (Not GA Year)	**Section:**	
	History	Nelson Costa Ribeiro
	Law	Loreto Corredoira and Rodrigo Cetina Presuel
	Mediated Communication, Public Opinion and Society	Susanne Eichner (Denmark)
	Journalism Research and Education	Sadia Jamil
	International Communication	Karen Arriaza Ibarra
	Communication Policy and Technology	Francesca Musiani and Julia Pohle
	Political Economy	Rodrigo Gómez
	Political Communication Research	Marie Grusell
	Gender and Communication	Carolina Matos and Wajiha Raza Rizvi
	Community Communication and Alternative Media	Amparo Cadavid and Vinod Pavarala
	Media Education Research	Sara Pereira, Ruchi Jaggi, Michael Hoechsmann, and Leena Ripatti-Torniainen
	Participatory Communication Research	Ana Duarte Melo and Dorismilda Flores-Márquez
	Audience	Asta Zelenkauskaite (US) and Miguel Vicente (Spain)
	Emerging Scholars Network	Sibo Chen, Ksenia Emoshina and Steph Hill (Canada)
	Media, Communication and Sport	Alina Bernstein and Xavier Ramón
	Working Group:	
	Music, Audio, Radio and Sound	Ignacio Gallego and Mia Lindgren
	Committee:	
	Environmental Impact	Graham Murdock
	Finance	Elske va de Fliert
	Legal	Philippe Maarek
	Conference	Gerard Goggin
	Membership	Helena Sousa
	Publications	Maria Michalis
	Scholarly Review	Thomas Jacobson
	Task Force on the Global Alliance for Media and Gender (GAMAG)	Aimée Vega Montiel

(*continued*)

(continued)

Established/ Confirmed by General Assembly	*Sections and Other Bodies* *Sections in order of founding year, others in alphabetical order*	*Heads and Conveners* *Nationality in brackets when first listed*
	Task Force on the Global Alliance for Social and Behavioural Change	Thomas Jacobson
	Committee for the Improvement of Academic Life	Chika Anyanwu
	Task Force on Conference Modeling	Eno Akpabio (Namibia)
	INTER/ACTIONS: Multimodal Academic Communication	Sandra Ristovska
	Evaluation Committee for the Section/Working Group and Committee Task Force Funds	Elske van de Fliert
	Clearinghouse for Public Statements	Robin Mansell
	Commission on IAMCR History	Jörg Becker

Author Index[1]

[1] Note: Page numbers followed by 'n' refer to notes.

© The Author(s), under exclusive license to Springer Nature Switzerland AG 2023

J. Becker, R. Mansell (eds.), *Reflections on the International Association for Media and Communication Research*,
https://doi.org/10.1007/978-3-031-16383-8

Subject Index[1]

[1] Note: Page numbers followed by 'n' refer to notes.

© The Author(s), under exclusive license to Springer Nature Switzerland AG 2023

J. Becker, R. Mansell (eds.), *Reflections on the International Association for Media and Communication Research*,
https://doi.org/10.1007/978-3-031-16383-8

E

The manufacturer's authorised representative in the EU is Springer Nature Customer Service Centre GmbH, Europaplatz 3, 69115 Heidelberg, Germany. If you have any concerns regarding our products, please contact ProductSafety@springernature.com

Printed and bound by CPI Group (UK) Ltd, Croydon, CR0 4YY
29/04/2026
02099470-0011